# Dramatic Version of Seven Major Upaniṣads

# Dramatic Version
# of
# Seven Major Upaniṣads

## Kena, Iśavāsya, Praśna, Muṇḍaka, Māṇḍukya, Taittirīya and Kaṭha Upaniṣads

(With Original Text, Transliteration and Translation)

Rama Venkataraman

D.K. Printworld (P) Ltd.
New Delhi

**Cataloging in Publication Data — DK**
[Courtesy: D.K. Agencies (P) Ltd. <docinfo@dkagencies.com>]

**Upanishads. English & Sanskrit. Selections.**
Dramatic Version of Seven Major Upaniṣads : Kena, Iśavāsya, Praśna, Muṇḍaka, Māṇḍukya, Taittirīya and Kaṭha Upaniṣads : with original text, transliteration and translation / Rama Venkataraman.
p. cm.
In Sanskrit (Devanagari and roman); translation and pref. in English.

ISBN 13: 9788124605219 (HB) ISBN 10: 8124605211
ISBN 13: 9788124605226 (PB) ISBN 10: 812460522X

1. Hinduism — Sacred books — Early works to 1800 — Drama. 2. Hindu drama. 3. Sanskrit drama. I. Venkataraman, Rama, 1952-. II. Title.

DDC 294.59218 22


*First published in India, 2009*

ISBN 13: 978-81-246-0521-9 (HB) ISBN 10: 81-246-0521-1
ISBN 13: 978-81-246-0522-6 (PB) ISBN 10: 81-246-0522-X



*Published and printed by:*
D.K. Printworld (P) Ltd.
*Regd. office* : *'Srikunj'*, F-52, Bali Nagar
Ramesh Nagar Metro Station
New Delhi – 110 015
*Phones* : (011) 2545 3975; 2546 6019; *Fax* : (011) 2546 5926
*E-mail*: dkprintworld@vsnl.net
*Web*: www.dkprintworld.com

# Preface

It is difficult to ascertain a time period for the origin of the Upaniṣads. The Upaniṣadic utterances in the form of cryptic and coded Sanskrit *śloka*s are the work of great *ṛṣi*s of yonder who, with the strength of their penance, could untie the knot of the mystery behind the working of the universe. They recorded their realizations in saṁhitās or *śloka*s. These were passed on from *guru* to disciple in *gurukula* tradition in a well-ordained way. Thus the knowledge and wisdom gained by the austere *tapas* (penance) of great *maharṣi*s filtered into the society and helped the living process of mankind steeped in ignorance and wrapped up in the world of phenomena brought forth by the antennae of their five senses.

The knowledge was passed on to the chosen ones who had the inclination as well as the capacity to decipher the codes in the Upaniṣadic *śloka*s and who had the integrity to pass it on to the next generations. Thus the values, the wisdom and precious pearls of truth continued to be handed over from generation to generation.

The sceneries of the living process are undergoing drastic changes. The people who lived their lives in pre-ordained roles as warriors, craftsmen, traders and priests and led the machinery of the society, well oiled by their respective occupations, and imbibed the truths of the Śāstras in their living process, have all changed in the present tapestry of living. The fine subtle layers and rhythms of the society are all shredded away. By opening of the windows to the wild winds which bring both good and bad in fresh gusts continuously, the old rhythm has changed for sure. But the new order has yet to be established. In this age of transition, where there is a bombardment of information with the entire mass of the population, trying to grapple with both trivial and grave ideas in the same breath, it is becoming increasingly difficult to sieve the essentials for proper and worthy living. The bombardment starts right from the cradle, and by the time the youth reach their prime they carry several encyclopedias of knowledge on diverse subjects. In all the din it is indeed difficult to differentiate between *vidyā* and *avidyā* as our seers have described knowledge. Any knowledge which leads to the understanding of *Brahman*, which alone is the truth in this universe of appearances, is true *vidyā* or education, and all the rest of knowledge is grouped under *avidyā*: "non-essential knowledge."

That raises the question as to what is this true *vidyā* or *Brahman*-knowing knowledge. That is what is discussed by the realized *ṛṣi*s in the Upaniṣads.

As I was going through the labyrinth of life like any person of this substratum and floundering about in the sea of knowledge, not knowing which direction to veer my boat, I came across these precious Upaniṣadic teachings rendered by Shri Mani Iyer in a drama form in Tamil. This format of Upaniṣadic writing attracted me. Time and again, prodded by the latent wish of every educated person, I had tried to read commentaries of great scholars about the sacred Upaniṣadic *ślokas*. However my limited intellect and pressures of other living process have always found me falling short of comprehending the full purport of the weighty words and commentaries. As the readings get heavy the brain has a habit of curling up to slumber. Thus the words of Upaniṣads were always recorded patchily and thus robbed me of the full impact of their words, which eventually leads a soul to its final objective of realization to get out of this repeated cycle of bondage or imprisonment in the ignorance-personified life.

Words of wisdom locked up in the Upaniṣads, which are the key to open the mystery of life and death, have to be brought to the light of scholars and laymen alike. Shri Mani Iyer had taken it upon himself this stupendous job and had brought out the sacred and difficult text in a lucid and clear format of drama. Here the great *ṛṣi*s of yonder and their equally erudite disciples are brought out in dramatic format, a way every ordinary reader can understand. Further the difficult-to-comprehend truths of Upaniṣads are brought out in a dialogue form where the disciples are ever full of doubts like each one of us. The lurking doubts of our minds, are brought out through questions of the disciples and the concepts are discussed threadbare. Seeing these Upaniṣadic dramas rendering the difficult treatise in an interesting and captivating way, inspired me to take up translating the work into English, so that it can reach a wider audience. The universal truths should find light in the present universal language English, so that the profound thoughts and findings of the *ṛṣi*s, which rightfully belong to the entire human race, can be understood in an easy-to-comprehend manner. Hence though my station in life is a humble one, prompted by the all-knowing spirit "the *Brahman*" around and within us, I took up this work of translating Shri Mani Iyer's seven Upaniṣad dramas into English. I have tried to bring out the work to the best of my capabilities. Very many scholars may find lacunae and deficiency in this work. My objective is to inform the public of the Upaniṣads in a drama form, who like me, are ignorant of the most important work of our *ṛṣi*s that lead us to *brahma-vidyā* and final liberation. Hence I request the more erudite brethren to bear with any lapses and bring them to my notice, so that I can stand corrected.

In this endeavour of mine I owe my thanks to the scholars who took pains to go through the work from time to time and gave their valuable suggestions during the progress of the work. Shri S. Ranga Ramanujacharyalu the ex-Principal of Kovur, Sanskrit Vidhyalaya near Rajahmudry at Andhra Pradesh is one of the scholars who got involved with the work. Shri M.V.N. Chari went through the text and did the initial editing of it. Shri A.V.V.S. Kamaraju, a senior officer with ONGC devoted his valuable time and talent to draw out the many illustrations and bring out the nuances of the text matter clearly to the reader. Professor P.K. Dixit of Lal Bahadur Shastri Sanskrit Vidyapeetham, New Delhi gave his valuable time in discussing some finer aspects of the play.

Last but not the least, I would not have been able to pen this voluminous translation with its attached works without the support of my ever supporting partner of life, my husband Shri K. Venkataraman. My dear daughter-in-laws Smt. Archana Krishnan and Smt. Prerna Ramanathan joined me at the concluding stage of the work pitching in for the final correction works.

Helping me in the Sanskrit typing work was Mr. Kiran Kumar who painstakingly did many DTP work connected with the manuscript.

# Contents

# ॥ केनोपनिषत् ॥
# Kenopaniṣad

## Introduction

*Kena Upaniṣad* is one of the oft read and discussed Upaniṣads. One of the reasons may be that it right away addresses the crux of Upaniṣadic discussion, namely the understanding and realization of the all-pervading *Brahman* who is the architect of all that we find around us including ourselves and the sense organs through which we understand and operate in this world.

The word *kena* (केन) asks precisely "by whom": that is, by whom is this world made and operated? In the first *mantra* itself the disciple asks the *guru*, "*kena*" — by whose help — do the *mana* (mind), *prāṇa* (vital breath), *vāc* (words), *cakṣu* (eyes), and *śrotra* (ears) operate?"

*Kenopaniṣad* is part of the *Sāmaveda*.

In the present play, these subtle truths are brought out in the form of a discussion between the *guru* and his disciples. The *guru* is Jaimini Maharṣi, a Sāmavedi. The enquiries are probing and persuasive. The disciples do not hesitate in asking the *guru* questions repetitively till they obtain a clear understanding.

Further, the ṛṣi has introduced a mythological story involving Lord Indra, *deva*s like Agni and Vāyu, *Brahman* in the form of a Yakṣa and Umādevi, the daughter of Himavān.

The story depicts how the entire world operates due to the inherent strength of *Brahman*. Without the backing of the trancedent being, everything comes to a standstill.

The play is set in the verdant slopes of the Himālayas. The *āśrama* of Jaimini Maharṣi is found along the banks of river Sarasvatī in the picturesque foothills of the Himālayas.

There are many disciples staying in the *āśrama* and trying to get *brahmajñāna* from the teachings of the revered Guru Jaimini. The senior disciples are Thalavakāra and Gautama. The play commences at a point where the teachings of *Kena Upaniṣad* are being discussed. The disciples are keen to know who operates our sense organs, through which we understand and operate in the world, and who operates the *prāṇa* in the body even when one is asleep. The *maharṣi* explains to the disciples that the operating power behind all that is *Brahman*. The disciples then want to know how to realise this *Brahman* which is behind all actions. Can it be known by the mind which is superior to everything? The *guru* patiently shows how it is not possible to know by the mind, as it is *Brahman* alone which operates the mind. Then the disciples are perplexed as to how else to know it as it has no name and form with which to identify.

One of the disciples comes forward saying, "revered *guru*, with the help of your teachings I contemplated on it deeply and I think I have understood it. However there is a doubt. And again I feel it has gone beyond my grasp." The *guru* smiles at the disciple and says "one should not assume one has understood it by a little contemplation," and gives the analogy of a man from the village who went to see the palace in the city and by just seeing the palace garden assumes he has seen the palace. In the same way *Brahman* which is beyond the mind cannot be grasped by limited means. Hence the statement of the person who says "he has understood what *Brahman* stands for, but again he has not really understood what *Brahman* is" will be the correct statement rather than the one who states he has understood the *Brahman* with limited contemplation. However the redeeming feature is that a man's mind seeks *Brahman* in its natural course just like a growing creeper gravitates towards the Sun or water runs down a slope.

There is, yet, one clear way to know *Brahman*. By reaching a state of *samādhi*, it will be possible to perceive *Brahman* though it may not be possible to describe the *Brahman* so perceived in *samādhi*, as *Brahman* is beyond mere speech and words. To explain this the *guru* takes the analogy of a salt doll which when put in the ocean becomes one with the ocean. In the same way in *samādhi*, the aspirant becomes one with *Brahman*. The *samādhi* can be obtained by an undistrubed mind which meditates on *Brahman*. Hearing these explanations of the preceptor about *Brahman*, the disciples are now assailed with the thought, to what end the *Brahman* knowledge is obtained?

Is it necessary for an *ātmā* (a person) to strive for knowing *Brahman*? Hence the disciples put this question to the preceptor, "O! Revered teacher do tell us; by acquiring *Brahman* knowledge what will one get?"

The *maharṣi* had anticipated such a question for though the disciples had come to the *āśrama* and are staying there to acquire the *Brahman* knowledge (like a creeper gravitates towards the Sun, an *ātmā* gravitates towards the knowledge of *Brahman*) still the rational mind, seeks gratification for the effort put in. Though everything in the world is verily *Brahman*, it is however clothed by names and forms. A man acting in the universe is conditioned by these appearances and rarely does his intellect go in search beyond the forms he sees around him. This puts a veil on the true nature of things and he is clouded by the illusion of what he sees in the world, which our seers called *māyā*. Working under the effects of this illusion or *māyā*, he acts conditioned by what he sees as true. He then gets caught in its web and the rules of *karma* and fruits which govern the world of *māyā*. This leads to the cause and effect cycle, which also govern birth and death. Thus tied to the *kālachakra* (wheel of time) the soul undergoes plurality of repeated birth and death, happiness and sorrow, ups and downs and stays anchored to the world of phenomena or illusion. This spell can be broken by the knowledge of *Brahman* which breaks the illusion and throws light on the reality and the truth. Thus, the knower of *Brahman* obtains immortality by breaking away from the chain of birth and death. This immortality or knowing the truth, becoming one with *Brahman* in turn leads to supreme happiness which the scriptures call "bliss." The feeling is akin to coming out of a bad dream and realizing at once that the entire life with its struggles and miseries was only but an illusion. Thus, the preceptor tells that after getting that *jñana* (realization) about *Brahman*, even other knowledges about the world and its working which were not known are revealed. Without striving for that knowledge, a human soul is destined to be chained to his world of illusion which he carries along, through his many lives. Thus he incurs a big loss. A human form with its intellect is endowed with the potential to know, perceive and realize *Brahman*. By not making use of the opportunity granted to him, he is at a great loss. Hence an intelligent person who lives a life controlled by senses (inputs and outputs) strives to know *Brahman* leading to immortality.

The play then proceeds to its next part where an interesting mythological story is being enacted. The story imparts the same theme; that it is *Brahman* who is behind all actions. Gods as well as humans are just forms which are empowered through *Brahman*. When *Brahman* chooses not to act, the mightiest also fall down and remain powerless to even move an atom. Hence in victory and defeat alike, men should remain *sāma* (equal) as all actions are but His *līlā* (play).

In the second part of the play, the prime disciples of Maharṣi Jaimini, Gautama and Talavakāra proceed to the forest to collect some requirements for a guest they were expecting in the *āśrama*. On their return they come across the dwellers of *devaloka* Lord Indra and his entourage consisting of some prime *devas* like Agni and Vāyu and the rest of the *devagaṇas*. It was in fact a rare treat for them, perhaps due to some blessings they had acquired in their previous births, for the persons in *bhūloka* (earth) are not destined to see the residents of *devaloka* (heaven).

The *devas* are in a victorious mood having won a war with *asuras*. The glorious looking Devendra (Indra) and the *devas* with him are in all their finery while the *devagaṇas* are shouting victory cries and hailing their master. Their faces look swelled with pride and their gait was a victory march showing off their undisputed leadership. As they march, hailing and shouting victory cries, right in front of their path appeared a huge terrifying form of a *yakṣa*. The *yakṣa* was none but the almighty *Brahman* Himself. But the *devas* could not recognize it, blinded by their victory and pride. Seeing the *yakṣa* abruptly on the way, they first sent Agnideva who is referred to as Jātavedas as he has the capacity to understand everything found in the universe. He goes with self-pride and asks the *yakṣa* to reveal its identity and give way for them to march ahead. The *yakṣa* in turn asks of the identity of Agni and his strength. Agni proudly states that he can burn and annihilate everything found in this world. *Yakṣa* then asks him to burn a small blade of grass lying in front of him. Agni ridicules his humble request and tries to burn it. But as it was not getting burnt he uses all his strength of annihilation applying the heat used for the final calamity.

But the blade of grass remains as such. Even the dew drops shining in the grass do not evaporate. The humbled Agni returns back crestfallen. The *devas* then request Vāyu referred to as Mātariśvan as he can reach every available space in the *prapañca* (universe) thus becoming *sarvavyāpin* (present everywhere). Vāyudeva then goes to the *yakṣa* to find out its true identity. The *yakṣa* asks Vāyu to state its true strength and warns not to boast unnecessarily like Agni. However Vāyu is not able to adopt any humility. He also boasts of his supremacy stating that he has the strength to lift everything in the world. He can lift and overturn even big mountains. *Yakṣa* then asks him to lift the small blade of grass in front of him. Vāyu too ridicules his humble request and first tries to lift the grass casually, failing which he applies the strength as in a hurricane but still the grass remains unmoved. Vāyu then returns humbled and humiliated. The *deva*s then ask their lord himself to find out who the *yakṣa* is. Lord Indra goes forth determined to find the truth behind that form. However the *yakṣa* suddenly vanishes from the scene as Lord Indra nears. Seeing this the *deva*s state the *yakṣa* indeed has got scared of our lord and has retreated from the scene. They suspect this as an illusion created by Śukrācārya (*guru* of *asura*s). They prod their king to return back to complete the victory march. But Indra feels he must go to the place and find the truth of the matter. As he approaches the place, suddenly in a blinding effulgence, Goddess Umādevī, daughter of Himavān descends down in her full magnificent form and appears in front of lord Indra.

The disciples of Maharṣi Jaimini, Gautama and Talavakāra who were witnessing the entire proceedings unable to stand the blinding brightness of the Goddess's form swoon and fall down. Goddess Umādevī reveals to Indra the identity of the *yakṣa* stating that it was none but *Brahman* the all-pervading Almighty. It had come to remind the *deva*s as to who is behind all their actions. The victory which they were proclaiming as theirs was actually *Brahman*'s work. *Brahman* showed the mighty *deva*s like Agni and Vāyu that they were unable to act even on a small blade of grass when they tried to do it with their ego thinking it was their power in action. Thus when the Almighty withdraws His support, all action ceases.

The story beyond doubt proves that all forms are merely the instruments of *Brahman*. It is He who acts behind the action of living beings including the functioning of their sense organs. Hence He is described as an ear to the ear, eye to the eye and so on. Realizing this all-pervading and almighty *Brahman* who is the cause behind all that is found here is the ultimate truth to be known.

The play concludes with Maharṣi Jaimini and the other *āśrama* residents coming in search of the prime disciples who had not returned for a long while to the *āśrama*. Maharṣi Jaimini with his power of intuition had known the arrival of *deva*s and the ensuing events that had occurred. He tells the disciples that the entire event should further reinforce the preachings already given about *Brahman*. He once again tells them about *Brahman* and the ways to know It. He tells them it is close and dear to all, as it is present in every breath and is the life-giver for all forms and should be worshipped as such.

# The Drama

**Characters**

| | | | |
|---|---|---|---|
| 1. | **Jaimini** | – | A Maharṣi having his *āśrama* in the Himālayan slopes close to Sarasvatī River. He teaches *brahma-jñāna* (wisdom of *Brahman*) to mature disciples and follows the discipline of *Brahmaniṣṭhā*. He is a *Sāmavedī*. |
| 2. | **Talavakāra & Gautama** | – | *Brahmachārī*s staying in *gurukula* and disciples who have come to learn from the *guru*. |
| 3. | **Umādevī** | – | Parāśakti. Consort of Lord Śiva. |
| 4. | **Yakṣa** | – | A being of the celestial world. |
| 5. | **Indra** | – | King of *deva*s. |
| 6. | **Vāyu & Agni** | – | *Deva*s (wind and fire gods). |
| 7. | **Devas** | – | Celestial beings who accompany Lord Indra. |
| 8. | **Sūtradhāra** | – | Narrator. |

Residents of the *āśrama* and animals residing there (like fawns, calves, peacocks, cuckoos, parrots, etc.).

**Venue**

Himālayan mountain and surroundings.

# PART I

## SCENE I

**(Behind the screen as the instrumental music is heard, the sūtradhāra enters).**

श्रुतिस्मृतिपुराणानामालयं करुणालयं ।
नमामि भगवत्पादशङ्करं लोकशङ्करं ॥

*śrutismṛtipurāṇānāmālayaṁ karuṇālayaṁ* |
*namāmi bhagavatpādaśaṅkaraṁ lokaśaṅkaraṁ* ||

He is the abode of vedas, smṛtis and purāṇas.
He is abode of compassion, my praṇāmas in the feet of lord Śaṅkara. He is the benefactor of the whole world.

— prayer to Śaṅkara

**Sūtradhāra** – True devotees, my *namaskāram* to you all. More elders than expected have assembled. The assumption that people enjoy only historical, mythological and social stories and they may not be keen about matters of Vedānta has been proved false. O Learned ones! kindly watch and enjoy this small drama enacted by us, and bless us. Give us encouragement to undertake more of such work. In this worldly life, everyone is looking for happiness. Where is the happiness? Is it really to be found? How to obtain it? Enquiring thus, every life is running behind it. Like a child trying to catch its own shadow, we fail in the attempts and get disappointed. However real happiness lies in knowing *Brahman*. The proverb tells "search for the distorted *Brahman* in *Kenam* (*Kena Upaniṣad*)." Though this is the smallest among Upaniṣads still it reveals the knowledge of *Brahman* like a gooseberry held in the palm. Hence, with the blessings of Śṛṅgerī Mahāpīṭham and with your affections we are presenting this drama. Kindly bear with the mistakes, appreciate the good points and bless us, that it should do well. Now the drama is going to start. The curtain will rise, so does your curtain of ignorance. Observe carefully with alertness. You will benefit.

***(The curtain opens)***

(The scene at the *āśrama* — Along the slope of the Himālayas, on the banks of river Sarasvatī the big *āśrama* is seen. Morning time. From inside Vedic chants are heard which are pleasing to the ears. The *āśrama* residents are attending to their work without hurry, moving here and there. Outside under a banyan tree Jaimini Maharṣi is sitting in *padmāsana* in a majestic way. On either side of him disciples are standing. On one side *homa* is taking place. Everywhere peace prevails.

The peacocks dance, parrots chatter and the cuckoo sings. Even baby deer are engrossed in the chants and stand transfixed. Hearing the Vedic recitals and learning it by heart, a bird is teaching it to its dear one.)

***fig* : Jaimini Maharṣi at his *āśrama* at the bank of river Sarasvatī**

Everyone together are saluting and praying for the welfare of everyone through *maṅgalācaraṇam āratī.*

*Oṁ Brahman,* please protect our *guru* and his disciples. Bless us to realize the eternal bliss. We shall stay in unity. Bless us so that our learning is inspiring. Let us stay in friendship without hostility to one another. Let us not be disturbed by personal, social and godly anxieties. Let us feel peace. Let happiness and peace prevail in the three worlds.

*oṁ śāntiḥ* | *śāntiḥ* | *śāntiḥ* ||

*Oṁ*! Let all my sense organs, the speech, *prāṇa*, eyes, ears and other senses be strong and work efficiently. Everything is *Brahman* as told in the Upaniṣads. I should not stray from *Brahman*. *Brahman* also should never leave me. This relationship should stay permanently. Let me also acquire the Upaniṣadic *dharma* of staying in the bliss of *ātmā*. I may be blessed that this *dharma* should stay with me constantly.

*oṁ śāntiḥ* । *śāntiḥ* । *śāntiḥ* ।।

(After salutations to god for general welfare, the disciples offer their respects to the *guru* and say *abhivādaye asmi bho*. *Guru* also blesses them "May you live long." Then with the permission of the *guru*, the disciples sit.)

**Jaimini** – Children. May you be blessed with all good things. Let us start the lesson. Dear Gautama, you can ask the first question.

**Gautama** – Master, after thinking and contemplating about this universe some things are very confusing to understand.

केनेषितं पतति प्रेषितं मनः केन प्राणः प्रथमः प्रैति युक्तः ।
केनेषितां वाचमिमां वदन्ति चक्षुः श्रोत्रं क उ देवो युनक्ति ॥ १ ॥

*oṁ keneṣitaṁ patati preṣitaṁ manaḥ kena prāṇaḥ prathamaḥ praiti yuktaḥ* ।
*keneṣitāṁ vācamimāṁ vadanti cakṣuḥ śrotraṁ ka u devo yunakti* ।।1।।

Who impels the mind to alight on its object? Enjoined by whom does the vital force proceed to function? At whose behest do men utter speech? Which divinity indeed directs the eyes and the ears?

Who causes my mind to enter into different matters? Even if I don't wish, mind operates at someone's wishes and orders. Who is He? Under whose prompting is the *prāṇa* doing my work. When I am in deep sleep, the *prāṇa* does its job properly. Who is the controller of it? Which God operates my eyes and ears? Under whose prompting does the tongue speak? Who is the cause of our speaking words infused with life? By whose prompting do people talk like this? What is the reason? For that matter, under whose orders and prompting is the present conversation taking place? Kindly tell us in detail and clearly.

**Jaimini** – My dear child, your question is a detailed one. Good, very good. I will tell you shortly and try to explain. Listen carefully.

श्रोत्रस्य श्रोत्रं मनसो मनो यद्वाचो ह वाचंꣳ स उ प्राणस्य प्राणः।
चक्षुषश्चक्षुरतिमुच्य धीराः प्रेत्यास्माल्लोकादमृता भवन्ति ॥ २ ॥

*śrotrasya śrotraṁ manaso mano yadvāco ha vācaṁ̐ sa u prāṇasya prāṇaḥ* |
*cakṣuṣaścakṣuratimucya dhīrāḥ pretyāsmāllokādamṛtā bhavanti* ||2||

That which is the Ear behind the ear, the Mind of the mind, the Word of the speech, Life of the life breath, Sight behind the sight. The wise men separate the guiding force *Brahman* from these functions, rise out of sense-life and attain immortality.

The *chaitanya*, the power which operates the ear, the one which controls the mind, intellect and speech is all *Brahman*. The same acts as an eye to the eye, *prāṇa* to the *prāṇa*, tongue to the tongue and prompts all of them to act. The perishable senses are the eye and ear. The inner strength of these organs and the constant prompting power *chaitanya* behind them are all *Brahman*. A person getting this knowledge of *Brahman* conquers death and enters an immortal state.

न तत्र चक्षुर्गच्छति न वाग्गच्छति नो मनः।
न विद्मो न विजानीमो यथैतदनुशिष्यात् ॥३॥

*na tatra cakṣur gacchati na vāg gacchati no manaḥ* |
*na vidmo na vijānīmo yathaitadanuśiṣyāt* ||3||

> The eye does not go there, nor speech, nor mind. We do not therefore know It, nor do we know any process of instructing about It.

The eyes cannot reach *ātmā* nor speech reach there, even the mind cannot reach the same. We cannot understand It as It is. Hence it is difficult to preach about it.

अन्यदेव तद्विदितादथो अविदितादधि ।
इति शुश्रुम पूर्वेषां ये नस्तद्व्याचचक्षिरे ॥४॥

*anyadeva tad viditādatho aviditādadhi* |
*iti śuśruma pūrveṣāṁ ye nastad vyācacakṣire* ||4||

> That is surely different from the known, and It is beyond the unknown. Thus we have heard from the ancients who expounded It to us.

Our past *ācārya*s (teachers) also described it as — "It is different from the things we know and is even beyond the things we don't know."

यद्वाचाऽनभ्युदितं येन वागभ्युद्यते ।
तदेव ब्रह्म त्वं विद्धि नेदं यदिदमुपासते ॥५॥

*yad vācā 'nabhyuditaṁ yena vāgabhyudyate* |
*tadeva brahma tvaṁ viddhi nedaṁ*
*yadidamupāsate* ||5||

> That, which speech cannot reveal, but what reveals speech, know That alone as *Brahman* and not "this" that people here worship.

The *Brahman* cannot be explained with a set of words as It is beyond words, and It only gives the power to the words or speech. Neither It can be represented as different gods which we worship here as It is beyond attributes. It can stand on its own, It cannot be seen by eyes because it only gives the power to the eye to see outside things. Similarly the ear can hear only by the power it derives from It. In the same way all other sense organs also derive their strength from *Brahman* alone. Hence they are not able to understand *Brahman*.

**Talavakāra** – Revered Guru! I understand. It is fascinating. Kindly tell me more about these.

**Gautama** – But there is a doubt. Master, is even mind unable to reach *Brahman*? Mind has great potential, is it not? It is much more powerful than the other sense organs.

**Jaimini** –

> यन्मनसा न मनुते येनाहुर्मनो मतम्।
> तदेव ब्रह्म त्वं विद्धि नेदं यदिदमुपासते ॥६॥
>
> *yanmanasā na manute yenāhur mano matam |*
> *tadeva brahma tvaṁ viddhi nedaṁ yadidamupāsate ||6||*
>
> That which cannot be comprehended by the mind but by which the mind is cognized, know that alone to be *Brahman*, and not this that people worship here.

Child, it is beyond the reach of the mind. It is the power of *Brahman* which orders the mind. That being so, can it understand the source? *Brahman* is the king of mind's kingdom. The sense organs are servants. Mind is the emperor, intellect is the minister. It is only due to orders of *Brahman* that the sense organs are operating. Hence the sense organs cannot see *Brahman* and also cannot understand It.

**Talavakāra** – In that case is there no way to understand *Brahman*? Your blessings are required, Svāmī, in making it clear.

**Jaimini** – *Brahman* can be known to some extent only in *samādhi*. It cannot be understood through argument or mere instructions. What cannot be explained in words but that gives expression to words is *Brahman*. What one cannot understand by mind but which gives expression to mind is *Brahman*.

> यच्चक्षुषा न पश्यति येन चक्षूंषि पश्यति।
> तदेव ब्रह्म त्वं विद्धि नेदं यदिदमुपासते ॥७॥

*yaccakṣuṣā napaśyati yena cakṣūṁṣi paśyati |*
*tadeva brahma tvaṁ viddhi nedaṁ yadidamupāsate ||7||*

That which sight fails to see, which perceives the sight, know That alone to be Brahman, and not this that people here worship.

What cannot be seen by the eye but that which makes the eye get the vision, is *Brahman.*

यच्छ्रोत्रेण न शृणोति येन श्रोत्रमिदं श्रुतम्।
तदेव ब्रह्म त्वं विद्धि नेदं यदिदमुपासते॥८॥

*yacchrotreṇa na śṛṇoti yena śrotramidaṁ śrutam |*
*tadeva brahma tvaṁ viddhi nedaṁ yadidamupāsate ||8||*

That which man fails to hear with the ear, that by which man perceives hearing, know That alone to be *Brahman*, and not this that people here worship.

What cannot be heard by the ear but that which is the cause of operating the ear is *Brahman.*

यत्प्राणेन न प्राणिति येन प्राणः प्रणीयते।
तदेव ब्रह्म त्वं विद्धि नेदं यदिदमुपासते॥९॥

*yatprāṇena na prāṇiti yena prāṇaḥ praṇīyate |*
*tadeva brahma tvaṁ viddhi nedaṁ yadidamupāsate ||9||*

That which breaths not the breath, but what leads the life breath forward, know That alone to be *Brahman*, and not this that people here worship.

What cannot be smelt but that which gives the power to the nose to smell is *Brahman.* The same should be understood by other sense organs. Say if it is told it is here, this is *Brahman,* then such a thing cannot be *Brahman.* Even if you feel you have understood *Brahman,* that cannot be *Brahman* because it is beyond the reach of mind and intellect.

**Gautama** – What you told is very interesting to hear, Svāmi. You told *Brahman* is beyond even unknown things. What are those unknown things?

**Jaimini** – Child, from your question it is seen you are listening very carefully. Yes, it is possible to understand about unknown things. For example, you don't know my age but it is possible to know this unknown thing, that is, my age. In the same way we can know about other unknown things. Beyond such unknown things is *Brahman*. It is also different from known things. It is different from the things of name and form as we know them in this world. It is not one with form or the one without form. That is, it is different from things with form yet it is apart from formless things. It is not tangible nor is it intangible. If you think you have known it then it is not *Brahman*. To think of having known *Brahman* itself is wrong. Children, the afternoon prayer time is nearing. Let us go for this regular ritual.

**(Disciples get up and salute the *guru*.)**

**All together recite –**

सर्वं ब्रह्मं। सत्चित् आनन्दं। ॥॥ ॐ ब्रह्मं ॥॥ ॐ ब्रह्मं ॥॥ ॐ शान्ति ॥

*sarvaṁ brahmaṁ | satcit ānandaṁ | oṁ brahmaṁ | oṁ brahmaṁ | oṁ śānti! | |*

*Brahman* is all-pervading. *Sat chit* – Everything is happiness. Everything is Brahman. Oṁ Brahmaṁ! Oṁ Brahmaṁ! Oṁ Brahmaṁ! Oṁ śāntiḥ | śāntiḥ | śāntiḥ ||

***(They all are singing. Curtain closes.)***

## SCENE 2

**Āśrama scene** – (In the *āśrama* at one side Jaimini Maharṣi is sitting on a tiger skin on a majestic throne made of tiger hide. A baby deer comes and stands by his side and he feeds it with grass. On another side a cat and a parrot are playing. From inside the *āśrama* melodious sounds of songs and pleasant smell of ghee are emanating and spreading everywhere.)

Gautama, Talavakāra and other disciples enter and invoke the *guru*.

गुरुर्ब्रह्म गुरुर्विश्नुः गुरुर्देवो महेश्वरः।
गुरुः साक्षात् परब्रह्म तस्मै श्री गुरवे नमः।

*gururbrahma gururviśnuḥ gururdevo maheśvaraḥ* ।
*guru sākṣāt parabrahma tasmai śrī gurave namaḥ* ॥

*Guru* is Brahmā, the creatar, *guru* is Viṣṇu, the protector, *guru* is Maheśvara, the destroyer. *Guru* is Parabrahman himself. To that *guru*, I salute with reverence.

(Chanting thus the disciples salute the *guru* and prostrate themselves on the ground. Jaimini blesses them and they get up, and chant all together.)

ॐ नमो ब्रह्मादिभ्यो ब्रह्मविद्या सम्प्रदायकर्तृभ्यो वंशऋषिभ्यो नमो गूरुभ्यः।
यो ब्रह्मणं विद्धाति पूर्वं यो वै वेदांश्च प्रहिणोति तस्मै।
तं ह देवमात्मबुद्धिप्रकाशं मुमुक्षुर्वै शरणमहं प्रपद्ये॥

ॐ शान्तिः। शान्तिः। शान्तिः

*oṁ namo brahmādibhyo brahmavidyā sampradāya-*
*kartṛbhyo vaṁśarṣibhyo namo gūrubhyaḥ* ।
*yo brahmaṇaṁ Vidadhāti pūrvaṁ yo vai vedāṁśca*
*prahiṇoti tasṁai* ।
*taṁ ha devamātmabuddhiprakāśaṁ mumukṣurvai*
*śaraṇamahaṁ prapadye* ।।

*oṁ śāntiḥ* । *śāntiḥ* । *śāntiḥ* ।।

Praṇāmas to lord Brahmā, praṇāmas to the once who hold the tradition of brahma vidyā, praṇāmas to ṛṣis whose lineage is followed, praṇāmas to the gurus.

Brahman who is the creator of Brahmā, Brahman who gave

vedic lessons to brahmā in olden times, brahman who enlightens the intellect the every ātmā, i who is the seeker of salvation offer my salutation to you.

(Thus they seek the well-being of all entities. All of them sit in their respective places.)

**Jaimini** – Children. Let Vedamātā bless you all with good fortune. Gautama! Whatever was taught previously did you contemplate on it?

**Gautama** – Master, as I think, the thought of *Brahman* gives me astonishment. At one time I seem to understand it properly, crystal clearly. The next moment I feel nothing is understood and the *Brahman* runs beyond the grasp of the mind.

**Talavakāra** – After hearing your preaching I have been thinking constantly about that and contemplating. I understand clearly. I have known *Brahman*.

**Jaimini** –

यदि मन्यसे सुवेदेति दभ्रमेवापि नूनं त्वं वेत्थ ब्रह्मणो रूपम्।
यदस्य त्वं यदस्य देवेष्वथ नु मीमांस्यमेव ते मन्ये विदितम् ॥ १॥

*yadi manyase suvedeti dabhramevāpi nūnaṁ tvaṁ*
*vettha brahmaṇo rūpam* |
*yadasya tvaṁ yadasya deveṣvatha nu mīmāṁsyameva*
*te manye viditam* ||1||

If you think, "I have known *Brahman* well enough," then you know little; for the form of *Brahman* you see as conditioned in living beings and deities is but a trifle. Therefore you should enquire further about *Brahman*.

Disciples, at the start itself I would like to warn you about one thing. Don't assume you have understood everything. What you feel you have known is miniscule. Talavakāra! my child, what you think you know well is not the full form of *Brahman*. Whatever you have known is very little, it is definite.

The form of *Brahman* you have understood from *devatās* is also little. Hence you are still only in the enquiring state about *Brahman*. Contemplate deeply and dwell in the inner state to enquire and understand *Brahman*. You are far from knowing it fully.

**Talavakāra** – Revered Guru! I am not knowing anything definitely. You who have sown the seed, you alone should put water and help it to grow. With your teachings which are like a flow of nectar, our fruit of knowledge would grow well for which you must bless us Svāmī.

**Jaimini** – There was once a poor countryman. He went from his village to the capital and then to the palace of the king. There he saw the garden in front of the palace and thought that was the palace and became supremely happy. He was wonderstruck seeing the decorations of the frontage itself. However the prosperity, wealth, ornaments, comforts, pleasures and entertainment of the palace were yet to be seen and experienced and it may be difficult to describe it. It is the same way with *Brahman* also. In the first learning itself, it may appear to have been understood. One should not be taken in by that and get fooled. One should carefully, continuously and consistently keep the enquiry of *ātmā* (Self) on till the true essence is understood.

**Gautama** – Respected Guru, we are listening carefully. Please explain at length.

**Jaimini** – As a growing creeper grows towards the Sun, and as water runs down a slope, in the same way a man's mind seeks the *Brahman*. However even the sense organs are unable to know *Brahman*. Whatever we understand through our experiences is only the reflection of the *Brahman*.

**Gautama** – In that case how to understand the non-reflective *Brahman*?

**Jaimini** – Child Talavakāra, just bring some milk for this cat to drink. (***Talavakāra* goes and brings some milk in a container and keeps it near the cat. The cat looks up at the *guru* for permission**

**to drink.**) Child! I told you to bring only milk. Why the container. Remove the container and bring only milk.

**Talavakāra** – (**Confused and surprised**) Svāmī! How is it possible? Without a container how to bring the liquid? Without a vessel it is not possible to bring the milk.

**Jaimini** – Let that be. Eh cat! Drink the milk and play happily with the parrot. Child Talavakāra, as you cannot just carry milk without a vessel, in the same way to bring *Brahman* to your knowledge a vessel is required. They are the set of sense organs as discussed previously (eye to the eye, so on). *Devatās* or gods having attributes are called *Saguṇa Brahman*, they are *Brahman* with attributes or quality. They help to show attributeless *Brahman*. Hence just by knowing *Saguṇa Brahman* don't feel elated that you have understood the truth.

**Talavakāra** – Then how to know the truth?

**Jaimini** – If properly enquired the truth can be understood in *samādhi*. (**For some time everyone sits silently in meditation. Then again the conversation gets started.**)

**Talavakāra** – Now *Brahman* has been well explained. However one should not say that one has understood it well or one has not understood it, etc. Among us, the one who realizes he has not understood *Brahman*, as well as thinks he has understood It, is the one who has realized It. It is beyond unknown things and different from known things. One can describe It as one has understood, but again one does not understand It fully.

**Gautama** – Svāmī! If I say I don't understand It and also say I have understood It, won't it be contradictory? Is It not a thing which will produce laughter?

**Jaimini** – Child, Gautama. Where is the place for laughter in that. *Brahman* is apart from both the states, hence what Talavakāra tells is completely true.

**Gautama** – Revered Guru, kindly tell us the same some more clearly and bless us.

**Jaimini** –

नाहं मन्ये सुवेदेति, नो न वेदेति, वेद च।
यो नस्तद्वेद तद्वेद नो न वेदेति वेद च ॥२॥

*nāhaṁ manye suvedeti, no na vedeti, veda ca* |
*yo nastad veda tad veda no na vedeti veda ca* ||2||

I do not think that "I know well." Nor that "I do not know"; I know too. Who amongst us comprehends It knows that he comprehends that It is not unknown to him.

Let us examine the statement: "I don't understand It and also I have understood It." As you understand, things which you are familiar with have a name and form. However in the same way it is not possible to know *Brahman*. *Brahman* does not have a particular form, nor does It have qualities like caste, character, action, and such *dharmas*. It is very vast. It does not have attributes and characters like small, big, short, long, birth, death, colour, shape, name, etc. It is just an illusion, if one tells one has known It by some attribute. Hence I don't understand It. Such a statement is completely correct. Now let us come to the next word. On further enquiry "now I understood, I think so." The meaning of this is, in *samādhi* it is possible to understand *Brahman*. Although it may not be possible to describe *Brahman*, you may know of some thing as *Brahman*. If a doll is made from the salt derived from the ocean and the salt doll is tied in a thread and put back in ocean and then the thread is pulled out after some time, will the doll be there? In the same way once in *samādhi* you become one with the *Brahman*, then is it possible to describe It? Even if a great poet like Vālmīki describes the milk pudding, is it possible to get the taste of it just by description? Each person has to sit separately in *samādhi* and experience It. Then alone will the person get the true knowledge of *Brahman*.

**Talavakāra** – By acquiring the *Brahman* knowledge what will one get? Kindly tell that clearly.

**Jaimini** –

यस्यामतं तस्य मतं मतं यस्य न वेद सः।
अविज्ञातं विजानतां विज्ञातमविजानताम् ॥३॥

*yasyāmataṁ tasya mataṁ mataṁ yasya na veda saḥ* |
*avijñātaṁ vijānatāṁ vijñātamavijānatām* | |3| |

He understands It, who conceives It not; and he understands It not, who conceives It. It is the unknown to the man of true knowledge, but to the ignorant It is the "known."

The one who thinks he cannot understand *Brahman,* is the one properly informed. The one who thinks he can understand *Brahman* is not properly informed. The knowledgeable ones know It is an unknown thing. The ignorant ones think It is a known thing. Though it is known in every breath yet it remains unknown.

प्रतिबोधविदितं मतममृतत्वं हि विन्दते।
आत्मना विन्दते वीर्यं विद्यया विन्दतेऽमृतम् ॥४॥

*pratibodhaviditaṁ matamamr̥tatvaṁ hi vindate* |
*ātmanā vindate vīryaṁ vidyayā vindate 'mr̥tam* | |4 | |

When the *Brahman* is known in and through every state of consciousness, it is rightly known, for one attains eternal state (by such knowledge). Through one's own self (or by oneself) one gains power, and through wisdom one gains immortality.

In case there is one who knows *Brahman* properly he attains immortality. He conquers death. He acquires the true strength from *ātman.* With the knowledge from It he attains a deathless state here, in this world itself. Thus by knowing It he becomes imperishable. Without this knowledge he is perishable. Over the time the ones who have enquired, researched and seen the *ātman,* such enduring persons have achieved immortality from this world. A person without strength cannot attain this knowledge. The true strength is Self (*ātman*) strength. From that strength alone the nectar, eternal blissful state will be attained. It is your birthright. You can attain it on consistent endeavour.

इह चेदवेदीदथ सत्यमस्ति न चेदिहावेदीन्महती विनष्टिः।
भूतेषु भूतेषु विचित्य धीराः प्रेत्यास्माल्लोकादमृता भवन्ति ॥५॥

*iha cedavedīdatha satyamasti na cedihāvedīnmahatī vinaṣṭiḥ* |
*bhūteṣu bhūteṣu vicitya dhīrāḥ pretyāsmāllokādamṛtā bhavanti* ||5||

If one has realized It here in this world, then there is true life, if he has not realized here, great is the destruction. Discerning the *ātmā* in every single being, the wise man rises from sense-life, and attains immortality.

Knowing that (even if other things are not known), one can be considered as having obtained everything. If one does not obtain that knowledge (even if you had obtained many things) you incur a big loss. It will be like you have gained nothing in this world. Hence intelligent persons who live life controlled by senses, learn to find *Brahman* in everything and attain immortality.

**Disciples – (Everybody gets up)** Revered Guru, with your teachings we become blessed. A many thousand salutations to you.

**(Then everybody sings together.)**

चिदानन्द रूपम् शिवोहम् शिवोहम्।

*cidānanda rūpam śivoham śivoham* |

With purity, full consciousness, and true understanding remove differences, destroy fear, realize the *Brahman* in *samādhi*. There catch it and hold on to It. Get your bliss in that experience. Remove the ignorance, attain happiness.

चिदानन्द रूपम् शिवोहम् शिवोहम्।

*cidānanda rūpam śivoham śivoham* |

***(Curtain falls)***

## SCENE 3

From Jaimini Maharṣi's *āśrama*, the route to Kailāsa mountain's deep forest. Gautama and Talavakāra are talking and walking along. They are bearing loads on their heads and shoulders.

**Gautama** – Friend, tomorrow our group leader, Kauśika is coming. To welcome him we have collected the required twigs from the sacred trees and plucked sufficient *durvā* grass. It is getting late. Have we lost the way?

**Talavakāra** – No, I don't think so, we are only going along the way our *pūjya guru* told. Here the *Śaptaśāla* trees are coming, after crossing them the *kadamba* forest comes.

**Gautama** – Friend, do you remember, near this forest only, last year's forest feast celebrations took place.

**Talavakāra** – Yes. How pleasant that day was! In our life it can be celebrated as a golden day. That day Devaguru Bṛhaspati had also come, had he not?

**Gautama** – Yes the *pūjya guru* had come. We all fell at his lotus feet and took his blessing. All this good fortune is due to the *āśīrvāda* of our teacher. **(Behind the curtain suddenly there is sound of festive activity.)**

**("Hail *devas*, down *asuras*, hail Devendra" such shouts are heard along with the sound of instruments.)**

**Talavakāra** – Friend! What sounds are being heard? Look our *āśrama*'s *koel* comes flying.

**Gautama** – Dear friend, yes it is our *āśrama*'s bird only. That shows we have reached near the *āśrama* and we are indeed following the correct path.

(Behind the curtain the sounds are increasing. Both are surprised, taking the load they go behind a big banyan tree and sit on a rock over there. The *koel* also sits on the branch of that tree. *Devas* with great enthusiasm, wearing grand clothes, blowing trumpets, beating drums, march and come.

Devendra also comes walking majestically. The fine silk shawl worn by him flutters wafted by the breeze. The scented flowers strewn on him fall all over the ground. Everywhere pleasant smell spreads. A white umbrella is held over his head to give shade and traditional splendour. He is fanned from either side by delicate feathered fans. The chieftain of *deva*s after winning over the *asura*s, intoxicated by the victory, with great fanfare comes along in a procession.)

**Gautama** – (**Pulling aside his friend**) Friend! What is this fanfare?

**Talavakāra** – Brother! The *deva*s have obtained victory in the *deva-asura* fight. Hence with great pride they are making victory sounds. A victorious man forgets himself, it is but natural.

**Gautama** – Whatever it may be, still it is not proper for the *deva*s to be so proud. Indra walks as though proclaiming he is above all.

ब्रह्म ह देवेभ्यो विजिग्ये तस्य ह ब्रह्मणो विजये देवा अमहीयन्त।
*brahma ha devebhyo vijigye tasya ha brahmaṇo vijaye devā amahīyanta* ||1a||

*Brahman* conquered for the gods and thus gods attained glory.

*fig :* **Talavakara and Gautama witnessing Devendra going in procession**

It looks like they have forgotten even God. It is God almighty who has helped them to conquer and because of that they have attained glory. However they don't seem to remember it. Instead of *tejas* is it not the expression of pride dancing in their faces. Do immortals have such pride? Good God! Where will this go and end? Let us see.

**Talavakāra** – Everything will end well. There is no need for you to worry. Just be quiet for a while. They are telling something. Let us listen.

**Gautama** – Alright. Let it be so.

**(Talavakāra and Gautama are listening to the conversation)**

**Devas** – Long live our king!

**Agni** – Our strong shoulders won the war. Hail our king Devendra! Let the side with more valour win.

**Vāyu** – With the strength of our army we defeated our enemies. Let our valour win. Let the crown of our king rise with honour.

**Devendra** –

त एक्षन्तास्माकमेवायं विजयोऽस्माकमेवायं महिमेति ॥१॥

*ta ekṣantāsmākamevāyaṁ vijayo 'smākamevāyaṁ mahimeti* | | 1b | |

"Ours indeed is this victory and ours indeed is the greatness."

With the strength of our shoulders, we made the enemies run taking to their heels. Hail our victory. The devas' strength is rising.

**Vāyu** – King of *deva*s is the immortal one, the *asura*s have been annihilated. Their entire sect has been destroyed. We have finished them right down to their roots.

**Agni** – Now our king Devendra is without enemies. He will be ruling all the three worlds as the one and only undisputed Emperor. Let his fame spread. Let his rule rise. Hail Devendra!

(Everybody shouts. Their victory cries made in high tone were sounding fearful shaking all the worlds. However that time, an astonishing event occurs there. Making a bigger sound, drowning the victory cries a huge fearful *yakṣa* appears.)

(That *yakṣa* which appeared in front of the *deva*s was actually a divine form. But the *deva*s with their brains overpowered by pride do not recognize it. Seeing the *yakṣa,* Gautama and Talavakāra are terrified and they hug one another out of fear. Initially they closed their eyes tight with fear and after a while they watch intently at the proceedings. They look spellbound at the scene unfolding in front of them. A very rare sight indeed for the denizens of the earth to see the *deva*s. Now added to that they are seeing this *yakṣa* also. They are transported to another realm and become completely oblivious of their surroundings and to the passage of time.

Here Jaimini Maharṣi, and the *āśrama* residents get anxious when the two prime disciples who had gone to the forest to collect some valuable herbs and *samidhā* for the *yajña* don't return in time. The worried *āśrama* residents urge the Maharṣi, to venture out and search for the disciples. The Maharṣi, an *antaryāmī* (knower of all happenings) is in knowledge of the happenings, however complies with the other disciples' requests and the entourage consisting of Jaimini Maharṣi, disciples, peacocks, deer, parrots, koels, starts from the *āśrama* towards the forest.)

**(Talavakāra and Gautama are conversing.)**

**Talavakāra** – Gautama! What we saw and heard was real wonder of wonders, wasn't it? It is unbelievable and astonishing; it has brought great peace to my mind.

**Gautama** – Yes my friend. Again and again thinking about this astonishing form of *yakṣa,* I am filled with great wonder. Further thinking about it gives me lot of happiness.

**Talavakāra** – Yes, a sight rare even to many *yogīs* and *munis*. What we saw, we could see only by the blessing of our *guru*. Let us prostrate in the direction where our *guru* stays.

(Both of them raise their hands and tell *praṇāmas* along the direction of the *āśrama*. Just then Jaimini Maharṣi and other disciples appear in front of them.)

**Talavakāra** – Pūjya Maharṣi *praṇāma*. With your blessings we witnessed presently the happenings of *devaloka*. What we saw further helped us to understand beyond doubt the supremacy of the *Brahman*.

*fig* : *Yakṣa* **talking to** *devas*

**Gautama** – **(With great excitement)** *Gurudeva*, we just now saw great *devas* like Agni and Vāyu humbled in front of the all-prevading and all powerful *Brahman*. Lord Devendra too could not realize the huge *yakṣa* was none other than *Brahman*. Umādevī herself came and told who the *yakṣa* was and erased the pride of the *devas*.

(The other disciples and the *āśrama* residents were unable to follow their utterings. They prod them to explain clearly all they witnessed.

They recount the arrival of *deva*s and their victory march full of pride and how the arrival of *yakṣa* right in front of their path halts their victory march and gives them a jolt.

The further scenes are explained very vividly by Talavakāra and Gautama as the *āśrama* residents listen.)

**Talavakāra –**

तद्धैषां विजज्ञौ, तेभ्यो ह प्रादुर्बभूव।
तन्न व्यजानन्त किमिदं यक्षमिति ॥२॥

*taddhaiṣāṁ vijajñau, tebhyo ha prādurbabhūva*।
*tanna vyajānanta kimidaṁ yakṣamiti* ।।2।।

*Brahman* indeed knew this conceit of theirs. He appeared before them, it is said. But they did not know, what adorable *yakṣa* it was.

**Gautama –**

तेऽग्निमब्रुवन्, जातवेद, एतद्विजानीहि किमेतद्यक्षमिति तथेति ॥३॥

*te 'gnimabruvan jātaveda etad vijānīhi kimetad yakṣamiti tatheti*।।3।।

They (the gods) said to *Agni*, the Fire-god,"*O* Jātavedas please find out what this *yakṣa* is." He said "Let it be so."

(**Devas address the Agnideva**) O! Jātaveda (a person who possesses the capacity to know all created things) What is the form of this *yakṣa*? Do go and find out? Why has it come in this place? Is it an illusion made by *asura*s? Ascertain everything properly and come back. Agni said Immortals! Let that be so. Here I am going in a second to find what illusory trick is that.

**(With pride he goes towards the Yakṣa)**

**Talavakāra –**

तदभ्यद्रवत् तमभ्यवदत् कोऽसीति।
अग्निर्वा अहमस्मीत्यब्रवीत् जातवेदा वा अहमस्मीति ॥४॥

*tadabhyadravat tamabhyavadat ko 'sīti* |
*agnirvā ahamasmītya-bravīt jātavedā vā ahamasmīti* ||4||

Agni hastened towards *Brahman*, *Brahman* asked him "who are you?" Agni said "I am Agni, indeed. I am known as Jātavedas."

Who are you? asked *yakṣa.* I am Jātaveda. I am also called Agni. I am famous for knowing all the things created, said Agni.

तस्मिंस्त्वयि किं वीर्यमिति।
अपीद् सर्वं दहेयं यदिदं पृथिव्यामिति ॥५॥

*tasmiṁstvayi kiṁ vīryamiti* |
*apīd sarvaṁ daheyaṁ yadidaṁ pṛthivyāmiti* ||5||

*Yakṣa* asked "what power is there in you?" Agni said, "I can burn everything whatever there is on the earth."

Such a person as you are, what is your inherent strength and how big is it? asked *yakṣa.*

**(Smiling)** Agni said, "you are asking questions like a small boy. Is there anyone who does not know my strength? I have the capacity of burning everything in this world."

*Yakṣa* took a small strand of grass and keeps it in front of Agni. Since it was morning time, small dew drops were shining like diamonds at the end of the grass.

**Gautama –**

तस्मै तृणं निदधावेतद्दहेति तदुपप्रेयाय सर्वजवेन तन्न शशाक दग्धुम्।
स तत एव निववृते नैतदशकं विज्ञातुं यदेतद्यक्षमिति ॥६॥

*tasmai tṛṇaṁ nidadhāvetad daheti tadupapreyāya sarvajavena tanna śaśāka dagdhum* |
*sa tata eva nivavṛte naitadaśakaṁ vijñātuṁ yadetad yakṣamiti* ||6||

> *Yakṣa* placed a blade of grass before him saying, "Burn this." Agni went towards it with all speed, but could not burn it. He withdrew immediately and said (to the *devas*). "I have not been able to find out what this *yakṣa* is."

O! God of Agni! You, who possess the strength to burn everything, burn this small piece of grass said the *yakṣa*.

Agni quickly pounces on that grass but was unable to burn it. Agni attacked the grass with the heat used at the time of final calamity (*pralaya*) but this small bit of grass did not burn. He was unable to understand who is this *yakṣa*? He who had never seen failure was now defeated. He lost his self-esteem and was embarrassed. Thinking of the fearful *yakṣa* itself gave them fright. His intelligence also seemed to get blunted. He felt the name given to him, Jātaveda (all-knowing being), seemed to be meaningless and an empty phrase, he thought. "Let me go to our king. Let me take asylum under the protector of immortals."

> (Agni defeated, head dropped in shame came running towards the *devas*. Devendra, the king embraced him and tried to pacify him.)

**Talavakāra** – *Devas* asked Agni, "What happened? Why are you running and coming in such a dishevelled manner."

Agni told "I am not able to understand as to who has come in the *yakṣa*'s form. I could not burn even the small blade of grass which it kept in front of me, I am defeated completely. You all ponder and do the needful."

> अथ वायुमब्रुवन्, वायवेतद्विजानीहि किमेतद्यक्षमिति; तथेति ॥७ ॥
> *atha vāyumabruvan vāyavetad vijānīhi kimetad yakṣamiti; tatheti* | |7| |

> Then *devas* said to Vāyu, the Wind-god, "O Vāyu, find this out — what this *yakṣa* is." He said, "Let it be so."

The *devas* said "Vāyu! You go and learn the truth of this matter. There is no place where you cannot reach. No senses which you cannot go through. There is no matter which you may not know. Hence kindly oblige us and find out."

Vāyu said, "Let that be so. Here in one instant I will learn about it and come. I will return with victory. You all don't have to worry." (**Vāyu goes running towards the *yakṣa*.**)

**Gautama –**

तदभ्यद्रवत् तमभ्यवदत् कोऽसीति ।
वायुर्वा अहमस्मीत्यब्रवीत् मातरिश्वा वा अहमस्मीति ॥८॥

*tadabhyadravat tamabhyavadat ko 'sīti* |
*vāyurvā ahamasmītyabravīt mātariśvā vā*
*ahamasmīti* | |8| |

Vāyu hastened towards the *yakṣa*. It asked him, "Who are you?" He said, "I am Vāyu, indeed. I am known as Mātariśvā."

*Yakṣa* addressed Vāyu, "Who are you? Why have you come?" "O! Fearful ghost form. I am Vāyudeva. I am well known as Mātariśvā. I move in the vast sky" said Vāyu proudly.

तस्मिंस्त्वयि किं वीर्यमिति ।
अपीदँ सर्वमाददीय यदिदं पृथिव्यामिति ॥९॥

*tasmiṁstvayi kiṁ vīryamiti* |
*apīdaṁ sarvam ādadīya yadidaṁ pṛthivyām iti* | |9| |

*Yakṣa* asked Vāyu, "What power is there in you?" Vāyu replied, "I can blow off everything whatever there is on the earth."

"Is that so?" exclaimed the *yakṣa*, "I am very happy. Let your arrival bring goodness. What is the strength you possess? Tell me correctly as it is. Not like Agni who came previously and boasted about something which he could not do and got into unnecessary trouble" said the *yakṣa*. Vāyu told proudly, "whatever is there in this world, I am capable of lifting it. I can lift, as well as throw them far. Mountains, I can lift and overturn. I can rotate like a ball, even the mighty mountains of Himālaya. Whatever help you want from me don't hesitate, go ahead and ask. I will do it."

तस्मै तृणं निदधावेतदादत्स्वेति।
तदुपप्रेयाय सर्वजवेन तन्न शशाकदातुम्।
स तत एव निववृते नैतदशकं विज्ञातुं यदेतद्यक्षमिति ॥१०॥

*tasmai tṛṇaṁ nidadhāvetad ādatsveti* |
*tadupapreyāya sarvajavena tanna śaśākādātum* |
*sa tata eva nivavṛte naitadaśakaṁ vijñātuṁ yadetad yakṣamiti* ||10||

*Yakṣa* placed a blade of grass before him and said, "you blow this off." Vāyu went towards it with all speed, but could not manage to blow it off. He immediately withdrew and said to the *deva*s. "I have not been able to find out what the *yakṣa* is."

"My greetings to you Vāyudeva. There is nothing in particular you have to do. Just lift this small blade of grass. That is enough" said the *yakṣa*.

Vāyu retorted, "What is so great about it? You have not asked a favour befitting my strength. What a pity! Your intellect is not as big as your size."

"Vāyudeva, you can make fun of me later. First you do the work I requested you to do" said the *yakṣa*. Vāyu then converted himself into a whirlwind and in great speed dived on the grass but he was not able to move it at all.

Vāyu was unable to understand as to who this ghost form was, having such astonishing strength. He felt utterly defeated and also was getting scared. Further he was embarrassed by the defeat and came running to Devendra.

Vāyu said "Immortal! *deva*! You must give me asylum. Annihilator of *asura*s! You must give me protection. Who is that *yakṣa,* what are his actions? I am unable to fathom. I also got defeated like my brother Agni and have come back. Further whatever action needs to be taken, we the *deva*s have to think properly and act." Hearing these words of Vāyu all the *deva*s sat and thought deeply.

**Talavakāra** –

अथेन्द्रमब्रुवन् मघवन्नेतद्विजानीहि किमेतद्यक्षमिति।
तथेति तदभ्यद्रवत् तस्मात्तिरोदधे ॥११॥

*athendramabruvan maghavannetad vijānīhi kimetad yakṣamiti* |
*tatheti tadabhyadravat tasmāt tirodadhe* | | 11 | |

*Deva*s said to Indra, "O, Meghavān, you find out what this *yakṣa* is." He said, "Yes. Let it be so." He hastened towards it, but it disappeared from his view.

*Deva*s then addressed Devendra, "Your majesty! Our Emperor! When we were having victory celebration after winning the *asura*s, this *yakṣa* has disrupted it, like a person disrupting during prayer time. Is it an illusion created by *asura*s? Or is it a plot conceived by Śukrācārya (*guru* of *asura*s)? We are not able to find the truth. You must only show us the way out from this danger and lead us towards the victorious path. Please do the needful, O leader of men! You must go and find out."

Devendra said "Immortals! Don't be scared, leave your worries. This second itself I will go and try to find out the truth."

Vāyu and Agni said "Protector of immortals! You must go and act very carefully. That ghost figure is like Bhīma, very strong. It possesses the tenacity of Bhīṣma. You must go with utmost care Master!"

Devendra said "Let it be so. I will be alert. I will try my best and try to investigate the truth." Then Devendra went towards the *yakṣa* without pride and without hurry. But suddenly the *yakṣa* form vanished from there and everybody was completely taken by surprise.

The *devas* said, "King you please come back. That fearful *yakṣa* has vanished. Let us go to heaven."

Agni said, "King of immortals! The ghost form got scared of you and ran away. You come back majesty, let us go."

Vāyu said, "Protector of all! Let us go back. O Majesty! Like a coward not able to face the opponent, it has vanished. Let us not search further for the ghost figure. It is time to start the dance entertainments. Urvaśī, Rambhā, Tilottamā and others will be waiting and pining for your arrival. We should not disappoint them. Let us go immediately."

**Gautama** – However Devendra retorted "*Devas*! What you are telling is not correct. I won't retrace my steps. If you all want you can go. I am not coming without knowing the truth behind this *yakṣa*. I am going further near to observe keenly and see. I feel there is some hidden thing in this."

स तस्मिन्नेवाकाशे स्त्रियमाजगाम बहु शोभमानामुमां ।
हैमवतीं ताꣳ होवाच किमेतद्यक्षमिति ॥१२॥

*sa tasminn evākāśe striyamājagāma bahu śobhamānāmumāṁ* |
*haimavatīṁ tām̐ hovāca kimetad yakṣamiti* ||12||

In the same region of the sky Indra came upon a lady, the most beautiful Umā, the daughter of Himavān. He asked her, "Who is this *yakṣa*?"

Devendra went with humility and reached the place where the *yakṣa* was standing. At that moment, from the sky the daughter of Himālayas; Umādevī, shining brightly with her remarkable beauty appeared in full form. Dressed with all kinds of ornaments and fineries, bright like molten gold, Umādevī shone forth. Devendra went near and prostrated fully on the ground and saluted Umādevī. He requested her help.

He saluted her thus –

Mother Komalavallī, many thousand salutations.

ईश्वरि। महेश्वरि पाहिमां। मातेश्वरि राजेश्वरि रक्षमां। उमादेवि महादेवि पाहिमां। विद्यादेवी दुर्गादेवि रक्षमां। भयहरिणि भवदारिणि पाहिमां। सर्वकारिणि दयापूरिणि रक्षमां।

*īśvari* | *maheśvari pāhimāṁ* | *māteśvari rājeśvari rakṣamāṁ* | *umādevi mahādevi pāhimāṁ* | *vidyādevī durgādevi rakṣamāṁ* | *bhayahariṇi bhavadāriṇi pāhimāṁ* | *sarvakāriṇi dayāpūriṇi rakṣamāṁ* | |

**(He sings and salutes)** Then addressing her he asked —

"Goddess, protector of the entire world Jagadambikā, you must protect and bless me. Who is this *yakṣa* form which vanished just now? Why did it appear? Now what is the reason for its disappearance?"

**(Once again Devendra falls at her lotus feet and salutes.)**

Umādevī answered Devendra: "Child! Indra! Get up. I will tell you everything. The *yakṣa* is none but *Brahman*. In the fight between *deva*s and *asura*s, it was *Brahman* which won the fight for you all *deva*s. Even though it was well known that this was the victory won with the help of *Brahman*, you have forgotten this in pride and ignorance and proclaimed "this victory is ours." *Brahman* realized this wrong notion and appeared as *yakṣa* in between you all. In spite of its appearance, you did not realize its greatness. Because of *yoga-śakti* of lord Parameśvara this astonishing form was created and it was worthy of worship. However, blinded by pride over the victory with *asura*s you all did not realize It. In front of *Brahman*, Agni and Vāyu lost their strength. Even then, you all did not realize who It was?"

**Talavakāra** – Hearing these words of wisdom Devendra prostrated in front of the *devī* and with all humility prayed thus "O Creater of the entire world! Jagat-jananī! My pride has been completely annihilated. Mother Parāśakti you must bless me. You bear with my mistakes and show me mercy and forgiveness."

## SCENE IV

Umādevī with compassion told,

सा ब्रह्मेति होवाच ब्रह्मणो वा एतद्विजये महीयध्वमिति।
ततो हैव विदाञ्चकार ब्रह्मेति ॥१॥

*sā brahmeti hovāca brahmaṇo vā etad vijaye*
*mahīyadhvamiti* |
*mtato haiva vidāñcakāra brahmeti* ||1||

Umādevī said, "It is *Brahman*. In the victory of *Brahman* indeed did you attain glory." Only thus Indra did know that it was *Brahman*.

"Devendra, I appreciate your devotion. The best wisdom is *Brahman* knowledge. With knowledge remove the fear. The victory you had is due to *Brahman*. Self-pride is due to ignorance. The *Brahman* is known as "delightful to all." Knowing that, destroying evil, live for long along with other *deva*s in the limitless, high heaven. Let all good tidings come to you," thus saying Umādevī retracted into the ether. Devendra returned happily. He came to the *deva*s and narrated what had happened.

*fig* : **Devendra salutes Umādevī**

Hearing him, the *deva*s reacted with excitement and exclaimed "Our majesty! Our king! Seeing you returning comfortably and happily we are very pleased. Because of Umādevī's blessing, we all have been enriched."

Devendra calmed the *deva*s and said "Don't feel great about yourselves. Let us leave self-pride. Let us not forget Mother. Let us always be in meditation of *Brahman*." Vedamātā is forgiveness personified.

कुपुत्रो जायेत। क्वचित् अपि कुमाता न भवति ।

*kuputro jāyeta* । *kvacit api kumātā na bhavati* ।

A child can do wrong but a mother never wrongs the child.

Akhilāṇḍeśvarī (ruler of all the worlds)! Umādevī! Himavatī! (Daughter of Himālaya), she will always be considerate to us and bless us. Let us praise her and worship her.

ईश्वरि महेश्वरि रक्षमां। मातेश्वरि राजेश्वरि पाहिमां।

*īśvari maheśvari rakṣamāṁ* । *māteśvari rājeśvari pāhimāṁ* ।

Goddess Īśvari, Maheśwari protect us. Goddess Māteśvari, Rajeśvarī protect us.

(Everybody sang together)

Narrating thus in detail the happenings they had witnessed, Talavakāra and Gautama prostrate fully and do *namaskārams* to the *guru* and repeatedly say, it was only due to the blessing of the *guru* they could witness such a *divya* scene. The *āśrama* residents dance with joy hearing these happenings. The *maharṣi* embraces them with affection and all of them sit below a banyan tree.

**Maharṣi** – Children! Since you were getting delayed all the *āśrama* residents were getting apprehensive. They were calmed and we all started and came here.

**Other disciples** – Friends! Without seeing you both our dear mother (wife of *guru*) became very much worried. With the consoling words of the *guru* she was pacified.

**Jaimini** – Dear Gautama! My child Talavakāra! You both are very fortunate. Whatever you now saw and heard are like explanations to my teachings. The *yakṣa* form was *Brahman.* This by now you would have realized. Vāyu is the fountainhead of wealth and prosperity. Agni is the seat of learning (*jātaveda* — he knows everything). Indra is the lord of the mind.

**Gautama** – Like a story it was, but how much philosophy is contained in this!

**Jaimini** – There is no surprise that Vāyu and Agni who went near *Brahman* were belittled. They went with lot of pride. They went to find who the *yakṣa* was. However, they could not even ask that question and they became dumb. The *yakṣa* asked them who they were and then alone were they even able to talk.

**Talavakāra** – Yes, Svāmī. In the presence of the *yakṣa* they could not move even a blade of grass.

**Gautama** – Because of the *Brahman*'s prompting only their tongues speak, words get life. Hence in front of that *Brahman* they got incapacitated, that was correct. Is it not?

**Jaimini** – What you are saying is correct. Devendra in order to know the truth, leaving his pride and feeling of self-achievement, with humility, wisdom and detachment approached the *yakṣa*. Seeing him in that state Vedamātā obliged him and appeared in front of him forgiving him and showering her blessing.

My dear disciples! Haimavatī addresses Indra and tells "in the fight between *deva*s and *asura*s, the one who won was *Brahman*." However, you *deva*s became proud thinking it was you who won the war. To remove that ignorance and teach a lesson to the *deva*s, the *Brahman* itself came taking the form of a *yakṣa*. Devendra! You leave your pride, control your senses, get over the temptations, sit in meditation and realize *Brahman.*

**Gautama** – Revered Guru, after that . . . . . .?

**Jaimini** –

> तस्माद्वा एते देवा अतितरामिवान्यान् देवान् यदग्निर्वायुरिन्द्रः ।
> ते ह्येनन्नेदिष्ठं पस्पर्शुस्ते ह्येनत् प्रथमो विदाञ्चकार ब्रह्मेति ॥२॥
>
> *tasmād vā ete devā atitarāmivānyān devān yadagnirvāyurindraḥ* |
> *te hyenannediṣṭhaṁ pasparśuste hyenat prathamo vidāñcakāra brahmeti* ||2||
>
> Therefore indeed these gods, Agni, Vāyu, and Indra are as if surpassing greatly the other gods. Because they indeed felt this *Brahman* closest. Because they, for the first time knew this as *Brahman.*

After that only did Indra realize it was *Brahman*. Having gone near *Brahman*, Indra, Vāyu and Agni, became more blessed. And it was *Brahman* in the form of the *yakṣa* who attracted the *deva*s towards him.

**Talavakāra** – Let these immortals become more and more excellent and let them shine.

**Jaimini** –

> तस्माद्वा इन्द्रोऽतितरामिवान्यान् देवान्, स ह्येनन्नेदिष्ठं पस्पर्श, स ह्येनत् प्रथमो विदाञ्चकार ब्रह्मेति ॥३॥
>
> *tasmād vā indro'titarāmivānyān devān, sa hyenannediṣṭhaṁ pasparśa, sa hyenat prathamo vidāñcakāra brahmeti* ||3||
>
> Therefore, indeed, Indra surpasses greatly, as it were, other gods. He indeed has come into close contact with this (*Brahman*). He indeed for the first time, knew that it (was) *Brahman.*

Indra went near it and with Umādevī's preaching he was the

first to understand it was *Brahman*. Hence he gained excellence in comparison to the other *devas*. He got benevolence of *brahma darśana*.

तस्यैष आदेशो यदेतद्विद्युतो व्यद्युतदा इतीन्न्यमीमिषदा इत्यधिदैवतम् ॥४॥

*tasyaiṣa ādeśo yadetad vidyuto vyadyutadā itīnnyamīmiṣadā ityadhidaivatam* ||4||

Of this *Brahman* there is this teaching: Such a *Brahman* is, as it were, like the lightning which flashes forth, or like the winking of the eye. Thus is the teaching based on the experience of brightness.

Some qualities of *Brahman* are preached here: It is like closing the eyelids and opening. Like a lightning seen between dark clouds, it is seen for a flash during meditation in the mind and vanishes. It is above the gods. Even when the lightning flashes for a short while, still its brightness and clarity gets spread everywhere and it can be seen clearly. In the same way *Brahman* also appears at times as a flash. Even for a second if seen, it can be observed with clarity. Just as the eyelids open and close without any effort, without our self willing, in the same way *Brahman* will also appear and vanish. In *samādhi*, during meditation without any disturbance of the mind, effortlessly it can be perceived. In this way only *Brahman* shines.

**Gautama** – Svāmī, Now I am able to appreciate your precious words that "knowledge of this *Brahman* which you have understood from the *devatās* is very small, very little."

**Jaimini** –

अथाध्यात्मं यदेतद्गच्छतीव च मनोऽनेन चैतदुपस्मरत्यभीक्ष्णं सङ्कल्पः ॥५॥

*athādhyātmaṁ yadetad gacchatīva ca mano'nena caitadupasmaratyabhīkṣṇaṁ saṅkalpaḥ* ||5||

And now the teaching based on the individual consciousness. It is thus: That *Brahman* is the one towards which mind appears to move. By the same *Brahman*, as mind, it is remembered. Repeated volition is also likewise.

When the mind makes a decision to get to know the *Brahman* those times one feels one has known the *Brahman*. That is, even when the mind is not able to catch up with the *Brahman* with the help of tools like thought, *Brahman* can be understood to some extent. This is a spiritual teaching to know *Brahman*.

**Talavakāra** – That which is mind to the mind, still mind is not able to reach it, and that which is a separate *ātmā*/spirit for all living things should rightly be called the fundamental spirit or *ātman*.

**Jaimini** –

तद्ध तद्वनं नाम तद्वनमित्युपासितव्यं; स य एतदेवं वेदाऽभिहैनं सर्वाणि भ
ूतानि संवाञ्छन्ति ॥६ ॥

*taddha tadvanaṁ nāma tadvanamityupāsitavyaṁ; sa ya etadevaṁ vedā 'bhihainaṁ sarvāṇi bhūtāni saṁvāñchanti* | | 6 | |

That (*Brahman*) verily is called the dearest of all. It is worshipped as the dearest of all. Whosoever knows it thus, him all beings seek for solace.

This *Brahman* is called *tadvanam*. That on which people can contemplate and that which is worthy of worship is the meaning of *tadvanam*. The one who meditates on it like that, that person will be liked by all living things and will look upon him with affection.

**Gautama** – The *Brahman* which is in the form of each person's inner *ātmā* if meditated as *tadvanam* is then the route to attain wisdom, to know the truth.

**Jaimini** –

उपनिषदं भो ब्रूहीति।
उक्ता त उपनिषद् ब्राह्मीं वाव त उपनिषदमब्रूमेति ॥ ७ ॥

*upaniṣadaṁ bho brūhīti* |
*uktā ta upaniṣad brāhmīṁ vāva ta*
*upaniṣadamabrūmeti* | |7| |

The secret wisdom has been taught to you. We have taught you the secret of *Brahman* indeed.

The secret of *Parabrahman* (to the extent I know) I have explained clearly. Now I will tell the ways to reach it.

तस्यै तपो दमः कर्मेति प्रतिष्ठा वेदाः सर्वाङ्गानि सत्यमायतनम् ॥ ८ ॥

*tasyai tapo damaḥ karmeti pratiṣṭhā vedāḥ sarvāṅgāni*
*satyamāyatanam* | |8| |

Austerity, self-control and action are its support. Scriptures constitute its limbs. Truth is its abode.

Penance, humility, *karma* are the feet of *Parabrahman*. As how man roots himself with his legs and stands, the same way only if the above qualities are there, will this understanding of *Brahman* stand firm. The Vedas are the different organs of *Brahman*. Truth is its armour.

यो वा एतामेवं वेदापहत्य पाप्मानमनन्ते स्वर्गे लोके ज्येये प्रतितिष्ठति प्रतितिष्ठति ॥९ ॥

*yo vā etāmevaṁ vedāpahatya pāpmānamanante svarge*
*loke jyeye pratitiṣṭhati pratitiṣṭhati* | |9| |

Whoever knows this *brahma-vidyā* thus, overcoming sin, is firmly established in the endless supreme world of heaven, overcoming all the sufferings.

The one who knows it like this, comes out of all negativity and bad things and stablizes himself in the limitless and exalted *svarga-loka*.

**Disciples** – Svāmī! What you have preached with love and affection, we receive with humility and devotion. With penance and daily regular prayer we will try to understand the *Brahman*. Since *Brahman* is attracted to and stays with persons not having deceit, untruth and selfishness, we will try to lead a life with these traits. Please bless us in this attempt. We are sure we will succeed with your blessings.

**Jaimini** – My dear disciples, what Umādevī preached Devendra and also the one I preached you is about the reflected *Brahman*. Now to receive the knowledge of non- reflecting *Brahman* and as to transform yourself into *Brahman* itself you will be helped by Vedamātā. She will be kind enough to bless you with the wisdom. I give you all complete benediction (*pūrṇa āśīrvāda*). Let good and blessed things happen.

(All disciples get up and worship the *guru*. *Guru* also blesses them individually. Later together they tell.)

ओम् आप्यायन्तु ममाङ्गानि। वाक् प्राणश्चक्षुः श्रोत्रमथो बलमिन्द्रियाणि च सर्वाणि। सर्वं ब्रह्मोपनिषदं। माऽहं ब्रह्म निराकुर्यां। मा मा ब्रह्म निराकरोदनिराकरणमस्त्वभनिराकरणं मेऽस्तु। तदात्मनि निरते य उपनिषत्सु धर्मास्ते मयि सन्तु ते मयि सन्तु॥

*oṁ āpyāyantu mamāṅgāni | vāk prāṇaścakṣuḥ śrotramatho balamindriyāṇi ca sarvāṇi | sarvaṁ brahmopaniṣadaṁ | mā 'haṁ brahma nirākuryāṁ | mā mā brahma nirākarodanirākaraṇamastvabhnirākaraṇaṁ me 'stu | tadātmani nirate ya upaniṣatsu dharmāste mayi santu te mayi santu | |*

Oṁ! May all our organs, speech, *prāṇa*, eyes, ears and other sense organs, let all function properly. *Brahman* should not leave us and go away. We also should not leave *Brahman*. Let this relationship remain stable and lasting.

The people who are happily immersed in *ātmā* knowledge should also bless us.

**Jaimini** – Children, it is getting late. Let us go to the *āśrama*.

ॐ तत् सत्

*Oṁ Tat sat*

***(Exit all)***

**Sūtradhāra** – (The person who conducts the drama — enters) O Elders! many many salutations to you all for being patient and alert, to have seen this small drama and to have given us enthusiasm. Our heartfelt thanks. We must see only good things with our eyes. We must hear only good things with our ears. Just as the swelling rivers lose their name and identity and mix with the sea and become one with it, in the same way we should know *Brahman* and become *Brahman* itself. Remove sin, go beyond grief and reach the exalted state. We should reach immortality. If even one person who sees this drama gets the inspiration to learn the main root knowledge of Upaniṣads then our purpose of enacting this drama would be achieved. Let the rising blessedness stay everywhere.

ॐ शान्तिः! शान्तिः! शान्तिः!!

*Oṁ śāntiḥ ! śāntiḥ ! śāntiḥ !!*

(Everybody sings together)

॥ॐ शंकर ॐ ॥॥ शंकर ॐ॥॥ शंकर ॐ॥

*||oṁ śaṅkara oṁ|| śaṅkara oṁ|| śaṅkara oṁ||*

सर्वं ब्रह्ममयं। रे। रे। सर्वं ब्रह्ममयं देवो नाहं। जीवो नाहं। प्रथ्यकबिन्न ब्रह्मैवाहं परिपूर्णोंहं। परमार्तोंहं। ब्रह्मैवाहं। ब्रह्माहं सर्वं आनन्दोहं। आनन्दोहं। आनन्दं। ब्रह्मानन्दं। व्यापक चेतन आत्म शिवोहं। व्यक्त। अव्यक्त स्वरूप शिवोहं साक्षि स्वप्रकाश निर्मलोहं नित्यमुक्त निराकार निर्गुण शिवोहं (आन)

*sarvaṁ brahmamayaṁ| re| re| sarvaṁ brahmamayaṁ devo nāhaṁ| jīvo nāhaṁ| prathyakabinna brahmaivāhaṁ paripūrṇohaṁ| paramārtohaṁ| bramaivāhaṁ| brahmāhaṁ (sarvaṁ) ānandohaṁ| ānandohaṁ| ānandaṁ| brahmānandaṁ| vyāpaka cetana ātma śivohaṁ| vyakta| avyakta svarūpa śivohaṁ śākṣi svaprakāśa nirmalohaṁ nityamukta nirākāra nirguṇa śivohaṁ (āna)*

***(Curtain falls)***

***(End of Kenopaniṣad Drama)***

॥ ईशावास्योपनिषद् ॥

# Īśavāsya Upaniṣad

## Introduction

*Īśavāsya Upaniṣad* is the last chapter of the *Śukla Yajurveda Saṁhitā.* The word *Īśavāsya,* by which the Upaniṣad is known, brings out the main theme of the Upaniṣad. The Upaniṣad starts with the statement "All the things which are seen and disappear in this unstable universe are all encircled by God Almighty."

Ṛṣi Yājñavalkya is the son of Brahmā, and the disciple and nephew of Ṛṣi Vaiśampāyana, who after a long penance for more than twelve years in the Mahāmeru mountains in the Himālayas was blessed with these truths preached by the Sun God who appeared with the face of *vāji* (a horse). Hence the Upaniṣad is called *Vājasaneyī Saṁhitā* and *Śukla Yajurveda Saṁhitā* as *Śukla* denotes the brightness of Sun god and the purity of the *Saṁhitā.*

The play opens in Mithilāpurī at the *āśrama* of Ṛṣi Vaiśampāyana. The *ṛṣi* is with his disciples staying in the *āśrama* and teaching them *Yajurveda*. The prime disciples are his two nephews. The senior one is Yājñavalkya who has been with the *ṛṣi* for a long time learning the Vedas and the junior one is a young lad, recently arrived. The other senior disciples are Bodhāyana, Triśaṅku, Vaikkānasa and Mahāsamasya.

Ṛṣi Vaiśampāyana is awaiting eagerly the arrival of Triśaṅku who had gone to a congregation of *maharṣi*s at Mahāmeru mountains, representing Ṛṣi Vaiśampāyana. The invitation had mentioned that all *ṛṣi*s are necessarily required to attend the meet and that no lapses would be tolerated. However Ṛṣi Vaiśampāyana chose to send his disciple in his place. Now he was waiting with trepidation as to the outcome of the meet to see if any strict measures were taken against the absentees. *Triśaṅku* arrives at the scene and relates the happenings at the meet. He informs that the meet was well attended by all the great *ṛṣi*s of the time. Vedavyāsa headed the meet while other great *ṛṣi*s like Vasiṣṭha Ṛṣi, other Saptarṣis, Ṛṣi Sadānanda from Mithilā, Durvāsā Maharṣi, Viśvāmitra Maharṣi, Devalāru Maharṣi and many other prominent *guru*s and clan teachers attended the congregation. However he had a bad news to deliver. Taking objection to the absence of Ṛṣi Vaiśampāyana, the prime *ṛṣi*s Viśvāmitra and Durvāsā have put the *brahmahatyā* curse on him equating the lapse to the killing of a brāhmaṇa. Though Vedavyāsa Maharṣi had tried to intervene and stop the curse, he could get only an atonement to the curse, according to which Ṛṣi Vaiśampāyana could come out of the curse in due course by following a *Chāndrāyaṇa*penance.

Ṛṣi Vaiśampāyana is crest-fallen hearing such a harsh curse had fallen on him. The *Chāndrāyaṇa vrata* was a difficult one to observe in his old age. Again, the disciple Triśaṅku tells him about the rejoinder his friend Vasiṣṭha and Maharṣi Vedavyāsa had got in his favour. He tells that considering his old age, he could get the help of his disciples to observe the *Chāndrāyaṇa* penance which would get him out of the curse. Ṛṣi Vaiśampāyana gradually reconciles himself to the curse and the happenings, which are going to befall him in seven days from then.

As the talk proceeds, the *ṛṣi* remembers that the daily *prasāda*s after the day's *Agnihotra pūjā* are to be sent to the king Janaka at his palace. He looks for his disciple Bodhāyana but as he had gone out on an errand at that time he asks his disciple Yājñavalkya to go and deliver the *prasāda*. A little lad, recent recruit, who has not yet seen the palace requests that he would also like to accompany Yājñavalkya. They both then depart to the palace. At the palace strange things take place. The King Janaka is not on his throne. The king's men request the holy men to leave the *prasāda,* but the short tempered and haughty Yājñavalkya refuses to either hand over the *prasāda* or wait. He chooses to keep it on the throne of the *mahārāja.* He then asks the young lad to keep it on the throne. However as the young lad climbs the throne to keep the *prasāda,* a voice is heard from the cosmos: "whoever ascends the throne of Mahārājā Janaka without prior permission is sure to die in seven days." The fearless lad as well as Yājñavalkya ignore this command and the lad, with the consent of Yājñavalkya ascends the throne and places the *prasāda* there. Later, they return to the *āśrama* and narrate the events as they happened. Now, Ṛṣi Vaiśampāyana already disturbed with the impending curse turns his wrath on his nephew Yājñavalkya who by acting without discrimination has now brought on a new curse on the young lad left in his care at the *āśrama.* The lad, of course is undisturbed and goes about with an air of non-chalance and jubilation stating "everyone who is born has to die either at a young age or old age."

In the meanwhile the king's soldiers arrive at the *āśrama* as they have been asked to bring in the disciple who had left the *akṣata prasāda* the other day on the throne. The grains in the *prasāda* had surprisingly grown manyfold in a day which had astonished the king. Hence he sent his men to invite the disciple to the *rāja-sabhā.* However the haughty Yājñavalkya again has his way. He refuses to go to the palace to see the king stating that he is not here to obey any orders of anyone even if it was the king and sends the soldiers back. Such a stand of Yājñavalkya further infuriates the Ṛṣi Vaiśampāyana who considers this as an insult to him.

The tension between the prime *guru* and the disciple further escalates when the lad, as foretold by the omen heard from the skies leaves the earthly abode to one in the heavens on the seventh day and the *guru* catches the *brahmahatyā* curse which transforms him into a hideous form having bloodshot eyes and red locks of curly hair that scares and repulses everyone. Seeing the *guru* thus, the only one who comes forward with strong loyalty and mental strength was his prime disciple Yājñavalkya. The rest of the disciples then take courage and go near their master, offering help as well as volunteering to undertake the difficult *Chāndrāyaṇa vrata* by which their master could come out of the curse. But Yājñavalkya in his anxiety to do the best to his master interrupt the proceedings saying, "it may be more proper for him alone to undertake the *vrata* singlehandedly rather than to delegate the task to some less deserving person."

But the *guru* who had been nursing a scathing anger against him at that time, instead of accepting his help pushes him away with strong words saying he does not want a headstrong and indisciplined disciple like him, who has belittled his other disciples calling them less deserving, to undertake the *Chāndrāyaṇa vrata.*

These words hurt the upright disciple Yājñavalkya who finally reacts strongly to Ṛṣi Vaiśampāyana's words telling him that if his *guru* feels so, he is prepared to go away immediately and he also does not want to keep the precious teachings of Vedas given by his *guru*. He was ready to spit all of it and go away without taking the debt of his teachings along with him. So saying, he goes and spits the *Yajurveda* so far taught to him. The *guru* and the rest of the disciples are taken aback at this sudden development. After Yājñavalkya leaves, the *guru* asks the rest of the disciples to partake those valuable teachings which Yājñavalkya had spat away and further instructs them to first become *ṭiṭṭirī* birds before partaking those parts of *Yajurveda* as it may be difficult to partake those regurgitated Vedas in a human form. The disciples obey their master and at once take the form of *ṭiṭṭirī* birds and assimilate those preachings. These *Yajurveda* preachings later became famous as the *Taittirīya* branch of *Yajurveda* and those disciples were called *Taittirīyas*.

Thus, the first part of the drama brings in an interesting human drama — the estrangement which occurred between two renowned masters of *Yajurveda*. One was responsible for giving the world the *Taittirīya* branch of *Yajurveda* while the estranged disciple later went on to become the master of *Śukla* branch of *Yajurveda*.

The human drama between the two giants was enacted for the eventual benefit of humanity, to bring out the knowledge and truth-filled Vedas to the people.

PART II

The second part of the play is held at Mahāmeru mountains in the Himālayas. It was here that the disciple Yājñavalkya becomes Maharṣi Yājñavalkya. The Sun god, pleased with his ardent penance of twelve long years blesses him with the preachings. Thus, the birth of *Śukla Yajurveda* and the *Īśavāsya Upaniṣad* which is the last chapter of *Śukla Yajurveda* came into being.

After getting estranged from his *guru* Ṛṣi Vaiśampāyana, a determined Yājñavalkya moves ahead in search of new frontiers of knowledge. Two disciples Kaṇva and Dadhyaṅga Atharvaṇa staying in the *āśrama* at Mithilā also accompany the adventurer to the Mahāmeru mountains at Himālayas. Yājñavalkya with a single-pointed mind and devotion spends his time in arduous penance in the rarefied and isolated regions of Himālayas at Mahāmeru mountains. The Sun god shows his benevolence towards the child of Brahmā — Yājñavalkya and comes out in his splendour. He tells Yājñavalkya, "Son, I was looking for the *uttama adhikārī* in whose bosom I can unload this great wisdom. I am highly pleased to find in you the fitting persona. Your dedication, keen intellect and fervent ardour to acquire the knowledge have assured me of your worthiness. I will come again in the auspicious form of *vāji* (horse) and impart this Veda unto you." So saying, he comes back in the form of *vāji* and imparted the wisdom to Yājñavalkya. In turn Yājñavalkya preached it first to his prime disciples Kaṇva and Dadhyaṅga Atharvaṇa. After getting the preaching of his *guru* Ṛṣi Yājñavalkya the disciple Dadhyaṅga Atharvaṇa expresses his wish to go back to Mithilā to see his aged parents and lead a life of a householder. The *guru* blesses him and sends him back saying the householder's life is indeed a worthy and important one.

PART III

This part takes place again at Mithilāpurī. Dadhyaṅga Atharvaṇa returns back to his home at Mithilāpurī. Obeying the wishes of his parents, he becomes a householder and begets a worthy son called Subodha. As Subodha grows up and becomes a young boy, the father thinks it is time to impart him the *Śukla Yajurveda* lessons he learned at the feet of Ṛṣi Yājñavalkya. Thus his son becomes his disciple. Here, the readers are blessed with the discussion between father and son of the most important and last chapter of *Śukla Yajurveda,* the *Īśavāsya Upaniṣad.*

The scene opens at Mithilāpurī in the household of Dadhyaṅga Atharvaṇa. He is talking to his son Subodha. The son implores the father to put on the mantle of *guru* and impart to him the lessons of the Vedas. The father is highly pleased with the request and starts imparting the teachings of *Śukla Yajurveda's* last chapter namely *Īśavāsya Upaniṣad.*

It starts with the *śānti-pāṭha* prayer giving oblations to the causative factor in the universe, the *Brahman.* It tells, the *paramātmā* (Almighty) is a whole entity. All that it creates has the same wholeness in them. Although *ātmā*s, which are whole, are created from the *paramātmā* which is whole, the *paramatma* even after the creation remains whole. Then the oblations conclude telling peace prevail for the continuation of the study of Vedas.

With the oblation to *paramātmā,* the study starts. All the eighteen stanzas of the *Upaniṣad* are discussed by the father and son.

After the preachings are over, the father asks his son to repeat the Upaniṣad preaching in brief to make sure if the son has grasped the knowledge. The son comes out with a clear commentary of the *Upaniṣad* in a concise form as follows —

> Present in all things is the God Almighty. This has to be understood well. Renouncing the desires, dedicating one's life to God and doing one's duties, is the best way to live. Forgetting that, if one leads a life of laziness, one will go to hell.
>
> *Ātmā* eludes the mind and sense organs. Differences like inside, outside, nearby, far off, one, and many will disappear once a person realizes *ātmā*. The true realized person is the one who sees everything in *ātmā* and *ātmā* in everything. Such a person can see no differences in things and people. He does not dislike anything and neither does he desires for anything. He is never unhappy. Without *ātmā*-knowledge, the *karma* and *upāsanā* of such a person will not help attain salvation.
>
> *Karma* and *bhakti* only, if followed together in a proper manner, can be of help. Otherwise one has to dwell in the darkness of ignorance.
>
> In the same way, worshipping the formless fundamental principal alone (unmanifested) or worshipping the one having name and form, the *kārya Brahman* (manifested) alone will not fetch results.
>
> However, by following both the *karma* and the *upāsanā* route combining it with worship of both formless and *Brahman* of name and form, the *sādhaka* or person will go gradually upon the path of salvation and finally obtain it. Father, please say if I am wrong anywhere.

The father is heartened that the son is indeed going on the right path and appreciates his keen intellect and grasping power. He further advises him for applying the teachings in the living process so he can expect to lead a worthy life.

The father and son conclude the *Upaniṣad* by repeating the prayer oblations to the supreme power, the *Brahman*.

# The Drama

**Characters**

| | | |
|---|---|---|
| **Vaiśampāyana** | – | A maharṣi staying in an *āśrama* near Mithilā. |
| **Yājñavalkya** | – | Principal disciple and nephew of Vaiśampāyana. |
| **Bodhāyana**<br>**Triśaṅku**<br>**Vaikhānasa**<br>**Mahāsamasya** | – | Disciples of Vaiśampāyana. |
| **A young boy** | – | Another nephew of Vaiśampāyana. |
| **Dadhyaṅga Atharvaṇa**<br>**Kaṇva** | | Disciples of Yājñavalkya |
| **Subodha** | – | Son of Dadhyaṅga Atharvaṇa |

Ministers, king's soldiers (includes king's retinue, bodyguards etc.), *ṛṣis*' wives, Residents of the *āśrama*.

| | | |
|---|---|---|
| **Venue** | – | Part I Mithilāpurī. |
| | | Part II Mahāmeru foot hills. |
| | | Part III Mithilāpurī. |

## PART I

### SCENE I

***(Curtain opens.)***

(*Āśrama* of Vaiśampāyana. The *maharṣi* is sitting on a reed mat. Disciple Yājñavalkya is fanning him with reverence.)

**Vaiśampāyana** – Dear child, has Triśaṅku arrived?

**Yājñavalkya** – No, uncle.

**Vaiśampāyana** – He should have arrived yesterday itself! His not coming till now is of some concern to me.

**Yājñavalkya** – Svāmī! Doesn't he have to go all the way to the Mahāmeru hills? On his way he may be visiting the *āśrama*s along the banks of the river Sarasvatī.

**Vaiśampāyana** – However I am keen to know about the intellectual transactions which would have taken place at Mahāmeru. Since morning my left eye and my left shoulder have been twitching. They seem to indicate the unfolding of some unfortunate events.

**(Triśaṅku enters.)**

**Vaiśampāyana** – Come, my child. (**Triśaṅku prostrates and does *namaskāra* expressing his respect. Vaiśampāyana hugs Triśaṅku affectionately and makes him sit near him.**) My mind was restless. Do tell me about the events that took place at Mahāmeru.

**Triśaṅku** – Vasiṣṭha Maharṣi and other *saptarṣi*s had come. Guru Sadānanda, the main clan teacher of Janaka Mahārāja had also come. The congregation of *maharṣi*s was headed by Vedavyāsa. Viśvāmitra Maharṣi and Devalāru Maharṣis were quietly observing who had come, and who had not honoured the invitation and were absent.

**Vaiśampāyana** – Who were the people who had not come?

**Triśaṅku** – My revered teacher, except you everybody had come.

**Vaiśampāyana** – Then what happened?

**Triśaṅku** – The names of the absentees were informed to the head. Vedavyāsa enquired in the *sabhā* as to what has to be done about the absentees? I then went to the podium and after paying my due respects to Vedavyāsa and other elders, explained the reasons which made you unable to be personally present. However Ṛṣi Durvāsā vehemently objected. He opined that if Ṛṣi Sadānanda has come from Mithilā, it is indeed wrong on the part of Vaiśampāyana not to have made it from the nearby *āśrama*. Ṛṣi Vedavyāsa tried to tone down the objection but it was not agreed to. The assembled congregation *en masse* gave the curse of *brahmahatyā* to the absentee.

*fig* : **Triśaṅku reporting to Vaiśampāyana**

**Vaiśampāyana** – There is no point blaming them. They had announced the repercussions beforehand. It is unfortunate I was not able to make it. But Triśaṅku, didn't my friend Vasiṣṭha Ṛṣi say anything in my favour?

**Triśaṅku** – He did get up and argue for your sake. However Ṛṣi Viśvāmitra took objection and argued against you. Once again Vedavyāsa Maharṣi tried to bring about a compromise but in vain.

**Vaiśampāyana** – Did they finally announce any atonement to the curse?

**Triśaṅku** – Yes, they said that by following strictly the *Chāndrāyaṇa vrata* the curse could be gradually removed.

**Vaiśampāyana** – Children, my disciples. The curse is one of the worst order. In seven days I will be caught up in *brahmahatyā*

*fig* : **Congregation of Maharṣis at Mahāmeru**

*doṣa*. In this old age, it may not be possible for me to observe a difficult penance like *chāndrāyaṇa*. I have no way but to submit to the curse of *brahmahatyā* without any redemption.

**Triśaṅku** – Svāmī! Don't feel so miserable. Your friend Vasiṣṭha Maharṣi has given a way out of this predicament too.

**Vaiśampāyana** – What is that? Do tell me quickly.

**Triśaṅku** – My lord. It was told in case you find it tough to observe the *chāndrāyaṇa vrata* due to old age, others close to you can observe it and pass on the fruits of their penance to you which will gradually bring you out of the curse.

**Yājñavalkya** - Svāmī! The greatness of Vasiṣṭha is remarkable. Even in an impossible situation, he is sure to come out with a just remedy.

**Vaiśampāyana** – Not only that my child. The amount of affection and respect he has for me cannot be gauged. I had assumed that as long as Vasiṣṭha is present in the congregation, nothing untoward would happen. But it is my ill fate that Viśvāmitra and Durvāsā opposed his words so vehemently and that he could not do anything.

**Yājñavalkya** – Honoured teacher, why should they oppose you? Do they have any hostility towards you?

**Vaiśampāyana** – They know me well and they have personally nothing against me. However Vasiṣṭha is a good friend of mine and Viśvāmitra has a habit of opposing whatever Vasiṣṭha says. Durvāsā too is impatient, full of anger and a strict disciplinarian. In their eyes whatever they had done is correct. It's only my fate, which has brought me this ill fortune.

**Yājñavalkya and Triśaṅku (together)** – Respected Sir, you should not be disturbed. We will follow the required penances and relieve you from this curse.

**Vaiśampāyana** – Children, my dear disciples! We will think about it later. Whose turn is it today to go to the palace?

**Yājñavalkya** – Uncle, it is the turn of Bodhāyana.

**Vaiśampāyana** – He has not come so far. Only today morning your aunt had sent him to the Gomatī River. Hence you go Yājñavalkya.

**Yājñavalkya** – Sir, yes! I will go as per your order.

**Vaiśampāyana** – Child, go immediately. Take the *prasāda* from the Agnihotri's sacrificial fireplace. Give them to the *mahārāja*.

Also don't forget to take the rice *akṣata* potent with *mantras*.

**Yājñavalkya** – Uncle, allow me to go and return. (**salutes**)

**Vaiśampāyana** – Child, do remember to take all the *prasādas*. Do take the holy water used for oblations and grains coated with holy ash and made potent by *mantras*. By the way the young lad said he wanted to see the palace. Do take him along.

**Yājñavalkya** – Svāmī! I will follow your instructions. Allow me to take leave. (**He goes**)

**Triśaṅku** – Respected Sir, please tell me what I should do. I await your orders.

**Vaiśampāyana** – (**thinking, meditating**) Child, please see whether Yājñavalkya has left. Till now I have not sent him to the palace. At times he acts in a hurry without any forethought. Hope nothing untoward happens by his going to the palace.

**Triśaṅku** – (**goes and sees outside**) He has left, Svāmī. The young lad has also gone along with him. Should I call him?

**Vaiśampāyana** – No, it's all right. Let him go. Whatever has to happen will happen. Nobody can fight fate. Let us go for the afternoon bath. Come, please hold my hand.

(The disciple holds his hand and Vaiśampāyana gets up.)

***(Scene closes.)***

## SCENE II

***(Curtain opens.)***

(In Mithilāpurī, Mahārājā Janaka's palace. The venue is the *darbāra* hall. In the middle a golden throne is kept. On either side, in high chairs ministers are seated. Soldiers with weapons are guarding the entrances and the throne. Yājñavalkya and the young lad enter.)

**Yājñavalkya** – Young lad, did you see everything? The palace filled with wealth, attractive silk garments worn by the palace inmates, people generally happy and prosperous roaming without a care. The scene here clearly brings out the saying that the entire world is a stage isn't it?

**Young lad** – Elder brother, what you say is correct indeed. However I am against the gaudy display of wealth.

**Yājñavalkya** – Then why did you insist that you should be brought here? Having come here let us look around and see the place.

**Young lad** – Elder brother, I was curious to see how Videha Mahārāja is keeping his palace from where he rules. I was thinking perhaps it will be different from the rest of the palaces. However, I find it is not different. It does not look like a residence of a person who knows the universal truth (*brahma-jñānī*). Why so many weapons and soldiers in this palace?

**Yājñavalkya** – Child, what you say is not correct. It is a critical observation. A man who is playing the part of a dog has to bark like a dog. As long as he is the king he has to follow the *dharma* of a king. By the way the king is not seen in the *darabāra* **(goes to the minister and talks)** "I am the main disciple of Maharṣi Vaiśampāyana and I have brought for Mahārāja, *akṣata* and *prasāda*s. Where is the king? I have to deliver this to him."

**Minister** – Please come. Take your seat. I am the prime minister of this country. Mahārāja is in meditation. Only when he comes out of meditation will the assembly start.

**Yājñavalkya** – We cannot wait till then. It is the order of our teacher to return immediately. However there seems to be a delay here. What to do?

**Minister** – Svāmī, the disciple who came yesterday did wait, met the *mahārāja* in person and gave the *akṣata*.

**Palace chief** – He also ate the feast served in the palace.

**Young lad** – The persons who have come today are different. We have to go immediately.

*fig:* **Yājñavalkya and the young boy hear a voice from the cosmos**

**Minister** – In that case, we will accept the *prasādas*. You can give it. . . .

**Yājñavalkya** – Honourable minister, we will give the *akṣata* (holy grains) made potent by *mantras* by *maharṣi* in the hands of *mahārāja* only, or else (**thinking, calls the lad and says something in his ears**) why don't we do like this?

**Young lad** – Elder brother, that seems to be a better way. Let us do that.

**Yājñavalkya** – As per the arrangement everyday one of *maharṣi*'s disciples has to deliver the *akṣata* to *mahārāja*. I have come today and have to return soon. Hence we will keep the *prasāda* on the king's throne.

**Chieftain** – Svāmī, you can do as you wish. However. . . .

**Young lad** – However what?

**Minister** – It is a divine throne. Except for the one belonging to Mahārāja Janaka's family, no one else is supposed to climb it.

**Yājñavalkya** – Even if you request me, I won't climb the throne. To touch a sort of metal like gold itself will accrue sin. I won't touch it. Child, keep the *prasāda* on the throne and let us go.

(The boy collects it and goes near the throne. That time a voice is heard from the cosmos: "The person who touches the throne of Mahārājā Janaka without permission will die in seven days." Hearing this the persons present there are perplexed and disturbed. The minister requests the lad not to go up to the throne. Yājñavalkya keeps quiet.)

**Young lad** – A person can die in youth or in old age, at six years or at hundred years, but death is certain. Getting scared of a sure thing like death, I won't retrace my steps. Elder brother, the death is only for this body, the soul does not get destroyed. (**Goes up to the throne, keeps the *prasāda* there and gets down.**)

**Yājñavalkya** – My dear brother, some ominous incident seems to await us. These are all signs of that.

**Young lad** – So you believe in those incoherent words uttered by some being from the cosmos.

**Yājñavalkya** – Dear brother, I am filled with some unexplainable uneasiness. Some bad fate seems to push us from heights of the mountain top into a deep ravine below.

**Young lad** – My elder brother, should such a small matter upset you? Of what use is all the knowledge you have gained from the Vedānta lessons learnt for so long?

**Yājñavalkya** – Dear child, it is aptly told that youth knows no fear. Whatever is going to happen is fate's play. We are helpless in this. Let us go and report to our teacher whatever happened. We will take asylum under his divine feet.

(**Within himself**) The young lad has got the curse that he will meet death. There our *guru* has got the curse of being caught by *brahmahatyā doṣa*. What is going to happen? Who knows? There is darkness everywhere. The teacher alone has to flash the light and show us the way. If I had shown some restraint such a thing would not have happened. O Lord! the young lad has to be saved somehow. You are our saviour. (**speaks out**) Child! let us go quickly and tell our uncle whatever events have happened.

**Young lad** – Yes, elder brother, let us go.

**(They are leaving.)**

***(Curtain closes.)***

## SCENE III

(It is the *āśrama* of Vaiśampāyana. The *maharṣi* and the disciples are sitting and conversing.)

**Vaiśampāyana** – My dear students, after hearing the events narrated by Yājñavalkya on his return from the palace, my mind is very disturbed. The young lad was given to me by his mother requesting me to take good care of him. I had given word that I will give him a good upbringing. However in four to five days, Yāma, the lord of death will snatch him from me. What a cruel fate?

**Mahāsamasya** – Revered Teacher, you should not get disheartened like this. You must pick up your spirits.

**Bodhāyana** – Svāmī, *smāraye tvāṁ na śikṣaye* (I am only reminding you but not teaching you.) You are aware of every wisdom. Still I am reminding you, *ātmā* or the soul does not have death. Just as a person discards his old clothes and wears new garments, in the same way, the *ātmā* discards the old body and takes a new form. Just as a snake which sheds out its skin, our body is discarded by the soul. You taught us this even yesterday. You should not be unduly disturbed. Please be brave.

**Vaiśampāyana** – All these happened because of Yājñavalkya. He is impatient and has no control on himself. If I had not sent him to the palace all these would not have happened.

(Yājñavalkya comes. He salutes the *guru* and stands near him. Vaiśampāyana ignores him and does not ask him to sit.)

**Triśaṅku** – Dear Revered Guru, we are getting unduly worried but the young lad seems to have no fear or worry. Like a prince about to be crowned, he walks around keeping his head high.

**Mahāsamasya** – Not only that, he is informing everyone about the impending happening and taking leave.

**Bodhāyana** – Like a student going for his studies to another country, he is moving with great enthusiasm.

**Yājñavalkya** – My brother is not like you all to shiver and get scared. He does not know the meaning of fear. Will a person having knowledge of Self get scared?

**Vaiśampāyana** – Hey! Yājñavalkya, stop your sermons and uncalled for comments. Who called you now here?

**Yājñavalkya** – A nephew has all the right to come near his uncle.

**Vaiśampāyana** – Hey, my brāhmaṇa relation. The relationship between you and me ended yesterday. When you were instrumental in pushing my younger nephew in the deep trench, any connection between you and me had been severed then and there.

(The young lad enters. Yājñavalkya is about to give an angry retort. The young lad gestures at him, asking him to keep calm.)

**Triśaṅku** – Revered Teacher, it is time for the evening *Agnihotra pūjā*. Shall we go inside?

**Vaiśampāyana** – Yes let us go. Come inside all of you.

(He is about to get up. That time a messenger comes from the palace and pays his respect. The *ṛṣi* sits down.)

**King's messenger** – Maharṣi! my *praṇāma*s. Yesterday the *akṣata* left by your disciple in the royal throne has grown well with great speed. The king was surprised seeing the unusual growth. He asked me to bring the disciple who brought it. Kindly send him.

**Vaiśampāyana** – King's soldier! (**pointing to Yājñavalkya**) He is standing there. You can come and take him along with you.

**King's messenger** – Svāmī, accept my *praṇāmas* (**goes near Yājñavalkya and pays him respect saluting him**). In the palace people have collected in large numbers and are keen to see you. The king has ordered to bring you soon along with me. He has also sent a chariot. You should kindly oblige.

*fig:* **Deliver me from death into immortality**

**Yājñavalkya** – O King's messenger! You can go and tell your king that it is not possible for me to come. I only obey my *guru*'s orders. Nobody else can order me. I cannot come now to the palace. If the king wants he can come here.

**Young lad** – Elder brother! I think in the present circumstances even if the king comes here he cannot see you. O! King's messenger it is sad indeed that you are going empty handed.

(The king's messenger salutes everyone and leaves for the palace.)

*fig* : **Vaiśampāyana under *brahmahatyā* curse.**

**Vaiśampāyana** – Eh! Yājñavalkya. We are all subjects of Janaka Mahārāja. It is our duty to obey the orders of the king. Most important, it is the king who protects and takes care of the brāhmaṇas and their *dharma*. Insulting the king's messenger is like insulting the king.

**Yājñavalkya** – *Pūjya guru*, if it is your wish that I should go, you should have just ordered me. I would have gone immediately.

**Vaiśampāyana** – I am ashamed to call you my disciple.

**Yājñavalkya** – My lord, I have not done any wrong knowingly. If I had done any mistake without my knowledge, kindly bear with me and forgive me. (**Falls flat on the ground and salutes the *guru*.**)

**Vaiśampāyana** – (**with uncontrollable anger**) Don't stand in front of me. Firstly you insulted my disciples and then you insulted the king. Don't further kindle my anger. My anger may burst and harm you. Before that, leave the place and don't stand in front of me.

**Young lad** – (**goes near and salutes**) Uncle, don't get angry. Where will your close kith and prime disciple go leaving you? Please forgive my elder brother and accept him. I will fall at your feet and pray "please accept him" (**falls flat on the ground and catches the *guru*'s legs**).

**Vaiśampāyana** – Leave, leave my leg. I have to go to the chamber where *agnihotra* has to be performed.

(He shakes off the lad from the leg and gets up. The lad is unable to bear such a reaction. He utters *mṛtyormā amṛtaṅgamaya* (Deliver me from death into immortality) and leaves his body embracing death. Yājñavalkya lifts him and takes him inside. There is a loud cry from the residents of the *āśrama* and the wives of *ṛṣis*. At the same moment the *brahmahatyā doṣa* catches the Maharṣi Vaiśampāyana. He gets converted to a hideous black figure. His hair changes to deep red locks and falls over the eyes, his eyes become blood shot — a figure invoking fear and repulsion.)

**Vaiśampāyana** – What an unbecoming and repulsive form. Well the young lad died and I am the cause of it. The curse *brahmahatyā* has caught me. Behind all these is the main person Yājñavalkya.

(His wife comes from inside, looks at him and runs away in fear telling it was not her husband. Other disciples don't come near seeing such a form. Triśaṅku is not sure and is in two minds to go near or to stay away. Yājñavalkya is the only person who approaches without fear and tries to be of service.)

**Vaiśampāyana** – O! O! The body feels like it is on fire. O, the body is getting dried and heated like glowing embers. (**cries out**) Thirst! Thirst! A thirst like this happens only during death. Give me water.

(Yājñavalkya fans him. Brings cool water to drink, without any aversion stands near and renders the required services. Seeing that the others also pluck up courage and come near.)

***(The curtain falls.)***

## SCENE IV

***(The curtain raises.)***

(Vaiśampāyana's *āśrama*. The disciples are sitting and talking.)

**Vaikhānasa** – Bodhāyana, did you hear the surprising and unbelievable news?

**Bodhāyana** – What is the news? Do tell me clearly.

**Mahāsamasya** – O! In our *āśrama* such wonders are happening like never before.

**Vaikhānasa** – Dear friend, what you are telling is in one way correct. A person knowing all the important disciplines, well-versed in learning, of high intelligence and keen to serve the *guru*, namely, the prime disciple Yājñavalkya, and the tiff between him and Maharṣi Vaiśampāyana is the prime news. However, presently I was not referring to that.

**Bodhāyana** – Then what else are you referring to? Please tell it clearly and not in a roundabout way.

**Vaikhānasa** – Yesterday, once the last rites of the young lad were over, he acquired a divine body and left in a chariot, which came from the heavens to take him. The gods were looking at it from the sky. They showered flowers and blew trumpets to express their blessings. It was a scene of great wonder.

**Mahāsamasya** – Is it? It is good news. There is a saying that people who die at a young age become dear to the *devas*. It has become correct in the young lad's case.

**Vaikhānasa** – Our *guru* is undergoing great difficulties. We should follow the prescribed penance quickly and get him out of the distress.

**Bodhāyana** – We ourselves should go to the *guru* and take permission. There should not be delay in this process.

**Vaikhānasa** – Friends, our *guru* himself is coming towards us.

(Maharṣi Vaiśampāyana was walking slowly and coming. On either side Triśaṅku and Yājñavalkya were holding him and coming.)

**Triśaṅku** – Svāmī, come slowly and carefully.

**Bodhāyana** – **(saying to himself)** Even good wood at times gets infected by insects. Everything should become all right in the course of time.

**Yājñavalkya** – Honourable Guru, please sit on this seat.

**Vaiśampāyana** – What a fate, it's only but the play of bad *karma*. Disciples, this unfortunate state has to be rectified. For that, help from all of you is required.

**Disciples** – Please order us, respected sir. We are ready to undertake any trouble and do the work immediately.

**Vaiśampāyana** – My most dear disciples, hearing your response I am very much pleased. Hearing it itself I am feeling half my trouble has taken leave of me and I am feeling better.

**Vaikhānasa** – Do order us quickly, honourable *guru*.

**Vaiśampāyana** – My dear disciples, listen carefully. There is only one way for me to get out of this *brahmahatyā doṣa*. That is to follow the route my dear friend Vasiṣṭha has advised. You have to follow the penance and help me to get rid of this curse. Without thinking about anything else, keeping the mind focussed, very carefully you must follow the *chāndrāyaṇa vrata*.

**Bodhāyana** – Let it be so, respected sir. As per your orders today itself we will start the penance. Do give us your blessings.

**Yājñavalkya** – Svāmī, why to trouble these brāhmaṇas who may not be having the required strength (*tejas*) to do the tough penances. I myself will do all the penances which are prescribed.

**Vaikhānasa** – Friend, don't be proud. We are also disciples of *maharṣi* like you. We are equally concerned to remove his sufferings. We also have equal right in giving our services and would like to put in our might too.

**Bodhāyana** – Yājñavalkya is filled with pride due to his superior knowledge. For a Self realized person this kind of pride will lead to destruction.

*fig :* **Tīiṭṭirī birds eat the Vedas spitten by Yājñavalkya.**

**Yājñavalkya** – Friends, I did not tell it due to pride. I only stated the truth.

**Vaiśampāyana** – (**angrily**) Eh! What is the truth? You told these brāhmaṇs were having less power (*tejas*). Is that the truth?

**Yājñavalkya** – Respected Sir, don't get angry. When many are doing the penance together, one person may tend to become careless and not follow the discipline, which may cause general harm. Hence allow me to do this single-handedly.

**Vaiśampāyana** – You are insulting the brāhmaṇas. If these people have low stamina then their *guru*, that means, I too have less *tejas*. It amounts to that.

**Yājñavalkya** – (**closing his ears**) Śiva, Śiva. I never thought like that. Even in my dreams I won't think of such a thing.

**Vaiśampāyana** – Enough! enough! Keep quiet. Stop your excessive and overbearing talk. First you belittled my sincere disciples. That day you were the cause of incurring the *rājā*'s displeasure. You invited the curse on my dear nephew. I don't want a disciple like this.

**Yājñavalkya** – (**with great humility**) Respected Sir, don't get angry. Be calm. Due to excess of *bhakti* and affection I have for you, I uttered such words. Otherwise I don't mean anything else. If I have told anything wrong please forgive me. Getting angry like this at this time will be harmful to your body.

**Vaiśampāyana** – Go away. I don't require any of your explanations. Against my orders you keep on talking. A person like you is not fit to be my disciple. Hence spit out the Vedas you have learnt from me.

**Bodhāyana and other disciples** – Respected Sir, please show some patience. Friend Yājñavalkya, go outside presently. By talking further you only will kindle his anger.

**Yājñavalkya** – (**angrily**) I am not going to gain anything from you, who is unnecessarily getting angry. I don't want the Vedas preached by you. I will give it back just now. (**Goes inside the curtain and comes back**) I have spitten out the *Yajurveda*. Like spitting out the consumed food I have spat out the Vedas.

You can collect it. Yourself and these disciples, stay in comfort. I am leaving the place.

(Seeing this harsh event, the disciples are surprised and the *maharṣi* is also for a moment taken aback. Then everybody becomes quiet.)

**Vaiśampāyana** – Eh, Yājñavalkya, you go peacefully. Son of lord Brahmā; you will live well. I am not blessing you now as a *guru* or as your uncle but as a brāhmaṇa. You leave the premises happily. In spite of the *brahmahatyā doṣa* I hope I am still having the *tejas* of a brāhmaṇa. I bless you, you will become successful in life as you wish.

**Yājñavalkya** – My teacher and preceptor, I am leaving. Forgive me for whatever happened. Many many *namaskārams* to you for blessing me (**falls prostate and pays his respects**). My friends, I am leaving. My *praṇāmas* to all of you (**he goes away.**)

**Vaiśampāyana** – My dear disciples. The burnt cinder has gone out. It is good in a way. You all take the Veda parts spat by him. I had taught him some very rare information. Those precious teachings should not go waste. You all collect it and eat it.

**Disciples** – How to eat what he has brought out? If you tell us the method we will do it.

**Vaiśampāyana** – Disciples. It may not be easy for you to eat them in this human form. You take the form of *ṭiṭṭirī* bird and eat them. That should be the best way.

(**Disciples go behind the curtain and come back.**)

**Disciples** – Honourable Teacher, as per your order we took the form of *ṭiṭṭirī* birds and ate the Veda parts brought out by our friend, without leaving a morsel.

**Vaiśampāyana** – Children! Since you ate those *Yajurveda* parts in the form *ṭiṭṭirī* birds, it will henceforth be known as *Taittirīya Saṁhitā* and you all will be called as *Taittirīyas*. Since you all pleased me and obeyed my orders, your fame will spread everywhere. These *Yajurveda* parts will be brought into practice in everyday *karma*. My full blessings will be with you all always.

**Disciples** – Now please give us permission to start the penances to remove your *doṣa* of *brahmahatyā*.

**Vaiśampāyana** – Alright my children, we will start today itself (**catches the hand of Triśaṅku and goes inside**).

**Bodhāyana** – Vaikhānasa, is it not sad that Yājñavalkya has left us?

**Mahāsamasya** – After staying together for fourteen years, leaving like this is indeed a sad thing.

**Vaikhānasa** – It started somewhere, leading to different things and finally it ended in an unfortunate way.

**Bodhāyana** – What to do? Fate does not leave anyone. However it is said that if elders get angry it will lead to the well being of the world.

**Mahāsamasya** – What you are saying is also correct. I have also heard that the quarrel initiated by Maharṣi Nārada will end in goodness.

**Vaikhānasa** – Let the unfortunate events end with this.

**Bodhāyana** – The clouds have cleared. The sun is shining. He will bring all prosperity and blessings.

**Triśaṅku** – (**coming along**) Friends, the *guru* asked me to call you all. The penances have to be started. He asked you all to take bath in the river Gomatī.

**Others** – We are all coming.

**(They are leaving.)**

***(The curtain falls.)***

## Part II

### SCENE I

***(Curtain opens.)***

(Yājñavalkya's *āśrama* on the eastern side of Mahāmeru Mountain. Seen behind the curtain, Yājñavalkya is standing in a one-legged penance and praying to the sun god. Outside, sitting under a banyan tree are Yājñavalkya's two disciples in conversation.)

**Kaṇva** – Friend, is it not 12 years since we have come here?

**Dadhyaṅga Atharvaṇa** – Yes, my dear friend. Now Jupiter is in the zodiac sign Libra. That time also it was in Libra. That makes it complete 12 years. How time has flown! It seems like today when we landed in Vaiśampāyana's *āśrama.*

**Kaṇva** – That time Yājñavalkya was coming out of Vaiśampāyana's *āśrama* estranged with his *guru.* We followed him along forests, wilderness, and deep jungles and reached this Meru mountain. Here our *guru* Yājñavalkya has undertaken deep penance. We have also been serving him since then.

**Dadhyaṅga Atharvaṇa** – Yes, We went to Maharṣi Vaiśampāyana's *āśrama* and decided to stay in the *gurukula* to learn *Yajurveda* lessons. However we have now got a different kind of experience. Our *guru* has undertaken a most difficult penance to know those branches of *Yajurveda* not preached by Vedavyāsa to Vaiśampāyana. We have got the good fortune of serving him.

**Kaṇva** – Friend, whatever happens, happens for the good. The son of Lord Brahmā, Yājñavalkya is not an ordinary *ṛṣi.* His penance will definitely end in success. He will come to know the knowledge of Vedas he is seeking. He will preach them to us. Let that be so. Well, you had been to Mithilā last month. Any particular news?

*fig* : **Yājñavalkya doing penance.**

**Dadhyaṅga Atharvaṇa** – At Mithilā I met my old parents. While returning I met Bodhāyana on the street near the palace. I told him the happenings here. He listened to it with a lot of interest. He told me about the happenings there.

**Kaṇva** – Friend, has our *guru* Vaiśampāyana come out of *brahmahatyā* curse?

**Dadhyaṅga Atharvaṇa** – After our *guru* Yājñavalkya left, other disciples together followed the required penance because of which Maharṣi Vaiśampāyana's curse got lifted and now he looks like his old glorious self, said Bodhāyana.

**Kaṇva** – What other news did he tell you?

**Dadhyaṅga Atharvaṇa** – Friend, apart from that he said the *ṛṣi* sons like Kātyāyana have also joined as disciples. Further Vaiśampāyana has divided *Yajurveda* into 27 branches and he is preaching it that way to them. He also told me about a surprising happening.

**Kaṇva** – What is that?

**Dadhyaṅga Atharvaṇa** – Mahārājā Janaka was blessed with a son having all the attributes a child can have.

**Kaṇva** – Dear friend, what is so surprising about a child being born, It would be better to tell it as good news?

**Dadhyaṅga Atharvaṇa** – Yes Kaṇva, it is indeed good news, giving lots of happiness. However what is surprising about it is that right from the time the child was born he is shining with *Brahman tejas*. He resembles the nephew of Vaiśampāyana, the young lad who met with an untimely death. People are talking that it seems the young lad himself has reincarnated as the son of Janaka Mahārāja.

**Kaṇva** – The ordinary folk will talk anything. But what is the opinion of the king, *maharṣi* and *rājguru*?

**Dadhyaṅga Atharvaṇa** – They also believe it. After *upanayana,* the prince will be sent to Vaiśampāyana's *āśrama* for *gurukula* stay, as Sadānanda Maharṣi himself said.

**Kaṇva** – It is indeed surprising, and happy news too. It is almost afternoon. Shall we go for bath?

**Dadhyaṅga Atharvaṇa** – Let it be so.

**(Both are getting up.)**

***(The curtain closes.)***

## SCENE II

***(The curtain raises.)***

(Yājñavalkya is seen doing penance behind the curtain. The Sun god presents himself in front of Yājñavalkya. Yājñavalkya prostrates and offers his *praṇāma*s to the Sun god and sings hymns in his praise.)

**Yājñavalkya** – O Sun god! My *praṇāma*s to you. The one who shows the way to salvation! You, who is the form of *Ṛg, Yajur* and *Sāmaveda! my namaskārams* to you. You, the lord who is the cause of the entire world, accept my salutations. You, who announces seconds, minutes and hours of the day; you, who are the form of the whole *praṇava* in the universe; who with your rays illuminate the moon; the protector of *deva*s and ancestors, I am saluting you.

**Sun God** – O Ascetic! I was pleased by your penance. You may ask for whatever boon you want.

*fig* : **Sungod blessing Yājñavalkya.**

**Yājñavalkya** – My revered god, I am saluting you in your entirety, to all the aspects of yours I am giving my *praṇāma*s. You must instruct me and bless me with the Vedas not known to Vaiśampāyana.

**Sun God** – Muni Yājñavalkya! I am highly pleased. You asked for a good boon. Here I am gifting it to you. The *mantra*s, which I am now going to preach to you have not been taught by Vedavyāsa to Vaiśampāyana. Hence, he does not know them. It is auspicious to instruct the *mantra*s in the form of Hayagrīva. Hence I will come back with the horse face and instruct you on this.

**Yājñavalkya** – God, do as per your wish.

**(Sun god returns with the face of a horse.)**

**Sun God** – My dear disciple, listen carefully. The *mantras* which I am going to tell you now are collectively known as *Śukla Yajurveda*. Initially they were taught to *Sañjīvanī*'s son Maṇḍūkayani and other *ṛṣis* by Prajāpati, and they preached it from generation to generation. Now you are getting this knowledge and are going to make it well known throughout the world. Hence your fame will stay till the world remains.

**Yājñavalkya** – God and preceptor, with your benevolence you must bless me to get a good understanding and expertise in this. With your blessing, there is nothing that cannot be attained. I am waiting, please show your consideration to me.

**Sun God** – O Ascetic! your penance, your devotion to your *guru*, your intellect, your knowledge and humility are all worthy of praise. In a way your leaving Vaiśampāyana with some differences was good for the world. I will also feel lightened unloading my heavy load of knowledge. There is nothing happier for a *guru* than to get a disciple who is an apt student to learn the knowledge of the teacher well.

**Yājñavalkya** – Respected Guru, everything is the act of the Lord who rules us. I have never differentiated between the God and the *guru*.

**Sun God** – Is that so my son, my disciple? I am very pleased.

**Yājñavalkya** – Respected Guru, if ever a situation arises when I have to decide between *guru* and God, I will be by the side of the *guru*. This is definite. This is the advice given by my honourable father Brahmā. Svāmī! Kindly enlighten me with your preaching.

**Sun God** – Listen carefully, Saumya!

ॐ पूर्णमदः पूर्णमिदं पूर्णात्पूर्णमुदच्यते ।
पूर्णस्य पूर्णमादाय पूर्णमेवावशिष्यते ॥

॥ ॐ शान्तिः । शान्तिः । शान्तिः ॥

*oṁ pūrṇamadaḥ pūrṇamidaṁ pūrṇāt pūrṇamudacyate* |
*pūrṇasya pūrṇamādāya pūrṇamevāvaśiṣyate* | |

*| | oṁ śāntiḥ | śāntiḥ | śāntiḥ | |*

*Oṁ* "that" (*Brahman*) is (infinite and) complete. This universe is complete. Out of "that", complete (*Parabrahman*) this (infinite) complete universe has come out. After manifestating this universe, the complete *Brahman* still remains complete.

(This is repeated by Yājñavalkya. The sun god continues to preach.)

***(The curtain falls.)***

## SCENE III

***(The curtain raises.)***

(Ṛṣi Yājñavalkya's *āśrama* in Mahāmeru mountain. On the reed mat the *muni* is sitting with *Brahma tejas*. On either side Kaṇva, Dadhyaṅga Atharvaṇa and other disciples are sitting. Conversation is taking place.)

**Yājñavalkya** – My dear disciples, the Vedas which the Sun god benevolently blessed me with, can be known as *Śukla Yajurveda* or *Vājasaneya Saṁhitā*. *Vāji* means horse. Since the Sun god came in the form of *vāji*, the horse, it got this name. The person who learns and practises these Vedas will be called as *vājasaneya*s.

**Kaṇva** – Such astonishing things are happening in our *guru*'s life. If somebody hears it merely, it may be hard to believe. But since I am with him all along, I know they are real happenings and I believe them.

**Yājñavalkya** – Children, there is nothing which is impossible in the world. Devotion to the teacher and continuous effort should be there. If it is so, there is nothing which man cannot achieve.

**Dadhyaṅga Atharvaṇa** – I have heard about the astonishing happening in the life of Viśvāmitra Maharṣi from my father. But now what is happening in our *guru*'s life is far more unbelievable.

**Yājñavalkya** – Disciples, all these are the blessings of the *guru*. In reality the Sun god gives his benevolence and reveals himself to everyone without differentiating between ordinary and learned, between sinners and ones who have done *puṇya*; further he induces everyone to do their *karma* (actions) and runs this universe. Is there any god equal to the Sun god whom we can look up to?

**Kaṇva** – Yes, Svāmī, the Sun god indeed is our protector and saviour. Our life here is due to his benevolence. Well, that apart, *gurujī*, my friend Dadhyaṅga Atharvaṇa wants to go home to see his parents. He hesitates to tell you this.

**Yājñavalkya** – My child, you may go comfortably. Go to Mithilā and give respects to your father and mother and lead your life doing service to them. But don't leave this learning process even for a single day. In due course with the wishes of your parents, you may marry a girl of good lineage and lead the life of a householder.

**Dadhyaṅga Atharvaṇa** – **(gets up and does *praṇāmas* to his *guru*)** Svāmī, I am disturbed in my mind that I have to leave you. Still I am not able to but obey the orders of my parents. It is a very difficult thing for me to decide. My mind is swinging in both directions.

**Yājñavalkya** – Child, don't be disturbed. Your going away saddens me too. Kaṇva will stay with me. He will remain a bachelor. You go home and lead the life of a householder. People taking to different paths of life — either an ardent *brahmachārī*, or the one who stays in forest and leads an austere life or the one who renounces and becomes a *sanyāsī* — all of them are dependent on the householder. Hence leading a life of a married man is also an important service to the society.

**Dadhyaṅga Atharvaṇa** – Svāmī, accept my salutations. Allow me to go. Friends, my *namaskārams* to all of you. I am leaving. (He gives respects to everybody and leaves. Everyone is saddened by his departure and wipes the tears caused by his leaving. He goes for some distance and comes back.) Svāmi! When can I see you next?

**Yājñavalkya** – Saumya! I have some more work left to do here in the Mahāmeru Mountain. I am planning to divide this *Śukla Yajurveda* into fifteen branches and teach it to my disciples. Later I will come to Mithilā along with these disciples. That time I will meet you and give you my blessings. You may leave with comfort. My wholehearted *āśīrvāda* is there for you and your descendants.

**(Dadhyaṅga Atharvaṇa again does *namaskārams* and leaves.)**

**Kaṇva** – Honourable *guru*, can I ask you one question?

**Yājñavalkya** – Child, why are you hesitant? I have won over my anger. You can ask me anything. Don't be afraid.

**Kaṇva** – If you go to Mithilā will you see Vaiśampāyana?

**Yājñavalkya** – Definitely, I will meet him. We will converse together forgetting our differences. I will pay him my respects with humility. He is also sure to bless me and embrace me. There is no doubt in my mind about this. Elders' anger will subside soon.

**Kaṇva** – Svāmī, please forgive me, if I had crossed my limits and questioned you. Somehow as it crossed my mind I asked you.

**Yājñavalkya** – There is nothing wrong about it. Time clears all differences and unhappiness. In due course all anger, differences, unhappiness, revenge, etc. vanish and melt away. Man has to learn to forget and forgive.

**Kaṇva** – Shall we go for the afternoon bath *gurudeva*? I think it is the time for it.

**Yājñavalkya** – Disciples, let us go. In the process of talking, time has passed off quickly.

**(All of them get up and leave.)**

***(The curtain falls.)***

***End of part II.***

# Part III

## SCENE I

**(Sound from behind the screen.)**

ईशिता सर्वभूतानां सर्वभूतमयश्च यः।
ईशावास्येन संबोध्यं ईश्वरं तं नमाम्यहम्॥

*īśitā sarvabhūtānāṁ sarvabhūtamayaśca yaḥ* |
*īśāvāsyena saṁbodhyaṁ īśvaraṁ taṁ namāmyaham* ||

The superior essence of all beings, being composed of all beings, to that divine power that is referred to as *Īśāvāsya*, do I humbly bow.

***(The curtain raises.)***

(It is the house of Dadhyaṅga Atharvaṇa. He and his son Subodha are sitting and talking.)

**Subodha** – Father, give me your blessing. The Vedas you had learnt from Yājñavalkya, you must kindly instruct me. Right from the time you told me about his life, I am very keen to know the knowledge he has imparted. Like a *chakam* bird keenly anticipating the rains, I am eager to acquire the knowledge.

**Dadhyaṅga Atharvaṇa** – Child Subodha, you have controlled your desires. You are following the disciplines of a householder with *niṣṭhā*. Further you have the aspiration to get salvation. Above all, you have come to my asylum. With great pleasure I will teach you the Vedas. Dear child, I will inform you in detail the sacred scriptures. Listen carefully. First let us recite the *śānti mantra.*

**(Both are reciting it.)**

॥ ॐ पूर्णमदः पूर्णमिदं पूर्णात्पूर्णमुदच्यते।
पूर्णस्य पूर्णमादाय पूर्णमेवावशिष्यते॥

॥ ॐ शान्तिः। शान्तिः। शान्तिः॥

*oṁ pūrṇamadaḥ pūrṇamidaṁ pūrṇāt pūrṇamudacyate* |
*pūrṇasya pūrṇamādāya pūrṇamevāvaśiṣyate* | |

| | *oṁ śāntiḥ* | *śāntiḥ* | *śāntiḥ* | |

**Subodha** – Revered Guru, kindly explain the meaning of this *śānti mantra.*

**Dadhyaṅga Atharvaṇa** – Saumya! (humble one), first let me explain the meaning of the words, then I will tell you clearly the in-depth meaning and philosophical concept behind it. "That is whole. This is whole. The whole comes out of the whole. Taking the whole from the whole, the whole remains whole. Let peace prevail."

**Subodha** – Svāmī, if from the whole, the whole is taken away nothing should remain, but you are saying in spite of it the whole remains. But this is against the precept of mathematics. How is it possible?

**Dadhyaṅga Atharvaṇa** – Young one, the principal matter of which the universe is made up is beyond the principles of mathematics. Let me explain clearly. "That is whole." "That" here denotes *Parabrahman*. That is the cause of the universe and "That" is whole. "That" is spread everywhere, filling everything and That is the material for all things in the universe. Everything in the universe is only but "That." There is nothing else apart from "That." "This" means the *Parabrahman* which has transformed itself into name and form. "That" which has become "this" *jīvātmā*, is also whole. The whole *Parabrahman* which is the cause of the creation has produced the *Brahman* of name and form. Though the creations of name and form may not be appearing whole, but if the disturbances and the blemishes in them are removed one can see the *chaitanya* form, which is whole, and thus *jīvātmā* is also whole. Listening and understanding the knowledge of Upaniṣads and words of the *parama guru*, the disturbances covering the name and form can be cleared. Once the ignorance is removed it can be seen, both "that and this" — that *paramātmā* and this *jīvātmā* — both are whole. What is appearing as

*fig* : **Dadhyaṅga Atharvaṇa preaching to his son Subodha.**

different forms can be realised as one whole. The meaning of many important scriptures can be known in this *mantra*.

**Subodha** – Let three kinds of peace prevail, you said. Please explain clearly the meaning of that too.

**Dadhyaṅga Atharvaṇa** – There can be three kinds of disturbances in our learning process. It can be *ādhidaivika,* from the heavens as natural calamities; it can be *ādhibhautika* by disease or caused by other beings around us; and *ādhyātmika* by disturbances in the mind as grief, fear, lack of interest, etc. It can be from unforeseen reasons or known reasons. Since our learning could be disturbed by any of these we say *śānti* (peace) three times. Today let me start discussing the *mantras* of *Īśavāsya Upaniṣad*.

॥ ॐ ईशावास्यमिदꣳ सर्वं यत् किञ्च च जगत्यां जगत्।
तेन त्यक्तेन भुञ्जीथा मा गृधः कस्य स्विद्धनम् ॥१॥

*oṁ īśāvāsyamidaṁ sarvaṁ yat kiñca jagatyāṁ jagat* |
*tena tyaktena bhuñjīthā mā gṛdhaḥ kasya svid dhanam*
||1||

> All this, whatsoever moves in this universe, including the universe, itself moving, is dwelt or pervaded by the Lord. Protect (your self) through detachment. Do not covet anybody's wealth (for whose is wealth?).

Child, let me tell you the meaning of this *mantra*. All the things which are seen and disappear in this unstable universe are all encircled by God Almighty. That is, all things virtually remain with God himself. Don't develop desires for other's things. Hence sacrifice everything and save yourself.

**Subodha** – Father, I understand this concept. That is, all things present in this universe belong to God and one should not covet or desire them. But can you explain the meaning of "save yourself by detachment?"

**Dadhyaṅga Atharvaṇa** – Everything is the form of *paramātmā*. In everything He is there. Without Him there is nothing. This you have understood clearly, isn't it? Once that thought is firm one sacrifices the feelings such as "that is my son, this is my wealth." Thus leaving desire, bondage and affection for all existing things, and only taking whatever is required to keep the life alive, as a gift from God Almighty, one has to lead one's life. Don't desire for anybody's things. Try to come out of the disturbance which plagues you in this universe with the thoughts of possessions. Continuously think and pray to God. Even if the article belongs to you, don't bind your mind to that.

**Subodha** – Not to desire for other's things is correct, but what is wrong in getting attached to one's own wealth?

**Dadhyaṅga Atharvaṇa** – Child, think properly about what I told you. How can any wealth be yours? Everything is *ātmā*. Everything is filled by God Almighty. Hence the concept of my wealth and other person's wealth itself is not correct. Mainly, you must not bind yourself with the things around you. There is nothing like a particular thing belongs to a particular person. There is nothing which is going to stay with us in this world. Everything is impermanent. Hence in these circumstances what is the point in desiring? To desire what? And for what purpose? This has to be given a serious thought.

**Subodha** – Father, now I understand. Once a person knows the truth of things, how he should act in his daily life becomes clear to him.

**Dadhyaṅga Atharvaṇa** – My Son, however this path of knowledge is not suitable for all. Only for a person who is ready to renounce everything, this will be useful.

**Subodha** – Svāmī! a person for whom it is not possible to embark upon the path of knowledge, how should he lead his life?

**Dadhyaṅga Atharvaṇa** – Child! a person who is taking the route of knowledge and understanding to know the Almighty should be firm in mind and should have depth of understanding. He should have a sacrificing temperament. Persons who are not having such a temperament should embark on *karma-mārga* (route of action). I will tell the *mantra* for that now.

कुर्वन्नेवेह कर्माणि जिजीविषेच्छतग्ं समाः।
एवं त्वयि नान्यथेतोऽस्ति न कर्म लिप्यते नरे ॥२॥

*kurvanneveha karmāṇi jijīviṣecchatagam samāḥ* ।
*evam tvayi nānyatheto 'sti na karma lipyate nare* ।।2।।

**(Both recite it together.)**

Child, the meaning of it is –

"The persons who wish to live in this world for hundred years can do so performing the *karmas* (actions) which are destined to them. Human being! this is the way for you not to get attached to action. There is no other way better than this."

**Subodha** – Father, what are the destined actions. Please explain clearly. Why should a person involved in *karm-mārga* want to live for hundred years.

**Dadhyaṅga Atharvaṇa** – Depending upon one's caste and

stage in life, the ordained action should be definitely done. The Veda states that the age of a person is hundred years. He can live up to a hundred years. It means till one is alive. Without dwelling on results one has to do the *karma* or action. Once you don't covet the results, the results won't get attached to you. There is no connection then between actions and the fruits of action. In this way you learn to live your entire life-span. Even if you happen to live for a hundred years just concentrate on your duties. Living a life of non-attachment to fruits of action for long will help you remove from your mind desire, hostility, selfishness, jealousy, the need to possess, etc. The mind becomes pure. Then with spiritual determination one can develop the temperament to follow the path of knowledge and truth.

**Subodha** – Revered Teacher, I have a doubt. What will be the status of a person who does not follow the path of knowledge and the path of *karma*? A person who falls from these two paths, what will happen to him?

**Dadhyaṅga Atharvaṇa** –

> असुर्या नाम ते लोकाः अन्धेन तमसाऽवृताः ।
> ताग्ंस्ते प्रेत्याभिगच्छन्ति ये के चात्महनो जनाः ॥३॥
>
> *asuryā nāma te lokāḥ andhena tamasā 'vr̥tāḥ* |
> *tāgaṁste pretyābhi-gacchanti ye ke cātmā-hano janāḥ*
> ||3||

A person not taking up the knowledge route or action route and conducts life as his mind dictates can be said to be doing annihilation of *ātmā*. The worlds they go to and reach after death will be filled with darkness, the worlds occupied by *asuras*.

**Subodha** – It is getting somewhat clear; still kindly explain in detail.

**Dadhyaṅga Atharvaṇa** – A person born as a human being should follow the path of knowledge to understand the truth or should keenly follow the path of *karma* where the fruits of action are renounced. If he is not following either of the paths, he is like an animal. They can be considered to have committed suicide. They will definitely fall in dark deep abyss and suffer. Both in moral conduct and spiritual evolution they will incur a deep fall. Just as a dead person does not show life expression, in the same way a person ignoring the knowledge-path will not show any presence of *ātmā* residing in him. They are persons devoid of *ātmā*-knowledge. They will be covered by the darkness of ignorance. After they die they will enter the form of *asura*s. Thus their journey is always downwards. Depending upon their bad *karma*s or actions they will attain birth in forms equal to their level.

**Subodha** – Father, I understand clearly now how to lead life in this universe and the results of not leading a life like that. Further what other things should I know? kindly instruct me.

**Wife of the ṛṣi** – **(enters)** Everything is ready for *pūjā* of Vaiśvadeva. You all can come inside.

**Dadhyaṅga Atharvaṇa** – Child, let us stop this discussion here. Tomorrow I will explain to you the concept of *Brahman*. Let us go inside my dear.

**(Both are getting up.)**

***(The curtain falls.)***

## SCENE II

***(The curtain raises.)***

(The house of Dadhyaṅga Atharvaṇa is seen. As before, both father and son are sitting and conversing.)

**Subodha** – My dear father, please accept my greetings. "A foolish person, disregarding the path of knowledge and who remains without self-effort in conducting properly the worldly affairs and who chooses living a life of laziness will be going on a path of self destruction," so you told yesterday. Today I am eager to know about *Brahman*. Please explain it in detail.

**Dadhyaṅga Atharvaṇa** – Child, as per your wish I will instruct you. However to explain a limitless concept in a limited language is a bit difficult. Still I will try my best. You hear it carefully, take the teachings in your mind, contemplate and accrue benefit from the wisdom.

**Subodha** – Svāmī, let it be so.

**Dadhyaṅga Atharvaṇa** – Saumya!

अनेजदेकं मनसो जवीयो नैनद्देवा आप्नुवन् पूर्वमर्षत्
तद्धावतोऽन्यानत्येति तिष्ठत्तस्मिन्नपो मातरिश्वा दधाति ॥४ ॥

*anejadekaṁ manaso javīyo nainad-devā āpnuvan pūrvamarṣat* |
*tad-dhāvato 'nyānatyeti tiṣṭhat tasmin-napo mātariśvā dadhāti* ||4||

**(Both recite it together.)**

The Self is the motionless one, swifter than the mind. The *devas* (senses) could not overtake; It ran ahead of them. Sitting, it goes faster than those who run after it. By it, Mātariśva (the element: Air) supports the activity of all living beings.

**Dadhyaṅga Atharvaṇa** – Child, *ātmā* is motionless and remains as one. It is faster than the mind. Even the *devas* (senses) cannot attain it. In spite of remaining in one place, it still moves fast and overtakes the things which move and goes further ahead. Due to its presence the god of movement *vāyu* is able to bring about all action.

**Subodha** – Father, everything is like a mystery. You said it is motionless. If so, is it a nonliving entity? Standing in one place, how can it go fast? Please explain each of its attributes clearly.

**Dadhyaṅga Atharvaṇa** – *Parabrahman* is motionless, that does not mean it is without strength. It only explains it is prevalent everywhere. *Ātman* is vast and is present here, there and everywhere. It is still and motionless. A person present only in one place can move to another place where he is not present. However there is no place where *paramātmā* is not there. Then how can it move? Where can it go? It is faster than the mind. In the world mind is considered to be the fastest. Faster than the mind means it cannot be attained by the mind. *Deva*s (senses) also are not able to grasp and know it. Here *deva*s mean our sense organs. Wherever the sense organs go *ātman* is seen there before. Hence it is said *ātman* goes ahead of the sense organs. Without itself undergoing any change with the help of Vāyudeva (god of movement), it conducts all actions in this world.The fundamental object is *ātman*. Staying in the sanctum of the *paramātmā*, procuring the strength from It the *prāṇa vāyu*, the main life force or Mātariśva (*vāyu)* is ruling over the living things.

**Subodha** – Father, I understand somewhat. *Ātman* is motionless and cannot be grasped by the mind. It is beyond the understanding of sense organs too. By the virtue of staying everywhere, it overtakes the things, even the ones which are on the run.

**Dadhyaṅga Atharvaṇa** – Saumya, very good. Hear the next mantra.

तदेजति तन्नैजति तद्दूरे तद्वन्तिके ।
तदन्तरस्य सर्वस्य तदु सर्वस्यास्य बाह्यतः ॥५॥

*tadejati tannaijati tad dūre tadvantike |*
*tad antarasya sarvasya tadu sarva-syāsya bāhyataḥ*
||5||

**(Both recite together.)**

It moves. It remains still, for those who don't have *ātmā* (*Brahman*) knowledge it is very far. For the knowledgeable, *ātmā* (*Brahman*) is very near. It is inside as well as outside of the entire universe.

**Subodha** – I think it is in continuation of the previous *śloka*. It remains as a moving thing as well as an immobile thing. *Ātmā* (*Brahman*) is seen in the form of a body by us with its attendant disturbances. Seeing the body moving we tell *ātmā* (*Brahman*) also moves. Without disturbance, we say that pure *ātmā* (*Brahman*) is motionless. For the knowledgeable, truth-seeking people, it is very near, for the ignorant and one embracing falsehood, it is very far. *Ātmā* (*Brahman*) remains inside and outside of everything. I understand clearly father. Please tell me further.

**Dadhyaṅga Atharvaṇa** – It is not so easy to understand *ātmā* (*Brahman*). I will tell you the characteristics of a person having *ātmā* (*Brahman*) *jñāna*. You can see for yourself the traits.

यस्तु सर्वाणि भूतान्यात्मन्येवानुपश्यति।
सर्वभूतेषु चात्मानं ततो न विजुगुप्सते ॥६॥

*yastu sarvāṇi bhūtāni ātmanyeva anupaśyati* |
*sarva-bhūteṣu cātmānaṁ tato na vijugupsate* ||6||

The person who sees everything in *ātmā* and everything as *ātmā* does not dislike anything. What is seen as different things in this world, he sees them as nothing else but *ātmā*.

He sees not only this body containing *ātmā*, he finds *ātmā* is present in everything. He is not indifferent or fed up with anything. If at all he sees something as apart from himself he may tend to find fault. If he sees the pure Self, present in himself, everywhere then how is it possible to dislike anything? I will tell you further, listen.

यस्मिन् सर्वाणि भूतान्यात्मैवाभूद्विजानतः।
तत्र को मोहः कः शोक एकत्वमनुपश्यतः ॥७॥

*yasmin sarvāṇi bhūtāni atmaivābhūd vijānataḥ* |
*tatra ko mohaḥ kaḥ śoka ekatvamanupaśyataḥ* ||7||

**(Both recite it together.)**

> When everything he sees becomes *ātmā* and he sees unity in objects then there is no attraction and no unhappiness.

Do you know how a man with Self-knowledge is? The one who remains equal both in happiness and unhappiness, the one who considers likes and dislikes as one, he alone is the true man with *ātmā*-knowledge. Since everything is in the form of *paramātmā* he won't find fault with anything. Once he acquires this even sight there is no ignorance or unhappiness, and nothing will affect him.

**Subodha** – Father, comparing the character traits explained by you, I find a whole of difference between me and a person possessed with true *ātmā* (Self-knowledge). Where is the wise person who sees unity in everything and who has no unhappiness or desires, and where am I? You must further tell me in detail a wise one's conduct and characteristics.

**Dadhyaṅga Atharvaṇa** – My dear child, think carefully. When does dislike and contempt happen? When something happens in the outside world which is different to one's wish and character, then the expression like, sadness, hatred, enmity, or at least one of them enters the mind. Such a thought of dislike is called *jugupsa*. Once such an unpleasant thought is removed, he sees unity in everything. The feeling that there is something different from oneself is the cause of hatred and fear. When one sees *ātmā* everywhere this contempt or *jugupsā* goes away. Once all things become his own *ātmā*, how can he get afraid of other things? The scientist who sees unity in everything cannot be gripped by sadness.

**Subodha** – Revered Guru, I understand. However to stabilize my knowledge please tell me about *ātmā* again.

**Dadhyaṅga Atharvaṇa** – I am very much pleased. I will tell you again.

> स पर्यगाच्छुक्रमकायमव्रणमस्नाविरगं् शुद्धमपापविद्धम्।
> कविर्मनीषी परिभूः स्वयम्भूर्याथातथ्यतोऽर्थान् व्यदधाच्छाश्वतीभ्यः
> समाभ्यः ॥८ ॥

*sa paryagāc-chukram-akāyam-avraṇam asnā-viragaṁ*
*śuddham apāpa-viddham* |
*kavir-manīṣī paribhūḥ svayambhūryāthātathyato 'rthān*
*vyadadhācchāśvatībhyaḥ samābhyaḥ* | | 8 | |

**(Both tell it together.)**

That *Paramātmā* is omnipresent. He shines brightly. He is without a body. He is unblemished. He does not have nerves. He is very pure. He is sinless. He is aware of everything. He rules the mind. He is transcendent to everything. He is self- created. He assigns the duty to permanent entities called Prajāpatis as to how to operate in the world.

**Subodha** – Father, *paramātmā* is all-pervading and has Its own self effulgence or *tejas*. However, kindly explain the expression "blemishless and without nerves" which you used for *paramātmā*.

**Dadhyaṅga Atharvaṇa** – Child, the *paramātmā* is filled in all places. It is self-effulgent. It is without a body, that is, It does not have *liṅga* form. It is beyond hurt and has no nerves, means, *ātmā* does not have a gross body. Only a physical body can get hurt. Only if there is body will there be disease. It is pure and does not possess wrong knowledge, means, It does not have a reasoning body either. Till now *ātmā* was described in negative mode as not this, not that and so on. In the above *śloka ātmā* is also described coherently as *kavi*. This word describes the quality of *ātmā*. *Kavi* means foreseer, a person who can see all the three time periods — past, present and future. *Ātmā* is the one who sees. Seeing, hearing, smelling tasting are not exactly by the eyes, nose and tongue. The execution of these activities by the sense organs is done by *ātmā*. In the same way, knowing everything is *ātmā*. *Ātmā* was not caused by any other thing. It was self-created. Hence it is also called *svayambhū*, self-established, and not an instrument made to work by another power. It is above everyone and It came about by Itself. It is all in all. It is the creator of Prajāpatis who are permanent entities. *Ātmā* dictates the *karma* for these permanent Prajāpatis (makers of the universe) as per their strength and the results of their *karma*. It regulates the creations, their proper functions and the works to be done. Due to Its truthful strength, planets move in regulated orbits and the seasons take place timely. Nature's different regulated work has been going on in the universe for crores of years systematically. Regulating things without an error, ruling with authority, power and efficiency is all the work of *ātmā*.

**Subodha** – Father, I understood many astonishing philosophies today. I want to be in solitude and contemplate about these things. Kindly give me the permission.

**Dadhyaṅga Atharvaṇa** – I am also getting late for *upāsanā*. Let us stop today's lessons here. Only by personal thinking and contemplation can one understand about the *ātmā*. Think deeply, repeat the *śloka*s, meditate and understand.

**(They arise.)**

***(The curtain falls.)***

## SCENE III

***(The curtain opens.)***

(Like in the previous scene, father and son are sitting and conversing.)

**Subodha** – Respected Father, *namaskāra*. I have a doubt. I have heard you talk about the path of knowledge, the path of *bhakti*, and the path of *karma* in different forms. However till now you instructed me about only knowledge and *karma*. You have not told me about *upāsanā*, why?

**Dadhyaṅga Atharvaṇa** – Child, it is a justified question. Doing different *karma* one has to live for hundred years, thus I have said in the beginning. In that the *bhakti* path is also included.

**Subodha** – In that case is it good only to do *karma*? or will *upāsanā* alone give good results or do both have to be done, combined in a proper manner?

**Dadhyaṅga Atharvaṇa** – My child, following only *karma* without *bhakti* or having only *bhakti* without proper *karma* is of no use. It is necessary for the bird which flies in the sky to have wings on both sides. Only with one wing can it fly high? Hence, persons having aspirations for *mokṣa* should not leave, either *bhakti* or *karma*. Now let us come to the *mantra*.

अन्धं तमः प्रविशन्ति येऽविद्यामुपासते।
ततो भूय इव ते तमो य उ विद्यायागं् रताः ॥९॥

*andhaṁ tamaḥ praviśanti ye 'vidyām upāsate* |
*tato bhūya iva te tamo ya u vidyāyāgaṁ ratāḥ* | |9| |

**(Both are reciting together.)**

They who worship *avidyā* (rites) alone enter into blinding darkness, and they, who are engaged in *vidyā* (meditation) alone verily fall into an even greater darkness.

Child here the word *vidyā* denotes *upāsanā* (meditation) and the word *avidyā* denotes *karma* (rites). A person who ignores his designated duties (*karma*) and spends his time in *upāsanā* invoking *devatā*s and keeps his desire only in that path, will enter into much more darkness. In the same way, without having knowledge of *devatā*s, if one does only *karma*, he will also enter into darkness.

**Subodha** – Are there differences between the results, accrued from *karma, bhakti* or following both together? Which of them will produce the proper goodness?

**Dadhyaṅga Atharvaṇa** – Child, I will tell you the results, listen!

अन्यदेवाहुर्विद्यया अन्यदाहुरविद्यया।
इति शुश्रुम धीराणां ये नस्तद्विचचक्षिरे ॥१०॥

*anyad-evāhur-vidyayā anya-dāhur-avidyayā* |
*iti śuśruma dhīrāṇāṁ ye nastad vica-cakṣire* | |10| |

One thing, they say, is verily obtained from *vidyā*. Another thing they say from *avidyā*: thus, we have heard from the wise who explained that to us.

Results obtained in life from knowledge or wisdom and results obtained in life from *karma* (action) are different. This truth has been shown by many wise ones from the days of yore. This is not anything known now as a new truth. For generations of *guru*-disciple traditions elders have accepted this.

**Subodha** – Revered Guru, kindly tell me the results when both the paths are followed in the proper combination.

**Dadhyaṅga Atharvaṇa** –

विद्यां चाविद्यां च यस्तद्वेदोभयगं् सह ।
अविद्यया मृत्युं तीर्त्वा विद्ययाऽमृतमश्नुते ॥११॥

*vidyāṁ cāvidyāṁ ca yastad vedo-bhayagṁ saha* |
*avidyayā mr̥tyuṁ tīrtvā vidyayā 'mr̥tam aśnute* | | 11 | |

**(Both recite together.)**

The person who understands both the knowledge-path and the *karma*-path, if he follows them in unison, then in this lifetime he can cross death by *karma*-path and by wisdom or knowledge he attains a deathless immortal state.

This Upaniṣad also tells us to combine *bhakti* and *karma* in life. In the world ruled by *karma*, it should be combined with wisdom, then in due course the path of salvation will be attained. Doing different *karma*s and *Agnihotra*s (prayer to the god fire) and following the *karma*-path diligently one can cross the impediments of death, and by doing *upāsanā* for *devatā*s he can attain the same mental state of *devatā*s. However, knowledge and action (*karma*) indulged in with selfish motives amount to the death of the *ātmā*. However, constant meditation with thought of the *devatā*s will help one to fetch *amr̥ta* (nectar), the most exalted state in life.

**Subodha** – I understand the importance of *karma* and *upāsanā*. Is it proper to worship a *deva* with form? Or is it proper to worship a *deva* without form? Please explain to me this too clearly.

**Dadhyaṅga Atharvaṇa** – Young one, I will tell you, listen carefully. This argument among devotees (*bhaktas*) did not occur just today or yesterday. Whether to worship a formless *deva* or the one with a form — this question has been raised from ages and has always been there. The Vedas speak definitely on the subject. Listen to it.

अन्धं तमः प्रविशन्ति येऽसम्भूतिमुपासते।
ततो भूय इव ते तमो य उ सम्भूत्याग्ं रताः ॥१२॥

*andhaṁ tamaḥ praviśanti ye 'sambhūtim upāsate* |
*tato bhūya iva te tamo ya u sambhūtyāgṁ ratāḥ* ||12||

**(Both are reciting it together.)**

Listen to the meaning.

> The persons who worship *asambhūti* (unmanifested–*prakṛti*) will fall into darkness. The persons who worship only *sambhūti* (manifested–God) will fall in deeper darkness.

**Subodha** – Svāmī. What is meant by *sambhūti*? What is *asambhūti*?

**Dadhyaṅga Atharvaṇa** – *Sambhūti*, the one which is manifested *Brahman*, is the one seen outside. This is the *Brahman* made for action *kārya Brahman*. *Asambhūti*, unmanifested *Brahman*, the one not seen outside. That is the force, the cause which produces the form. The person worshipping one alone, that is *asambhūti* or the fundamental cause alone or *sambhūti* that is *Brahman* of action alone, also called Hiraṇyagarbha, will continue to be steeped in ignorance. Hence he should worship both together. He should not consider one lesser than the other.

अन्यदेवाहुः सम्भवादन्यदाहुरसम्भवात्।
इति शुश्रुम धीराणां ये नस्तद्विचचक्षिरे ॥१३॥

*anyad-evāhuḥ sambhavāt anyad-āhurasambhavāt* ।
*iti śuśruma dhīrāṇāṁ ye nastad vicacakṣire* ।।13।।

सम्भूतिं च विनाशं च यस्तद्वेदोभयगं्‌ सह।
विनाशेन मृत्युं तीर्त्वा सम्भूत्याऽमृतमश्नुते ॥१४॥

*sambhūtiṁ ca vināśaṁ ca yastad vedo-bhayagṁ saha* ।
*vināśena mṛtyuṁ tīrtvā sambhūtyā 'mṛtam-aśnute* ।।14।।

**(Both are reciting together.)**

He who worships the Impersonal Godhead and the Personal God together, overcomes death through the worship of the Personal and obtains immortality through the worship of the Impersonal.

Worshipping *sambhūti* (manifested) what is obtained is different, and by worshipping *asambhūti* (unmanifested) what is obtained is something still different, thus the wise ones have explained the truth in the scriptures. However only the person who worships both can be considered a truly wise one. He will cross death by worshipping *sambhūti* and attain immortality by worshipping *asambhūti*. From this *mantra*, it is seen that the argument to determine the superior one between *bhakti* and wisdom is futile. Initially devotion should be shown to the God having name and form. Finally, sitting in high meditation and stabilizing in that, the formless *Brahman* should be meditated upon and at the same time, the one with form also has to be thought about. Both *bhakti* and wisdom should be combined prudently and learned to be followed together. One who learns to follow that path, by worshipping *sambhūti*, he will conquer death and sins accrued from wrong desires. By worshipping *asambhūti*, he will become one with nature and obtain the nectar.

**Subodha** – Father, your words which are like a shower of nectar and by your divine instructions I feel a great well being. Kindly instruct me further as to what I should know.

**Dadhyaṅga Atharvaṇa** – This *Upaniṣad* is coming to an end.

Further we can sing devotional songs and give salutation to the Sun god and end this session. You said you felt a great sense of well being on hearing these teachings. Whatever you heard, do tell them in short. Let us see?

**Subodha** – My dear father, is it possible for me to do it?

**Dadhyaṅga Atharvaṇa** – With practice, you must learn and perfect the ability to recall. The practice should not be done for the student by the teacher. My blessings are with you, do come out and tell me boldly.

**Subodha** – Svāmī, I will tell **(thinks for a while, then gets up tells *abhivādaye* and does *namaskāra* to the *guru*)**. I will try to tell without leaving out any basic concepts. Present in all things is God Almighty; this has to be understood well. The best way to live is renouncing the desires, dedicating one's life to God, and doing one's duties. Forgetting that, if one leads a life of laziness, one will go to hell. *Ātmā* eludes mind and sense organs. The differences like inside-outside, nearby-far off, one-many will disappear once a person realizes *ātmā*. The true realised person is the one who sees everything in *ātmā* and *ātmā* in everything. Such a person can see no differences in different things and people. He does not dislike anything, neither has he desire for anything. He is never unhappy. Without *ātmā*-knowledge, the *karma* and *upāsanā* of such a person will not help him achieve salvation. *Karma* and *bhakti*, if followed together in a proper manner can be of help or else one has to dwell in the darkness of ignorance. In the same way, worshipping the formless fundamental principle alone (unmanifested) or worshipping the one having name and form, the *kārya Brahman* (manifested), alone will not fetch results. However by following *karma* and *upāsanā* route combining it with worship of both formless *Brahman* and *Brahman* of name and form, the *sādhaka* or the person on the path of endevour will go gradually up towards salvation and finally obtain it. Father, please tell me if I am wrong anywhere.

**Dadhyaṅga Atharvaṇa** – Child, you made it clear in a very good and short way. I am very proud to have you as my son and disciple. Now let us sing devotional songs. You also sing along with me. I will tell you further.

हिरण्मयेन पात्रेण सत्यस्यापिहितं मुखम् ।
तत्त्वं पूषन्नपावृणु सत्यधर्माय दृष्टये ॥१५॥

*hiraṇmayena pātreṇa satya-syāpi-hitaṁ mukham* |
*tattvaṁ pūṣanna pāvṛṇu satya-dharmāya dṛṣṭaye* ||15||

O Sun god! With a glittering gold lid the face of truth has been hidden. You Pūṣan, the fosterer! remove the lid, so that I can visualise the Truth.

पूषन्नेकर्षे यम सूर्य प्राजापत्य व्यूह रश्मीन् समूह तेजः ।
यत्ते रूपं कल्याणतमं तत्ते पश्यामि योऽसावसौ पुरुषः सोऽहमस्मि ॥१६॥

*pūṣanne karṣe yama sūrya prājāpatya vyūha raśmīn samūha tejaḥ* |
*yatte rūpaṁ kalyāṇatamaṁ tatte paśyāmi yo 'sāvasau puruṣaḥ so 'ham asmi* ||16||

O God! Who takes care of this world, the universe, the One Who moves alone in the outer space, as per His regulation controls everything and rules the world, kindly decrease the power of your rays and show your inner brilliance. Bless me to see your exalted, pure prosperity-producing form. In your Sun orbit I am the form of *puruṣa* representation of *ātmā*.

**Subodha** – Father, I have not heard such heart-moving prayers about the Sun god. He alone takes care of all the worlds. Even for a second if the Sun is not there, what will happen to this world?

**Dadhyaṅga Atharvaṇa** - It is said that this prayer is recited in death bed by a person. However it need not be thought of as a prayer by an old person in his death bed. The feeling of "I" and the pride associated with it is nullified on realizing the meaning of this *mantra*.

*fig* : **The Virāṭ-rūpa**

A person filled with the feeling of "I," when he enters meditation will realise that such separate entity feeling has to die. This prayer will be the last prayer when his ego dies. Behind the limited knowledge lies the complete, pure knowledge. However it is covered by ignorance. To reach the true *Brahman*, there is a brilliant cover. I, who is the truth seeker, for my sight, for me to go ahead on that route kindly open the cover or clear the way. Hearing the heart-felt prayers, once you relent and open the cover I see your real form. Seeing that I get very surprised because I see myself there. I am that, the *puruṣa* inside you.

**Subodha** – The one who knows *Brahman* becomes *Brahman* himself. However it is not anything which is difficult to be experienced. It is a concrete truth. It is possible to experience and further live life. But the one who knows *Brahman* is not the same man. He just moves around with the body received due to his *karma*. In reality he is *Brahman*. *Brahman* can be understood only by *Brahman*.

**Dadhyaṅga Atharvaṇa** – Child, listen to the other two devotional songs.

वायुरनिलममृतमथेदं भस्मान्तग्ं शरीरम्।
ॐ क्रतो स्मर कृतꣳ स्मर क्रतो स्मर कृतग्ं स्मर ॥१७॥

*vāyur-anilam amṛtam athedaṁ bhasmāntagṁ śarīram |*
*oṁ krato smara kṛtaṁ smara krato smara kṛtagṁ smara | | 17 | |*

अग्ने नय सुपथा राये अस्मान् विश्वानि देव वयुनानि विद्वान्।
युयोध्यस्मज्जुहुराणमेनो भूयिष्ठां ते नमउक्तिं विधेम ॥१८॥

*agne naya supathā rāye-asmān viśvāni deva vayunāni vidvān |*
*yuyo-dhyas-majjuhu-rāṇa-meno bhūyiṣṭhāṁ te nam-uktiṁ vidhema | | 18 | |*

Let my *prāṇa* (breath) become one with the outside indestructible *prāṇa*. Then let this body turn into ashes. O Almighty! In the form of *oṁkāra* think of me, think of the actions done by me.

O! fire the wealth obtained by destiny, help me to use it in a good way! *Deva,* you are aware of all the thoughts. Kindly destroy the sin accruing from the unknown hidden way. I surrender my oblations to you and pray to you.

**Subodha** – Father, these devotional songs can one recite in his dying state? When a person undergoes death, his *prāṇa* will naturally mingle in the outside *prāṇa* which is present everywhere. After the breath leaves the body, the body only has to become ashes. That time the *jīvātmā* has to think and pray to *paramātmā,* the *oṁkāra.* He has to contemplate on the actions already done by him. That time the mighty God who is also the fire, who is aware of everything (the deliberations and actions), He must take the person along the right path in order to get the fruits of actions. He must help him to get rid of his sins. For Him our numerous salutations are due. What a supreme prayer! It raises the level of mind and the man.

**Dadhyaṅga Atharvaṇa** – Child, this prayer can also be interpreted in a different way. "Eh! determined and decisive *jīva*, keep repeating the name of god. Think of His actions. Eh! *jīva* leave your individualness and think about His actions. Eh! brilliant fire, who is the director of the right path, you are aware of all philosophies in the world. Take us through an easy path to realize eternal bliss. Remove the sins which take us along the round about path. I request you again and again with great humbleness, since I am in my death bed I cannot do any service now. Only I can repeat the word *namaskāra*."

**Subodha** – My dear father, many *namaskāra*s to you. Today and everyday take me along the righteous path. Further please instruct me as to how should I conduct myself.

**Dadhyaṅga Atharvaṇa** – My affectionate child, I appreciate your intellect and grasping power. You have exceeded me in wisdom. Once having learned your lessons thoroughly, you stand as per those teachings. Live in the path shown by this Upaniṣad and be blessed with well-being in multiples. Let us chant the *śānti-pāṭha*.

॥ ॐ पूर्णमदः पूर्णमिदं पूर्णात् पूर्णमुदच्यते।
पूर्णस्य पूर्णमादाय पूर्णमेवावशिष्यते॥
॥ ॐ शान्तिः। शान्तिः। शान्तिः॥

*oṁ pūrṇamadaḥ pūrṇamidaṁ pūrṇāt pūrṇamudacyate* |
*pūrṇasya pūrṇamādāya pūrṇamevāvaśiṣyate* | |

| | *oṁ śāntiḥ* | *śāntiḥ* | *śāntiḥ* | |

***(The curtain falls.)***

**End of *Īśavāsya Upaniṣad***

॥ प्रश्नोपनिषत् ॥

# Praśna Upaniṣad

## Introduction

The Upaniṣad is aptly named *Praśna* (question). There are six ardent seekers of *brahma-vidyā*. They are assailed with numerous questions as any seeker will be, when he tries to understand the ultimate reality — *parabrahman*. The play starts at Bhāradvāja *āśrama* in Prayāga. On the invitation of Bhāradvāja muni's son Sukeśa, his five companions had arrived at the *āśrama*. They are Satyakāma son of Śibi, Gārgya (Sauryāyaṇi) grandson of Sūrya, Kauśalya son of Ṛṣi Aśvala, Bhārgava from the Vidarbha country and Kabandhi son of Ṛṣi Kātya, each one of them learned and accomplished. They spent some pleasant days together in each other's company, having *satsaṅga* and taking bath in the sacred confluence of the three rivers Gaṅgā, Yamunā, and Sarasvatī at Prayāga, during the auspicious *mahodaya* time.

The young learned ones, as they sit discussing various matters, are stirred by the thirst of knowing the ultimate. They feel whatever knowledge they have acquired so far does not lead them towards *parabrahman*. Some of them feel, by being complacent and spending their time in Veda *pāṭha* and *karmaniṣṭha* they have succeeded in dwelling on *aparabrahman* only so far, and like missing the kernel in between the chaff, they have not devoted time for the understanding of *Brahman*. To redeem this, they decide to approach a *brahmarṣi* who will lead them to *brahma-vidyā*. They first decide to approach the *mahāguru* Ṛṣi Bhāradvāja in whose *āśrama* they were staying. Taking the advise of Sukeśa, the son of Bhāradvāja and their companion, they meet the Ṛṣi Bhāradvāja and request him to take them as his disciples. However Bhāradvāja Muni expresses his inability to take them as his disciples as he himself was going to Vālmīki Muni's *āśrama* as a disciple to help him write the great *kāvyam* called *Rāmāyaṇa.* But he guides them to go to his friend Maharṣi Pippalāda at Haridwar, who may take them as his disciples and impart to them the *brahma-vidyā.* The six seekers charged with enthusiasm and ardent desire to get the *brahma-jñāna* decide to travel to Haridwar immediately to seek Maharṣi Pippalāda's blessing.

As they were planning to travel, Hiraṇyanābha, the prince of Kosala country and a close childhood friend of Sukeśa arrives. The prince is in a state of agitation. He is troubled in mind, trying to get an answer to a question that has been occupying his mind as an unsolved riddle. Hoping his learned friend Sukeśa, will definitely know the answer, he had come in his chariot all the way from the Kosala country to meet him. Full of hope of getting the reply he asks Bhāradvāja "I would like to know about the *puruṣa* who has sixteen forms." Sukeśa has no inkling of the answer. He tells his friend he does not know its answer. This angers the prince who initially thinks his friend knowing the answer, does not want to divulge it. Without knowing the answer he has no peace of mind. In the meanwhile he comes to know that the group is going to Haridwar to meet Maharṣi Pippalāda. Restless and keen to know the answer, he decides to join them in disguise as he thinks going as a prince will be an impediment to seek knowledge. He hence disguises as his charioteer Aśvakośa and joins them on their trail in the forest enroute to Haridwar and volunteers his services as a co-traveller and a kshatriya. The naïve disciples get taken in by the disguise and readily agree to his joining them. Thus it is not six but seven of them who reach Haridwar at Maharṣi Pippalāda's *āśrama* where along with Pippalāda, they find his friend Sumantu Maharṣi also welcoming them.

Maharṣi Pippalāda after giving them a patient hearing decides it may not be prudent to right away impart them the *brahma-vidyā*, as he knows it is equally important for the disciples to be well prepared and tuned to understand the important knowledge. Hence he asks them to stay in the *āśrama* for one year following certain disciplines and austerities before imparting them the preachings. The disciples agree to the *guru*'s orders and spend the next one year in perfect obedience getting them physically and mentally prepared to receive the teachings.

The play leads the reader through the *āśrama* life with various interesting incidents and exchange of thoughts happening during that time. As the one year period gets over, noticed by the blooming of the *gajapuṣpa* flowers, the disciples with their thirst for *brahma-vidyā* are now prepared with intelligent and articulate questions or *praśna*s. One by one these questions are put to Maharṣi Pippalāda. These questions cover the three important aspects of life *sṛṣṭi* (creation), living (*sthiti*) and destruction (*saṁhāra* or *laya*) of life in the universe. The order of six questions is as follows:

The **first** question was by Kabanti son of Ṛṣi Kātya.

He asks, Bhagavān! Who has created the people or *praja*s we see around us?

For this, Ṛṣi Pippalāda replies:

*Brahman* is only Prajāpati. That only becomes the couple called Sūrya and Chandra. It only becomes *prāṇa* (life) and *rayi* (matter). Different kinds of *prajas* were brought about by *mithunams*, that is unions of these two. It becomes year, month, day, food and everything. Prajāpati which is the child grows eating the *annam* which is also Prajāpati. From that comes the Prajāpati which is sperm (*retas*). The mother Prajāpati conceives and gives birth to a child. That is also Prajāpati. That way everything is Prajāpati.

The **second** question is asked by Bhārgava from Vidarbha.

He is interested to know how the people so formed are maintained. Revered Guru! How many *deva*s are holding up the body? In them how many show their strength openly? Who is the best among them?

For this Ṛṣi Pippalāda replies thus:

Child! space (*ākāśa*), air (*vāyu*), fire (*agni*), water (*jalam*), earth (*pṛthivī*) are the five elements. The organs associated with action (*karmendriya*) are five, the organs helping to get knowledge (*jñānendriyas*) are five, the inner organs of perception (*antaḥkaraṇa*) are four. Thus, totally nineteen *deva*s are holding the body. Each of them show their capacities and help the body to run properly without any hindrance. In them who is best? In them *vāyu* or *prāṇa* known by the name *ekarṣi* (*Brahman*) is the lord of the entire world.

Then it was the turn of Kauśalya son of Ṛṣi Aśvala to put forth the **third** query. Coming to know the supreme importance of *prāṇa* in running the body of all living things, he wants to know how this *prāṇa* gets formed and enters the body. Hence he asks, "Respected Guru, how does this *prāṇa* get formed? from where is it born? How does it come into this body? How does it stabilize in the body? How does it go out? How does it hold the outside world (the basic elements in the universe)? How does it hold the inside world (physical body). Kindly explain these in detail, respected one!

For this Ṛṣi Pippalāda replies thus:

This *prāṇa* gets born from *ātmā*. As how a shadow rises from the human body, in the same way *prāṇa* also rises from the *ātmā*. It is like the shadow of *ātmā*. As per the intention (*saṁkalpa*) of the mind it enters the body.

There it splits into five. In the name of *apāna* it stabilizes in lower regions below navel. The *prāṇa* coming out of the face and nose stabilizes in eyes and ears. Near the navel it is known as *samāna*, here it takes the food partaken equally to all the organs. In the heart there are 101 important *nāḍīs*. Each one separates into hundreds of branches. Each of these branches further separates and they total to 72,000 smaller branches. In all these *nāḍīs*, *vyāna* moves. Among these thousands of *nāḍīs*, one goes upwards. That is called *suṣumnā nāḍī*. In that *udāna* moves. Because of this *udāna*, the *prāṇa* is able to leave the body. The main *prāṇa* comes from the sun, *apāna* originates from earth, *samāna* originates from space, *vyāna* originates from air (*vāyu*) and *udāna* originates from *tejas* such as stars, lightning, etc. Thus, the five outside *prāṇa*s are connected to the inside *prāṇa*s.

Knowing about the *prāṇa* in such details now, the son of Sūrya, Sauryāyaṇi or Gārgya is disturbed with the following query. If *prāṇa* is doing all these activities in the body, then during sleep what happens? Who sleeps in the body? During sleep, one finds the body working. That being so, who operates the body in sleep or who remains awake in the body when the master sleeps? Who does the dreaming and sees dreams? Who enjoys sound sleep? Hence, he approaches the learned *guru* and asks:

Respected Sir, what are the things sleeping in this body? What are awake? In this, who is seeing *svapna*? Who gets the enjoyment of *suṣupti* (subtle state)? What is the time when everybody joins together as one? You must kindly answer these questions of mine in detail.

For this, Ṛṣi Pippalāda replies thus:

During sleep all the sense organs join, together with the most exalted *deva*, the *tattvam* (mind). When the Sun's rays reach the *Sūryamaṇḍala* when he sets, the same way, the sense organs reach the mind and become one with that.

In this city, consisting of nine entrances (that is in the body where *puruṣa* lives) the five *prāṇa*s are the ones which are awake. They burn continuously like the fire. The five *prāṇa*s alone continue to do their work.

When a person sleeps, all sense organs mingle in the mind. At that time the minds *deva* enjoys, the experience of *svapna*. Whatever the mind had seen during waking time, it sees them again in *svapna*/dream.

When mind is filled with *brahma-tejas*, it does not see dreams. At that time, the body gets the comfort of deep sleep (*suṣupti*). At that time, the dreamless state is experienced. Ignorance, desire and *karma* of which the body is made along with its sense organs become quiet. The mind rests with the *ātmā*.

The four questions and Maharṣi Pippalāda's detailed teachings brought to light to the disciples clearly the working of *Brahman* through the tool of *prāṇa* in the human body; the making of the *prajas* with the help of *mithunam* (coupling) of *prāṇa* and *rayi;* as well as the system of working of the human body during three states of living — namely waking, dream and deep-sleep. The disciples now wanted to know the *sādhana* they have to do to reach the *Brahman* which is the ultimate truth. Being already well-versed in Vedas, they knew the importance of *praṇava mantra oṁ* in reaching the *Brahman*.

Hence Satyakāma, son of Śibi whose turn it was to put the **fifth** query to Ṛṣi Pippalāda, asks, Revered Guru! *namaskāra*. With your teaching all doubts have been cleared. I would like to know the result of the *praṇava upāsanā*. Respected one! Which *loka* does a man reach by doing *praṇava* meditation throughout his life? What status does he get on doing this *upāsanā*.

For this Ṛṣi Pippalāda replies thus:

Hey Satyakāma! *oṁkāra* is the *parabrahman* and also the *aparabrahman*. The one who continuously meditates on this becomes one of that. In that there are three *mātrā*s — *A* (अ), *U* (उ) and *M* (म्). These three *mātrā*s are the form of three Vedas. These are the three levels, three time periods, three worlds, three *guṇa*s/nature. The *Ṛgveda* recital sings the praise of *paramātmā*/almighty. The *Yajurveda* explains the *kriyā*s to be done to worship the *paramātmā*. The *Sāmaveda* is wisdom-incarnate. It provides great wisdom. Thus, understanding the inside meaning, if a person does *upāsanā* of *oṁkāra* he gets salvation from *karmas*.

The one who meditates on *aparabrahman* due to *Ṛgveda* obtains this human world, due to *Yajurveda* obtains *somaloka*, and due to *Sāmaveda* obtains *brahmaloka*.

If a person considers this *praṇava mantra* as *Brahman* and meditates on *parabrahman* he becomes very peaceful and attains *turīya* state which does not have states like waking, sleeping, etc. and reaches the *parabrahman* in which there is no birth and death.

It is Sukeśa, son of Bhāradvāja's turn to ask the **sixth** question.

Sukeśa, and his friend, the prince of Kosala country Hiraṇyanābha who had joined the group of seekers in disguise as Aśvakośa, the charioteer have been vexed for one year with the question about the *puruṣa* who holds in him the sixteen *kalās* (creations). The question has been weighing in their heart and soul for the last one year and the time had finally arrived to pose the question to the *param guru* Pippalāda. Sukeśa comes forth and talks:

Bhagavān! The prince of Kosala kingdom Hiraṇyanābha came to me and asked "do you know the *puruṣa* having sixteen forms?" For that I told "I don't know about that *puruṣa*." Now Svāmī, I am asking the same question to you. Who is that *puruṣa*? Where is he? Kindly give explanation for this.

For this Ṛṣi Pippalāda replies thus:

Sukeśa, the *puruṣa* you asked about is *paramātmā* himself. That *puruṣa* alone has sixteen forms. The *puruṣa* in whom sixteen forms are present is this body itself, that is the Self.

He is called *puruṣa*, where, *pura* is the body and *īṣa* means controller.

This *puruṣa* who is *paramātmā* created *prāṇa* with *samaṣṭi*/all-knowing qualities. Creating *prāṇa* then in proper order, He created the 15 forms or creations in the *prāṇā*.

The sixteen creations are as follows:

| | | | |
|---|---|---|---|
| 1. | *prāṇa,* from *prāṇa,* | 2. | mind |
| 3. | *śraddhā* (faith) | 4. | *rayi* (food), |
| 5. | *ākāśa* (space) | 6. | vitality/strength |
| 7. | *vāyu* (air) | 8. | penance (*tapas*) |
| 9. | *agni* (fire) | 10. | Vedas/hymns |
| 11. | water | 12. | *karmas* (action) |
| 13. | earth | 14. | *svarga* and other *lokas* |
| 15. | sense organs | 16. | names |

Later, all these get merged with that *puruṣa* just as the rivers which flow having different names, in the end merge in the ocean.

The answers to the six questions quenched the thirst of the seekers. They get enlightened by the wisdom filled preachings of the *maharṣi*. It is now time to take leave. Around this time the disguise of prince Hiraṇyanābha of Kosala country as charioteer Aśvakośa is also revealed. The prince with humility reveals his disguise and asks the pardon for such a deceit. The *brahma-jñāna* filled companions do not think ill of his act and pardon him with grace. Each of the disciples take leave of the Maharṣis Pippalāda and Sumantu and rest of the *āśrama* residents with a heavy heart.

By prior arrangement with Maharṣi Pippalāda, chariots arrive from the Kosala kingdom to take the honoured and graduated disciples back to Bhāradvāja's *āśrama* from where prince Hiraṇyanābha volunteers to take each them to their respective places. Thus the drama ends with the *Praśna* "questions" pertaining to *brahma-jñāna* answered for both the disciples and the viewers.

# The Drama

## Characters

| | | |
|---|---|---|
| **Pippalāda** | – | A *brahmarṣi* residing in an *āśrama* in Haridwar near the banks of the holy river Ganges. |
| **Sumantu** | – | A *maharṣi* and a friend of Pippalāda. He is an expert on the Vedas. |
| **Bhāradvāja** | – | A *maharṣi* residing in Prayāga. |
| **Sukeśa** | – | Son of Ṛṣi Bhāradvāja. |
| **Satyakāma** | – | Son of Śibi. He is a *ṛṣi.* |
| **Sauryāyaṇi (also called Gārgya)** | – | A *ṛṣi* born in the Gārgya *gotra;* grandson of Sūrya. |
| **Kauśalya** | – | Son of Ṛṣi Aśvala. |
| **Bhārgava** | – | A resident of the Vidarbha country. |
| **Kabandhi** | – | Son of Ṛṣi Katya. |
| **Hiraṇyanābha** | – | A friend of Sukeśa. He is the prince of Kosala country. |

In addition, residents of the *āśrama,* wives of sages, charioteer, etc.

*Venue* – First part in Prayāga and surrounding places. Other parts in Haridwar and surrounding places.

# PART I

## SCENE I

***(From behind the curtains.)***

यथा पूर्णं तथा पूर्णं पूर्णात् पूर्ण परात् परं।
पूर्णानन्दं प्रपन्द्ये हम् सत्गुरुम् शन्करम् स्वयं॥

*yathā pūrṇaṁ tathā pūrṇaṁ*
*pūrṇāt pūrṇa parāt paraṁ* ।
*pūrṇānandaṁ prapandye ham*
*satgurum śankaram svayaṁ* ।।

***(Curtains are raised.)***

(In Prayāga, it is Ṛṣi Bhāradvāja's *āśrama*. Outside, under a huge banyan tree, six *ṛṣis* are sitting on reed mats and conversing. A pleasant breeze is blowing. From the *agni-kuṇḍa* where *homas* are conducted, the smell of burnt ghee combined with smoke from the *homa* is emitting. The active chirping of birds is heard and as though in response to it, from distant place the gurgling sound of the rivers Gaṅgā, Yamunā, Sarasvatī flowing in a *saṅgam*, is heard.)

**Satyakāma** – Friend Sukeśa! We all came to take bath in this sacred river during the auspicious *mahodaya* time. With the blessings of almighty and due to the merits of previous lives, we have got this opportunity to stay in your *āśrama*. We had good company, discussed old historical information, got the knowledge of the secrets of Veda *mantras* along with doing other good deeds. We were not aware of how the time passes. Now kindly give us permission to return home.

**Sauryāyaṇi** – Yes, my friend, you have said correctly. The hospitality and affection we received here will be difficult to find anywhere else. The food which was sweeter than nectar, sweet words and gracious treatment immersed us in a sea of happiness. We have nothing to give in return for this hospitality.

**Sukeśa** – Friends, *ṛṣis*! Don't exaggerate. You have not stayed here for so many days. We took care of you as per our abilities. This *āśrama* is your house indeed. You all must definitely be here till the coming *iṣṭi*. Later on you can think about going.

**Bhārgava** – It is difficult to get a person like you as a friend. Coming here and receiving your friendship was our good fortune. Very soon I will be going to the Vidarbha country and telling my father about the festivities and incidents which took place here.

**Kauśalya** – O Bhārgava! do go and tell everything, but be cautious about revealing one matter.

**Bhārgava** – What is that?

**Kauśalya** – Don't put in the ears of the Vidarbha king that in the Bhāradvāja *āśrama* is the cow Kāmadhenu which is serving us, granting all boons without hesitation and that it is providing us not only food but also all kinds of pleasurable items. It would be better if this matter does not reach the king's ears.

**Bhārgava** – What is wrong in telling him? Hearing this, the king will also become happy. Our friend Sukeśa's name and his father's name and fame should spread till the Himālayas. That is only proper.

**Sauryāyaṇi** – Not only his fame but the truth about the *karma*s ordained in Vedas will be known to the people. The fruits one will get by performing the *Agnihotra homa*s and its greatness and strength will also be known to the people.

**Kauśalya** – I did not mean that.

**Bhārgava** – Then what did you mean?

**Kauśalya** – If the king hears of it and becomes happy it is alright. However by misfortune, if he gets jealous and like the son of Gādhi, if he tries to take the Kāmadhenu, then, what will happen? Unnecessary bitterness of mind, fights and differences may occur. That is what I meant.

**Sukeśa** – O! There is nothing to worry. It will be established that the strength obtained from worshipping *Brahman* is many times more than the kshatriya's strength. Hence only good will comes out by telling the happenings here, including the blessings obtained from the cow Kāmadhenu.

**Kabandhi** – Friends! Let that be so, till now we have been spending our time and effort only in following the daily *karmas*, eating and sleeping. We have thus wasted our time in mere *karma* or routine. We have not acquired any new wisdom. I have no peace in my mind due to that.

**Satyakāma** – What Kabandhi says is correct. We were just merely doing Veda *pāṭha* and following the *karma* or routine mentioned in that. This may help us in getting rewards and experience the bliss of heavens. For, the goal of our *karma* was that alone. We have remained complacent. Isn't this our ignorance?

**Kabandhi** – Yes. We believed the *aparabrahman* is the truth and spent our time learning that and did not make any enquiry about *parabrahman*. We spent our time unfruitfully.

**Kauśalya** – Friends! I can think of a way to make corrections for our ways.

**Kabandhi** – How is that?

**Kauśalya** – Having affinity towards understanding *aparabrahman*, we spent our concentration and attention on *aparabrahman*. As a result, we did not seek the knowledge of *parabrahman*. As retribution for that we can follow a *prājāpatya kṛcchram* and get ourselves purified. If you all agree to this we can do it.

**Kabandhi** – Your affinity for *karma* has not left you still. To gain wisdom the only way is to meet a proper teacher and learn under his guidance. Following the *chāndrāyaṇa vrata* and doing charity, are not going to be of any use.

**Kauśalya** – If that is so, whom should we approach?

**Kabandhi** – Keeping the butter in hand, will anybody go around searching for ghee? Leaving the herbs which are readily available, will anybody go and search for herbs in the forest?

**Sauryāyaṇi** – Friend! Is the *guru* close by? Who is he? Kindly clarify in detail.

**Kabandhi** – We can learn our lessons from the renowned *mahān* Bhāradvāja Maharṣi at this *āśrama,* itself.

**Everyone** – Let us do that! Yes let us do that!

**Sukeśa** – I am happy to hear that you are all planning to learn from my father. I will also join you all. Let us all stay together happily. (**thinking a little**) First I will approach my father and seek his willingness.

**Kabandhi** – Let us do that. Shall we approach him right away, as the elders say "To do a thing early is doing it well?"

**Sukeśa** – My father has gone to *kulapati* Aṅgīrā's *āśrama*. As soon as he returns we will request him.

**Kauśalya** – It is time for our evening prayers. Let us go to the river bank.

**Every one** – Let it be so. (**They depart**)

***(Curtain closes.)***

## SCENE 2

***(Curtain opens.)***

(The scene is outside Bhāradvāja's *āśrama*. Sukeśa is standing alone and feeding the birds food grains. The birds, one by one, were coming near and picking up the grains. Some come and pick it from the hands, some birds circle above his head and from time to time come down, sit and pick.)

**Sukeśa** – (**To himself**) Today nature is looking very beautiful. Even Devendra's *karpaka nandavana* will not be an equal to this scented flower garden. Here, the earth is so fertile and the people are happy. The reason for this is the adherence to *dharma*. The king of the Kosala country, whose foundation is *dharma,* is ruling the country justly. The king's greatness has to be acknowledged. Let the king live long. Let his noble rule rise. His son, the prince Hiraṇyanābha has not visited the *āśrama* after his *gurukula* stay. How affectionate he was towards me during those days of learning. Due to the duties of governance, he has probably forgotten me. Why am I suddenly remembering him today? (**a chariot is coming from afar and he listens keenly**) Who is coming at this time here? (**the chariot draws near**). There the chariot has come. Who is inside? (**looking at it keenly**). The flag of the Kosala country, the *kovīdara* flag is shining and fluttering in the wind. Who is coming? Is it the king or my dear friend?

(**The chariot comes near and stops suddenly. Hiraṇyanābha jumps outside.**)

**Sukeśa** – Welcome! Welcome! Let your coming bring good tidings.

**Hiraṇyanābha** – Friend! Is everybody keeping well? (**they embrace each other**).

**Sukeśa** – Friend! only now was I thinking about you. Immediately you have come. You will indeed live long. May you live for a hundred years.

**Hiraṇyanābha** – Honoured Brāhmaṇa! *Namaskāra*. I have come only to see you.

**Sukeśa** – Do come inside. Do accept *arghya pādya pūjā* as a token of our respect.

**Hiraṇyanābha** – Friend! I do not have much time to stay. Your words are like nectar, I will accept it as *pūjā* for the guest. (**with excitement**) I have come to ask you one question. Will you answer me frankly?

**Sukeśa** – Have I ever denied you whatever you have asked? If I know, I will definitely tell you.

**Hiraṇyanābha** – There is nothing that you don't know. Your father is a great scholar. You would have learnt everything from him.

**Sukeśa** – Enough friend. Don't praise me so much. Come to the point and ask me the question.

**Hiraṇyanābha** – You have not yet agreed to give me an answer to my question. Your evasive reply is causing anxiety in my mind. Shall I ask you the question?

**Sukeśa** – "Suspicious men are doomed" thus our *guru* often used to tell us. Have you forgotten that? Ask me without hesitation.

**Hiraṇyanābha** – Bhāradvāja! I would like to know about the *puruṣa* who has sixteen forms.

**Sukeśa** – What, a *puruṣa* having sixteen forms? Well I have never heard about such a *puruṣa*.

**Hiraṇyanābha** – (**does not believe**) It is impossible that you are not aware of it. Please tell me the answer without hiding.

**Sukeśa** – Friend! I really don't know. If I knew would I not tell you?

**Hiraṇyanābha** – O Ṛṣikumāra! Even if you don't tell the entire thing clearly at least give me a hint. Am I not your close friend?

**Sukeśa** – O, prince, please believe me.

**Hiraṇyanābha** – Friend! I do not believe that you don't know. Do give me the answer to the question. I will give you whatever you ask for. If required, I will give you half of the kingdom.

**Sukeśa** – (**within himself**) What to do about this embarrassing situation? Is it correct to tell a thing unknown as a known thing? To speak like that will not be in keeping with the precepts of *dharma*. (**speaking out**) Friend! A person who tells lies will wither from his root, trunk and stem. I won't tell a lie. Young prince, believe me. Whatever you may think, I do not know anything about the *puruṣa* of sixteen forms. I have no inkling of him. This is the truth.

(The prince without answering, angrily gets into the chariot. The charioteer also drives off the chariot fast. Sukeśa roams around and looks sadly at the chariot till it goes out of sight.)

**(Within himself)** "It pains me to see my friend going disturbed. I must find the answer to his question. Let me ask my father." **(He goes.)**

***(Curtain falls.)***

## SCENE 3

***(The screen opens.)***

(From Bhāradvāja's *āśrama,* it is the way to go to the Kosala kingdom. A chariot is going fast and suddenly stops. From the chariot the prince Hiraṇyanābha jumps out. From the driver's seat the charioteer also gets down.)

**Charioteer** – **(Folding his hands)** Mahārāja! Why did you order me to stop the chariot? Why did you get down so fast from the chariot?

**Hiraṇyanābha** – O Charioteer! You drive the chariot and go home. I am not coming home without knowing the answer to my question. Inform my parents about this with due respect.

**Charioteer** – Svāmī! What you are saying is surprising. For this small matter should you lose your peace of mind? Let us go to the capital. We can think about the matter calmly and find an answer.

**Hiraṇyanābha** – Charioteer! It is not like that. This is very important. Since my dear friend denied me the answer my mind is very disturbed. Without knowing the answer to this critical and important question, I will not like to come back.

**Charioteer** – Mahārāja! What you say is not correct. Perhaps your friend himself may not know the answer and your assumption that he has refused to tell you may not be correct. Hence let us go home. There are other teachers and seers who have the knowledge of *Brahman*. You can go and get wisdom from them. There are sages like Aṣṭāvakra and Yājñavalkya. Let us approach them and get an answer to the question. Do kindly get rid of your grief master.

**Hiraṇyanābha** – My dear charioteer. I also think sometimes as you tell. But this devil of a doubt has entered my mind. When I think of the greatness of Bhāradvāja Maharṣi, my doubt becomes stronger. Further something in my mind tells me that very soon I will get the answer to my question.

**Charioteer** – Master! If that is so, let us return immediately. Along the way we can go to the Maharājā Vidarbha's kingdom and ask Mahārājā Janaka the question and get proper explanation.

**Hiraṇyanābha** – Hey, charioteer! repeatedly you are countering me. Without knowing the truth I won't return to the palace. This is definite. You can leave.

**Charioteer** – Svāmī! Please forgive me. Do not be stubborn. It may not be proper to drown your elderly mother and father in sorrow. Please come back with me (**falls at the master's feet and requests desperately**).

**Hiraṇyanābha** – My dear charioteer ! Please get up. Either victory or failure! Once I have put my leg forward in the matter, I don't want to retreat. This is definite, a promise. However I want to go as a commoner this time in search of the answer. You give me your clothes and wear mine and go to the capital. This is my order. (**The charioteer reluctantly obeys the order and exchanges his clothes.**)

**Charioteer** – Maharāja! I am taking leave. As per your orders, I am going. Do come as early as possible. I will be looking forward to your return like the lotus awaiting the arrival of the sun. O forest *devatās*! Please protect the prince. Let all blessings be showered on him. (**He gets into the chariot and**

**goes. The horses neigh continuously as though expressing their grief on the parting. The chariot gradually moves off.)**

**Hiraṇyanābha** – The charioteer make up does suit me. In the world true persons are still there. However at times the gratitude and faithfulness which the horses have is not found in high-born people. Even the charioteer is having such affection and concern towards me. Before I get the answer to this Vedānta question, it appears I will be getting plenty of worldly experiences. (**thinks**) Let me go directly to Bhāradvāja *āśrama* and see what is happening. Observing Sukeśa's movement may put light on the truth. I went as a prince and could not get wisdom and knowledge. Now I am going in a different garb. Will I get the result? I will go with humility, love and fortitude. I am sure to get success. I believed in power, pride and went ahead. I encountered failure and returned. Now I have confidence and no fear in mind. (**On the way in a stream he washes his legs, hands and face. Sitting cross-legged he inspects the reflection of his face in the clear water.**) In this make up I look very much like the charioteer. My friend Sukeśa too may not be able to identify me. O! mind, be careful. Now you are not the prince. You are a poor charioteer. Remember that. Be careful that your act is not discovered. Say, if somebody asks my name what should I tell? (**thinking a bit**), alright Aśvakośa thus I will tell. Good name. O *devatā*s! who are close to me! Forest *devatā*s give me victory. I am submitting thousands of salutations to you (**goes with hesitation**).

***(Curtain closes.)***

## SCENE 4

***(The curtain is raised.)***

(Outside of Bhāradvāja's *āśrama*, nature is at its best. Under the expanse of the banyan tree in the prime place, Maharṣi Bhāradvāja is sitting in *padmāsana*, cross-legged. Sukeśa and his friends, six of them are offering their *praṇāma*s to the *maharṣi*.)

**Bhāradvāja** – Children! Let all the blessings be showered on you. Kabandhi! What is the news? The expression on your beautiful face indicates that you want to tell me something. Do tell it without fear.

**Kabandhi** – Revered Guru! Do accept my *praṇāma*s! We are keen to get the wisdom of *parabrahman*. You must show consideration on us and bless us with your teachings.

**All others** – Svāmī! Our wish is also that. You must kindly bless us. (**Hiraṇyanābha in a different make-up is standing behind the tree and listening. Nobody takes any notice of him.**)

**Sukeśa** – My dear Father! I asked a question in the morning, didn't I? You must kindly bless us by giving us the answers for that question.

**Bhāradvāja** – My dear children! Let all blessings be on you. Your question indeed is very important. It is a big matter like learning literature, Śāstras, etc. It is not easy to understand it, as soon as you wish to learn it. Only a disciple who fulfils the prerequisites of undergoing penance, following the rules of *brahmacarya,* staying in a *gurukula* can be preached this great wisdom. Hence to teach it now is not proper.

**Satyakāma** – Svāmī! Order me. Now on, from this second, we will start following the *vrata*s.

**Hiraṇyanābha** – (**slowly within himself**) What did my friend ask in the morning? It is not known. Perhaps it is possible that my doubt was misplaced. Sukeśa's face is downcast. As time passes I will know the truth.

**Bhāradvāja** – Children! Now there is no time for that. I am going immediately to Vālmīki Muni's *āśrama*. Hence it is not possible now to stay here and teach you all the lessons.

**Bhārgava** – If that is so, we will also come with you Revered Guru. We will be at the banks of river Tamasā and learn the lessons.

**Bhāradvāja** – Child! It is not possible to do that. I am going there now for some religious matter, as a disciple to do service.

**All six** – (**surprised**) What? What? You as a disciple! Svāmī! We are not able to believe it.

**Bhāradvāja** – Children! Yes indeed it is a surprise. It is a secret of the *deva*s to give the world a great *kāvyam* (literature). I am taking part in this divine and sacred work. I am going to be the disciple of enlightened Muni Vālmīki who proposes to write the primordial literature *Rāmāyaṇa* for his divine devotees. Hence your coming now may not be apt. This is not the right time.

**Kabandhi** – Prabhu! we felt happy hearing the nectar like words from you. Do order us as to what we have to do?

**Bhāradvāja** – Dear disciples! You go to Maharṣi Pippalāda. He is a great saint. An enlightened soul. He will preach to you all in detail and clearly.

**Hiraṇyanābha** – (**within himself**) Everything is strange. The king becomes the charioteer. The master *guru* becomes the disciple. Before getting the answer I think I will undergo a lot of new experiences.

**Kabandhi and the remaining five** – Your decision is our fortune. When do we have to start?

**Bhāradvāja** – Children! Today is a good day. It is said "the earlier the better." Get started today itself. Sukeśa! You go to your mother and ask her to make the required arrangements for their going.

**Sukeśa** – (**stands hesitantly**).

**Bhāradvāja** – Child! I forgot about your matter. You also can go along with them.

**Sukeśa** – (**within himself**) My friend's act is continuously coming to my mind. Let me ask for the answer from my father. (**speaking out**) Dear Father! I had asked a question in the morning about the *puruṣa* of sixteen forms. If you tell me about that in detail, I can go with some peace of mind.

**Hiraṇyanābha** – (**within himself**) I wrongly suspected my dear friend. I have done a grave mistake which cannot be pardoned. I must go directly and fall at his feet and ask for pardon. However now the situation is not correct. O! mind, be happy. You will soon get the answer to your questions. Maharṣi Bhāradvāja will open his mouth and tell the answer to the question which has been rising in my mind so persistently. To hear the nectar of his words, let me make my ears sharp.

**Bhāradvāja** – Sukeśa! Don't worry. You also go along with your friends today itself. Your question will be answered by Maharṣi Pippalāda himself. My wholehearted blessings to all of you.

**Sukeśa** – Dear Father! I will do as you bid. My *praṇāma*s to you. I will take care of the arrangements for the journey. (**goes inside**)

**Hiraṇyanābha** – (**within himself**) What a disappointment? The thing which reached the hand could not reach the mouth. For thinking wrongly of a good friend, I deserve this and more. There they are going inside. It is not possible to go running and ask for forgiveness. How unfortunate!

**Bhāradvāja** – Disciples, I am also going to the Tamasā River bank. You all go to Pippalāda and get *brahma-jñāna* and come back with its *tejas*. Do convey my affectionate *namaskāram*s to Pippalāda.

(All are going inside.)

**Hiraṇyanābha** – (**coming outside**) Going one step forward leads three steps backwards. What to do? Now it looks like one has to go to Maharṣi Pippalāda to get the answer? Should I go like this or in my true form? Let there not be a king's grandeur. This form of a charioteer is the one suitable for me to go. Hence let me go like that. Where does Ṛṣi Pippalāda stay? O Yes! He stays in Haridwar. Isn't that what Vasiṣṭha said? Let me go there earlier and wait for these people. That is only correct. Let me go.

"There is confidence and no fear in my mind"

**(He sings and goes.)**

***(Curtain falls.)***

***(End of Part I.)***

## PART II

### SCENE I

(Curtain opens.)

(On the way to Haridwar, below a banyan tree, Hiraṇyanābha is sitting and thinking.)

**Hiraṇyanābha** – It's a long time since I have come here. The sons of the *ṛṣis* are not to be seen. Perhaps thinking this way is rough, have they gone by some other way? However will those who are keen on acquiring *Brahman*-knowledge be attracted to comfort? Even the farmer told me this is a shortcut. Those who are in a hurry to achieve their goal would only come by this way (**gets up and walks around**). *Deva*s who are attached to Indra! Forest *devatā*s! All of you should bless me. There! I can hear the sound of footsteps. They are coming (**Sukeśa, Kabandhi and all the six enter**) they have come. Let me give my salutations to them. Then I will ask permission to join them.

(Hiraṇyanābha falls prostrate and does *namaskāram*s to the group. Kabandhi who was standing in the front lifts him up, offers *āśīrvāda* and questions him. Sukeśa without paying attention to this, is plucking the *gajapuṣpa* flowers which had bloomed nearby.)

**Kabandhi** – Who are you? What's your name? From where have you come?

**Hiraṇyanābha** – Svāmī! my name is Aśvakośa. I am a kshatriya. I have come from the Kosala kingdom.

**Kauśalya** – Aśvakośa! I also belong to Kosala kingdom. Seeing you I am very happy. Are all well in the country? What do you do there?

**Hiraṇyanābha** – I know how to drive chariots. I stay in the palace.

**Kauśalya** – If that is so, you must have seen my father Aśvala (*rājaguru*).

**Hiraṇyanābha** – Yes. I recollect seeing you somewhere. Now it is clear. In the palace I have seen your father several times.

**Satyakāma** – Aśvakośa! Now where are you going?

**Hiraṇyanābha** – To Haridwar.

**Sauryāyaṇi** – Is that so? We are also going there.

**Hiraṇyanābha** – I would like to come with you all, if you all permit and allow me. I can be of great help to you along the way. If wild animals will trouble you, I will protect you. If any other kind of service is required, I am ready to do it. Svāmī! Kindly permit me to join you all. You must show me consideration and allow me to come with all of you.

**All of them** – O! definitely. You can come. You can lead the path and as a person showing the way, you can walk in front.

**Bhārgava** – Aśvakośa! To get a kshatriya like you as a companion to guide us along the way is our good fortune indeed.

**Kabandhi** – Sukeśa! Enough of collecting flowers. Let us start.

**Sukeśa** – (**coming near**) Friends! Who is this? Looks like a new person.

**Sauryāyaṇi** – His name is Aśvakośa. He is coming from Kosala kingdom. He works in the palace. It seems he is going to Haridwar.

**Bhārgava** – He says he will come with us. We told him it is alright with us.

**Sukeśa** – Aśvakośa! Since you are staying in the palace of the Kosala kingdom you might know the prince Hiraṇyanābha.

**Hiraṇyanābha** – Svāmī! I know him well. I have also heard him mentioning your name several times. (Within himself, Sukeśa did not identify me. In spite of that I should be very careful. I should not become very friendly with him. In close quarters there is always a possibility that he can make out my camouflage.)

**Sukeśa** – Is the prince there now in the palace? Is everybody keeping well?

**Hiraṇyanābha** – Everybody is well. The prince is not there now in the palace. He has gone out of station for more than a month. It was told, he had gone to meet you. He has not come back as yet.

**Sukeśa** – (**with a great sigh**) He has not come back as yet? After seeing me without halting he went back. It is only to get an answer to his question that I am going to Haridwar along with these people.

**Hiraṇyanābha** – (**within himself**). What a superior friendship! What consideration for a friend! I suspected such a noble person. (**speaking out**) O Exalted brāhmaṇas! You must give me blessings to come there as I too want to acquire the *Brahman*-knowledge.

**Kabandhi** – Alright, let us do like that. (**All of them collect small twigs of jackfruit and other trees.**)

**Hiraṇyanābha** – Why are you collecting the twigs here itself. For the daily offering is it not enough to take them from Haridwar?

**Sauryāyaṇi** – When we go to meet the king, *guru* or God, we should not go empty-handed. When we go to Haridwar to meet Maharṣi Pippalāda, as an offering to his lotus feet, we should take these twigs used for the daily holy fire. Aśvakośa you could also collect some wood and twigs for the offering.

**Hiraṇyanābha** – Let that be so, Svāmī! If for this act any inner meaning is there you must explain it.

**Kabandhi** – It is the duty of the disciples to collect dry twigs to help in lighting the holy fire of the *guru* everyday. As it is required for the twigs to be dry without moisture so too it is necessary for the mind to be free of negative emotions like desire and hostility in order to attain *vairāgya.*

**Sukeśa** – My father used to tell us how, the twigs immediately catch fire on lighting, in the same way the mind of the disciple should be so prepared that as soon as he listens to the preaching of the *guru,* he should be able to catch on to it.

**Kauśalya** – Like the twigs are surrendered to the fire, the disciple surrenders himself completely to the teacher. This is also implied in this act of collecting firewood.

**Hiraṇyanābha** – Indeed how many philosophies lie behind collecting these dry twigs! It is surprising, Svāmī!

**Satyakāma** – Our *Sanātana Dharma* is like this. As firewood contains fire inside it, in the same way our daily duties contain deep concepts behind the acts.

**Kabandhi** – After mutual discussion, contemplation and penance, the truth is revealed by the *ṛṣis* who are visionaries. Aśvakośa! They are working for the welfare of the world and for the people's stock to improve. Do you understand that?

**Sukeśa** – Yes! Their efforts to help the people do not stop with a country. It is for the welfare of the entire world.

**Kauśalya** – Yes, that is correct. Their intention is to let the whole world prosper *lokaṣ samastā sukhino bhavantu.*

**Hiraṇyanābha** – Ṛṣikumāras! It is nearing sunset. Let us make haste.

**Everyone** – Let us do that.

**(Picking the bundles of the dry twigs they walk fast.)**

***(Curtain falls.)***

## SCENE II

***(Curtain opens.)***

(In Haridwar: Pippalāda Maharṣi's expansive *āśrama*. In a *parṇaśālā,* Pippalāda and Sumantu Maharṣis are sitting and conversing. From inside the *parṇaśālā* the Veda *mantras* are heard being recited.)

ॐ भद्रं कर्णेभिः शृणुयाम देवाः भद्रं पश्येमाक्षभिर्यजत्राः।
स्थिरैरङ्गैस्तुष्टुवाꣳसस्तनूभिर् व्यशेम देवहितं यदायुः॥

*oṁ bhadraṁ karnebhiḥ śṛṇuyāma devāḥ bhadraṁ paśyemākṣabhir yajatrāḥ* |
*sthirair aṅgais tuṣṭuvāṁsastanūbhir vyaśema devahitam yadayuḥ* | |

स्वस्ति न इन्द्रो वृद्धश्रवाः स्वस्ति नः पूषा विश्ववेदाः।
स्वस्ति नस्तार्क्ष्यो अरिष्टनेमिः स्वस्ति नो बृहस्पतिर् दधातु॥

*svasti na indro vṛddhaśravāḥ svasti naḥ pūṣā viśvavedāḥ* |
*svasti nas tarkṣyo ariṣṭanemiḥ svasti no bṛhaspatir dadhātu* | |

॥ॐ शान्तिः। शान्तिः। शान्तिः॥

| |*oṁ śāntiḥ*| *śāntiḥ*| *śāntiḥ*| |

*AUM*, May we, with our ears hear that which is auspicious, O gods. And may we, habitually offering oblations, see with our eyes that which is auspicious. With strong bodies, singing your praises, may we live out the span of life destined to us by the gods. May Indra of mature learning bestow well-being on us. May Pūṣā (the sun), the knower of all, bestow well-being on us. May Tārkṣya (Garuḍa) the annihilator of danger, bestow. wellbeing on us. May Bṛhaspati bestow well-being on us. *AUM,* Peace! Peace! Peace!

**Pippalāda** – Friend Sumantu! Today the *suprabhāta* is sounding very peaceful and full of happiness. It looks like some guests may arrive continuously in our *āśrama* because from the morning the crow is continuously cawing.

**Sumantu** – Maharṣi Pippalāda! I also noticed that. Further, from the *mandāra* tree, the *krauñca* bird came and sat on the branches of the *āśrama* trees repeatedly seven times, indicating seven people may come to the *āśrama*.

**Pippalāda** – Friend! You who are an expert in astrology, from your predictive capacities can you also tell me who they are? Why are they coming? Isn't it possible to make that clear?

**Sumantu** – Let it be so. Observing the colour of the branches of the mango tree it appears that six of them will be brāhmaṇas and another will be a kshatriya. Observing the direction from which the *krauñca* bird has flown in, it appears that they have started from *Prayāga* and are coming here. Why are they coming to your *āśrama*? To tell you that, there is no need of astrology. Even a small child will be able to tell it.

**Pippalāda** – What is that? Do tell me that.

**Sumantu** – Why will people come to the *āśrama* of the prime *guru*? Students from all over the Bhārata country are coming continuously for learning. Today also the students who are going to be here seeking knowledge are coming after being aware of your scholarship, teaching capacities and the varied experiences they get in the *āśrama*. Seeing your erudition and the *brahmarṣi tejas* exhibited by you even I have a desire to stay back in the *gurukula*.

**Pippalāda** – Enough of praise. Now I remember, two days ago Aṅgiras who went along this way to Gaṅgotrī had said that from Bhāradvāja Maharṣi's *āśrama,* with his permission, six *ṛṣi* sons are coming over here.

**Sumantu** – Knowing everything, your majesty tested me, this humble one.

At that time –

सुकेशा च भारद्वाजः शैब्यश्च सत्यकामः सौर्यायणी च गार्ग्यः कौशल्यश्चाश्वलायनो भार्गवो वैदर्भिः कबन्धी कात्यायनस्ते हैते ब्रह्मपरा ब्रह्मनिष्ठाः परं ब्रह्मान्वेषमाणा। एष ह वै तत्सर्वं वक्ष्यतीति । ते ह समित्पाणयो भगवन्तं पिप्पलादमुपसन्नाः ॥१.१॥

*sukeśā ca bhāradvājaḥ śaibyaś ca satyakāmaḥ, sauryāyaṇī ca gargyaḥ kauśalyaścāśvalāyano bhārgavo vaidarbhiḥ kabandhī kātyāyanas te haite brahmaparā brahmaniṣṭhāḥ paraṁ brahmānveṣamāṇā eṣa ha vai tatsarvaṁ vakṣayatīti, te ha samitpāṇayo bhagavantaṁ pippalādam upasannāḥ* | |1.1| |

Sukeśa son of Bhāradvāja, Satyakāma son of Śibi, Gārgya grandson of Sūrya, Kauśalya son of Aśvala, Bhārgava of the Vidarbha country, Kabandhi son of Kātya, all considering *Brahman* as the supreme Goal, firmly intent on *Brahman*, seeking the highest *Brahman*, sacrificial fuel in hand, approached the revered Pippalāda, thinking, "He verily will teach us all."

(Including Sukeśa six of them arrive along with the bundle of dry twigs. Hiraṇyanābha also comes with his *durvā* grass and firewood. Each of them place the bundle of twigs in front of Maharṣi Pippalāda, introduce themselves and do *namaskārams*. Then they pay their salutations to Sumantu Maharṣi also.)

**Kabandhi** – My *namaskārams* to Maharṣi Pippalāda! The one who diverted his mind from going to the *pañcabhūta* (five elements) that rule the world and went into contemplation and the understanding of *Brahman*. I am the son of Kātya. My name is Kabandhi.

**Pippalāda** – May you live long, young scholar! Come, sit here. Is your father keeping good health?

(Yes, replies Kabandhi and sits in a seat close to the *ṛṣi*.)

**Kauśalya** – O Bhagavān! The one who is having in himself complete knowledge, strength, *tejas*, wealth, strength and vitality! I pay a crore salutations to you. I am the son of Aśvala.

**Pippalāda** – A person possessed with a beautiful mind! Come and sit here. Is your father keeping well?

**Kauśalya** – Yes Sir. (**Sits on one side**).

**Sukeśa** – O Exalted Muni! The one who is revered by everyone in Bhāratadeśam! I am Sukeśa, the son of Prayāg's Bhāradvāja Muni. I offer my salutations to you.

**Pippalāda** – Sukeśa! Let your arrival bring good tidings. Is your father alright? Is the *Agnihotra homa* being conducted regularly? Come sit here.

(Sukeśa says, "yes, everything is going on properly" and goes and sits.)

**Bhārgava** – O Svāmī! "The great soul who has understood the truth of the Vedas! Many thousand salutations. My name is Bhārgava. I am from the Vidarbha kingdom. (**stands with folded hands.**)

**Pippalāda** – My affectionate child! Come here. Take your seat. (**Nodding in agreement he goes and sits.**)

**Sauryāyaṇi** – "O Knowledgeable Tejasvī! The one who is capable of clearing the doubts of even renowned *maharṣis*," I am Gārgya. I offer my many thousand salutations to you. I am the grandson of Sūrya.

**Pippalāda** – Dear Gārgya! Come and sit closer to me. (**Saying,** "let it be so", **Sauryāyaṇi comes and sits.**)

**Satyakāma** – The one who is having great expertise in Self-knowledge, I submit my prayers to you. My name is Satyakāma. I am the son of Śibi.

**Pippalāda** – Child, come! Your father is well, isn't he? Come, sit here.

**Satyakāma** – "Yes, he is well". (saying that Satyakāma sits.)

(Seeing Hiraṇyanābha standing far and paying his respects, Pippalāda asks).

Who is standing there aloof? Has he come with you all?

**Kabandhi** – Svāmī! He is a kshatriya, his name is Aśvakośa. We brought him as a companion for the way. He wishes to see you the "holy soul" and pay his respects.

**Pippalāda** – Is that so? Very happy to know. Come close by Aśvakośa. (Hiraṇyanābha prostrates completely in front of Pippalāda, pays his respects and stands separately on one side.) Children! What is the reason for you all to have joined together and come here.

**All six together** – Bhagavān, to have the *darśana* of yourself and with your blessings to get *brahma*-knowledge. You must kindly bestow your grace on us and teach us.

**Pippalāda** – May your arrival here bring good tidings. First go inside, take rest, have food and then come. Brahmadatta! Take them and perform the necessary hospitality.

(a disciple comes running and stands folding his hands. The seven of them go inside the *parnaśālā* along with Brahmadatta.)

**Sumantu** – Friend! The youngsters all appear to be well educated and possessing humility. Will you start teaching them from tomorrow itself?

**Pippalāda** – No, they still have attachment in *karma*. Those six are followers of *aparabrahman*. They have been so far following *apara-Brahma* disciplines. They have come here to know about *parabrahman*. Let them stay in the *gurukula* for some time. That is my opinion.

**Sumantu** – As you are telling, these disciples have learned the four Vedas and six Śāstras belonging to *aparabrahman*. They have learned it well. As per sanctions of the *karma* part of the Veda they have been following an orderly life. They have done their duties without fear. Still they have not had peace of mind and are wishing to know the philosophy higher than that, hence they have come here. Then why the delay?

**Pippalāda** – Friend! Whatever you are saying is all true. Still, for the teachings to establish it is necessary they stay here for some time. Then alone can the teachings be imparted. There, they themselves have come. (**Kabandhi and others come and sit**) Children! Was everything comfortable?

**All six** – (**with folded hands**) With your blessings everything is comfortable.

**Pippalāda** – As per your request I have accepted you all as my disciples.

**All the six** – We are very happy to hear this. We have become blessed.

**Pippalāda** – However, before imparting the teachings there is a condition.

**Hiraṇyanābha** – (**within himself**) Is my misfortune following me here also?

**All the six** – Honourable Guru. What is the condition? We will fulfil it as soon as you spell it out.

**Pippalāda** –

> तान्ह स ऋषिरुवाच — भूय एव तपसा ब्रह्मचर्येण श्रद्धया संवत्सरं संवत्स्यथ यथाकामं प्रश्नान् पृच्छत। यदि विज्ञास्यामः सर्वं ह वो वक्ष्याम इति॥१.२॥
>
> *tān ha sa ṛṣiruvāca — bhūya eva tapasā brahmacaryeṇa śraddhayā saṁvatsaraṁ saṁvatsyatha yathākāmaṁ praśnān pṛcchata, yadi vijñāsyāmaḥ sarvaṁ ha vo vakṣyāma iti* ||1.2||
>
> To them that seer said: Live with me another year with austerity, *brahmacarya* and faith. Then ask what questions you will. If we know we shall indeed tell you all.

**Pippalāda** – It is not anything so big. For one year all of you have to stay here, following the rules and regulations of this *āśrama*, keeping up the *brahmacarya vrata* with great care and doing penance. After completion of one year each one of you can ask your doubts and questions. I will answer as much as I know. I will tell you everything in detail.

**Sumantu** – Children! Don't worry. One year will pass off like a second.

**All the six** – Revered Guru! Maharṣi, we will do as you bid. It is our good fortune to follow your orders.

**Sumantu** – Did you notice Maharṣi Pippalāda's humility? O Sons of *ṛṣis*! "He who is having great *tejas*! Is there any matter he does not know? Still he said, I will teach you as much as I know. As you do one year of *gurukula* stay, you will come to learn various lessons. You may come to know things which will be useful for this worldly life also.

**Pippalāda** – Sumantu, the sun has gone behind the mountains. It is getting late. Shall we go for the evening prayers?

(**He gets up. All of them get up and go along with him.**)

**Sumantu** – Friend! I am also departing to my *āśrama*. Do give me permission.

**Pippalāda** – Alright, take leave. But be coming here from time to time and give encouragement to the children.

**Sumantu** – Yes, I will be coming from time to time. Sons of *ṛṣis*! My *āśrama* is nearby. You all should come there also when you have the time. I am taking leave. Let good tidings be bestowed on you and may things end well.

**All the six** – We will do as you say, Svāmī!

**Sumantu** – Aśvakośa! Why are you standing quietly? You also should come.

**Hiraṇyanābha** – So be it! (**telling that, he gives his salutations.**)

***(Curtain falls.)***

SCENE 3

***(Curtain rises.)***

(It is the *āśrama* of Sumantu Maharṣi. The *maharṣi,* Kabandhi,

Satyakāma, Kauśalya are all sitting together and conversing.)

**Kabandhi** – Svāmī! We are already doing *vrata* (penance) with great involvement. What can be the reason for *maharṣi* ordering us to follow the path of penance for one more year?

**Sumantu** – All for your good only. When gold is heated in fire it becomes purer and shines more.

**Kauśalya** – Yes it is true. Presently we are assailed with some doubts. Can you clarify them? Kindly explain the meaning of *śānti-pāṭha* (the *mantra* of peace) in detail.

**Sumantu** – I shall do so. Listen carefully. *Oṁ*! *deva*s, the ones worthy of worship. May we always hear with our ears good words. May we always see with our eyes good things. With strong organs and body we should sing and praise the *deva*s. Let us live well the complete span of life, which they offer us, with pleasure. Let the greatly renowned Indra bless us with good tidings. The sun is aware of everything, may he bless us with goodness. Let the bird Garuḍa, the incarnation of Vedas, which dispels the hurdles of knowledge, do good to us. Let Bṛhaspati bless us with good tidings.

*oṁ śāntiḥ* । *śāntiḥ* । *śāntiḥ* ।

**Kabandhi** – Svāmī! During the prayer you mentioned about goodness. Kindly explain the meaning of that fully.

**Sumantu** – Goodness is *bhadram*. For this word many kinds of meanings can be given according to the circumstances. The ear must always hear Veda *mantras*, Upaniṣads, etc. The eyes should always see good sights like *pūjā*, *yajña*, etc.

**Kauśalya** – In the same way the *svasti* also means many things, isn't it?

**Sumantu** – Yes. The ancient man of great fame and good name, the Devendra should bless us with good intellect. He should help us understand the Vedas and help us act according to their dictates. The sun who nurses the entire universe should bestow good tidings on us. He should give us desire for *upāsanā* and bless us with perfect health. Let the divine bird Garuḍa save us from diseases, difficulties, hindrances and give us the stature to do *pūjā*s. The *guru* of *deva*s, Bṛhaspati, let him give us the ability to learn *Brahman*-knowledge and bless us with prosperity.

**Satyakāma** – Svāmī, a small word is having so much meaning embedded in it. It is indeed a wonder.

**Sumantu** – Children! Don't think this is just a prayer. This is the common offering given by *guru* and *śiṣya* before starting the lessons, lest any hindrances in the learning process should occur. The *śānti-pāṭha* is chanted for that.

**Kabandhi** – This *pāṭha* is a prayer, it is required to learn the lessons thoroughly and after learning to stand by that. This we have understood. However, isn't it enough to say *oṁ śānti* once? Why should one recite it three times?

**Kauśalya** – Saying it only once may not be enough to remove hindrances? Is that the intention?

**Sumantu** – Kauśalya! What you are thinking is wrong. For any work, three kinds of obstacles can arise. To clear them one by one the *śānti pāṭha* is repeated thrice.

**Satyakāma** – To remove three types of obstacles, it is required to recite it three times. However, what are those three types of obstacles?

**Sumantu** – Children! Listen carefully. The first one is due to the gods or by fate (*ādhidaivika*), the second one from entities around (*ādhibhautika*) and the third can be from one's own self (*ādhyātmika*).

**Kauśalya** – This is not still understood clearly. Kindly explain it with examples *maharṣi.*

**Sumantu** – The obstacles from the gods are natural calamities like lightning, thunder, earthquake, etc. The obstacles from the outer world are the ones coming from other beings as well as the elements like heat, cold, humidity, etc. The obstacles coming from one's own self are the ones like diseases, sleepiness, laziness, lack of concentration, disbelief, etc.

**Kabandhi** – Revered Muni. Among the three hindrances, the third one causes more problems. One should be very careful regarding that.

**Sumantu** – Yes, it may be so. Haven't your other friends come today?

**Satyakāma** – Sukeśa has gone to fetch flowers for the *maharṣi*'s *pūjā*. Bhārgava has taken the cattle to the banks of the Ganges. Aśvakośa! where did he go? Do you know Kauśalya?

**Kauśalya** – I don't know. This morning the teacher had called him and was telling him something. He might have asked him to go somewhere. (**addressing Kabandhi**) Friend! Do you know?

**Kabandhi** – In the coming *amāvāsyā*, the solar eclipse is due. That time a huge gathering will assemble near the river Ganges to take bath. The necessary arrangements have to be made for that. The *guru* has given that responsibility to Aśvakośa.

**Kauśalya** – He is the correct person to carry out this work.

**Sumantu** – In what work is Sauryāyaṇi involved?

**Satyakāma** – He is helping the *guru*'s wife in carrying out her different jobs in the *āśrama*.

**Sumantu** – Is that so? I am very happy. Convey these discussions to them in detail.

**Kabandhi** – So be it *maharṣi*! We will do as you say.

**Sumantu** – Now it is time for the afternoon bath. I am going to the river. You may all proceed to the *āśrama*. To Maharṣi Pippalāda do give my *praṇāma*s. May all good tidings be bestowed on you.

(The three *ṛṣi* sons give their salutation and go)

***(Curtain falls.)***

***(IInd Part Gets Over.)***

# PART III

## SCENE I

***(Curtain opens.)***

(It is the *āśrama* of Sumantu Maharṣi. Sukeśa and the other disciples are sitting and conversing. Hiraṇyanābha comes running. He salutes everyone and begins to talk excitedly.)

**Hiraṇyanābha** – Svāmī! Today, the one year period is coming to an end. On the way I noticed the *gajapuṣpa* flowers in bunches, full blossomed. It occurred to me that last year during this very spring season we came here. Immediately I came running to inform this to my friends.

**Kabandhi** – Aśvakośa! We have also not forgotten it. We are talking to *maharṣi* about that only.

**Kauśalya** – Sukeśa had also seen the *gajapuṣpa* blossoms and he has plucked some flowers and brought them here, did you notice them?

**Hiraṇyanābha** – Our friend Sukeśa derives a lot of pleasure from nature. Well, let that be. O Ṛṣikumāras! You were saying that you have been talking about something. Can I also join in?

**Sauryāyaṇi** – Assuredly. You can also join in.

**Sukeśa** – Indeed you have accompanied us also to participate in these discussions, isn't it?

**Sumantu** – Aśvakośa! You also sit here. I am explaining to them about penance, *brahmacarya*, concentration and such concepts. Since you have come now I will tell you about it once again from the beginning.

**Hiraṇyanābha** – Svāmī! Your will is our command. I will listen carefully.

**Sumantu** – Last year when you came here, do you remember what Maharṣi Pippalāda had said?

**Hiraṇyanābha** – I remember very well. The honoured Pippalāda blessed us with his divine words. He had said that for one year "you must remain following penance, *brahmacarya, śraddhā* and live in a disciplined manner."

**Kabandhi** – That time we were worried. We thought, we had come with great desire and thirst to know about *para-Brahmam,* but *maharṣi* was putting a condition to teach.

**Kauśalya** – That time you pacified us saying that it is not an obstacle.

**Sumantu** – Yes! Just as the honeybees come towards a beautiful scented flower, you all came here, searching for a preceptor. But only if you subdue the senses and learn with great aspiration it is possible to obtain Self-knowledge. Hence *maharṣi* made such a rule.

**Sukeśa** – Once Vasiṣṭha Maharṣi paid a visit to our *āśrama.* He said that "when you give charity, it is important to know the quality of the one to whom it is given. In the same way it is important to know the quality of the disciple before preaching to him. Disregarding such an equation will end in the teaching disappearing like water in a desert. Only the seeds sown in fertile land will grow well and give good benefit. The seeds falling in an infertile ground will go waste. Hence, it is necessary to test the disciple before preaching to him." I am recollecting these significant words said by the great *mahātmā.*

**Sumantu** – Sukeśa! Very good. It gives worth to the person who sows only if the seeds sprout well. The ones who get benefited can consider themselves fortunate and blessed. For *brahmachārīs*, service to *guru* is the best penance. Not thinking of evil is the penance done through mind. *Ahiṁsā* is the penance done by *karma*. It is not necessary to do this penance living in a forest, it can be done living in any place.

**Kauśalya** – Svāmī! What you are telling appears very easy but only when one practises, is its difficulty known.

**Satyakāma** – Maharṣi! Do tell us about the discipline of *brahmacarya* in detail.

**Sumantu** – Subduing the sexual feeling alone is not *brahamacarya.* To control all senses and keep them under one's command is true practice of *brahamacarya.* To follow it correctly, it is necessary to eschew eight kinds of deeds.

**Sauryāyaṇi** – Revered Guru! What are those deeds to be avoided? Kindly tell us in detail.

**Sumantu** –

1. To think about sexual things.
2. To talk about it.
3. To become close to a person of the opposite sex.
4. To see it.
5. To converse on that.
6. To get drawn to it.
7. Aspiring to get it.
8. The sexual action itself.

Generally everyone thinks the eighth, the sexual act, is the one to be avoided and then it is *brhamacarya*. But all the eight will cause equal harm. All of them have to be avoided. Like an iron gets attached to the magnet, even if one of them is allowed, the other acts will be attracted and drawn in.

**Kabandhi** – Svāmī! We are blessed with these explanations. Kindly also explain *śraddhā.*

**Sumantu** – First there should be belief in oneself. At the same time, there should be complete belief in the *guru* without any doubt. Only when these exist is there complete *śraddhā.* Even if a little doubt persists, it will be the cause of destruction.

**Hiraṇyanābha** – Hearing these words makes one very happy. I feel like staying here one more year to hear all this.

**Satyakāma** – I also feel like that. With *bhakti* and *śraddhā,* controlling the senses, and doing service to the *guru,* I think I can spend the rest of my life here.

**Sukeśa** – Then the purpose of our coming is not served.

**Kauśalya** – Satyakāma! Even if you are carried away by circumstances, don't take your eyes away from the purpose.

**Satyakāma** – Staying on the holy banks of Ganges and remaining with the very sacred Maharṣi Pippalāda is such a bliss, better than *mokṣa.* Still, I am not suggesting that we should forget about the job for which we have come.

**Kabandhi** – These sacred surroundings are benefiting us a lot. Still, it is necessary that we receive our teachings and go back home. My grandfather is in his old age and will be worried and looking in the northern direction for my arrival. Waiting and looking with expectation his eyes would have become strained. Should I not go and see him?

**Sumantu** – Ṛṣikumāras! Tomorrow you have to ask the questions. Who is going to ask the first question?

**(The six of them thinking within themselves.)**

**Kabandhi** – Svāmī!, I am going to ask the first question.

**Hiraṇyanābha** – What question? About what?

**Kabandhi** – Tomorrow morning I will ask Maharṣi Pippalāda. Why should I say it now?

**Sumantu** – You can ask it in front of Maharṣi Pippalāda tomorrow. But to think among yourselves now is not wrong. The doubts each one has can be told outside and discussed, then the remaining ones can be asked to the *guru.*

**Kabandhi** – **(He is thinking what to ask.)**

**Hiraṇyanābha** – Svāmī! I have a doubt.

**Satyakāma** – What is that?

**Sumantu** – Aśvakośa! I know your doubt. Why are the explanations of penance, *bramacarya* and *śraddhā* being discussed now. They should have been told before the year started. Isn't that your doubt?

**Hiraṇyanābha** – Yes, Svāmī!

**Sukeśa** – There is a proper reason for that.

**Sumantu** – Child Sukeśa! You clear the doubt of your friend.

**Sukeśa** – Svāmī! I shall do so. You must correct me if there is a mistake.

**Kauśalya** – Sukeśa! Do tell us the reason, we are eager to hear it.

**Sukeśa** – In the holy *āśrama* of Maharṣi Pippalāda it was definite we would achieve the three things namely *vrata, brahmacarya* and *śraddhā.* Hence there was no need of explanation in the beginning.

**Hiraṇyanābha** – Then where is the need now?

**Sukeśa** – Now we must test ourselves and find out our advancement. After hearing the explanation, we can find out how far we have gone ahead. Have we conducted ourselves properly? Thus a self-testing can be done. It is only for that reason that the *maharṣi* gave us the teachings now.

**Sumantu** – My affectionate ones! There is no need for you to harbour a doubt. You have passed in the examination. This can be made out from the *tejas* you all exhibit in your face and the magnetism you all exhibit in the body. Tomorrow early morning you may go to *maharṣi* and ask your doubts. That time I shall also come along.

**Kauśalya** – Our friend has kept his mouth closed and gone into silence. Only when this silence is broken will it be possible to know the first question he intends to ask.

**Kabandhi** – My dear friends hear, I will discuss the question. You listen to it and give me your approval. I am pondering seriously to know the principal cause of this universe? When and by whom was it created? I am eager to know the fundmental reason for this. On the sight of this, it appears dual. Is it really so? or is it only one? The reason for this we must know? Further, what is the connection between *upāsanā* and *karma*. To know that also my mind is very eager. Without *upāsanā*, the *karmas* we do, will they fetch any result? What are the results of the *karmas* which we do with *bhakti*? Based on these concepts I am going to ask questions tomorrow.

**Sumantu** – Child! Kabandhi! Your thoughts are beautiful and intelligent. The first doubt has become the first question. The Almighty God will bless you all. Tomorrow we will meet in the presence of Maharṣi Pippalāda.

**(All seven of them do *namaskārams* to *maharṣi* and take leave.)**

***(Curtain closes.)***

## SCENE 2

***(The curtain opens.)***

(Pippalāda's *āśrama* is seen outside, under the shade of the banyan tree Maharṣi Pippalāda and Sumantu Maharṣi are sitting on reed mats. Along the side, the six young *ṛṣikumāras* and Hiraṇyanābha are standing. From inside the curtain the sound of Vedic chanting is heard. All disciples pay their respects to the *maharṣi* by doing their *namaskārams* and reciting *oṁ namo paraṁdhāmane hari oṁ* and then take the *ṛṣis*, permission to sit.)

**Pippalāda** – Children! Let there be good tidings everywhere. In this one year of your *brahmacarya* you must have controlled your mind very well. By penance you must have won over the five senses. By *śraddhā* you must have brought around your intellect in the proper form. Now you have become ready to hear the teachings which will lead you to understanding *Brahman*.

**Sumantu** – You, who are having beautiful *chit*, seeing you all with shining faces full of *ojas* and *tejas*, it appears like seven glittering suns have arisen and shining at the same time. You can now ask your questions to Maharṣi Pippalāda.

**Pippalāda** – It will be good if one by one, each of you come near and ask.

**Kātya's son Kabandhi** – Svāmī! I request you to allow me to ask the question today. Please show your consideration O great one!

**Pippalāda** – Child! by all means. I will answer as much as I know.

**Kabandhi** – **(Others are looking at his face eagerly!)**

> भगवन् कुतो ह वा इमाः प्रजाः प्रजायन्त इति ॥१.३॥
>
> *bhagavan kuto ha vā imāḥ prajāḥ prajāyanta iti* ||1.3||

> Venerable Sir, Whence verily are all these creatures born? Bhagavān! From what these people have been created? This you must tell me in detail and bless me.

**Sumantu** – Well done, Kabandhi! This is a very apt question! The intellect which is lulled in ignorance, before it understands the undifferentiated *Brahman*, is required to know the appearance of this differentiated world. O My friend! all the creatures found in this world as well all the human beings, how did they come about? For what? How? When? From what has creation happened? This is being asked by Kātya's son Kabandhi.

**Kabandhi** – Please do answer this revered being.

**Pippalāda** –

> तस्मै स होवाच — प्रजाकामो वै प्रजापतिः स तपोऽतप्यत स तपस्तप्त्वा, स मिथुनमुत्पादयते रयिं च प्राणं चेत्ये तौ मे बहुधा प्रजाः करिष्यत इति ॥१.४॥
>
> *tasmai sa hovāca — prajākāmo vai prajāpatiḥ sa tapo 'tapyata sa tapas taptvā, sa mithunam utpādayate rayiṁ ca prāṇaṁ cety etau me bahudhā prajāḥ kariṣyata iti* ||1.4||

He (Pippalāda) said to him:

> Prajāpati, verily, was desirous of offspring. He underwent *tapas*. Having undergone *tapas*, he produced the couple *rayi* and *prāṇa*, expecting them to produce offspring of various kinds for him.

**Pippalāda** – Prajāpati, not wishing to stay alone got the desire to create *prajās* (people) and did penance. After penance he made the couple, *rayi* (matter) and *prāṇa* (life). Thinking this pair together would make different kinds of *prajās* for him, he brought about *mithunams*, that is unions of these two.

**Kabandhi** – Revered Guru! Who is Prajāpati? What are the details of the penance he did?

**Pippalāda** – The meaning of Prajāpati is that he is the creator of *prajās*. He is the form of all creation. He is also known as Hiraṇyanābha. I will tell you one small example. It will make it very clear. Let us take ourselves. When our mind is awake, its thoughts, actions, and their reflections, these are the universe which we see outside. Once the mind becomes quiet, the outside world is not there. The mind which is *samaṣṭi* (all-pervading) is only Prajāpati. When *samaṣṭi* becomes *vyaṣṭi* (individual) then *sṛṣṭi* happens. The penance is the thought that the *samaṣṭi* has to become *vyaṣṭi*. During each *kalpam* at the end of the *pralaya*, Hiraṇyanābha thinks of creating. He declares "I will remain as *sarvātmā* and create this world" and brings the matters of the previous *kalpa* into the memory of this *kalpa*. Then He brings about the couples having capacity for union and production, the *rayi* and *prāṇa*. These two together create all kinds of *prajās*. Thus He conceptualized the duality and their *mithunam* (union).

**Kabandhi** – Svāmī! You must tell us in detail about *rayi* and *prāṇa*.

**Pippalāda** –

आदित्यो ह वै प्राणो रयिरेव चन्द्रमाः रयिर्वा एतत् सर्वं यन्मूर्तं
चामूर्तं च तस्मान्मूर्तिरेव रयिः ॥१.५॥

*āditya ha vai prāṇo rayireva chandramāḥ rayir vā etat sarvaṁ yan mūrtaṁ cāmūrtaṁ ca tasmānmūrtireva rayiḥ* ||1.5||

*Prāṇa* is the sun indeed, and *rayi* the moon. All that is

materialized and non-materialized is *rayi* indeed. Whatever is concrete is therefore *rayi*.

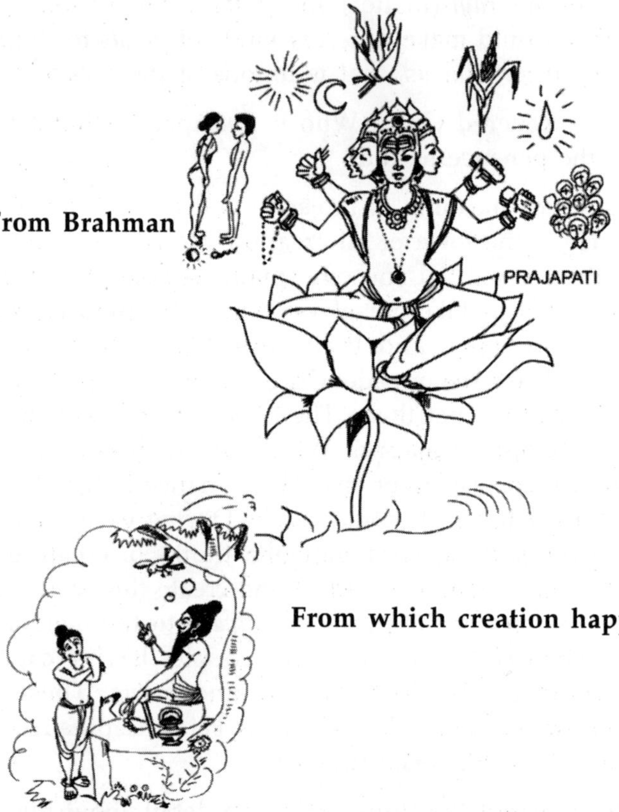


*Rayi* means matter. That is a thing of *bhoga* (enjoyment, consumption). It can also be termed as cereal or fuel (*dahyam*). Here *annam* or *rayi* means anything which is gross, subtle, having form or formless. As this *rayi* is in all *ātmās* it is part of Prajāpati. However the ones having forms are called *rayi-annam* and the formless are called *pirāṇan-atta*.

*Prāṇan* means *bhoktā* (the one who enjoys/experiences), also represents *agni* or *āditya* (fire or sun). For all *annam* the ruling deity is moon. For all *prāṇan* the ruling deity is the sun. In short Prajāpati becomes the sun–moon union (*mithunam*) and appears as this universe.

**When *prajās* die.**
**Northwards - Mokṣa route.**
**Southwards - Pitṛ route.**

**Sukeśa** – Svāmī! Initially you told us about creation. When did the first creation take place?

**Kauśalya** – I have heard my father talking about creation of *prajās* in a different manner.

**Sauryāyaṇi** – Revered Guru, my father also has described the formation of creation in a different manner. You must kindly give the explanation for these differences.

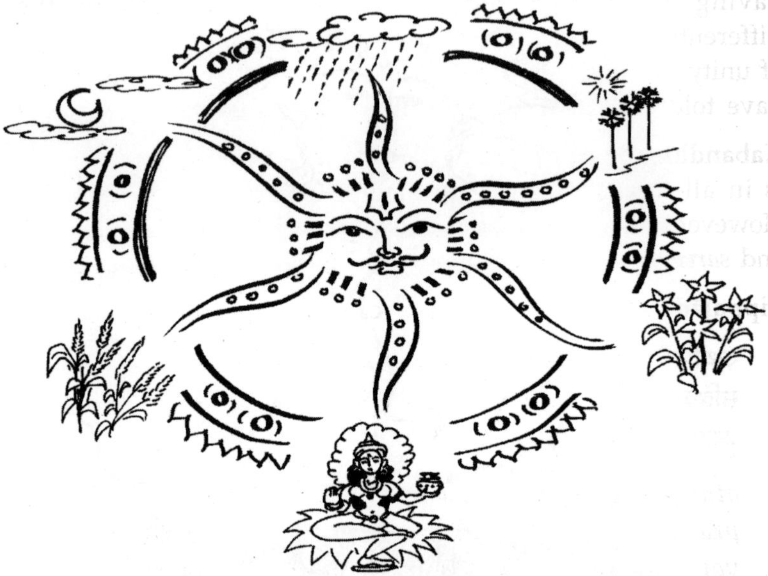

*fig* : **Time scale is Sun bringing in seasons and 12 months**

**Pippalāda** – Friend, kindly remove these doubts of the children.

**Sumantu** – Child Sukeśa. It is not possible to state when creation took place, in which particular *kalpa,* in which *yuga* or in which particular year, month and date. It is one without a beginning. It is true that the creation without beginning is described differently in different Upaniṣads by different *ṛṣis.* However, it should not be considered that they are contradicting one another. Each teacher, depending upon the capacity of the students and the circumstances, has explained it in a manner they can understand by employing different means. When seen superficially there may seem differences between one's word, another's language and another one's description. This is natural. Further for this, state a light-hearted explanation can be given. The *brahma-jñānī,* the one having knowledge of *Brahman,* one who abhors the differentiated knowledge and stays steeped in the knowledge of unity and not having involvement about this creation, might have told about it differently in a joking manner.

**Kabandhi** – Since everything in this world is *annam-rayi* which is in all *ātmās,* it can be termed as *sarvātmā* and Prajāpati. However how can *prāṇa* which is the sun be termed as Prajāpati and *sarvātmā?* You must kindly tell us this in detail.

**Pippalāda** – I will tell you my child, listen carefully.

> अथादित्य उदयन्यत्प्राचीं दिशं प्रविशति तेन प्राच्यान् प्राणान् रश्मिषु सन्निधत्ते। यद्दक्षिणां यत्प्रतीचीं यदुदीचीं यदधो यदूर्ध्वं यदन्तरा दिशो यत्सर्वं प्रकाशयति तेन सर्वान्प्राणान्रश्मिषु संनिधत्ते ॥१.६॥
>
> *atha āditya udayan yat prācīṁ diśaṁ praviśati tena prācyān prāṇān raśmiṣu sannidhatte। yad dakṣiṇāṁ yat pratīcīṁ yad udīcīṁ yad adho yad ūrdhvaṁ yad antarā diśo yat sarvaṁ prakāśayati tena sarvān prāṇān raśmiṣu saṁnidhatte ।।1.6।।*
>
> Now then, the sun on rising, enters the eastern horizon, thus bathing all life in the east with his rays. So too, on his illumining the directions of the south, the west, the north, below, above, in between, he bathes all living beings with his rays.

The sun rises in the east and it brightens all the *prāṇa* found in that side, with the result that all the *prāṇa* there existing in the *annam* form is contained by its rays and gets its form and characteristics. In the same way by penetrating and brightening all forms in south, west, north, up, down, corners, every direction and every place, all the forms are contained in the sun and get its form. Hence He who penetrates everything is the *sarvātmā* and *viśva-rūpa* (all the forms). He is the *prāṇa,* the *agni.* Daily He rises high. This concept is also given by the *Ṛgveda mantra.*

**Sumantu** – The sun spreads its rays in all directions, penetrates all the living things and brightens them. With His bright rays He is omnipresent and wraps all the living things completely and makes them do their different acts. Hence He is *prāṇa*. He is the *jīva* (life) in everything.

**Kabandhi** – Do tell us the *Ṛgveda mantra,* Revered Guru.

**Pippalāda** –

> स एष वैश्वानरो विश्वरूपः प्राणोऽग्निरुदयते।
> तदेतदृचाऽभ्युक्तम् ॥१.७ ॥
> *sa eṣa vaiśvānaro viśvarūpaḥ prāṇo 'gnirudayate* |
> *tadetadṛcābhyuktam* ||1.7||

> विश्वरूपं हरिणं जातवेदसं परायणं ज्योतिरेकं तपन्तम्।
> सहस्त्ररश्मिः शतधा वर्तमानः प्राणः प्रजानामुदयत्येष सूर्यः ॥१.८ ॥

> *viśvarūpaṁ hariṇaṁ jātavedasaṁ parāyaṇaṁ*
> *jyotirekaṁ tapantam* |
> *sahasraraśmiḥ śatadhā vartamānaḥ prāṇaḥ*
> *prajānāmudayatyeṣa sūryaḥ* ||1.8||

This sun, the Vaiśvānara assuming every form, life and fire, rises (everyday). This very truth has been declared in the *Ṛgveda* thus: This sun, who has everything for its form, constituted of rays, the all-knowing, the goal (of all), the sole effulgence, the giver of heat, the possessor of thousands of rays, existing in hundreds of ways, the life of all creation, rises.

The sun is seen by the elders as *viśva-rūpa,* lustre filled rays, as preceptor, eyes of all the creatures and the only one. He has many thousand rays. He is the form of hundreds of living things. The rising sun is *prāṇa* of the *prajās*.

**Kabandhi** – Svāmī! You described the sun and moon as Prajāpati. How do both of them together create *prajās*? You must tell us about this in detail.

**Pippalāda** –

संवत्सरो वै प्रजापतिस्तस्यायने दक्षिणं चोत्तरं च। तद्ये ह वै तदिष्टापूर्ते कृतमित्युपासते। ते चान्द्रमसमेव लोकमभिजयन्ते। त एव पुनरावर्तन्ते। तस्मादेते ऋषयः प्रजाकामा दक्षिणं प्रतिपद्यन्ते। एष ह वै रयिर्यः पितृयाणः ॥१.९॥

*saṁvatsaro vai prajāpati stasyāyane dakṣiṇaṁ cottaraṁ ca | tadye ha vai tad iṣṭā-pūrte kṛtamityupāsate | te cāndramasam eva lokam abhijayante | ta eva punarāvartante | tasmād ete ṛṣayaḥ prajākāmā dakṣiṇaṁ pratipadyante | eṣa ha vai rayiryaḥ pitṛyāṇaḥ* ||1.9||

The year verily is Prajāpati; emerging of him are two paths: the southern and the northern. Now, those who perform *iṣṭa pūrta* thinking of those rituals as of supreme value, they attain the world of the moon, certainly returning again. The sages desirous of offspring therefore take to the southern path. This is called the path of manes, is verily *rayi.*

The sun and the moon together created the time scale. This time scale is also Prajāpati. That is, Time is *Brahman*. It has two routes. One southward, another northward. Whoever does *upāsanā* by the acts of *iṣṭa* and *pūrta* they reach *chandra-loka.* They are born again. These *prajā*s depending on the *iṣṭa pūrta* acts they have indulged in go southwards. The southward route is also called, *pitṛ-yāna* (route taken by ancestors).

**Kabandhi** – Respected one. What exactly is meant by *iṣṭa pūrta*?

**Sumantu** – *Iṣṭa* is the *karma* act as laid out in the Smṛtis. It is more pertaining to *nimitta karma* (ordained *karma*) like doing *Agnihotra-pūjā*, penance, truth, *pūjā* to the *deva*s, *pūjā* to the guests, etc. *Pūrta* pertains more to *kāmya karma* as told in Smṛtis. That is, digging well, pond, lake, building temples, feeding people, etc. which are done for common good.

**Kabandhi** – Svāmī! You must explain the benefit attained by people doing this *iṣṭa* and *pūrta karma*s. As also what *karma* should persons having desire for *mokṣa* do?

**Pippalāda** – Child! The people who are doing *karma*s like *iṣṭa, pūrta* will move along the southern route and reach *chandra-loka.* They are the ones who aspire for comforts of this world. They do *karma* with a wish for its benefits and with great desire in that. They will get fame, happiness in this world and then they will enjoy a good heavenly life. When their *karma* benefits get over they will be again born in this world as per the aspirations of their previous life.

अथोत्तरेण तपसा ब्रह्मचर्येण श्रद्धया विद्ययाऽऽत्मानमन्विष्यादित्यमभि जयन्ते। एतद्वै प्राणानामायतनमेतदमृतमभयमेतत्। परायणमेतस्मान्न पुनरावर्तन्त इत्येष निरोधस्तदेष श्लोकः ॥१.१०॥

*athottareṇa tapasā brahmacaryeṇa śraddhayā vidyātmānam anviṣyādityam abhijayante* | *etadvai prāṇānām āyatanam etad amṛtam abhayam etat* | *parāyaṇam etasmān na punarāvartanta ity eṣa nirodhaḥ* | *tad eṣa ślokaḥ* ||1.10||

But those who seek the Self by *tapas*, *brahmacarya*, faith and knowledge, they attain the world of the sun by the northern path. That verily is the abode of *prāṇa*s, that is the immortal; that is the place of fearlessness, that is the final goal from where there is no return, for it is the termination. About that, there is this verse.

The persons who are interested in *mokṣa* will consider wisdom as the highest value and worship Sūrya by austerity (*tapas*), purity (*brahmacarya*), faith (*śraddhā*), go along the path of gods (*devayāna*) and reach the world of sun. This is only the fate of all living things. The final abode. This is the only nectar, indestructible, an asylum to be sought. The people who go there don't come back. But people with incorrect knowledge cannot reach there. Their incomplete knowledge or ignorance will be a block for them. There is a *mantra* describing its time scale.

**Kabandhi** – Svāmī! Kindly tell us the *mantra* pertaining to it.

**Pippalāda** –

> पञ्चपादं पितरं द्वादशाकृतिं दिव आहुः परे अर्धे पुरीषिणम्।
> अथेमे अन्य उ परे विचक्षणं सप्तचक्रे षडर आहुरर्पितमिति ॥१.११॥

> *pañca-pādaṁ pitaraṁ dvādaśākr̥tiṁ diva āhuḥ pare ardhe purīṣiṇam* |
> *atheme anya u pare vicakṣaṇaṁ sapta-cakre ṣaḍara āhur arpitam iti* ||1.11||

> He is spoken of as the father having five feet and twelve forms, seated in the higher half of heaven full of water. Still others speak of him as a genius set on (a chariot) of seven wheels and six spokes.

The Āditya which is the most exalted abode for all and which represents the time scale in the world has five legs and twelve forms. He is the father who is the cause of everyone's birth. His position is above the *devatās*. He who stays above everything is described by some as "the sun who holds the water" and "the Sun who is the knower of Time." Some others term it as an entity having complete knowledge and He is the *paramātmā*. He has seven horses and six spokes. He is the one who is in constant motion and in his form the entire world is contained. He is the one who gives asylum to the entire world. He is the form of time and year and He is the Prajāpati. He is also the form of Chandra, the moon. The nights formed by moon and the days formed by the sun both are together the cause of Time and formation of years.

**Sumantu** – The sun or *ravi* whom we see daily with our eyes is described in such beauty. I am sure such a description is not there in other literature. The seasons are described as *pādam* or legs, the months are described as organs or forms. It is very apt. Since the sun is the cause of rains, he is described as possessing the liquid-water. It is also correct.

**Kabandhi** – *Pādams* are told as five, however the seasons are six, isn't it?

**Sumantu** – The two cold seasons *hemanta* and *śiśiram* are combined as one and said to be five *pādams*. In the next line it is said that wheel has six spokes. The seven colours in the rainbow are only described as seven horses.

**Pippalāda** – Child Kabandhi! Now I will describe how the months are termed as Prajāpatis.

मासो वै प्राजपतिस्तस्य कृष्णपक्ष एव रयिः शुक्लः प्राणस्तस्मादेते
ऋषयः शुक्ल इष्टं कुर्वन्तीतर इतरस्मिन् ॥१.१२॥

*māso vai prājapatis tasya kr̥ṣṇa-pakṣa eva rayiḥ śuklaḥ prāṇas tasmād ete r̥ṣayaḥ śukla iṣṭaṁ kurvantī tara itarasmin* ||1.12||

Month verily is Prajāpati, emerging of it are the darker fortnight as *rayi* and the brighter fortnight as *prāṇa.* The *r̥ṣi*s therefore perform sacrifices in the brighter fortnight and others in the other fortnight.

The months here are understood as Prajāpatis. In that the waning moon period *kr̥ṣṇa-pakṣa* is *rayi* and waxing moon period *śukla-pakṣa* is *prāṇa*. However for these *r̥ṣi*s all are *śukla-pakṣa.* The *kr̥ṣṇa-pakṣa* is also meditated as a form of *śukla-pakṣa* or *prāṇa*. The *prāṇa* is seen in the form of *śukla-pakṣa* only by them. Apart from that they cannot see anything else. Hence the *yajña* they do in *kr̥ṣṇa-pakṣa* is also considered as being done in *śukla-pakṣa*. The one who doesn't understand the form of *prāṇa*s will be filled with the darkness of ignorance. Such people even if they perform *yajña* in *śukla-pakṣa* will still be considered as having done it in *kr̥ṣṇa-pakṣa*. Here *śukla-pakṣa* denotes enlightenment and *kr̥ṣṇa-pakṣa* denotes ignorance. Now, a day made up of day and night is also Prajāpati.

अहोरात्रो वै प्रजापतिस्तस्याहरेव प्राणो रात्रिरेव रयिः प्राणं वा एते
प्रस्कन्दन्ति ।
ये दिवा रत्या संयुज्यन्ते ब्रह्मचर्यमेव तद्यद्रात्रौ रत्या संयुज्यन्ते ॥१.१३॥

*aho-rātro vai prajāpatistasyāhar eva prāṇo rātrireva rayiḥ prāṇaṁ vā ete praskandanti* |

*ye divā ratyā saṁyujyante brahmacaryameva*
*tadyadrātrau ratyā saṁyujyante* ||1.13||

Day is verily Prajāpati, emerging of it, day time is indeed *prāṇa* and night indeed is *rayi*. Couple uniting in love by day time are dissipating their own *prāṇa*, couples uniting in love by night are practising *brahmacarya* indeed.

The day is understood as Prajāpati. In that the day is *prāṇa* and night is considered *rayi.* Whoever have a union in the night will be considered as having retained the *vrata* of *brahmacarya.* This is the great boon of *vedamāta*. Even persons in *gṛhasthāśrama* following this rule will get the benefit of *brahmacarya.* Child! Now I will answer your question further, listen.

अन्नं वै प्रजापतिस्ततो ह वै तद्रेतस्तस्मादिमाः प्रजाः प्रजायन्त इति ॥१.१४॥

*annaṁ vai prajāpatis tato ha vai tad retas tasmād imāḥ prajāḥ prajāyanta iti* ||1.14||

Food indeed is Prajāpati, emerging of it is semen from which creatures here are born.

तद्ये ह वै तत्प्रजापतिव्रतं चरन्ति ते मिथुनमुत्पादयन्ते।
तेषामेवैष ब्रह्मलोको येषां तपो ब्रह्मचर्यं येषु सत्यं प्रतिष्ठितम्॥१.१५॥

*tad ye ha vai tat prajāpati vrataṁ caranti te mithunam utpādayante*|
*teṣām evaiṣa brahmaloko yeṣāṁ tapo brahmacaryaṁ yeṣu satyaṁ pratiṣṭhitam* ||1.15 ||

Those who thus take the vow of Prajāpati beget couples. To them alone is given this word of *Brahman*; theirs alone is *tapas* and *brahmacarya*; in them alone is Reality well-founded.

*Annam* is Prajāpati! From that, sperm (*retas*) is produced. From that these *prajā*s are formed. If a married man (*gṛhastha*) does the *vrata* of Prajāpati (has union with wife in *ṛtu* season at night), he will produce sons and daughters. Thus the wheel of *saṁsāra* rotates. The world created in this way is what we see.

**Sumantu** – Dear children! I will tell now the teachings of *satguru* in short. Listen carefully, *Brahman* is only Prajāpati. That only becomes the couple called *sūrya* and *chandra*. It only becomes *prāṇa* (life) and *rayi* (matter). It becomes year, month, day, food and everything. Prajāpati which is a child grows eating the *annam* which is also Prajāpati. From that comes the Prajāpati which is sperm (*retas*). The mother Prajāpati conceives and gives birth to a child. That is also Prajāpati.

**Pippalāda** – We make small rings with gold. The rings are all gold. Then many rings are joined together to make a chain. That way everything is Prajāpati. People who concentrate only on *karma* will attain *chandraloka* (*pitṛloka*). And –

तेषामसौ विरजो ब्रह्मलोको न येषु जिह्ममनृतं न माया चेति ॥१.१६ ॥

*teṣām asau virajo brahma-loko na yeṣu jihmam anṛtaṁ na māyā ceti* ||1.16||

To them is given that blameless world of *Brahman*, in whom there is no crookedness, no falsehood, no trickery. The ones who do penance (*tapas*), austerity (*brahmacarya)*, follows purity, truth and do not have cunning thoughts, lies, deceit, they will attain *sūryaloka.* That is, the ones who have thought of the *deva*s and wisdom and are out of ignorance will attain the *sūryaloka*.

*oṁ tat sat*! Let goodness prevail everywhere.

(The disciples get up and salute the *maharṣi* and one by one leave the place.)

***(The curtain falls.)***

## SCENE 3

***(The curtain opens.)***

(Maharṣi Pippalāda's *āśrama*. All are sitting and conversing with one another.)

**Sumantu** – Children, let goodness prevail everywhere. Who is going to ask the question today?

**Bhārgava** – (**gets up and does *namaskārams***) Svāmī! I am thinking of asking a question.

**Pippalāda** – Child! Come and sit near. You may ask. I will give you the answer.

अथ हैनं भार्गवो वैदर्भि पप्रच्छः ।

*atha hainaṁ bhārgavo vaidarbhiḥ papracchaḥ* ।

Then Bhārgava of Vidarbha asked Pippalāda —

**Bhārgava** –

भगवन् कत्येव देवाः प्रजां विधारयन्ते कतर एतत्
प्रकाशयन्ते? कः पुनरेषां वरिष्ठ इति ॥२.१॥

*bhagavan katyeva devāḥ prajāṁ vidhārayante* ।
*katara etat prakāśayante? kaḥ punar eṣāṁ variṣṭha iti* ।।2.1।।

Venerable Sir, how many *deva*s sustain created beings? How many of them make themselves manifest? And who again is the principal among them?

Revered Guru! How many *deva*s are holding up the body? In them how many show their strength openly? Who is the best among them?

**Sumantu** – Sabāsh, a good question. It is matching properly with the first question. We learned about creator (Prajāpati), life (*prāṇa*), matter (*rayi*) and how they are present in the outside world. Now one should know how this Prajāpati is operating in the body.

तस्मै स होवाच

*tasmai sa hovāca*

To him, he (Pippalāda) said:

**Pippalāda** –

आकाशो ह वा एष देवो वायुरग्निरापः पृथिवी वाङ्मनश्चक्षुः श्रोत्रम् च।
ते प्रकाश्याभिवदन्ति वयमेतद्बाणं अवष्टभ्य विधारयामः॥२.२॥

*ākāśo ha vā eṣa devo vāyur agnir āpaḥ pṛthivī vāṅ manaś cakṣuḥ śrotram ca* ।
*te prakāśyābhivadanti vayam etad bāṇam avaṣṭabhya vidhārayāmaḥ* ।।2.2।।

Space verily is such a god, so too are wind, fire, water, earth, speech, mind, eye, ear. They, becoming illumined declare: "We sustain this arrow in coherence."

Child! space (*ākāśa*), air (*vāyu*), fire (*agni*), earth (*pṛthivī*), water (*āpaḥ*) are the five elements. The organs associated with action (*karmendriyas*) are five. The organs helping to get knowledge (*jñānendriyas*) are four. The inner organs of perception (*antaḥkaraṇa*) are five. Thus there are nineteen *devas* in all sustaining the body. Each of them show their capacities and help the body to function properly without any hindrance. Of them who is the best? I will answer the question by telling you a story.

**Sumantu** – Children! Hearing that it is a story don't be careless in listening. An important philosopy will be contained in each sentence. To explain those philosophies only *maharṣi* is telling this way.

**Bhārgava** – Respected one! We will listen very carefully.

**Pippalāda** – Once all these *devatās* who stay in the body fought with one another. Each one having become very proud, stated "I only am holding the body together." They thus proudly shouted. Seeing this the main *prāṇa* told, "due to ignorance you are all getting unnecessarily proud. Really, none of you are holding the body. I only have split my form into five and am holding the body firmly."

The *prāṇa* says –

तान् वरिष्ठः प्राण उवाच मा मोहमापद्यथाहमेवैतत्पञ्चधात्मानं
प्रविभज्यैतद्बाणमवष्टभ्य विधारयामीति। तेऽश्रद्दधाना बभूवुः ॥२.३॥

*tān variṣṭhaḥ prāṇa uvāca* | *mā moham āpadyatha aham evaitat pañcadhātmānaṁ pravibhajyyaitad bāṇam avaṣṭabhya vidhārayāmīti te 'śraddadhānā babhūvuḥ* ||2.3||

To them the chief *prāṇa* said: Do not be deluded; I alone, dividing myself fivefold, sustain this arrow. But they became faithless in him.

In spite of *prāṇa* telling them this calmly in different ways, they were not ready to listen to the *prāṇa*. They were only thinking of their own greatness and behaving in a headstrong manner.

**Bhārgava** – Then what happened?

**Hiraṇyanābha** – Bhagavan! The story is very interesting. Do continue and tell us the rest.

**Pippalāda** – Then the *prāṇa* decided to teach the *devatā*s, who claimed to be the cause of running the body, a proper lesson.

सोऽभिमानादूर्ध्वमुत्क्रमत इव। तस्मिनुत्क्रामत्यथेतरे सर्व
एवोत्क्रामन्ते तस्मिंश्च प्रतिष्ठमाने सर्व एव प्रतिष्ठन्ते ॥४a॥

*so 'bhimānād ūrdhvam utkramata iva tasmin utkrāmatyathetare sarvam evotkrāmante, tasmiṁśca pratiṣṭhamāne sarva eva pratiṣṭhante* ||2.4a||

He from indignation pretented to rise up (from the body). At his rising up all other (gods) were also found rising up. On his settling down they were also found settling down.

He mockingly started to move out of the body and rise above. The minute he started going out all *devatā*s who were triumphantly claiming their supremacy lost their strength and were forced to leave the body and follow the *prāṇa* to rise above.

**Sumantu** – Did you notice the fate of the senses who had swelled with pride? Children, these senses blinded in their pride did not accept that all of them were together holding the body. Instead, each one thought he was the one most important and indulged in an unnecessary fight. Even when the truth was explained by the main *prāṇa*, they chose to ignore it. Though they behaved so badly, the *prāṇa* was sad rather than being angry. It showed mock anger and acted as if it was leaving the body. If really it had left the body, the story would have ended and there would not have been any place for further conversation.

**Bhārgava** – Svāmī! Afterwards what happened?

**Pippalāda** – The *prāṇa* which thought of leaving the body took pity on them and remained back in the body. Because of that the others also could stay back in the body. They got involved in their respective work. They behaved like honey bees following the queen bee.

**Kauśalya** – How does the honey bee follow the queen bee? Kindly explain in detail.

**Pippalāda** –

> तद्यथा मक्षिका मधुकरराजानमुत्क्रमन्तं सर्वा एवोत्क्रामन्ते। तस्मिꣳश्च प्रतिष्ठमाने सर्वा एव प्रातिष्ठन्त। एवं वाङ्मनश्चक्षुःश्रोत्रं च ते प्रीताः प्राणं स्तुन्वन्ति ॥२.४b ॥
>
> *tad yathā makṣikā madhukara rājānam utkramantaṁ sarvā evotkrāmante। tasmiṁśca pratiṣṭhamāne sarvā eva prātiṣṭhanta evaṁ vāṅmanaś cakṣuḥ śrotraṁ ca te prītāḥ prāṇaṁ stunvanti* ||2.4b||
>
> On the queen bee's rising up all bees rise up, and all settle down when the queen bee settles down. Even so are speech, mind, sight, hearing and so on. Satisfied, they praise *prāṇa* thus: If the queen bee deserts the beehive and leaves, all

the honey bees will follow suit. Later, if the honey bee goes to another beehive or returns to the same beehive, the other honey bees also return there.

**Sumantu** – Like that, till *prāṇa* remains in the body, the others will remain there. If *prāṇa* goes out they also have to go out. They cannot anymore stay there. When this truth was clearly known, understanding the greatness of the *prāṇas*, the *devatās* left their pride.

**Hiraṇyanābha** – Respected one! I have heard a story like this narrated by Maharṣi Vasiṣṭha at the palace.

**Sukeśa** – Is that so, Aśvakośa, do tell us that now.

**Sumantu** – Child Aśvakośa! We are also eager to know that. Do tell us that story.

**Hiraṇyanābha** – Elders! Friends please accept my *praṇāmas*. Where does a person of my standing have a right to talk in this exalted gathering? However this is the statement of Maharṣi Vasiṣṭha and hence I am narrating it with some confidence. Once the sense organs, the eyes, ears, nose, mouth, hands, legs all of them joined together and thought, "we are taking a lot of effort in bringing food and filling the stomach. The stomach like a lazy one stays where it is and eats everything. It asks for more and more. From now onwards we need not work ourselves for this stomach. Let us stop our work." So saying they stopped work. The stomach advised variously, but the sense organs filled with self-pride continued to strike work. Two or three days passed. Since the stomach was starved all the sense organs also started becoming weak. The leg could not be moved here or there. The eyes got sunk in the socket. Likewise, each one lost its strength and was suffering. Then they realized the situation. They left their fight with the stomach and without much loss of time resumed their respective works.

**Kauśalya** – Friend! The story is indeed very interesting.

**Bhārgava** – Bhagavan! What did the the *devatās* do thereafter?

**Pippalāda** – The *devatās* who proudly shouted learned the lesson taught by *prāṇa* and sang in praise of it. "Like a palace is held by the pillars we only hold this body and see that it does not fall down and get damaged and thus we only look after it."

**Sumantu** – When an indifferent attitude and pride left, happiness and gratitude took its place. After realizing the truth, to express it the best way is to sing devotional songs praising the *prāṇa*.

**Bhārgava** – How did they express them in songs? How did they tell and sing in praise?

**Pippalāda** – I have answered the question raised by you. *Prāṇa* is the greatest. That truth you must have understood by this story. Still, to further reinforce this information, I will recite the song sung in praise of *prāṇa*. With great *bhakti* the senses chanted —

> एषोऽग्निस्तपत्येष सूर्य एष पर्जन्यो मघवानेष वायुः एष पृथिवी रयिर्देवः सदसच्चामृतं च यत्॥२.५॥
>
> *eṣo 'gnis tapaty eṣa sūrya eṣa parjanyo maghavāneṣa vāyuḥ* | *eṣa pr̥thivī rayirdevaḥ sadasaccāmr̥taṁ ca yat* ||2.5||
>
> As fire He burns; He is the sun; He is rain as well as Raingod (Maghavān); He is the wind; He is the earth, *rayi* and gods. He is being and non-being and the Immortal too.

O *prāṇa*! You act as *agni* (fire). You burn and cook everything. You are the sun, the cloud, Indra, *vāyu*, *pr̥thivī* (earth), *chandra* (moon) and water. Existing things or non-existing things which are in proper form and not in proper form are none else but you. The indestructible nectar-like *parabrahman* is you.

**Sumantu** – The main *prāṇa* acts as *agni* and burns. It takes the form of sun and gives light. The same *prāṇa* becomes cloud and pours down rain. It becomes Indra and takes care of the *prajās*. It destroys the *asura* (evil forces) and protects the *devas* (good forces). The different *vāyus* as *āvāham, pravāham, nivāham,* also belong to the main *prāṇa*. The *prāṇa* also acts as earth and holds the whole world. He is only *rayi* — matter (*chandra*). He is the nurturer of the entire world. He is the gross and subtle form.

**Pippalāda** – Children! I will recite the devotional prayer further.

> अरा इव रथनाभौ प्राणे सर्वं प्रतिष्ठितम्।
> ऋचो यजूंषि सामानि यज्ञः क्षत्रं ब्रह्म च ॥२.६॥
>
> *arā iva ratha-nābhau prāṇe sarvaṁ pratiṣṭhitaṁ* ।
> *ṛco yajūṁṣi sāmāni yajñaḥ kṣatraṁ brahma ca* ।।2.6।।
>
> Like spokes in the hub of a wheel, all are well fixed in *prāṇa* — the *Ṛg* (verses) the *Yajus* (formulas) and the *Sāman* (chants), as also sacrifice, valour and wisdom.

Like the spokes in the axle of the wheel everything is fitted in you. You are the *Ṛgveda, Yajurveda, Sāmaveda,* the *yajña, Brahman* and all. You are the Prajāpati. You are the one inside the womb. You are the one born outside. O *prāṇa*! These *prajā*s bring you sacrifical offerings. You are also seen with all the sense organs.

**Sumantu** – With this devotional prayer, *prāṇa*'s paramount importance has been explained. Just as in the centre of the wheel spokes are joined, in the same way in this universe all the substances are connected with *prāṇa*. The three Vedas and *yajña*s done through that, the kshatriyas who are the rulers and the protectors of everyone, the brāhmaṇas who do the *yajña*s are all this *prāṇa*.

> प्रजापतिश्चरसि गर्भे त्वमेव प्रतिजायसे।
> तुभ्यं प्राणः प्रजास्त्विमा बलिं हरन्ति यः प्राणैः प्रतितिष्ठसि ॥२.७॥
>
> *prajāpatiś carasi garbhe tvam eva pratijāyase* ।
> *tubhyaṁ prāṇaḥ prajāstvimā baliṁ haranti yaḥ prāṇaiḥ pratitiṣṭhasi* ।।2.7।।

O *prāṇa*, as Prajāpati you move within wombs; you yourself are born repeatedly. These creatures, in each of whom you dwell along with *prāṇa*s, bring offerings to you.

The body and the holder of the body, the mother and father, the womb, the foetus and the child are all *prāṇa*. He is the *sarvātmā* (everybody's *ātmā*). The human beings who are *prajā*s are doing sacrificial *pūjā* with their sense organs like eyes, ears, nose, and tongue. The pleasures enjoyed by the sense organs are all but sacrificial offerings to *prāṇa*. Satisfied with the offerings of these sense organs, you embrace them. The sense organs become happy with the embrace and again get ready for the *pūjā* which is only just. It is correct also because *prāṇa* is the *bhoktā* (enjoyer). The rest are only objects of enjoyment.

**Kabandhi** – Respected Guru, these answers explain my question.

**Sumantu** – Yes, your enquiry's continuation is only the second question.

**Pippalāda** –

देवानामसि वह्नितमः पितॄणां प्रथमा स्वधा ।
ऋषीणां चरितं सत्यमथर्वाङ्गिरसामसि ॥२.८॥

*devanām asi vahnitamaḥ pitṝṇāṁ prathamā svadhā* |
*ṛṣīṇāṁ caritaṁ satyam atharvāṅgirasām asi* ||2.8||

Among gods you are the best carrier (of offerings). Among manes you are the first *svadhā* offering. Of *ṛṣi*s like Atharvan and Aṅgiras you are their truthful conducts.

O *prāṇa*! You are the supreme fire and you take the *havis* to *devas*. You take the *annam to pitṛ*s (ancestors). You are the functionary in the sense organs as well as the power which makes the sense organs function.

इन्द्रस्त्वं प्राण तेजसा रुद्रोऽसि परिरक्षिता ।
त्वमन्तरिक्षे चरसि सूर्यस्त्वं ज्योतिषां पतिः ॥२.९॥

*indrastvaṁ prāṇa tejasā rudro 'si parirakṣitā* |
*tvam antarikṣe carasi sūryastvaṁ jyotiṣāṁ patiḥ*
||2.9||

O *prāṇa*, you are Indra by your valour; you are Rudra, the protector; you are the sun orbiting in the atmosphere, the lord of the luminaries.

Hey *prāṇa*! You are Indra representing the *tejas*. You are Rudra who annihilates the world. You are also the protector. You are the sun moving in the sky who is supreme of all lights.

यदा त्वमभिवर्षस्यथेमाः प्राण ते प्रजाः।
आनन्दरूपास्तिष्ठन्ति कामायान्नं भविष्यतीति ॥२.१०॥

*yadā tvam abhivarṣasyathemāḥ prāṇa te prajāḥ* |
*ānanda-rūpāstiṣṭhanti kāmāyānnaṁ bhaviṣyatīti*
||2.10||

O *prāṇa* these creatures of yours live as embodiments of happiness on seeing you pouring down as rain, thinking of the possibility of sufficient food.

When you pour the rain at that time these *prajā*s become happy thinking they will now get enough food. It is all the result of your mercy.

**Sumantu** – If there is no *prāṇa* the body will dry up. Hence it is *prāṇa* which gives secretions in the organs and keeps them alive.

**Pippalāda** – The *śloka* in praise of *prāṇa* continues further,

व्रात्यस्त्वं प्राणैकऋषिरत्ता विश्वस्य सत्पतिः।
वयमाद्यस्य दातारः पिता त्वं मातरिश्व नः॥२.११॥

*vrātyas tvaṁ prāṇaika ṛṣir attā viśvasya satpatiḥ* |
*vayam ādyasya dātāraḥ pitā tvaṁ mātariśva naḥ*
||2.11||

Untouched by initiatory rites, O *prāṇa*, you are the one seer, the enjoyer, the Lord of all existence. O Mātariśvan, you are our father, we the givers of enjoyables.

O *prāṇa* you are known by the name of *ekarṣi* (the only *ṛṣi*) who consumes everything.You are lord of the entire world. We are all the one who give you material for consumption.

**Bhārgava** – Svāmī! What is meant by *vrātyaḥ*?

**Pippalāda** – *Vrātyaḥ* means the one who has not been tainted by *saṁskāra* (the previous *karmas*). Each *prajā* as soon as it is born is already tainted by some *saṁskāras* done by his father, mother and by himself in the previous birth. However, *prāṇa* is the first Prajāpati, the first member of the world. He does not have any parents. The one who has no *saṁskāras* is *vrātyaḥ*. Here the concept is that the Self is only the pure one.

The *śloka* elobarates about *prāṇa* –

या ते तनूर्वाचि प्रतिष्ठिता या श्रोत्रे या च चक्षुषि।
या च मनसि सन्तता शिवां तां कुरु मोत्क्रमीः ॥२.१२॥

*yā te tanūr vāci pratiṣṭhitā yā śrotre yā ca cakṣuṣi* |
*yā ca manasi santatā śivāṁ tāṁ kuru motkramīḥ*
||2.12||

That subtle form of yours, the firm basis of speech, ears and eyes, which pervades mind too incessantly, please make it auspicious; do not depart.

O Vāyu! You have mingled with us in our body, eyes and mind. Combining with our body you have kept it as *Śivam*. Let it be blessed always. You should not rise and go up. If you detach yourself from the body the blessedness will go away and this body will become a corpse. Hence kindly be considerate. Don't leave the body and rise up.

**Bhārgava** – Respected one, the *ślokas* sound very beautiful and are full of knowledge-giving words. Please continue the *ślokas*.

**Pippalāda** –

प्राणस्येदं वशे सर्वं त्रिदिवे यत्प्रतिष्ठितम्।
मातेव पुत्रान् रक्षस्व श्रीश्च प्रज्ञाम् च विधेहि नः इति॥२.१३॥

*prāṇasyedaṁ vaśe sarvaṁ tridive yat pratiṣṭhitam*।
*māteva putrān rakṣasva śrīśca prajñām ca vidhehi naḥ iti*।।2.13।।

Everything in this world is under the control of *prāṇa*. All that exists in the three worlds is under the control of *prāṇa*. O *prāṇa*, protect us as a mother does her children. Please grant to us prosperity and wisdom.

"In this entire world, both the inner world and outer world belong to you. Protect us like a mother. Give us prosperity and wisdom," thus the *devatā*s prayed to the main *prāṇa*.

**Bhārgava** – Respected one! What is the reason the *devatā*s asked for prosperity and wisdom? Kindly explain in detail.

**Sumantu** – The capacity to understand good information and make use of it; then an opportunity to come across the wisdom bearing information, these are called prosperity by the good people. This is the real wealth and education. The feeling for good thought is wisdom. A person getting such wealth of education can conduct his sense organs in a good path and conduct his life in a proper and disciplined way.

**Kabandhi** – At the beginning of the lesson we recited the *śānti-pāṭha*. It has the same meaning.

**Bhārgava** – We remember it very well. We should hear good things. We should see only good things. Thus we sang in the beginning.

**Sumantu** – Children! Once they had been beaten these *devatā*s lost confidence in their strength and intellect. Hence they were asking a boon very carefully. They pray to *prāṇa*, "Protect us, O *prāṇa* just as a mother protects her children." Ordinarily three people take care of us. The king, father and mother. Of them the first two, the king and father give whatever is asked for and take care of us. Only the mother gives without asking. Thus, in comparison to the other two, the mother's affection is superior. There is no comparison to mother in showing love and sympathy. Hence we say motherland and Vedamāta in praise of the mother's role. The *devatās* say at the end of the devotional prayer song, "We are asking the things required for us. If those things will give us solace kindly give them, like a proud mother who nurtures and brings up children and like a mother who forgives a thousand mistakes and patiently bears them, in the same way you must protect us."

**Pippalāda** – Children! Friend! Today let us stop it here.

**Sumantu** – Let us do so. The noon prayer time is nearing. Let us go.

***(They get up and go. The curtain closes.)***

## SCENE 4

***(Curtain opens.)***

(The scene is as before, Pippalāda and others are sitting and conversing.)

**Kauśalya** – Svāmī, kindly allow me to ask questions today.

**Pippalāda** – Child, you may ask with all the liberty.

अथ हैनं कौसल्यश्चाश्वलायनः पप्रच्छ ।

*atha hainaṁ Kauśalyaścāśvalāyanaḥ papraccha* |

Then Kauśalya, the son of Aśvala, asked Pippalāda:

**Kauśalya** –

भगवन्कुत एष प्राणो जायते कथमायात्यस्मिञ्छरीरे? आत्मानं वा प्रविभज्य कथं प्रातिष्ठते केनोत्क्रमते? कथं बाह्यमभिधत्ते? कथमध्यात्ममिति ॥३.१॥

*bhagavan kuta eṣa prāṇo jāyate kathamāyāty asmiñcharīre? ātmānaṁ vā pravibhajya kathaṁ prātiṣṭhate? kenotkramate? kathaṁ bāhyam abhidhatte? katham adhyātmam iti* ||3.1||

Venerable Sir, whence is this *prāṇa* born? How does he come into this body? Himself divided, how does he find stability? By what means does he sustain the external? How does he sustain the self-based?

Respected Guru, how does this *prāṇa* get formed? From where is it born? How it came into this body? How does it stabilize in the body? How does it go out? How does it hold the external world (the basic elements in the universe)? How does it hold the inside world (physical body)? Kindly tell all this in detail, respected one.

तस्मै स होवाचा

*tasmai sa hovācā*
He then said to him:

**Pippalāda –**

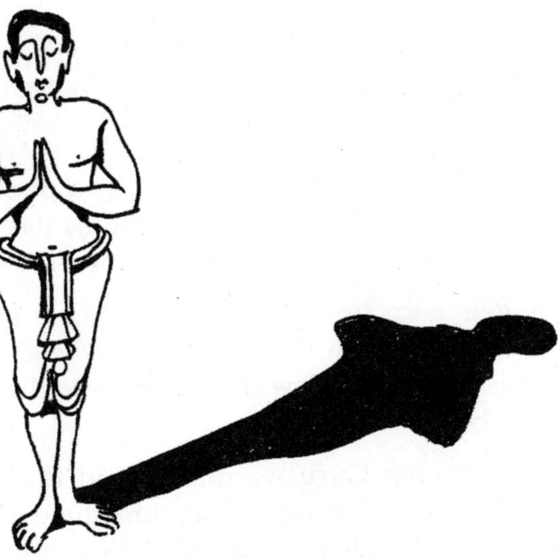

*fig* : **Prāṇa is like a shadow from Ātmā**

तिप्रश्नान्पृच्छसि ब्रह्मिष्ठोऽसीति तस्मात्तेऽहं ब्रवीमि ॥३.२॥

*tipraśnān pṛcchasi brahmiṣṭho 'sīti tasmāt te 'haṁ bravīmi* ||3.2||

The question you are asking is beyond limits. Yet, seeing you yearning for nothing but *Brahman*, I shall answer you.

Child! You are asking a difficult and complicated question. However you are a disciplined brāhmaṇa, *Brahman* knowledge follower and a keen enquirer. You are an exalted and deserving person. I will answer your enquiries in detail, listen.

**Sumantu** – In the second question we heard praises of *prāṇa*. In this question we will understand how it operates, how it splits and spreads into the entities and how it later goes out and where it reaches. Friend! this third question is aptly related and in continuation of the earlier questions.

**Pippalāda** –

आत्मन एष प्राणो जायते। यथैषा पुरुषे छायैतस्मिन्नेतदाततं
मनोकृतेनायात्यस्मिञ्छरीरे ॥३.३॥

*ātmana eṣa prāṇo jāyate | yathaiṣā puruṣe chāyaitasminnetadātataṁ manokṛtenāyātyasmin śarīre | |3.3| |*

This *prāṇa* is born of the Self (*ātman*). As a person has a shadow, so too this (*prāṇa*) is pervaded by this (Self). It comes into this body through (its own) mind-activity.

This *prāṇa* gets born from *ātmā*. Just as how a shadow rises from the human body, in the same way *prāṇa* also rises from the *ātmā*. It is like the shadow of *ātmā*. Due to the act of mind it enters the body.

**Bhārgava** – Revered Guru we understand that the *ātmā* is changeless. It does not change in the three time periods (past, present and future). This being so how does *prāṇa* get created from *ātmā*?

**Sumantu** – Child, didn't you observe properly the example given by the *maharṣi*? Depending on the position of the sun in the sky and the position of man standing in front of it, the shadows are formed short or long. In the same way, from one *ātmā* the *prāṇa*s come out and reach different bodies. If the shadow forms the *puruṣa* does not get changed in any manner.

**Kabandhi** – Kindly explain in detail the role of *ātmā* in the creation of a human being?

**Sumantu** – My child! During the full moon night if different vessels of small and big sizes are kept on the ground and filled with water, the full moon will shine in all of them. In a small vessel it will be seen as small, in a big vessel it will be seen as big, in a moving vessel it will be seen as a moving thing. The changes in reflections however do not bring any change in the moon in the sky. Now imagine the *ātmā* in place of the moon, the body in place of the water and think. The truth will become clear.

**Sauryāyaṇi** – Svāmī! The example you narrated gave us a good understanding.

**Kauśalya** – Respected one, we understood that rising from the immortal being (*akṣara-Brahman*) *prāṇa*s enter the human body due to man's *karma*s formed as per his intention and wish. Later, how does it operate in the human body? Kindly explain this clearly.

**Kabandhi** – Who is the one who separates this *vāyu* and stabilizes them in different places. Is there any philosophy or concept for this placement.

**Pippalāda** –

> यथा सम्राडेवाधिकृतान्विनियुङ्क्ते एतान्ग्रामानेतान्ग्रामानधितिष्ठस्वेत्येवमेवैष प्राण इतरान्प्राणान्पृथक् पृथगेव सन्निधत्ते ॥३.४ ॥
>
> *yathā samrāḍevādhikṛtān viniyuṅkte* । *etān grāmānetān grāmānadhi tiṣṭhasvety evam evaiṣa prāṇa itarān prāṇān pṛthak pṛthag eva sannidhatte* ।।3.4।।
>
> As an emperor commands his officials saying, "Superintendent such and such districts," even so this *prāṇa* directs other *prāṇa*s in their respective functions.

As a king appoints his representative officers and each one is given a duty to show his authority in different parts of the country, in the same way the main *prāṇa* sends as its representatives the other *prāṇa*s and commands the different parts. Initially I explained how the main *prāṇa* separates as *prāṇa, apāna* and *samāna* and how it spreads in the body. I also explained their places of functioning. Now I will tell about the other *prāṇa*s as *vyāna* and *udāna*.

**Kabandhi** – Respected Sir. Do bless us with more knowledgeable words.

**Pippalāda** – O! The one having a beautiful mind, the *prāṇa* enters the body and splits into five. They are *prāṇa, apāna samāna, udāna* and *vyāna*.

> पायूपस्थेऽपानं चक्षुःश्रोत्रे मुखनासिकाभ्यां प्राणः स्वयं प्रातिष्ठते मध्ये तु समानः। एष ह्येतद्धुमन्नं समं नयति तस्मादेताः सप्तार्चिषो भवन्ति ॥३.५॥
>
> *pāyūpasthe 'pānaṁ cakṣuḥ śrotre mukha nāsikābhyāṁ prāṇaḥ svayaṁ prātiṣṭhate madhye tu samānaḥ | eṣa hyetad hutaṁ annaṁ samaṁ nayati tasmād etāḥ saptārcciṣo bhavanti ||3.5||*
>
> To the excretory organ and genitals (is directed) *apāna* (the downward vital function). *Prāṇa* himself functions in the eyes and ears, in the mouth and nose. *Samāna* (equalizing vital function) that distributes Indeed equitably whatever is offered as food, is directed to the middle region; from it arises the seven flames.

By the name of *apāna* it stabilizes in the lower regions below the navel. The *prāṇa* coming out of the face and nose stabilizes in the eyes and ears. Near the navel it is known as *samāna*; from here it distributes the food partaken equally to all the organs. That is why seven flames are rising up.

**Kabandhi** – Which are the seven flames?

**Sumantu** – Two eyes, two ears, two nostrils, one mouth, thus making a total of seven flames. Through the sense organs connected to the seven holes the *prāṇa* gets the knowledge of sight, hearing, etc. The food which is coming to the stomach is distributed equally by the *samāna* to all the organs. Because of that the sense organs gain strength and the brightness of seeing, etc. takes place. If food is not there, all remain depleted. Here the food is considered as *havis* (fodder), the process of eating is *homa* and the sense organs are regarded as flames.

**Pippalāda** –

हृदि ह्येष आत्मा। अत्रैतदेकशतं नाडीनां तासां शतं शतमेकैकस्यां द्वासप्ततिर्द्वासप्ततिः प्रतिशाखानाडीसहस्राणि भवन्त्यासु व्यानश्चरति ॥३.६॥

*hṛdi hy eṣa ātmā | atraitat ekaśataṁ nāḍīnāṁ tāsāṁ śataṁ śatam ekaikasyāṁ dvāsaptatir dvāsaptatiḥ pratiśākhānāḍīsahasrāṇi bhavanty āsu vyānaś carati ||3.6||*

In the heart is this self. From here are issued one hundred and one arteries. From each one of them are issued a hundred smaller arteries. From each of these branches are issued seventy-two thousand sub-branches. Within all these moves *vyāna* (the diffused breath).

This *jīvātmā* gets fixed in the heart. In the heart there are 101 important *nāḍīs*. Each one separates into a hundred branches. Each of these branches further separates and they total 72,000 smaller branches. In all these *nāḍīs*, *vyāna* moves. Among these thousands of *nāḍīs* one goes upwards. That is called *suṣumnā nāḍī*. In that *udāna* moves. Because of this *udāna* the *prāṇa* is able to leave the body.

**Kauśalya** – What happens to the life which leaves the body?

**Pippalāda** –

अथैकयोर्ध्व उदानः पुण्येन पुण्यं लोकं नयति पापेन पापं उभाभ्यामेव मनुष्यलोकम् ॥७॥

*athaikayordhva udānaḥ puṇyena puṇyaṁ lokaṁ nayati | pāpena pāpaṁ ubhābhyām eva manuṣyalokam ||3.7||*

Now, *udāna* (the upward breath) is that which moves upwards alone. Following meritorious deeds it leads to the world of merits; following sinful deeds it leads to the world of sins. Following both kinds of deeds it leads to the human world.

Those who do *puṇya,* they are taken to *puṇyaloka* by *udāna.* Those who act according to the scriptures they are *puṇyātmās.* They are born as *devas.* Those who do mixed *karma* reach the human world. It is the job of *udāna* to take the life force to the different worlds.

**Kauśalya** – Svāmī! We understand about *prāṇa*'s appearence, its coming inside, its passage in the body and leaving the body. Now do tell us how *prāṇa* holds itself in the outside world and inside world.

**Pippalāda** – Children! Listen carefully. I will tell you the relationship between the outside *prāṇa* which is *samaṣṭi* (all-pervading) in form and the *prāṇa* which is inside the body which is *vyaṣṭi* (individual) in form. The *prāṇa* in different *samaṣṭi* forms operates the individual *prāṇas* in the body pertaining to different functions. For example, the outside *prāṇa* is the sun. This operates the *prāṇa* of the eyes. The *prāṇa* of the sun which is *samaṣṭi* blesses the *prāṇa* of the eyes which is *prāṇa* of the physical body and is *vyaṣṭi.* In the same way outside *prāṇas* operate the other *prāṇas* in the body along with the related controlling *devatās.*

आदित्यो ह वै बाह्यः प्राण उदयत्येष ह्येनं चाक्षुषं प्राणमनुगृह्णानः।
पृथिव्यां या देवता सैषा पुरुषस्यापानमवष्टभ्यान्तराः यदाकाशः स
समानो वायुर्व्यानः ॥३.८॥

*ādityo ha vai bāhyaḥ prāṇa udayatyeṣa hyenaṁ cākṣuṣaṁ prāṇam anugṛhṇānaḥ* | *pṛthivyāṁ yā devatā saiṣā puruṣasyāpānam avaṣṭabhyāntarāḥ yadākāśaḥ sa samāno vāyur vyānaḥ* ||3.8||

तेजो ह वाव उदनस्तस्मादुपशान्ततेजाः
पुनर्भवमिन्द्रियैर्मनसि सम्पद्यमानैः ॥३.९॥

*tejo ha vāva udanas tasmād upaśāntatejāḥ*
*punarbhavam indriyair manasi sampadyamānaiḥ* ||3.9||

The sun, verily, as the externally manifest *prāṇa* rises gracing the *prāṇa* of the eyes. The divinity in the earth seizes *apāna* in man. What is in between (the sun and the earth) is *samāna,* and air is *vyāna.*

Fire verily is *udāna.* One, whose lustre has died out with senses sunk in the mind, re-emerges.

For example, the *devatā* in earth operates the *apāna* of the body. *Apāna vāyu* has an attraction towards going down. This is the gravitational force of the earth. It is due to this that the body stays in the ground without going up or falling down. The *vāyu* in space operates the *samāna* in the body. The air which moves outside blesses the *vyāna*. Just like the air is spread everywhere outside, *vyāna* is spread all over the body.

**Sumantu** – The main *prāṇa* comes from the sun, *apāna* originates from earth, *samāna* originates from space, *vyāna* originates from air (*vāyu*), *udāna* originates from *tejas* such as stars, lightening, etc. Thus the five outside *prāṇa*s are connected to the inside *prāṇa*s. Isn't that so, my friend?

**Pippalāda** – Yes Maharṣi! When the *udāna vāyu* goes out of the body, then it is told *tejas* has gone out of the body (*tejas* means brightness). When *udāna vāyu* leaves, the life ebbs out. The body starts cooling. It is then called a corpse. This *tejas* only is born again. The sense organs like speech which are bottled inside the mind are also born again.

यच्चित्तस्तेनैष प्राणमायाति प्राणस्तेजसा युक्तः।
सहात्मना यथा संकल्पितं लोकं नयति ॥३.१०॥

*yac cittas tenaiṣa prāṇam āyāti prāṇas tejasā yuktaḥ* |
*sahātmanā yathā saṁkalpitaṁ lokaṁ nayati* ||3.10||

> As one's thinking is so, he attains *prāṇa. Prāṇa* functions undifferentiated from lustre. Along with *ātmā*, it leads the world as mind conceives.

During the time of death with whatever intention (*saṁkalpa*) a person leaves the body with those thoughts he joins with the main *prāṇa*. That *prāṇa* joining with *udāna* along with the life force reaches the world of intention (*saṁkalpa*) at the time of death. That is, he reaches the world in accordance with the thoughts at the time of death.

**Sauryāyaṇi** – Respected Sir, as you say according to a person's intention at the time of the death he goes to *pāpaloka* or *puṇyaloka*. In that case, if a person who does good deeds throughout life but slips during the period of death, will he then reach the world of sin — *pāpaloka*? In the same way, a person who wastes his time in bad ways and in the last stages alone holds some good thoughts, will he reach *puṇyaloka*? This idea is very disturbing, please explain.

**Sukeśa** – I am also getting this doubt. Kindly explain this anomaly.

**Pippalāda** – Friend, do clear the doubt of these children.

**Sumantu** – During the final stages whatever a person thinks and leaves the body, he is destined to reach that thing. There is no doubt regarding this. What is learned in the cradle will come till the graveyard. What is seen in *svapna* is sometimes thought during waking time (*jāgar̥ta avasthā*) isn't it? Whatever has been thought deeply and long during this lifetime, that alone will come to the forefront during death. It would not happen otherwise as Sauryāyaṇi fears. Whatever is thought of during death is the seed for the next *janma* or next birth. The birth which will be coming is only the gross form of that thought.

**Pippalāda** –

> य एवं विद्वान्प्राणं वेद। न हास्य प्रजा हीयतेऽमृतो भवति तदेष
> श्लोकः ॥३.११॥

*ya evaṁ vidvān prāṇaṁ veda* | *na hāsya prajā*
*hīyate 'mṛto bhavati tad eṣa ślokaḥ* ||3.11||

The wise one, knowing *prāṇa* thus, his progeny never terminates. He becomes immortal. As to this there is this verse:

उत्पत्तिमायतिं स्थानं विभुत्वं चैव पञ्चधा।
अध्यात्मं चैव प्राणस्य विज्ञायामृतमश्नुते।
विज्ञायामृतमश्नुत इति ॥३.१२॥

*utpattim āyati sthānaṁ vibhutvaṁ caiva pañcadhā* |
*adhyātmaṁ caiva prāṇasya vijñāyāmṛtam aśnute* |
*vijñāyāmṛtam aśnuta iti* ||3.12||

Knowing *prāṇa*'s birth, entrance, abode, fivefold all-pervasiveness and relation to the Self in detail, one becomes immortal! On knowing in detail one becomes immortal!

A person who understands *prāṇa* like this, a person who contemplates and understands the origin of *prāṇa* and who does *upāsanā* on this will attain the nectar-filled path. That is, the one who understands the orgin of *prāṇa,* its entry into the body, its place in the different parts of the body, how it splits into five and rules the body, who understands this physical relationship of the outside and the inside, reaches the deathless state, so says this *mantra*.

**Sumantu** – Children! The *maharṣi* answered the question raised by Kauśalya. I hope you all understood it very well. What Kauśalya! Can you tell us in brief what you understand.

**Pippalāda** – Child! I am giving my blessings to you. You are a student of brāhmaṇa. Explain it in short and make it clear.

**Kauśalya** – *Maharṣis, namaskāram*. I will tell you as much as I have understood. This *prāṇa* was formed like a shadow from *paramātmā*. As per the intention (*saṁkalpa*) of a mind it enters the body, splits and reaches the sense organs such as eyes, ears and other parts. Like the officials appointed by the king they perform the job designated to them. Once the mind's intention (*saṁkalpa*) is over, it leaves the gross body for the outside along with *suṣumnā* and *karma* bodies. The thoughts which rise in the mind towards the end form the base for the next life.

**Pippalāda** – Child, you have explained it very well. You are a deserving person. I am fortunate to have a disciple like you.

**Kauśalya** – All this is your blessing, Svāmī.

**Pippalāda** – Children! Let us stop today's lesson here. What do you say, my friend?

**Sumantu** – Let it be so, my friend.

(The disciples get up and pay their respects. Both *maharṣis* give their blessing.)

## PART IV

### SCENE I

***(Curtain opens.)***

(The *pūjā* room in Pippalāda's *āśrama*. The young disciples are sitting and segregating *pūjā* flowers into the *pūjā* trays. Some are making garlands. Some are singing and dancing. Some are giving beat to the songs. Suddenly a hissing sound is heard from a corner where lots of of *pūjā* flowers are collected in a heap. Hearing that one young lad throws a *pūjā* spoon in that direction. A huge snake comes out and with great hissing, raises its hood poised to sink its fangs. Seeing this all of them become alarmed and run amok in all directions. The hissing snake moves forward and drives everyone around. At that time Hiraṇyanābha enters.)

**Hiraṇyanābha** – What is the commotion? Why is everybody running about in panic?

**One person** – (**His tongue slipping with fear.**) See that, Aśvakośa (trembles in fear, points to the snake)

**Another person** – **(crying)** I am scared. **(Again cries with great alarm.)**

**Third person** – There in the *pūjā* room, s. . . . s. . . . snake, I. . . . I. . . . am. . . . very afraid. . . .

**Hiraṇyanābha** – **(looks around the *pūjā* room and understands the situation.)** O! That? It can be beaten by a stick and put to death. Don't be scared. I will protect you all.

**One young lad** – How to beat it? Our insides are shaking even with the thought of getting close to it.

**Hiraṇyanābha** – No need to get scared. I will beat it. **(Picks up a brass vessel from the ground and is about to go inside the *pūjā* room. At that time Sumantu comes running and catches his hand.)**

**Sumantu** – Stop! stop! Aśvakośa! This is the *āśrama* of Pippalāda. Did you forget that? Here the killing of a living thing is prohibited, whatever the reasons may be. Stop, don't beat the snake.

**Hiraṇyanābha** – Svāmī! Even if a cow comes to kill one, it is only proper to kill the cow. This is a poisonous snake. If we leave it this way it might attack any of these children. Because of that many people may die. To save many lives it is only good to kill one creature. Please give me way! I humbly request you. **(The poisonous snake is dancing showing its hood)**.

**Children** – **(Getting very scared)** Aśvakośa! Don't delay. Now itself half of our *prāṇa* has gone. As time passes, even if the snake does not touch us, because of fear, our life will pass away.

**Hiraṇyanābha** – Svāmī! Please show mercy. Did you hear what the children are saying? Don't you feel sorry for them? Please don't stop me.

**Sumantu** – Aśvakośa! The life of a man and the life of a snake are both the same to me. Looking at it evenly, both the lives are valuable. Same fill, same cast. If we only think, we will find that the snake's life is more valuable than a human being's life.

**Hiraṇyanābha** – Where is a man's position having six senses and where is the position of this poisonous snake? Why are you talking in riddles? Svāmī, please leave my hand.

**Sumantu** – Aśvakośa! Don't get annoyed, I won't leave your hand (**he catches his hand tightly**).

**Hiraṇyanābha** – Svāmī! You must excuse me. You must pardon the act which I am going to do now. I have to act against your order.

(He tries to relieve himself from his grip. The confusion increases and the children cry out in alarm. Maharṣi Pippalāda after completing his afternoon bath and *pūjā* is coming down from the river. In his face the brightness of *tejas* is seen. Compassion shines in his face. In one hand is a *pūjā* vessel and in another hand he holds the *japamālā* strung with prayer beads. Seeing him, everybody gives way. Sumantu and Hiraṇyanābha also stand on one side. However Sumantu does not leave his grip on Hiraṇyanābha.)

**Pippalāda** – Is this an *āśrama* or is it a place of entertainment? It is full of noise and shouting? What is the matter, my friend?

**Sumantu** – Revered Master, a snake has come into the *pūjā* room. The disciples are trembling with fear. Aśvakośa wanted to kill it. I was holding him back and stopping him in that act.

**Pippalāda** – What you did was very good. In the dwelling of *Brahman*-knowledgeable people, where is the place for differences? If there is no difference where is enmity? Without enmity why the killing? Aśvakośa! Keep away the *kamaṇḍala*; I will take care of the snake. (**Hiraṇyanābha obeys the order of the *guru* and keeps the *kamaṇḍala* down and stands on one side.**)

**Hiraṇyanābha** – I am scared. What will be the result of this action?

**Sumantu** – Don't be scared, my son, nothing will happen. Only something good will be done. You will see Maharṣi

Pippalāda's *Brahman*-strength now, right in front of your eyes.

**Pippalāda** – (**Calls the disciples who were coming behind him.**) Hey young one! Go and keep my reed mat for sitting and *pūjā* vessel inside the *pūjā* room (**the disciple hesitates**) O Saumya! there is no need to be scared. Go bravely. The snake won't touch you.

(Takes some holy water and sprinkles it on the snake. The snake becomes quiet. The disciple keeps the reed mat and *kamaṇḍala* near it in the front. Pippalāda goes and sits down.)

**Pippalāda** – Hey *nāga,* the messenger of Nāgarāja, the replica of Ādiśeṣa the descendant of Vāsuki! there is no difference in this *āśrama* between one life form and another. Hence there is no anger or killing. You need not be scared. We are not your enemies. Don't consider us as your enemies. Lower the hood which you have spread. Be in peace.

(Pippalāda with concentration puts his glance on the snake. The snake becomes subdued. The people who were looking on are very much surprised. Pippalāda enters into meditation.)

**Sumantu** – Did you see that, Aśvakośa! The strength of the *tejas* of a *brahma-jñānī.*

**Hiraṇyanābha** – Svāmī, kindly excuse me for my faults.

**Sumantu** – There is no fault at all from your side. Anybody else in your place would have reacted exactly like that.

**Pippalāda** – (**Comes out of meditation**) O poisonous snake! I am considering you as a good snake. O snake! let good things happen to you. You are the bed of Lord Viṣṇu, you are the ornament of Paramaśiva and you are the handband of Pārvatīdevī. Don't stay here. Go away. All of you leave way. The snake will go quietly without making any noise.

(As all of them give way and stand by a side, the snake wriggles and goes round the *maharṣi,* later it climbs the fence and goes out of the *āśrama.*)

Children! The snake has left the place. Now you can take care of your things. Aśvakośa! for no reason should there be any kind of killing of any creature. Be comfortable and do your duties, my child (**goes inside. Except Sumantu and Hiraṇyanābha everybody else takes leave.**)

**Hiraṇyanābha** – I got a new insight today. Svāmī! It is a very new experience for me.

**Sumantu** – Why, are you speaking like this? Haven't you heard of the tigress giving milk to the calf of the cow, the goat and tiger drinking water from the same water spot together, the snake holding its hood as an umbrella to the pregnant frog?

**Hiraṇyanābha** – I too have heard. However I did not believe in them. I thought of them to be the imagination of poets. Only today I saw things right in front of my eyes. Svāmī please give me permission to leave. The Revered Guru had asked me to go to the Mandākinī riverside and bring Mṛkandu Maharṣi. I came inside to take my woollen drape and seeing the incidents here I stayed back. I am taking leave, respected one.

**Sumantu** – Go carefully and come back. Give my *praṇāma*s to Mṛkandu Maharṣi and convey my enquiries to him. (**Hiraṇyanābha gives his salutations and leaves.**)

**Sumantu** – What a surprise? This Aśvakośa's walk is so majestic. Similar to the walk of an elephant, a lion's gait and a bull's walk, how majestic he looks. He is not an ordinary chariot driver. This is sure. I caught his hands. What strong hands! They are not the hands which have caught only the reins of a horse. It is the hand which has handled various weapons, heavy bow and arrows and other armours of war. His hands are seasoned hands. He is definitely a kshatriya's son. Why is he in this camouflage? Everything will be known in due course of time. Let me enquire from Kauśalya who is from the Kosala kingdom. Till then it is better to maintain silence.

***(Curtain falls.)***

## SCENE 2

***(Curtain opens.)***

(Pippalāda Maharṣi's *āśrama*. Maharṣi is seated facing northwards. The six disciples are sitting in front of him facing east. In front of them Sumantu Maharṣi is also seated. Conversation is taking place.)

**Sumantu** – Children! Today who is going to ask the question?

**Sukeśa** – I am thinking of asking.

**Pippalāda** – Child! Today Aśvakośa is not here, isn't he? After he comes you can ask. Let Sauryāyaṇi or Satyakāma ask today.

**Sukeśa** – Respected Guru! I will do as you bid (within himself. What can be the connection between my question and Aśvakośa's presence, I am not able to understand this. I must ask the *guru* the reason for this.)

**Sauryāyaṇi** – Svāmī! As per your bidding today I will ask the question. Kindly answer it.

**Sumantu** – Child! Let there not be any further delay. Ask immediately. *Maharṣi* has already given you permission.

**Satyakāma** – Friend, we are all eager to hear your question.

अथ हैनं सौर्यायणी गार्ग्यः पप्रच्छ।

*atha hainaṁ sauryāyaṇī gārgyaḥ papraccha* |

Then Gārgya, the son of Sūrya, asked

**Sauryāyaṇi (Gārgya)** –

भगवनेतस्मिन्पुरुषे कानि स्वपन्ति? कान्यस्मिन् जाग्रति? कतर एष देवः स्वप्नान् पश्यति? कस्यैतत् सुखं भवति? कस्मिन्नु सर्वे सम्प्रतिष्ठिता भवन्ति इति ॥४.१॥

*bhagavan etasmin puruṣe kāni svapanti? kānyasmiñjāgrati* | *katara eṣa devaḥ svapnān paśyati? kasyaitat sukhaṁ bhavati? kasmin nu sarve sampratiṣṭhitā bhavanti iti* ||4.1||

> Venerable Sir, what are they that sleep in this *puruṣa* (person)? What are they that keep awake in him? Which one of the gods dreams? Whose is this happiness (*sukham*)? In whom are all these well-founded?

Respected Sir, what are the things sleeping in this body? What are awake? In this who is seeing *svapna*? Who gets the enjoyment of *suṣupti*/subtle state? What is the time when everybody joins together as one? You must kindly answer these five questions of mine in detail.

**Sumantu** – *sādhu*! *sādhu*! Child! These are very good questions. Your friends before asked questions about the *jāgarita* or waking state and the things taking place inside and outside. Also, they enquired about who is conducting these affairs. Now you are asking questions on happenings in dream, during sleep and in a state more subtle than that. This is a very apt enquiry.

***fig.:* The things sleeping in the body — sense organs**
**Things awake in sleeping state — *prāṇa*, mind and *Brahman***

**Pippalāda** – Child! Gārgya! Let us take the first question you asked first. The body consisting of a head, hands, legs, eyes, ears, etc. among them which sense organs go to sleep? That is, stopping their respective activities, do they go to sleep? This is your first question. I will answer. Listen carefully.

**Gārgya (Sauryāyaṇi)** – Let it be so, Svāmī.

तस्मै स होवाच

*tasmai sa hovāca* ।

*To him then he said:*

**Pippalāda** –

यथा गार्ग्य मरीचयोऽर्कस्यास्तं गच्छतः सर्वा एतस्मिन्स्तेजोमण्डल एकीभवन्ति। ताः पुनः पुनरुदयतः प्रचरन्त्येवं ह वै तत्॥४.२a॥

*yathā gārgya marīcayo 'rkasyāstaṁ gacchataḥ sarvā etasmin tejomaṇḍala ekībhavanti* । *tāḥ punaḥ punar udayataḥ pracarantyevaṁ ha vai tat* ।।4.2a।।

सर्वं परे देवे मनस्येकीभवति। तेन तर्ह्येष पुरुषो न शृणोति न पश्यति न जिघ्रति न रसयते न स्पृशते। नाभिवदते नादत्ते नानन्दयते न विसृजते नेयायते स्वपितीत्याचक्षते॥४.२b॥

*sarvaṁ pare deve manasyekī-bhavati* । *tena tarhyeṣa puruṣo na śṛṇoti na paśyati na jighrati na rasayate na spṛśate nābhivadate nādatte nānandayate na visṛjate, neyāyate svapiti iti acakṣate* ।।4.2b।।

O Gārgya, as all the rays of the setting sun become one with the orb of brilliances, and as they spread forth when he rises again and again, even so does all this become one with the mind, the transcendental god. The *puruṣa* in that state, therefore, hears not, sees not, smells not, tastes not, touches not, speaks not, takes not, rejoices not, moves not. It is therefore said, "He sleeps."

All the sense organs join together with the most exalted *deva*, the *tattvam*/mind. Just as the sun's rays reach the *sūryamaṇḍala* when he sets, the same way, the sense organs reach the mind and become one with that. Just as again when the sun rises the rays spread, in the same way again the sense organs come out to do their respective functions. When all the senses coalesce into the mind, the *puruṣa* does not hear, does not see, does not taste, does not touch or feel, does not talk, he is then considered to be sleeping.

**Sumantu** – Children! Do understand this properly. When the sun dips behind the mountain all his rays get wrapped up in the sun's *tejomaṇḍala*. You might have observed this when you do your evening prayers. In the same way, when the *puruṣa* goes to sleep, his sense organs get enclosed in the very powerful concept of mind. Then he is said to be sleeping.

**Kabandhi** – Svāmī! I have a doubt.

**Sumantu** – What is that? Ask?

**Kabandhi** – We can also assume that the sense organs after doing their respective functions are resting by themselves. For example, we cut the wood with the axe. We cut the leaves with the knife. The axe or the knife after doing the work is laid down and is not connected to the hand which operates it. In the same way, the sense organs can rest separately and why should they go and wrap themselves in the mind.

**Pippalāda** – Kabandhi! Your doubt is a sensible one indeed. However the example is not correct. For things like the axe, apart from the connection with the hand at the time of its use, it has a separate existence. However, the sense organs are always under the control of the mind. They don't act independently. Even in the waking state, they are under the control of the mind. Hence, during sleep they go back to the mind. Here it should not be thought that they get merged with the mind. Once they stop their respective work, they come under the control of the mind and it appears like they have merged with it; however, they soon become separate entities when awake.

**Kauśalya** – My friend's question and the reply of the revered *guru* have cleared everybody's doubts.

**Pippalāda** – Now let us come to the next question. While

sleeping, which is the one keeping awake? In this city consisting of nine entrances (that is in the body where *puruṣa* lives) the five *prāṇa*s are the ones which are awake. They burn continuously. The five *prāṇa*s alone continue to do their work.

**Gārgya** – You told us the similarity between *prāṇa* and *agni*. Kindly tell us that in more detail.

**Pippalāda** –

> प्राणाग्नय एवैतस्मिन् पुरे जाग्रति। गार्हपत्यो हवा एषोऽपानो
> व्यानोऽन्वाहार्यपचनो यद्गार्हपत्यात्प्रणीयते प्रणयनादाहवनीयः प्राणः ॥४.३॥
>
> *prāṇāgnaya evaitasmin pure jāgrati* | *gārhapatyo ha vā eṣo 'pāno* |
> *vyāno 'nvāhārya-pacano yad gārhapatyāt praṇīyate praṇayanādāhavanīyaḥ prāṇaḥ* ||4.3||
>
> The fires of *prāṇa* indeed are wakeful in this city (*pura*). Of these, *apāna* is the householder's fire (*gārhapatya agni*), *vyāna* the southern sacrificial fire (*anvāhārya agni*). *Prāṇa*, called so because it is kindled (*prāṇāyānat*) from *gārhapatya agni*, is the *āhavanīya agni*.

**Satyakāma** – you kindly explain, why are they called so?

**Pippalāda** – Friend! Do clear the doubts of the children.

**Sumantu** – Let it be so, my friend.

*Gārhapatya* is the *agnikuṇḍa* which is circular in shape lying behind the master. It is related to householder's life. It is the central fire. From this *apāna vāyu* originates. *Apāna* is seated in the organs of excretion and procreation and just as *apāna* is always alive in a living body, so too *gārhapatya agni* is always alive. The other two *agni*s come out from this.

*Āhavanīyam* is the *agnikuṇḍa* in front of the master in a square shape. This represents *prāṇa* or vitality which energises the senses. This is kindled by the act of *prāṇāyāma* (breathing) from *gārhapatya agni*. It is called *āhavanīyam* because like offering to gods done by *āhvāna*, the *prāṇa* does offerings to sense organs and activates them.

South of him is *dakṣiṇa agni* which is *anvāhārya pācana*. This represents *vyāna*. It is equated with the circulatory and nervous system. *Vyāna*'s function is to reach the vitality to every part of the body through circulation. It is given the name *anvāhārya* meaning ancestors. Our ancestors branch intricately like our father, mother having two fathers and mothers between them and theirs having eight fathers and mothers between them. In the same way the *agni* from *vyāna* branches endlessly reaching each and every part. It also implies that offerings we make to ancestors branch off like *vyāna* and reach our ancestors.

Since *apāna* is in the back it is called *gārhapatyam*. As *prāṇa* is like offerings it is called *āhavanīya*. *Vyāna* is the right *nāḍī* of the heart, hence it is called *dakṣiṇa agni*.

**Gārgya** – What roles are the remaining two *prāṇa*s given in the *yajña*. As you explain it, even sleep is a worship to the Almighty. It is like a *yajña*, so it appears. What is the role of the mind? What is the benefit of the *yajña*?

**Sumantu** – Yes, my child! Each and every *karma* done by man is worship to the Almighty. There is no doubt in this.

**Pippalāda** –

> यदुच्छ्वासनिश्वासावेतावाहुती समं नयतीति स समानः। मनो ह वाव यजमान इष्ट-फलमेवोदानः स एनं यजमानमहरहर्ब्रह्म गमयति ॥४.४॥
>
> *yad ucchvāsaniḥ śvāsāvetāv āhutī samaṁ nayatīti sa samānaḥ | mano ha vāva yajamāna iṣṭa-phalam evodānaḥ sa enaṁ yajamānan ahar ahar brahma gamayati | | 4.4 | |*
>
> As the one who keeps the two oblations of breathing In and breathing out in perfect balance, he is called *samāna*. The sacrificer is but the mind. *Udāna* is the favourable result attained.

Taking the air in and leaving the air out are offerings/*āhuti*.

As both these offerings are done in balance, *samāna vāyu* remains in balance. Mind is the master; the individual who represents it, is said to be doing the offering. He is also called *yajamāna,* the master. The *udāna vāyu* is the benefit of the *yajña.* This only takes the master (mind) to the *Brahman* daily while sleeping.

**Sumantu** – The wise one should never be thought of as a lazy one. Even while sleeping he observes *yajña* and works for the good of the world. This is certain.

**Pippalāda** – Now let us see who is the one who dreams?

> अत्रैष देवः स्वप्ने महिमानमनुभवति। यद्दृष्टं दृष्टमनुपश्यति; श्रुतं च श्रुतमेवार्थमनुशृणोति; देशदिगन्तरैश्च प्रत्यनुभूतं पुनः पुनः प्रत्यनुभवति; दृष्टं चादृष्टं च श्रुतं चाश्रुतं चानुभूतं चाननुभूतं च सच्चासच्च सर्वं पश्यति सर्वः पश्यति ॥४.५॥
>
> *atraiṣa devaḥ svapne mahimānam anubhavati । yad dṛṣṭaṁ dṛṣṭam anupaśyati; śrutaṁ ca śrutaṁ evārtham anuśṛṇoti; deśa digantaraiś ca praty anubhūtaṁ punaḥ punaḥ pratyanubhavati; dṛṣṭaṁ ca adṛṣṭaṁ ca śrutaṁ ca aśrutaṁ ca anubhūtaṁ ca ananubhūtaṁ ca saccāsacca sarvaṁ paśyati sarvaḥ paśyati* ||4.5||
>
> This god in the dreaming state experiences (its own) greatness, for he sees again what had once been seen, for he hears again what had once been heard, for he experiences again what had once been experienced repeatedly at various places in different directions. What has been seen and not seen, what has been heard and not heard, what has been experienced and not experienced, what is existent and non-existent — he sees everything, as everything.

When a person sleeps, all sense organs mingle in the mind. At that time, the mind's *deva* enjoys the experience of *svapna.* Whatever he had seen while awake, he sees them again in *svapna* (dream). Whatever he had heard while awake he hears them again in *svapna.* Whatever he had experienced in different places and different directions, all that he experiences again. Seen and not seen, heard and not heard, experienced and not experienced, present and not present, he himself becomes all that and sees everything.

**Sumantu** – Friend! I have not heard anyone describing *svapna* so beautifully. After all the senses take shelter in the mind, the five *prāṇa*s remain awake and function, and before deep sleep (*suṣupti*) state, *svapna* take place. Whatever the mind has seen, heard, experienced while being awake as well as the aspirations in the mind get form during *svapna*. Thus, it sees the scenes as they happened while awake and also with imagination sees their extension.

**Gārgya** – I have one doubt, Svāmī! If dreams are incidences seen while awake, how do we see in dreams, certain things not seen, not possible to be seen. How is that possible?

**Pippalāda** – My dear Gārgya, your doubt is a just one. I will explain it. Listen to it. When a person is awake and has an experience of talking with his friend or son, that experience makes him see the friend or son in the *svapna*. In the same way, while awake, if he hears thunder, Vedas being recited, a child crying, he may again hear these sounds in his dreams. The experience he has had in several places and various incidences are again being experienced in his dreams. Not only does he see whatever he has seen during the waking time in this birth, but also those experiences which have occurred in several previous births. It is those experiences which I told as neither those heard nor seen.

**Satyakāma** – However, Revered Guru, at times we see scenes which we cannot imagine and which are most inappropriate. Some time we see things which we may not be fortunate to see in this *janma* or may not have seen in any previous birth. What is the reason for that?

**Kauśalya** – Respected Guru, for example I saw an elephant having four horns in a dream. It was frightening. It was eating a snake with many hoods. It was taking out and eating each hood. At least we have heard about a white elephant in Purāṇas. Elephants eat only leaves and other plant material. It is very improbable for an elephant to eat a black snake. Hence this dream is a false scene, isn't it? It might not have been possible to see such things even in previous births.

**Sumantu** – The dreams which the mind see need not be real. One can see the real things like water and even unreal things like a mirage. Mind, which is the dwelling place of our sense organs, is the one which sees the dreams. Hence it can be related to real as well as unreal.

**Gārgya** – How does a mind which creates such a lot of commotion, later go to sleep?

**Pippalāda** –

स यदा तेजसाऽभिभूतो भवति। अत्रैष देवः स्वप्नान्न पश्यत्यथ तदैतस्मिञ्छरीरे एतत्सुखं भवति ॥४.६॥

*sa yadā tejasā bhibhūto bhavati | atraiṣa devaḥ svapnān na paśyaty atha tadaitasmin śarīre etat sukhaṁ bhavati | |4.6| |*

Overcome with brilliance (*tejas*) this god (mind) then sees no dream. Confined thus to the concerned body, arises pleasure (and pain).

When the mind is filled with *brahmatejas*, it does not see dreams. At that time the body gets the comfort of deep sleep (*suṣupti*). Dear one! Just as the birds reach their dwelling tree, in the same way everything goes and takes abode in the *ātmā.*

**Sumantu** – The *Brahman* which is *chit* due to its *tejas* closes the inclinations of the mind which is responsible for dreams. That time the dreamless state is experienced and *suṣupti* state is reached. Also ignorance, desire, *karma,* because of which the body is made, and its sense organs become quiet.

स यथा सोम्य वयांसि वासवृक्षं संप्रतिष्ठन्ते।
एवं ह वै तत्सर्वं पर आत्मनि संप्रतिष्ठते ॥४.७॥

*sa yathā saumya vayāṁsi vāso-vṛkṣaṁ sampratiṣṭhante* |
*evaṁ ha vai tat sarvaṁ para ātmani sampratiṣṭhate*
||4.7||

Even as birds, O Dear, have trees for their dwelling so does everything here have the transcendental Self for a dwelling. Again, like the birds resting in the dwelling tree, the mind rests within the *ātmā*.

**Gārgya** – Everything becomes quiet, you said. What do you mean by that? Kindly explain in detail.

**Pippalāda** – The things which become quiet are:

पृथिवी च पृथिवी-मात्रा चापश्चापोमात्रा च, तेजश्च तेजोमात्रा च, वायुश्च वायुमात्रा चाकाश्चाकाशमात्रा च, चक्षुश्च द्रष्टव्यं च, श्रोत्रं च श्रोतव्यं च, घ्राणं च घ्रातव्यं च, रसश्च रसयितव्यं च, त्वक्च स्पर्शयितव्यं च, वाक्च वक्तव्यं च, हस्तौ चादातव्यं चोपस्थश्चानन्दयितव्यं च, पायुश्च विसर्जयितव्यं च, पादौ च गन्तव्यं च। मनश्च मन्तव्यं च, बुद्धिश्च बोद्धव्यं चाहंकारश्चाहंकर्तव्यं च चित्तं च चेतयितव्यं च, तेजश्च विद्योतयितव्यं च, प्राणश्च विधारयितव्यं च ॥४.८॥

*pṛthivī ca pṛthivī-mātrā ca āpaś ca āpo-mātrā ca, tejaś ca tejo-mātrā ca, vāyuś ca vāyu-mātrā ca ākāśa ca ākāśa-mātrā ca, cakṣuś ca draṣṭavyaṁ ca, śrotraṁ ca śrotavyaṁ ca, ghrāṇaṁ ca ghrātavyaṁ ca, rasaś ca rasayitavyaṁ ca, tvak ca sparśayitavyaṁ ca vāk ca vaktavyaṁ ca, hastau ca adātavyaṁ ca upasthaś ca anandayitavyaṁ ca, pāyuś ca visarjayitavyaṁ ca, pādau ca gantavyaṁ ca, manaś ca mantavyaṁ ca, buddhiś ca boddhavyaṁ ca ahaṁkāraś ca ahaṁkartavyaṁ ca, cittaṁ ca cetayitavyaṁ ca, tejaś ca vidyotayitavyaṁ ca, prāṇaś ca vidhārayitavyaṁ ca* ||4.8||

The gross element earth and its subtle aspect, the gross element water and its subtle aspect, the gross element fire and its subtle aspect, the gross element air and its subtle aspect, the gross element space and its subtle aspect, sight

> and what can be seen, hearing and what can be heard, smell and what can be smelt, taste and what can be tasted, touch and what can be touched, speech and what can be spoken, hands and what can be handled, genitals and what can be enjoyed, organ of defecation and what can be defecated, feet and what can be walked to, mind and what can mind be applied on, intellect and what can be conceived, the "I" sense and what can be sensed as "I," memory factor and what can be memorized, effulgence and what can be illumined, *prāṇa* and what can be supported by it — all these have the transcendental Self for their dwelling.

The five cosmic aspects –

The *pṛthivī* and the subtle form of that, responsible for the gravitational pull;

The water and the subtle form of that, responsible for the secretions;

The fire and the subtle form of that, responsible for the forms;

The air and the subtle form of that, responsible for touch;

The space and the subtle form of that, responsible for sound;

The five senses and their objects which are individual facilities, each having a quality of one of the five cosmic aspects:

The eye and sight having the quality of fire;

The ear and hearing having the quality of space;

The nose and smell having the quality of earth;

The tongue and taste, having the quality of water;

The skin and touch having the quality of air:

The organs of action which are five in number:

The words and speech involved in it;

The hand and the lifting of things;

The organs of procreation and the enjoyment from it;

The organs of excretion and the matter to be discarded;

The feet and the going to places;

The four mental faculties which are called *antaḥkaraṇas*:

The mind and the contemplatable things;

The intellect and the decision-making things;

The ego and matters connected with that;

The memory and things remembered with that;

The still interior factors like *tejas* and *prāṇa*. The *tejas* (self-effulgence) which illuminates everything. The *prāṇa* which holds everything together. All these abide in the *ātmā*.

**Sumantu** – The five elements and their subtle form, the ten organs (the knowledge-giving ones and the functional ones) and the things connected with them, the *antaḥkaraṇas* with four parts, all those which are the products of cause and effect and go join the *ātmā*. During sleep all this thus merge with the *ātmā*.

**Pippalāda** –

> एष हि द्रष्टा स्प्रष्टा श्रोता घ्राता रसयिता मन्ता बोद्धा कर्ता विज्ञानात्मा पुरुषः। स परेऽक्षरे आत्मनि सम्प्रतिष्ठते॥४.९॥
>
> *eṣa hi draṣṭā spraṣṭā śrotā ghrātā rasayitā mantā boddhā kartā vijñānātmā puruṣaḥ | sa pare 'kṣare ātmani sampratiṣṭhate | | 4.9 | |*
>
> He verily is the *puruṣa*, the seer, the one who touches, the hearer, the smeller, the taster, the perceiver, the knower, the doer, specifically knowing self. He is well seated in the transcendental, undecaying Self.

That time the *jīvātmā* who actually sees, touches, hears, smells, tastes, thinks, knows, and acts, He only is the *puruṣa*. He stabilizes with the *paramātmā* which has no destruction. He gets installed in the *parabrahman*.

**Gārgya** – We became very blessed. We are full of gratitude after hearing the answers.

**Pippalāda** – You, a person with a beautiful mind, I will tell you now the benefits accrued by hearing these teachings. The sun's reflection is seen in the vessel which contains water. Once the water is thrown out and as the disturbance called water is removed, the reflection goes and unites with the sun found in the sky. In the same way for the *puruṣa* living in the body, when disturbances of cause and effect holding the *jīvātmā* in the body get removed, it unites with *paramātmā*. Whoever realizes Him (the *parabrahman*) as the one without ignorance, without a body, without colour and as a pure entity, he becomes one with the *parabrahman*. There is an important *mantra* also explaining this.

**Sukeśa** – What is that *mantra*, Svāmī?

**Pippalāda** –

> परमेवाक्षरं प्रतिपद्यते स यो ह वै तदच्छायमशरीरमलोहितं
> शुभ्रमक्षरं वेदयते यस्तु सोम्य। स सर्वज्ञः सर्वो भवति। तदेष श्लोकः ॥४.१०॥
>
> *paraṁ evākṣaraṁ pratipadyate, sa yo ha vai tad acchāyaṁ aśarīraṁ alohitaṁ śubhraṁ akṣaraṁ vedayate yas tu somya | sa sarvajñaḥ sarvo bhavati | tad eṣa ślokaḥ* ||4.10||
>
> One who knows That as the shadowless, the bodiless, the colourless, the pure, the imperishable, O dear, He is the knower of everything; he is everything. As to this there is this verse.

A person is said to understand *Brahman* when he realizes that the *vijñānātmā* (*jīvātmā*) is present in all *devas*, all sense organs, all elements and It is an indestructible thing. With this realization he becomes all-knowing. He enters everything and fills everything.

**Sumantu** – Children, you must understand about *Brahman* as a thing without a shadow, body, colour, very pure and indestructible. It does not have a shadow called ignorance. Thus there is no causal body, no subtle body. Since there is no colour or form, a gross body is also not there. *Śubhram* means very pure. There is absolutely no blemish. Since it does not have any attributes, it is beyond the reach of the mind. Thus *parabrahman* is omniscient, truth, *śivaṁ*, *śāntaṁ* and beyond the mind's comprehension.

विज्ञानात्मा सह देवैश्च सर्वैः प्राणा भूतानि संप्रतिष्ठन्ति यत्र।
तदक्षरं वेदयते यस्तु सोम्य स सर्वज्ञः सर्वमेवाविवेश इति ॥४.११॥

*vijñānātmā saha devaiś ca sarvaiḥ prāṇā bhūtāni*
*saṁpratiṣṭhanti yatra* ।
*tad akṣaraṁ vedayate yastu saumya sa sarvajñaḥ*
*sarvam eva aviveśa iti* ।।4.11।।

Aware of the Imperishable in which dwell the knowing Self (*vijñānātmā*), *prāṇa*s and all beings along with all gods, one becomes, O dear, the omniscient pervading everything.

If a person knows or realizes it like this, he becomes all-knowing. Then there is nothing which he does not know. Embroiled in ignorance he had not known the truth. However learning *brahma-vidyā* he becomes all-knowing.

**Kauśalya** – Revered Guru! Today an important teaching has been given. We are a bit sorry Aśvakośa could not come.

**Sumantu** – As soon as Aśvakośa comes one of you must tell him all this in detail.

**Gārgya** – However much all of us together explain to him still it wouldn't be like the *guru* himself explaining.

**Pippalāda** – Children! You need not feel sorry. I myself will bless Aśvakośa so that he will come to know everything.

**Kabandhi** – Respected one, indeed we are very happy.

**Sumantu** – Friend! Shall we stop our conversation here?

**Pippalāda** – Let us do so.

*(All of them get up.)*

*(Curtain falls.)*

## SCENE 3

***(Curtain opens.)***

(In Sumantu Maharṣi's *āśrama,* Sumantu, Sukeśa, Kauśalya, Satyakāma are sitting and conversing.)

**Sukeśa** – Svāmī! Did you observe what the revered *guru* said yesterday?

**Sumantu** – Child, what are you referring to?

**Sukeśa** – Respected One! I am referring to his reply when I asked permission to ask a question.

**Kauśalya** – I also observed that.

**Sumantu** – Can you tell us about what he said about Aśvakośa. Even I did not understand the meaning behind his words.

**Sukeśa** – Svāmī! What about asking *maharṣi* directly.

**Satyakāma** – Since Aśvakośa did not come from Mr̥kandu's *āśrama,* our friend Sukeśa lost an opportunity to ask a question. I am feeling very bad for that.

**Kauśalya** – Why should you feel bad for that? After you ask your questions, when Aśvakośa returns, it can be asked as the last question.

**Satyakāma** – However there will be some disappointment that the question could not be asked when initially thought of.

**Sukeśa** – Friends, thanks for your sympathies. Svāmī! You did not answer anything about my query.

**Sumantu** – **(thinking)** Child! It may not be proper to ask the *maharṣi* directly. The reason will be known when the time comes. Otherwise he will tell you himself. Let us not be in haste. To show patience in these kinds of matters is our duty.

**Sukeśa** – Let it be so, respected Sir.

**Sumantu** – I wanted to ask Kauśalya about Aśvakośa. Later I totally forgot about it.

**Kauśalya** – Svāmī! You wanted to ask me something? Please do so. I will tell you if I know.

**Sumantu** – That day in the *āśrama* a snake came and there was some confusion, isn't it? At that time I stopped Aśvakośa by catching his hands. I felt then, his hands were like those of a prince, not those of a charioteer. Since you told us you are coming from the Kosala kingdom, I was wondering if you might have known him. Do you know him?

**Kauśalya** – My father belongs to the Kosala kingdom. However I stayed most of the time in my mother's country, Magadha. I don't know anything about Aśvakośa.

**Satyakāma** – Perhaps our friend Sukeśa might know him. Sukeśa is the friend of the Kosala kingdom's prince Hiraṇyanābha. He has gone to the palace many times. Hence I feel he might know him.

**Sumantu** – Child Sukeśa! Do you know him? If so you can clear my doubt.

**Sukeśa** – Aśvakośa does not move with me closely. Even if I go near and ask any questions, he turns his face, answers and leaves immediately. Hence I also move with him indifferently. Sometimes I feel I have seen him somewhere. However I feel it is my mind's illusion, I control such thoughts. He looks and sounds like a close friend of mine. But I am neither able to express it clearly nor ignore it, and I am troubled by it.

**Sumantu** – Whom do you feel, he is like?

**Sukeśa** – He appears like my friend Hiraṇyanābha. However, why should my close friend move with me so indifferently? Since there is no reason, I decided he cannot be my friend. But after what you said, my doubts are getting stronger.

**Sumantu** - (**within himself**) He should be Hiraṇyanābha. (**outside**) Everything will be known as time passes. There is no need to worry unnecessarily. Tomorrow what question are you going to ask, Satyakāma?

**Satyakāma** – I am thinking about that only, Svāmī.

**Kauśalya** – Respected One. We came here to acquire *Brahman-*

**A-Kāra** *Bhūloka, Ṛgveda,* **waking state**

**U-Kāra** *Chandraloka, Yajurveda,* **dream state**

**M-kāra** *Sāmaloka, Sāmaveda,* **deep sleep state**

*fig :* **Meditaing Oṁ**

knowledge. Asking questions we cleared our doubts. Now, I think there is nothing to ask.

**Sumantu** – *Sādhu*! Kauśalya! As far as you are concerned it might be correct. However Satyakāma may have some doubts.

**Satyakāma** – Respected One, if anything has to be asked further, the ways to reach *Brahman*-knowledge and the *sādhanās* to be done for that, is what needs to be asked.

**Sumantu** – Very correct. Ask that. Ask about *oṁkāra* and its benefits.

**Satyakāma** – Let it be so. Your kind presence is also needed.

**Sumantu** - Children! I will always be there. Now it is getting time for doing *pūjā*. You can all go and come back. (**The disciples pay their respects and take leave.**)

## SCENE 4

***(Curtain opens.)***

(Maharṣi Pippalāda is sitting on the reed mat. On either side Sukeśa and other disciples are sitting. Sumantu Maharṣi is also sitting. Conversation is going on.)

**Pippalāda** – Children! Today also Aśvakośa has not come. Hence let Satyakāma ask the question. Sukeśa can ask last. Child, Satyakāma! Ask your doubts. I will clear your doubts.

अथ हैनं शैब्यः सत्यकामः पप्रच्छ ।
*atha hainaṁ śaibyaḥ satyakāmaḥ papraccha*

Then Satyakāma, son of Śibi, asked him (Pippalāda):

**Satyakāma** –

स यो ह वै तद्भगवन्मनुष्येषु प्रायणान्तमोंकारमभिध्यायीत । कतमं वाव स तेन लोकं जयतीति ॥५.१ ॥

*sa yo ha vai tat bhagavan manuṣyeṣu prāyaṇāntaoṁkāram abhidhyāyīta* | *katamaṁ vāva sa tena lokaṁ jayatīti* ||5.1||

Then Satyakāma, son of Śibi, asked him (Pippalāda): Venerable Sir, which of the many worlds does he among men conquer by meditation on *AUM* till death?

Revered Guru! *namaskāra*. With your teaching all doubts have been cleared. I would like to know the result of *oṁkāra upāsanā*. Respected one! Which *loka* does a man reach by doing *oṁkāra* meditation throughout his life? What status does he get on doing this *upāsanā*.

**Sumantu** - Satyakāma! Śibi's son! Desiring for the attainment of the ultimate you have asked this apt question.

तस्मै स होवाच ।
*tasmai sa hovāca* |

To him Pippalāda said:

**Pippalāda -**

एतद् वै सत्यकाम परं चापरं च ब्रह्म यदोङ्कारः तस्माद्विद्वानेतेनैभ वायतनेनैकतरमन्वेति ॥५.२ ॥

*etad vai satyakāma paraṁ ca aparaṁ ca brahma yad oṁkāraḥ | tasmād vidvān etenaivāyatanenaikataram anveti | |5.2| |*

That which is (meant by) the sound *AUM*, O Satyakāma, is verily the transcendental and immanent *Brahman*. With it alone, therefore, for means, the wise one pursues and attains either of the two.

O Satyakāma! *oṁkāra* is the *parabrahman* and also the *aparabrahman*. The one who continuously meditates on this becomes one of that. The one who keeps the sense organs in control and does not allow them to wander, keeps the mind one-pointed, meditates with *bhakti*, he will definitely reach a good state. *Oṁkāra* has to be meditated following the path of truth, *brahmacarya*, *ahiṁsā*, sacrifice, good habits, happiness and with a clear mind.

**Satyakāma** – Svāmī! How is it that one who meditates on *oṁkāra* reaches *parabrahman* and another one following the same path reaches *aparabrahman*. All the *upāsika*s of *oṁkāra* should get the same kind of benefit, isn't it? Why is there a difference in the results?

**Pippalāda** – Child, what you asked is correct. *Brahman* is a very dear thing. Even mind cannot know it. Still, just as how *śāligrāma* is worshipped as Viṣṇu, to worship *Brahman* many things in our knowledge can be used, say Śāstras. Among these things the best is *oṁkāra* which is close to *parabrahman* and it is His name. The one who meditates on this as *parabrahman* following the required mental discipline reaches *brahmaloka* and gets *mukti* or salvation. A person not having strength for this and meditates on it as *aparabrahman* does not get *mukti* or salvation but gets other benefits. Thus though for both the persons *oṁkāra* was the same, depending on the nature of meditation the benefits differ. Not only that, even if the entire *oṁkāra* is not done in *upāsanā* and only part of it is meditated upon that too will bring good results. Good deeds will never go waste.

**Sukeśa** – Svāmī! Kindly explain the *upāsanā* of *oṁkāra* when done in parts.

**Pippalāda** –

स यद्येकमात्रमभिध्यायीत स तेनैव संवेदितस्तूर्णमेव जगत्यामभिसंपद्यते। तमृचो मनुष्यलोकमुपनयन्ते स तत्र तपसा ब्रह्मचर्येण श्रद्धया सम्पन्नो महिमानमनुभवति ॥५.३॥

*sa yady eka mātram abhidhyāyīta sa tenaiva saṁveditas tūrṇam eva jagatyām abhisaṁpadyate* | *tam ṛco manuṣyalokam upanayante sa tatra tapasā brahmacaryeṇa śraddhayā sampanno mahimānam anubhavati* ||5.3||

Meditating on sound unit (अ — A), one, enlightened accordingly, no sooner attains this world of changefulness (*jagat*). The *Ṛgveda* verses lead him unto the human world. Endowed with *tapas*, *brahmacarya* and *śraddhā*, there he enjoys greatness.

In *oṁkāra* there are three *mātrās*. *A* (अ), *U* (उ) and *M* (म्). Instead of meditating on all portions if a person only meditates on *A* (अ), he will attain in this *bhūloka* itself a superior birth. In this *praṇava,* the first vowel form is the *Ṛgveda* which will bring him back to this world of human beings. However, he gets an exalted human birth again after death. With penance, *brahmacarya* and faith he enjoys this worlds pleasures. This is the benefit a person gets by meditating on the first portion *A* (अ).

**Satyakāma** – Bhagavan! Now you must explain the importance of the second *mātrā U* (उ) of the *praṇavam.*

**Pippalāda** –

अथ यदि द्विमात्रेण मनसि सम्पद्यते सोऽन्तरिक्षं यजुभिरुन्नीत्यते सोमलोकम्।
स सोमलोके विभूतिमनुभूय पुनरावर्तते ॥५.४ ॥

*atha yadi dvi-mātreṇa manasi sampadyate so 'ntarikṣaṁ yajubhir unnītyate somalokam | sa somaloke vibhūtim anubhūya punar āvartate | | 5.4 | |*

Meditating on the units (of *AUM*), one attains mind (*manas*). The formulas of the *Yajurveda* lead him up to *somaloka*, the mid-world. Having experienced prosperity there, he returns.

Child! Listen carefully. Whoever meditates on the second *mātrā U* (उ) goes to the *somaloka*. The second vowel form *U* (उ) is the *Yajurveda*. After death it takes him to *chandraloka* in *antarikṣa* (space). There, after enjoying the prosperity of that world he comes back. After completion of the *puṇya* (merit) acquired by his meditative strength, he again comes back and is born in the human world.

**Kabandhi** – What are the benefits obtained by the meditation on the third portion?

**Pippalāda** –

यः पुनरेतं त्रिमात्रेणैवोमित्येतेनैवाक्षरेण परं पुरुषमभिध्यायीत स तेजसि सूर्ये संपन्नः यथा पादोदरस्त्वचा विनिर्मुच्यत एवं ह वै स पाप्मना विनिर्मुक्तः स सामभिरुन्नीयते ब्रह्मलोकं स एतस्माज्जीवघनात्परात्परं पुरिशयं पुरुषमीक्षते, तदेतौ श्लोकौ भवतः ॥५.५ ॥

*yaḥ punar etaṁ tri-mātreṇaiv om iti etenaivākṣareṇa paraṁ puruṣam abhidhyāyīta sa tejasi sūrye sampannaḥ | yathā pādodaras tvacā vinirmucyata evaṁ ha vai sa pāpmanā vinirmuktaḥ sa sāmabhirunnīyate brahmalokaṁ sa etasmāj jīvaghanāt parāt-paraṁ puriśayaṁ puruṣamīkṣate, tad etau ślokau bhavataḥ | | 5.5 | |*

Meditating on the highest *puruṣa* as the syllable *AUM* with

> its three *mātrās*, one finds himself in the Sun, the world of effulgence. Even as snakes get rid of their slough, so too he becomes free of sin. He is led by the *Sāma* chants to the world of *brahman*. He, as a living entity, sees the higher than the highest *puruṣa*, the dweller in the city. As to this there are these two verses.

Considering the third *mātrā* as important and concentrating on that and all the three portions combined a person who meditates on *oṁkāra* as *paramātmā* reaches the *sūryamaṇḍala*. Unlike the person going to *chandramaṇḍala* and comes back he does not come back. Just as a snake sheds his skin, he is relieved of all the sins. The *M* (मं) *mātrā* is the form of *Sāmaveda* and that takes him to *brahamaloka*. Lord Brhamā represents all living things, a complete form. Hence, he is termed as the provider of life. He is the *Hiraṇyagarbha*. Because of *oṁkāras*' greatness he even reaches a state above *Hiraṇyagarbha*, a blemishless omnipresent state and becomes witness of all living things. In this state, the *parama puruṣa* is realized as one's self form and the person is relieved of the bondage of *karmas*. The person attains salvation (*mukti*). *Oṁkāra upāsanā,* even if it does not give *mukti* in this *bhūloka* it takes the *upāsaka* to *brahmaloka*. There he realizes the concept of this world and attains *mukti*. To explain this concept there are two *mantras*.

**Satyakāma** – You explained the three *mātrās* present in *oṁkāra* as the three Vedas. Kindly explain these vowels a little more elaborately.

**Sauryāyaṇi** – Bhagavan! Hearing the nectar filled words from your mouth we have become blessed. You must further show your mercy on us.

**Pippalāda** – My friend! Do clear the doubts of these children.

**Sumantu** – Let it be so friend. Satyakāma as you asked, I will explain the three *mātrās* of the *praṇava* more elaborately.

> तिस्रो मात्रा मृत्युमत्यः प्रयुक्ता अन्योन्यसक्ता अनविप्रयुक्ताः ।
> क्रियासु बाह्याभ्यन्तरमध्यमासु सम्यक्प्रयुक्तासु न कम्पते ज्ञः ॥५.६॥

*tisro mātrā mṛtyumatyaḥ prayuktā anyonya saktā anaviprayuktāḥ* | *kriyāsu bāhyābhyantara madhyamāsu samyak-prayuktāsu na kampate jñaḥ* ||5.6||

The three *mātrās*, put to use separately, lead to death. Seen thus as mutually attached, each is not inapplicable separately in activities properly performed, whether within, without or midway.

Actually it is only one word. In that there are three *mātrās*. *A* (अ), *U* (उ) and *M* (म्) *mātrās*. These three *mātrās* are the form of three Vedas. These are the three levels, three time periods, three worlds, three *guṇas* (nature). The *Ṛgveda* recital sings the praise of *paramātmā* (almighty). The *Yajurveda* explains the *kriyās* to be done to worship the *paramātmā*. The *Sāmaveda* is wisdom- incarnate. It provides great wisdom. Thus, understanding the inner meaning, if a person does *upāsanā* of *oṁkāra* he gets salvation from *karmas*.

**Pippalāda** –

ऋग्भिरेतं यजुर्भिरन्तरिक्षं सामभिर्यत्तत्कवयो वेदयन्ते ।
तमोंकारेणैवायतनेनान्वेति विद्वान्यत्तच्छान्तमजरममृतमभयं परं चेति ॥५.७॥

*ṛgbhiretaṁ yajurbhir antarikṣaṁ sāmabhir yat tat kavayo vedayante* | *tam oṁkāreṇaivāyatanenānveti vidvān yat tac chāntam ajaram amṛtam abhayaṁ paraṁ ceti* ||5.7||

Through *Ṛg* verses (is attained) this world, through *Yajur* formulas the mid-region, through *Sāma* chants is attained that which the seers know. The wise one, with *AUM* alone as means, seeks and attains the tranquil, the unageing, the immortal, the fearless, the supreme. Thus are the verses.

Now I will explain the meaning of this *mantra-śloka*. Listen, further if the three portions of the *oṁkāra* are separately meditated upon they will give only partial benefits which will eventually get over. If *upāsanā* is done on all three portions together the benefits will not get over. The one who does meditation with the help of *oṁkāra* on the *puruṣa* of inside, middle and outside, which are well joined, becomes fearless. The one who meditates on *aparabrahman,* due to *Ṛgveda* obtains this human world, due to *Yajurveda* obtains *somaloka,* and due to *Sāmaveda* obtains *brahmaloka.* Such is the greatness of *oṁkāra* the elders have known. If a person considers this *praṇava mantra* as *Brahman* and meditates on *parabrahman* he becomes very peaceful and attains *turīya* state which does not have states like waking, sleeping, etc. and reaches the *parabrahman* in which there is no birth and death. A person meditating on *aparabrahman* through *oṁkāra* reaches *svarga* and other *lokas.*

**Satyakāma** – Do explain the concept of inside, middle, outside.

**Sumantu** – Inside means *suṣupti* (deep sleep state) represented by *M* (मृ) *mātrā* and causal body. In this *vyaṣṭi* form is *prajñan, samaṣṭi* form is *Īśvaran.*

Middle means *svapna* (dream) state represented by *U* (उ) *mātrā* and subtle body. In this *vyaṣṭi* form is *taijasan, samaṣṭi* form is *hiraṇyagarbha.*

Outside means *jāgarita* (waking state) represented by *A* (अ) *mātrā* and gross body. In this *vyaṣṭi* form is *viśvan, samaṣṭi* form is *vaiśvānaran.* These states though are not seen separately. However the *vyaṣṭi, samaṣṭi* forms present in these states have separate identities.

The *vyaṣṭi, samṣṭi* forms are:

*Viśvan — Vaiśvānaran, Taijasan — Hiraṇyagarbha, Prajñānīśvaran* all of them in their respective levels have respective bodies. In the form of *paramātmā* they are present. That *paramātmā* is *oṁkāra.* Thus knowing it well if a person does *upāsanā* he becomes *sarvātmā.* He never then slips from that state.

**Pippalāda** – Children! Now I will tell it in short, listen. Perceived by the great (*mahāns*), it is known that one can reach due to *Ṛgveda* this world, due to *Yajurveda* the *chandraloka,* due to *Sāmaveda* the *brahmaloka.* All these benefits are due to a person who meditates on *oṁkāra.* Here meditation of *oṁkāra's A* (अ),

*U* (उ) and *M* (म्) *mātrās* are discussed separately only to show the greatness of *oṁkāra*. Even if the *upāsanās* are separately done then also one gets a result, and if the *upāsanā oṁkāra* is done together, how much more good benefits will be obtained? This shows *oṁkāra*'s potential. However *oṁkāra upāsanā* is generally done together only. In that, if *aparabrahman* is meditated upon, even if one get benefits it is not possible to come out of *saṁskāra* wheel. Hence, understanding clearly the concept of other portions, *jāgarita*, dreaming and deep sleep states, equating them with their respective *puruṣas*, one gradually perceives that all are but *paramātmā*'s *svarūpa*. He is only *oṁkāra*. Realizing these, if one meditates on *parabrahman* one reaches *brahmaloka*, gets *Brahman* knowledge, reaches *turīya* state and attains real bliss.

**Sukeśa** – *Bhagavan*, today also you have revealed an important precept. However I feel sad that my friend Aśvakośa did not hear it.

**Sumantu** – No need to feel bad. The *guru* will bless him in such a way that all matters will be known to him. A *mantra* which does not have *praṇava* has no *prāṇa*. Hence all as per the teachings of the *guru*, do *upāsanā* of *praṇava* and accrue the benefits.

**Disciples** – We will do so Revered Guru. (Get up and salute both of them and leave.)

***(Curtain closes.)***

## PART V

### SCENE I

***(Curtain opens.)***

(It is the *āśrama* of Sumantu Maharṣi. Maharṣi, Sukeśa and the rest five disciples are sitting and talking.)

**Kauśalya** – Respected one, till now Aśvakośa has not come. Tomorrow Sukeśa has to ask his question, isn't it?

**Sumantu** – Child, there is no need to worry. Aśvakośa will definitely come today. Tomorrow there may not be any objection for the young one Sukeśa to ask the question.

**Sukeśa** – Revered Guru, hearing your solace-filled words I feel happy.

**Satyakāma** – Svāmī, I have a doubt.

**Sumantu** – What is that? Do ask, I will try to clear it.

**Satyakāma** – When Maharṣi Pippalāda preaches, he says, "There is a *śloka* for this, there is a *śloka* for that." Thus time to time he blesses us. What is the intention of that?

**Kabandhi** – Revered *guru*, I also have that same doubt. Are there any words above *maharṣi*'s uttering? Why should he cite examples.

**Sumantu** – Children! Your doubt is just. However for him to bless like that there is a proper reason. **(Aśvakośa enters and offers his salutations to everyone. After the *guru* asks him to sit, he sits.)**

**Sumantu** – Come Aśvakośa! Was your journey comfortable?

**Aśvakośa/Hiraṇyanābha** – Respected one! With your kindness and *maharṣi*'s blessing the journey went off comfortably.

**Sumantu** – Child, now they had asked a doubt. That is, "whenever *maharṣi*s preaches, he says 'There is a *mantra* (*śloka*) for this' to cite an example. What is the intention of that?" I had started to explain that when you also came by then.

**Aṣvakośa/Hiraṇyanābha** – Svāmī! I am also eager to know about this.

**Sumantu** – There are two types of Upaniṣads. One is the *Brahmanopaniṣad*, another one is the *Mantropaniṣad*. The *Mantropaniṣad* is in the form of *sūtrams*. The *Brahmanopaniṣad* is the explanation for that. The *Muṇḍaka Upaniṣad* belongs to *Atharvaveda* and is a *Mantropaniṣad*. The *Praśna Upaniṣad* also belongs to the same *Atharvaveda* and is a *Brahmanopaniṣad*. The explanation of *Muṇḍaka Upaniṣad* is the *Praśnopaniṣad*. That is why Maharṣi Pippalāda quoted some important *mantras* from *Muṇḍaka-mantropaniṣad* and cited them to explain the matter clearly.

**Kabandhi** – Respected one. Our doubts are cleared.

**Satyakāma** – Svāmī, we are indeed very grateful.

**Sauryāyaṇi** – Aśvakośa, do tell us all the news about the places you had been to.

**Aśvakośa/Hiraṇyanābha** – **(He expects the order from the *guru* and hence is hesitant.)**

**Sumantu** – Child, do tell us everything in detail.

**Aśvakośa/Hiraṇyanābha** – Revered Guru, In Mṛkaṇḍu *āśrama* a big gathering had assembled. A number of great people had come. They discussed about Veda, philosophy and Śāstras. The *yajñas* also were performed properly. With *maharṣi's* blessing and my previous life's *puṇya* I got an opportunity to take part in that.

**Kabandhi** – Aśvakośa! You are indeed lucky. Do tell us more about matters which took place there.

**Aśvakośa/Hiraṇyanābha** – All the people assembled there talked highly about Ṛṣi Pippalāda. When they came to know that I am his disciple they took special care of me.

**Satyakāma** – What happened afterwards?

**Aśvakośa/Hiraṇyanābha** – In the *yajña-maṇḍapa* there was a discourse on *Śrīmad Rāmāyaṇa.* The *Śrīmad Rāmāyaṇa* which is present in *devaloka* as hundred crore *ślokas* was preached in *bhūloka* by Nārada and Brahmā to Vālmīki Maharṣi. Accordingly Vālmīki Muni wrote the long epic poem of *Śrīmad Rāmāyaṇa* consisting of 24,000 *ślokas*. The discourse took place unceasingly in the *yajña* place. Everybody praised the *ādi kāvya* of Vālmīki Maharṣi, and his disciple Bhāradvāja Maharṣi talked highly about them.

**Sukeśa** – When we were coming here the words of my father are coming to my mind. Aśvakośa! What more did they tell?

**Aśvakośa/Hiraṇyanābha** – Ṛṣikumāras! It is not possible even for the thousand-tongued *Ādiśeṣa* to praise that epic.

**Sumantu** – In this composition of *Rāmāyaṇa*, Bhāradvāja Maharṣi part is very important. Sukeśa, your father by becoming the disciple of Vālmīki Maharṣi has obtained a lot of fame.

**Kabandhi** – Respected one, you must tell us the story of *Rāmāyaṇa*.

**Sumantu** – Children! Aśvakoṣa will tell you at leisure. Later you can hear and come to know of it. *Rāmāyaṇa* is an immortal story. Even if the earth, mountains, rivers and deep sea get destroyed, still this story will remain. When Kosala kingdom's *chakravarti*'s (emperor's) past story was being discussed, it was very appropriate that you who belong to Kosala kingdom had gone there.

**Kauśalya** – Dear Aśvakośa! You are lucky that you got this good opportunity.

**Satyakāma** – Aśvakośa! In your absence many happenings took place here too.

**Aśvakośa/Hiraṇyanābha** – **(quickly)** What? What happened? **(within himself)** Did Sukeśa get the answer for that question?

**Kabandhi** – Don't be scared. When you were not there Sauryāyaṇi and Satyakāma asked questions. The *guru* answered them. That is all.

**Aśvakośa/Hiraṇyanābha** – Those questions and the teachings, I perceived that day only with *guru*'s blessing.

**Sukeśa** – Friend, tell us how that happened, in detail.

**Aśvakośa/Hiraṇyanābha** – One morning I was sitting in meditation. That time all that happened here was seen by me. All the talk was heard very clearly, as though I was seeing directly and observing, I could see everything. I heard the questions and answers, I became blessed.

**Kabandhi** – Aśvakośa you are indeed fortunate.

**Aśvakośa/Hiraṇyanābha** – Friend, Sukeśa has not asked the question yet, has he?

**Sukeśa** – I wanted to ask that day itself. However the respected *guru* did not give permission.

**Aśvakośa/Hiraṇyanābha** – (**within himself**) O! Misfortune (**speaking out**) Why did he deny? Did he ask to search for someone else and ask to enquire from him?

**Sumantu** – He did not say anything like that. He gave a proper reason and then only denied it.

*fig* : **The *puruṣa* of sixteen *kalās***

**Aśvakośa/Hiraṇyanābha** – (**anxiously**) What reason did he give?

**Sukeśa** – Since you were not there, he did not give permission. He told "You can ask after Aśvakośa comes, I will give the reply then."

**Aśvakośa** – (**very happily**) Did the *guru* say that? I must have done *puṇya*. I am blessed, I am blessed. (**He dances and sings. With great happiness he salutes everyone again and again.**)

**Sumantu** – (**within himself**) He is Hiraṇyanābha, there is no doubt about it, (**speaking out**) Aśvakośa, enough, stop it. After knowing the matter there should be room for more happiness, hence be quiet now.

**Kabandhi** – It has been a long time since we came. Don't we have to go? Friends.

**Sumantu** – Alright, depart, and come again. Tomorrow morning we will meet in the *maharṣi āśrama*.

**(All of them get up and give their *praṇāmas*.)**

***(Curtain falls.)***

## SCENE 2

***(Scene opens.)***

(Pippalādā's *āśrama*. Pippalāda and Sumantu are sitting. In front Sukeśa and all the six disciples are sitting. Aśvakośa with a hand fan, fanning the *guru*, is standing.)

**Sumantu** – Child Sukeśa! today you can ask any question.

**Pippalāda** – Young one! Now Aśvakośa has come. You can now ask your question by all means.

अथ हैनं सुकेशा भारद्वाजः पप्रच्छ ।
*atha hainaṁ sukeśā bhāradvājaḥ papraccha* |

*Sukeśa, the son of Bhāradvāja, then asked Pippalāda.*

**Sukeśa –**

भगवन्हिरन्यनाभः कौसल्यो राजपुत्रो मामुपेत्यैतं प्रश्नमपृच्छत। षोडशकलं भरद्वाज पुरुषं वेत्थ। तमहं कुमारमब्रुवं नाहमिमं वेद यद्यहमिममवेदिषं कथं ते नावक्ष्यमिति। समूलो वा एष परिशुष्यति योऽनृतमभिवदति। तस्मान्नार्हाम्यनृतं वक्तुम्। स तूष्णीं रथमारुह्य प्रवव्राज। तं त्वा पृच्छामि क्वासौ पुरुष इति॥६.१॥

*bhagavan hiranyanābhaḥ kausalyo rājaputro mām upetyaitaṁ praśnam apṛcchata | ṣoḍaśa-kalaṁ bharadvāja puruṣaṁ vettha? tam ahaṁ kumāram abruvaṁ nāham imaṁ veda yadyahami mamavediṣaṁ kathaṁ te nāvakṣyaṁ iti | samūlo vā eṣa pariśuṣyati yo 'nṛtam abhivadati | tasmān nārhāmy anṛtaṁ vaktuṁ | sa tūṣṇīṁ ratham āruhya pravavrāja | taṁ tvā pṛcchāmi kvāsau puruṣa iti* ||6.1||

Venerable Sir, Hiraṇyanābha, the son of the king of Kosala, approached me and asked, "Bhāradvāja, do you know the *puruṣa* of sixteen *kalā*s?" I replied, "I know him not. If known to me why should I not tell you of him? Telling untruth, one verily becomes dried up right unto his root. I will not therefore, tell you untruth." Mounting his chariot, he departed silently. Now I ask you of Him: Wherein is that *puruṣa*?

O Bhagavan! The prince of Kosala kingdom, Hiraṇyanābha came to me and asked "do you know the *puruṣa* having sixteen forms?" I said, "I don't know about that *puruṣa*."

He did not believe my words. "It is a wonder a learned person like you don't know about it," said the prince. "If I had known would not I tell a close friend like you?," I told him.

However he still did not believe me. "Not to reveal the answer only, you are telling me you don't know and hiding the answer from me" said he.

I again repeatedly told him "In fact, I don't know, if I tell I know it will be a lie. A person who tells lies will not get any peace in this world or in heaven. As I know it very well, I will never tell a lie. Believe my words, really I don't know about the *puruṣa*." After saying so much he believed me.

He then fell embarrassed that he had asked a person like me who didn't know the answer. Later he climbed up in his chariot and without talking further went off. From then that question has been disturbing my mind. Only if I get the answer for it will my mind get peace. Now sir, I am asking the same question to you. Who is that *puruṣa*? Where is he? Kindly give us an explanation for this.

**Sumantu** – O Truthful person! a person having a beautiful mind, a very good question. Among the questions asked this is the prime question. To establish truth what involvement you have! You could see the basic destruction of human being in telling a lie." How much ever one praises you it will still not be enough.

**Kabandhi** – Not only that Svāmī, in order to get the answer for his friend's question, how much trouble Sukeśa has taken. The greatness of such a friendship is to be appreciated.

**Satyakāma** – Sukeśa is a personification of truth. He is the abode of friendship. To clear the doubt of his friend, he has taken undue pains.

**Aśvakośa/Hiraṇyanābha** – Ṛṣikumāras! Kindly stop this conversation. Give an opportunity for the *maharṣi* to answer.

**Pippalāda** – Children! Listen carefully.

इहैवान्तःशरीरे सोम्य स पुरुषो यस्मिन्नेताः षोडशकलाः प्रभवन्तीति ॥६.२॥

*ihaivāntaḥ śarīre somya sa puruṣo yasminnetāḥ ṣoḍaśa kalāḥ prabhavanti iti* | |6.2| |

Here indeed, within the body,
O dear, is that *puruṣa*, from Him arise these sixteen *kalās*.

Sukeśa, the *puruṣa* you asked about is *paramātmā* himself. That *puruṣa* alone has sixteen forms. The *puruṣa* in whom sixteen forms are present is this body itself, that is the Self.

**Sukeśa** – What are the sixteen forms? How did they come about? In which order did they come?

**Pippalāda** – Child, I will explain in detail.

स ईक्षांचक्रे। कस्मिन्नहमुत्क्रान्त उत्क्रान्तो भविष्यामि कस्मिन् वा प्रतिष्ठिते प्रतिष्ठास्यामीति ॥६.३॥

*sa īkṣāṁcakre | kasminnaham utkrānta utkrānto bhaviṣyāmi kasmin vā pratiṣṭhite pratiṣṭhāsyāmi iti ||6.3||*

He (the *puruṣa*) thought (of Himself); Whose departing makes me also depart? Whose settling down makes me also settle down?

This *puruṣa* who is *paramātmā* thought as follows. Staying inside the body, coming out of the body, these jobs have to be done. These I can do only with the help of some other person. Who is capable of this act? Thinking this way he created *prāṇa* with *samaṣṭi*/all-knowing qualities.

In this world also the kings themselves don't go and do all jobs. They appoint a chieftain having all powers. He alone supervizes and does all jobs. However, in the world everyone tells the work is done by the king. In the same way, *paramātmā* does not do everything. It is the *prāṇa*'s job to enter the body, stay there and later come out of the body. However it is told in the world that the *ātmā* is inside the body and *ātmā* leaves the body. Thus first creating *prāṇa,* then in proper order He created the fifteen forms or creations in the *prāṇa.*

**Kabandhi** – Revered Guru, I request you to tell us the names of the arts created in the *prāṇa* in detail.

**Pippalāda** –

स प्राणमसृजत। प्राणाच्छ्रद्धां खं वायुर्ज्योतिरापः पृथिवीन्द्रियं मनः। अन्नमन्नाद्वीर्यं तपो मन्त्राः कर्म लोका लोकेषु च नाम च ॥६.४॥

*sa prāṇam asṛjata* | *prāṇāc chraddhāṁ khaṁ vāyur jyotir āpaḥ pṛthivīndriyaṁ manaḥ* | *annam annād vīryaṁ tapo mantrāḥ karma lokā lokeṣu ca nāma ca* || 6.4 ||

He created *prāṇa;* from *prāṇa* faith, space, air, fire, water, earth, sense organs, mind and food; from food, vitality, austerity, hymns, actions, worlds, and in the worlds, names too.

The sixteen creations are as follows:

| | |
|---|---|
| 1. *prāṇa* | 9. mind |
| 2. faith | 10. *rayi* (food), from food |
| 3. sky/space | 11. vitality/strength |
| 4. *vāyu* (air) | 12. penance (*tapas*) |
| 5. *agni* (fire) | 13. Vedas/hymns |
| 6. water | 14. *karma*s (action) |
| 7. earth | 15. *svarga* and other *loka*s, |
| 8. sense organs | 16. names |

**Sukeśa** – Svāmī! The *Brahman* is present everywhere. Then is it proper to say it is within the body? You must kindly explain.

**Sauryāyaṇi** – A thing which is the cause of making a thing, how can that cause be contained in the effect (final thing produced)?

**Aśvakośa** – Ṛṣikumāras! The mango seed is the cause of the mango tree. However, in the mango tree both the thing which is the effect, namely the ripe mango is there, along with the seed which was the original cause. Both coexist.

**Pippalāda** – Children! Your doubts are only just. I am proud to have disciples having doubts like you. The example cited by Aśvakośa is not completely correct. The mango seed is the cause of the mango tree. However the seed which is the cause of the mango tree is different from the ripe mango and seed obtained from the mango tree. Apart from that, the tree and the seed are connected to each other as organs in a body are connected. However the *puruṣa* is without any organ. The creations and body have organs. Hence the *puruṣa* inside the body is similar to the truth of deathless moon.

**Sukeśa** – Deathless moon! What does that mean?

**Sumantu** – Child! In the night when pointing to the moon and showing it, it is told, there it is seen in the tree; now see above the tree, near that branch which is slightly curved, etc. However the moon is somewhere else. There is little connection between the moon and the branch of the tree. Still as the branch of the tree shows a reference point to the moon, to understand the moon and its position we use the branch of the tree. Likewise the *puruṣa* and the body have no connection. Since he is everywhere, it can be said that he is inside the body too. Further, the *ātmā* is seen inside the body, in other places *ātmā*'s presence is not seen. From this it is said that *ātmā* is inside the body. Actually just as the moon is referred as seen behind the branch of the tree, in the same way it is told that *ātmā* is inside the body though *paramātmā/parabrahman* is present everywhere.

**Sukeśa** – Svāmī! Do tell in mcre clear terms about the sixteen forms.

**Pippalāda** – Friend, complete the wish of the children and explain to them.

**Sumantu** – Let it be so *maharṣi*. Children listen; initially for the cause of all creatures, the *prāṇa* was created which was *samaṣṭi* (all-knowing). From that *prāṇa,* for all creatures to indulge in good *karma,* a conducive factor *śraddhā* (faith) was created. Then the five elements were created. Among them first the sound-containing factor the *akāśa* (space) was created. Afterwards, *vāyu* (air) was created containing the two factors sound and touch, then *agni* was created containing the three factors, sound, touch and form. From that combining the three factors and joining the *rasa* factor, water was created.

Combining the four factors of the water with the magnetic factor, the five-characteristic earth was created. From these five sense organs and five *karma* organs, a total of ten functioning organs were made. Then the master of these functioning organs the mind having intention and disturbances was created. After making the *kārya kāraṇaṁ* (functioning organs) of the living things then for them to eat and live God made *annam* (rice, wheat and other cereals were made). From the food partaken *vīryaṁ* (strength) was obtained. By eating the food and gaining strength many kinds of *karma* doing abilities were created. Then for the improvement of those living entities *tapas* (penance) was created. Because of penance the inside and outside got purified. For helping such purified souls, to do the right *karma* (action) *Ṛg, Yajur, Sāma, Atharvaveda mantra*s were made. Then with the help of these *mantra*s, *yajña, agnihotra* and such *karma*s were done. To give right rewards for the *karma*s, the other worlds or *loka*s were created. For those who had done *puṇya, svarga* (heaven) and for *pāpī*s (sinners), *naraka* (hell) are created. For people doing mixed *karma, bhūloka* (earth) was created. For the living beings in the different *loka*s, different lords were created. Lord Indra for *svarga*, Lord Yama for *naraka*, Lord Brahmā for earth. Such entities/names were made. Later all these get merged with *puruṣa* just as the rivers which flow having different names, in the end merge in the ocean. This is told in the *śloka* –

स यथेमा नद्यः स्यन्दमानाः समुद्रायणाः समुद्रं प्राप्यास्तं गच्छन्ति भिद्येते तासां नामरूपे समुद्र इत्येवं प्रोच्यते। एवमेवास्य परिद्रष्टुरिमाः षोडश कलाः पुरुषायणाः पुरुषं प्राप्यास्तं गच्छन्ति। भिद्येते तासां नामरूपे पुरुष इत्येवं प्रोच्यते स एषोऽकलोमृतो भवति तदेष श्लोकः ॥६.५॥

*sa yathemā nadyaḥ syandamānāḥ samudrāyaṇāḥ samudraṁ prāpyāstaṁ gacchanti bhidyete tāsāṁ nāmarūpe samudra ity evaṁ procyate evam evāsya paridraṣṭur imāḥ ṣoḍaśa-kalāḥ puruṣāyaṇāḥ puruṣaṁ prāpyāstaṁ gacchanti | bhidyete tāsāṁ nāma-rūpe puruṣa ity evaṁ procyate sa eṣo 'kalomṛto bhavati tad eṣa ślokaḥ ||6.5||*

Just as these flowing rivers heading for the ocean, on reaching it, disappear with their names and forms diffused, and are simply called ocean, even so, of this *puruṣa,* these sixteen *kalās*, heading for Him the perceiver, their names and forms diffused, are called simply the *puruṣa,* the *kalā*-less, the immortal. As to it, there is this verse:

**Sukeśa** – Paramaguru! For your teachings to clearly register in our minds this example is very useful.

**Pippalāda** – Just as a person having double vision disease of the eyes, sees everything double and when he gets cured of the disease his vision gets corrected, in the same way, due to *avidyā* all of what appears as different forms, merge into *puruṣa* once *avidyā* is removed. They get destroyed and the one which remains indestructible is called by *Brahman*-knowledgeable people as *puruṣa*. That *puruṣa* is undifferentiated, It is without creation, nectar-filled and is deathless. There is a *śloka* for this.

**Aśvakośa/Hiraṇyanābha** - Svāmī! Do tell us the *śloka.* Your teachings never pale even as we hear more and more.

**Pippalāda** –

अरा इव रथनाभौ कला यस्मिन् प्रतिष्ठिताः।
तं वेद्यं पुरुषं वेद यथा मा वो मृत्युः परिव्यथाः इति ॥६.६॥

*arā iva ratha-nābhau kalā yasmin pratiṣṭhitāḥ* |
*taṁ vedyaṁ puruṣaṁ veda yathā mā vo mṛtyuḥ parivyathāḥ iti* ||6.6||

Wherein the *kalās* rest firm, like spokes on the hub of a wheel — know Him as the *puruṣa* to be known! Death thus disturbs you not!

Just as the spokes of the chariot wheel remain attached to the axle, in the same way these creations remain attached to *puruṣa*. Knowing such a *puruṣa* means that one won't get caught by the fear of death. Like spokes in the wheel of a chariot, the sixteen *kalās* are fixed in the *puruṣa*. *Prāṇa, śraddhā* (faith) and such sixteen *kalās* depend on the *puruṣa* for their creation, stability and action. The main founder for these creations is *parabrahman.* Since He is completely and fully present everywhere and also lives in the place called body, He is called *puruṣa* where *pura* is the body and *isa* means dwells. O disciples! You come to know Him. Once you know Him you will have no fear of death as the *puruṣa* which dwells in you is immortal, but if you don't know this *puruṣa* you may get caught in fear of death. You will think as the body dies you also die. Hence to relieve you of this ordeal also I preached you these things.

**Sumantu** – Children, today all of you have become fully blessed. Aśvakośa, Sukeśa did you get to know now the answer for the question? (**Aśvakośa keeps quiet.**)

**Sukeśa** – Gurudeva, it has become very clear. Anything more?

तान् होवाच ।
*tān hovāca* |

*To them then Pippalāda said:*

**Pippalāda** –

एतावदेवाहमेतत्परं ब्रह्म वेद । नातः परमस्तीति ॥६.७ ॥

*etāvad evāham etat paraṁ brahma veda* | *nātaḥ paramasti iti* | | 6.7 | |

This much only do I know of that supreme *Brahman.* Nothing is there beyond this.

Children, I have informed you all I know about *parabrahman.*

**(The disciples are looking at each others faces.)**

**Sumantu** – My dear friend, whatever you told them, these young ones have taken it in a different meaning. They are wondering whether you are giving order to go to somebody else and take his help to know further. Kindly tell your opinion clearly without an element of doubt.

**Pippalāda** – What I have known from exalted and learned *ṛṣis* is this much. Above this there is nothing more to be known. You all need not have any doubt. Now there is nothing further to be known. Beyond this there is nothing more important.

**All disciples** – **(Get up and worship *maharṣi* and give their salutations.)** You are our father who has helped us to cross the river of *avidyā* and reach the banks of *mokṣa* (salvation). We again and again give our *namskārams* to you.

ते तमर्चयन्तस्त्वं हि नः।
*te tam arcayantastvaṁ hi naḥ* ।

Praising him they said.

**Pippalāda and Sumantu** – **(standing)** Disciples! Let us all together give our *praṇāmas* to the *brahmarṣis* who have been most benevolent to help you all to learn these.

पिता योऽस्माकमविद्यायाः परं पारं तारयसीति।
नमः परमऋषिभ्यो नमः परमऋषिभ्यः ॥६.८॥

*pitā yo asmākam avidhyāyāḥ paraṁ pāraṁ tārayasi iti* ।
*namaḥ parama ṛṣibhyo namaḥ parama ṛṣibhyaḥ* ।।6.8।।

You are truly our father;
You are taking us across the ocean of ignorance.
Adoration to the Supreme Seers!
Adoration to the Supreme Seers!

**(All sing together.)**

॥ ॐ भद्रं कर्णेभिः शृणुयाम देवाः भद्रं पश्येमाक्षभिर्यजत्राः।
स्थिरैरंगैस्तुष्टुवाꣳसस्तनूभिर् व्यशेम देवहितं यदायुः॥

*oṁ bhadraṁ karṇebhiḥ śṛṇuyāma devāḥ bhadraṁ paśyemākṣabhiryajatrāḥ* ।

*sthirair aṅgaistuṣṭuvām̐ sastanūbhirvyaśema devahitaṁ yadāyuḥ* | |

स्वस्ति न इन्द्रो वृद्धश्रवाः स्वस्ति नः पूषा विश्ववेदाः ।
स्वस्ति नस्तार्क्ष्यो अरिष्ठनेमिः स्वस्ति नो बृहस्पतिर् दधातु ॥

*svasti na indro vr̥ddhaśravāḥ svasti naḥ pūṣā viśvavedaḥ* |
*svasti nastārkṣyo ariṣṭhanemiḥ svasti no br̥haspatir dadhātu* | |

॥ ॐ शान्तिः । शान्तिः । शान्तिः ॥

| | *oṁ śāntiḥ* | *śāntiḥ* | *śāntiḥ* | |

*AUM,* May we, with our ears hear that which is auspicious, O gods.
And may we, habitually offering oblations, see with our eyes that which is auspicious.
With strong bodies, singing your praises, may we live our span of life destined to us by the gods.
May Indra of mature learning bestow well-being on us.
May Pūṣā (the sun), the knower of all, bestow well-being on us.
May Tārkṣya (Garuḍa), the annihilator of danger, bestow well-being on us.
May Br̥haspati bestow well-being on us.

*AUM,* Peace! Peace! Peace!

## SCENE 3

***(Curtain opens.)***

(Pippalāda's *āśrama* is seen. The door is closed. From outside Sukeśa is coming towards the *āśrama.*)

**Sukeśa** – In life a big wonder has taken place. The incidents are taking place like *indrajāla* (tricks played by lord Indra). Everything is strange. Only after Maharṣi Sumantu told in detail, I have come to the conclusion that Aśvakośa and Hiraṇyanābha are one. (**walking along**) I am not able to believe it. I did doubt seeing the familiar face. Finally it turned out to be correct. Everything is God Almighty's work who rules us. Now our *gurukula* stay is over. It is time to take leave of the preceptor and depart to our respective places. Before that I must see Hiraṇyanābha. Let me see if he is inside (**as he opens the *āśrama* door, Aśvakośa comes running and falls on Sukeśa's feet and gives his salutations.**)

**Sukeśa** – Dear one, Aśva-Hiraṇyanābha! Get up (**embraces him**).

**Hiraṇyanābha** – (**getting up**) Ṛṣikumāra! Do tell you have forgiven me at least once. Unless I hear those nectar-filled words my mind won't become quiet.

**Sukeśa** – Friend! You have not committed any mistake for me to forgive you. Who has to forgive whom? Everyone commits some mistake or the other. The blemishless *guru* of great character will forgive everyone and give his blessings.

**Hiraṇyanābha** – I have taken forgiveness and blessing from Maharṣi Pippalāda with humility. You also must forgive me for the deceit drama which I enacted. Otherwise I won't leave your feet. (**Once again about to fall at his feet. Sukeśa stops him and tells "I forgive you." Sumantu and the five *ṛṣikumāra*s enter.**)

**Sumantu** – Did you see! Children, what to say if separated men join again? Did you watch Hiraṇyanābha and Sukeśa talking animatedly?

**Kabandhi** – Yes, Svāmī! I noticed. They are very dear friends, aren't they?

**Kauśalya** – That too, from childhood they are close friends.

**Satyakāma** – In spite of that Sukeśa did not recognize the prince which is a bit surprising.

**Sauryāyaṇi** – There is nothing to be surprised. It only shows Hiraṇyanābha's talent for acting.

**Bhārgava** – For more than one year he fooled all of us. Hiraṇyanābha is indeed a good actor.

**Sumantu** – (**smiling**) This world itself is a stage, we are all but actors in it. On behalf of you all, shall we give the title "The star actor" to Hiraṇyanābha?

**Kabandhi** – The title *nāṭaka-kesarī* will also be apt.

**Satyakāma** – We shall ask Sukeśa to perform the award cermony. (**All come close and converse. Hiraṇyanābha falls on others' feet and asks for forgiveness.**)

**Sumantu** – O Prince! There is no mistake on your part. Trying to search for knowledge is not a crime. Seeing the eagerness of your search for knowledge, we all praise you. (**From the *āśrama,* Maharṣi Pippalāda and other disciples come. As one disciple spreads the reed mat Pippalāda and Sumantu sit down. Sumantu addresses Maharṣi Pippalāda**), Friend, the *gurukula* stay for the children is over, isn't it? They are waiting to take leave of you.

**Pippalāda** – Children, let good tidings befall on all of you. Now you are standing at an important turning point of your lives. You must speak the truth. You must walk on the path of *dharma.* Don't stop reciting Vedas. Now each one of you can come and take leave.

**Sukeśa** – O Great one! You helped us to cross the *avidyā* and bestowed immortal life. Here I give my respects to you and offer my *dakṣiṇā* with lot of affection. (**Deposits the *gurudakṣiṇā* at his feet and gives his salutations.**)

**Kabandhi** – Revered Guru, removing the darkness, the one who showed the sun of wisdom, O! merciful one, I give my salutations to you. (**Keeps the *dakṣiṇā* and does *namaskāram.***)

**Kauśalya** – O Merciful lord! I bow my head and salute you. You have helped me in crossing the wordly ocean. You have helped us to be unaffected and untouched from evil crocodiles of this ocean of life, like birth, death, disease, sorrow, etc. (**Lays his offerings and offers his worship.**)

**Bhārgava** – O Benevolent one! my salutations to you for making us climb in the boat of knowledge and helping us to reach the banks of *mokṣa*/salvation. (**Keeps the offering and gives his *praṇāmas*.**)

**Sauryāyaṇi** – You are our father. You are even above the father who gave us birth. With great humility I pay my respects to you. (**Gives the *dakṣiṇā* and does *namaskāram*.**)

**Hiraṇyanābha** – Today only we realized the benefit of having eyes, the benefit of having ears. Forgive our shortcomings and give your *āśirvāda*, respected one. (**Gives the *dakṣiṇā* and gives his salutations. Then all together give *praṇāmas* to Sumantu Maharṣi and other elders.**)

**Pippalāda** – Children, let me tell you all a good news. I had informed the Kosala kingdom about your journey earlier itself. Now in a short time chariots will come. All of you can go together to Bhāradvāja Muni's *āśrama*, give your respects to him, take his blessings and then go to your respective places. Let good tidings be bestowed on everyone. You may all go happily.

**Disciples** – We will do as you say.

(Pippalāda and Sumantu go inside. The chariots come and stand. The charioteer comes running and gives his repects to Hiraṇyanābha. Hiraṇyanābha also comes out of his camouflage and wears the dress of the king.)

**Sukeśa** – Friends, as per our *guru*'s order we shall all go to Prayag.

**Hiraṇyanābha** – R̥ṣikumāras, do climb into the chariot.

**Kabandhi** – We are saved the walk. On the way we can hear the *Rāmāyaṇa* also.

**Kauśalya** – I can go up to the house.

**Hiraṇyanābha** – I will make arrangements for everyone to go to their respective *āśramas*. Enough number of chariots have come.

**Satyakāma** – Very happy to know.

(The ladies of the *āśrama* come and do *āratī*. Sukeśa and others climb into the chariot, they move slowly from the *āśrama*, the following *śloka* is heard.)

ॐ पूर्णमदः पूर्णमिदं पूर्णात् पूर्णमुदच्यते ।
पूर्णस्य पूर्णमादाय पूर्णमेवावशिष्यते ॥
॥ ॐ शान्तिः शान्तिः शान्तिः ॥

*oṁ pūrṇamadaḥ pūrṇamidaṁ pūrṇāt pūrṇamudacyate* |
*pūrṇasya pūrṇamādāya pūrṇamevāvaśiṣyate* | |
| | *oṁ śāntiḥ śāntiḥ śāntiḥ* | |

**(*Curtain falls.*)**

**End of *Praśṇa Upaniṣad.***

## ॥ मुण्डकोपनिषत् ॥

# Muṇḍaka Upaniṣad

### Introduction

UPANIṢADS are revelations by realized and enlightened *ṛṣi*s about working behind the world of appearances. They again and again state about the all-pervading *Brahman* which is the only unalterable truth behind the names and forms. However, for souls who go through life in ignorance of this fact, it is difficult to fathom and realize the import of this *Brahman* which cannot be understood by any of the senses, and for humans they are the main inputs for understanding the universe.

The *Muṇḍaka Upaniṣad* reveals these facts as well as it is possible to put forth. Hence, symbolically it is called *Muṇḍaka*. As like shaving off the hair and leaving the scalp bare all the facts are stated in very clear terms to the extent of condemning even the rituals associated with Vedic religion. The *ṛṣi* asks the aspirant to concentrate on bare facts and take to ways of renunciation to know the truth.

Śaunaka is the *mahā gṛhastha* (the householder). The play opens with Śaunaka's discontent, a disturbing unhappiness in spite of having an ideal life set-up. He is blessed with wealth, a good wife, children and a good disposition to do Vedic rites as written in scriptures. He is aided by the *purohita* who provides him all the guidance to the rituals which are conducted with an objective of gaining merit and reach heaven. Śaunaka is further aided by two close friends Vājapeyī and Saumya.

As Śaunaka laments about his state of restlessness to his friends, Maharṣi Gopāda arrives at his abode. He learns about the discontent plaguing the mind of Śaunaka, in spite of doing *yajñas* and following Vedic rituals as per rules. Maharṣi Gopāda states with his wisdom, this restlessness can be put to rest only on learning *brahma-vidyā* which is the ultimate knowledge. He directs him to the *āśrama* of his friend and *Brahman*-realized Maharṣi Aṅgiras at Rishikesh.

Śaunaka and his friends hence reach the *āśrama* of Maharṣi Aṅgiras in search of *brahma-vidyā*. Ṛṣi Aṅgiras accepts them as his disciples and imparts *brahma-vidyā,* that is knowledge of knowing and understanding *Brahman.*

Right at the onset, he tells them, among knowledge there are two types *parā* and *aparā*. *Parā* is transcendental knowledge, that is knowledge which talks about *Brahman* which is behind all appearances of the world. *Aparā* is non-transcendental, that which is seen around the world. The *ṛṣi* even includes all the four Vedas also in *aparā-vidyā* as they may only lead towards the *Brahman* knowldege and not amount to actual *brahma-vidyā.* Thus, this *Muṇḍaka Upaniṣad* minces no words and excludes even the sacred Vedic rituals from the Knowledge which can directly reveal *Brahman*. This gives a jolt to Vedic scholars as well as ritualists who follow faithfully the *yajñas* and other rituals subscribed in Vedas, also with an eye on incurring merits which will help them to gain better life in this world and the next. However a seeker of *Brahman* has to realize that all these worlds are only apparent and realization of *Brahman* is beyond the wants and needs of these worlds. The *Upaniṣad* advocates the path of renunciation without passions and attachments as the true way to get enlightenment.

*Brahman* (the Creator) was the first preceptor who taught the *brahma-vidyā* to his elder son Atharva. He, in turn, taught it to Aṅgiras who taught it to Satyavaha and so on.

By knowing *brahma-vidyā* one realizes *Brahman* is one reality behind all animate and inanimate things in this universe.

It is the inner urge for self-expression of *Brahman* which has brought about all the names and forms we see around us. They have emerged spontaneously like the web coming out of a spider, the plants coming out of the earth, hair coming out of the body or sparks coming out of a blazing fire. However this *Brahman* eludes the medium of words, thoughts and mind as it is beyond all these and is an all-prevading reality. To bring this concept to the intellect of the seekers, the *ṛṣi* variously tries to describe the intangible and unfathomable unity behind all the worlds and the actions (*karma*) of the beings.

The *Brahman*'s essence is effulgence. He exists both internally and externally. He has no birth or death. He is not sustained by birth; thus he is birthless. He alone gives rise to all the five elements, the mind and senses which we are familiar with. The entire cosmos is but the invisible *Brahman* which has visibly manifested.

How to realize this all-prevading *Brahman* by our limited power of intellect and mind? Is it possible to know one's own spark as an individual self who has emerged from the bigger "Self"? Is the great goal (*mahatpādam*) attainable? This question is answered by the *ṛṣi*.

The perceiver and perceived are the effulgence of one and the same consciousness. Thus the enquirer on enquiring about the one Reality, the *Brahman,* should himself become like an arrow aimed at the realization of *Brahman* and contemplate with deep concentration taking the help of knowledge gained from the Upaniṣads. When such an arrow gets released, he and *Brahman* can become one.

When it is said he becomes one with *Brahman* it means there is a change in the vision or perception while the present existence remains the same. This concentration can also be achieved by chanting of *praṇava mantra oṁ* which symbolically denotes *Brahman*.

*Brahman* can be imagined like a hub in a wheel. From the hub emanates the spokes. So also all the creatures in the

Universe emanate from Him. When we are well entrenched in this concept, that is, we are part of the whole and not a separate entity, we can find peace and tranquillity.

The thing which separates us from the reality around us from which we emanate are various conditioning factors such as mind, thoughts or body form, etc. All these are termed as — *upādhi* in *Upaniṣad*. At the zenith of meditation these *upādhi*s fall off and one sees oneself not as a separate entity but as a part of overall reality.

On getting the vision of oneness all the bondages and obligations which bind a human being fall off and one gets liberated from them, which is called *mukti*. One realizes one's soul's self-content. Then one does one's action in a relaxed manner as an agent of *Brahman* without any personal expectations. A person is then relieved of fruits of actions and the bondages of cause and effect.

Though *Brahman* is found in each and every living entity, man fails to realize it. Here the *Upaniṣad* explains the position by the analogue of two similar birds on the same tree. One is the perishable "I" and the other the imperishable *Brahman* who is the witness but not affected by the cause-effect cycle. Once the person realises the *guru* or witness *Brahman* within him he understands the truth. This realization should stay with him *nityam* (always).

Thus viewing life as an unfolding of *Brahman* one gets the true perspective of life and the substance behind it.

The *Upaniṣad* giving explanation about *Brahman* says, for a seeker who has realized "IT" it is nearest and for the one who is ignorant it is farthest as though hiding in a cave. The scripture further elaborates, to know the *Brahman* which is beyond the senses one must meditate. Here, meditation implies intuitively perceiving the *Brahman* and conducting life always in that perception. In that perception, the uncontaminated state of consiousness is met with and one understands one's soul's self-content.

A realized person is synonymous with *Brahman* itself. Hence, such a realized person should be venerated, who in turn can instruct less-evolved souls and help them in realization and liberation from the bondage of life and death.

However, the *Upaniṣad* warns the path is not very easy. It cannot be had just by following some instructions or by superior intellectual power, learning the scriptures, heavy discussions, etc. One should pursue the goal with single minded devotion and seek the Self as the only value of life. The wisdom is realized then.

As he becomes one with the Almighty, one with the cosmic being, the different parts by which a human is made, which are enumerated here as fifteen, find their union with their fifteen cosmic counterparts. That is, the microcosm finds unity with the macrocosm in all aspects. This brings an eternal wisdom and peace in the being, which is a state of everlasting bliss.

Thus, the *Muṇḍaka Upaniṣad* like an arrow sharply pointed to the correct object, guides the seeker clearly away from the labryinth of all unclear paths directly to the wisdom of *Brahman* uncovering the veil of ignorance.

# The Drama

**Characters**

| | | | |
|---|---|---|---|
| 1. | **Gopāda** | – | Brahmarṣi |
| 2. | **Aṅgiras** | – | Brahmarṣi |
| 3. | **Śaunaka** | – | *Mahā gṛhastha* |
| 4. | **Devadatta, Saumya, Brahmadatta, Vājapeyī** | – | The friends of Śaunaka |
| 5. | **Yajñasenī** | – | Śaunaka's wife |

***Purohita*, Ṛtviks and other *āśrama* residents**

## PART I

### SCENE I

**(From behind the screen.)**

ॐ भद्रं कर्णेभिः शृणुयाम देवाः। भद्रं पश्येमाक्षभिर्यजत्राः।
स्थिरैरङ्गैस्तुष्टुवाँसस्तनूभिः। व्यशेम देवहितं यदायुः॥

*oṁ bhadraṁ karṇebhiḥ śṛṇuyāma devāḥ | bhadraṁ paśyemākṣabhiryajatrāḥ |*
*sthirairaṅgaistuṣṭuvām̐sastanūbhi | vyaśema devahitaṁ yadāyuḥ ||*

स्वस्ति न इन्द्रो वृद्धश्रवाः। स्वस्ति नः पूषा विश्ववेदाः।
स्वस्ति नस्तार्क्ष्यो अरिष्टनेमिः स्वस्ति नो बृहस्पतिर्दधातु॥

*svasti na indro vṛddhaśravāḥ | svasti naḥ pūṣā viśvavedāḥ |*
*svasti nastārkṣyo ariṣṭanemiḥ svasti no bṛhaspatir-dadhātu ||*

॥ ॐ शान्तिः। शान्तिः। शान्तिः॥

॥ *oṁ śāntiḥ | śāntiḥ | śāntiḥ* ॥

*Auṁ*, May we, with our ears hear that which is auspicious, O gods. And may we, habitually offering oblations, see with our eyes that which is auspicious with strong bodies, singing your praises, may we live out our span of life destined to us by the gods. May Indra of mature learning bestow well-being on us. May Pūṣā (the sun), the knower of all, bestow well-being on us. May Tārkṣya (Garuḍa) the annihilator of danger bestow well-being on us. May Bṛhaspati bestow well-being on us.

*Auṁ* Peace! Peace! Peace!

(***Curtain opens.***)

(Śaunaka is sitting and conversing with his friends and the *purohita*)

**Śaunaka** – *Purohita*! I was able to do different *yajña*s with your help. You have taken great pains in helping to complete them. I am truly indebted to you.

**Purohita** – Friend! I did not have any strain due to these. It is only due to your *śraddhā* all the *yajña*s were conducted in an exemplary manner.

**Saumya** – Friends, I myself have done a number of *yajña*s and *iṣṭi*s. I have also seen many *yajña*s being conducted. However, I have not seen anybody doing *yajña*s with such *śraddhā* and elaboration like Śaunaka. *Na bhūto na bhaviṣyati* (न भूतो न भविष्यति – not happened in past nor will happen in future). There is no one equal to Śaunaka in present or even in future.

**Vājapeyī** – Undoubtedly! Since he is doing *yajña*s every year like this in a very exemplary manner, he has been conferred the title *mahāśāla*.

**Purohita** – Yes indeed.

प्रत्यब्दं यज्ञकMत् महाशालः प्रकीर्तितः
*pratyabdaṁ yajñakṛt mahāśālaḥ prakīrtitaḥ*

Every year the one who does this yajña is called as Mahāśālā.

This has been stated by the elders. I consider it as a great fortune to be his *purohita*, and do the *yajña*s for him.

**Śaunaka** – Friends! Don't praise me in excess. Everything is happening due to the blessings of *deva*s. (**Thinking a little**) I have a lot of wealth, a good and affectionate wife. She is good-natured and obedient. Also I have many children who are blessed with good nature. I am living with all comforts and fortunes. I have also the company of good friends. I am trying not to commit any sins and do only good (*puṇya*) deeds. To do the good *karma*s in a good manner I have a *purohita* to help me. However, though I have everything, still I feel there is something which is lacking, not allowing me to complete the whole picture. I cannot even describe it as something wrong. I get a feeling which cannot be described, a kind of dissatisfaction. At times I feel, what is the use of this life?

**Vājapeyī** – Friend! You lack nothing. It is only a false feeling. You should not feel disheartened. Let us go ahead with the preparations for the next *yajña*.

**Saumya** – That is only correct. A mind which has nothing to do will imagine something. कर्मण्येवाधिकारस्ते (*karmaṇyevādhikāraste*, our rights are limited to do *karma*s only), therefore we should continue to do our duties constantly.

**Purohita** – Śaunaka, what the friends are saying is correct. You are performing *yajña*s. You are sure to reach *svarga* (heaven). You collect money by good means. You are having enough wealth. You are doing the rites prescribed in the Vedas without fail. There are definite fruits for these actions. You need not be scared of anything. Leave aside the worries. Let us make arrangements for the next *yajña*.

**Vājapeyī** – Yes, my friend. After finishing *yajña* in one place another *yajña* should be done nearby and next one close to that. Like this the entire earth should be made *yajña* place. Only then will we get the blessing of Yajña Varāhamūrti.

**Saumya** – Not only that, we should also fill the world with *durvā* grass keeping them facing eastwards.

**Purohita** – Then we can call our friend as "*prācīna* Śaunaka."

**Śaunaka** – Friends, what you say is correct. The *devatās* get satisfied by *yajñas*. Because they are getting satisfied we get rain. By rain the yield of crops is good. The land becomes prosperous. We enjoy that. In return we offer our grateful gratitude to gods and perform *yajñas*. We should do them continuously. Respected *purohita*, what *yajña* can we do next? Friends, please tell me your ideas too. I will consult my wife and decide the date.

**Purohita** – We will do so. Looks like somebody is coming.

(One *āśrama* person comes and informs "Brahmarṣi Gopāda is coming." Immediately everybody gets up and goes to welcome him. Yajñasenī goes to bring from inside the required things for doing *arghyapādya ācamanam* and the welcome. After receiving the *maharṣi* all return. Brahmarṣi Gopāda is offered a high seat and all of them sit down taking his permission. Conversation continues.)

**Śaunaka** – Svāmī! With your arrival all of us have become blessed. You a *maharṣi* of such a big stature coming to my humble abode, a mere house of a householder is indeed due to the fortune earned by our ancestors. I am thankful for your arrival. You must accept our small welcome and hospitality with an open mind.

**Purohita** – Brahmarṣi, let your arrival bring good tidings. You have come at the correct time. Mahāśāla Śaunaka wanted to perform a *yajña*. He has already done many *yajñas*. Now he is thinking as to what *yajña* can be done next. Since you have also come it is a good omen.

**Vājapeyī** – Maharṣi, it is like a rare herb we were searching is found right here. Your arrival is indeed a good fortune for us. You have come at the right time. You must kindly instruct us what *yajña* we have to do now?

**Śaunaka** – Svāmī, you must kindly with your holy words bless us and tell us what we have to do now.

**Saumya** – Friends! It is already decided that a *yajña* has to be done. In what order it has to be done? How it has to be done? Only these things have to be asked of the *maharṣi*.

**Gopāda** – O Good men! allow Śaunaka to talk for a while. When we see his face we can make out, his mind is disturbed. Let him ask his doubts himself. Let no one talk in between. Is that clear?

*fig* : **Maharaṣi Gopāda being received by Śaunaka**

**All of them** – Alright, so be it.

**Gopāda** – Śaunaka! Mahāśāla! The one who has acquired a lot of fame by spreading all over the world the *dūrbā* grass facing eastwards and converting the entire place into a *yajñaśālā,* do ask me your doubt. I will answer as well as I can.

**Śaunaka** – Svāmī, accept my *praṇāma*s. I have become blessed with your arrival. In spite of doing many *yajña*s my mind has not got peace. I constantly have some dissatisfaction. I feel something lacking. Although I feel I have all the *bhoga*s (enjoyment) and all kind of prosperity still I feel something which I am not able to describe, a kind of incompleteness. When I do the *yajña*s properly I do get some peace of mind, I do not deny it, but that is only for a short while.

**Purohita** – Friend, that is just a delusion. There is no one who does *yajña* like you, with such *śraddhā*. Some people who are jealous might have wished some evil for you. That may be the reason your mind has been disturbed like this.

**Gopāda** – (**angrily**) *Purohita*! Didn't I ask everyone of you to be quiet for a short while and allow Śaunaka to talk? That request is for you also. Be calm for a while and allow Śaunaka to talk. Let Śaunaka open his mind and tell his opinions. After that you can talk. Śaunaka, you may ask boldly your doubts.

**Śaunaka** – Svāmī! I have told my doubts already. Though I am living with no dearth of wealth and prosperity, still I feel something lacking. There is some other need pulling me. Is this feeling real or just an imagination. If it is real how to remove this feeling. What I have to do? Kindly preach to me with consideration.

**Gopāda** – The feeling of something lacking is indeed true. You are doing different kinds of *yajña*s. However because of that you are not going to incur any special benefit. Only by true knowledge the sadness will be wiped off, and true happiness and comfort can be obtained. Just by doing your duties alone you cannot get lasting comfort.

**Purohita** – O Learned one! The statement that *karma* does not have the ability to give happiness is strongly objected to by me. This is against the utterances of Vedas.

**Saumya and Vājapeyī** – We also admonish it strongly.

**Śaunaka** – Svāmī, you continue to talk. You need not stop your sayings just because the friends are raising objection.

**Gopāda** – Friend! I am not going to stop. Your mind was burdened in spite of doing the *karma*s. Now is a good opportunity. It has awakened. This might be a good turn.

**Śaunaka** – Yes, as you are telling me, I was immersed in *karma*s. I don't know if any goodness is accruing. What should I do now? Do preach to me the philosophy. As *pravṛtti dharma*s continue *saṁsāra* increases. What should I do to come out of these.

**Gopāda** – Desiring the comfort of *svargaloka* the various *yajña*s have been performed till now. You must have killed and sacrificed many thousands of animals. They, remembering the torture you have given them, keep waiting for you to die to take their revenge. As soon as you die, they, with their iron like horns, may poke you and torture you with great anger.

**Purohita** – (**closing both the ears**) Here insult of Vedas and insult of *yajña*s are taking place. I will leave this congregation and go out.

(He goes out. "We are also going" say Saumya and Vājapeyī as they also exit.)

**Śaunaka** – Svāmī! My friends have gone. What to do?

**Gopāda** – They don't want to hear, and they are going. What can we do? You need not be scared of anything. Further *yajña*s need not be done. You must try to realize the *ātmasvarūpa.*

**Śaunaka** – Svāmī! I will do as you say. I will come out of the act of performing *yajña*s. To realize *ātmasvarūpa* what more has to be done?

**Gopāda** – Leaving aside *yajña*s you must try to achieve *brahma-jñāna.* You must go and take asylum under the feet of *maharṣi*s. They will teach you.

**Śaunaka** – Svāmī! Can't you teach me? Keeping the butter in hand, where is the need to go around for the ghee? You are the best person to teach me.

**Gopāda** – Śaunaka, I am not as learned and competent as to preach you. The one capable of that is Maharṣi Aṅgiras. You come to Rishikesh to his *āśrama*. Your questions and doubts will be cleared there.

(Then Yajñasenī is coming and inviting for *vaiśvadeva*. All are getting up and going.)

***(Curtain closes.)***

## SCENE 2

***(Curtain opens.)***

(Gopāda and Śaunaka are sitting. Yajñasenī is standing nearby with humility.)

**Śaunaka** – Svāmī! My wife also wishes to come to Rishikesh along with me. With your permission I thought I would bring her.

**Gopāda** – Mahāśāla! Though it is not proper for couples who have done *yajña* together to get separated, still in the place where you are going for *brahma-jñāna,* it may not be proper for your wife to come along.

**Yajñasenī** – Svāmī, please don't say that I should not go. Right from the age of eight when I got married I have not left my husband. Kindly give me permission to come along.

**Gopāda** – Child, Yajñasenī, your devotion to the husband and *dharma* of *pativratā* you follow are indeed of very high order and are worthy of praise and emulation. Still it may not be proper to be adamant at this juncture.

**Śaunaka** – Brahmarṣi, my wife is also keen on acquiring *brahma-jñāna.* Hope there is no restriction on it.

**Gopāda** – There is no such restriction. The ladies have full rights to acquire knowledge. Haven't you heard about Gārgī, Maitreyī and such other noble ladies who had acquired knowledge?

**Yajñasenī** – Svāmī, if that is so, can I also go with my husband and get the preaching? Can I also accompany him?

**Gopāda** – Seeing such united couples like you, with mutual love, feeling of duty to one another, I am also getting attracted towards householder's life. Though I said that ladies can acquire this knowledge still it may not be proper for ladies to accompany their husbands to learn this knowledge. There is much difference in both the situations.

**Yajñasenī** – Svāmī, the difference between the two situations is not very clear. Kindly tell me in detail.

**Gopāda** – For ladies to acquire *brahma-jñāna* they need not approach another *guru*. They can get their preaching from their husbands themselves. Now let Śaunaka alone come along with me. Let him get the teachings and later he can come back and preach to you. That is the proper order and ideal way for householders. Hope you understood that well.

**Both of them** – Svāmī, we will act as per your orders.

**Gopāda** – Now the arrangements for the travel have to be made.

**Śaunaka** – Brahmarṣi! When do we have to start?

**Gopāda** – Day after tomorrow is a good day. We can start during *abhijita muhūrta*.

**Śaunaka** – We will do as you say. Before that do give orders for the jobs to be done.

**Gopāda** – Nothing much has to be done. An *agnihoma* called *ekarṣi* has to be done. For that as per rule, *śirovrata* has to be done. This *homa* and *vrata* can be done tomorrow and we can start the day after tomorrow.

**Śaunaka** – I will make all the arrangements. Dear Yajñasenī! Make all the preparations for tomorrow's *homa* and *vrata*, with the help of the disciples.

(Yajñasenī leaves. Saumya comes running and falls at the feet of Gopāda and does *namaskārams*.)

**Saumya** – Brahmarṣi! You must kindly pardon the mistakes I have done. If you don't do so I will be in great anguish.

**Gopāda** – Friend, do get up. You have not done any mistakes for me to pardon you. You have not done anything wrong. Do tell clearly so that I can understand.

**Saumya** – Brahmarṣi! Due to your magnanimous nature you are not able to find anything wrong. That day I left the *sabhā* proclaiming loudly my objections. Isn't that wrong? Is it not a sin? I am realizing my mistake and am repenting. You must kindly bless me.

**Śaunaka** – Svāmī! My friend Saumya is a highly emotional person. On impulse he talks something. Then he realizes the mistake and repents.

**Gopāda** – Saumya you have not done any mistake. Everyone has a right to walk out of the *sabhā* if they feel matters against their liking are discussed. Whatever you felt that day you did boldly. There is no mistake or sin in this. Still if you feel so much, for your consolation, I can tell I have pardoned you. That is all.

**Saumya** – As you say you have pardoned me, I now feel at peace.

**Gopāda** – I have pardoned you from my heart, come and sit near me. To get peace of mind you must get *brahma-jñāna*. By my pardoning alone there is no use as just by *mantra*s alone the mango does not fall.

**Śaunaka** – Friend, I am going to Rishikesh with the Brahmarṣi Gopāda to get preaching from Brahmarṣi Aṅgiras. The required things for that are going to be done tomorrow.

**Saumya** – I am also coming. Please take me along with you. Allow me to do the jobs required for tomorrow's *pūjā*.

**Gopāda** – I am very happy. Brahmarṣi Aṅgiras's *āśrama* doors will be open always for everyone. The disciples like you who are keen on doing the right *karma* are always sought after by the *guru*. Persons who are learning Vedas are also favoured. Saumya you can also come along with us.

**Śaunaka** – Svāmī! I am keen about knowing Brahmarṣi Aṅgīras's greatness. Kindly tell me about him in detail.

**Saumya** – Svāmī, kindly inform with your blessing words.

**Gopāda** – Listen, I will tell you. The greatness of Aṅgiras is *brahma-jñāna*'s greatness. By making you all understand about *brahma-jñāna*'s greatness, you can also understand Aṅgiras's greatness.

**Śaunaka** – Svāmī, if that is so tell about the greatness of *brahma-vidyā* in detail.

**Gopāda** –

ओं ब्रह्मा देवानां प्रथमः सम्बभूव विश्वस्य कर्ता भुवनस्य गोप्ता।
स ब्रह्मविद्यां सर्वविद्याप्रतिष्ठांअथर्वाय ज्येष्ठपुत्राय प्राह ॥१॥

*oṁ brahmā devānāṁ prathamaḥ sambabhūva viśvasya kartā bhuvanasya goptā |*
*sa brahmavidyāṁ sarvavidyāpratiṣṭhāmatharvāya jyeṣṭhaputrāya prāha ||1||*

Brahmā, the creator of all and the sustainer of the world, emerged as the first of gods. He taught the science of *Brahman* (*brahma-vidyā*), the basis of all sciences, to Atharva, his eldest son.

*Oṁ*! The one who has made the world is Brahmā; the one who protects the world is also He. Such a Brahmadeva came about before all *deva*s. The *vidyā* first preached by Him is *brahma-vidyā*. To his first human son Atharva He preached *brahma-vidyā*. It is the basis of all *vidyā*s. By knowing that everything else is known. That is the knowledge worth knowing and is the basis of all knowledge.

**Saumya** – Why is it named as *brahma-vidyā*? Is there any concept behind it?

**Gopāda** – The words from the Vedas have deep meaning. There won't be any empty words in this without meaning. The *brahma-vidyā* can have two kinds of meaning. It can mean it is the first *vidyā* (knowledge) preached by Brahmā. Also it can mean the knowledge about *Brahman*.

**Śaunaka** – Is there inside meaning in giving the preaching first to one's son?

**Gopāda** – It is there. A father wishes to give one's wealth and knowledge to one's son. That which will enrich only will be preached. Only that which will give blessing and prosperity will be told to the son.

**Śaunaka** – Svāmī, thereafter who all learned that exalted knowledge?

**Saumya** – How did Brahmarṣi Aṅgiras obtain it? Tell us in detail.

अथर्वणे यां प्रवदेत ब्रह्माथर्वा तां पुरोवाचाङ्गिरे ब्रह्मविद्यां।
स भारद्वाजाय सत्यवाहाय प्राह भारद्वाजोऽङ्गिरसे परावराम् ॥२॥

*atharvaṇe yāṁ pravadeta brahmātharvā tāṁ*
*purovācāṅgire brahmavidyāṁ* |
*sa bhāradvājāya satyavāhāya prāha bhāradvājo 'ṅgirase*
*parāvarām* ||2||

What Brahmā imparted to Atharva, that science of *Brahman* Atharva taught to Aṅgir long ago; he in turn taught it to Satyavāha of the Bhāradvāja clan; and Bhāradvāja (Satyavāha) imparted this hierarchical wisdom to Aṅgiras.

The *brahma-vidyā* was preached by Brahmā to Atharva. Atharva taught it first to a person called Aṅgir. He taught it to Satyavāha who was from the Bhāradvāja clan. Thus the knowledge was passed from one generation to another. It contains both *parā-vidyā* and *aparā-vidyā* Such *brahma-vidyā* Satyavāha taught to Aṅgiras.

**Śaunaka** – Svāmī! I am indeed happy to know this. That *brahma-vidyā* started from Brahmā and was protected by Atharva and other *maharṣis*. Now it is being taught by Aṅgiras. Kindly continue.

**Saumya** – Svāmī! What is the meaning of *parā-vidyā* and *aparā-vidyā*?

**Gopāda** – There is nothing more for me to tell. If you go and question Aṅgiras he will teach everything in a proper order. It is almost afternoon. Let us go for bath. Do come.

***(The curtain falls.)***

SCENE 3

***(The curtain opens.)***

(In Rishikesh near the banks of river Gaṅgā, under a *maṇḍapa*, Devadatta, Saumya, Brahmadatta and Vājapeyī are sitting and conversing.)

**Saumya** – Friend! Your coming here is indeed very good. How did you know of our arrival here? What is the news over there? What is the purpose of coming here? Do tell me everything in detail.

**Vājapeyī** – Devadatta! The other day after leaving the *sabhā* in haste I was very much disturbed. I sat alone and thought. However it only increased the confusion and did not provide any clarity. I decided to meet you. I enquired at your place and came to know that you had gone out of station. From mother Yajñasenī I got all the information and came here. In between this the *purohita* came and he stopped me from going. He tried to tell various reasons and the correctness of the situation. I did not listen to him and came here.

**Saumya** – I am very happy. If Śaunaka knows of your arrival here he will also be very happy.

**Vājapeyī** – We have been living together in the same place since childhood. Hence staying separately is difficult. I also want to go to *gurudeva* and get his blessings. You must recommend me through Śaunaka.

**Saumya** – Brahmadatta, after coming here for the first two or three days we were enjoying the natural beauty of this place. Only yesterday we met the Gurudeva Aṅgiras. In his face *brahma tejas* is shining. Just by seeing him the doubts are getting cleared. He talks with the majesty of Himālayas, with the clarity of rising Gaṅgā and the depth of river Yamunā. Listening to his words is a great pleasure.

**Vājapeyī** – You have kindled my curiosity. Do tell me in detail, my friend.

**Saumya** – Yesterday my friend Śaunaka and I were taken to Brahmarṣi Aṅgiras by Gopāda. After doing the *vrata*s as per rules and taking *samidhā* in hand we went to the sanctum of *gurudeva* and gave our respects to him. He gave us blessings and with great affection asked us to sit near him.

**Vājapeyī** – Then what happened?

**Saumya** –

> शौनको ह वै महाशालोऽङ्गिरसं विधिवदुपसन्नः पप्रच्छ ।
> कस्मिन्नु भगवो विज्ञाते सर्वमिदं विज्ञातं भवतीति ॥३॥

> *śaunako ha vai mahāśālo 'ṅgirasaṁ vidhivadupasannaḥ paprаccha* |
> *kasminnu bhagavo vijñāte sarvamidaṁ vijñātaṁ bhavatīti* ||3||

> Śaunaka, the great householder approaching Aṅgiras as enjoined asked: "Venerable Sir, knowing what does all this world become known?"

Our friend Śaunaka who is known as Mahāśāla approached Aṅgiras in a proper manner of a disciple approaching a *guru* and did *namaskāram*s and gave his respects and asked "Respected Sir, by knowing what, it can be said that everything can be understood"?

**Vājapeyī** – I did not understand the meaning of this question clearly.

**Saumya** – The meaning of what Śaunaka asked was, "till now we read the Vedas carefully and the *karma*s as recommended in the Vedas we did as per rule. However this did not bring peace of mind. Hence to get peace of mind what has to be done? After knowing which it may not be necessary to acquire other knowledge? By knowing which a person becomes all knowledgeable?

**Vājapeyī** – Hearing the question, it looks like there is a strong feeling that for all things happening in the universe there is a fundamental cause. In fact, the first question should be, is there a fundamental cause for all the things? Is there a knowledge encompassing all the knowledge? A question like this can be asked only after knowing that it is there.

**Saumya** – In a way what you are saying is correct. However there is nothing wrong in this way of questioning too. In the question "by knowing which a person becomes all knowledgeable?" the expression "by which?" itself denotes the meaning if it is there? Hence the question is a good and proper one. We are doing many ornaments of gold. Even though the ornaments may vary, they all happen to be of gold. The fundamental causative thing is gold, is it not? Similarly even though knowledge may vary still the one which penetrates all knowledge and the fundamental knowledge should be one. Is it not? What is that? That is the question to be asked.

**Vājapeyī** – Alright, I accept it. What answer did gurudeva give?

**Saumya** –

> तस्मै स होवाच। द्वे विद्ये वेदितव्ये इति ह स्म यद्ब्रह्मविदो वदन्ति परा चैवापरा च ॥४॥
>
> *tasmai sa hovāca* | *dve vidye veditavye iti ha sma yad brahmavido vadanti parā caivāparā ca* ||4||
>
> To him then he said: Two kinds of knowledge are there to know, as indeed *Brahman*-knowers are wont to say: the transcendental (*parā*) and the immanent (*aparā*).

**Aṅgiras told Śaunaka** – There are two kinds of knowledge which one should know *parā* and *aparā*, thus have told *brahmajñānīs*.

**Vājapeyī** – There is a doubt in this answer too, dear friend! For the question of Śaunaka "by knowing this you become knowledgeable" will be the apt kind of answer. Leaving that, to give as an answer the unheard of things is not clear. Kindly, you must explain them in detail.

**Saumya** – Brahmadatta! There is nothing wrong about the answer. To the question "what has to be known?" the answer was given as "two kinds of knowledge have to be known." One named *parā-vidyā* and the other *aparā-vidyā*. That also he did not tell all by himself. He told with humility, "I am only telling you what the *brahmarṣi*s have been saying for generations." What is wrong about this? Where is the doubt? There is nothing. The question is asked in short. The answer is with clarity in detail, that is all.

**Vājapeyī** – Devadatta, the explanation is good. However to my small intellect it is felt that the answer should not be round-about. These kinds of answers only create more confusion.

**Saumya** – There is some justice in what our friend says. Though there is nothing wrong in giving such an answer, one question may have the answer in one word, for another the answer may have to be given in lengthy words. This answer however is given very cryptically. The person who wants to know about *brahma-vidyā* teachings has to be told step by step only. Now we should know about *parā* knowledge. However before that we should know the meaning of *parā* knowledge. It is only proper to know things in complete order. Hence the knowledge is mentioned as two and he explains this as "one is *aparā* and the other is *parā*."

**Vājapeyī** – Friend, my doubts have been cleared. Please continue to explain further.

**Saumya** – Brahmadatta! The teachings were stopped yesterday with this. Now tomorrow only he will continue. Tomorrow you can also come along with us and listen.

**Vājapeyī** – Devadatta, I am very happy. When you are telling itself it is very good to hear. When *gurudeva* explains it will be indeed nice. Everything is due to the blessings of Vedamātā. Now our friend *purohita* is not here.

**Saumya** – Everything is done due to the blessings of *gurudeva*. It is also due to the blessing of Brahmarṣi Gopāda. There need be no thought of *purohita* now. Let us go to the *āśrama.*

***(The curtain falls.)***

***(The First Part Ends.)***

## PART II

### SCENE 1

***(Curtain opens)***

(In Rishikesh Brahmarṣi's *āśrama*. On the seat covered by tiger skin Aṅgiras and Gopāda are sitting. On either side disciples such as Śaunaka, Brahmadatta, and Devadatta are standing. Obtaining the permission from gurudeva, after everybody sits, *śānti pāṭha* is recited).

**Aṅgiras** – Dear Saumya! Let good tidings befall you. Let Śaunaka tell us whatever he has learned till now.

***fig* : Ṛṣi Aṅgiras at Rishikesh**

**Śaunaka** – Respected Sir! I shall do so. Brahmā who is the head of all *deva*s initially came first before *deva*s of Indra clan. He was more exalted in qualities such as wisdom, *dharma*, prosperity, *vairāgya*, etc. than other *deva*s. He was not bound to the rules of *karma* like us. He came about by himself. He is the creator of all the worlds. Further the worlds he created were protected, ruled and taken care of by him. Such a great Brahmā taught the *brahma-vidyā* to his eldest son Atharva.

**Vājapeyī** – Friend! I have heard hundreds of *yogī*s were created by Brahmā. However you are telling Atharva was created first?

**Śaunaka** – What you are telling is that which happened in Svayambhuva *manvantaram* but in Vaivasvata *manvantaram* Atharva only came first. From him began *Atharvaveda*.

**Vājapeyī** – Is that so? Do continue.

**Gopāda** – Śaunaka tells very beautifully. I am very happy.

**Śaunaka** – Atharva taught the *brahma-vidyā* learned by him to a person called Aṅgiras. He in turn taught it to Satyavāha belonging to Bhāradvāja *gotram*. Thus from *guru* to disciple in that order this *brahma-vidyā* was taught. Now let us approach the gurudeva and get his preaching.

**Aṅgiras** – Children, I am very happy. The explanation was done very well.

**Saumya** – Friend, further continue to tell us other matters.

**Vājapeyī** – To disciples who came later like me, do repeat what you asked *gurudeva* and the answer he gave for the same.

**Śaunaka** – I will do so dear friends. I asked *gurudeva* "Knowing which everything will be known *Bhagavān*. You must bless me with that information." *Gurudeva* told us you must know two kinds of knowledge *parā* and *aparā* as preached by *brahma-jñānī*s.

**Gopāda** – Śaunaka tells very shortly without leaving a single one. I request friend Aṅgiras to continue to preach that.

**Disciples** – We also pray the same thing. What is *parā-vidyā*? What is *aparā-vidyā*?

**Aṅgiras** – Friend! Saumya, I will continue to tell. Listen carefully.

> तत्रापरा ऋग्वेदो यजुर्वेदः सामवेदोऽथर्ववेदः शिक्षा कल्पो व्याकरणं
> निरुक्तं छन्दो ज्योतिषमिति। अथ परा यया तदक्षरमधिगम्यते ॥५॥
>
> *tatrāparā ṛgvedo yajurvedaḥ sāmavedo 'tharvavedaḥ śikṣā kalpo vyākaraṇaṁ niruktaṁ chando jyotiṣamiti* ।
> *atha parā yayā tadakṣaramadhigamyate* ।।5।।
>
> Of these, the immanent consists of the *Ṛgveda, Yajurveda, Sāmaveda* and *Atharvaveda;* Pronunciation (*Śikṣā*), Ritual (*Kalpam*), Grammar (*Vyākaraṇam*), Etymology (*Niruktam*), Metrics (*Chandam*) and Astrology (*Jyotiṣam*). And the transcendental is that whereby the Imperishable is comprehended.

I said that there were two kinds of knowledge, isn't it? In *aparā* is included *Ṛgveda, Yajurveda, Sāmaveda, Atharvaveda, Śikṣā, Kalpam, Vyākaraṇam, Niruktam, Chandas, Jyotiṣam,* etc. That's, four Vedas and six Vedāṅgas. *Parā* is that knowledge which leads one to the indestructible *Brahman.*

**Vājapeyī** – Svāmī! Do Vedas and Vedāṅgas belong to *aparā-vidyā*? It is very surprising but disappointing.

**Saumya** – We thought that the Vedas are very exalted.

**Gopāda** – Saumya, you need not think less about Vedas. It is, in comparison to other *vidyā*s, much exalted. However when compared with *brahma-vidyā* it is indeed placed below, otherwise not. It won't serve any purpose however to relinquish the path of wisdom.

**Śaunaka** – Thanks for the explanation. To understand well *parā-vidyā* do tell us in detail about *aparā-vidyā.*

**Gopāda** – So be it. *Aparā-vidyā* is the one through which the knowledge of the matters of this world is known, knowledge of *anātmā* objects (not belonging to *ātmā* knowledge) is understood, and thus all things connected with and to *saṁsāra* constitute *aparā-vidyā*. *Saṁsāra*'s nature will be turned towards that. Because of that, the knowledge leading to the concept of the world's existence won't be known. Only knowledge which are *amūśmika* (non-*Brahman* knowing) will be known. Actually *aparā-vidyā* is a form of non-wisdom knowledge (*avidyā*). Since it is in everyday usage it is mentioned as knowledge just to differentiate it from other regular things. Those who are interested in knowing the concept of the world, *ātmā*, etc. have to leave the *aparā-vidyā*.

**Śaunaka** – Svāmī, now kindly tell us about *parā-vidyā* in some detail.

**Gopāda** – *Parā-vidyā* is the one through which the philosophy of *Paramātmā* is learned, that which is indestructible, that which constitutes the entire world, that which is the cause of the blemishless universe, that only is the foundation of the entire wisdom. Once that knowledge is understood then there is nothing more to be known in the universe.

**Vājapeyī** – Gurudeva! I request you to tell us about Vedas and Vedāṅgas a little more in detail.

**Aṅgiras** – Saumya! Listen. I will tell you. From Vedavyāsa, the *R̥gveda* was received by Paila, *Yajurveda* by Vaiśampāyana, *Sāmaveda* by Jaimini, and *Atharvaveda* by Sumanta. For each of them there were a number of disciples. Through them many branches of Vedas multiplied. Brahmā preached to his first son Atharva *brahma-vidyā*. That only I am telling you all now. To learn Vedas properly and to understand the concept in them, Vedāṅgas came to the fore. They are as follows:

1. *Śikṣā* – It is *Śikṣā* which tells about the formation of words and their pronunciation.
2. *Kalpa* – The rules for doing *karma*.
3. *Vyākaraṇam* – It is the grammar about words and sentences.

4. *Niruktam* – It is the explanation of the Vedas.
5. *Chandas* – It is the grammar of the songs coming in Vedas.
6. *Jyotiṣam* – The knowledge of time as per the position of the sun and the moon.

All these are *aparā-vidyā*. As my friend Gopāda told, they can be termed as "no knowledge" (*avidyā*) too.

**Śaunaka** – Gurudeva, now kindly preach about *parā-vidyā*.

**Aṅgiras** – *Parā-vidyā* is the one from which *Brahman* which is *akṣara* (imperishable) is understood.

**Vājapeyī** – What is meant by *akṣara*?

**Aṅgiras** – *Akṣara* means indestructible. "The one which is spread everywhere" is another meaning.

**Saumya** – Will both the meanings be apt for describing *Brahman*?

**Aṅgiras** – Definitely they will fit. *Brahman* is indestructible. It is filled everywhere. Hence *Brahman* is described as *akṣara*.

**Śaunaka** – I request you to continue to preach further.

**Vājapeyī** – Gurudeva, one doubt. We are all bounded by *karmas*. We consider the things which are not in accordance with Vedas as of no strength and equivalent to hell. When Vedas are counted in *aparā-vidyā*, will Upaniṣads also be contained in that, are not Upaniṣads explanations (*bhāṣyam*) to Vedas? Then the wisdom which is told in the Upaniṣads will be considered in accordance with Vedas and as having no strength and they will get counted in *aparā-vidyā*. Then which is *parā-vidyā*?

**Aṅgiras** – I request friend Gopāda to give an explanation for this.

**Gopāda** – Upaniṣads are connected to the Vedas. The *brahma-jñāna* told in that is only discussed here. The *brahma-jñāna* understood from Upaniṣads is only *parā-vidyā*. However just learning words of Upaniṣads and understanding of the word meanings from them, which can be done by all, will not be *parā-vidyā*. After learning the Upaniṣadic truths with *vairāgya* a *guru* has to be approached, and the required services done to him. Then the preachings obtained from the *guru* have to be contemplated upon and understood; that is *brahma-vidyā*. To differentiate that, Vedas are called *aparā-vidyā* and *brahma-tatva sākṣātkāram* (to understand *Brahman* in reality) is explained as *parā-vidyā*.

**Śaunaka** – Svāmī! Our doubts have been cleared. Please continue to preach.

**Aṅgiras** – Now I shall tell you in detail about *parā-vidyā*.

यत्तदद्रेश्यमग्राह्यमगोत्रमवर्णमचक्षुःश्रोत्रं तदपाणिपादम् ।
नित्यं विभुं सर्वगतं सुसूक्ष्मं तदव्ययं यद्भूतयोनिं परिपश्यन्ति धीराः ॥६॥

*yattadadreśyamagrāhyamagotramavarṇamacakṣuḥśrotraṁ tadapāṇipādam* |
*nityaṁ vibhuṁ sarvagataṁ susūkṣmaṁ tadavyayaṁ yad bhūtayoniṁ paripaśyanti dhīrāḥ* ||6||

Invisible, ungraspable, having no family line, colourless, sightless, hearingless, it is, the handless and feetless, eternal, omnipresent, all-pervading, exceedingly subtle, undecaying, perceived all over by the wise as the source of all that has emerged.

This cannot be seen by anyone, This cannot be grasped by anyone, It does not have any colour, has no eyes or ears, no hands or legs. However It is a permanent thing – *vibhu* – filled everywhere. It is very subtle, blemishless. It is the cause of all elements. The wise ones see It everywhere always. This is the meaning of the *mantra* I just recited.

**Śaunaka** – Gurudeva, the matters you have told us now are creating in the mind a lot of confusion. We pray, please tell in a detailed manner so that we can understand.

**Vājapeyī** – Svāmī, we are like blindfolded people left in the forest. Nothing is clear to our brains. You must kindly explain things again.

**Saumya** – Respected Sir, at one place you said that It cannot be seen. In another place you say they are seeing It well. It sounds contradictory.

**Aṅgiras** – Saumya! There is nothing contradictory. Initially it may appear confusing and contradictory. If you think deeply it will become clear. I will explain in detail. Listen carefully. Let us take each characteristic separately. By stating that It cannot be seen, etc. we mean that all the sense organs are not equipped to know this. *Brahman* cannot be known by the five *jñānendriyas*. It cannot be heard by the ear, It cannot be smelt by the nose. It cannot be tasted by the tongue. It cannot be felt by sense of touch.

That which cannot be known by *jñānendriyas*, doesn't mean that it can be known by *karmendriyas*. It is apart from *karmendriyas*. *Agotram* means It is one without a fundamental or foundation. There is nothing which is the cause of *Brahman*. *Avarṇam* means It is without any characteristics or colours. It cannot be described. It is beyond the description of words. Only if It has characteristics it can be described. It is without attributes such as being short, stout, fat, lean, white, black, etc.

**Śaunaka** – I can understand well, Svāmī, please continue to tell.

**Aṅgiras** – The first *śruti* states, It cannot be reached by *jñānendriyas* and *karmendriyas*. Now you might think, though others are not able to understand It, That is able to understand everything. Hence does It have *indriyas* for perceiving things around It? However *Brahman* does not have *jñānaendriyas* like eyes and ears. Nor can It be perceived by sense organs. That is, It does not have sense organs, nor by sense organs can we understand It. But It understands everything by its *svarūpachaitanya*. *Paśyatyacakṣuḥ sa śṛṇotyakarṇaḥ* (पश्यत्यचक्षुः स शृणोत्यकर्णः — he can see without eyes, hear without ears). Hence It remains indestructible. It is called *vibhu* because It is spread everywhere. It is more subtle than *ākāśa* (sky). It does not diminish. Just as how earth is the cause of *sthavara jaṅgamam* (all life), in same way It is the cause for everything. Just by describing It like this don't think It can be understood. With contemplation, as thinking process, gets clarity It can be understood. The intelligent seers discovered It in Its true form. Not as a fleeting phenomenon but they found It everywhere, encompassing all things. It is possible for you all also to realize It as such.

**Gopāda** – Friend, let us stop the lessons here. Let the disciples think about It and come.

**Aṅgiras** – So be it.

(The disciples prostrate and say their respects.)

***(The curtain falls.)***

## SCENE 2

***(Curtain opens.)***

(The conversation takes place like the previous scene)

**Gopāda** – Saumyas, did you think clearly? Is there any doubt about whatever you learnt yesterday? If so you can ask?

**Disciples** – We thought over well, there is no doubt.

**Śaunaka** – What cannot be explained, you described in detail and made us understand. The *Brahman* is the *yoni* of all *bhūta*s (lives). It is the cause factor. But how did It becomes the cause factor? Kindly explain the creation's characteristics.

**Aṅgiras** – It is a good question. I will give you the reply.

यथोर्णनाभिः सृजते गृह्णते च यथा पृथिव्यामोषधयः सम्भवन्ति।
यथा सतः पुरुषात्केशलोमानि तथाऽक्षरात्सम्भवतीह विश्वम्॥७॥

*yathorṇanābhiḥ sṛjate gṛhṇate ca yathā*
*pṛthivyāmoṣadhayaḥ sambhavanti* |
*yathā sataḥ puruṣātkeśalomāni tathā 'kṣarāt*
*sambhavatīha viśvam* | |7| |

Spider emits out and absorbs back (its thread); herbs emerge out of the earth; hair grows out of the head and body of a living person; likewise too emerges this universe out of the imperishable.

Just as how the spider makes the thread and spins the web around itself, just as how plants come out of the earth, just as hair grows on living things in the same way the world is formed from *Akṣara Brahman*.

**Śaunaka** – The examples are very apt and interesting.

**Vājapeyī** – Still I require some more examples to understand.

**Aṅgiras** – We have seen the spider spinning the web and wrapping it around itself. In the same way the *Brahman* spins the *prapañca* (universe) from itself and encompasses within Itself. For a potter to make a mud pot, he will require the mud wheel and other things. However in a spider's case it does not go out in search of yarn to make the web. From its body itself it brings out the yarn and makes the web. Later it draws it in its own body. In the same way *Brahman* also does not go out looking out for anything else. Remaining as a single entity It makes the entire universe and carries out its destruction also. *Brahman* is nature's cause and apparent cause of the universe.

**Saumya** – What does the second example explain?

**Aṅgiras** – The spider made the web for its own needs. For staying in it made the house. Here *Brahman* does not have any self-welfare or needs. To show this only, the second example is cited. That is, the plants and trees coming out of the earth are not for its self needs. In the same way *Brahman* makes the universe.

The meaning can be told for this example in another way. The earth as per the nature of seeds makes the plants. In the same way as per each person's *karma* the birth takes place. Because of that God does not have the fault of prejudiced discrimination of its creations.

**Saumya** – Svāmī, what aspect does the third example personify?

**Aṅgiras** – In the second example, the earth which is the cause of the plants, and the plants, both are perishable. The resultant and the cause for it have the same characteristic. Considering this example the universe which is perishable, which is the resultant and the cause of it, the *Brahman* may also be thought to be perishable. To clear this, the third example is given. Just as how from living persons non-living hair grows out, in the same way from the non-perishable *Brahman* the perishable world comes out.

**Gopāda** – Friend, I am very pleased. The concept of how creation took place was described by you very beautifully and wonderfully. I have never heard anyone else describing it with such clarity.

**Aṅgiras** –

तपसा चीयते ब्रह्म ततोऽन्नमभिजायते ।
अन्नात्प्राणो मनः सत्यं लोकाः कर्मसु चामृतम् ॥८॥

*tapasā cīyate brahma tato 'nnamabhijāyate* |
*annātprāṇo manaḥ satyaṁ lokāḥ karmasu*
*cāmṛtam* | |8| |

By *tapas*, *Brahman* swells up, and thus is produced food; and from food emerges *prāṇa* (life-breath); mind; the elements; and the worlds; and even the attainment of immortality implicit in self-efforts.

In this *mantra* the sequence of creation is explained. It is not as if the world was made like scattering fruits from a tree. It was made step by step in an order. This is explained by this *mantra*. Initially *Brahman* performs *tapas,* connects with *jñāna,* and expands. From that *annam* (food) gets formed. From *annam, prāṇa* (life-breath) gets formed. From *prāṇa,* mind, *satyam* (truth), world elements, *karma* and nectar-like fruits of *karma* were formed in sequence.

**Vājapeyī** – However, you say, *Brahman* does not have a body, then how did it perform the *tapas*?

**Gopāda** – *Tapas* does not mean going to the forest and holding one's breath. *Tapas* is remaining with an one-pointed mind. To think intensely about the act of creation is the *tapas* of *Brahman*. As soon as the wish was formed for creation the *Brahman* of neutral characteristics (without attributes) acquired multi-faceted characteristics (having many attributes). This is expansion and feeling of great happiness. In daily occurrence we see the father expanding with great happiness when he gets a child.

**Śaunaka** – How did the attributes of *Brahman* change later?

**Gopāda** – From the *Brahman* of attributes – the *saguṇa Brahman* – the *annam* came out. *Annam* denotes the *avyākṛta tattva* or *māyāśakti*. From that was made *prāṇa* (life-breath) which is the Hiraṇyagarbha or the creator of all living things. From that emerged the mind. From that the *satyam* (truth) came out, which are nothing but the five elements. From the five elements, the seven worlds came about. From that the *karma*s suitable for people came out. The resultant effect of *karma*s, the concept of *svarga,* arose. These cause and effect of *karma*s are termed as *amṛta* (nectar). Thus from the *Brahman* the world came to be formed in this process.

**Vājapeyī** – When *karma* and its effect are temporary why are they called nectar or imperishable? Is it correct to call them thus?

**Aṅgiras** – As per the *varṇa* (caste/group of people) the *karma*s change. The effect of *karma*s also changes accordingly. Even if many years elapse it is not possible to escape the effects of *karma*. Even if crores of years are past the fruits of *karma* will not be erased. For the actions performed the effects have to be experienced. Since the *karma*s are never erased and their effect always remains, the fruits of the *karma*s are called *amṛta* (imperishable).

**Vājapeyī** – Gurudeva, I understand very well, however!

**Gopāda** – Saumya! However what? Ask your doubt.

**Vājapeyī** – The word *satyam* was interpreted as *pañca-bhūta* (five elements). How does that fit?

**Saumya** – I also got the doubt. You must make it clear, Svāmī.

**Gopāda** – This world made up of names and forms came out of the *pañca-bhūta*s (five elements). In comparison to the resultants — the name and form — the cause of it, the *pañca-bhūta*s, are permanent, ever present. Further the gross things seen by the eyes: the earth, the water, and the *tejas*, all these three are called *sat*. The one which is not seen by eyes, the subtle *vāyu* (air) and *ākāśa* (space) are called *tyat*. Both these combined — *sat* and *tya* — is *satyam*. Hence they are termed as *satyam* by Upaniṣads.

**Śaunaka** – Kindly continue preaching.

**Aṅgiras** –

यः सर्वज्ञः सर्वविद्यस्य ज्ञानमयं तपः।
तस्मादेतद् ब्रह्म नाम रूपमन्नं च जायते॥९॥

*yaḥ sarvajñaḥ sarvavidyasya jñānamayaṁ tapaḥ* |
*tasmādetad brahma nāma rūpamannaṁ ca jāyate* | |9| |

All-knowledge, all-knowing, Its *tapa*s is the act of "knowing" in essence; out of It emerge this *Brahman*, names, forms and food as well.

The *Brahman* which generally knows everything and also knows everything in particular, and whose *tapas* is wisdom personified, from that *Brahman* names, forms and *annam* (food) arose. This *mantra* summarizes what has been told so far.

**Śaunaka** – Gurudeva, you must explain clearly yet again.

**Vājapeyī** – Is there any difference between the words *sarvajñaḥ* and *sarvavid.*

**Aṅgiras** – The *Brahman* using *māyā* as a deception or *upādhi* creates the universe. *Māyā* is a general phenomenon. It is also called *samiṣṭi* (all encompassing). The meaning of the word *sarvajñaḥ* is all-knowing. By the *upādhi* called *māyā* the universe is understood and it is termed as *sarvajñaḥ*. The same *Brahman* becomes *jīva* and becomes individual entities and with the *upādhi* termed as *avidyā* understands the various things of the universe. This is the meaning of *sarvavid* (all-knowledge). Here the *tapas* (penance) of *Brahman* is not like a *tapa*s done by an individual by putting the body to harness and austerity. From the *sarvajñaḥ* (all knowledge) *Īśvara* (God) the Hiraṇyagarbha who is *kriyābrahman* comes out. From that the names such as Devadatta, Yajñadatta, etc. and forms such as white, blue, etc. and *annam* such as rice, wheat, etc. emerge. This *mantra* is only the previous *mantra*'s short form.

**Saumya** – Gurudeva, daily we recite *śānti pāṭha*. The meaning of that is not clearly known. Kindly bless us and explain the meaning in detail.

**Aṅgiras** – So be it. Let us recite the *śānti pāṭha.* I will tell you the meaning.

**(All the disciples recite it together.)**

॥ ॐ भद्रं कर्णेभिः शृणुयाम देवाः। भद्रं पश्येमाक्षभिर्यजत्राः।
स्थिरैरङ्गैस्तुष्टुवाꣳसस्तनूभिः व्यशेम देवहितं यदायुः॥

*oṁ bhadraṁ karnebhiḥ śṛnuyāma devāḥ* | *bhadraṁ paśyemākṣabhiryajatrāḥ* |
*sthirairaṅgaistuṣṭuvāṁsastanūbhiḥ vyaśema devahitaṁ yadāyuḥ* | |

स्वस्ति न इन्द्रो वृद्धश्रवाः। स्वस्ति नः पूषा विश्ववेदाः।
स्वस्ति नस्तार्क्ष्यो अरिष्टनेमिः। स्वस्ति नो बृहस्पतिर्दधातु॥

*svasti na indro vṛddhaśravāḥ | svasti naḥ pūṣā viśvavedāḥ |*
*svasti nastārkṣyo ariṣṭanemiḥ svasti no bṛhaspatir-dadhātu | |*

॥ ॐ शान्तिः। शान्तिः। शान्तिः॥
| | *oṁ śāntiḥ* | *śāntiḥ* | *śāntiḥ* | |

**Aṅgiras** – *Oṁ*! *Deva*s, we may hear with the ears *maṅgalam* (good things). O! ones worthy of worship! With the eyes we should see good things. With strong organs and body we should praise and sing about you and live for a long time. May we acquire as much life span as we desire. Our life span should be beneficial to the *deva*s. Lord Indra of great fame, let him bless us with goodness. Let the Lord Sun who knows everything bring us good tidings. Let the Lord Garuḍa who moves without hindrance remove the obstacles from our path and bring us good tidings. That is, let fame, strength, goodness, and intellect be bestowed on us. Let *śānti* or peace prevail in three ways. Let no hindrances occur from three fronts, namely God, natural causes and one's nature. With this, today's lesson is completed. (**He gets up**).

***(The curtain falls.)***

## SCENE 3

***(Curtain opens.)***

(Brahmarṣi Aṅgiras's *āśrama*. Like in the previous scene, teachings are going on.)

**Aṅgiras** – Saumya! In whatever you heard till now, if any doubt is there you may enquire. I will give the explanation and proceed with the next lesson.

**Vājapeyī** – Since Vedas belong to *aparā-vidyā,* were the *yajña*s and other *karma*s we were performing till now as per Vedic scriptures, of no use?

**Saumya** – Did we waste our precious birth in a worthless manner. O! Our lifetime came to a mere naught. Svāmī! You must clear our doubts in this matter.

**Aṅgiras** – Gold is more precious and costly. Silver is comparatively of less value. However it is not as if silver does not have any value. It is only termed of less value compared to gold. Isn't it? Compared to copper, silver is still considered precious. In the same way, *Brahmajñāna* which is *parā-vidyā* is higher than *aparā-vidyā* which is the knowledge from Vedas. However it does not mean *aparā-vidyā* is of no use. Such a thing is not told anywhere. This only means that in comparison to one the other is lower. There are many *karma*s which lead to distress for others and cater to selfishness. Compared to that *yajña*s are many times superior. Hence you need not have any doubt about the *karma*s prescribed in the Vedas.

**Śaunaka** – Gurudeva! In support of what you told now, are there any corresponding verses in the Upaniṣads. If so kindly preach them.

**Gopāda** – Friend, in the *Muṇḍaka Upaniṣad* from the first *Muṇḍakam*, if the **second *khaṇḍa*** is told in detail the disciple's doubts will be cleared.

**Aṅgiras** – Friend, I will do so. Saumya, listen.

> तदेतत्सत्यम् मन्त्रेषु कर्माणि कवयो यान्यपश्यंस्तानि त्रेतायां बहुधा सन्ततानि ।
> तान्याचरथ नियतं सत्यकामा एष वः पन्थाः सुकMतस्य लोके ॥१॥
>
> *tadetat satyam mantreṣu karmaṇi kavayo yānyapaśyaṁstāni tretāyāṁ bahudhā santatāni |*
> *tānyācaratha niyataṁ satyakāmā eṣa vaḥ panthāḥ sukṛtasya loke ||1||*
>
> This is the truth: Rituals the sages conceived are variously elaborated on in the *mantra* part of the three Vedas. Perform them constantly, ye desire-mongers, thinking of this path to be to the world of merits.

What is being told now is *satyam,* the truth. The *karma*s which are mentioned in Vedas were taught by great sages as Maharṣi Vasiṣṭha and others. Those Vedic scriptures belong to three groups of Vedas and in course of time they were further expanded in their domain. If the *karma*s are done being desirous of the definite benefit to be accrued from them, then the benefits will be received. To get *puṇya* (fruits) this is the best way. This is the meaning of this *mantra.* Now I will explain in detail.

**Vājapeyī** – Svāmī! Do preach us accordingly.

**Aṅgiras** – *Brahman* is called *satyam.* As it is at all times unchanging and imperishable, it is called *akṣara.* However the *karma*s are also called *satyam* but not with that meaning. If a *karma* is done the fruits of that *karma* are definite to occur, in that sense only it is termed as *satyam.* The wise ones through Veda *mantra* found various *karma*s. They are described variously in *Ṛg, Yajur* and *Sāma* Vedas. If you seek the fruits of the *karma,* you observe those *karma*s without fail. Then definitely you will obtain the fruits or results of the *karma.* For going to the *puṇya* worlds this is only the best for you, the only route.

**Śaunaka** – Gurudeva! I had thought that the word *tretāyam* meant belonging to the Tretāyuga. Is there anything wrong about it?

**Gopāda** – There is nothing wrong about it. Actually the three types of Vedas were mentioned because the *karma*s of *hotā*s are described in *Ṛgveda, āthvarya karma*s in *Yajurveda* and *udgātha karma*s in *Sāmaveda.* However as our friend is telling, if the meaning is understood as Tretāyuga then it will mean in Tretāyuga *karma*s expanded in different ways and were done elaborately. This interpretation can also be correct.

**Saumya** – The *karma*s spoken of in the Vedas are worthy of following and those desirous of its fruits can reach the *puṇya loka*s and this is the only route. This we understand. I request you to kindly preach further.

**Aṅgiras** – Saumya, to perform the *karma*s is indeed very tough. The required fruits of action can be expected only if done properly. If any mistake or lapse occurs then good rewards cannot be had, and also bad effects have to be borne. Hence the *karma*s have to be done very carefully with full attention without any excess or depletion in the deeds. For example, *agnihotra* is an ordinary *karma*. That also has to be done very attentively, thus tells the Śruti. Then what to tell of the *yajña*s?

**Saumya** – Svāmī, what does Veda say about *agnihotra*?

**Aṅgiras** –

> यदा लेलायते ह्यर्चिः समिद्धे हव्यवाहने।
> तदाज्यभागावन्तरेणाहुतीः प्रतिपादयेत् श्रद्धया हुतम्॥२॥

> *yadā lelāyate hyarciḥ samiddhe havyavāhane* ।
> *tadājyabhāgāvantareṇāhutīḥ pratipādayet śradhyā hutam* ।।2।।

> Into the kindled fire, at the very moment the flame blazes, should the oblations be offered with full faith, at the very middle of the two halves of the melted butter.

When the fire is in the form of smoking cinder the offerings should not be done. Only when it burns as a bright flame between the two parts in the centre, the offering has to be done either in the early morning or evening (sunset) time.

**Gopāda** – Saumya! The *ājya* parts are facing north where the offerings are given to *agni* (fire) saying *agni svāhā*, and the other offerings are given to *saumya* (moon) telling *somya svāhā* facing south. In between these two parts *agnihotra* offerings have to be done. Śaunaka and his friends will know this information very well. I explained it for the benefit of other disciples.

**Śaunaka** – Svāmī! Yes we know about this. Kindly continue preaching further.

**Aṅgiras** –

यस्याग्निहोत्रमदर्शमपौर्णमासमचातुर्मास्यमनाग्रयणमतिथिवर्जितं च ।
अहुतमवैश्वदेवमविधिना हुतमासप्तमांस्तस्य लोकान्हिनस्ति ॥३॥

*yasyāgnihotramadarśamapaurṇamāsamacāturmāsyamanāgra-
yaṇamatithivarjitaṁ ca* |
*ahutamavaiśvadevamavidhinā hutamāsaptamāṁstasya
lokānhinasti* ||3||

He whose *agnihotra* sacrifice is unaccompanied by *darśa* sacrifice (new moon sacrifice), the *pūrṇamāsa* sacrifice (full moon sacrifice), the *cāturmāsya* sacrifice (four months sacrifice), the *agrāyaṇa* sacrifice (harvest sacrifice), without honouring guests, of unoffered oblations, without offerings to *viśvedeva*s (all gods), or of wrongly offered oblations, he thus destroys all his worlds up to the seventh.

It is instructed that the person who does *agnihotra* has to do certain *karma*s necessarily till his *prāṇa* is there in his body. The important ones are the two *iṣṭi*s (*pūjā*) to be done — one a day after *amāvasyā* (new moon day) and another a day after *pūrṇimā* (full moon day) — three *yajña*s to be done in *cāturmāsya* (four-month period), the *agrāyaṇa karma* to be done during *śarada* season and the *aditi pūjā* to be done daily. If these are not done or in due time the prescribed *homa*s are not done, and if *viśvadeva pūjā*s are not done and only *agnihotra* is done, that will create obstacles in seven *loka*s. If *karma*s are done in order without any lapse then without fail the fruits of the *karma* can be obtained. Even if some aberration is there, fruits of *karma* cannot be accrued and it will only result in wasteful effort. To do as per rule is indeed very difficult.

**Śaunaka** – O! The fate of *karma*s is alarming. It is like you go to dig a well for water and a ghost comes out of it. Is it so difficult to do *agnihotra*?

**Vājapeyī** – The *purohita* had told us that even by just changing the *svara* (tone), very bad things can happen. In *yajña* conducted to create Vṛtran for killing Indra as the *svara* changed and the Vṛtran created was of less strength, he could be annihilated by Indra.

**Saumya** – Yes, I have also heard about it.

**Śaunaka** – You told us that it will create destruction in seven *loka*s. What are those seven *loka*s?

**Aṅgiras** – From *bhūloka* to *satyaloka* there are seven *loka*s. *Puṇya* benefit will be deprived if the *karma*s are done wrongly. The ones connected by virtue of *piṇḍadāna* are father, grandfather, great grandfather, it accounts for three. Then son, grandson, great grandson thus three. Thus the benefit to be acquired by seven people will be destroyed. If *agnihotra karma*s are not done correctly the bad effects are not only for us but the three generations before and three generations after will also be affected.

काली कराली च मनोजवा च सुलोहिता या च सुधूम्रवर्णा।
स्फुलिङ्गिनी विश्वरुची च देवी लेलायमाना इति सप्त जिह्वाः ॥४॥

*kālī karālī ca manojavā ca sulohitā yā ca sudhūmravarṇā* |
*sfuliṅginī viśvarucī ca devī lelāyamānā iti sapta jihvāḥ* | |4| |

The black (*kālī*), the terrible (*karālī*), the mind-like swift (*manojavā*), the bright red (*sulohitā*), the copper-brownish (*sudhūmravarṇā*), the scintillating (*sfuliṅginī*), the All-devouring (*viśvarucī*) are the seven flickering tongues of the (sacrificial) fire.

*Agni* has seven tongues: *kālī, karālī, manojavā, sulohitā, sudhūmravarṇā, sfuliṅginī* and *viśvarucī*. These flames absorb the offerings like *ghee, havis* (cooked rice), etc.

**Vājapeyī** – Kindly explain the meaning of those names.

**Gopāda** – The seven dancing flames are as follows:

| | | |
|---|---|---|
| *Kālī* | – | Black colour |
| *Karālī* | – | Terrifying |
| *Manojavā* | – | Like the mind moving fast |
| *Sulohitā* | – | Red colour |
| *Sudhūmravarṇā* | – | Smoky colour |
| *Sfuliṅginī* | – | Having a number of fire sparks |
| *Viśvarucī* | – | All devouring |

Nowhere are the flames of fire described in such detail.

**Śaunaka** – You explained the results accrued if *karma*s are not done correctly, also kindly tell us the results to be obtained if *karmas* are done correctly.

**Aṅgiras** –

एतेषु यश्चरते भ्राजमानेषु यथाकालं चाहुतयो ह्याददायन्।
तं नयन्त्येताः सूर्यस्य रश्मयो यत्र देवानां पतिरेकोऽधिवासः ॥५॥

*eteṣu yaścarate bhrājamāneṣu yathākālaṁ cāhutayo hyādadāyan* |
*taṁ nayantyetāḥ sūryasya raśmayo yatra devānāṁ patireko 'dhivāsaḥ* ||5||

The one (sacrificer) who offers oblations at the proper time whilst these tongues are ablaze, led by them (oblations) through sun-rays. He reaches the abode of the one Lord of all gods.

As told before when the fire is burning well, if the offerings are done at the correct time that will take the offerer through the sun's rays to the king of *deva*s Lord Indra in the *svargaloka*.

**Vājapeyī and Saumya** – We are very happy. The *yajña*s we did won't go waste. Śaunaka you also need not worry. You will definitely reach *svargaloka*. You will get a seat near Lord Indra himself.

**Gopāda** – Saumya, not only that. Hear further, the kind of welcome and reception you will be accorded.

एह्येहीति तमाहुतयः सुवर्चसः सूर्यस्य रश्मिभिर्यजमानं वहन्ति।
प्रियां वाचमभिवदन्त्योऽर्चयन्त्य एष वः पुण्यः सुकृतो ब्रह्मलोकः॥६॥

*ehyehīti tamāhutayaḥ suvarcasaḥ sūryasya*
*raśmibhiryajamānaṁ vahanti* |
*priyāṁ vācamabhivadantyo 'rcayantya eṣa vaḥ puṇyaḥ*
*sukṛto brahmalokaḥ* ||6||

Saying to him "come come" the splendid oblations carry the sacrificer along the sun-rays, honouring him and saluting him with pleasing words: "Here is the *Brahma-loka* attained through your merits and good deeds."

The brightly shining offerings welcome him. "Welcome due to your special *karma*s. This is the *svargaloka* you have been destined to have," they tell you affectionate words and will receive the master along through the rays of the sun.

**Śaunaka** – *Sabhāsa*, very good reception. I was afraid the *karma*s prescribed in Vedas were redundant or useless acts. However, knowing there are benefits to be accrued for it, I feel very happy.

**Vājapeyī** – The offerings done in a proper manner call the master "welcome, welcome," carry him on their back along the sun's rays, say affectionate words and offer him respects. What more is required? What the *purohita* told us seems to be correct.

**Saumya** – In the entire lifetime if these *karma*s are done as prescribed, then permanent stay in *svarga* will be obtained, I suppose.

**Aṅgiras** – Saumya, I will further continue to preach. Listen. These *karma*s are temporary, so tell the *śruti* (couplet). Don't come to a conclusion in a hurry.

प्लवा ह्येते अदृढा यज्ञरूपा अष्टादशोक्तमवरं येषु कर्म।
एतच्छ्रेयो येऽभिनन्दन्ति मूढा जरामृत्युं ते पुनरेवापि यन्ति ॥७॥

*plavā hyete adṛḍhā yajñarūpā aṣṭādaśoktamavaraṁ yeṣu karma* |
*etacchreyo ye 'bhinandanti mūḍhā jarāmṛtyuṁ te punarevāpi yanti* ||7||

Unsafe boats indeed are these eighteenfold sacrificial forms, said to be founded whereon are rituals the inferior. Fools, esteeming it as leading to good, fall back into the very evils of old age and death they intended to cross over.

These *karma*s are to be done in the form of *yajña* collectively. Eighteen people are required to do this. However these *yajña* boats are not strong, they will get drowned in the ocean of *saṁsāra* finally one day. The ones who consider this alone as a most exalted virtue and are pleased with it are mere fools. They again and again go through the process of birth and death.

**Saumya** – Who are the eighteen people?

**Gopāda** – Ṛtviks – 16, master – 1, his wife – 1, total eighteen people together have to perform the *yajña.* The ones who do the *yajña*s enjoy the fruits of the *puṇya* deeds for some days in *svarga,* then they return to *saṁsāra* consisting of birth and death.

**Aṅgiras** –

अविद्यायामन्तरे वर्तमानाः स्वयं धीराः पण्डितम्मन्यमानाः।
जङ्घन्यमानाः परियन्ति मूढा अन्धेनैव नीयमाना यथान्धाः ॥८॥

*avidyāyāmantare vartamānāḥ svayaṁ dhīrāḥ paṇḍitam manyamānāḥ* |
*jaṅghanyamānāḥ pariyanti mūḍhā andhenaiva nīyamānā yathāndhāḥ* ||8||

Abiding in the midst of ignorance, the self-styled wise, esteeming themselves as learned, do move around, trouble-inflicted fools as they are, like blind men led by one who himself is blind.

Though the people are in the midst of *avidyā,* still without any wisdom, they consider themselves as *paṇḍit*s and knowledgeable people and get fooled. Are there any bigger fools than them? Like a blind person following another blind person, they come across the thorns and pits and suffer. Thus doing the *karma* without the necessary wisdom, showing path to one another fall into the pit of *saṁsāra* filled with pain, old age and death and get deeply troubled. They find no way to come out and are trapped in the net of birth and death.

**Vājapeyī** – We were in that state only some time before.

**Saumya** – This Veda has drawn a picture of our state itself.

**Aṅgiras** –

अविद्यायां बहुधा वर्त्तमाना वयं कृतार्था इत्यभिमन्यन्ति बालाः।
यत्कर्मिणो न प्रवेदयन्ति रागात् तेनातुराः क्षीणलोकाश्च्यवन्ते ॥९॥

*avidyāyāṁ bahudhā varttamānā vayaṁ kṛtārthā*
*ityabhimanyanti bālāḥ* ।
*yat karmiṇo na pravedayanti rāgāt tenāturāḥ*
*kṣīṇalokāścyavante* ।।9।।

Immature and variously living in ignorance, they think of themselves, "we have accomplished, we are content"; ritualists' understanding, attached to pleasure as they are, they sink down wretched.

Like children these people who are steeped in ignorance consider themselves blessed and do holy *karma*s. They who are attached to the fruits of the *karma,* prodded by desire, do their *karma*s but don't realize the truth. They who are interested in pleasure, fame and position lose their wisdom. The stable intellect will never dawn in their minds.

**Śaunaka** – Gurudeva! You explained beautifully the *karma* follower's lack of wisdom. What does *śruti* further tell about them?

**Aṅgiras** –

इष्टापूर्तं मन्यमाना वरिष्ठं नान्यच्छ्रेयो वेदयन्ते प्रमूढाः ।
नाकस्य पृष्ठे ते सुकृतेऽनुभूत्वा इमं लोकं हीनतरं वा विशन्ति ॥१० ॥

*iṣṭāpūrtaṁ manyamānā variṣṭhaṁ nānyacchreyo vedayante pramūḍhāḥ* |
*nākasya pṛṣṭhe te sukṛte 'nubhūtvā imaṁ lokaṁ hīnataraṁ vā viśanti* ||10||

Considering rituals and charity works as paramount, the deluded are unaware of values still higher. Having had enjoyment of the good results of their good deeds at the acme of heaven they re-enter this world, or a still lower one.

They are great fools. This is because they consider the *karma*s like *iṣṭa* prescribed in the Vedas and *karma*s like *pūrtam* prescribed in the *smṛti* as the most superior *karma*s. They don't consider anything else worthy. Hence in the *svarga* after enjoying pleasures as a result of the deeds of their *karma*s they return back to human world or attain even lower birth.

**Saumya** – Svāmī, kindly describe about *iṣṭa* and *pūrta karma*s.

**Aṅgiras** – *Iṣṭa* (rituals) is *śrotra karma*, and *pūrta* (charity) such as digging wells and ponds are *smārtta karma*s. Those who consider that only the *iṣṭa* and *pūrta karma*s are of importance and others are of no consequence are fools. They think whatever good deeds we intend to do will be contained in these. They enjoy the fruits of their *karma*s for some time in *svarga* and subsequently they take the human birth or still lower birth in this world. Thus they go around in circles again and again of birth and death.

**Gopāda** – Friends, let us stop today's lessons with this. Let Saumyas think about what they learnt and come.

**Aṅgiras** – So be it.

***(The curtain falls)***

## SCENE 4

***(The curtain opens, similar to the previous scene)***

**Śaunaka** – Gurudeva! By following the *karma*s properly with faith as prescribed in the Vedas one can reach the exalted *puṇya loka*s. However you told us that these benefits are perishable. If we have to reach the imperishable *Brahman* what we have to do? Kindly tell us about it in detail.

**Aṅgiras** – Saumya! I will continue to tell, listen carefully. Till now I told you all about the fruits of the person who goes along the *pravṛtti* (action) route. Today I will tell the *nivṛtti* (inaction) route.

तपःश्रद्धे ये ह्युपवसन्त्यरण्ये शान्ता विद्वांसो भैक्षचर्यां चरन्तः।
सूर्यद्वारेण ते विरजाः प्रयान्ति यत्रामृतः स पुरुषो ह्यव्ययात्मा ॥११॥

*tapaḥśraddhe ye hyupavasantyaraṇye śāntā vidvāṁso bhaikṣacaryāṁ carantaḥ* |
*sūryadvāreṇa te virajāḥ prayānti yatrāmṛtaḥ sa puruṣo hyavyayātmā* ||11||

Undergoing *tapa*s and full of faith, those who live in forests, tranquil in mind, erudite and living on alms, having no passions and attachments — they attain through the door of the sun the abode of immortal *puruṣa*, the undecaying *ātmā* (Self).

An intelligent person will leave the *pravṛtti* route. They remain as peace lovers and forest dwellers, partake their food by taking alms and spend their life. This way they follow with faith the *dharma* of dwelling in forest (*vānaprastha*) and *sanyāsa dharma* which results in their becoming *virājar* (having no affliction of *pāpa or puṇya*) and when they meet death they travel along the *sūrya-maṇḍala* and reach the *puruṣa* who is indestructible and imperishable.

**Vājapeyī** – Is this the state of *mokṣa*?

**Gopāda** – This is only *Brahmaloka*. The person who dies can take one out of the two routes. One is southward bound. This is also termed *chandramārga* or *pitṛpatha*. Another is called *sūryamārga* or *devayāna*. Persons who have controlled the senses and are peaceful of mind and full of wisdom satisfied in partaking what is obtained by alms, staying in forests, following one's *āśrama dharma* and *upāsanā*s connected to it, *sanyāsī*s (renounced persons) and also householders who do Hiraṇyagarbha *upāsanā*s, who have blemishless minds go along *devayānam* and reach the *Brahmaloka* where unchanging Hiraṇyagarbha *puruṣa* is there. Till *mahāpralaya* they are not destroyed. They also don't return back to *bhūloka* till then. Such persons who get *mokṣa* from this *loka* can obtain *mukti* very easily.

**Vājapeyī** – Who goes along *pitṛmārga*? What happens to them?

**Aṅgiras** – About them it has been told in previous lessons. They again and again go through birth and death and remain in this *chakra* of *saṁsāra*.

**Śaunaka** – Gurudeva, if so what should persons who have desire for *mokṣa* do?

**Aṅgiras** –

परीक्ष्य लोकान् कर्मचितान् ब्राह्मणो निर्वेदमायान्नास्त्यकृतः कृतेन।
तद्विज्ञानार्थं स गुरुमेवाभिगच्छेत् समित्पाणिः श्रोत्रियं ब्रह्मनिष्ठम्॥१२॥

*parīkṣya lokān karmacitān brāhmaṇo*
*nirvedamāyānnāstyakṛtaḥ kṛtena* ।
*tadvijñānārthaṁ sa gurumevābhigacchet samitpāṇiḥ*
*śrotriyaṁ brahmaniṣṭham* ।।12।।

Having well scrutinized the worlds built by rituals a brāhmaṇa should naturally grow indifferent to them; not-made is never attained through made-up means; for the sake of attaining that (the not-made), let him go, fuel in hand, to a *guru* well learned in scriptures and well stabilized in *Brahman*.

*Parā-vidyā*
**(Brahmavidyā)**

*fig* : *Aparā-Vidyā* — **All worldly knowledge and four Vedas**

The brāhmaṇa who is worthy of *mokṣa* as described above, after examining the *loka*s obtained by the *karma*s should come to the conclusion that there is nothing to be gained by this *saṁsāra*. Hence leaving that path he must tread the path of *vairāgyam* (desireless state). He must understand that by these temporary result-producing *karma*s he cannot reach the permanent lasting *Brahman*. To know such a *Brahman* he must reach a *guru* who is *śrotriya* (follower of Vedas) and having *brahmaniṣṭhā*.

**Gopāda** – Saumya! That is what you have done now.

**Vājapeyī** – What is wrong in doing independent enquiry of *Brahman* without a *guru*? After all, wisdom is the most important factor.

**Aṅgiras** – It is not like that. By use of the word *gurumeva* the *śruti* orders, it is imperative to approach a *guru*. Without the blessings of a *guru* it is not possible to get *brahma-jñāna*. Further without approaching a *guru* whatever is self learnt (like mere bookish knowledge is not enough to fill the stomach) will not shine. That kind of learning is like a lady trying to get pregnant from a unisex male.

**Gopāda** – Here the *śruti* tells us two important and necessary characteristics the *guru* should posses. Did you all observe?

**Śaunaka** – Svāmī! I did observe. A *guru* should have mastered well the Vedas and should be having *brahmaniṣṭhā*.

**Gopāda** – Saumya! The other day you requested me to preach to you; however, I refused. The reason was that though being *śrotriya* (*veda upāsaka*) I cannot call myself *brahmaniṣṭha*.

**Aṅgiras** – Friend! If you are not *brahmaniṣṭha,* then who else has that capacity? There is no one. You are just saying this in humility.

**Śaunaka** – Gurudeva, I request you to further preach to me in this direction.

**Aṅgiras** –

तस्मै स विद्वानुपसन्नाय सम्यक् प्रशान्तचित्ताय शमान्विताय ।
येनाक्षरं पुरुषं वेद सत्यं प्रोवाच तां तत्त्वतो ब्रह्मविद्याम् ॥१३॥

*tasmai sa vidvānupasannāya samyak praśāntacittāya*
*śamānvitāya* |
*yenākṣaraṁ puruṣaṁ veda satyaṁ provāca tāṁ tattvato*
*brahmavidyām* | | 13 | |

Unto one who has thus duly approached, with thoughts

> tranquil and mind restrained, such an enlightened master teaches *brahma-vidyā* down to its basics, whereby one gets enlightened to *puruṣa* the imperishable reality.

In this *mantra* it is told how the disciples have to be. A disciple who approaches the *guru* in a proper manner, who is possessed of peaceful mindset and whose sense organs are well under control, for such a disciple that *guru* who is wisdom personified will instruct and inform about the *brahma-jñāna* and make him realize the *parama puruṣa* who is in the state of *satyam* and *akṣara*.

**Vājapeyī** – Why should the disciple carry the *samidhā* (twigs) for making fire? Is there any inner meaning?

**Saumya** – What qualities should the disciple possess? Do tell us about it in detail.

**Aṅgiras** – Like the *guru,* the disciple also should possess two characteristics necessarily. He should have a peaceful *chit* (mind). Without having blemishes like pride, he should be calm and composed. Further he should possess equanimity. That is, his senses and desires should be under control and should have *virakti* (non-attachment) in every thing. "I have become peaceful; I have attained equanimity," without uttering these words he should imply the same by taking dried *samidhā* (twigs) in the hand. Like the dried *samidhā*, the disciple's desires and pulls should have dried up. This is symbolically implied by the dried *samidhā*.

**Gopāda** – Thus when a deserving disciple approaches and surrenders himself to a *guru* who is both *śrotriya* (exponent of Vedas) and *brahmaniṣṭha* (follower of the path leading to realization of *Brahman*), then that *satguru* has to preach *brahma-jñāna* to the disciple, so orders the *śruti*. This is a rule. To a deserving disciple, the *guru* cannot refuse to preach.

**Aṅgiras** – Saumya! Till now I explained in detail about *aparā-vidyā*. Now I must preach about *parā-vidyā,* that is, about the *Brahman*. As the *śruti* mentioned, you are deserving disciples.

I consider myself to be fortunate to preach to you. True disciples have to be helped to be brought out of *avidyā* and restored. This is the duty of a *guru*. That I will do as far as I know. I will try to do it. To get success in that I request my dear friend Gopāda's co-operation.

**Gopāda** – Just as a fruit slips into the milk or rain pours in a sugar cane field, a good *guru* and deserving disciple have come together. Getting an opportunity to participate in this *sabhā* itself is a great fortunate thing for me.

**Aṅgiras** – It is our friend Gopāda who brought along the disciples. The praise and pride for it should go to him. It is mid-afternoon time. Let us stop the lesson here.

***(Curtain falls.)***
***(The Second Part Ends.)***

## PART III

### SCENE 1

***(Curtain opens.)***

(Like the previous scene all are sitting together and conversing)

**Gopāda** – Friend! A deserving disciple who reaches the *guru* has to be preached *brahma-vidyā*. This is a duty of *satguru* as you told us yesterday. Śaunaka and others well versed and deserving disciples have come to receive *brahmopadeśa*. Already enquiry has been conducted. You must kindly now preach the holy words and bless them.

**Aṅgiras** – Friend! Wisdom-filled dear ones, I will do so. Saumya! Listen carefully. Till now I told you about *aparā-vidyā* in detail. The *Brahman* which is imperishable and in the form of *akṣara* gave rise to this *saṁsāra*. The *saṁsāra* rises in that, stays wrapped in that and finally merges into that. That *Akṣara Brahman* is the truth. A person who knows that will be the knower of all. This same concept I have explained again and again from different angles, in different ways and with different examples. If there is any lapse in my explanations I kindly request friend Gopāda to amend the same. Now let us come to the *śruti.*

तदेतत्सत्यम् यथा सुदीप्तात् पावकाद्विस्फुलिङ्गाः सहस्रशः प्रभवन्ते सरूपाः ।
तथाऽक्षराद्विविधाः सोम्य भावाः प्रजायन्ते तत्र चैवापि यन्ति ॥१॥

*tadetat satyam yathā sudīptāt pāvakād visphuliṅgāḥ*
*sahastraśaḥ prabhavante sarūpāḥ* ।
*tathā 'kṣarād vividhāḥ saumya bhāvāḥ prajāyante tatra*
*caivāpi yanti* ।।1।।

That Reality is such: As, from a well-blazing bonfire, sparks by the thousands issue forth, yet the same fire in essence, so from the imperishable, my dear, apparent forms many a kind emerge and therein re-merge too.

That is, It is the truth. Just as a blazing fire gives out thousands of sparks, in the same way from *Akṣara Brahman* numerous *jīva* (life forms) emerge and they finally are merging in that only.

**Gopāda** – Very apt example. From a big fire which burns fiercely the sparks fly out when the wind blows. After flying for a while it turns into ash and falls back into the big fire. Same way when the wind called *māyā* blows the creations come out of *Brahman*. Saumya, did you follow this concept clearly? If any doubt is there, you can ask.

**Śaunaka** – Svāmī! When you talked about *aparā-vidyā* you mentioned that as truth. Now when you are talking about *Akṣara Brahman* you describe that as truth. At the same time how can both be the truth?

**Aṅgiras** – *Sabhāsa* Śaunaka! It is a good question. I will give you the answer. Let everybody listen carefully. The *saṁsāra* which is the resultant of *aparā-vidyā* whose fundamental reason is *Akṣara-Brahman* and finally the *saṁsāra* also merges into it. That *Akṣara puruṣa*, the *Brahman*, is only the truth. The subject of *aparā-vidyā*, the *saṁsāra*, is *Āpekṣa Brahman*. The subject of *parā-vidyā* is the *Nirapekṣa Brahman*. That is *satyasya satyaṁ paramārtha satyaṁ* (सत्यस्य सत्यं परमार्थ सत्यं) meaning *Brahman* is ultimate truth. *Saṁsāra* is *vyavahāra satyam* (a temporary truth in the present context). That is only the difference.

**Vājapeyī** – Gurudeva! If that is so, how can results of *karma* be termed as *satyaṁ*.

**Aṅgiras** – Due to the compassion Vedamātā has on us she has said that, so that everyone of us may cross the ocean of *saṁsāra*. However only after doing one's duties as per the caste one belongs to and with that the *chit* (mind) getting pure, can one approach the path of knowledge. Instead of that if it is said *karma* and its results as untruth in the beginning itself then nobody will follow it. Everyone will think that for *mokṣa* what is required is only wisdom or knowledge and will sit down for meditation. But instead of meditating and getting knowledge they will become silent and go to sleep. To save them from the situation only, *śruti* preaches step by step.

**Śaunaka** – Svāmī! It is very clearly understood. Kindly continue to preach.

**Aṅgiras** – Now I will explain the supreme thing — *Brahman*'s expanded form.

दिव्यो ह्यमूर्त्तः पुरुषः स बाह्याभ्यन्तरो ह्यजः।
अप्राणो ह्यमनाः शुभ्रो ह्यक्षरात् परतः परः॥२॥

*divyo hyamūrttaḥ puruṣaḥ sa bāhyābhyantaro hyajaḥ* |
*aprāṇo hyamanāḥ śubhro hyakṣarāt parataḥ*
*paraḥ* | |2| |

Effulgence in essence and abstract is that *puruṣa*; existing internally and externally, He is the unborn; breathless and mindless, He is the pure; even higher than the highest imperishable is He. That *parama puruṣa* is filled with holy light, formless and blemishless, it exists in the inside and outside of all beings. He is above *akṣara* and *avyākṛtam.*

**Saumya** – Respected Sir! You have told us the meaning of the *mantras*. You must kindly explain the concept in detail.

**Vājapeyī** – Apart from the descriptions of phrases such as "filled with light," "blemishless," etc. kindly give special explanations.

**Śaunaka** – Svāmī! What is meant by "superior to *avyākṛtam*?" Kindly explain in detail.

**Aṅgiras** – The meaning of holy light is a brightness which emits by itself. Without depending on other objects, unlike the lamp, sun, moon, etc. to emit brightness and light by itself. That is filled with light which is out of the world. Blemishless means without any *upādhi*s (attachments). Hence It does not have mind, *prāṇa*, etc. In the word "mind" sense organs are included, and in the word *prāṇa* the *karma* organs are contained. *Avyākṛta* means before creation, the formless state. The *parama puruṣa* is still beyond that.

**Vājapeyī** – We should like to know the explanation for the word *puruṣa*. Do kindly tell us about it clearly.

**Aṅgiras** – *Puruṣa* means completeness. It can also mean He resides in the space called body within the heart space; since he is inside and outside he is filled everywhere. The *puruṣa* is the one not just here or there but is filled everywhere and spreads his light.

**Śaunaka** – Gurudeva, kindly continue to preach.

**Aṅgiras** – Saumya! In the previous *śruti* it was told that He does not have a mind, *prāṇa*, etc. Isn't that so? The reason for this is told in this *Ṛk*.

एतस्माज्जायते प्राणो मनः सर्वेन्द्रियाणि च।
खं वायुर्ज्योतिरापः पृथिवी विश्वस्य धारिणी ॥३॥

*etasmāj jāyate prāṇo manaḥ sarvendriyāṇi ca* |
*khaṁ vāyurjyotirāpaḥ pūthivī viśvasya dhāriṇī* ||3||

From It is born breath, mind and all the senses, space, air, fire, water, and earth, the all-supporting.

From Him the *prāṇa*, mind and other sense organs as also *ākāśa, vāyu, agni*, water, and the earth which holds the world all these came about.

**Vājapeyī** – Respected Sir! It is a bit confusing. Initially you told, *Brahman* does not possess *prāṇa* and other things. Now you tell that *prāṇa*, mind and the rest came about from Him. This is not understood. If they are created from Him how can it be said that He does not have them.

**Gopāda** – Saumya! The *Brahma puruṣa* does not have *prāṇa* and the rest. This is the truth. When it is in a blemishless state without any *upādhi*s (attachment) then there are no distortions. However when It gets connected with *māyā* then *prāṇa* and the rest are produced, so it is told. Hence the perishable *prāṇa* came about as a result of *avidyā*. However this does not mean pure *Brahman* contains the *prāṇa* within it.

**Aṅgiras** – Yes, yes, what our friend tells is very correct. If a childless person gets a child in a dream he cannot be supposed to have the child in the waking state. In the same way like a dream child, *prāṇa*, all sense organs, *pañca-bhūta* (elements) everything was created from *Brahma puruṣa*. Hence before mind, *prāṇa*, etc. came about, *Brahman* was *asat*. After they ultimately merge into the *Brahman*, then again *Brahman* is *asat*. In between for some time it appears different. That is all.

**Śaunaka** – You have told about *Brahma puruṣa* in short. Kindly tell us about it in greater detail.

**Aṅgiras** – So be it.

अग्निर्मूर्द्धा चक्षुषी चन्द्रसूर्यौ दिशः श्रोत्रे वाग्विवृताश्च वेदाः ।
वायुः प्राणो हृदयं विश्वमस्य पद्भ्यां पृथिवी ह्येष सर्वभूतान्तरात्मा ॥४॥

*agnirmūrdhā cakṣuṣī candrasūryau diśaḥ śrotre vāg*
*vivṛtāśca vedāḥ* |

*vāyuḥ prāṇo hṛdayaṁ viśvamasya padbhyāṁ pṛthivī hyeṣa sarvabhūtāntarātmā | |4| |*

Fire is His crown point of head; The sun and the moon form His eyes; The direction of the compass His ears; Multifarious knowledge His speech; Air is His life-breath (*prāṇa*); and "the all" constitute his heart. Out of His feet emerges the earth; He indeed is the all-pervading substance (*ātman*). Of all that has come into being (*bhūta*s).

For whom the *agni* is the head, Chandra, Sūrya are the eyes, the directions are the ears, the famous Vedas are words, *vāyu* is *prāṇa*, the world is mind and from whose feet the earth arose, He only is the inner *ātmā* of all beings in the world. Here the *śruti* is describing the *virāṭa puruṣa*. He contains the three worlds and all the things held in them as *upādhi* (attachment). The *virāṭa puruṣa* who has come out of the *Hiraṇyagarbha* acts as inner *ātmā* of all *bhūta*s (living things). Though He appears different, the previously mentioned *parama puruṣa* also came out from Him. Not only this, the *virāṭa puruṣa* which is the cause of everything acts as the seeing, hearing, and knowing being in everyone.

**Śaunaka** – What is the meaning of describing the world as the mind.

**Aṅgiras** – Without the connection of mind there is no activity. Hence the entire universe is the sight of the mind. During sleep these scenes vanish in the mind, and as soon as we get up like the sparks coming out of the fire, they rise out of the mind. Hence the world becomes the mind.

**Vājapeyī** – Respected Sir! we are struck with wonder as we hear these. You must continue to tell further.

**Aṅgiras** –

तस्मादग्निः समिधो यस्य सूर्यः सोमात् पर्जन्य ओषधयः पृथिव्याम्।
पुमान् रेतः सिञ्चति योषितायां बह्वीः प्रजाः पुरुषात् संप्रसूताः ॥५॥

*tasmāt agniḥ samidho yasya sūryaḥ somāt parjanya oṣadhayaḥ pṛthivyām* |
*pumān retaḥ siñcati yoṣitāyāṁ bahvīḥ prajāḥ puruṣāt saṁprasūtāḥ* ||5||

From Him proceeds fire whose fuel is the sun; from Soma, rain and herbs on the earth; males pour seeds in females, manifold creatures are thus born of the *puruṣa*.

The fire came out of Him. The *samidhā* (firewood) for that is sun. From Him came the moon and the clouds. From the clouds came the rain. The rain brought out the plants in the earth. From the *puruṣa* who partook it came *vīryam* (sperm). On getting connection with woman many persons were born. This way from *Brahma puruṣa* all lives came about. Thus, in proper order from the attributeless *akṣara puruṣa* many creations arose.

**Śaunaka** – What is the meaning of the expression sun is the *samidhā* (firewood) for *agni*?

**Gopāda** – Here *agni* is *dhiyoloka*. Just as how *agni* (fire) burns well in the (*samidhā*) firewood, in the same way due to the sun the *dhiyoloka* appears well lit and bright. Hence the sun is termed as *samidhā*. From the moon which has come out of *dhiyoloka*, the second *agni* as also the clouds, came about. Due to that, in the third *agni*, the earth, the plants have been produced. From them the fourth *agni*, virility of *puruṣa*, the sperms arose. They, when combined in the fifth *agni*, the women form, a variety of lives came about. The *dhiyoloka*, sun and moon, earth, *puruṣa*, women, all these five should be considered as *agni* and *prajā*s are being made by *homa*s done on them. If one meditates on this concept, such a meditation is called as *pañcāgni vidyā*. This is being told in other *śruti*s also. When meditated like this the purity of *chit* (mind) comes about.

**Aṅgiras** – After the *prajā*s are made, can they be lazy? Don't they have to do *karma*s? The instrument to perform the *karma* and the fruits of the *karma* also came about from *parama puruṣa*.

तस्मादृचः साम यजूंषि दीक्षा यज्ञाश्च सर्वे क्रतवो दक्षिणाश्च।
संवत्सरश्च यजमानश्च लोकाः सोमो यत्र पवते यत्र सूर्यः ॥६॥

*tasmādṛcaḥ sāma yajūṁṣi dīkṣā yajñāśca sarve kratavo dakṣiṇāśca* |
*saṁvatsaraśca yajamānaśca lokāḥ somo yatra pavate yatra sūryaḥ* ||6||

The *yajus* formulas, the initiation rites, and all the *yajña*s, all the *kratu*s, all sacrifical rites, the year, the sacrificer too, and the worlds attainable, where for purification shine the moon and the sun too.

From Him only emerged *Ṛgveda, Yajurveda, Sāmaveda,* rules of *dīkṣā* (directions), *yajñas, kratu*s (sacrifice), *dakṣiṇā*s (offerings), seasons, master, *sūrya,* and *chandra loka*s.

Further –

तस्माच्च देवा बहुधा सम्प्रसूताः साध्या मनुष्याः पशवो वयांसि।
प्राणापानौ व्रीहियवौ तपश्च श्रद्धा सत्यं ब्रह्मचर्यं विधिश्च ॥७॥

*tasmācca devā bahudhā samprasūtāḥ sādhyā manuṣyāḥ paśavo vayāṁsi* |
*prāṇāpānau vrīhiyavau tapaśca śraddhā satyaṁ brahmacaryaṁ vidhiśca* ||7||

From Him are manifoldly born, Gods, *sādhya*s, men, cattle, birds, in-breath and out-breath, rice and barley, austerity, faith, truth, *brahmacharya* and moral codes.

From Him only arose many *deva*s — the *deva*s who are called *satyaguṇa*s — men, animals, birds, the *vāyu*s like *prāṇa, apāna,* the cereals like rice, barley, further qualities like austerity, faith, truth, *brahmacharya* and moral codes came forth.

**Śaunaka** – We understand the explanation of the *mantra.* We kindly request a more detailed explanation.

**Aṅgiras** – After the *prajā*s came forth, in order to do the important *karma*s like *yajñas,* the three Vedas, the rules and regulations for doing the *yajña* and the *yajña*s like *agnihotra*s and big *kratu*s (big sacrifices) were formed. Then, to give at the *yajñas,* the *dakṣiṇā*s (offerings) like cow and *dakṣiṇā*s came about.

Further the different time periods for doing the *karma*s, the subject to do the *karma,* the master (*yajamāna)* and for him to enjoy the fruits of *karma,* the *svargaloka* came forth. As per the *karma upāsanā* adopted by each person as preached in the previous teachings the southward route (*dakṣiṇāyana mārga*) and northern route (*uttarāyana mārga*) were created. Going in these different routes the persons reach the respective worlds and experience the fruits of their *karma*s. For the sake of *havis* (offerings) to the *deva*s who are called *vasu*s staying in those worlds; for the human beings who are the ones entitled to do the *karmas;* for the animals who live in the forest and villages; for different types of birds; and for the *vāyu*s like *prāṇa* and *apāna* and which we intake during breathing process, various cereals came about.

Not only this the concepts which lead a man on the right path to live his *saṁsāra* life, the austerity, faith, truth and *brahmacharya vrata* all these came about. In this way different types of rules and regulations came about from Him.

**Śaunaka** – Svāmī, from your preaching it is clearly understood that everything is *Brahman.* As we keep hearing its greatness we are astonished. Do continue to preach.

**Aṅgiras** –

सप्त प्राणाः प्रभवन्ति तस्मात् सप्तार्चिषः समिधः सप्त होमाः।
सप्तेमे लोका येषु चरन्ति प्राणा गुहाशया निहिताः सप्त सप्त ॥८॥

*sapta prāṇāḥ prabhavanti tasmāt saptārciṣaḥ samidhaḥ sapta homāḥ* |
*sapta ime lokā yeṣu caranti prāṇā guhāśayā nihitāḥ sapta sapta* | |8| |

> From Him came forth the seven *prāṇa*s, the seven flames, their seven fuels, the seven oblations, these seven worlds wherein move the *prāṇa*s, inhabiting a secret abode of seven in human system.

From Him only seven *prāṇa*s and their seven brightnesses, seven *samidhā*s, seven *homa*s and seven *loka*s came about. All these which get settled in the heart are thus found as seven in each living thing.

**Vājapeyī** – Svāmī, we are not able to understand anything. Kindly explain it to us in detail.

**Aṅgiras** – Seven *prāṇa*s denote the seven sense organs in the face (that is, two eyes, two ears, two nose, and one tongue making a total of seven). Each sense organ brightens one aspect of sensing. Thus the seven brightnesses denote the particular strength of each sense organ. The tongue is also a sense organ. The brightness of that is its tasting ability. *Samidhā* means fire evoking things. Each of the sense organs evokes and provides that particular sense. The seven *homa*s are the knowledge or ability inherent in the sense organs. One sense organ cannot have the ability of another sense organ. The eyes cannot hear. The ear cannot see. Hence the abilities are also different. In the same way the place from where they operate is different. They are only the seven worlds (*loka*s).

**Gopāda** – Saumya. Till now we understood that the *karma*s of the learned and their results and the *karma*s of the ignorant and their results also emanated from the *parama puruṣa.* If you have any further doubts you may ask.

**Vājapeyī** – Gurudeva, till now the *śruti* told us about the creation of living things only in detail. However aren't the mountains seen in front of us and the rivers flowing close by formed from the *parama puruṣa*.

**Aṅgiras** – Where is the doubt about it? He is only everything. He is the centre for all creation, and all creations take their final abode in Him.

अतः समुद्रा गिरयश्च सर्वेऽस्मात् स्यन्दन्ते सिन्धवः सर्वरूपाः।
अतश्च सर्वा ओषधयो रसश्च येनैष भूतैस्तिष्ठते ह्यन्तरात्मा ॥९॥

*ataḥ samudrā girayaśca sarve 'smāt syandante*
*sindhavaḥ sarvarūpāḥ* ।
*ataśca sarvā oṣadhayo rasaśca yenaiṣa bhūtaistiṣṭhate*
*hyantarātmā* ।।9।।

From Him arise all the seas and mountains, from Him roll out rivers of every kind; and from Him all herbs, their sap whereby is upheld the interior self (the *puruṣa*) along with His manifest forms.

From him only the sea, the mountains, the many rivers, all kinds of plants and their different tastes came about.

**Gopāda** – Saumya, the great oceans, the mountains like the Himālayas, the rivers like Gaṅgā, and Kāverī, all came out from Him. From Him only all the food and their six different tastes came about. Thus was everything created from *parama puruṣa*. To enjoy the taste the *suṣumnā* body functions with the five elements between *ātmā* and gross body and acts like the *ātmā* in each being. However all these are impermanent. Only the *parama puruṣa* is the truth.

**Aṅgiras** –

पुरुष एवेदं विश्वं कर्म तपो ब्रह्म परामृतम्।
एतद्यो वेद निहितं गुहायां सोऽविद्याग्रन्थिं विकिरतीह सोम्य ॥१०॥

*puruṣa evedaṁ viśvaṁ karma tapo brahma parāmṛtam* ।
*etad yo veda nihitaṁ guhāyāṁ so 'vidyāgranthiṁ*
*vikiratīha saumya* ।।10।।

*Puruṣa* indeed is all this — (Vedic) rituals, (Vedāntic) austere self-enquiry, the transcendental and immortal *Brahman*, he who knows Him as abiding in their secret abode, he here on earth, my dear, rends asunder the knots of ignorance.

Śaunaka! I will give the answer now for the question which

you asked initially. By knowing what do we know everything? For this question the answer is that by knowing the *paramātmā* who is the *parama puruṣa* and is the cause of everything, one comes to know everything. That *parama puruṣa* is only this entire world. *Karmas, tapa* are all but Him. That *Brahman* is the excellent nectar. He resides in the cave of our heart and the one who sees Him, immediately unties the knot of ignorance.

**Gopāda** – Dear ones, this *parama puruṣa* is this world. Beyond Him there is no other world. The answer for your question is now known. It is only wise to know Him. By knowing Him one knows everything.

**Śaunaka** – Gurudeva! We have become blessed. We are greatly indebted to you.

**Vājapeyī** – Svāmī! Kindly explain the meaning of this *mantra.*

**Aṅgiras** – *Karma* is also Him. Here *tapa* means knowledge. *Tapa* is also Him. He is *parama puruṣa.* He is nectar personified and indestructible *Brahman.* He only stays as all the living things' inner being. One who knows Him like that in this world itself (not after death) unties the knot of ignorance. He reaches a permanent state without life and death. Shall we stop today's lesson with this?

**Gopāda** – Already I had thought of telling you that. Time has exceeded. Let us stop. Let *saumya* meditate well on what has been told.

***(Curtain falls.)***

## SCENE 2

***(Curtain opens.)***

(It is the *āśrama* of Gopāda. Brahmarṣi Gopāda, Śaunaka and their friends are sitting and talking.)

**Gopāda** – Śaunaka! Did you think about the things taught yesterday? Can you tell them in short?

**Śaunaka** – Svāmī! As much as I know I will tell. If there is any mistake you must kindly correct me. *Parama puruṣa* is filled with light. However He is without form. He is there both inside and outside. He does not have *prāṇa* and mind. He is blemishless. He is beyond *akṣara.* He is the inner soul of every living thing. From Him just as sparks come out of a big fire, the human beings, *deva*s and all other living things emerge. Our *karma* is the penance we have to do to understand Him. He is everything in this universe. The one who realizes this *parama puruṣa* as the one stabilized in his heart, becomes free from ignorance in this life itself.

**Gopāda** – *Sabhāsa*! You have explained it very well. Śaunaka! Your friend has answered the question asked by you. What more are you going to ask? I had called you here to think about that only.

**Vājapeyī** – Svāmī! What do we know? You only help us to ask the right question.

**Gopāda** – Saumya! For me to tell you is not correct. You only should think and ask what comes to your mind. Think quickly and come to a decision. I have called friend Aṅgiras to come over here. He has also agreed. Today's lesson will be conducted in this *āśrama.*

**Śaunaka** – Is that so, we are very happy (within himself), what to ask? What have we understood till now? What more do we have to know? I understood that *vidyā* is of two types. The four Vedas and other knowledge are contained in *aparā-vidyā,* and *parā-vidyā* is only *brahma-jñāna.* Then I came to know about the *Brahman* and its connection with the universe. Now I must find out the way to reach this *Brahman*. That should be my next question.

**Gopāda** – Śaunaka! Have you finished thinking over ? The *gurudeva* is coming here. Let us welcome him.

(Aṅgiras enters. Everybody gets up and welcomes him, wishes him and brings him inside. Everybody sits in their respective places and starts conversation.)

**Aṅgiras** – Friend! Saumya! The places surrounding the *āśrama* are very clean, beautiful and pleasing. I think our friend alone is responsible for it being so clean. What? Am I correct, my friend?

**Gopāda** – Play and fun will never leave a man. However old he becomes, the sense of humour will be with him, I suppose. Our friend Aṅgiras is a good example of this.

**Aṅgiras** – I did not tell it just in humour. I only said the truth. I think our friend did not like to be praised on the face. If so, I will stop praising.

**Gopāda** – Thank you for your kind words, my dear friend. The disciples are waiting keenly to get your preaching. You must bless them first with your holy preaching.

**Śaunaka** – Gurudeva, you explained the formless, the one which is beyond form, the *akṣara Brahman.* What we have to do to reach that? Kindly bless us with that knowledge.

**Vājapeyī** – What kind of *sādhanā* do we have to do? What all does one who aspires to realize *Brahman* have to follow? Respected Sir, kindly explain that in detail.

**Aṅgiras** – Saumya! The *Brahman,* though it is beyond mind and word, one can still realize it by thought and meditation. There need not be any doubt that. It can be properly realized.

**Saumya** – Respected Sir, what is the thought process one should follow? Kindly explain the meditation methods.

**Vājapeyī** – Is there any *japa* or *mantra* to be repeated?

**Aṅgiras** –

आविः सन्निहितं गुहाचरन्नाम महत्पदमत्रैतत्समर्पितम्।
एजत्प्राणन्निमिषच्च यदेतज्जानथ सदसद्वरेण्यं परं विज्ञानाद्यद्वरिष्ठं प्रजानाम्॥१॥

*āviḥ sannihitaṁ guhācaraṁ nāma mahat padamatraitat samarpitam* |
*ejat prāṇannimiṣacca yadetajjānatha sadasadvareṇyaṁ paraṁ vijñānād yadvariṣṭhaṁ prajānām* ||1||

> Intimately manifest and well-known as moving in the heart. Is the great goal attainable? In it reposes all that moves, breathes and blinks; know It as reality as well as appearance. The best of all desirables for all, the transcendental, beyond man's all-specific knowledge.

The *Brahman* is bright. It is very close, stabilized in everybody's heart and has the name *guhācaram*. This is the most significant word. In that *guhācaram* is kept the entire world. The ones which move, the ones which breathe, the ones which blink and the ones which don't blink, all these things are contained in this. It is seen as *sat* and *asat*. It is worthy of everybody's worship and beyond the common knowledge of the *prajā*s. It is supreme to everything. It should be imagined as such and meditated upon to realize it.

**Gopāda** – The *Brahman* shines in the world through all things that we perceive around us. It is there everywhere and in everything. It shines by itself like a lamp. This thought is a good tool for the persons who want to realize the true state of *ātmā/Brahman*.

**Vājapeyī** – We understood it very well, however we require detailed explanations for some words.

**Aṅgiras** – You may ask and I shall explain..

**Vājapeyī** – Kindly explain the *sannihitaṁ guhācaraṁ nāma mahat padam* in detail.

**Saumya** – What is the meaning of *variṣṭhaṁ?*

**Aṅgiras** – *Sannihitaṁ* means that which is very close. Just as a person hears sound wih sense organs like ears, in the same way It can be perceived very close. Like when seeing, hearing, etc. are done one can perceive *chaitanya* existing there, that is *sannihitaṁ* (very close). Combining with the *upādhi* mind, It moves around in the abode of the mind, namely the heart, and is called *guhācaram*. Here *guha* denotes the heart. *Mahat* denotes a big thing. However since no limit is prescribed for it, here the word *mahat* stands for *Brahman* and means that it is bigger than everything and there is nothing bigger than this. It is the fundamental support for everything. Just as all the spokes of the wheel are fitted in the axle of a wheel in the same way everything is fitted in *Brahman* which is the fundamental support similar to an axle. Hence it is called *mahat padam* (support).

**Gopāda** – All the birds which fly, the breathing men, cows and other cattle, all the blinking living things, non-blinking living things and all other living beings are based in *Brahman*. Hence It is called *mahat padam* (the big support). Everything is dependent on It. The ones having form — gross things, one without form — subtle things, everything is That. Beyond That there is nothing else. It cannot be known by common worldly knowledge. It is called *variṣṭhaṁ*, meaning fully exalted. It is above all the exalted things known. It is without blemish or mistakes. Hence it is most exalted, and the permanent thing. Know That as your *ātma-svarūpa*. Thus say the Vedas like a teacher.

**Śaunaka** – Gurudeva, Do continue to preach. It is very interesting to hear.

**Aṅgiras** –

> यदर्चिमद्यदणुभ्योऽणु च यस्मिन्ल्लोका निहिता लोकिनश्च ।
> तदेतदक्षर ब्रह्म स प्राणस्तदु वाङ्मनः तदेतत्सत्यं तदमृतं तद्वेद्धव्यं सोम्य विद्धि ॥२॥

> *yad arcimad yadaṇubhyo 'ṇu ca yasmiṁlllokā nihitā lokinaśca |*
> *tadetadakṣara brahma sa prāṇastadu vāṅ manaḥ tadetat satyaṁ tadamṛtaṁ tat veddhavyaṁ saumya viddhi ||2||*

Spontaneously ablaze, subtler than the subtle is it; in it are set all the observable worlds and their observers; It is the Imperishable *Brahman*; It appears as *prāṇa*; It appears as speech and mind; It is the Real; It is the immortal; That is

> the target (that is to be known); my dear, do aim at That (do know That).

That which is most attractive, that which is smaller than the smallest particle, That in which all the world and its people are kept, That only is the *Akṣara Brahman. Prāṇa,* word, mind, everything is That. It is the fundamental support for everything. It should be thus imagined and realized. Saumya, know It with your thought.

**Gopāda** – That only is the true thing. To understand That which is indestructible, It should be aimed at like a thing aimed at by an arrow.

**Vājapeyī** – Gurudeva, It is very surprising. How to shoot the *Akṣara Brahman.* You must tell us about it in detail.

**Aṅgiras** –

> धनुर्गृहीत्वौपनिषदं महास्त्रं शरं ह्युपासानिशितं सन्दधीत।
> आयम्य तद्भावगतेन चेतसा लक्ष्यं तदेवाक्षरं सोम्य विद्धि ॥३॥
>
> *dhanur gṛhītvaupaniṣadaṁ mahāstraṁ śaraṁ*
> *hyupāsāniśitaṁ sandadhīta* |
> *āyamya tadbhāvagatena cetasā lakṣyaṁ tadevākṣaraṁ*
> *saumya viddhi* ||3||
>
> Holding the great Upaniṣadic weapon as bow firmly should one put on to it the arrow sharpenend by intense contemplative self-effort. Pulling the bowstring back, with consciousness lost in That, hit at That, the imperishable Target, my dear.

Dear one, take the big bow of the Upaniṣad in hand, well sharpened by *upāsanā,* think about the target *Akṣara Brahman* in the mind and shoot the arrow.

**Śaunaka** – Which is the bow? Which is the arrow? Which is the air? How to shoot the *Akṣara Brahman.* Kindly bless us with detailed teachings.

**Aṅgiras** –

प्रणवो धनुः शरो ह्यात्मा ब्रह्म तल्लक्ष्यमुच्यते।
अप्रमत्तेन वेद्धव्यं शरवत्तन्मयो भवेत्॥४॥

*praṇavo dhanuḥ śaro hyātmā brahma*
*tallakṣyamucyate* |
*apramattena veddhavyaṁ śaravat tanmayo*
*bhavet* | |4| |

*Praṇava* is the bow, and oneself the arrow; *Brahman* spoken of as That, is the target. Unerringly is It to be shot at, and, like an arrow, should come to be one with That.

The *Praṇava* is the bow; *ātmā* is the arrow, the target *Brahman*. As how a carefully aimed arrow hits the target, in the same way the arrow should hit the *Brahman* by meditation.

**Vājapeyī** – It is very nice to hear. However the meaning is not understood well.

**Saumya** – Like the one described in literature the examples and synonyms are nice to hear and give great pleasure. However the inner meaning is not clearly known.

**Gopāda** – Ones having beautiful mind! I will explain in detail. In the Upaniṣad a good method is described to reach *Brahman*. To get rid of the *saṁsāra* which is the demon of ignorance a good weapon is available in the Upaniṣad. That is the *mahāmantra* called *praṇava*. That only is the bow. Taking the bow of *oṁkāra*, the arrow called *jīvātmā* should be strung in that. Keeping the *Brahman* as the target without losing one's concentration, the arrow should be aimed carefully. That is, meditation should be carried out. Just as the arrow hits the target, in the same way the *ātmā* also will strike the *Brahman* and become encompassed in that.

**Vājapeyī** – Is there so much greatness for the *praṇava oṁ*?

**Aṅgiras** – Yes. A *mantra* which does not join with *praṇava* is a *mantra* without *prāṇa*.

**Gopāda** – Śaunaka! All the *prāṇa*s (sense organs) are made to worship the *paramātmā* by the *praṇava*. Did you understand this well.

**Śaunaka** – By the blessing of *gurudeva* we understood it very well. You must continue to preach to us more and more, Svāmī.

**Vājapeyī** – One doubt. Kindly explain the meaning of the word *apramattena*.

**Aṅgiras** – Here the *śruti* means the condition of not allowing the mind to roam in matters belonging to outer world, lose oneself in the happiness and sorrow they represent and also not feel attracted towards them. Such a state of mind is called *apramattena*. When we leave the arrow, if our hand trembles then won't the aim get spoilt? The same applies here. Hence to succeed in aiming and shooting well the *Brahman*, one has to control the senses and dispassionately with total one-pointed concentration, has to leave the arrow, that is, the meditation to be done to achieve the goal.

**Saumya** – Svāmī! It appears very difficult to know and meditate on absolute *Brahman*. Hence, again you must preach in a way it makes a firm impression in our minds.

**Aṅgiras** – Saumya, The Vedamātā has again and again told about this with great compassion. I will repeat her saying to you all and bless you all.

यस्मिन् द्यौः पृथिवी च अन्तरिक्षमोतं मनः सह प्राणैश्च सर्वैः ।
तमेवैकं जानथ आत्मानमन्या वाचो विमुञ्चथामृतस्यैष सेतुः ॥५॥

*yasmin dyauḥ pṛthivī ca antarikṣamotaṁ manaḥ saha prāṇaiśca sarvaiḥ* |
*tamevaikaṁ jānatha ātmānamanyā vāco vimuñcathāmṛtasyaiṣa setuḥ* ||5||

He into whom are woven the sky, the earth and the interspace, and also mind along with all the *prāṇa*s, know Him alone as yourself; and do dismiss all else, He alone is the bridge to Immortality.

The heaven, world below the *antarikṣa*, the mind which consists of all *prāṇa*, all these are threaded to the one and only *paramātmā*. Let you all know Him and leave out the other matters. This is only the bridge to *mokṣa* (salvation). My dear disciples! In the *akṣara Brahman* the upper world (heaven), the earth, and the sky which is in between, are all contained.

**Gopāda** – Like the cloth is contained in the thread, all these are contained in the *akṣara Brahman.* The thread is the base of the cloth. Once the thread is removed there won't be any cloth. Actually, if observed keenly the thread only goes criss-cross and appears as the cloth. Without the thread the cloth is not a separate product.

In the same way the basis of the entire universe is *akṣara Brahman*. This only appears as the universe. There is no universe apart from the *Brahman*. That is the only thing which is really true. All others are mere appearances. One should know the *akṣara Brahman* as the *ātmā* present in oneself and all other living things. One should discard all other knowledge that is in the form of *aparā-vidyā*. Leaving the unwanted, one should seek the *ātmā* knowledge which is the bridge for the *mokṣa* state which is indestructible. Hence accept this *ātmā* knowledge; this is the best bridge to cross the river of death. There is no other than this.

**Śaunaka** – Kindly tell us about *praṇava* meditation further.

**Aṅgiras** –

अरा इव रथनाभौ संहता यत्र नाड्यः स एषोऽन्तश्चरते बहुधा जायमानः।
ओमित्येवं ध्यायथ आत्मानं स्वस्ति वः पाराय तमसः परस्तात् ॥ ६ ॥

*arā iva rathanābhau saṁhatā yatra nāḍyaḥ sa*
*eṣo 'ntaścarate bahudhā jāyamānaḥ* |
*omityevaṁ dhyāyathātmānaṁ svasti vaḥ pārāya*
*tamasaḥ parastāt* ||6||

> He, wherein all nerves meet together, like spokes in the hub of a wheel, being such, becoming multitudinous, lives and moves within everything. Meditate therefore yourself as *AUM*. May you succeed in crossing over to the shore farther from darkness.

Just as the spokes are connected to the axle of a chariot wheel, all the *nāḍī*s are connected in the heart's seat. There listening and seeing, further being witness to the intellect, resides the that *ātmā*. Due to various changes which occur in the inner mind it appears that *ātmā* also undergoes various changes. This *ātmā* has to be thought of separately and meditated upon with the *praṇava oṁ*. If so meditated the *tamas* or inertia called ignorance can easily be removed. For that no obstacles should come your way. I give my blessings for that, so tells the *śruti*.

**Gopāda** – Saumya! There is a deep meaning for the *śruti "svasti* saying." The teacher will only preach to the disciples what has to be known and tell them in short and explain it. With that, his task is over. By saying that one should meditate on the *oṁkāra* his duty is over. After that, to meditate, continue to enquire and to think deeply is the duty of the disciple. In that there is no role for the teacher. Hence he blesses the disciples so that there are not any obstacles in the disciple's advancement. He blesses "let good tidings come about."

**Śaunaka** – Svāmī! I request you to further preach to us.

**Aṅgiras** –

> यः सर्वज्ञः सर्वविद्यस्यैष महिमा भुवि ।
> दिव्ये ब्रह्मपुरे ह्येष व्योम्न्यात्मा प्रतिष्ठितः ॥
> मनोमयः प्राणशरीरनेता प्रतिष्ठितोऽन्ने हृदयं सन्निधाय ।
> तद्विज्ञानेन परिपश्यन्ति धीरा आनन्दरूपममृतं यद्विभाति ॥७॥
>
> *yaḥ sarvajñaḥ sarvavidyasyaiṣa mahimā bhuvi* |
> *divye brahmapure hyeṣa vyomnyātmā pratiṣṭhitaḥ* ||
> *manomayaḥ prāṇaśarīranetā pratiṣṭhito 'nne hṛdayaṁ sannidhāya* |

*tadvijñānena paripaśyanti dhīrā ānandarūpamamṛtaṁ yadvibhāti* ||7||

He is all-knowledge and all-knowing, whose greatness is what appears as this world? In the firmament of the effulgent city of *Brahman* is the Self-wellfounded. He appears as mind, He appears as the controller of *prāṇa*s and body. With heart well-placed in food, Is He well-founded? The inflexibly wise visualizes Him holistically, perceiving Him in all the specific forms, immortal *ānanda* in essence, manifesting specifically as all.

The one who is *sarvajña* (all-knowledge), *sarva-vit* (all-knowing), He is installed in the divine *Brahmapura,* in the *cidākāsa* (the firmament of consciousness). He is the one who conducts the *prāṇa* and the body and the one who is *annam* (food). The wise one keeping the intellect in the *cidākāsa* with keen knowledge sees this *akṣara Brahman* which is bliss personified and indestructible.

**Vājapeyī** – The meaning of the *mantra* is not clearly understood. Kindly tell it in detail, Svāmī.

**Aṅgiras** – Saumya! The *śruti* tells, the *akṣara Brahman* shines everywhere. To realize that one has to meditate on the *oṁkāra,* so says the *śruti.* It explains how the person sees things when he gains expertise in practising meditation. *Brahman* understands everything ordinarily and specially. As explained above, it possesses all exalted qualities. The one which remain in the macro sphere (universe) can also be seen in the micro sphere (individual level) by meditation. *Brahmapura* is the lotus of the heart which is the seat of *chit* (mind). The mental changes which occur here shine due to *chaitanya* (power of the *Brahman*). Since it is known by the changes of the mind, the *Brahman* is termed as *manonmaya*. The *Brahman* retains His individuality owing to the conditioning factors such as body form, senses, mind, intellect, and the animating vitality, etc. all together known as *upādhi*s. From one gross body to another gross body the *Brahman* only carries the *prāṇa* (soul). Since He is seen to shine in the heart of the gross body which is formed by *annam* (food), *Brahman* is also considered to be the *annam* (food).

Keeping the intellect in the *chidākāsa* and doing meditation and concentration with mental traits like equality, equanimity, determination and holding on to the knowledge preached by the teachers, one realizes all phenomena appearing as the Self-expression of the creative urge inherent in the *Brahman*. They then come face to face with the indestructible, bliss-personified *Brahman*. With this let us stop today's lesson.

**Gopāda** – Let us do so. I request you to partake your food after finishing your routine.

***(Curtain closes.)***

## SCENE 3

(**The curtain opens**. Like the previous scene conversation is taking place in Maharṣi Gopāda's *āśrama*.)

**Gopāda** – Śaunaka! Do tell us in short the previous lesson which was taught.

**Śaunaka** – Gurudeva! *Namaskāra*. The route for reaching *akṣara Brahman* was taught. Taking the bow of *oṁkāra*, stringing on to that the arrow of *jīva* sharpened by *upāsanā* and released by *chit* (mind) filled with thought about *Brahman* and aimed towards *akṣara Brahman*, it will pierce it like an arrow piercing its target. It is our prime duty to know of the one and only thing filling the universe, the *Brahman*. The other things should be of lesser importance. Only this is the bridge for *mokṣa*.

**Vājapeyī** – Respected Sir, you described about *oṁkāra dhyāna* (meditation) and the vision which people in meditation can see. Further, kindly tell us about the benefit the people who see this vision acquire.

**Aṅgiras** – Saumya! As I continue to preach to persons like you who are most deserving, I become very enthusiastic. The one who has acquired wisdom by knowledge from *śāstras* and knowledge received from the teachings of the teacher and also the wisdom obtained from the mental state of equality, equanimity, meditation, sacrifice, austerity, determination, etc. will get to see the *Brahman* concept. The *śruti* tells us what happens during the realization of *Brahman*:

भिद्यते हृदयग्रन्थिश्छिद्यन्ते सर्वसंशयाः ।
क्षीयन्ते चास्य कर्माणि तस्मिन्दृष्टे परावरे ॥८॥

*bhidyate hṛdayagranthiśchidyante sarvasaṁśayāḥ* |
*kṣīyante cāsya karmāṇi tasmindṛṣṭe parāvare* ||8||

The knots of heart shatter, all doubts get dispelled, and all deeds (*karma*s) get exhausted, on visualizing Him — the transcendental and the Immanent.

Once the *parāvara* (truth) is seen, the *sādhaka*'s heart's knot gets loosened. All the doubts get cleared. All *karma*s get destroyed.

**Vājapeyī** – It is very difficult to believe that all these wonderful things can happen.

**Aṅgiras** – Why won't it happen? You don't have to believe because I am telling you. You will know it yourself by experience, by wisdom acquired by realizing the *Brahman*. In the wise one's mind the roots of ignorance are removed. Just as how the blazing fire reduces the firewood to ash, the fire of wisdom burns away all the *karma*s into ash.

**Gopāda** – Saumya, if a small light is lit in a room which was filled with darkness for many years, the darkness is driven away, likewise when the *parāvara* (the *ātmā* which is both cause and effect) is realized, all *karma*s get destroyed. The knot of ignorance in the heart gets opened up. All doubts get cleared.

**Śaunaka** – Gurudeva! We pray, you continue to preach further.

**Aṅgiras** – Disciples, so be it. In the next *śruti* the thing which is told previously is repeated in short so that it will get firmly fixed in one's mind.

हिरण्मये परे कोशे विरजं ब्रह्म निष्कलम्।
तच्छुभ्रं ज्योतिषां ज्योतिस्तद्यदात्मविदो विदुः ॥९॥

*hiraṇmaye pare kośe virajaṁ brahma niṣkalam* |
*tacchubhraṁ jyotiṣāṁ jyotistadyadātmavido viduḥ* | |9| |

In the Transcendental golden treasury is *Brahman*, the actionless and partless; pure is it, Light of lights, what the Self-knowers perceive.

The clear, formless, bright and effulgent *Brahman* which is present in the *kośa*s is very pure. It is the light of all lights. The *ātmavit*s (Self-knowledgeable) are the persons knowing this.

**Śaunaka** – Gurudeva! Is this *brahmajyoti* brighter than the brightness of the sun, lightning, etc. which we see around us?

**Aṅgiras** – Yes, the *śruti* says as follows.

न तत्र सूर्यो भाति न चन्द्रतारकं नेमा विद्युतो भान्ति कुतोऽयमग्निः।
तमेव भान्तमनुभाति सर्वं तस्य भासा सर्वमिदं विभाति ॥१०॥

*na tatra sūryo bhāti na candratārakaṁ nemā vidyuto bhānti kuto 'yamagniḥ* |
*tameva bhāntamanubhāti sarvaṁ tasya bhāsā sarvamidaṁ vibhāti* | |10| |

The sun illumines It not, nor the moon and stars; these lightnings illumine It not, much less this fire! Following Its shining indeed all is luminous; by Its light everything specifically shines.

In front of the *ātmā*, light of the sun won't shine. The fire is of no consequence. That also won't shine. The reason why they won't shine is given by the *śruti* itself. All these lights are alive because of the light of the *Brahman*. Because of that only, the universe also is there.

**Gopāda** – The sun which gives light during the day also loses its brightness in front of (*ātmasvarūpa*) the dazzling light of *Brahman*. The moon and the stars which give us light during the night time also lose their light in front of *ātmasvarūpa*. When, during day time the sun shines will the light of fireflies be seen? Even lightning and big fires (*agni*) also lose their lustre in front of the sun. Similarly the sun, moon, stars, and fire also lose their lustre in front of *Brahman* which is self-shining. Now we can see this water jug (*kamaṇḍala*) with our eyes. However can this water jug see the eye? It is not possible. Likewise the *ātmasvarūpa, Brahman* brightens everything but we are not able to see it. Further, the other objects, apart from *Brahman*, like the sun, moon, etc. do not have the ability to shine by themselves. In the same way the world also.

**Saumya** – I have heard this *ṛk* from time to time during *pūjā*. Now only I understand the meaning correctly.

**Aṅgiras** –

> ब्रह्मैवेदममृतं पुरस्ताद् ब्रह्म पश्चाद्ब्रह्म दक्षिणतश्चोत्तरेण।
> अधश्चोर्ध्वं च प्रसृतं ब्रह्मैवेदं विश्वमिदं वरिष्ठम्॥११॥
>
> *brahmaivedamamṛtaṁ purastād brahma paścād-*
> *brahma dakṣiṇataścottareṇa* |
> *adhaścordhvaṁ ca prasṛtam brahmaivedaṁ viśvamidaṁ*
> *variṣṭham* | | 11 | |
>
> *Brahman* indeed is all this! It is the immortal! *Brahman* before, *Brahman* behind, to the right, to the left too! It spreads forth below and above! *Brahman*, the best of desirables, indeed, is this whole world!

This *mantra* talks about *Brahman*'s presence everywhere. The world which is seen differently in front of us is the permanent *Brahman*. It is *Brahman* everywhere. To the left is *Brahman*, right is *Brahman*, and below is *Brahman*, above also *Brahman*. This universe is full of *Brahman*. It is spread everywhere and it is *variṣṭham*.

**Gopāda** – Disciples! did you understand how *Brahman* is found everywhere?

**Vājapeyī** – We understood there is *Brahman* everywhere and it is present in all places in an entwined way. However to experience that concept is a bit difficult.

**Aṅgiras** – For that only, this *śruti* preaches to us, who are immersed in ignorance, about this permanent, indestructible *Brahman*. Whatever is there in front of us, behind us, above, below in the sides and in all directions we see, everything is *Brahman*. Thus we have to understand.

The *Brahman* is the cause of the name and forms which are but effects and are in essence *Brahman*. It penetrates and spreads everywhere. This entire world is nothing but this exalted *Brahman*. Due to our ignorance or *avidyā* we don't understand it. The *Brahman* alone is the true thing. That only is the supreme cause and meaning of all the things.

**Śaunaka** – Respected Sir! Now everything is known clearly. Gradually with enquiry and meditation it should be experienced.

**Gopāda** – Yes. "The wood is hidden by the elephant and the elephant hides behind the wood," in the same way the supreme is hidden by the earth and the earth in turn gets hidden by the supreme." Thus tell the elders in a proverbial manner. There is much truth in that.

> An expert sculptor makes an elephant with a wood piece. It looks exactly like a real elephant. It looks like it comes forward in heat. Seeing that a young boy thinks an elephant really is coming towards him. Here he is not seeing the wood. He only sees the elephant. However an elder coming there sees only a piece of wood. In the same way when the universe with the five elements, earth, water, fire, air, and sky is seen we are not able to see the *Brahman*. When *Brahman* is seen the universe is not seen.

**Śaunaka** – What beautiful proverbs have come down over

ages. Initially in an ignorant state the elephant hides the wood. Similarly the earth and other elements hide the supreme. In the state of enlightenment just as the wood is seen the elephant gets hidden. In the same way the *Brahman* is seen and the universe gets hidden. We understand this very well, Svāmī.

**Aṅgiras** – This is told by the elders in a proverb as "when you see the dog the stone is not located and when the stone is found the dog is not seen."

**Vājapeyī** – Gurudeva! Through these examples we understand the concept very well. Kindly preach further to us.

**Gopāda** – Disciples, if any doubt is there, you can ask. I will clear it.

**Saumya** – You mentioned that as soon as the *parāvara* thing (*Brahman*) is seen, all the *karma*s get destroyed. For a person reaching such a state, won't the results of *karma* affect him?

**Gopāda** – It won't affect him. Will the seeds which are fried germinate? In the same way, the *karma*s done by him won't affect him. When the sun shines at one place, *yajña* takes place in another place, a murder may take place in yet another place. However the sun is not affected by both these *karma*s. In the same way the enlightened is not affected by the *karma*s.

**Aṅgiras** – Saumya, I will tell yet another example to explain the *Brahman*'s omnipresent characteristic. Let us take the mud pot present here. There is mud above, mud below, mud in the right side, mud on the left side, in short the entire pot is mud. Apart from mud nothing else the pot contains. The pot has come about from the mud. It remains as mud; after it breaks also it becomes mud. Mud only is the result and cause factor for it. In the same way, the *Brahman* becomes result and it is the cause of the universe also. It is present everywhere, penetrates into everything and appears as everything.

(Gopāda's wife enters. She stands aside. She gives her *praṇāma*s to her husband and Aṅgiras.)

**Gopāda** – Friend, do you know why my wife has come?

**Aṅgiras** – I do not know, do tell me.

**Gopāda** – We are immersed in the lessons and are not aware of the time. The afternoon time is nearing. Everything is ready for *vaiśvadeva pūjā*. It is time for making the offerings, she has come to tell that.

**Aṅgiras** – Is that so? I am very happy indeed. Let us stop today's lessons here. Disciples! The coming three days are holidays. There will be no lessons on these days. You may all take rest and enjoy nature. After that the lessons will start in my *āśrama* as usual.

**Śaunaka** – Gurudeva! We will do as you order.

**(All get up.)**

***(Curtain Falls.)***

**(Part Three Ends.)**

## PART IV

### SCENE 1

(**Curtain opens.** It is Aṅgiras *āśrama*. The conversation is taking place)

**Aṅgiras** – Friends (*saumya*)! Till now many ways of realizing *akṣara Brahman* are being talked about. However since it is very difficult to understand the *Brahman* concept, here I will today try to explain it in yet another way.

**Śaunaka** – Gurudeva! Your *chitta* (will) is our fortune. We will listen carefully.

**Aṅgiras** –

द्वा सुपर्णा सयुजा सखाया समानं वृक्षं परिषस्वजाते।
तयोरन्यः पिप्पलं स्वाद्वत्तिअनश्नन्नन्योऽभिचाकशीति ॥१॥

*dvā suparṇā sayujā sakhāyā samānaṁ vr̥kṣaṁ*
*pariṣasvajāte* ।

*tayoranyaḥ pippalaṁ svādvattyanaśnannanyo*
*'bhicākaśīti* ||1||

Two beautiful winged-ones, fast bound companions, cling to the self-same tree. Of the two, one eats delicious berries while the other looks on, not eating.

Two birds with beautiful wings which always stay coupled and never leave each other's company reach the same tree. They both are of equal status. Out of them one eats the fruits enjoying its taste. The other one without eating is just looking at the other bird.

**Saumya** – Svāmī! I am not able to understand anything. Everything sounds like a riddle.

**Vājapeyī** – Gurudeva! I also don't understand. The tree denotes what? Who are the birds? What is meant by fruits? You must explain it clearly.

**Aṅgiras** – Here the two birds denote the *jīva* and *Īśvara* (God). Like two birds stay together in one tree, the *jīva* and *Īśvara* stay together in the body which is equated to the tree. However among the two birds only the *jīva* eats the fruits which ripen in this tree. The other bird *Īśvara* sees what *jīva* eats as a witness. It does not eat anything.

**Śaunaka** – The fruits mean the effects of good and bad deeds, is it not?

**Gopāda** – Yes.

**Vājapeyī** – The fruits are the happiness and pain incurred due to one's deeds or *karma*. Enjoys and eats, it does not mean eats only the tasty fruits. Even if it is tasteless, it assumes them as tasty and eats.

**Aṅgiras** – The banyan tree which arises from *avyakta* (अव्यक्त) is the foundation for the fruits of *karma*s of living things. This has root in the sky and branches facing down. In this tree the *jīva* bird stays having the gross body and the *upādhi*s (attachment), whose basis is desire, *karma vāsanā* (inclinations).

There the *jīva* bird eats the fruits which have been produced as a result of its deeds and enjoys both happiness and sorrow found in the fruits. That is, the *jīva* experiences the fruits of its *karma*s which are *prāpta* (destined). However the other bird which is *Īśvara* (God) does not eat the fruits. He does not experience or enjoy them. It remains as the witness between *bhokta* (the one who enjoys) and *bhogyam* (the things which are enjoyed). He appears like the king who sits back and observes the servants who run about and work. It is under the gaze of *Īśvara* that all the deeds in the world occur. However he does not carry out any manoeuvres to bring about that.

**Śaunaka** – The *jīva* bird has always to partake the fruits of his deeds. When it will get freedom? Does not the *Īśvara* bird which keeps seeing it have any compassion?

**Aṅgiras** – The *jīva* definitely gets his freedom. However to get such a freedom it does not require any sympathy from *Īśvara*. Self-help is the best help, meaning thus the *śruti* tells as follows that in good and bad situation its life also is in its own hands.

समाने वृक्षे पुरुषो निमग्नोऽनीशया शोचति मुह्यमानः।
जुष्टं यदा पश्यत्यन्यमीशमस्य महिमानमिति वीतशोकः ॥२॥

*samāne vṛkṣe puruṣonimagno 'nīśayā śocati muhyamānaḥ* |
*juṣṭaṁ yadā paśyatyanyamīśamasya mahimānamiti vītaśokaḥ* ||2||

On the same tree, the one *puruṣa* engrossed as he is in eating, Finding himself not its controller, gets confused and grieves. Seeing the other, the controller, contented he becomes devoid of sorrow, wondering, "How Great He is !"

Though *Īśvara* and *jīva* have the same dwelling place, still the *jīva* has a lower status. Drowned in its senses and losing its abilities it suffers. When it sees the other bird having higher capacity and having ruling abilities, it realizes its own greatness and leaves sorrow.

**Śaunaka** – Do kindly tell this in detail.

**Vājapeyī** – You must preach how the *jīva* suffers in different ways, in detail Svāmī.

**Aṅgiras** – Friend, do explain the status of this *jīva*.

**Gopāda** – I will do so. The tree denotes the living body. The *jīva* is weighed down by things like ignorance, desire, fruits of the deeds, likes, and dislikes, and he struggles like a heavy boat which is about to drown in a sea. The *jīva* equates his body as himself and thinks "I am only myself, I am the son of such a person, grandson of another, father of somebody, having this relationship, I am now happy, now sad, now very much bloated and fat, now very thin," thus variously thinking he gets disturbed. There is nothing apart from this body thinking thus, taking birth, living, getting along with relations and friends, becoming happy at times, at times separated, becoming sad, growing old, and meeting death; thus continuously jostled between pain and pleasure it suffers.

**Aṅgiras** – Thus the *jīva* suffers in different ways and comes to a pitiable lowly state. Assuming that nothing is possible by oneself, it comes to a very sad state. In this way it gets birth in different forms as ghost, animal, man, etc. In different lives little by little by the dint of the good deeds done, it reaches a *satguru* and by his consideration goes along the good path, follows good principles like *ahiṁsā* (no harm to other living things), truth, *brahmacharya* (celibacy), sacrifice, etc. Through such good moral standards the different blemishes of the mind get removed and he is able to see the *Īśvara* (God). As soon as he sees the *Īśvara* (God) who has no *upādhi* (blemishes) and who is purity personified he comes out of all sorrow and desire and becomes blessed.

**Vājapeyī** – Svāmī! As soon as he sees the *Īśvara* how does he come out of the sorrow?

**Gopāda** – Seeing *Īśvara* means, understanding the greatness of the inner *ātmā* — the *Īśvara* who has all the ruling abilities and greatness.

**Aṅgiras** – Not only that, he comes to the conclusion that *Īśvara* form is none but oneself. Then he comes to realize that since there is no difference between *Īśvara* and *jīva* where is the place for suffering and desire? In the next *ṛk* also *śruti* tells this in detail.

यदा पश्यः पश्यते रुक्मवर्णं कर्तारमीशं पुरुषं ब्रह्मयोनिम्।
तदा विद्वान् पुण्यपापे विधूय निरञ्जनः परमं साम्यमुपैति॥३॥

*yadā paśyaḥ paśyate rukmavarṇaṁ kartāramīśaṁ puruṣaṁ brahmayonim* |
*tadā vidvān puṇyapāpe vidhūya nirañjanaḥ paramaṁ sāmyamupaiti* ||3||

Visualizing the *puruṣa*, the golden-hued all-doer, all controller, source of Brahmā (the creator), the wise one shakes off both sin and merit, and thus, blemishless, attains supreme sameness.

When *jīva* sees the *puruṣa* filled with light, who is the creator – God and — *Brahman*'s form, that learned soul leaves the *pāpa* and *puṇya* cycles, becomes purified and reaches the supreme goal.

**Gopāda** – Saumyas! In this *ṛk,* leaving the simile of the birds the *śruti* explains directly, who is the one seen. The *jīva,* the *sādhaka* helped by the compassion of the *satguru,* becomes a *yogī.* He sees the *Īśvara* (God) the omnilighted shining like gold, possessing the indestructible brightness, he comes to know the *Īśvara* who is the creator of the entire world and the cause of Brahmā himself. He realizes him as the ruler and controller of everything. A person who acquires such knowledge is the truly learned person, thus say the Vedas and call him *vidvān* (learned one). As soon as he acquires that knowledge then he comes out of the *pāpa puṇya karma*s which are the causes of attachment. He becomes blemishless, devoid of any aberration and gets unified with the *paramātmā*, the complete God form.

**Aṅgiras** – Just as when coal is put into the fire, it gets the heat and light and becomes the fire itself, in the same way when *jīvātmā* joins the *paramātmā*, it comes out of the dual state and acquires *sāmya*, the unified state.

*fig* : **Two birds on the same tree, Īśvara and Jīva.**

**Śaunaka** – The *jīvātmā,* tossed and changed in different ways, finally acquiring the true knowledge, realizes its true state. This we understood. Do kindly continue to preach.

**Aṅgiras** –

प्राणो ह्येष यः सर्वभूतैर्विभाति विजानन् विद्वान् भवते नातिवादी ।
आत्मक्रीड आत्मरतिः क्रियावानेष ब्रह्मविदां वरिष्ठः ॥४ ॥

*prāṇo hyeṣa yaḥ sarvabhūtairvibhāti vijānan vidvān bhavate nātivādī* |
*ātmakrīḍa ātmaratiḥ kriyāvāneṣa brahmavidāṁ variṣṭhaḥ* ||4||

> Truly It is the one that shines out as and through everything; It is the one *prāṇa* in everything. The wise one, seeing It in all specific manifestations, remains reticent. Sporting in the Self, all his actions having become the Self's delighting in the Self, he is the greatest of all *Brahman*-knowers.

The *parameśvara* who is *prāṇa* to the *prāṇa* itself contains all *bhūta* (living things) and is the *ātmā* of all living things. The *vidvān* (learned one) who knows him as his *ātmasvarūpa* (Self) won't unnecessarily argue. He will be the one playing with *ātmā,* enjoys the bliss of the *ātmā* and considers that as the doer of deeds. Such a person will be the best among *brahma-jñānī*s.

**Gopāda** – Yes, the one who knows what he has to know won't argue unnecessarily. He won't talk much. He won't give long lectures. That is because, once he knows the *paramātmā* which is *prāṇa* to *prāṇa* (life of the life force) and is contained in all *bhūta*s (living things), then what is there to tell? After knowing that everything is *ātmā*, right from the Brahmā-creator to created, everything is *ātmā* and is nothing else apart from that, what can he talk about? If there are differences between two entities, castes, high-low status, then he can talk and argue about the various aspects and differences. However once he sees everything as *ātmā* and does not see, hear or understand anything else, then there is nothing much to argue about.

**Śaunaka** – Respected Sir, we understand why an *ātma-jñānī* (Self-knowledgable) person will remain silent.

**Vājapeyī** – Now kindly explain these parts — "how he plays in the *ātmā,* and he enjoys the *ātmā.*"

**Aṅgiras** – Saumya! The one who comes to know *Brahman* plays in that only. He has no interest in other outer things. With great belief he immerses in that only and becomes happy. He does not indulge in his wife, children, wealth, etc. and he does not derive happiness from them. The word *krīḍa* implies happiness derived from outer products. The word *rati* means happiness which comes by itself without the help of outer things. Both for him means *ātmā*.

**Saumya** – The word *kriyāvān* means one who keeps doing some deeds, isn't it? In those *karmas*, are *agnihotra*, *yajña*, etc. also included?

**Aṅgiras** – No, they are not included. The one who does *yajña* and similar *karmas* is supposed to do *bāhya karma*. There is no connection between this and *brahma-jñānī*. The one who does *bāhya karma* (बाह्य कर्म) will never be the one who gets immersed in *ātmā* and enjoys *ātmā*-knowing deeds. They are contradictory. There is a difference as much as between light and darkness. How can both stay together? He will be having no deeds apart from seeking *ātmarati* (*ātmā* beauty) and will be considered supreme among the *brahma-jñānīs*.

**Gopāda** – However, due to that don't think that an *ātma-jñānī* is completely lazy and a sleepy person. He always remains a person who does deeds. He sees happiness, play and brightness inside. He does not discard or neglect the daily living, knowledge and meditation. At the same time he becomes a *sanyāsī* who has discarded all worldly pleasures and stays as a sacrificing ascetic. We are now fortunate to get preachings from such a good strict follower of the path of *Brahman*.

**Aṅgiras** – Friend, with this we shall stop today's lessons.

***(Curtain falls.)***

## SCENE 2

(**The curtain opens**. Like the previous scene the conversation takes place.)

**Gopāda** – Friend! Do continue to tell us further.

सत्येन लभ्यस्तपसा ह्येष आत्मा सम्यग्ज्ञानेन ब्रह्मचर्येण नित्यम्।
अन्तःशरीरे ज्योतिर्मयो हि शुभ्रो यं पश्यन्ति यतयः क्षीणदोषाः ॥५॥

*satyena labhyastapasā hyeṣa ātmā samyagjñānena*
*brahmacaryeṇa nityam* |

*antaḥśarīre jyotirmayo hi śubhro yaṁ paśyanti yatayaḥ kṣīṇadoṣāḥ* ||5||

Obtainable through Truth (*satya*) and *tapas* is that *ātmā* as also through proper knowledge (*jñāna*) and proper studentship constantly practised; within the perishable appearance (*śarīra*) is that *ātmā*, Effulgence in essence, the Pure, perceived by those of self-restraint and weakened blemishes.

To acquire *ātmā* knowledge and for that to stabilize it is necessary to possess truthfulness, *tapas* and *brahmacharya*. Only this is told in detail in this *ṛk*. That *ātma-jñāna* will be obtained with unbroken *brahmacharya*, consistent *tapas* (penance) and by truthfulness. As told earlier the renounced ones, *sanyāsīs* reaching a state of equanimity after all the blemishes in *chit* get removed, see the *ātmā* thing which is bright light within the body itself.

**Gopāda** – Saumya! In this *ṛk* the word *nityam* (consistent) is very important. It is not only important to follow *brahmacharya* but all other states denoted also should be followed in a consistent manner like a lamp kept in between the two points.

**Vājapeyī** – What is the meaning of "a lamp being kept in between the two points."

**Gopāda** – It means the lamp kept at the doorstep giving light both inside and outside; likewise these principles should be followed both in the inner conduct and external conduct. Always one should speak and think truthfully, always one should be in penance (control) both inside and outside, always the intellect should be alert and sharp, and consistent *vrata* of *brahmacharya* should also be followed. Here *brahmacharya* means not only celibacy, the important thing in a *brahmacharya*'s life is viewing all life as a manifestation of *ātmā* or *Brahman*. Having such a vision is part of the *brahmacharya*'s *vrata*.

**Saumya** – Kindly explain what is the meaning of seeing inside the body?

**Aṅgiras** – Following the above *sādhanās* a person is able to see in his inside, in the inner sky, the light-filled golden coloured self-effulgent *ātmā*. Who sees that? Not everyone, only the ones who do not have blemishes like desire, anger, etc. and who follow the principles of truth, penance, etc. as a daily routine.

**Śaunaka** – The greatness of truth is really exalted. You must continue to preach it, Respected Sir.

**Aṅgiras** –

सत्यमेव जयते नानृतं सत्येन पन्था विततो देवयानः।
येनाक्रमन्त्यृषयो ह्याप्तकामा यत्र तत्सत्यस्य परमं निधानम्॥६॥

*satyameva jayate nānṛtaṁ satyena panthā vitato devayānaḥ* ।
*yenākramantyṛṣayo hyāptakāmā yatra tatsatyasya paramaṁ nidhānam* ।।6।।

Truth alone succeeds; not untruth. By truth is laid out the path of gods, the path through which the seers with fulfilled desires cross over to where exists the supreme repository of that very same truth.

Only truth will succeed. Not untruth. The *ṛṣis* whose desires are completed travel towards the end of truth whose route is again laid on acts of truth itself.

**Saumya** – We followed the literal meaning. Kindly explain the meaning behind the words.

**Aṅgiras** – Only the truthful person will win. He will succeed in everything. The untruthful person will not succeed. The concept of *Brahman* is truth. To reach that, the route followed by *ṛṣis* is again laid on truth alone. The *ṛṣis* whose desires are contained, and the wise ones who have quitened after experiencing the desires, aspire to get *mokṣa* which is but truth. They have no other desire. The path they have to follow is also truth.

**Śaunaka** – In short, truthful souls tread the path of truth following truthful ways and reach truth-personified *Brahman*. This is only the truth.

**Gopāda** – *Sabhāsa* Śaunaka! You are an expert in telling in short and making things clear. There is no doubt about it.

**Saumya** – Yes, Śaunaka is an expert in talking to the point. This is truth, not a lie.

**Aṅgiras** – Listen further to what the Vedas say about the truth-personified *Brahman*.

बृहच्च तद् दिव्यमचिन्त्यरूपं सूक्ष्माच्च तत् सुक्ष्मतरं विभाति।
दूरात्सुदूरे तदिहान्तिके च पश्यत्स्विहैव निहितं गुहायाम्॥७॥

*bṛhacca tad divyamacintyarūpaṁ sūkṣmācca tat sukṣmataraṁ vibhāti* I
*dūrātsudūre tadihāntike ca paśyatsvihaiva nihitaṁ guhāyām* I I7I I

The far-extended, the self-effulgent, of inconceivable form, minuter than the minutest, It becomes visible as all. Farther away from the farthest, yet here near at hand, It is perceived by those who perceive intuitively, as remaining here itself, as if in a secret abode.

*Brahman* is self-effulgent and big. It cannot be thought about by the mind. It is subtler than the subtlest of the things known. It is very far and also very close by. It dwells in the heart cave of people who are able to see it.

**Gopāda** – The *Brahman* which is obtained by truth, equanimity and *brahmacharya*, is spread everywhere and it is considered big. As it has its own effulgence it is called divine. Since it is beyond the reach of mind (cannot be thought about) it is termed as *acintya* — beyond thinking process. It is more subtler than the subtle things like sky. It shines brighter than the sun and moon. As it cannot be realized by the ignorant it is considered to be very far from them. It is very close to the wise learned ones. As it shines as their *ātmā* within the body, It is seen very close. By *yoga* It is seen in the cave of their intellect. The learned ones also see It. However the ignorant, unwise ones are not able to see it, as it is covered by ignorance. For those ones who try hard to get a glimpse of It, It stays far.

**Śaunaka** – Is there any easy method to see the *Brahman* which is in the cave of the intellect? Kindly bless us with this information.

**Aṅgiras** – As told before, all the blemishes in *chit* (mind) have to go. In a mirror well coated with the reflector a person's face gets well reflected. Similarly an intellect well coated with strength, purity, *brahmacharya* and truth can see the *Brahman* very easily. There is no other method than this.

न चक्षुषा गृह्यते नापि वाचा नान्यैर्देवैस्तपसा कर्मणा वा।
ज्ञानप्रसादेन विशुद्धसत्त्वस्ततस्तु तं पश्यते निष्कलं ध्यायमानः॥८॥

*na cakṣuṣā gṛhyate nāpi vācā nānyairdevaistapasā karmaṇā vā |*
*jñānaprasādena viśuddhasattvastatastu taṁ paśyati niṣkalaṁ dhyāyamānaḥ ||8||*

Not by the eyes is It grasped, nor even by speech! Not by other sense organs, *tapas* or *karma*; beyond all this, however, purified in mind by the graciousness of wisdom, one meditating, intuitively perceives It, the partless.

*Brahman* cannot be seen by the eyes, by talk or other sense organs. Nor can it be known by *karma*s or penance. A person having a mind which is pure and an intellect which is clear can see the blemishless *Brahman* in meditation.

**Gopāda** – This is an important *mantra*. Its meaning has to be well thought over and done by heart. Why cannot the *Brahman* be seen by the eyes? let me see if anyone can tell me.

**Śaunaka** – As it does not have a form it cannot be seen by the eyes.

**Aṅgiras** – Why cannot it be understood by words? Do tell, Vājapeyī.

**Vājapeyī** – **(thinking)** *Brahman* cannot be explained in words. It is like this, like this — that is, it is beyond words.

**Aṅgiras** – Yes, *Brahman* cannot be explained by words; not only that, it cannot be understood by the other sense organs. It may be possible to get many things by penance (control). However *Brahman* cannot be understood by penance also. By doing *agnihotra* and other religious rites also *Brahman* cannot be understood.

**Saumya** – Respected Sir, then by what means can it be known? How it can be understood?

**Aṅgiras** – To make things known to dull heads like us with great compassion the *śruti* recites it again and again. It can be known by the *prasāda* (blessing) of wisdom.

**Gopāda** – The *Brahman* which cannot be known by eyes, words and other sense organs, *karma*s and *tapas* can be known by *jñāna* (wisdom). It can be seen by intellect. The intellect also should be enlightened. The inner being should be pure, then it can be seen through meditation.

**Aṅgiras** – Our intellect, by its inherent nature leads us to *ātmā*. However, with the desires and attachment one acquires with the outside world, the intellect loses its clarity and gets disturbed. Hence though the *ātmā* is near, the intellect loses its ability to recognize It. In a mirror which is covered with dirt is it possible to see one's face? Once the dirt is wiped off, the face can be seen clearly. In the same way, once the blemishes in the mind are removed, the intellect becomes clear. This only is called wisdom's blessing. By the blessing of the wisdom whosoever's inner world becomes pure only he gets the capacity to see the *Brahman*. Thus by taking the help of moral principles like truth, controlling the senses and with an one-pointed mind as a person meditates, he sees the formless *Brahman* directly inside himself.

**Gopāda** – Here it will be apt if an example is given. The sun is shining. The group of clouds comes and covers the sun. It is then not possible to see the sun. At that time if the wind blows, the clouds are dispersed and the sun is seen clearly. Here the wind has not brought a new sun. It is the sun which already exists. The job of the wind is only to remove the clouds. In the same way, if we remove the cover by meditation and other methods, then we can see the *Brahman* which is found everywhere.

**Vājapeyī** – Respected Sir! The matter has been well understood due to the example.

**Aṅgiras** – Saumyas! I will also tell an example as our friend has told. We pound the paddy and get rice. Here as we pound the paddy, new rice is not being made. Only the husk or the covering of the rice is removed.

**Gopāda** – The example my friend cited is still better than the example I told. We shall stop the lesson here with this now.

**Aṅgiras** – Let us recite this one *ṛk* and tell the meaning before stopping the lesson. This is connected to what we have been discussing.

एषोऽणुरात्मा चेतसा वेदितव्यो यस्मिन् प्राणः पञ्चधा संविवेश ।
प्राणैश्चित्तं सर्वमोतं प्रजानां यस्मिन् विशुद्धे विभवत्येष आत्मा ॥९॥

*eṣo 'ṇurātmā cetasā veditavyo yasmin prāṇaḥ pañcadhā saṁviveśa* |
*prāṇaiścittaṁ sarvamotaṁ prajānāṁ yasmin viśuddhe vibhavatyeṣa ātmā* | |9| |

Realizable is this subtlest Self as the consciousness into which are infused the fivefold *prāṇa*s. Woven by the fivefold *prāṇa*s. Is this functional Consciousness (*chit*) of all born beings! To that consciousness, when blemishless, is this Self self-revealed.

The *ātmā* is very subtle. The pure awareness of this *ātmā* is called *chetas*. In the body *prāṇa* enters in five different forms. Then the *chetas* is known as *chetanā/chaitanya*. It is in the *chaitanya/ātma-svarūpa* that all the *chit* (mind) of the *praja*s and the *prāṇa*s of all beings is established. The *ātma-svarupa* reveals its Self in a pure *chit* (mind) of the *jīva*. If the thinking facility is halted *chit* gets purified into pure *chetanā*. When the *prāṇa*s are not involved the *chetanā* gets purified into *chetas* — the pure mind (*viśuddha-sattva*). In that state the seeker through meditation perceives his own real self-content.

**Gopāda** - In the previous *ṛk*, since *Brahman* is spread everywhere the *śruti* described it as big. Here we are describing that aspect of *Brahman* which penetrates everything. It cannot be seen by the senses and is very subtle. Hence here it is described as small (atom). Since it is like an atom and very subtle, only by wisdom which is very pure it can be understood. In a body in which the five *prāṇa*s like the *prāṇa vāyu, apāna vāyu*, etc. are moving equally, it can be seen inside the cave of the heart. Just as the clarified butter is found mixed with the milk and the fire is found mixed in the cinder, the *ātmā-chetas* is found mixed in the *chit* (mind) and *prāṇa*, etc. That is why the *chit* (mind) appears to be having *chaitanya*. In a *chit* which is pure, devoid of any sludge-like blemishes the *Brahman* shines forth and can be perceived.

**Śaunaka** - What is meant by sludge-like blemishes?

**Aṅgiras** - There are five kinds of blemishes

1. *Avidyā* — lack of knowledge
2. *Ahaṁkāra* — Ego
3. *Rāgam* — desire
4. *Dveṣam* — anger
5. *Abhimānam* — pride

Saumya, let us stop today's lesson with this. However I wish one of you tell in short the summary of the lesson.

**Vājapeyī** – Śaunaka! Do tell us.

**Śaunaka** – Friend Vājapeyī, today you only must tell us.

**Saumya** – Yes today Vājapeyī only should tell us.

**Vājapeyī** – I wonder if I have the capacity to tell that.

**Gopāda** – Only by telling often it has to be practised. Do say boldly.

**Vājapeyī** – Respected Sir! As per your order here I am telling. **(thinking)** Leave my faults, accept my strength and bless me. In the body which is likened to the tree, the *jīva* and *Īśvara* are settled like two beautiful coupled birds. The bird which is *jīva* gets completely swayed eating the sweet and bitter fruits. The bird which is *Īśvara* stays as a witness and does not partake of any fruits. Finally the *jīva* sees the bright golden lighted *Īśvara* bird. It leaves the fruits which are but *pāpa* and *puṇya* and merges with the bird attaining an equanimous state with it. The indestructible *ātmā* can be won by *brahamcarya,* clear wisdom, penance, truth, etc. Untruth will never prevail over it. It cannot be obtained by mere talk, by sense organs or by *karmas.* A person having a pure *chit* by the virtue of his clear wisdom can know it by meditation.

**Others** – It is explained very well. Very good, very good.

**Aṅgiras** – Saumyas! I will describe the characteristics of a *brahma-jñānī,* the results accrued by worshipping him and the fruits of wisdom.

**Śaunaka** – Gurudeva! We are ready to hear

यं यं लोकं मनसा संविभाति विशुद्धसत्त्वः कामयते यांश्च कामान्।
तं तं लोकं जयते तांश्च कामांस्तस्मादात्मज्ञं ह्यर्चयेद्भूतिकामः ॥१०॥

*yaṁ yaṁ lokaṁ manasā saṁvibhāti viśuddhasattvaḥ*
*kāmayate yāṁśca kāmān* |
*taṁ taṁ lokaṁ jayate tāṁśca kāmāṁstasmādātmajñaṁ*
*hyarcayedbhūtikāmaḥ* | | 10 | |

> Whichever world the purified in mind perceives clearly in his mind, whichever the desire that arises in him (as Self's unfoldment), those worlds he wins over, those desires as well. Those desirous of welfare, therefore, should adore the Self-knowers.

A person having a clear *chit* is an *ātma-jñānī* (Self-knower). Whichever world he thinks about with his mind and whatever enjoyment he desires in those worlds, he obtains those worlds and enjoyment. Hence a person aspiring for great things should worship that *ātma-jñānī.*

**Gopāda** – The *ātma-jñānī* is the one possessing a clear *chit* (mind), From *pitṛloka* to *brahmaloka* whichever world he desires and whichever he determines to have, he obtains that. In the same way whatever enjoyment wealth and desire he aspires, he will get it immediately. Why? Because he is a true soul. His thoughts and wishes never get wasted. The other worlds and enjoyments he can aspire not for himself alone but also for some other person also. That time the other person will get it. Hence a person who is desirous of wealth and aspires to get *svarga* and such kind of worlds and enjoyment should worship an *ātma-jñānī.*

**Vājapeyī** – Gurudeva! How should he worship him?

**Aṅgiras** – *Ātma-jñānī* can be prayed to, *namaskārams* can be offered at his feet, giving him *bhikṣa* (alms), by taking care of him, etc. He is truth-personified. Hence he is worthy of worship.

***(The curtain falls.)***

## SCENE 3

(As **the curtain opens** like the previous scene, conversation is taking place.)

**Śaunaka** – Svāmī! You have explained the benefits obtained by worshipping a *brahma-jñānī* by persons desirous of worldly things and enjoyment. However if there is a person who is a *niṣkāmī* and is not desiring anything and if he worships a *brahma-jñānī* what will he obtain? Kindly tell us today, respected Sir.

**Aṅgiras** – Saumyas! I will tell, you listen.

स वेदैतत्परमं ब्रह्म धाम यत्र विश्वं निहितं भाति शुभ्रम्।
उपासते पुरुषं ये ह्यकामास्ते शुक्रमेतदतिवर्तन्ति धीराः ॥१॥

*sa vedaitatparamaṁ brahma dhāma yatra viśvaṁ nihitaṁ bhāti śubhram* |
*upāsate puruṣaṁ ye hyakāmāste śukrametadativartanti dhīrāḥ* ||1||

Founded wherein this world shines in its purity, that Supreme abode, *Brahman*, is known to him. Those desireless who adore that person, wise and firm-in mind, they leave behind the seed of birth.

A person having no desires and who does *upāsanā* of a *brahma-jñānī* crosses even *śukram* (the seed). They are indeed great achievers. The *parabrahmaṁ* is the dwelling place of everything. The world itself is kept in That. It appears as *śubhram* — pure. A person doing *upāsanā* of a *brahma-jñānī* without desires is not born again. They do not reach *narabījam*, seed of man again which is the cause of birth.

**Gopāda** – A *brahma-jñānī* is the one who realizes the *Brahman*, which is the cause of this entire world as well as the aspirations. He sees the *Brahman* which shines in its Self-light. If this *brahma-jñānī* is worshipped, it is like worshipping the *parama deva* with a desireless attitude without seeking for wealth, etc. with a wish for getting *mokṣa*, then they, by crossing over the brightness of the seed, and without reaching it, escape form the cycle of birth and death. They don't obtain *yoni*s (forms) again. Hence persons who are aspiring to learn about *Brahman* without any personal desire, they should worship *brahma-jñānī*s.

**Aṅgiras** – A person having a wish to get *mokṣa*, to become independent, should sacrifice all *karmas*. That is because the *śruti* states as follows.

कामान् यः कामायते मन्यमानः स कामभिर्जायते तत्र तत्र।
पर्याप्तकामस्य कृतात्मनस्तु इहैव सर्वे प्रविलीयन्ति कामाः ॥२॥

*kāmān yaḥ kāmāyate manyamānaḥ sa kāmabhirjāyate tatra tatra* |
*paryāptakāmasya kṛtātmanastu ihaiva sarve pravilīyanti kāmāḥ* ||2||

Resolutely desiring the enjoyables, one is born again in accordance with one's desires accompanied by the very desires. With the one of fulfilled desires, on the other hand, himself transformed as the Self, all the desires die out here and now.

The one who keeps the wishes in mind and aspires to fulfil them, gets born with these wishes. However, for a person fully satisfied with his desires and who has completed whatever he wants to do here in this life itself, such a person's wishes get completed and destroyed here.

**Vājapeyī** – A person losing his mind on the attraction of things around him keeps thinking about his desired things, is born again with those desires. Prodded by those desires he then tries to get his wishes fulfilled. Through that he comes to possess things and fulfil his desires. Whoever gets desirous of whichever things, he gets born in a place where these things are available and gets born with those desires. Thus the *purohita* has said from time to time and I have heard it.

**Śaunaka** – When we are doing *karmas* with desire, we are sowing the seed for the next life. Hence one should be without getting attracted to things and should aspire to know the Self. Such a person will be a fully contented person. Since he does not aspire to get anything his desires are not roused for anything.

**Saumya** – Yes friend! Such a victorious person who has satisfied his desires is a fully contented person. All his wishes get destroyed here (in this life) itself. Hence he does not have a cause for being born again. He reaches the state where he won't be born again.

**Gopāda** – Friend! Did you see! The disciples following the matter are themselves giving explanation and understanding. It is really commendable.

**Aṅgiras** – A *guru* cannot have anything which gives him more happiness than this. I am thankful to you, my friend, for bringing me such disciples.

**Śaunaka** – Respected Sir! Kindly continue to preach further.

**Aṅgiras** –

नायमात्मा प्रवचनेन लभ्यो न मेधया न बहुना श्रुतेन।
यमेवैष वृणुते तेन लभ्यस्तस्यैष आत्मा विवृणुते तनुं स्वाम्॥३॥

*nāyamātmā pravacanena labhyo na medhayā na bahunā śrutena* |
*yamevaiṣa vr̥ṇute tena labhyastasyaiṣa ātmā vivr̥ṇute tanuṁ svām* | |3| |

This (Self) is unattainable by instruction; nor by intellectual power, nor even by much learning of scriptures. One chooses (the Self) alone as such, and thus alone is unattainable. To him the Self unveils Itself.

As told in the previous *śruti* it is understood that compared to all other good results a man can accrue in life, advancing in the knowledge of Self and realization of Self is most exalted. To reach that how much ever effort is put it will be worth it. That is because to reach that is not that easy. It is told so in Vedic words "this realization of Self cannot be reached by Vedic studies, sharp memory or consistent enquiry only." This learned person, that is the one desirous of reaching the Self-realization can reach it only by intense longing to obtain it. Then the *ātmā* reveals itself to this learned one in its true form.

That is, it makes him know It.

**Gopāda** – Saumya! But don't assume that for *ātmā*-knowledge the Vedic studies, knowledge and enquiries are not needed. Here what *śruti* tries to stress is, just by doing these only one cannot obtain wisdom. Apart from this a person should be possessed with a keen desire to obtain *mokṣa* and become independent. Then only it will be possible to obtain *ātmā*-knowledge. For such a person the *ātmā* lies open in its true form.

**Śaunaka** – Gurudeva! It is clearly understood. Do continue to preach.

**Aṅgiras** –

> नायमात्मा बलहीनेन लभ्यो न च प्रमादात्तपसो वाप्यलिङ्गात्।
> एतैरुपायैर्यतते यस्तु विद्वांस्तस्यैष आत्मा विशते ब्रह्मधाम ॥४॥

> *nāyamātmā balahīnena labhyo na ca pramādāt tapaso vāpyaliṅgāt* |
> *etairupāyairyatate yastu vidvāṁstasyaiṣa ātmā viśate brahmadhāma* ||4||

> This Self is not to be obtained by one destitute of fortitude; nor is It obtainable by the heedless; neither through austerity devoid of external signs. Yet the one who strives by these means, provided he is learned and an intent seeker, he finds himself (the Self) already in the *Brahman* abode.

This *ātmā* cannot be reached by a weak person. It cannot be obtained by *pramādāt* (प्रमादात्) — lack of concentration and a *tapas* (austerity) which does not include *sanyāsa* (renunciation). A *vidvān* who tries truly in the right way with the knowledge that *ātmā* alone is his sole objective realizes the *Brahma-svarūpa.*

**Vājapeyī** – Svāmī! Nothing is clearly understood.

**Saumya** – Strength means, is it body strength or mental strength? Or is it both? What is the meaning of *pramādāt*?

**Śaunaka** – *Sanyāsa* means renunciation. Is it not enough to have inner renunciation? Is it necessary to show with outer garments?

**Gopāda** – Saumyas! First Svāmī will explain the *ṛk,* then he will clear your doubts.

**Aṅgiras** – This *ātmā* cannot be understood by a person without strength. To some extent the physical strength is required, but what is being said is not only that. Due to discipline adhered for knowing *ātma-jñāna* the mental strength acquired is told as "strength" here. *Pramādāt* means lack of concentration or forgetfulness, that is, getting embroiled in *saṁsāra* and with excessive attachment to wife and children, not doing the correct things at the correct time, and doing the uncalled-for things will all be included in *pramādāt.* Further the wisdom acquired by *sanyāsa* (renunciation) is very important. How to know that the mind is in a renounced state? For that the ascetic's outside dress is also important. Like erecting a fence for the crops it becomes necessary to wear saffron to indicate inner renunciation as a security. That only the *śruti* tells as *sanyāsa.* Thus to get *ātma*-knowledge these methods are being told. First mental strength, then *apramādāt* (concentration), finally *liṅgāt* (renunciation) and wisdom connected with such renunciation. In this way a *vidvān* with *viveka* (discrimination) has to try. Then his *ātmā* enters *Brahma-svarūpa.*

**Vājapeyī** – For acquiring *ātma-jñāna,* is it necessary to employ different methods? Isn't wisdom the most important?

**Gopāda** – Without following proper diet the medicine won't benefit. In the same way an effort without discipline and determination will not fetch proper result.

**Śaunaka** – We understand that with mental strength, determination, consistent efforts without fatigue and the wisdom combined with renunciation (*sanyāsa*), one can realize *ātmā.*

**Saumya** – You told that the *ātmā* of these learned ones enters into *Brahman.* Kindly give a little more explanation to it. How it enters? Does it build a palace or *parṇaśālā* and do *gṛhapraveśam*?

**Aṅgiras** – The *paramātmā* is present everywhere. It is mentioned as an *ātmā* entering *paramātmā* only as a sort of a way to make the concept clear. It can be considered as a phrase than a fact. Listen carefully what the *śruti* tells more.

संप्राप्यैनमृषयो ज्ञानतृप्ताः कृतात्मानो वीतरागाः प्रशान्ताः ।
ते सर्वगं सर्वतः प्राप्य धीरा युक्तात्मानः सर्वमेवाविशन्ति ॥५॥

*saṁprāpyainamṛṣayo jñānatṛptāḥ kṛtātmāno vītarāgāḥ praśāntāḥ* |
*te sarvagaṁ sarvataḥ prāpya dhīrā yuktātmānaḥ sarvamevāviśanti* ||5||

Duly attaining *Brahman*, the seers, already transformed as the Self, free from attachments and tranquil in mind, become content in wisdom. Having become one with the all-pervasive One everywhere, they, of unitive Self-content, get merged with all.

Persons who are contented with the wisdom acquired, the persons who have realized themselves as *ātmā*, the persons who are without desires (*rāgam*) and the ones who have controlled their senses and have become peaceful, after realizing *ātmā* properly enter freely all these things present everywhere in an effortless way.

**Gopāda** – The *ṛṣi*s who have followed the ways as described above, content with the wisdom acquired, possessing *virakti* (detachment), peacefully do whatever that has to be done and stay blessed. These strong *puruṣa*s see *Brahman* everywhere, in everything. At that time they become one with *Brahman* in an indistinguishable way.

**Saumya** – It is not followed properly. Kindly explain further.

**Aṅgiras** – With this today's lesson is over. You also think deeply and contemplate on it. I will continue the teachings tomorrow.

**(Everybody gets up.)**

***(The curtain falls.)***

## SCENE 4

(**The scene opens**. The conversation takes place like the previous scene.)

**Gopāda** – Saumyas! Tell the previous lesson's summary one after another.

**Saumya** – If the *ātma-jñānī* is worshipped with desires for *bhoga* (experience/enjoyment) then one can obtain all the *bhogas*. If he is worshipped without wishes in a desireless way then one can get *ātma-jñāna*. It will then be possible to cross *saṁsāra*. One can be relieved from the cycle of birth and death.

**Vājapeyī** – Whoever yearns for whichever desires is born in those places where he can enjoy those desires. However an *ātma-jñānī*'s desires get destroyed here itself. He has no necessity to reach and come back again to this world. Thus birth and death is not there.

**Śaunaka** – To obtain *ātma-jñāna* one requires strong *chit* (mind). That is, a good mental strength is required. He can acquire it by following properly daily routine and discipline, pure practices, etc. It is not enough if one sways under the feeling that he has left worldly pleasures. Truly he should be with- out yearning for those things (wife, children, house, cattle, etc.). He should possess the strength of *tapas* (penance). For that he should have wisdom combined with *sanyāsa* (renunciation). A person following these methods is a strong person. He is not a coward. In such a knowledgeable person's heart in the *brahmapūra* the *ātmā* dwells. How the *ṛṣi*s who have reached such a state will be, the *śruti* describes. They will be without getting torn by attractions, very peaceful in full control of senses and fully contented in *ātma-jñāna*. They then become the *ātma-svarūpa, ātmā* form itself. They become one with the *parama* thing found everywhere. Their greatness indeed is indescribable.

**Aṅgiras** – Saumya! The persons having *ātma-jñāna* are indeed very great ones. What the *śruti* tells about them, I will explain further, listen carefully.

वेदान्तविज्ञानसुनिश्चितार्थाः संन्यासयोगाद्यतयः शुद्धसत्त्वाः ।
ते ब्रह्मलोकेषु परान्तकाले परामृताः परिमुच्यन्ति सर्वे ॥६॥

*vedāntavijñānasuniścitārthāḥ sanyāsayogād yatayaḥ śuddhasattvāḥ* ।
*te brahmalokeṣu parāntakāle parāmr̥tāḥ parimucyanti sarve* ।।6।।

With what Vedānta teaches having become a certitude those of self-restraint, through the *yoga* of renunciation, attain pure existence. Absolutely immortal as they all are, liberated in all respects into the *Brahman*-world they become.

Those who have definitely known the *paramātmā*, the mendicants, ascetics, *sanyāsīs*, the pure-minded person, such people in *parānta* (ultimate) time get merged with *Brahman* and freed from bondages.

**Śaunaka** – Svāmī! The explanation of the *śruti* is understood. However kindly explain in detail.

**Aṅgiras** – The knowledge obtained by Veda is Veda knowledge. That is, the understanding of knowledge personified *Parābrahman*. That is what is inside the Vedas, Upaniṣads and the proper understanding of the *mantras* written in them. The one who knows them well are the truly wise persons. It is not enough knowing them in a very superficial manner. It should get properly registered in the mind. That is the Veda and Upaniṣad known from the *guru* should first be repeated and by hearing and contemplating upon it *Parabrahman* should be grasped without even a little bit of doubt, and one should get an experienced wisdom about it. These only the *śruti* describes as *vedānta vijñāna suniścitārthāḥ* (as what Vedānta teaches).

**Gopāda** – Friend! The discourse is very wonderful. *Sabhāsa*. Do continue to tell further.

**Aṅgiras** – It is not only enough just knowing the Vedānta's inner meaning, that is, the *Brahman*. It is also essential to live a life of *sanyāsa* (renunciation). The main identity of having obtained such a knowledge is *sanyāsa*. Hence it is necessary to sacrifice all the *karma*s one does and do *yoga* of renunciations. Such persons further have to be immersed in *brahma-jñāna* and obtain *samādhi* in that state. Their *chit* becomes very pure in that state. Such *puruṣa*s having *chit* (mind) which are pure, having no blemishes and impurities reach *Brahmaloka* in *parānta* time and become immortal. As soon as they reach the indestructible *Brahman*-state they get freed from everything. Just as a pot breaks and the inside of the pot joins the outer big sky, in the same way the *jñānī* also gets *mukti* (salvation).

**Śaunaka** – Svāmī! You mentioned about *parānta* time. What is the meaning of that?

**Vājapeyī** – *Parānta* time means the end, that is, the time of death. That is the meaning, isn't it?

**Saumya** – It isn't like that. If so, it will mean that *mokṣa* can happen only at the time of death.

**Śaunaka** – Gurudeva! Kindly explain this at length.

**Aṅgiras** – Saumyas! You need not take *parānta* time as the time of death. When ordinary people die it is termed as *aparānta* time. Here for the *jñānī* (wise one) when the time of *saṁsāra* gets completed that time is called *parānta* time, so say the Vedas. It is not necessary that when *saṁsāra* ends death follows. If such a meaning is taken there cannot be anyone who can be termed as *jīvanmukta* (released from life). It need not be thought that a *jñānī* gets *mukti* only when he leaves the body. *Mukti* is obtained as soon as he gets the realization (*jñāna*). There is no doubt about it. Here "*parānta* time" means, *vāsanā*s or attractions end, or the end of ego and feeling of separateness, or end of results from *karma* (action).

**Gopāda** – What our friend tells is very true. That a *jñānī* (wise one) will get *mokṣa* only after death is not a correct statement.

If *jīvanmukta*s are not there who will preach *brahma-jñāna*? A *satguru* should be well versed and also a follower of *Brahman*-understanding disciplines. This has been repeatedly told by the *śruti* in the previous *ṛk*s. That being so, how can it be considered that *mokṣa* will be obtained only at the time of death. If so, there won't be any teachers teaching this.

**Śaunaka** – There is only one *Brahma-svarūpa* (*Brahman*'s form). Advaita does not preach two supremes, that being so, why does *śruti* mention *Brahmaloka*s indicating many worlds of *Brahman*. What is the concept behind such a statement?

**Aṅgiras** – Many disciples, that is many *sādhaka*s get preaching. Each one sees the same *Brahman* as his own, or he sees it as himself. They reach it accordingly. Hence *Brahmaloka*s are spoken in plural. In fact, the meaning of *Brahmaloka*s is "in *Brahman*." Further if we think of them as different worlds then it amounts to going from one place and reaching those different worlds. However, this is not true. That is because *Brahman* does not have differentiation as worlds, differentiation as time, and differentiation as things. It remains in all places at all times as everything. To reach such a *Brahman* which is everywhere there is no need to go to another place.

**Gopāda** – Friend! Do continue to preach further.

**Aṅgiras** –

गताः कलाः पञ्चदश प्रतिष्ठा देवाश्च सर्वे प्रतिदेवतासु ।
कर्माणि विज्ञानमयश्च आत्मा परेऽव्यये सर्व एकीभवन्ति ॥७॥

*gatāḥ kalāḥ pañcadaśa pratiṣṭhā devāśca sarve pratidevatāsu* ।
*karmāṇi vijñānamayaśca ātmā pare 'vyaye sarva ekībhavanti* ।।7।।

The fifteen constituent minute parts go to their basic abodes; all the senses (*deva*s) too to their respective deities; one's deeds and self of the essence of specific consciousness, all become unified in the Imperishable Supreme.

As told in the previous *ṛk* at the time of getting *mukti* (liberation) all the fifteen arts reach their respective places. The ones which used to dwell in the sense organs to which the *deva*s had been doing services, come out and join with the fundamental form outside. All *karma*s (actions) and the *ātmā* which is *vijñānam* (knowledge) unite with *Brahman* as one.

**Vājapeyī** – What are the fifteen parts? You must explain in detail Gurudeva.

**Gopāda** – In this *ṛk* the happenings during *mokṣa* time are explained like a picture. For this body to form, there are fifteen parts which are its root cause. They are:

1. *prāṇa* (vital breath)
2. *śraddhā* (faith)
3. *ākāśa* (sky)
4. *vāyu* (air)
5. *agni* (fire)
6. *āpaḥ* (water)
7. *Pṛthvī* (earth)
8. senses
9. mind
10. *annam* (food)
11. strength
12. penanace (austerity)
13. *mantra*s
14. *karma*s (actions)
15. the result of *karma*s.

At the time of *mokṣa* all these reach their respective forms. The *deva*s who had been in the body supported by the senses also reach their respective places. For example, the *deva* helping the eyes, who is the component of seeing, reaches the sun.

**Śaunaka** – The *karma*s wont leave without showing the results. How to end that?

**Gopāda** – The *karma*s discussed here are *sañchita karmas*. They can be burnt by the fruits of wisdom. After *karma*s leave the body, the *ātmā* which had so far been considering the body as its abode and was steeped in ignorance, comes out of that state and gets merged in *Parabrahman*. Once the *upādhi*s (blemishes) leave, it joins the *Brahman* which is formless, *akṣaraṁ* (अक्षरं), *ajayaṁ* (अजयं), *ajaraṁ* (अजरं), *amṛt* ( अमृत् ), *abhayaṁ* (अभयं), *athvayaṁ* (अथ्वयं), *śivaṁ* (शिवं), and *śāntam* ( शान्तम् ). The reflection of the sun seen in the water joins the sun when the water is removed. In the same way, *ātmā* joins the *paramātmā*.

**Vājapeyī** – We understand the matter well by the help of the examples. Kindly continue to preach, Svāmī.

**Aṅgiras** –

> यथा नद्यः स्यन्दमानाः समुद्रेऽस्तं गच्छन्ति नामरूपे विहाय।
> तथा विद्वान् नामरुपाद्विमुक्तः परात्परं पुरुषमुपैति दिव्यम्॥८॥
>
> *yathā nadyaḥ syandamānāḥ samudre 'staṁ gacchanti nāmarūpe vihāya* |
> *tathā vidvān nāmarūpādvimuktaḥ parātparaṁ puruṣamupaiti divyam* ||8||
>
> As flowing rivers, casting off their names and forms, disappear in the ocean, even so does the awakened one, Freed from name and form, attain the efflugent *puruṣa*, higher than the highest.

Just as the rivers which are flowing leave their strength and mingle into the sea, the *vidvān* (learned one) at the time of *mokṣa* (liberation) leaves the name and form and reaches the *divya puruṣa* which is above the *parama* things.

**Śaunaka** – This example is better than what was told before.

**Gopāda** – In comparison to what we explain the *śruti*'s preachings will be more apt indeed. Where is our little knowledge? And where is the knowledge filled saying of the *śruti.*

**Aṅgiras** – It is almost afternoon. I think, it is time to stop the lessons now.

**Gopāda** – Friend! Before that, can we ask the students to tell the summary of the lessons?

**Aṅgiras** – We will do so. Saumya! Do tell the summary of today's lessons. Let Saumya tell.

**Saumya** – Today you explained the state of a *brahma-jñānī*: how he becomes one with *Brahman* during *mokṣa* (liberation) time. I will tell in brief what I understand, kindly bless me. The persons who have stabilized in *ātmā*-knowledge as a result of experience in Vedānta wisdom and who possess pure *chit* which they have acquired by following *sanyāsa yoga* (renunciation route) get stabilized in the immortal *Brahman* and get freed from attractions and desires. At the time of liberation the fifteen parts which make up the body reach their respective places. The *deva*s who do service to the sense organs also reach their places of origin. All *karma*s and the knowledge filled *ātmā* combine with the indestructible *parama* thing. Just as the swelling waters of a river leave its name and form and vanish in the ocean, the wise ones also leave the name and form and reach the most exalted and *tejas*-filled *puruṣa.*

**Gopāda** – *Sabhāsa*! Saumya! You explained very well. Just as the river seeks the ocean after running its course and mixes with it in an undifferentiated manner, the wise ones surrender themselves to *Brahman* and merge with *Brahman* and get liberated.

**Aṅgiras** – Yes friend! The water in the sea gets converted into cloud, pours as rain and takes various names and runs as rivers finally reaching its original place, namely the ocean and completes its journey. When they are rivers they are differently called as Gaṅgā, Kāverī, Godāvarī, and Yamunā. When they mix in the sea they are all the same water. The universe, *saṁsāra* (world) are all like this only. How apt! With this today's lesson is getting over.

(The disciples get up and tell *śānti pāṭha* and do *namaskārams*).

***(The curtain falls.)***

***(Part IV ends.)***

## Part V

### SCENE 1

***(Curtain opens.)***

(Like the previous scene in the *āśrama* of Aṅgiras, preaching is going on.)

**Aṅgiras** – Saumya! With today's lessons we will almost be completing the teachings. Before starting today's teachings if you have any doubt you may ask.

**Śaunaka** – Gurudeva! For good work some obstacles may crop up often. Everybody is aware of this. Hence for attaining *Brahman*-realization, will some obstacles arise? Will *deva*s or others create any obstruction in the path?

**Aṅgiras** – A person who does hundred *aśvamedha yajña*s will reach the position of lord Indra, so says *karma-kāṇḍa*. Hence Indra and other *deva*s, becoming jealous and afraid that their position may be lost, try to create obstacles to different *yajña*s. Here *brahma-prāpti* is not obtained due to *karma*s but only by wisdom. This wisdom alone will help one cross all obstacles. In this route *deva*s won't create any hindrance.

**Gopāda** – The obstacle to *mokṣa* is ignorance alone. That ignorance will be removed by wisdom (*jñāna*). Hence whoever realizes the exalted *Brahman* as himself and declares "I and He are one" becomes that *Brahman* itself. He does not then revert to any other state. The *deva*s also do not create any hindrances to him.

**Saumya** – Why don't the *devatā*s come in his way?

**Gopāda** – In the matter of obtaining *Brahman* the *devatā*s cannot create any obstacles.

**Vājapeyī** – How may the all-powerful *devatā*s lose their power? They are stronger and superior to us.

**Aṅgiras** – Yes, the *devatā*s are more superior to us. However they are not above a *brahma-jñānī*. For *devatā*s also He only remains as *ātmā*. Hence a person knowing *Brahman* becomes *Brahman* itself. Now I recite the Vedic chantings, listen.

स यो ह वै तत्परमं ब्रह्म वेद ब्रह्मैव भवति। नास्याब्रह्मवित्कुले भवति।
तरति शोकं तरति पाप्मानं गुहाग्रन्थिभ्यो विमुक्तोऽमृतो भवति ॥९॥

*sa yo ha vai tatparamaṁ brahma veda brahmaiva*
*bhavatināsyābrahmavitkule bhavati* |
*tarati śokaṁ tarati pāpmānaṁ guhāgranthibhyo*
*vimukto 'mr̥to bhavati* || 9 ||

The knower of Transcendental *Brahman* becomes *Brahman* indeed. In his line is never born a non-*Brahman*-knower. He, crossing over sorrows, crossing over sins, becomes freed from all knots of heart. He becomes immortal.

The one, who knows this *Parabrahman* becomes the *Brahman* itself. In his lineage there won't be anyone who will be without *brahma-jñāna*. Further he crosses the sorrow and crosses all sins. Getting out of the knot of the heart he reaches the immortal state.

**Gopāda** – Disciples, you need not have any doubts. The Veda speaks with authority and assuredly. The one who knows the

*Parabrahman* comes to know that the *Brahman* which is Reality is none but oneself. Initially he understands it as *parokṣam* and then later as *aparokṣam*. He comes out of all sorrows. He is not affected by loss of things dear to him or loss of the dear persons does not unduly trouble him. Further in his family no one gets born who is not seeker of *brahma-jñāna*. The ones who are born in his lineage are all usually aspirants of *brahma-jñāna*.

**Vājapeyī** – Svāmī! How is that possible?

**Aṅgiras** – There is nothing to be surprised about this. It is seen from generation to generation that in good families good people are born, and in families having evil habits persons with similar nature are born. This is a thing happening routinely.

**Śaunaka** – Yes, one or two may be exceptions to the general rule. However, that is the norm. Hence, friend, there is no doubt about this kind of happening.

**Aṅgiras** – The *brahma-jñānī*, apart from crossing *saṁsāra*, also comes out of sins. The *pāpa*s and *puṇya*s are like coins with two sides. By crossing the *pāpa*s and *puṇya*s one is liberated from birth and death. A person gets released from heart knots, from afflictions and attractions and attains an immortal state.

**Gopāda** – In the previous *ṛk* the knots holding the heart get loosened, the doubts get cleared and the *karma*s get destroyed. These words were told. Do you remember? Let one of you repeat what was told.

**Śaunaka – (while the others are thinking)**

भिद्यते हृदयग्रन्थिश्छिद्यन्ते सर्वसंशयाः।
क्षीयन्ते चास्य कर्माणि तस्मिन् दृष्टे परावरे।

*bhidyate hṛdayagranthirichhadyante sarvasaṁśayāḥ* |
*kṣīyante cāsya karmāṇi tasmin dṛṣṭe parāvare* |

Once the brahman is realised, knots of the heart get opened, all doubts get cleared, all *karma* get annihilated.

**Aṅgiras** – *Sabhāsa*! Śaunaka! I am very happy. It is indeed fortunate to get a disciple like you.

**Gopāda** – Yes, friend . . . *na bhūto na bhaviśyanti* (never in the past, nor in the future).

**Śaunaka** – (**a bit embarrassed**) Respected Sir ! It is all due to your blessings. Do kindly bless us more.

**Aṅgiras** – Now, I will tell how the chosen one should conduct himself. That is, the one who has received *Brahma-upadeśa*. This *śruti* describes it as written in *karma-kāṇḍa*.

तदेतदृचाभ्युक्तं क्रियावन्तः श्रोत्रिया ब्रह्मनिष्ठाः स्वयं जुह्वत एकर्षिं श्रद्धयन्तः ।
तेषामेवैतां ब्रह्मविद्यां वदेत शिरोव्रतं विधिवद्यैस्तु चीर्णम् ॥१० ॥

*tatetatṛcābhyuktaṁ kriyāvantaḥ śrotriyā brahmaniṣṭhāḥ*
*svayaṁ juhvata ekarṣiṁ śraddhayantaḥ* |
*teṣāmevaitāṁ brahmavidyāṁ vadeta śirovrataṁ*
*vidhivad yaistu cīrṇam* | |10| |

Concerning this very teaching is it declared in a Ṛgvedic verse: Those who practise what they learn, well versed in scriptures, those intent on *Brahman* to the exclusion of all else, who make oblation of themselves to the sole seer with full faith, to them alone is to be imparted this secret *Brahman*-wisdom, when the head-related rites have been duly performed as per injunctions.

What was told now has also been told in the *mantra*. That is, only to the ones who follow the rules of *karma* and who are learned in Vedas, who are *brahmaniṣṭhas* (follower of *Brahman*-realization methods), those *śraddhā* (faithful) ones, and the ones who do *homa* as *ekarṣi* in the *agni* (fire) and also as per rule who have done *śirovrataṁ* (clean shaven of the head hair), the *brahma-vidyā* is to be taught.

**Gopāda** – Saumyas, here the disciples have been told to follow six kinds of salient principles.

1. Followers of the rules of *karma* (*karmaniṣṭha*)
2. Learning the *vedas* (*veda adhyayana*)
3. Following *Brahman*-realization methods (*brahmaniṣṭha*)
4. Unshaken faith (*śraddhā*)
5. To do *homa* in *agni* as *ekarṣi* (*ekarṣi homa*)
6. To shave off the head hair (*śirovrataṁ*)

**Vājapeyī** – Respected Sir, in the beginning itself there is a doubt.

**Gopāda** – What is that? Do tell immediately. I will try to weed it by the root itself.

**Vājapeyī** – Usually in the Vedas it is said that the Upaniṣad *mantras* are more potent than the ones told in *karma-kāṇḍa.* That being so why the *karma-kāṇḍa mantras* are advised to be recited here.

**Gopāda** – There is nothing wrong about that. Only when one contradicts, the questions such as which is superior and which is inferior arise. When both are similar it is better to take the help of one another. For disciples, like you who have been immersed in *karma-kāṇḍa,* it is better to tell the *mantras* you are familiar with.

**Śaunaka** – Svāmī! Now kindly tell in detail about the six salient qualities to be possessed and as to how they help in the attainment of *Brahman.*

**Aṅgiras** – If a person does his *karmas* as told in Vedas with devotion and having no interest in the fruits of *karmas,* then his *chit* becomes pure. His nature and qualities become exalted. The bad nature like selfishness gets removed. The Vedas have to be studied properly and contemplated upon. Then the meditation on *Brahman* has to be done. Here *brahmaniṣṭhaka* is not told as a person who knows *Brahman* and gets stabilized in that, but as a person who is in the process of knowing *Brahman* and follows a discipline to realize it. Further, *śraddhā* (faith) is very important. With *śraddhā* the *homa*s as told in the *Atharvaveda* have to be done in the *agni* (fire) called *ekarṣi*. Another most important thing to be followed is *śirovratam*, that is, to hold the *agni* in the head. This *vrata* is told in high praise in *Atharvaveda*. Thus, only to those people who are worthy as per Śāstras and following all the disciplines, the *brahma-vidyā* is to be taught.

**Gopāda** – Saumyas! You have fulfilled these requisite qualifications. Bhagavān Aṅgiras has preached to you. Let the light of knowledge emitting from the Upaniṣad stay with you without diminishing its brightness over the generations to come. Return to your native place and preach to the desiring disciples. That time you have to observe keenly and see if they have the requisite qualities as told by *satguru* for learning the *brahma-vidyā*.

**Aṅgiras** – With this the teaching on *Brahma-jñāna* is complete. Tomorrow is a good day. After doing your *avāpūtha* bath, you can return home as realized souls. I am giving you my best wishes. Let the disciples increase in strength and wisdom and let Upaniṣad-knowledge grow and passed from generation to generation. I pray for that and also give my blessing for that to happen. Like a lamp kept on a hill, let the brightness of your knowledge spread everywhere.

**Gopāda** – Śaunaka! The time for us to part has come. In your *āśrama* your wife will be anxiously looking out for your arrival. Go immediately to the lady of virtue who is a *pativratā* and preach the *brahma-vidyā*. Also you must preach to Saumya, Vājapeyī, *purohita* and other deserving disciples.

**Saumya** – Gurudeva! May I summarize today's lessons?

**Aṅgiras** – Very good. You may definitely do so.

**Saumya** – Whoever comes to know of *Brahman* becomes himself the *Brahman*. In his family there won't be born a person who does not strive to realize the *Brahman*. He crosses all sorrows. He crosses all sins. He gets freedom from the knots of his heart, that is freedom from desires. He becomes immortal.

**Śaunaka** – A person who is devoid of the pride caused by the feeling that he is freed from all desires and the feeling of greatness of one's own *yoga-siddhi* and other negative traits like anger and feeling of possession, becomes *Brahman*. He does not feel sad and does not desire. Hence he does not do any sin. He has equal feeling with all lives and reaches the unparalleled *Brahman* and attains the immortal state.

**Vājapeyī** – Such an exalted education learnt with great interest should not be preached to undeserving people. Only to persons who are truly deserving, it should be preached. The truly deserving persons are the ones who follow good *karmas*, learned in Vedas, follow discipline of *Brahman*-realization, have *śraddhā* and along with that do the *agni homa* called *ekarṣi* and do the *Atharvaveda* ritual called *śirovratam*. The persons following them and so deserving should be taught this *brahma-jñāna*.

**Aṅgiras** – Saumyas! I am very happy. Let the *upaniṣad-jñāna* get well protected by you all and spread widely. It will gain wide acceptance and I give my blessings for the same.

(All recite *śānti pāṭha* together. The disciples each get up and tell *abhivādaye* and prostrate fully and do *namaskārams*. The *guru* blesses them.)

## SCENE 2

***(The curtain opens.)***

(The *āśrama* of Śaunaka. Śaunaka and his wife, his friends and other disciples are sitting and conversing).

**Vājapeyī** – Friends! Today it is one year since we came to Rishikesh. How time has flown! It appears like yesterday.

**Saumya** – The important matters and incidents which have become close will not leave the minds screen so easily. Hence these incidents remain firmly in the memory.

**Śaunaka** – Yes friends! Gopāda Brahmarṣi coming here and taking us to Rishikesh. There Bhagavān Aṅgiras imparting us teachings. All that is very much in front of our eyes as though it happened today. Everything is the blessing of *satguru*.

**Purohita** –

> तदेतत्सत्यमृषिरङ्गिराः पुरोवाच। नैतदचीर्णव्रतोऽधीते।
> नमः परमऋषिभ्यो नमः परमऋषिभ्यः ॥११॥
>
> *tat etat satyam ṛṣi aṅgirāḥ purovāca* ।
> *naitadacīrṇavrato 'dhīte* ।
> *namaḥ paramarṣibhyo namaḥ paramarṣibhyaḥ* ।।11।।
>
> This Truth, being such, was declared in olden days by the seer Aṅgiras. None of unobserved vows is to read this. Adoration to the Supreme Seers! Adoration to the Supreme Seers!

Aṅgiras Maharṣi preached to you all the truthful teachings about the *parama* thing. You also with great consideration preached to people like us. This Upaniṣad should not be received by persons who have not followed the requisite discipline to obtain it. Our salutation to great *ṛṣis*. Our salutations to great *ṛṣis*.

**Yajñasenī** – Āryaputra! Why are the *namaskārams* told two times in this *ṛk*?

**Śaunaka** – Dear, even if we give our salutations a crore times to the *brahmarṣis* who gave these preachings, it won't be considered more. To show our regard and respect, *praṇāmas* are being told two times. Further it can be considered that the salutations are being recited two times to indicate that this *Muṇḍaka Upaniṣad* is getting completed with this.

**Purohita** – What is the meaning of *Muṇḍaka Upaniṣad*. Kindly describe.

**Vājapeyī** – *Purohita,* listen to what I say. *Muṇḍaka* means bald head. This is the sign of *vairāgyam* (determination). Only persons who are ready to put their head completely for life of wisdom are worthy to learn this *Upaniṣad*. Persons who are fulfilling *śirovratam* only are deserving to get its teachings. Hence this *Upaniṣad* is called *Muṇḍaka Upaniṣad*. There are three parts (*muṇḍakams*) and in each part two *kāṇḍa*s (chapters) are there.

**Yajñasenī** – Is it! Very happy. In each *muṇḍakam* what matters are being described?

**Śaunaka** – I have already preached to you before them all the matters of *Muṇḍaka Upaniṣad*. I have not separated and preached part by part. Here I am telling you. In the first part it is mentioned, there are two *vidyā*s (knowledge). The four Vedas and all other knowledge are contained in *aparā-vidyā*, and *parā-vidyā* is *brahma-jñāna*.

**Vājapeyī** – In the second *muṇḍakam* the connection between *Brahman* and *prapañcam* (universe) and the ways to reach *Brahman* are explained.

**Saumya** – In the third *muṇḍakam* the characteristic of *brahma-jñānī* and the fruits of wisdom are described.

**Yajñasenī** – Respected Sir! We are blessed. I will keep everything ready for Vaiśvadeva. Kindly complete your afternoon bath and come (**gets up and goes inside**).

**Śaunaka** – *Purohita*! Shall we go to the river?

**Purohita** – Friend! You were previously itself well learned and well considered. Today as Kulapati Śaunaka you are still more renowned and thought of with great regard. Earlier many people used to come to you to perform *yajña*. Today, to get *brahma-upadeśa* the disciples are continuously coming. Earlier you were an example for family *dharma*. Today you are a great example for *akṣara dharma* and *gurukula* life. We are indeed fortunate just as the thread also gets the smell joining the flowers in a garland, with your friendship we are also acquiring good qualities. We are proud of your friendship. Both myself and other disciples offer our great gratitude and many many thanks to you. We are indeed indebted to you.

**Vājapeyī** – Friend, whatever you said is very correct. Śaunaka indeed has risen to be a great soul.

**Saumya** – I also agree. Let Kulapati Śaunaka live long (**Everybody together** — Let Kulapati Śaunaka live long, Let Brahmarṣi Śaunaka's fame grow.)

**Śaunaka** – Friends, getting emotional and with great regard for me you are praising me highly. I don't deserve such praise. Everything is the blessing and good wishes of *brahmarṣi*s Gopāda and Aṅgiras. Let us give them our thanks humbly and gratefully. Those *brahmarṣi*s first reached *Brahman*-realization. To those great souls who did such noble trials and succeeded in their effort, for them let us give our *praṇāma*s. They did not keep quiet after reaching the *Brahman*. They preached with great compassion to the disciples who approached them in the proper manner. Our *namaskāram*s to such compassionate *brahmarṣi*s. Let us follow their footsteps. We will preach to those disciples who approach us. Only the food eaten with hunger will get digested. Likewise, only the one who has followed the discipline and done proper *vrata* the *brahma-vidyā* will benefit. Hence to deserving disciples only this should be preached. This way only we can show the salutations and gratitude to the *brahmarṣi*s. Friends let us tell *śānti-pāṭha* and go for the afternoon bath. Let good tidings befall every one.

**(Everybody together recite the śānti-pāṭha.)**

॥ ॐ भद्रं कर्णेभिः शृणुयाम देवाः। भद्रं पश्येमाक्षभिर्यजत्राः।
स्थिरैरङ्गैस्तुष्टुवाꣳसस्तनूभिः। व्यशेम देवहितं यदायुः॥

*oṁ bhadraṁ karnebhiḥ śṛnuyāma devāḥ bhadraṁ paśyemākṣabhir yajatrāḥ* |
*sthirair aṅgais tuṣṭuvām̐ sastanūbhi vyaśema devahitaṁ yadayuḥ* | |

स्वस्ति न इन्द्रो वृद्धश्रवाः। स्वस्ति नः पूषा विश्ववेदाः।
स्वस्ति नस्तार्क्ष्यो अरिष्टनेमिः। स्वस्ति नो बृहस्पतिर्दधातु॥

*svasti na indro vṛddaśravāḥ svasti naḥ pūṣā viśvavedāḥ* ।

*svasti nas tārkṣyo ariṣṭanemiḥ svasti no bṛhaspatir dadhātu* ।।

॥ॐ शान्तिः। ॐ शान्तिः। ॐ शान्तिः॥

॥*oṁ śāntiḥ* । *oṁ śāntiḥ* । *oṁ śāntiḥ* ॥

(The disciples one by one tell *abhivādaye* to Kulapati Śaunaka and does *namaskāra* prostrating fully on the ground. He also blesses each one telling *dīrghāyuṣmān bhava*.)

***(The curtain falls.)***

**(End of *Muṇḍaka Upaniṣad*.)**

## ॥ माण्डूक्योपनिषत् ॥

# Māṇḍūkya Upaniṣad

### Introduction

*Māṇḍūkya Upaniṣad* is one of the smallest but important and well-read Upaniṣad among the 125 or so well-known Upaniṣads. It belongs to *Atharvaveda.*

The word *maṇḍūka* meaning frog is indeed an odd name for a treatise which speaks with all brevity about the Ultimate truth. There are two reasons cited for the title. One, Lord Varuṇa who came to preach this *Upaniṣad* to Satyakāma after the latter's year-long penance on the banks of Mānasarovara lake in the Himālayās, came in the guise of a *maṇḍūka*, the "frog." Another reason cited is a *maṇḍūka* has the characteristic of jumping from place to place unlike the other many four-legged creatures who move step by step after being sure of the next step. This *Upaniṣad* talks mainly about different states of consciousness of human beings, that is, waking, dreaming, sleeping where men move from one state to another similar to a *maṇḍūka*. Thus the title implies the abruptly changing states of human consciousness.

The play opens at the breathtaking Himālayan mountain slopes close to Mānasarovar lake most conducive for meditation and contemplation. Satyakāma, Ṛṣi Śibi's son and disciple of Maharṣi Pippalāda had undertaken a severe penance, seeking the blessings of Lord Varuṇa to obtain the preachings of the higher truths and get enlightened. As he sits on the banks of the lake in a contemplative mood, he is joined by

Brahmadatta, the disciple of Maharṣi Gopāda. Satyakāma is pleased to meet Brahmadatta, a fellow traveller on the path, yearning to get *brahma-jñāna.* He greets him joyously and both the ardent seekers settle down again for some prayer and meditation.

Soon they espy a huge *maṇḍūka* coming towards them in large hops. Brahmadatta becomes alarmed that it is an attack by the giant *maṇḍūka* and gets ready with sticks for a counter-attack. However Satyakāma is calm and he even suspects it may be Lord Varuṇa in disguise, whose arrival he had been eagerly awaiting. Anyway he puts his lot in Lord Varuṇa's hand and continues his prayer. To their surprise the *maṇḍūka,* reaching near, abruptly changes into Lord Varuṇa. Both the disciples are speechless with wonder and prostrate in front of Lord Varuṇa seeking his blessings. Soon Gopāda Maharṣi also enters the scene. They all retire to Gopāda's *āśrama* where Lord Varuṇa preaches the *Māṇḍūkya Upaniṣad* totalling just twelve verses which incisively and with great precision talk about the Truth, about the reality surrounding us. The *Māṇḍūkya Upaniṣad* is the one which very clearly talks about the Advaita or non-dual state of this universe. Many scholars have tried to make people understand the import of these twelve verses. The most acknowledged among the explanatory commentaries called *Kārika* is the one by Mahāguru Gauḍapāda who is the grand *guru* of Ādi Śaṅkara.

The *ṛṣi* of *Māṇḍūkya Upaniṣad* adopts an exemplary way to make the pupil understand the *Brahman* which is beyond the mind. He relates it to the word *oṁ* and says that by meditating on the word *oṁ* in all its entirety the *Brahman* can be understood. The disciples are surprised. They are unable to grasp how a word can be related to *Brahman*? Lord Varuṇa explains that a sound and what it represents are inseparable. By relating every *mantra* by which *oṁkāra* is pronounced to *Brahman* it is possible to understand *Brahman,* states the *ṛṣi* emphatically. Going on a parallel path it is explained the *ātmā* which is *jīva* is part of *Brahman* (*paramātmā*). This *jīva/ātmā* has four states, *jāgarita, svapna, suṣupti* and *turīya* or it also can be termed as waking, dream, deep sleep and *turīya*. These four states of *ātmā* can be related with the letter *oṁ*. The letter *oṁ* has four *mātrās*.

They are *A, U, M* and a silence in the end. These correspond to the *jāgarita, svapna, suṣupti* and *turīya* state of the *jīva/ātmā*. From the third *mantra* to seventh *mantra* the equation of *oṁkāra* to the four states of *jīvātmā* is explained vividly. The *A-kāra* representing the *jāgarita* state is termed as Vaiśvānara. He is consious of the external world and enjoys the gross objects. The *U-kāra* representing the *svapna* state is termed as *taijasa*. He is the dream state who is consious of the internal world and enjoys the subtle objects of the mental world.

The *M-kāra* representing the *suṣupti* state is termed as *prajñā*. It is the deep sleep state in which all experiences become unified in an undifferentiated, homogeneous mass of consciousness.

The fourth silent state is related to *turīya*. As this state is pure *ātman* and difficult to describe, as it is beyond words, it is described by a negation method. It is neither a mass of consciousness nor unconsciousness. Some positive descriptions are also given. It is peaceful, auspicious, non-dual and that is the *ātmā* which has to be understood.

Thus it is seen that *turīya* is the real state which has to be known. But still the other three states are described because only by negating the *dharma* of the three states it is possible to know *turīya* which is the true thing and all others are unreal. It is not only *svapna* state which is unreal and can be easily understood and agreed to by any lay person, but the *jāgarita* state where we see gross objects is also equally unreal says the Upaniṣad. Thus there is no creation and no dissolution as everything is in the realm of imagination. These emphatic statements of Advaita are difficult to fathom by the disciples who are conditioned to regard the world and the objects around them as real. Hence they want to know, if they are not real how they are seen, felt and heard. It is a difficult task to drive home the Advaita philosophy where both the *guru* and the *śiṣya* are engulfed by the world of *māyā* or illusion. Only through a seer who has experienced the *turīya* state and known the truth of non-dual status of the world can one know that the first three states are not real.

Then the disciples want to know, how then the non-real gross objects are created. Lord Varuṇa explains how the *māyā śakti* operates. The *ātmā* is self-effulgent, illuminating and it is also called consciousness. This consiousness is the womb of all things. Through the instruments of mind and intellect this consciousness is projected outwards creating gross objects and it is projected inside creating dream objects. However all things are in the world of imagination only and they have no reality. Without consicousness there is no sun, moon or stars. A dead man having no consciousness to project cannot perceive the sun even if it shines right in front of him. Thus without consciousness acting through the mind and intellect, the world does not exist. The *jīva* is lulled into wakefulness, sleep, dream and sufferings. Crossing that, once he reaches the soundless *turīya,* then he comes out of the cause-effect cycle and also out of *jāgarita, svapna* and *suṣupti* states and reaches *Brahman.* Thus by relating *Brahma*-knowledge to *oṁkāra* the seer has succeeded in explaining the incomprehensible *Brahman.*

The *oṁkāra* is split into four parts, the *A, U, M mātrā*s and a silent part in the end. Now the *ātmā* is also described in four parts, the waking, dreaming, sleeping states represented by *A, U, M* and the last silent part is *turīya.* Then the seer has gently brought out the startling fact that the first three states are not real, as they are not permanent and they are mere projections of our consciousness through the instrument of mind and intellect. The last one alone is real which is the all-pervasive *Brahman,* and it is non-dual as well as bliss personified. This essence of the scripture is beautifully explained thus: "In the body the *jīva* has three states, *jāgarita, svapna* and *suṣupti,* and apart from that, has also the state of *turīya.* During *jāgarita* state the outside world is known by sense organs. In *svapna* he comes to know the mind-induced things and their forms. In sleep there is nothing to see, no forms which are attached to any thought attractions. However there is wisdom and happiness which cannot be described. In *turīya* the *jīva* comes to know its true state. For doing *upāsanā*, *oṁkāra* is the most exalted representation. If *upāsanā* is done on *oṁkāra* with *Brahman* in mind then it will act as an apt tool to reach *Brahman.* Staying in *samādhi* when the *oṁkāra* is visualized with gross as *A-ātmasvarūpa* (*jāgarita* state), subtle as *U-kāra* (*svapna* state), the cause of both as *M-kāra* (*suṣupti* state) and the cause and effect of all of them as *turīya* state, then the *ātma-jñānī* gets immersed in that and becomes one with the Self, a non-dual state.

# The Drama

**Characters**

**Lord Varuṇa** – The Lord who preaches.

**Satyakāma** – A disciple of the Maharṣi Pippalāda, and Ṛṣi Śibi's son.

**Brahmadatta** – A disciple of the Maharṣi Gopāda.

**Gopāda** – Brahmarṣi.

(Other actors, Sūtradhāra, *āśrama* residents and the rest.)

**Venue** – The first scene and the last scene are in Śaṅkara Maṭha. Other scenes are in Himālayan mountain regions.

## SCENE 1

### *(At Śaṅkara Maṭha)*

(Behind the screen the *Śānti pāṭha* is being recited.)

॥ॐ भद्रं कर्णेभिः श्रृणुयाम देवाः। भद्रं पश्येमाक्षभिर्यजत्राः।
स्थिरैरङ्गैस्तुष्टुवाꣳसस्तनूभिः। व्यशेम देवहितं यदायुः॥

*oṁ bhadraṁ karnebhiḥ śṛṇuyāma devāḥ bhadraṁ paśyemākṣabhir yajatrāḥ* ।
*sthirair aṅgais tuṣṭuvāṁ̐ sastanūbhiḥ vyaśema devahitaṁ yadāyuḥ* ।।

स्वस्ति न इन्द्रो वृद्धश्रवाः। स्वस्ति नः पूषा विश्ववेदाः।
स्वस्ति नस्ताक्ष्र्यो अरिष्टनेमिः। स्वस्ति नो बृहस्पतिर्दधातु॥

*svasti na indro vṛddhaśravāḥ svasti naḥ pūṣā viśvavedāḥ* ।
*svasti nas tārkṣyo ariṣṭanemiḥ svasti no bṛhaspatir dadhātu* ।।

॥ॐ शान्तिः। शान्तिः। शान्तिः॥

।। *oṁ śāntiḥ* । *śāntiḥ* । *śāntiḥ* ।।

*AUM*, May we, with our ears hear that which is auspicious, O Gods! may we, habitually offering oblations, see with our eyes that which is auspicious.

With strong bodies, singing your praises, may we live out our span of life destined to us by the gods.

May Indra of mature learning bestow well-being on us. May Pūṣā (the sun), the knower of all, bestow well-being on us. May Tārkṣya (Garuḍa) the annihilator of danger bestow well-being on us. May Bṛhaspati bestow well-being on us.

*AUM*, Peace! Peace! Peace!

(As the curtain opens Śaṅkara Maṭha is seen. From the right side Sūtradhāra and from the left side the actors are entering.)

**Sūtradhāra** – My *praṇāmas*, friend.

**Actor** – Accept my respects Sir.

**Sūtradhāra** – Have all preparations been completed for Śaṅkara *Jayantī*? Has the *dharmādhikārī* told you that a drama has to be enacted?

**Actor** – Almost all preparations have been carried out. Regarding the drama, he has asked me to consult with you and decide.

**Sūtradhāra** – Is that so! Very good. As per his wish we will enact a good drama.

**Actor** – Which drama can be enacted in a short time? All the dramas, which our group enacted took more than two hours. Now the *dharmādhikārī* is telling us that since *upanyāsa* and other programmes are there, not more than half an hour can be alloted for this drama.

**Sūtradhāra** – The drama we have proposed is a small one, even half an hour may not be required for this new drama. Many actors are also not required. Also, a lot of costumes and scenes are not required as it can be completed in one part.

**Actor** – Friend, Āha! what an ability you have. Do tell me the details of this short drama.

**Sūtradhāra** – Alright, friend. The title of this drama is *Māṇḍūkya Upaniṣad*. It is the smallest of all the Upaniṣads and it has an interesting name. The word *maṇḍūka* means "a frog." It belongs to *Atharvaveda*. It consists of only twelve *mantras*. It has been preached by Lord Varuṇa. It is difficult to extol all its virtue. To get salvation for seekers of *mokṣa* this one *Māṇḍūkya* itself is enough, so say *brahma-jñānīs*.

**Actor** – Very well. We are grateful to you for getting ready to enact such a fine Upaniṣad drama. What could be the reason it is called *Māṇḍūkya Upaniṣad?*

**Sūtradhāra** – Many reasons can be stated for this name. The *ṛṣi* of this *Upaniṣad* is Lord Varuṇa. It is said that he came in the *maṇḍūka* (frog) form and preached it. Hence such a name could have come for this Upaniṣad. Another reason can be the mind of the *yogī* jumps like a frog, crosses three different states and when it reaches the fourth state; the experience it has is described here. Hence, it could have got such a name.

**Actor** – Let the name be anything. The jackfruit can be called by any name, still it will be sweet. Likewise, the lotus flower even if it is called by another name, it will emit its fragrance. What we require is a drama having a good theme. We will co-operate and act, win the love and respect of the viewers and get their blessings also.

**Sūtradhāra** – Friend, as per your wish we will do it. The audiences are waiting. The worship and *āratī* is going on. Once it gets over with *jagadguru*'s blessing we will start the drama.

***(They leave, the curtain falls.)***

## SCENE 2

***(Curtain opens)***

(The Mānasarovara is seen in the Himālayas. Sitting along its banks Satyakāma is in deep contemplation. Brahmadatta enters.)

**Brahmadatta** – (**walking around**) This place is so beautiful. The Mānasarovara lake is so soothing and wonderful to look at. Like the mind of the people doing *tapas* (penance) it is very clear. Mother Nature, with unsurpassable beauty is present here. Indeed it is a majestic appearance and a rare beauty. The swans are looking so peaceful and playing about. In the north, Mount Kailāsa is shining like a silver mountain. This mountain path seen here, this should be the place where the Pāṇḍavas must have travelled during *Dvāparayuga*. Far-off to the east we can see the Paśupatinātha mountains. To the south are the Nārāyaṇa mountains. Far-off to the west are Amaranātha mountains. Everywhere, nature's scenery is giving lot of peace of mind. It is a healthy and peaceful place both for the body and the mind. Once, if we get immersed in this beauty (*saundaryalaharī*) then we will forget ourselves and will be immersed in the ocean of happiness. Well, who is the one sitting on the banks of the lake? Is he Satyakāma? (goes near and sees). Yes, It is he only. What *tejas*! The *brahma-jñāna* is flowing in his face like a bright river. Indeed, it is the greatness of penance. It is the strength of *brahmacharya vrata* and the knowledge acquired from learning Vedas. All together is shining in his blissful soul. He must be a *puṇya ātmā* no doubt. What my Gurudeva Gopāda told won't go wrong. Going near and giving salutations let me enquire about his welfare. "Holy sir, salutations, I think you must be Satyakāma? Please bless this humble Brahmadatta (**going near tells *abhivādaye* and salutes**).

**Satyakāma** – (**startled, gets up a bit confused**) You? — How did you come to know me? Who are you? I am the disciple of Maharṣi Pippalāda and the great sage Śibi's son Satyakāma.

**Brahmadatta** – I am the disciple of Gopāda Brahmarṣi. Gopāda's *āśrama* is at Gaṅgotrī. I came here yesterday. My *guru* has sent me here to understand still higher principles of *praṇava upāsanā*. While coming my *guru* told me "Satyakāma has come to Mānasarovara and for the last one year, he is doing penance to know the higher truths. He may receive preaching very soon. If you go there you will also get benefited." Hence I have come here and got the fortune of seeing you in person. I am blessed indeed.

**Satyakāma** – (**with great joy**) I am very happy to hear that. Did Maharṣi Gopāda say that I may receive preaching today? I came here last rainy season. When I asked my *guru* he directed me to come here and do *upāsanā* of Lord Varuṇa. Following that I am doing penance here. I am chanting the *mantra* **इमं मे वरुण श्रुधीहवं** (*imaṁ me varuṇa śrudhīhavaṁ*) constantly. I am happy to see you. Do come and sit here. Let us do the *japa* together.

(Both are doing *pāda prakṣālaṇam* (washing the feet) and *ācamanam* (ablutions), then sitting facing north, they start doing the *japa*. Maharṣi Gopāda along with the *āśrama* residents is standing behind the *devadāra* tree and hearing it. He is not noticed by the two doing *japa*.)

**Brahmadatta** – Friend, did you notice this? The frogs are jumping here and there. Usually, if any living being has to leave a place it will do so only after getting hold of another place. However the *maṇḍūka* (frog) is not like that.

**Satyakāma** – Yes, I have also noticed. A worm, when it travels from one leaf to another leaf, crawls slowly, rises up, elongates itself and catches the new leaf gradually and then leaves the old leaf. However the frogs non-chalantly jump and move about. See that one big frog is coming from inside the *sarovara*. Seeing that, the other frogs are getting scared and jump about.

**Brahmadatta** – Yes, my friend. That huge frog is coming towards us. As it is coming, it is getting bigger and bigger. How fearful its eyes and legs are! It comes eating the small fish, bees and other insects with its long tongue.

**Satyakāma** – It is seen bigger and bigger. Is it increasing in size? Or is it because it is coming nearer and nearer? Anyway, our *japa* has been disturbed. Let us get up and see. (**Both get up and observe keenly the *maṇḍūka*.**)

**Brahmadatta** – My dear friend, it is not an ordinary frog. I think it is some plot of the demons to disturb our penance and *japa yajña*. I think one *rākṣasa* is coming over here in the form of this frog. See that when it opens its mouth how scary it looks. We should attack it. Let us go and bring a stick from the nearby *devadāra* tree and beat it.

**Gopāda** – (**within himself**) Brahmadatta is a man who suspects easily and he is a bit gusty too. In truth isn't it Lord Varuṇa himself in *maṇḍūka* form? Before he spoils the matter I must go near. Well, well, let it be. Let me see what Satyakāma is going to do.

**Satyakāma** – Friend, don't come to some hasty conclusion. A person who makes hasty decisions will come to regret them. One can't predict what is hiding behind an appearance. Perhaps Lord Varuṇa has come in disguise in *maṇḍūka* form. Let us not lose our cool. Let us wait and watch.

**Brahmadatta** – Why should the one who is coming to preach us, come like this? He should rise and come in a divine form on a crocodile vehicle. Isn't that more fitting? I have no doubt that this frog in front of us is a *rākṣasa*. It is becoming bigger and bigger like a huge whale. Seeing this frog itself is very fearful. Only our preceptor can save us. If you don't want to come, be here. I will go and bring the sticks from the *devadāra* tree.

(The *maṇḍūka* opens its mouth widely, protrudes its tongue, rolls its eyes and raises a huge terrifying sound. Brahmadatta is about to fall down. Satyakāma holds him.)

**Satyakāma** – Don't be afraid, friend! The one who doubts will get destroyed. Leave off suspicion. Let us again do *ācamanam* and continue the *japa*. If the *maṇḍūka* who is coming is Lord Varuṇa he will come near and initiate us gracefully. In case what you say is true then also we will surrender to Lord Varuṇa and continue the *japa*. It is his duty to protect us.

**Brahmadatta** – Friend! As per your wish we will do. (Both washing their hands and face, do *ācamanam* and continue the *japa*.)

**Gopāda** – (**within himself**) Well done! Satyakāma is very smart. He has done everything correctly. Now Lord Varuṇa will reveal his presence. Let us also do *japa*. (**He and other *āśrama* residents sit below the *devadāra* tree and do *japa*.**)

(That time, like thousand lights shining at once, a bright light is seen in Mānasarovara. The huge *māṇḍūka* changes its shape and becomes Lord Varuṇa in his crocodile vehicle. Everybody seeing this wonder becomes very happy and offer their salutations. Gopāda also comes out from behind the tree.)

*fig* : **Maṇḍūka becomes lord Varuṇa**

**Gopāda** – Lord Varuṇa, let your arrival bring good tidings. You, with your divine holy words kindly preach to the disciples and enlighten them.

**Satyakāma** – O divine Lord Varuṇa! Salutations. I salute you with all humility. You must kindly heed to this humble being's prayers and bless us. You must clear our doubts. You must show us your grace. By preaching to us, you must make us the blessed ones. You must forgive our misgivings if any and bless us. You must make us deserving of your grace and blessings. Eh! Master, our *praṇāmas* to you again and again.

**Brahmadatta** – O god of gods! Protector of the entire world, our *namaskārams* to you. You must forgive our misapprehensions and preach to us. You must kindly pardon the utterings I did some time back due to my ignorance. Save me, the sinner. Eh, lord, possesser of noose in the hand! The one who has great affection for the devotees, kindly protect us and save us. Once again I offer my salutations and pray to you to forgive us. O Lord! Master! Even as the father forbears the son's fault and protects him, so also you must protect us and bless us.

**Varuṇa** – Children, don't worry. I have come to protect you. You have not done any such mistakes which call for forgiveness (addressing Gopāda) friend, my *praṇāmas* to you. Are *dhyāna, samādhi, yoga* (meditation, concentration, contemplation) practised properly? Is your *āśrama* always open for disciples' arrival? Is every one keeping well?

*fig :* **Lord Varuṇa is preaching.**

**Gopāda** – My dear friend. By the grace of the lord and with your blessings everything is going on well. From all sides lots of disciples keep coming. Whatever you are going to preach to them, I request you to kindly do in the *āśrama* so that it will help the other disciples too. You must kindly shower your kindness, dear one.

**Varuṇa** – We will do so. I consider it my great fortune to do the preaching in the *āśrama* of Brahmarṣi Gopāda.

**Gopāda** – I am immensely pleased. Come, let us go to the *āśrama*.

**(They leave.)**

***(Curtain falls.)***

SCENE 3

(Maharṣi Gopāda's *āśrama* is seen. Facing north Lord Varuṇa and Maharṣi Gopāda are sitting. Satyakāma, Brahmadatta and other disciples are seated nearby. The conversation is continuing.)

**Varuṇa** – Dear children, now I am going to preach to you all about *oṁkāra*. Listen carefully. If you have any doubt ask immediately. I will clear it. Friends! You also listen and correct whatever mistakes arise.

हरिः ओम्। ओमित्येतदक्षरमिदꣳ सर्वं तस्योपव्याख्यानं भूतं भवद्भविष्यदिति सर्वमोङ्कार एव। यच्चान्यत्त्रिकालातीतं तदप्योङ्कार एव ॥१॥

*hariḥ aum, aum-ityetad-akṣaram-idaṁ sarvaṁ tasyopavyākhyānaṁ bhūtaṁ bhavad-bhaviṣyad iti sarvam-oṁkāra eva, yac-cānyat-trikālātītaṁ tadapyoṁkāra eva* ॥ 1 ॥

*Hariḥ oṁ*, *oṁ*, the word is all this. A clear explanation of it is (the following): All that is past, present and future, verily, is *oṁ*. That which is beyond the three periods of time is also, indeed *oṁ*.

Now I will explain it. *Oṁ*, this word is everything. The explanation of that is whatever happened, is happening and is going to happen, everything is *oṁkāra*. What is beyond the three periods of time all these also is *oṁkāra*.

**Satyakāma** – Sadguru, what does "all these" mean! Do tell more elaborately and in detail.

**Varuṇa** – "All these" means — whatever is being seen. Whatever things we know, are nothing but this *oṁ,* that is, everything is contained in *praṇava.*

**Brahmadatta** – Svāmī, when you tell a thing is contained in a word, the meaning is not clear. Please do explain it further.

**Varuṇa** – This universe and all its creation is *Brahman*'s act. *Praṇava* is told as the symbolic representative of *Brahman.* The sound *oṁ* is the body of *Brahman,* the lustre inside it is *Brahman.* From the sound *oṁ* arose all other sounds in the universe. With these sounds all objects are named. Since all things have been named with the sounds emanating from *praṇava,* those things are contained in *praṇava,* so says the Veda.

**Gopāda** – Yes. A very wonderful explanation. *Oṁ* and the sound related to that are all the words which we use. *Oṁ* and the things which are named by these words, that is, the words or the sounds and the things they represent, both are inseparable. This we should understand.

**Varuṇa** – Thanks for the explanation given by our friend. Here this *kamaṇḍalam* (water jug) is the *ka-ma-ṇ-ḍa-la-m,* these letters join together and become a word *kamaṇḍalam.* One cannot separate from this *kamaṇḍalam* the letters *ka-ma-ṇ-ḍa-la-m.* Thus the sound and the thing it represents are inseparable. These letters have originated from the *praṇava-oṁ.* Hence everything is termed *oṁ.* This will also apply to all three periods of time, according to *śruti*s. Further, what is past is over, now what is happening is present, what is going to happen is future and all that is *oṁkāra.* Further, anything beyond this time period is also *oṁkāra.*

**Satyakāma** – What is beyond the three time periods?

**Varuṇa** – The one which crosses the three time periods is *avyaktam* in nature, that is it merges into *Brahman.* This is responsible for time and other things. That is also *oṁkāra,* so say the *śruti*s.

**Satyakāma** – You told us that all the things we see and know are things which have names having sounds arising from *oṁkāra,* they all are contained in *oṁkāra*. Hence to know all things *oṁkāra* becomes a way. That is what I understand. But how will this be useful to understand *Brahman*?

**Varuṇa** – I will tell you about this in detail. The entire universe is *oṁkāra.* The world which is *praṇava* and the matter which is universe is one and the same. This universe which is termed as *oṁkāra* sound is nothing but *Brahman*. As all the universe is contained in *oṁkāra,* and if grasping that one crosses over then the all-encompassing *Brahman* can be easily understood. However don't think this *Brahman* is somewhere far. That *Brahman* is in our body as a reality always shining brightly. The *ātmā* of ours has four parts.

सर्वं᳭ ह्येतद् ब्रह्मायमात्मा ब्रह्म सोऽयमात्मा चतुष्पात् ॥२॥

*sarvaṁ hyetad brahma ayamātmā brahma | so 'yamātmā catuṣpāt* | |2| |

All this is verily *Brahman*. This *ātman* is *Brahman*. This *ātman* has four quarters (parts).

**Brahmadatta** – Sadguru, after having said that everything is undifferentiated, how can it be said that *ātmā* has four parts. I do not understand the meaning.

**Varuṇa** – This *ātmā* that is *jīva* is *Brahman*. This *jīva* is in four states. *Śruti* is explaining about all the four states in detail.

**Gopāda** – Children, four parts does not mean that like a cow has four legs, the *ātmā* has four parts. Now friend, kindly preach further.

**Varuṇa** –

जागरितस्थानो बहिः प्रज्ञः सप्ताङ्ग एकोनविंशतिमुखः स्थूलभुग्वैश्वानरः प्रथमः पादः ॥३॥

*jāgarita-sthāno bahiḥ-prajñaḥ saptāṅga ekonaviṁśati mukhaḥ sthūla-bhuk vaiśvānaraḥ prathamaḥ pādaḥ* | |3| |

> The first quarter (*pāda*) is Vaiśvānaraḥ whose sphere of activity is the waking state, who is conscious of the external world of objects, who has seven limbs and nineteen mouths, and who enjoys the gross objects of the world.

The first part is Vaiśvānara who represents the gross. He has seven organs, nineteen faces and feeling of outer things and has a resting place in waking consciousness. Among the four states, the first state is in *jāgarita* — waking state. He is the one who is interested in external things. He has head, eye, *prāṇa*, body, urinary point, feet, face thus seven body parts. Further five *jñāna* (sense) *indriyas*, five *karma indriyas*, five *prāṇas*, four *antaḥkaraṇas* (mind, intellect, ego, and *chit*) thus having nineteen faces. Since with these he enjoys the pleasures of the world they are termed as faces.

**Satyakāma** – Svāmī! If there is any special meaning for the word *vaiśvānara* do kindly tell.

**Varuṇa** – The *virāṭ puruṣa* who is *samiṣṭi* of everything gross and is in the form of *nara* (man) is called Vaiśvānara (Universal ego). For all *naras* (humans) as per their fruits of *karma* they are made to enjoy happiness and sorrow. Now we will see the second *pādam*.

स्वप्नस्थानोऽन्तःप्रज्ञः सप्ताङ्ग एकोनविंशतिमुखः प्रविविक्तभुक् तैजसो द्वितीयः पादः ॥४॥

*svapna-sthāno 'ntaḥ-prajñaḥ saptāṅga ekona-viṁśati-mukhaḥ pravi-vikta-bhuk taijaso dvitīyaḥ pādaḥ* ||4||

> The second quarter (*pāda*) is Taijasa, whose sphere of activity is the dream-state, who is conscious of the internal world of objects, who has seven limbs and nineteen mouths and who enjoys the subtle objects of the mental world.

The second part's resting place is dream (*svapna*). The name is Taijasa. He has inner knowledge. However he has no outside consciousness. He has seven organs and nineteen faces like Vaiśvānara. He experiences the subtle field.

**Brahmadatta** – I suppose there is not much difference between Taijasa and Vaiśvānara.

**Gopāda** – There are some similarities and some differences. For both, the organs are seven and the faces nineteen, but for the rest everything else is different. As Vaiśvānara is in the conscious state and experiences the outside world, Taijasa experiences the subtle world in dreams. During *jāgarita* (waking) state the experience is by all the sense organs while in *svapna* state the experience is by the mind.

**Varuṇa** – Now let us see what the Veda tells us about the third part.

यत्र सुप्तो न कंचन कामं कामयते। न कंचन स्वप्नं पश्यति तत्सुषुप्तम्।
सुषुप्तस्थान एकीभूतः प्रज्ञानघन एवानन्दमयो ह्यानन्दभुक् चेतोमुखः प्राज्ञ-
तृतीयः पादः ॥५॥

*yatra supto na kañcana kāmaṁ kāmayate na kañcana svapnaṁ paśyati, tat suṣuptam | suṣupta-sthāna ekībhūtaḥ prajñāna-ghana evā-nandamayo hyānanda-bhuk ceto-mukhaḥ prājña tṛtīyaḥ pādaḥ ||5||*

That is the state of deep-sleep wherein the sleeper does not desire any objects, nor does he see any dream. The third quarter (*pāda*) is the *prājña* whose sphere is deep-sleep, in whom all (experiences) become unified or undifferentiated, who is verily a homogeneous mass of entire consciousness, who is full of bliss, who is indeed an enjoyer of bliss and who is the very gateway for the projection of consciousness into the other two planes of consciousness — the dream and the waking.

The third part is the *prājña,* the one who enjoys happiness. He stands as a single entity. It is the resting place of happiness (*ānandamaya*). It is also called the *suṣupti* state. It is a state where there is no desire, no dreams, and the deep-sleep state is *suṣupti.*

**Satyakāma** – Sadguru, it is not understood properly. Kindly explain it clearly.

**Gopāda** – Children, I will tell you about it more clearly. The state in which a person without desiring anything, without seeing any dreams, sleeps deeply that is the state of *suṣupti*. This is the third state of *ātmā*. This is called *prajñā*. He is the personification of happiness hence called *ānandamaya*. His face is *chit*. In this state he becomes one with *Brahman*.

**Satyakāma** – I realized at the time of deep sleep there are no wishes and dreams. However what is the meaning of becoming one with *Brahman*, called as *ānandamaya* and *chit* has its face, etc.

**Gopāda** – The things we see in the day, when night comes cannot be differentiated and become one with the darkness. However they don't lose their characteristics, they don't lose their identity. For example, what we see in front of us during day light here, this *kamaṇḍala* (water jug), the reed mat, wooden seat, *pañcapātra* (*pūjā* vessel) here cannot be distinguished in the night and become one homogeneous darkness with the night. When light comes, they are seen again distinctly as separate things. Likewise the acts and things seen during *jāgarita* (waking state) and *svapna* (dream) becomes undifferentiated during *suṣupti* (deep sleep). *Ānanda* means one devoid of sorrow. Since there is no desire there is no sorrow. It is a sorrowless state, hence he enjoys happiness in this state. That is why when he gets up he tells he slept fitfully or happily. This is expressed by the *śruti* by saying that he experiences happiness.

**Satyakāma** – What is the meaning of calling *prajña* as *cheta*s faced ?

**Gopāda** – The word *chetas* represents *svapna* and *jāgarita* states. However the route or the passage to these states is *suṣupti*. This is the base for the other two states. If the basic cause factor *suṣupti* is not there the resultant *jāgarita* and *svapna* state also won't be there. To go from *suṣupti* state to *svapna* state and through that to go to *jāgarita* state the *chetas* (*chaitanya*) is the route. Whatever experience one gets in waking and *svapna* state gets mingled in the *chaitanya* form and is undifferentiated in sleep which remains as *prajñā* (wisdom). This *prajñā* (wisdom) is the base of all imaginations. But in sleep one may tend to say there is no knowledge, that is because in *suṣupti* along with the brightness, ignorance is also combined. The brightness is like a small lamp lit in a dark house. Here when viewed only the lamp light is seen in the darkness and nothing else can be made out hence the *śruti* denotes this state as *prajñā* (light of wisdom) state.

**Varuṇa** – Let us further hear what the *śruti* has to say.

> एष सर्वेश्वर एष सर्वज्ञ एषोऽन्तर्याम्येष योनिः सर्वस्य प्रभवाप्ययौ हि भूतानाम्
> ॥६॥
>
> *eṣa sarveśvara eṣa sarvajña eṣo 'ntaryāmy-eṣa yonīḥ*
> *sarvasya prabha-vāpyayau hi bhūtānām* ||6||
>
> This is the Lord of all, this is the knower of all, this is the inner controller, and this is the source of all. And, this is that from which all things originate and in which they finally dissolve themselves.

He is the *Īśvara* (lord) who rules everything. He is the one who knows everything. He is the one who conducts all life from inside. He is the source for everything, the appearance of everything born and final destination of everything.

**Gopāda** – The *śruti* further tells us about the *prajñā* which is the third state. It is the cause of every living thing. It is the *Īśvara* which creates, protects the living state and causes destruction. It is the *prajñā* which acts as *antaryāmī,* that is the one who knows everything inside out. Even as the world gets created from *Īśvara,* gets stabilized in Him during living process and finally gets annihilated and becomes one with Him, the states of *jāgarita* and *svapna* comes out of *suṣupti* and finally becomes one with it.

**Varuṇa** – Today the explanations of the three states have been told. The lessons about the fourth state can be told tomorrow. Children, think well about whatever you learned today, discuss among yourselves and if any doubt arises ask tomorrow. Is it alright, my friend?

**Gopāda** – Very much alright. The afternoon is approaching. Let us go to the river.

*(They get up. The curtain falls.)*

## SCENE 4

***(Curtain opens.)***

(As in the previous scene all are sitting and conversing.)

**Varuṇa** – Children! Did you think well about the lessons taught yesterday?

**Satyakāma** – Sadguru! We thought well. We also discussed among ourselves. We understand the truth to some extent.

**Gopāda** – Can you tell in brief what you have understood?

**Satyakāma** – Inside our minds everything is clear. But how to describe it seems to be difficult.

**Brahmadatta** – Svāmī! Everything of course appears clear. But to express it seems to be difficult. You must only again kindly tell it in short.

**Gopāda** – Children! Don't worry. I will only tell you in short and try to further clarify it. Listen carefully. Everything is *Brahman*. The word and the thing it represents is all *Brahman*. There is no difference between them. This *ātmā* and *jīva* is *Brahman*. *Ayam ātmā brahman* this is one of the salient *mantras* of *Atharvaveda*. This *ātmā* is known by different names as Vaiśvānara, Taijasa, Prajñā, etc. Vaiśvānara is the one having outer consciousness. He is the right eye; the resting place is the waking state. He enjoys gross experiences (*sthūla bhogas*). He gets satisfied with that. This is the first stage. The second stage is dream with inner consciousness. He enjoys the subtle experiences (*sūkṣma bhogas*). He gets satisfied with that. The third stage is the sleep with *prajñā* form of consciousness. *Prajñā* does not have any special desire. He enjoys happiness. He has no desire for experiences and forms. He is the only one. He is the *Brahman.* Crossing these three stages the fourth stage is *turīya*. The *oṁkāra upāsanā* helps the *sādhaka* to reach that state.

**Satyakāma** – Sadguru! It is clearly understood. Now kindly tell us about the fourth stage.

**Gopāda** – Friend! Do preach, the disciples are eager to listen.

**Varuṇa** – So be it. I shall teach.

> नान्तःप्रज्ञं न बहिःप्रज्ञं नोभयतःप्रज्ञं न प्रज्ञानघनं न प्रज्ञं नाप्रज्ञम्।
> अदृष्टमव्यवहार्यमग्राह्यमलक्षणमचिन्त्यमव्यपदेश्यमेकात्मप्रत्ययसारं
> प्रपञ्चोपशमं शान्तं शिवमद्वैतं चतुर्थं मन्यन्ते स आत्मा स विज्ञेयः ॥७॥
>
> *nāntaḥprajñaṁ na bahiḥprajñaṁ nobhayataḥprajñaṁ na prajñāna-ghanaṁ na prajñaṁ nāprajñam | adr̥ṣṭam-avyavahāryam-agrāhyam-alakṣaṇam-acintyam-avyapad eśyam-ekātmapratyaya-sāraṁ prapañcopaśamaṁ śāntaṁ śivam-advaitaṁ caturthaṁ manyante sa ātmā sa vijñeyaḥ ||7||*
>
> It is not that which is conscious of the internal subjective world or the outer world, nor that which is conscious of both, nor that which is a mass of consciousness, nor that which is simple consciousness, nor is it unconsciousness. It is unseen by any sense-organ, beyond empirical dealings, incomprehensible by the mind, uninferable, unthinkable, and indescribable, but, could be understood essentially by the knowledge of the Self alone, negation of all phenomena, the peaceful, the auspicious and the non- dual. This is what is considered as the Fourth (*turīya*). This is the *ātman* and this is to be realised.

The one that is considered the fourth part (*pāda*) state is not conscious of the internal subjective world nor of the outer. It is unseen by any sense organ, beyond empirical dealings, incomprehensible by the mind, uninferable, unthinkable and indescribable. However it could be understood essentially by the knowledge that the Self is only one, negation of all phenomena, the peaceful, the auspicious and non-dual. This is what is considered as the fourth (*turīya*). He is the *ātman* and he should be realized. All the teachings are only to know Him. The one who is considered the fourth part has no outer consciousness, no inner consciousness. He is not a form of consciousness neither is he unconciousness. He is not the knower. He is not the one who has *chetana*. He cannot be seen. He cannot be described. He cannot be grasped. He does not have any characteristic. He cannot be thought about. He cannot be pointed out and shown. Only through the knowledge that there is only one *ātmā,* he can be known. He does not have any *prapañca* (worlds). He is peace, Śiva, undifferentiated one. He is only *ātmā.* He is the one worthy to be understood. All these preachings are to know Him.

**Satyakāma** – *Parama guru,* nothing is understood.

**Brahmadatta** – Everything is in confusion. Kindly tell us the meaning of all these and bless us.

**Gopāda** – The *turīya* state cannot be contained in counting. Still to show it is different from the other three states it was mentioned as the fourth state. I will tell you one example by which you can easily understand. You must have seen the magic shown by the magician.

**Brahmadatta** – Yes I have seen it. When we went to Mithilā city there in the street leading to the king's palace, I have seen these acts.

**Satyakāma** – I have also seen. Once when I went to the *Kumbha-melā* with my father I have seen it.

**Gopāda** – The magician comes. He throws a rope in the sky. He takes various weapons and walks over it. Then he is cut by those weapons and falls down into many pieces. However finally he gets up without any wound and walks about. We conclude that all this is *māyā*, just magic. The magician is just standing, the acts right from throwing the rope in the air till cutting himself into pieces, later getting up, all that are just magic. Some way of hoodwinking us. In the same way, *jāgarita* (waking), *svapna* (dream) and *suṣupti* (sleep) these stages are just passing phases. The fourth state is the *paramārtha tattva* (the real *ātmā*). We can see the three states — *jāgarita, svapna,* and *suṣupti.* The fourth state is different from them. It is not seen. To show that, it is termed as fourth by the *Upaniṣad.* Only for practical usage it is named *turīya.* But in reality the first three states being false, it may not be correct to call this as the fourth. It is the ultimate real and *paramārtha* state.

**Satyakāma** – It is somewhat understood. Still to understand it well kindly explain each word. I humbly request you, O good preceptor! Be kind enough.

**Varuṇa** – Children! I will explain that.

*Na antaḥprajñam* (न अन्तःप्रज्ञम्) — Not conscious of the internal world. This tells us that *turīya* is not *taijasa* which is in the state of *svapna.*

*Na bahiḥprajñam* (न बहिः प्रज्ञम्) — Not conscious of the external world. This tells us that *turīya* is not *jāgarita* state which is in the state of waking.

*Na ubhayataḥprajñam* (न उभयतःप्रज्ञम्) — Not in the state in between *jāgarita* and *svapna.*

*Na prajñāna ghanam* (न प्रज्ञान घनम्) — Not a mass of consciousness. This tells that *turīya* is not *suṣupti* state which is the state of deep sleep.

*Na prajñam* (न प्रज्ञम्) — Not the all-knowing consciousness. However since it is considered *na prajñam* it should not be thought of as an inert thing. Hence it is also described as *na aprajñam* (न अप्रज्ञम्) — Not unconsciousness.

Let us find out further what the *śruti* says. Since it cannot be seen by our sense organs or mind it is beyond perception.

Since it has no identity it cannot be cognized. It cannot be thought of by mind and cannot be explained by sounds or words.

**Brahmadatta** – If it is continued to be described like this won't it end in *śūnya* or emptiness.

**Varuṇa** – Child, there is no *śūnya* or emptiness, thus *śruti* confirms clearly. *Ekātma-pratyaya-sāram* (एकात्मप्रत्ययसारम्) traceable through unbroken Self-awareness. That is, by wisdom the *turīya* state can be understood. By perceiving by wisdom that it is the same *ātmā* which penetrates the three stages, the *jāgarita, svapna,* and *suṣupti,* one can know *turīya* state. This state is devoid of *prapañca* (worlds) which is the expansion of the *pañcabhūta* (five elements).

**Gopāda** – *Turīya* does not have the *dharma* which *prajña* and others have. This *śruti* describes by the word *prapañcopaśamam* (प्रपञ्च उपशामम्) free from the world of phenomena.

**Varuṇa** – Hence the *turīya* is described as tranquil, *śāntam* (शान्तम्), unchanging and he is *advaitam* (अद्वैतम्) one without differentiation — non-dual. He is *śivaṁ* (शिवम्) auspicious, full of bliss. He is only *ātmā.* He is told as the fourth one. One should know Him only. These teachings are only for that.

**Satyakāma** – Sadguru, I have a doubt.

**Varuṇa** – Child, I am happy you are getting some doubts. I felt sorry when you told nothing was understood. Now since you have understood something, the doubts arise. Do ask, I will explain.

**Satyakāma** – Svāmī, you preached *so 'yam — ātmā catuṣpath* (सोऽयम् आत्मा चतुष्पथ्), that is, *ātmā* has four parts. First you described the three parts, since the fourth part is present how it can be described as *na antaḥ prajñam* (न अन्तः प्रज्ञम्) not conscious of the internal world.

**Varuṇa** – The one who has beautiful *chit,* it is a good question. The rope in dim light is seen in various ways as a snake, a stick, a crack on the face of earth. However these forms are not different from the rope. The rope only is seen as various forms. Here how can the rope be known as the rope? By negating that it is not the snake, it is not the stick, it is not the crack we can understand the true form of rope. That is, "what is seen as snake is not a snake but the rope."

Likewise, *jāgarita, svapna,* and *suṣupti,* in these states the *ātmā* which is present is the *turīya*. To preach this true state it is told that *ātmā* is not Vaiśvānara, it is not Taijasa, thus the *Upaniṣad* continues to negate. By these negations we are able to understand *turīya tattvam*. Instead of telling like that, if *turīya* is described as having different characteristics it may not be correct. Since there is no method in *Upaniṣad* to describe this self-effulgent *turīya,* it has to be described by negation. Further, since it is not known through preaching the *sādhaka* may think such a *tattva* is not there and he will subscribe to the *śūnya* principle. However it is told that the first three states are not the truth, by negating the three states one can understand the *turīya tattva* present in that. Thus, the *śruti* first describes the three state, of human beings and then tells *ātmā* does not have these three states and that the same *ātmā* when it detaches itself from the three states becomes *turīya*. Hence, to remove the *dharma* of the three states is the only way of knowing *turīya*.

**Satyakāma** – Sadguru! The doubt is cleared. Do continue to preach.

**Brahmadatta** – Svāmī, I have a doubt.

**Varuṇa** – Child, what is that? Do tell me.

**Brahmadatta** – Nothing much. Just . . .

**Varuṇa** – Don't be scared, do ask me.

**Brahmadatta** – When we told you we didn't understand anything then you said you were very much saddened. For our foolishness why should you feel unhappy? This is only my doubt.

**Varuṇa** – It is not anything difficult to preach an intelligent disciple. For that you don't require much expertise or sharp intellect. However to preach a person of dull intellect the *guru* requires good teaching abilities. But you are ideal and exalted disciples. You have learnt from great (*mahāns*). To such disciples of repute if I am not able to make something clear then it does not speak high of my expertise in teaching. Seeing my state only I felt saddened.

**Gopāda** – Friend, your humble talk indeed thrills me. There is no one who is capable of preaching like you, *na bhūto na bhaviśyati* (न भूतो न भविश्यति). Still you are telling this without any pride and with great humility. A full vessel does not make noise, whereas a half empty vessel makes a lot of noise. Child Satyakāma, tell us in short what you understood today.

**Satyakāma** – Master, I will do so. *Turīya* is not Taijasa, nor is he Vaiśvānara, nor is he the state in between them. He is also not *prajñana*. He does not have *prajñā* (consciousness), nor is he *aprajñā* (without consciousness). He cannot be seen, He cannot be described. He cannot be perceived, He cannot be identified. He can be understood only by the concept that there is only one *ātmā*. He is not involved in daily affairs of the world. He is *śāntam*, he is bliss, he is undifferentiated. He is only *ātmā*. He is the one to be known. Guru, if there are any mistakes please forgive me.

**Varuṇa** – Child! You have told in a very brief way but without anything being missed, without any mistakes. Well done! I praise you. With this, todays lesson is complete. Let, good prevail everywhere.

***(Everybody leaves. The curtain falls.)***

## SCENE 5

(As the curtain opens, as in the previous scene all are sitting and the preaching is taking place.)

**Brahmadatta** – Sadguru, we would like to know the *turīya* state a little more clearly. For that I would kindly request you to explain the characteristics of Vaiśvānara, Taijasa and *prajñā*.

**Varuṇa** – Saumya! What you are asking is a very good question. Once the characteristics of those three are properly stated then the status of *turīya* will emerge and shine by itself. I will tell you in detail, listen carefully. Once when you realize *turīya* you will be released from all sorrows. That is because *turīya* is the *prabhu* (lord), the one who rules, he has no changes. All other things are false. He is only the true thing. He is one having self-brightness, he is spread everywhere. The Vaiśvānara and Taijasa are conditioned by cause and effect factors. *Prajñā* is conditioned by cause alone. These conditions, that is, cause and effect both, are not there in *turīya.*

**Brahmadatta** – Svāmī! Kindly explain the condition of cause and effect.

**Varuṇa** – Action is the effect. Cause is the seed. That is, whatever acted on is the effect and the causative factor for it is the seed. First the truth gets hidden. Then it appears as different. When truth is known then one does not imbibe wrong knowledge. Since truth is not known, wrong assumptions and knowledge are accumulated. Thus the state of not grasping the right knowledge is the cause-seed. Because of that the wrong knowledge is acquired, namely *anāyata grahaṇam* (अनायत ग्रहणम्), grasping something apart from the truth is the cause which produces the effect of wrong action. The state of *jāgarita* (waking) and *svapna* (dream) are conditioned by the cause which is *anāyata grahaṇam* — wrong knowledge. In *prajñā* state also the truth is hidden. However there is no wrong knowledge. Hence *prajñā* is conditioned only by cause and not by effect. However in *turīya* state since the truth is known and as there is no wrong knowledge the *turīya* is not affected by cause and effect.

**Satyakāma** – Svāmī! We understood it very well. Do kindly continue to preach.

**Varuṇa** – *Prajñā* does not realize himself or anything else nor differentiates between truth and false. That is because he is in a state of sleep. In *prajñā* only the cause, *tattva grahaṇam* (तत्त्व ग्रहणम्), is there. Hence *prajña* is conditioned only by cause. Since the effect, the wrong knowledge, is not there *prajñā* is not conditioned by effect. However *turīya* has crossed *suṣupti* — *prajñā* — he knows everything all the time. As just in the sun which is always bright it is difficult to see the darkness or any kind of false brightness, in the same way the *turīya* which is ever-present, everywhere remains as wisdom personified bright entity and not conditioned by cause and effect. The first two, that is, Vaiśvānara and Taijasa are states of ignorance. In the first state the reality is in sleep and hence named as *tattva* ignorance. In the second state, the dream state, in which one is seen as another and this state of sleep is also named as *tattva ajñāna* (*tattva* ignorance). *Prajñā-suṣupti* state is without dreams and has only dreamless ignorant sleep. In *turīya* state there is no sleep and no dream. When one sees one thing as another he is said to be dreaming. A person who does not know the *tattva* or truth is lulled into the sleep of ignorance. When both these are destroyed the fourth state is reached. In *suṣupti* (*prajñā*) and *turīya* there is no wrong knowledge. However in *suṣupti* (*prajñā*) there is sleep in ignorance. In *turīya* the ignorance is removed.

**Gopāda** – Friend, your explanation is indeed exemplary. The *jīva* is lulled into *māyā* and is in a state of sleep in ignorance. When he rises from the state then he realizes the birthless, sleepless, dreamless, non-dual (Advaita) form of *turīya*.

**Varuṇa** – Yes, friend. The *jīva* which for a long time was immersed in *saṁsāra* is unaware of the original state. He meets sorrow in *jāgarita* and *svapna* states. "He is my son, she is my daughter, she is my wife, they are my parents, and this is my house, my cattle," thus thinking variedly he experiences happiness and sorrow. Thus he remains in the sleep of ignorance. When a kind-hearted *guru* who is well-versed in Vedānta *tattvas* approach him and preaches to him thus, "you are apart from the cause and effect cycle" then he wakes up, comes out of his unconscious state, understands his true state, and reaches the same by realizing the state.

**Brahmadatta** – Respected Sir, now I understand it very well. Do kindly continue to preach.

**Varuṇa** – Dear disciple, till now I have described the three states of *Brahman* and also a state which is apart from the three states. You may remember, initially I mentioned "*oṁkāra* is *Brahman.*" In that case the fourth state *Brahman* should also be fitted into *oṁkāra,* isn't it? Now I will preach about that.

> सोऽयमात्माऽध्यक्षरमोङ्काराऽधिमात्रं पादा मात्रा मात्राश्च पादा अकार उकारो मकार इति ॥८॥
>
> *so 'yam-ātmā 'dhyakṣaram-oṁkāro 'dhimātraṁ pada mātrā mātrāś-ca pada akāra ukāro makāra iti* ||8||
>
> The same *ātman* is again *AUM* from the point of view of the syllables. The *aum* with parts is viewed from the standpoint of its sounds or letters. The quarters are the letters (morae) and the letters are the quarters. The letters here are *A*, *U*, and *M*.

That *ātmā* that is *Brahman* when described by *oṁkāra* it is the *akṣara* or word *oṁ*. When *oṁkāra* is divided into parts it becomes *mātrā*s/morae. Those *mātrā*s are the parts of *ātmā.* Those *mātrā*s are *A-kāra, U-kāra* and *M-kāra.*

**Satyakāma** – It is not clearly understood, Master.

**Gopāda** – To persons belonging to *uttama* school of thoughts and *madhyama* school of thoughts who have more capacity to understand the truth, the true state of *ātmā* is explained by *atyāropa* (non-superimposition) methods, that is denial of wrong attributions to *ātmasvarūpa.* However those who don't have wisdom to understand the the true *tattva, ātma-tattva* is presented with *āropa* (superimpositon) methods. They are initiated into *dhyāna* and *ātma-tattva* is explained by *praṇava* concepts. The word representation of *ātmā* is *oṁ* which is *praṇava.* This is the name of the *ātmā.* By the argument the word and what it represents are one, it can be said the word *oṁ* which is the *praṇava* and the *ātmā* it represents are not different from each other. The *ātmā* has four *padas*, so is *oṁkāra* word which represents it in sound. The four parts of *oṁkāra* are represented by three *mātrās*/morae and the last part is silent. Thus *oṁkāra* has *A-kāra, U-kāra*, and *M-kāra* representing the three *pādas* of *ātmā*. Initially the *pādas* of *ātmā* were explained as Vaiśvānara, Taijasa, and *prajñā*. Hence here the *praṇava A-kāra* is Vaiśvānara, the *U-kāra* is Taijasa and *M-kāra* is *prajñā* and the silent last part is *turīya*.

**Varuṇa** – Children, I will now continue to preach to you all.

> जागरितस्थानो वैश्वानरोऽकारः प्रथमा मात्राप्तेरादिमत्त्वाद्वा आप्नोति ह वै सर्वान्कामानादिश्च भवति य एवं वेद ॥९॥
>
> *jāgarita-sthāno vaiśvānaro 'kāraḥ prathamā mātrā pterādi-matt-vād-vā āpnoti ha vai sarvān-kāmān-ādiśca bhavati ya evaṁ veda* | |9| |
>
> He who is Vaiśvānara having for his sphere of activity the waking state is *A* (अ), the first letter of *AUM*, on account of its "all-pervasiveness" or on account of "being the first" — these two are the common features in both. One who knows thus surely attains the fulfi'ment of all his desires and becomes the first or the fore·nost among all.

The first *mātrā, A-kāra* is the *jāgarita*'s (waking state) place whose lord is Vaiśvānara. That is because both have a spreading nature and also it is the first *mātra*. Whoever knows him this way attains all his wishes and becomes foremost in every sphere. Now I will tell you the next *mantra*.

> स्वप्नस्थानस्तैजस उकारो द्वितीया मात्रोत्कर्षादुभयत्वाद्वा उत्कर्षति ह वै ज्ञानसन्ततिं समानश्च भवति नास्याब्रह्मवित् कुले भवति य एवं वेद ॥१०॥
>
> *svapna-sthānas-taijasa ukāro dvitīyā mātrot-karṣād-ubhayatvādvā utkarṣati ha vai jñāna-santatiṁ samānaś-ca bhavati-nāsyā brahmavit kule bhavati ya evaṁ veda* | |10| |

> He who is Taijasa, having for his sphere of activity the dream state is *U* (उ) the second letter of *AUM;* on account of "superiority" or on account of "being in between the two." He who knows thus heightens to a superior knowledge and becomes equal to all and finds no one in his line of descendants who is not a knower of *Brahman.*

As it is higher and connected with *ubhaya,* the second *mātra U-kāra* is *svapna*'s place whose lord is Taijasa. The one who knows this, he develops his wisdom. Further he will be equal to all. In his lineage there won't be born anyone who will not have *brahma-jñāna.*

**Brahmadatta** – Sir, I kindly pray to you to explain the words like *ubhaya* connection and higher plane, etc.

**Varuṇa** – Child Brahmadatta, I will tell first the third *mantra* also. Then friend Gopāda will give explanations for all together. What? Is it not correct what I have told?

**Gopāda** – My dear friend, yes, I will explain as per your wish.

**Varuṇa** –

> सुषुप्तस्थानः प्राज्ञो मकारस्तृतीया मात्रा मितेरपीतेर्वा मिनोति ह वा
> इदꣳ सर्वमपीतिश्च भवति य एवं वेद ॥११ ॥
>
> *suṣupta-sthānaḥ prājño makāras-tṛtīyā mātrā miter-apītervā minoti ha vā idaṁ sarvam-apītiś-ca bhavati ya evaṁ veda ||11||*
>
> *Prajñā*, whose sphere of activity is the deep-sleep state, is *M* (म), the third letter of *AUM,* because, it is both the "measure" and also "that wherein all become one." One who knows this identity of *prajñā* and *M* (म) is able to know the real nature of the things and beings, and also come to realize as being the Self of all.

The third letter is *M-kāra* which gives the measure and which lulls into becoming one with *ātmā*. It is the *suṣupti*'s place whose lord is *prajñā*. The one who knows it gains the capacity to measure/gauge everything and has the capacity to hide everything. I have told the *mantra*s and corresponding meanings. Now my friend will give the explanation. Listen carefully.

**Gopāda** – The *A-kāra* represents Vaiśvānara who has *jāgarita* (wakefulness, consciousness) as the resting place. The reason being *A-kāra* is *oṁkāra*'s first syllable. In the same way, it is Vaiśvānara which is the first part of the *ātmā*. Further both have the same characteristics of spreading everywhere; *A-kāra* spreads over all sounds and Vaiśvānara spreads over all *jāgarita* worlds. Both have the first place. The *A-kāra* is the first among all *akṣara*s; when the mouth is opened for talking the first sound pronounced is *A* (अ). In the same way, Vaiśvānara is the first among all creations. The waking state is before the state of sleep and dream. A person who realizes this attains all his wishes. Further he becomes first among all *mahān*s/great souls.

**Brahmadatta** – Svāmī! I understand it very well. Now kindly tell about Taijasa and *U-kāra*.

**Gopāda** – The one who is in the *svapna* (dream) state is Taijasa. He is the second part of *oṁkāra*; the *U-kāra* is the second syllable. Both Taijasa and *U-kāra* are in an elevated state. Compared to *A-kāra*, *U-kāra* is of a higher note and compared to Vaiśvānara, the Taijasa has a higher status. This is an elevated state. This *U-kāra* is in between *A-kāra* and *M-kāra*, thus it is said to be a state of *ubhayatvādva* (उभयत्वाद्व) where it is helped in its existence by two factors on its either side. Taijasa is in between Vaiśvānara and *prajñā* and he is cushioned by both states. A person who realizes this state increases his wisdom. He gets great wisdom as greatest seer (*mahājñānī*). He becomes dear to everyone. In his lineage there won't be anyone without *brahma-jñāna*. That is, he produces *brahmavit* (*Brahman*-realizing individuals) and multiplies such persons. In successive lineages only *brahmavit*s will be seen. His disciple dynasty also will flourish unbroken.

**Satyakāma** – Sadguru, we understand very well. Kindly tell the third state, *prajñā* and *M-kāra* in detail.

**Gopāda** – *Prajñā* who is placed as *suṣupti* is represented by *M-kāra*, the third letter of *oṁkāra* and the third part of *ātmā*. When *praṇava* is pronounced the *A-kāra* and *U-kāra* end in *M-kāra*. Like after a good sleep we see in everyday experience the waking state and dream state gets ended into sleep. One realizes this, gets the capacity to measure the entire world, that is, he realizes the truth and becomes the *ātmā* which is the cause of the world. Vaiśvānara and Taijasa get into the fold of *prajñā* and come out again. This the *śruti* says "measuring" (taking hold and letting off afterwards) like the act of measuring the grains into the measuring vessels. Hereafter we see getting absorbed or absolved. The *A-kāra* and *U-kāra* get absolved in *M-kāra* at the end, so also Vaiśvānara and Taijasa get into oneness with *prajñā* at the end.

**Varuṇa** – Well done! friend, many thanks for your explanations. With this, today's lessons are over. We will meet again tomorrow.

**Disciples** – Your will is our fortune.

***(The curtain falls.)***

## SCENE 6

(As the curtain opens, like the previous scene, conversation continues.)

**Varuṇa** – Children, friend, *āśrama* residents! With today's preaching this *Upaniṣad* is coming to an end. Thank you all for making all the arrangements here for me.

**Gopāda** – Dear friend, please don't differentiate between your *āśrama* and this *āśrama*. We all belong to you. Your coming here so gracefully acceding to my request and preaching to us is indeed laudable. It is we who have to express our gratitude to you. However you have outwitted us even in this.

**Satyakāma** – Pūjya Gurujī! please excuse me for interrupting while two *gurudevas* are talking. Only we want to express our thanks to both of you, the great teachers, here.

**Varuṇa** – The one who has a beautiful mind, according to the deep import of the *Upaniṣad,* the differentiating nomenelatures such as *guru,* disciple, *Śāstras* are only aberrations to true knowledge. Once realization dawns all the labels get nullified, the *guru-śiṣya* differences are only for preaching and knowing. When the wisdom is acquired such differences are not required. There is no duality or any difference. Hence there is no room to thank or praise one another.

**Brahmadatta** – Svāmī! I request you to kindly continue preaching. I have still not reached that wisdom. I feel I am still steeped in the cycle of *saṁsāra.* You must kindly show your consideration and teach us.

**Varuṇa** – Saumyas! Listen carefully.

अमात्रश्चतुर्थोऽव्यवहार्यः प्रपञ्चोपशमः शिवोऽद्वैतः एवमोंकार
आत्मैव संविशत्यात्मनात्मानं य एवं वेद य एवं वेद ॥१२॥

*amātraś-caturtho 'vyavahāryaḥ prapañcopaśamaḥ śivo'dvaitaḥ evam-oṁkāra ātmaiva saṁviśaty-ātmanātmānaṁ, ya evaṁ veda, ya evaṁ veda* ||12||

That which has no parts, the soundless, the incomprehensible, beyond all the senses, the cessation of all phenomena, all blissful and non-dual aspects of *oṁ*, the fourth part of it verily is the same as the *ātman*. He, who knows this, merges his self in the Supreme Self — the individual in the Total.

The fourth place is occupied by the undivided one which is known as Śiva where the *prapañca* (the entire universe) rests, and that which cannot be described. It is not represented by any sound. However the entire *oṁkāra* represents *ātmā*. If a person realizes this he himself becomes *ātmā*.

**Satyakāma** – Sadguru, the meaning is somewhat clear.

However kindly explain in detail.

**Varuṇa** – Till now Vaiśvānara, Taijasa, *prajñā* the three lords and *jāgarita, svapna, suṣupti* the three states *A, U, M,* the three *mātrā*s were explained in detail. Now about *turīya,* the fourth state as described in this *mantra* is being explained. It has no *mātrā* (sound unit). It is immeasurable. It cannot be comprehended or spoken about. It is the abode of the entire universe. It is bliss personified and is an unified state. The one who realizes it in this way gets mingled with *ātmā* and becomes one with that.

**Gopāda** – Initially the equation between the three letters of *oṁkāra* and the three states of *ātmā* has been brought out. In fact the fourth place does not come under any counting. It is described as the fourth only in the sense that it is different from the other three states.

**Satyakāma** – Sadguru! We have understood everything very well. Still do explain further with examples so that it enters firmly in the mind.

**Brahmadatta** – Sir, I also request the same.

**Gopāda** – Children, I will tell further, listen carefully. First you must understand that the states of *jāgarita* and *svapna* are false. Both these states are neither true nor permanent. In the same way it has to be understood that the *suṣupti* state is also false.

**Brahmadatta** – Svāmī! It is easy to understand that the dream state is false. However is it correct to think the wakeful state in the same way? Do explain it in detail.

**Gopāda** – Like *svapna, jāgarita* is also false. By comparing both states, truth will come to light. Let us take *svapna* first. Since all objects are seen inside the body in *svapna* they are false. In *svapna* we see elephants, horses, mansions, towers, the Himālayas, the Gaṅgotrī, the fourfold armies, the congregation at *Kumbha-melā* and the like. How could these objects, seen within ourselves in the space wherein we are contained, be true? Therefore they are false. Further we see in the dream journeying from Kailāsa to Kanyākumārī. It is beyond reasoning that a person lying in an *āśrama* goes to those places. The period of dreaming in the sleeping state is only for a short time while the period of travel could be for many days or months. After getting up from sleep all the objects seen in the dream are found not actually present. In dreams we talk to friends, relatives, enemies, etc. Later we do not see them. Hence whatever is seen or happenned in the dream is false. They are not seen in the state of *jāgarita* or in the state of *suṣupti.* They are seen only in the state of dream. Hence in the dream the body is false. The non-dual mind is seen as dual in *svapna*. It itself provides all imaginations.

**Satyakāma** – My benefactor! We have clearly learnt about the state of dream. I request you to explain about the state of *jāgarita*/wakeful state.

**Brahmadatta** – O noble preceptor! Kindly speak, we will hear attentively.

**Gopāda** – Whatever we see around us is only in the field of thought and imagination. Mind is the main reason behind it. This everyday world around us is only seen by the mind. The *Brahman* which has no birth and which has no names and forms is seen by the mind as different things purely by imagination. If mind does not think, the things are not perceived and they do not exist. The things are felt by the senses. For the wise and realized these forms are known as false assumptions. That is because, what is not there in the beginning and in the end has no permanent value. If a thing has to be true and permanent it should be seen in three states that is *jāgarita, svapna* and *suṣupti.* The thing we see during *jāgarita* (wakefulness) is not there in *svapna* (dream), and in sleep it is not there at all. Similarly, what we see in dream is not there in *jāgarita* and *suṣupti*. Hence they are not the everlasting things. The one which has beginning and end is considered false.

**Satyakāma** – If the things in both the states are false who is the one who brings them about?

**Varuṇa** – The *ātmā* which is self-effulgent teaches himself with his own *māyā-śakti*. The dream happens when the all-powerful *ātmā* sees inwards and creates *bhāvanā* or thought process. Likewise, looking outwards and creating outer things is what is called *jāgarita*. Whatever is thought by the *chit* (mind) and remains for a short period either in the dream state or in both states of *jāgarita* and *svapna* are all but imaginations and not real. They are not permanent nor the truth. *Ātmā* first creates *jīva* and then creates various things which are seen both inside (dream) and outside (outer world). He creates them through the instrument of mind, however they are all in the world of imaginations only and not real. As per the knowledge in the mind, the present rises in mind and as per the wishes in mind, knowledge crops up in the intellect, and this cycle goes on. This *jīva* is lulled into a trip of wakefulness, sleep, dream and sufferings. However all this state is not permanent. The experience got there is imagination and false.

**Brahmadatta** – Sadguru! When will *jīva* be released from this? When will he get *mukti*?

**Gopāda** – The *jīva* which is sleeping in the rootless *māyā* awakes when the rising moon in the form of *sadguru* rises on the horizon. Then he reaches the Advaita *rūpa* of *turīya* which does not have birth, sleep and dream. The one which is the same and unchangeable in the three states should definitely be known. *A-kāra* takes him to Vaiśvānara, *U-kāra* takes him to Taijasa, and *M-kāra* takes him to *prajñā*. Crossing that once he reaches the soundless *turīya*, then he comes out of the cause-effect cycle and also out of the *jāgarita, svapna* and *suṣupti* states and reaches *Brahman avasthā*.

**Varuṇa** – Children! Hence the mind should be joined in *praṇava*. *Praṇava* is the fearless *Brahma-svarūpa*. The one who worships *praṇava* always, does not have any fear. *Praṇava* is *aparabrahman*, also *praṇava* is *Parabrahman*.

**Satyakāma** – Svāmī! What I studied earlier is coming to the mind. Guru Pipplāda also preached the same thing.

**Gopāda** – Child! tell us what the *paramaguru* told us.

**Satyakāma** –

एतद्वै सत्यकाम परं चापरं च ब्रह्म यदोंकारः।

*etad vai satyakāma paraṁ cāparaṁ ca brahma yadoṁkāraḥ* ।

The *oṁkāra* is both *Parabrahman* and *Aparbrahman.*

**Brahmadatta** – Sadguru, do continue to preach.

**Varuṇa** – *Praṇava* does not have a cause, it has no effect. It has no inside or outside. It is indestructible. The *praṇava* which is present in the hearts of all living things should be known. The one who knows it does not fall into grief.

**Gopāda** – Just how the dream and *māyā* are looked into, how *gandharva* city is looked into, in the same way the *jñānī*s (wise ones) understand the reality of this world. In truth there is no production, no destruction, no *sādhaka*s, no *mumukṣū*s (*brahma-jñānī*s). One should know the *ātmā* which is blemishless, without any *prapañca* (worlds) and which is Advaita (non-dual). Knowing that the thoughts should be stabilized in Advaita, inside the mind the *ātma-tattva* should be seen and viewed and the same *tattva* should be seen outside and one should become that *tattva* itself and get *paramānanda* or great bliss in it. Further one should never slip from the *ātma-tattva,* once it is realized.

**Varuṇa** – Children! The teachings are over with this. However those concepts are not the ones which can be understood just by hearing. You have to contemplate on whatever you have learnt, discuss with one another, sit in *dhyāna samādhi* and realize the concepts. Let all good tidings befall you. My *āśīrvādam*s. I am taking leave. *Bhadram astu* (भद्रं अस्तु) — let you get all the good tidings.

(Lord Varuṇa disappears.)

**Gopāda** – Children! Due to *puṇya*s of previous births you all got the fortune of Varuṇadeva giving you the teachings. From Mahārājā Janaka an invitation has come that a Vedānta *pariṣad* is going on. Let all of us go there. We will give discourses there about *Māṇḍūkya Upaniṣad*. Satyakāma is good at telling concisely and clearly. Disciples, what are your opinions?

**Disciples** – Sadguru, as per your wish, we will also come to Mithilā. If Satyakāma tells in brief now only then it will be useful to *āśrama* residents also who won't be able to come.

**Brahmadatta** – I also thought the same. Satyakāma should kindly tell in brief now itself. Then it will be helpful.

**Satyakāma** – Respected Sir, As per the wish of the friend, wish of others, above all *sadguru*'s orders I will tell. Kindly bless me so that I may tell it with devotion and in short.

(Does *namaskārams*, gets up and tells with humility.)

In the body the *jīva* has three states: *jāgarita, svapna* and *suṣupti* and apart from that, has also the state of *turīya*. During *jāgarita* state by sense organs the outside world is known. In *svapna* he comes to know the mind-induced things and their forms. In sleep there is nothing to see — no forms which are attached to any thought attractions. However, there is wisdom and happiness which cannot be described. In *turīya* the *jīva* comes to know its true state the *ātma-svarūpa*. For doing *upāsanā*, *oṁkāra* is the most exalted representation. If *upāsanā* is done on *oṁkāra* with *Brahman* in mind then it will act as an apt tool to reach *Brahman*. Staying in *samādhi* the *oṁkāra* should be visualized, with gross as *A-kāra* (*jāgarita* state), subtle as *U-kāra* (*svapna* state), the cause of both as *M-kāra* (*suṣupti* state), and the cause and effect of all the things as *turīya* state. Then the *ātmajñānī* gets immersed in that and becomes one with the Self, a non-dual state. Do kindly forgive me if any faults are there. My *namaskārams*.

**Gopāda** – Child, You did very well. Let good tidings befall you all. Let us all go to Mithila.

***(Curtain falls)***

## SCENE 7

(As the curtain opens the Śaṅkara Maṭha is seen. The Sūtradhāra enters. Soon the actor arrives with great excitement.)

**Sūtradhāra** – Yes, my friend! What is the hurry? Even after the drama has got over, is such excitement required?

**The actor** – Friend, my *namaskārams*. The *dharmādhikārī* has sent a messenger requesting us to come immediately. Well that be so. How was the drama? Was everybody satisfied?

**Sūtradhāra** – Are you asking if people were satisfied? It was indeed very good. It can be described as a wonderful act. To describe it in old style of praise, it was *paramānanda*. My congratulations to everyone.

**The actor** – Friend, a lot of thanks for the praise. For a person like you, who is well-read, a scholar and cultured one, the drama may appeal greatly. But I wonder how the common public enjoyed it.

**Sūtradhāra** – You need not have any doubt on that. The public also liked and enjoyed the drama. Their happiness could be seen in the expression on their faces. In between they also clapped their hands and expressed their appreciation. At times they were exclaiming "fine!" "very good!" Such reactions clearly showed the public enjoyed the drama very well.

(The *dharmādhikārī* is coming.)

**The actor** – There the *dharmādhikārī* himself has come. The person whom we were seeking has himself come in front of us. Accept our greetings, respected sir. We were just coming to see you.

**Dharmādhikārī** – My *namaskāram* to you all. The *mahāsannidhāna* was very pleased with your drama and the performance. He has ordered me to give presents to you and the writer of the drama.

**The actor** – Is that so? Very happy to know that. The *sadgurū*'s blessing itself is equal to many thousand presents. Still we are immensely happy to receive presents from the *sadguru* along with his blessings. (Sings and dances with great happiness.)

**Sūtradhāra** – Friend! Which drama are you going to enact next?

**The actor** – I don't know that. I should ask the drama director.

**Dharmādhikārī** – Sūtradhāra! I will answer your question. Very soon *Taittirīya Upaniṣad* will be getting ready.

**Sūtradhāra** – Very happy. *Taittirīya* will be a big drama, is it not so? The scenes, costumes and actors may be more. The preparation should be started from now itself, I think.

**The actor** – Yes. today, now itself I will start the work. When I am having the support and affection of the public, the co-operation of the friends and *sadgurū's* blesssings, then what should I worry about? Is it anything which cannot be done? My *namaskāram*.

**Sūtradhāra** – My *praṇāma*s too.

**Dharmādhikārī** – *Namaskāram*. Before we part ways let us also say our *praṇāma*s to the people who are seeing and the ones who are reading. Let us also tell *namaskāram* to the *ātmā* which is mentioned in this drama. Let all actors and the writers of the drama come to the stage.

(The director and the actors of the drama come over to the stage and offer the following prayer.)

प्रज्ञानांशुप्रतानैः स्थिरचरनिकरव्यापिभिर्व्याप्य लोकान्२। भुक्त्वा भोगान्स्थविष्ठान्पुनरपि धिषणोद्भासितान्कामजन्यान्। पीत्वा सर्वान्विशेषान्स्वपिति मधुरभुङ्भायया भोजयन्नो मायासंख्यातुरीयं परममृतमजं ब्रह्म यत्तन्नतोऽस्मि ॥

*prajñānāṁśupratānaiḥ sthiracaranikaravyāpibhirvyāpya lokān | bhuktvā bhogānsthaviṣṭānpunarapi dhiṣaṇodbhāsitānkāmajanyān | pītvā sarvānviśoṣānkhapiti madhurabhuṅbhāyayā bhojayanno māyāsaṁkhyā-*

*turīyaṁ paramamṛtamajaṁ brahma yattannato 'smi* । ।

यो विश्वात्मा विधिजविषयान्प्राश्य भोगान्स्थविष्ठान्पश्चाच्चान्यान्स्वमतिविभ-वाञ्ज्योतिषा स्वेन सूक्ष्मान्। सर्वानेतान्पुनरपि शनैः स्वात्मनि स्थापयित्वा हित्वा सर्वान्विशोषान्विगतगुणगणः पात्वसौ नस्तुरीयः॥ न कश्चिज्जायते जीवः संभवोऽस्य न विद्यते। एतत्तदुत्तमं सत्यं यत्र किंचिन्न जायते॥

*yo viśvātmā vidhijaviṣayānprāśya bhogānstha-viṣṭhānpaścāccānyā nsvamativibhavāñjyotiṣā svena sūkṣmān* । *sarvānetānpunarapi śanaiḥ svātmani sthāpayitvā hitvā sarvānviśoṣānvigataguṇagaṇaḥ pātvasau nasturīyaḥ* । । *na kaściñjāyate jīvaḥ sambhavo 'sya na vidyate* । *etattaduttamaṁ satyaṁ yatra kiñcinna jāyate* । ।

Spreading its self-effulgent rays of wisdom and knowledge, the *Brahman* enjoys in *jāgarita* state the gross, in dream it enjoys the mind and *vāsanā* (impressions)-induced acts, and later in deep sleep all phenomena vanish and it just enjoys the bliss. Our gratitude-filled *praṇāma*s to the immortal, nectar filled, birth-and-deathless *Brahman* which is found clearly in *turīya* state. In conscious waking state it experiences the resultant of good and bad deeds done in the past. In subtle state of dream it enjoys the mind induced impressions formed by its own self-effulgence. Then in deep sleep everything is contained in itself. Finally, leaving all these mind-induced imaginary states it reaches the *nirguṇa* — attributeless state to the *paramātmā*. Let him protect us. The pure effulgent *ātmā* which is realized by doing *oṁkāra upāsanā*, the one which is beyond the three known states of living but penetrating into the three states of living, to that *ātmā* we offer our gratitude-filled *praṇāma*s. There are no *jīva*s created and there is no reason for him to create them. The one in which nothing gets created, the *Brahman* is the exalted Truth. All the phenomena which are seen and known are in the realm of imagination and are false assumptions or ignorance. Let the *ātmā* show light unto us.

***(The curtain falls.)***

|| तैत्तिरीयोपनिषत् ||

# Taittirīya Upaniṣad

## Introduction

AMONG Upaniṣads, *Taittirīya Upaniṣad* is well known for its systematic renderings in a recital form and thus, is the oft-repeated one. One of the reasons for its popularity can be apart from the philosophical and spiritual teachings, it addresses the problems and life of a *Brahmachārī* and a householder. It has clear teachings for an orderly ideal *gṛhastha* life in tune with a person's spiritual aspirations.

It belongs to *Yajurveda*. Ṛṣi Vaiśampāyana, Varuṇa and Bhṛgu are the main architects of the preparation. The name *Taittirīya* is attributed due to two reasons. One, the teacher Taitri was instrumental in spreading the teachings, and another because, the desciples of Ṛṣi Vaiśampāyana changed themselves into *ṭiṭṭirī* birds and ate the part of the teachings which was vomitted by the estranged disciple Yājñavalkya. Thus, the word *taittirīya* came from *ṭiṭṭirī*.

The teachings are divided into three main sections or *vallī*s named "Śikṣā Vallī," "Brahmānanda Vallī" and "Bhṛgu Vallī" dealing with the social, intellectual, and spiritual aspects of living.

### ŚIKṢĀ VALLĪ

The word *śikṣā* means education. In the first part, the *Upaniṣad* talks about the fundamental principles of science and education.

The play starts at Ṛṣi Vaiśampāyana's *āśrama* at Mithilā during the time of Mahārājā Janaka's reign. Ṛṣi Vaiśampāyana is surrounded by numerous disciples. Some of the prime disciples are Mahācamasya, Bodhāyana, Prācīnayogya, Triśaṅku and Vaikhānasa. The group is joined by another illustrious disciple Bhṛgu from Haridwar, the son of Ṛṣi Varuṇa. The disciples chant *śānti-pāṭha* and discuss the meaning of the same. Then they have a discussion on *ṛtam* rules ordained in Śāstras and *satyam* (truth) words. Later, the play moves to the important content of Śikṣā Vallī which deals with language and pronunciation. The primary tool for education or *śikṣā* is speech and hearing. For correct speech, pronunciation is an important factor, this in turn depends on correct voice production. In this the pronunciation aspect is discussed in detail. The following, aspects namely, *varṇa* (quality), *svara* (pitch), *mātra* (measure), *bala* (emphasis), *sama* (modulation) and *saṁdhāna* (combination) have to be taken into account for correct pronunciation. For the words so pronounced a correct joining, *sandhi*, is important to make it meaningful. Such combination is called "Saṁhitā."

Thus explaining, the seer shifts his enquiry to a larger field of Saṁhitās (combinations) and talks about the language of life and its combinations referring them as Mahāsaṁhitās. As examples of Mahāsaṁhitā in life, he explains five combinations pertaining to different aspects. For a *sandhi* (connection) to be fruitful it is important to have a proper *saṁdhāna* (connecting link). The five Mahāsaṁhitās or combinations which he refers are:

(1) In connection with the visible world, earth and heaven join, where sky is the *sandhi* and air is the *saṁdhāna* or connecting link.

(2) In connection with shining entities, fire and sun join where water is the *sandhi* and lightning is *saṁdhāna* or connecting link.

(3) In connection with knowledge, teacher and pupil join where knowledge is *sandhi* and instructions are

*saṁdhāna* or connecting links.

(4) In connection with progeny, mother and father join where child is the *sandhi* and birth is *saṁdhāna* or connecting link.

(5) In connection with soul (human being), where lower jaw and upper jaw join is the *sandhi* and tongue is the *saṁdhāna* or connecting link.

Thus, talking about the combination of words, the seer is putting forth a broader picture of understanding the working of the universe.

Then the teaching moves on to *Śrī Kāma Yajña* and the *oṁkāra* or *Brahman* concept hidden in that. Then again, reverting back to the use of words, the *ṛṣi* talks about grouping of five words termed *pāṅktam*. This grouping then again is extended to the larger life picture where grouping of matter takes place. Thus, there are *lokapāṅktam*, *devapāṅktam*, and *bhūta* (element) *pāṅktam*. These *pāṅktam* counterparts are found inside the body also, showing "*aṇḍam* (macrocosm)" and "*piṇḍam* (microcosm)" which are the same thing. The *ṛṣi* says on doing *upāsanā* on this concept, the universal *Brahman* in everything will be more clearly understood.

Then the instructions of the *ṛṣi* attempt to correct parameters to lead a householder's life. The Śikṣā Vallī is also a parting advice to *brahmachārī*s who are leaving the *gurukula* and going back home to lead a householder's life. Hence, the *ṛṣi* tells how each human being comes to the world with three debts: one for the *deva*s, one for the *ṛṣi*s, and one for the *pitṛ*s. Debt to *deva*s is paid back by doing *pūjā*, *yajña*, etc. Debt to *ṛṣi*s is paid back by listening to scriptures. Debt to *pitṛ*s or ancestors is paid back by making good *prajā*s (children). However, if one choses to be a *brahmachārī*, then it is his duty to prepare a lineage of good disciples and offer services to mankind. The preachings also explain the methods of living in charity, how to conduct oneself gently in public, among the learned, and the *dhārmika* ways of doing one's *karma*s in the society, etc.

BRAHMĀNANDA VALLĪ

In the second part of the *Upaniṣad,* the preceptor is Ṛṣi Varuṇa. Ṛṣi Vaiśampāyana along with his wife undertakes a pilgrimage giving the charge of his *āśrama* to his friend Ṛṣi Varuṇa who arrives in Mithilā from Haridwar. However, Varuṇa's son Bhṛgu staying in the *āśrama* also accompanies Ṛṣi Vaiśampāyana on his piligrimage.

Later, the teachings of understanding *Brahman* are given by Varuṇa to the rest of the disciples present in the *āśrama*. These preachings are known as Brahmānanda Vallī. The crux of the teachings is as follows: "Whatever we see around us has come out of *Brahman*. The sky, Vāyu, Agni, water, earth, plants, food, all of them step by step have come out of *Brahman*. The body which is sustained on food is like a sheath to the *ātmā*. This body hence is called *annamaya-kośa*. More subtle than *annamaya-kośa* is the *prāṇamaya-kośa* which is described to be contained in that; within that is *manomaya-kośa*; within that is *vijñānamaya-kośa*; and within that is *ānandamaya-kośa*. If thought deeply we can understand that the basis for all these five *kośa*s is *Brahman* only. As the seed is there within the fruit, we should understand the *Brahman* is within the *kośa*s and it is the only truth. Thus, if a person understands that (the *Brahman*) he himself becomes *sat*. A person not knowing this, becomes *asat*. *Brahman* by His own *saṁkalpa* (decision) enters everything. In life this is the only essence of happiness. *Brahman* Himself is the form and formless, *saguṇa* and *nirguṇa*, *chit* and *achit*, stable and unstable. Its *ānanda-svarūpa* is in every breath, in every act and each person reaches it in every breath, in every act and every moment without fail.

Further to drive home the feeling of *ānanda* or bliss which *Brahman* personifies, Varuṇa explains that the *Brahman* is the essence (*rasa*) which nourishes a person. In every birth, every action, every thought, each and every word, He is present and His nature is happiness.

On hearing him the disciples want to know how to understand this *rasa* or happiness. Is it possible to know this *rasa* through worldly happiness which is the stimulant of the senses? The disciples question the *guru*. The *guru* tells them, it is possible because that is also a part of *brahmānandam*. Taking the height of worldly happiness as yardstick — that is, happiness felt in the world with youth, goodness, knowledge, ability to act, bravery, strength, ability to rule the world — as one measure, it can be said the happiness felt by human *gandharva* is hundred times the happeness felt by the human beings. Hundred times the happiness of human *gandharva* is *deva gandharva*'s happiness. Hundred times the happiness of *deva gandharva* is the happiness felt by gods. Hundred times the happiness of gods is the happiness felt by Indra. Hundred times to that is the happiness felt by Prajāpati. Hundred times the happiness of Prajāpati is the happiness felt by *Brahman*. However, if a seeker of *Brahman* leaves all the desires and with one-pointed concentration tries to be one with *Brahman*, he also obtains all these measures of happiness. This happiness so felt is a drop in the ocean of *brahmānanda,* hence, it is difficult to measure *brahmānanda*, though through these measures the infinite bliss experience can be imagined.

BHṚGU VALLĪ

This part is the dialogue that takes between Lord Varuṇa and his son Bhṛgu in understanding the concept of *Brahman*. The young Bhṛgu was accompanying his teacher Vaiśampāyana on a pilgrimage when his father Lord Varuṇa was preaching *brahma-vidyā* to other disciples and had missed out on the preachings.

Hence on returning, charged with a burning desire to acquire the knowldge of *brahma-vidyā* he approaches his father and humbly requests him to preach him too. However his father takes a different approach. Every indvidual is a *brahma-svarūpa* made of the *sat* which is *Brahman;* however this aspect is not realized by an ordinary human being. Hence he goes in search of the *Brahman* elsewhere. On contemplation and meditation with deep concentration *Brahman* can be understood and realized. To bring home this fact and to tap the hidden source of every human being to educate himself Lord Varuṇa adopts this approach to his eminently deserving son Bhṛgu and guides him in his quest for the eternal.

Lord Varuṇa tells his son Bhṛgu that *Brahman* is "That from which everything is born, because of which everything lives and into which everything goes back and merges." Bhṛgu then meditates on this deeply and comes out with the realization that food (*annam*) is *Brahman*. Thus he understands the *annamaya-kośa,* or the body made of food, is nothing but *Brahman*. However he feels it is not the final answer to his query, as both the food and the *annamaya-kośa* or the physical body is perishable whereas *Brahman* is not.

Hence he approaches his father and asks his clarification. His father again sends him back asking him to dwell on himself and meditate. Bhṛgu then meditates and finds that permeating into the food/body sheath is the vital breath or *prāṇa* which the *pañca-bhūta*s are structured into. Discovering the *prāṇamaya-kośa* of vital breath in all living things, he comes to the conclusion that it is the *Brahman*.

However he feels this too is not the final answer as the all-pervading *prāṇa* in the living things is not intelligent, thus being not a ruling factor. Hence there must be more to be understood as to the presence of *Brahman*.

His father again sends him back on the route of meditation. On doing so he discovers permeating into the vital breath (*prāṇa*) are the thoughts and emotions making the mind. Thus the mind ruling above the *prāṇa* making the *manomaya-kośa*/ the mind sheath can be the ultimate *Brahman,* as all the things in the universe have come about from mind.

However he doubts if it is wholly correct, as there is an intellect which is the ruler of thoughts. It is the intelligence in each being which decides what to think. Thus permeating into the mind is the *vijñanam* or intelligence, making the *vijñanamaya-kośa*. Thus the all-prevading intelligence is the ultimate *Brahman,* he decides.

He approaches his father and tells his conclusion. But his father tells him to continue his penance and meditate further. Bhṛgu then thinks the intellect may not be the ultimate. As all living things are *Brahman*, there is a common *sūtra* or binding among all living things. In fact, all living things are part of the whole as well as the whole itself. Thus everyone is *Brahman* or instruments of *Brahman*. Realization of this common web is *ānanda* or bliss. *Brahman* is *ānanda* or bliss and happiness. Thus on realizing about this *ānandamaya-kośa* the quest of Bhṛgu is complete.

He then approaches his father and tells him about his realization. On knowing from his father his penance has fetched the correct results, Bhṛgu becomes an enlightened soul. He then establishes himself in the *ānandamaya Brahman* and becomes the blemishless *Brahman-svarūpa*.

This part gives confidence to every aspirer that to realize *Brahman* is not an impossibility. It can be done in this life itself. With proper *śraddhā*, discipline and one-pointed meditation it is possible to know the ultimate Truth.

# The Drama

## Characters

| | |
|---|---|
| **Vaiśampāyana** | – Maharṣi |
| **Varuṇa** | – Maharṣi |
| **Mahācamasya**<br>**Bodhāyana**<br>**Bhṛgu**<br>**Prācīnayogya**<br>**Vaikhānasa**<br>**Triśaṅku** | Six disciples |
| **Vaiśampāyana Ṛṣi's wife**<br>**Ṛṣi Varuṇa's wife** | Ṛṣipatni |
| **Āśrama residents** | – Resident 1, Resident 2 |

## Part I

### Śikṣā Vallī

SCENE 1

(Curtain opens)

(It is the *āśrama* of Maharṣi Vaiśampāyana. He is sitting on the tiger skin in *padmāsana* posture. Bodhāyana and six disciples are sitting on either side of the *maharṣi*. All of them together tell *śānti-pāṭha*).

ॐ शं नो मित्रः शं वरुणः। शं नो भवत्वर्यमा। शं न इन्द्रो बृहस्पतिः। शं नो विष्णुरुरुक्रमः। नमो ब्रह्मणे। नमस्ते वायो। त्वमेव प्रत्यक्षं ब्रह्मासि। त्वमेव प्रत्यक्षं ब्रह्म वदिष्यामि। ऋतं वदिष्यामि। सत्यं वदिष्यामि। तन्मामवतु। तद्वक्तारमवतु। अवतु माम्। अवतु वक्तारम्।

॥ॐ शान्तिः शान्तिः शान्तिः॥१॥

*oṁ śaṁ no mitraḥ śaṁ varuṇaḥ* | *śaṁ no bhavatvaryamā* | *śaṁ na indro bṛhaspatiḥ* | *śaṁ no viṣṇururukramaḥ* | *namo brahmaṇe* | *namaste vāyo* |

*tvameva pratyakṣaṁ brahmāsi* । *tvameva pratyakṣaṁ brahma vadiṣyāmi* । *r̥taṁ vadiṣyāmi* । *satyaṁ vadiṣyāmi* । *tanmāmavatu* । *tadvaktāramavatu* । *avatu mām* । *avatu vaktāram* ।

।। *oṁ śāntiḥ śāntiḥ śāntmiḥ* ।। 1 ।।

*AUM* May Mitra (the Sun) be propitious to us. May Varuṇa (be) propitious (to us). May Aryamā (a form of the Sun) be propitious to us. May Indra and Br̥haspati be propitious to us. May Viṣṇu of wide strides be propitious to us. Salutations to *Brahman*. Salutations to you, O Vāyu! You indeed are the perceptible *Brahman*. Of you indeed, the perceptible *Brahman*, will I speak of the right. I'll speak of the truth. May that protect me. May that protect the speaker. Let that protect me. Let that protect the speaker. AUM. Peace! Peace! Peace!

**Vaiśampāyana** – Children! May you get the blessings of all good tidings. Mahācamasya, explain clearly the *śānti pāṭha* to the new students of our *gurukula;* to Bhr̥gu, Prācīnayogya and others.

**Mahācamasya** – (**Folds both his hands and offers his salutations**) I will explain to them, revered *guru.*

May Mitra give his blessings to us.
May Varuṇa give us comforts.
May Aryamā give his blessings to us.
Indra and Br̥haspati should bring us with good tidings.
May the all-encompassing Viṣṇu shower us with good tidings.

**Vaiśampāyana** – You told the meaning well. However, if you explain the particular field, in which *devatā*s like Mitra and Varuṇa help us then the concept can be understood better. Bodhāyana you explain to them.

**Bodhāyana** – (**Gives his salutations with folded hands**) Svāmī, I will do as you asked.

The Mitra Devatā helps in functioning of day and *prāṇa.*

The Varuṇa Devatā helps in functioning of night and *apāna vāyu.*

The Aryamā Devatā helps in functioning of eyes and it is dear to Lord Sūrya.

The Lord Indra for strength and Bṛhaspati for intellect and speech.

Lord Viṣṇu is the cause of functioning of everything, true to the saying "everything in the world is Viṣṇu."

Viṣṇu is also called Urukrama because when he incarnated as Trivikrama he had big feet.

If we praise and worship them we will get all the blessings.

**Vaiśampāyana** – Child! Prācīnayogya and young one Bhṛgu, did you understand everything well.

**Bhṛgu** – Revered Guru, I understood everything well.

**Prācīnayogya** – Respected Sir! When we pray "kindly bless us" does it imply the disciples should get the blessings?

**Vaiśampāyana** – Child! It implies both *guru* and the disciples. At the end of the prayer it will be understood more clearly. Mahācamasya! Do tell the meaning for the rest of the *śānti-pāṭha.*

**Mahācamasya** – As per your order I would do. My *namaskārams* to *Brahman.* My salutations to Vāyu Devatā. You are only the *Brahman* which we can see (which can be perceived). I worship you as *Brahman* only. You alone are *ṛtam.* You alone are the truth. Let this Vāyu *Brahman* which is *sarvātmā* protect me. Let it protect the teacher also (**the prayer is repeated**). Let it take care of me and my teacher. *Oṁ śānti* is repeated three times and the prayer gets over.

**Bhṛgu** – Friend! What is the use of telling three times *śānti*?

**Mahācamasya** – Friend! To acquire knowledge three types of obstacles can happen. To remove that, three times *oṁ*! *śānti* is told as prayer.

**Prācīnayogya** – Is that so? What are the three types of obstacles? kindly explain.

**Mahācamasya** – Pertaining to the body (*ādhyātmika*), pertaining to worldly things (*ādibhautika*) and pertaining to gods (*ādidaivika*). Thus three kinds of difficulties can happen.

The disease, laziness, etc. which are the obstacles to the well-being of the physical body (*ādhyātmika*).

The obstacles from the atmosphere are rain, thunder, strong winds, etc. They pertain to worldly things. They can be experienced through our senses (*ādibhautika*).

Not included in these two categories, and the ones beyond understanding, are the obstacles happening unexpectedly from unknown sources that are pertaining to gods (*ādidaivika*).

May the three obstacles get completely removed. Let us have peace and happiness (**thus the prayer is ended**).

**Vaiśampāyana** – Children! The meaning has been explained well. I think the new students must have understood well.

**Bhṛgu** – Respected Sir, I understood the *śānti-pāṭha* well. I am keen to hear more lessons. You must kindly bless me.

**Vaiśampāyana** – Child! Your father Varuṇa is my close friend. We both have together learned *veda-pāṭha* from Vedavyāsa Bhagavān. Later listening to Mahārājā Janaka's request I came here. Varuṇa stayed back at Haridwar. He is a great teacher. In spite of that he has sent his only son as a student to my *āśrama* for *gurukula* stay. It is surprising indeed.

**Prācīnayogya** – Svāmī! It is necessary to stay away from parents to learn disciplined lessons. Only to stress this great truth Bhṛgu has been sent here. They have sent me also along with him to keep him company.

**Bhṛgu** – Not only that. Everybody knows that the quality of education and discipline here is very high.

**Vaiśampāyana** – Whatever may be the reason, I am giving you both my blessings, and may your arrival bring good tidings. I am feeling proud of the fact that my erudite friend has sent you here. I will teach you whatever I know. You also learn carefully and without any difference of feelings should live in friendship and unity.

**Disciples** – We will do as you say, Revered Guru.

**Vaiśampāyana** – Child Triśaṅku (**Triśaṅku who was in meditation gets startled and responds to the call**). Bodhāyana! today you must welcome and perform the hospitality *pūjā* to the new guests who have come to our *āśrama*. You must take Bhr̥gu and Prācīnayogya to the forest and bring twigs and firewood. However don't put the new disciples to too much of strain in the beginning. Everything should be put to practice gradually. Further Bhr̥gu has been brought up comfortably and he is not used to *āśrama* ways.

**Bodhāyana** – Svāmī! I will do as per your orders.

**Vaiśampāyana** – Mahācamasya! You need not go out. You be near me and attend to the matters. Hey Vaikhānasa!

**Vaikhānasa** – Svāmī! Do give your orders for me.

**Vaiśampāyana** – Child! Didn't I tell you in the morning? As per that, be of help in place of cooking. A number of guests have come. Hence there will be more work there.

**Vaikhānasa** – I will do so.

**Vaiśampāyana** – Children! Let us stop the lessons today here. Afternoon time is nearing. We will start the lessons tomorrow morning.

***(All of them get up and tell śānti-pāṭha)***

***(Scene closes.)***

## SCENE 2

(It is the *āśrama* of Vaiśampāyana. The *guru* is teaching to the disciples.)

**Bhṛgu** – Revered Guru! A doubt!

**Vaiśampāyana** – What is that? Do tell immediately. I will try to clear it.

**Bhṛgu** – Svāmī! Yesterday when telling the meaning of *śānti-pāṭha* it was told "You are only *ṛtam*, you are only truth." What is the meaning of *ṛtam* and what is the meaning of "truth"? Both have the same meaning isn't it? Kindly tell the difference in detail.

**Vaiśampāyana** – Yesterday itself I noticed. Nobody took it up for discussion. Hence I thought perhaps it is understood. Bodhāyana! Do tell the explanations of that clearly.

**Bodhāyana** – Revered Guru! Salutations to you. I will explain as you bid. Seeing superficially both *ṛtam* and *satyam* (truth) may look like one. However, without necessity Veda won't give two words to explain the meaning of one concept. If observed keenly the difference in meaning will be understood. *Ṛtam* means whatever is told in the Śāstras (scriptures) will be followed without any change. Such a determination is made up in mind. Such a thing which is so determined when acted upon practically is the truth. The order and beauty seen in the world is bounded by rules of Śāstras. That is only *ṛtam*. There is a basis for this order and beauty. That is only truth.

**Vaiśampāyana** – Children! Now we will start the lesson.

शिक्षां व्याख्यास्यामः। वर्णः स्वरः। मात्रा बलम्। साम सन्तानः।
इत्युक्तः शिक्षाध्यायः ॥२॥

*śikṣāṁ vyākhyāsyāmaḥ* । *varṇaḥ svaraḥ* । *mātrā balam* । *sāma santānaḥ* । *ityuktaḥ śikṣādhyāyaḥ* ॥2॥

We will expound the science of pronunciation: the syllables, sounds, measure of the sound, emphasis of the sound, uniformity of the sound, juxtapostion of the sound. Thus has been declared the lesson on pronunciation.

**(As the *guru* recites first, the disciples repeat.)**

In *Upaniṣad* the meaning is most important. However the pronunciation norm used for it I have told before. But to inform the new entrants and to remind you of that, I will tell in short. 1. *varṇam* 2. *svaram* 3. *mātrā* 4. strength 5. *śamam* 6. *santānam,* like this *śikṣā* chapter of veda has differentiated about the pronunciation norms. These you also must know definitely. Vaikhānasa! Do explain in detail about *varṇam, svaram* to your friends.

**Vaikhānasa** – It is my fortune to follow Svāmī's *chit.* Friends listen, *varṇam* are syllbles of language (both consonants and vowels). *Svaram* is of three types. They are *udātta, anudātta, svaritam.* If *svara* changes the meaning itself changes.

**Prācinayogya** – Yes, Lord Varuṇa has told. In the story of Vṛtrāsura how a change of *svaram* has brought a lot of harm.

**Vaikhānasa** – *Mātrā* — this is also of three types: *hrasvam, dhīrgam, plutam.*

**Bhṛgu** – What is meant by strength in this context?

**Vaikhānasa** – The clarity used in pronouncing the words and how strongly the words are pronounced is the strength element here. Most important is pronunciation, that is what *śamam* stands for. *Śāntānam* is the combination of *varṇams.* Thus this *śikṣā* chapter is very important.

**Prācīnayogya** – Is *śikṣā* the correct way or *śīkṣā* is the correct way to pronounce with stress on *śī*? (Vaikhānasa is not able to give an answer.)

**Vaiśampāyana** – Bodhāyana! If you know the answer for your friend's question, do give the answer.

**Bodhāyana** – I don't know. *Śikṣā* and *śīkṣā* should mean the same thing, isn't it?

*fig.:* **Mahāsaṁhitās.**

**Vaiśampāyana** – The question of meaning does not arise here. What is the reason for using a longer vowel in that word? Mahācamasya! Where is he? Not to be seen.

**Bhr̥gu** – He has gone to the riverside along with the guests who had come in the morning.

**Vaiśampāyana** – Well I forgot, tomorrow is Kr̥ttikā and Sunday. I had told to make arrangements for food to be partaken in the forest. He has gone for that. Triśaṅku is in meditation. Only after he wakes up we can ask him. Child! Bhr̥gu if you know tell the answer.

**Bhr̥gu** – I am a bit doubtful. I have learned grammar from my Respected Father.

**Vaiśampāyana** – Yes. What you are thinking may be correct. Do tell it out boldly.

**Bhr̥gu** – The grammar used in language is different and the grammar used for Vedas is different. In Veda grammar instead of *E-kāra Eii-kāra* is used. As per religious order *śikṣā* when told in longer vowels as *śīkṣā* it is a more effective pronunciation. Is it correct, revered *guru*?

**Vaiśampāyana** – Very correct. I am very happy. When we were studying those days your father was very intelligent. You are also like him. Your coming to learn here is indeed fortunate. Children! Now onwards all of you learn grammar from Bhṛgu. Any doubts you have, you can get it cleared.

**Disciples** – Yes we will do so.

**Vaiśampāyana** – I will start the lesson. Tell the prayer. (The disciples recite.)

सह नौ यशः। सह नौ ब्रह्मवर्चसम्।

*saha nau yaśaḥ* | *saha nau brahmavarcasam* |

May glory be with us both. May the splendour of the Wisdom of *Brahman* be with us both.

**Vaiśampāyana** – Children! I will tell the meaning, listen carefully. The teacher and the *āśrama* boarders, may both of us get the blessings together. Let *Brahman-tejas* also we beget together. Now I am going to tell *Samhitopaniṣad*. Saṁhitā means joining of words, that is, sounds. Before going to enquire of the meaning it is better to exercise the sound. After hearing the pronunciation and the sounds of the words it will be easier to enter the meaning of words. Let the glory acquired by learning lessons reach us. The *yaśa* is the glory received by what is rightfully got doing the right deed. Let us also get *Brahman-tejas* as a result of reciting Vedas during our lifetime.

अथातः सꣳहिताया उपनिषदं व्याख्यास्यामः। पञ्चस्वधिकरणेषु। अधिलोकमधिज्यौतिषमधिविद्यमधिप्रजमध्यात्मम्। ता महासꣳहिता इत्याचक्षते ॥३.१॥

*athātaḥ saṁhitāyā upaniṣadaṁ vyākhyāsyāmaḥ* | *pañcasvadhikaraṇeṣu* | *adhilokam adhijyautiṣam adhividyam adhiprajam adhyātmam* | *tā mahāsaṁhitā ityācakṣate* | | 3.1 | |

Now, therefore, we shall expound the sacred (secret) teaching of the juxtaposition (the state of being inseparably together of various factors) as coming under five contexts. They are the contexts of the visible world, of the shining entities, of knowledge, of progeny, and of oneself. These are known as the great combinations (*mahāsaṁhitā*). *Saṁhitā* means combining, that is, joining. *Adhilokam, adhijyautiṣam, adhividyam, adhiprajam, adhyātmam,* these are five kinds of *ācāryam*. They are called *adhikaraṇam.*

As how *liṅga* is worshipped as Paramaśiva and Śāligrāma is worshipped as Mahāviṣṇu, in the same way we have to see in the words, their inferences, and on that *upāsanā* has to be done. The order of the words should be considered a *pratīka,* and *upāsanā* should be done. By doing like this on gross matter we will get the ability to see the subtle concept.

**Bodhāyana** – Svāmī! Kindly tell about the five *adhikaraṇam* in more detail.

**Vaiśampāyana** –

| | | |
|---|---|---|
| *adhilokam* | – | It is connected to the world. |
| *adhijyautiṣam* | – | It is connected to light and splendour. |
| *adhividyam* | – | It is connected to knowledge. |
| *adhiprajam* | – | It is connected to progeny (offspring). |
| *adhyātmam* | – | It is connected to the soul. |

All these five are *mahāsaṁhitā*s (big union) as elders used to tell.

Now I will tell the secret information found in each of these. Accordingly the *upāsanā* has to be done.

अथाधिलोकम्। पृथिवी पूर्वरूपम्। द्यौरुत्तररूपम्। आकाशः सन्धिः।
वायुः सन्धानम् इत्यधिलोकम् अथाधिज्यौतिषम्॥३.२॥

*athādhilokam* | *pṛthivī pūrvarūpam* | *dyauruttararūpam* |
*ākāśaḥ sandhiḥ* | *vāyuḥ saṁdhānam ityadhilokam*
*athādhijyautiṣam* | |3.2| |

Now with reference to the context of the visible world: The earth is the prior form; the heaven is the latter form; space is the meeting place, and air is the connecting link. Thus is the nature of the *mahāsaṁhitā*, with reference to the context of the visible world.

When told about the world, the earth is the first form, the heaven is the second form, the sky is the *sandhi* (connecting place), Vāyu induces this connection, and thus *ādiloka* can be described. O Bodhāyana! You do the *upāsanā* of this.

**Vaiśampāyana** –

अग्निः पूर्वरूपम्। आदित्य उत्तररूपम्। आपः सन्धिः।
वैद्युता सन्धानम्। इत्यधिज्यौतिषम्। ॥३.३॥

*agniḥ pūrvarūpam* | *āditya uttararūpam* | *āpaḥ sandhiḥ* | *vaidyutā saṁdhānam* |
*ityadhijyautiṣam* | |3.3| |

Now with reference to the context of the shining entities: fire is the prior form; sun is the latter form; water is the meeting place and lightning is the connecting link. Thus is the nature of the *mahāsaṁhitā*, with reference to the context of the shining entities.

When described about *jyoti* (light), Agni belongs to earlier form, Āditya belongs to the later form. The joining place for both is water. The *sandhi* (connecting thing) is lightning. Thus *ādhijyautiṣam* is described. Hey Vaikhānasa, you meditate on this.

**Vaikhānasa** – I will do so, Svāmī.

**Vaiśampāyana** – Now I will tell about *vidyā* (education).

अथाधिविद्यम्। आचार्यः पूर्वरूपम्। अन्तेवास्युत्तररूपम्। विद्याः सन्धिः।
प्रवचनमꣳ सन्धानम्। इत्यधिविद्यम्। ॥३.४॥

*athādhividyam* | *ācāryaḥ pūrvarūpam* | *antevāsy-uttararūpam* | *vidyāḥ sandhiḥ* | *pravacanaṁ saṁdhānam* | *ityadhividyam* | |3.4| |

> Now with reference to the context of knowledge: the teacher is the prior form; the pupil is the later form; knowledge is the meeting place, and instruction is the connecting link. Thus is the nature of the *mahāsaṁhitā*, with reference to the context of knowledge.

*Guru* is the first form, the disciple the next form, *sandhi* (connection) is *vidyā* (education). The preaching is the connector.

This way each word is to be understood as gross, subtle and *kāraṇa* (reason), then gradually the bigger concepts will be understood. In each stage one can see the *parama* matter (*Brahman*). Dear Bhṛgu, you do the *upāsanā* of this as such.

**Bhṛgu** – As per your order I will do the *upāsanā*, revered *guru*.

**Vaiśampāyana** –

> अथाधिप्रजम्। माता पूर्वरूपम्। पिता उत्तररूपम्। प्रजा सन्धिः । प्रजननम्ँ सन्धानम्। इत्यधिप्रजम्। ॥३.५॥
>
> *athādhiprajam* | *mātā pūrvarūpam* | *pitā uttararūpam* | *prajā sandhiḥ* | *prajananaṁ saṁdhānam* | *ityadhiprajam* | | 3.5 | |
>
> Now with reference to the context of progeny: the mother is the prior form; the father is the later form; progeny is the meeting place and procreation is the connecting link. Thus is the nature of the *mahāsaṁhitā*, with reference to the context of progeny.

When talking about *praja* (child), mother comes first, father comes next, *praja* is the joining place, and birth is the connecting thing. Hey Prācīnayogya, you meditate like this.

**Prācīnayogya** – Svāmī! I will do as you say, however one doubt.

**Vaiśampāyana** – What is that? Ask it, son.

**Prācīnayogya** – In the *mahān* (great) *Upaniṣad* when they are talking about *Brahmam,* how to do *upāsanā* of *praja*? How is it proper to talk about child and birth?

**Other disciples** – We also wanted to ask about this.

**Vaiśampāyana** – My dear children. It is better to ask your doubts in the beginning itself. Instead of keeping it in mind and getting restless, if it is told outside it will do good. Our ancestors the *maharṣi*s did not belittle a householder's life. They considered it as a good thing to lead householder's life and they supported it. *Brahmacaryam* (bachelorhood), *gṛhastham* (householder), *vānaprastham* (going to the forest), and *sanyas* (renunciation) — in these four *āśrama*s the life was divided and to support the three *āśrama*s was the job of the *gṛhastha* (householder). The women were given an important status. Without wife a *yajña* cannot be conducted. None of the religious work can be done without the wife. The husband and wife union was considered a holy one. To bring about the growth of *prapañca* (world) the support of women was thought imperative. Rather than giving advice on how to control unwanted sexual expression, the mode of union was considered a route for longer bliss. The sexual instincts, instead of keeping in wraps and allowed to grow in the wrong direction, must be allowed to grow properly and hence the institution of marriage was created and *dharma* was safeguarded. (Mahācamasya comes and does his salutations.)

**Vaiśampāyana** – Child! Mahācamasya, sit. In what state are the arrangements for food to be served in the forest (*vana bhojana*) going on?

**Mahācamasya** – Svāmī! Everything is in readiness.

(He sits down).

**Vaiśampāyana** –

अथाध्यात्मम्। अधरा हनुः पूर्वरूपम्। उत्तरा हनुरुत्तररूपम्।
वाक् सन्धिः। जिह्वा सन्धानम्। इत्यध्यात्मम्। ॥३.६॥

*athādhyātmam | adharā hanuḥ pūrvarūpam | uttarā hanuruttararūpam | vāk sandhiḥ | jihvā saṁdhānam | ityadhyātmam* | | 3.6 | |

Now with reference to the context of oneself: the lower jaw is the prior form: the upper jaw is the later form; speech is the meeting place and the tongue is the connecting link. Thus is (the nature of the *mahāsaṁhitā*) with reference to the context of oneself.

*Athādhyātmam* is about the body. When describing about it the lower lip is *pūrvarūpam,* the upper lip is *uttararūpam,* the talk is the connection (*sandhi*), and the connecting link is tongue. This is only *athādhyātmam.* Mahācamasya, you do *upāsanā* like this.

**Mahācamasya** – I will do so, Respected Sir.

**Vaiśampāyana** –

इतीमा महासꣳहिताः। य एवमेता महासꣳहिता व्याख्याता वेद।
सन्धीयते प्रजया पशुभिः। ब्रह्मवर्चसेनान्नद्येन सुवर्गेण लोकेन। ॥३.७॥

*itīmā mahāsaṁhitāḥ | ya evametā mahāsaṁ 'hitā vyākhyātā veda | sandhīyate prajayā paśubhiḥ | brahmavarcasenānnadyena suvargeṇa lokena* | | 3.7 | |

These are the great combinations. He who knows these great combinations thus expounded, becomes endowed with progeny, cattle, with the splendour of *Brahman*-knowledge, with food to eat and with the heavenly world.

Like this *mahāsaṁhitā*s were preached by me. Likewise, the words should be understood. Take the particular thing like *pṛthivī* as world, the first letter, and so on. A person who understands the *mahāsaṁhitā*s and does *upāsanā* of them as told, he will get a life blessed with good *praja*s (children), cows, *brahman-tejas, annam, svargaloka,* etc.

That is, if a person desires for the results and does *upāsanā* he gets those *bhoga*s. However if a person does *upāsanā* but without desiring he will qualify to obtain *brahma-vidyā*. Children! With this let us stop today's lesson.

***(Curtain falls.)***

SCENE 3

***(Curtain opens.)***

(It is the *āśrama* of Vaiśampāyana. In the place where *yajña* has to take place Triśaṅku and Vaikhānasa are making a *homa-kuṇḍa* (fire place for conducting *yajña*). The *homa-kuṇḍa* is made in the form of bird Garuḍa. To do *Śrīkāma yajña* Bodhāyana keeps out the ghee, *havis* and other things required. The *ṛṣi*'s wife also helps him in these jobs. Vaiśampāyana enters with Mahācamasya).

**Vaiśampāyana** – Dear! Has everything been arranged for the *homa* (*yajña*)?

**Wife of the *ṛṣi*** — *Āryaputra*! Everything is ready. The *homa* can be started in *śubha-muhurtta* (auspicious time).

**Vaiśampāyana** – Dear! Let it be so. It can be started in another hour's time. By the time Bhṛgu and others will come back.

**Triśaṅku** – Revered Guru! Where have they gone?

**Vaiśampāyana** – The important guests who had come for *vana bhojana* are returning today. I told Bhṛgu and others to see them off by escorting them till the river bank.

**Vaikhānasa** – Svāmī! Have all the guests departed?

**Vaiśampāyana** – The sons of Radhira, Satyavaca and Pūṣṭi's son Taponitya are going today. Mahanagar and others are going tomorrow.

**Bodhāyana** – The three of them came together, isn't it? Now why Mahānagara is separated and going tomorrow alone?

**Ṛṣipatnī** – You don't know that? Mahānagara as per the request of King Janaka is going to give a discourse in the *rāja-sabhā* today evening. Hence he is staying back.

**Vaikhānasa** – Is that so! Very happy to know it. We also can go there and hear it.

**Vaiśampāyana** – We all will go. Now attend to the *homa* requirements. Hey Bodhāyana! *Samidhā* (firewood) is not enough. Bring a little more. Hey dear, the *ghee* is of cows isn't it? Vaikhānasa, keep this holy grass bundle (*dūrbā*) a little this side and keep the wooden seat for sitting that side. Hey Triśaṅku bright the *ṛtvigs*.

(Vaiśampāyana goes around the *yajña* place and supervises the proceedings. Later he goes and sits in one corner of the *āśrama*. Mahācamasya also goes and joins him.)

**Vaiśampāyana** – Child! Mahācamasya! Come near. I am going to teach you one *mantra* now. After you do *japa* of this *mantra* properly and get *siddhi*, the other disciples also have to be taught.

**Mahācamasya** – **(gives his respects by telling *praṇāmas*)** Reverend Guru, *dhanyosmi*, your *chit* is my fortune.

**Vaiśampāyana** – Come near and sit (**the disciple sits**). I am telling, listen.

यश्छन्दसामृषभो विश्वरूपः। छन्दोभ्योऽध्यमृतात्सम्बभूव। स मेन्द्रो मेधया स्पृणोतु। अमृतस्य देव धारणो भूयासम्। शरीरं मे विचर्षणम्। जिह्वा मे मधुमत्तमा। कर्णाभ्यां भूरि विश्रुवम्। ब्रह्मणः कोशोऽसि मेधया पिहितः। श्रुतं मे गोपाय। ॥४॥१॥

*yaśchandasāmṛṣabho viśvarūpaḥ | chandobhyo 'dhyamṛtātsambabhūva | sa mendro medhayā spṛṇotu | amṛtasya deva dhāraṇo bhūyāsam | śarīraṁ me vicarṣaṇam | jihvā me madhumattamā | karṇābhyāṁ bhūri viśruvam | brahmaṇaḥ kośo 'si medhayā pihitaḥ | śrutaṁ me gopāya | |4.1| |*

He who is the bull (the mightiest) in the Vedic hymns, who has the cosmos as his form, who has sprung up from the immortal Vedic hymns, may that Indra *AUM* cheer me with intelligence. O God! may I be the possessor of immortality. May my body be vigorous; may my tongue be exceedingly sweet; may I hear (learn) rich words with my ears. Thou art the sheath of *Brahman* veiled with intelligence; guard for me what I have learned.

(As the *ācārya* tells, the disciples repeat.)

**Vaiśampāyana** – Now I will tell the meaning listen. The one which is exalted among Vedas and manifests as *viśvarūpam;* the one which has been formed from the nectar of Vedas that *oṁkāra,* give me consciousness and perception. Hey *deva*! You must help me to acquire *brahma-jñāna* whose concept is as sweet as nectar. May my body become strong and capable to receive such wisdom. Let my tongue become sweet like honey. Let it talk always sweet words. Let my ears hear always only sweet words and good things. Hey *oṁkāra*! You are like a wrap for *Brahman.* Due to *saṁsāra* you are hidden. Protect my knowledge about *brahma-jñāna.* Whatever Self-knowledge I have heard kindly protect it. That is, let me not forget what I have learnt.

**Mahācamasya** – Svāmī! You told *oṁkāra*'s meaning in these *mantras*. However that word itself has not come in the *mantras*.

**Vaiśampāyana** – Child! What you are asking is a good question. I will answer you, listen. The word Indra is only told. Like a *ṛṣabha* among a herd of cows, among the *mantras* the one who is supreme, the Indra itself means *oṁkāra.* It is *viśvarūpam* and has come out of nectar of Vedas in a special way. From the mention of these and other adjectives it is *oṁkāra* that is mentioned in this *mantra* which is definite. Hence the *oṁkāra rūpam,* the Indra who is the lord of all. May he give me erudition and good memory which is important for students.

**Mahācamasya** – *Oṁkāra* is the cover of *Brahman,* you told. I am not able to understand that. Kindly explain it in detail.

**Vaiśampāyana** – Just like for a shining sword a protective cover is there, in the same way *oṁkāra* acts as the cover for *paramātmā* (*Brahman*). Similarly as cover of the sword leads to the sword itself, in the same way *oṁkāra* leads to *Brahman.*

Meditating on *oṁkāra* or meditating on *Brahman* is the same. Even when we talk ordinarily we give importance to the holder. For example water is kept in a *kamaṇḍala.* If water is required we ask the *kamaṇḍala* to be brought. Out here water means *Brahman. Kamaṇḍala* is *oṁkāra*. Inside *oṁkāra* the *Brahman* is contained, he is enclosed. Hence meditating on *oṁkāra* is very good. Carefully do *japa* of these *mantras*.

**Mahācamasya** – Let that be so, Svāmī.

**Vaiśampāyana** – Go immediately and sit under the gooseberry tree where *vana-bhojana* took place and do *japa* of this *mantra* for one *maṇḍala* (Mahācamasya is about to get up). Before you leave whatever you have learned, do tell in short.

**Mahācamasya** – As per your order I will do. The *medhakāma japa* is to be done thinking about *oṁkāra*. O! king of *mantras*, the one discovered by Brahmā from Veda which is like nectar and can be considered as its essence.

"I must stay high in my intellect. I must reach the indestructible wealth of Self-knowledge. My body should be made capable for that. I must speak as sweetly as the honey. My words should flow like honey drops full of sweetness. I must stay high in enquiries. In front of elders, without talking too much, I must keep my ears sharp to hear what they tell. You are covering the *Brahman* like a sheath. Kindly give me *Brahman* knowledge and save me. You must bless me as not to forget it. *Oṁkāra,* I give my salutations to you.

**Vaiśampāyana** – *Sabhāsa*! You told very well. In a short time you will outdo me in giving discourse. I am very proud of you. (within himself) My disciples all are like that. Yājñavalkya went away, but how intelligent he was? Triśaṅku is also not ordinary. He is also very knowledgeable. Now Mahācamasya also has progressed well. I am indeed very happy. Child! By repeating this *mantra,* brain power, memory power and strength of the body will increase. A person not having intelligence but only body strength will only cause harm. Hence only after praying for brain power the body strength is to be prayed for. After that only *aiśvaryam* (wealth) is being requested. Go do the *japa* and come back with *siddhi* (capability). I am giving you my *āśīrvāda* for it. Do go and come.

(Mahācamasya does *namaskāra* and departs. Bhṛgu and Prācīnayogya are coming. Triśaṅku comes with *ṛtvigs*.)

**Vaiśampāyana** – Come all of you. Let us start the *homa* (around *homa-kuṇḍa* Vaiśampāyana and *ṛtvigs* are sitting. Nearby disciples, *ṛṣi-patnī* and the ladies of the *āśrama* are standing.

**Vaikhānasa** – Here I am giving ghee (*ājyam*) separately to each one.

**Vaiśampāyana** –

ॐ आवहन्ती वितन्वाना। कुर्वाणाऽचीरमात्मनः। वासाꣳसि मम गावश्च। अन्नपाने च सर्वदा। ततो मे श्रियमावह। लोमशां पशुभिः सह स्वाहा। आ मा यन्तु ब्रह्मचारिणः स्वाहा। वि मा यन्तु ब्रह्मचारिणः स्वाहा। प्र मा यन्तु ब्रह्मचारिणः स्वाहा। दमायन्तु ब्रह्मचारिणः स्वाहा। शमायन्तु ब्रह्मचारिणः स्वाहा। ॥४.२॥

*āvahantī vitanvānā | kurvāṇā 'cīramātmanaḥ | vāsāṁsi mama gāvaśca | annapāne ca sarvadā | tato me śriyamavaha | lomaśāṁ paśubhiḥ saha svāhā | ā mā yantu brahmacāriṇaḥ svāhā | vi mā yantu brahmacāriṇaḥ svāhā | pra mā yantu brahmacāriṇaḥ svāhā | damāyantu brahmacāriṇaḥ svāhā | śamāyantu brahmacāriṇaḥ svāhā | |4.2| |*

Then vouchsafe to me who is the Self, the prosperity which brings, increases and accomplishes quickly for me clothes, cattle, food and drink forever, and which is associated with furry and other animals. May seekers of Truth approach me. May seekers of Truth approach me variously. Hail! May seekers of Truth approach me undisturbed by external influences. Hail! May seekers of Truth approach me with mental self-control.

यशो जनेऽसानि स्वाहा। श्रेयान् वस्यसोऽसानि स्वाहा। तं त्वा भग प्रविशानि स्वाहा। स मा भग प्रविश स्वाहा। तस्मिन् सहस्रशाखे। नि भगाहं त्वयि मृजे स्वाहा। यथापः प्रवता यन्ति। यथा मासा अहर्जरम्। एवं मां ब्रह्मचारिणः। धातरायन्तु सर्वतः स्वाहा। प्रतिवेशोऽसि प्र मा भाहि प्र मा पद्यस्व॥४.३॥

*yaśo jane 'sāni svāhā | śreyān vasyaso 'sāni svāhā | taṁ tvā bhaga praviśāni svāhā | sa mā bhaga praviśa svāhā | tasmin sahasraśākhe | ni bhagāhaṁ tvayi mṛje svāhā | yathāpaḥ pravatā yanti yathā māsā aharjaram | evaṁ māṁ brahmacāriṇaḥ | dhātarāyantu sarvataḥ svāhā | prativeśo 'si pra mā bhāhi pra mā padyasva* ||4.3||

May I become famous among people.
May I become more renowned than the very rich.
O Gracious Lord, may I enter into you, as you are,
In that self of yours, of a thousand branches, O Gracious Lord, am I cleansed.
As waters run downwards, as months into the year, so unto me may seekers come.
O Disposer of all, come from every side.
You are a refuge, so you do shine forth to me, unto me do you come.

(Whenever *svāhā* is pronounced the *homam* is done by ghee.)

**The first ṛtvig** – Maharṣi, kindly tell the meaning of these *mantras*.

**Vaiśampāyana** – Child Bodhāyana, you stay back to do *Aiyathi homa* and other *homa*s and do the *pūjā*s and complete the *yajña* proceedings. Others come over here. Let us stay away. I will tell the meaning.

(Taking them to the side *maharṣi* is telling the meaning). This *homa karma* is pertaining to a person desiring for wealth. If *śrīkāma* (one desirous of things) does this *homa* all the good fortune will come and reach him. There is no doubt about this. First prayer is for knowledge and brain strength, then body strength has to be gained, then the prayer should be directed for wealth. "Bless me with all the prosperity (*saubhāgya*). May Lakṣmī (Goddess of Wealth) give me cloth, cattle, food and drink. May I be blessed with healthy goats having strong hair. Let the cattle wealth be multiplied and grow. The word *svāhā* should be told when doing the *homa. Brahmachārin*s should come seeking me (telling thus I am doing the *homa*). The *brahmachārin*s should come from all directions and far-off places. Such *brahmachārin*s should come who can control the senses. *Brahmachārin*s having peaceful character should come in large numbers. Let me be a very famous and wealthy person. Respected *oṁkārā,* I enter in you. You also enter in me. That is, I must sublime into you. You who have thousand branches, I clean myself in you and remove my blemishes. Just like the water flows towards deep basins, just like the months join together and complete the year, in the same way let *brahmachārin*s come from all four sides to me. You are the asylum for everyone. You are the place where all sorrow and sin can be drowned. Hence come and reach me and bless me. By brightening me you brighten yourself.

**The first ṛtvig** – Maharṣi, my salutations. Very wonderful *mantra*s. It is filled with poetic essence and deep meaning.

**Bhṛgu** – Svāmī! We understand how the water moves to the deep basins, in the same way the disciples by themselves should seek the *guru* and come. However kindly tell the meaning of the word *aharjaram* and the meaning for the simile, that the disciples should come like months. Do explain.

**Vaiśampāyana** – Child! I will tell. Do listen carefully. As how the year should get completed by months in the same way the *guru*'s life will be complete only by good disciples. Just like how months are contained in the year and do not go away from the year, in the same way the disciples should not go away from the *guru*. Only by *brahmachārin*s who have good control of senses and have peaceful nature, good deeds can be attempted. Because of that, sins will get mitigated and wisdom will come. The meaning of *ahas* is a day. *Aharjaram* means *saṁvatsaram* (year). In the form of day and night the world is digested. Hence the word *aharjaram* (to digest) is very apt for the year.

**Prācīnayogya** – The request for wealth and *brahmachārins* are together prayed for. Is there any special meaning in this?

**Vaiśampāyana** – The wealth prayed for is not for self-use. There is no selfish motive here. *Brahmachārins* should come in large numbers. They should do *gurukula* stay in the *āśrama*, learn lessons, live disciplined in *brahmaniṣṭhā,* then like Rājā Janaka they should enter *gṛhasthāśrama.* To give the necessary comforts for them wealth is prayed for. It is prayed that the wealthy one should be exalted, meaning of this is he should possess good *dharma* and should be a generous donor, a philanthropist. To get wealth, this *homa* is done. To do the deeds of *dharma* and for the sins to be mitigated. When sins decrease then wisdom dawns. On this basis only this *homa* is being done. Finally just like how a metal piece when melted mixes with *rasa* and changes, in the same way I must combine with *Brahman* and become one with it. Praying thus the *mantra* gets completed.

**Ṛṣipatnī** – It is time for food. All of you come inside.

**Bodhāyana** – **(getting up and coming)** I have completed the *homa,* revered Guru.

**Vaiśampāyana** – Alright, let us go inside, come.

**(All are going inside.)**

***(Curtain falls.)***

## SCENE – 4

***(Curtain opens.)***

(Mahācamasya is sitting under the gooseberry tree where *vana-bhojana* took place. In his face *ojas* and *tejas* are shining. Prācīnayogya and Vaikhānasa are entering.)

**Prācīnayogya** – Friend! This early morning you have called me in great hurry and brought me here. What is the reason?

**Vaikhānasa** – Yes, it is very important indeed. Yesterday our *guru* called me alone and ordered.

**Prācīnayogya** – What is that order? It is about whom? And about what?

**Vaikhānasa** – All about you only.

**Prācīnayogya** – Is that so! About me, tell me fast, what it is? I am ready to act accordingly.

**Vaikhānasa** – No need to hurry. I am telling you, my friend. It is about *vyāhṛti*s. How many *vyāhṛti*s are there? What are their names? Do you know?

**Prācīnayogya** – Friend! This is an ordinary question. I will tell you the answer in detail.

भूर्भुवः सुवरिति वा एतास्तिस्रो व्याहृतयः।

*bhūrbhuvaḥ suvariti vā etāstisro vyāhṛtayaḥ* ।

*Bhūr, bhuvaḥ, suvaḥ* verily these are the three utterances (*vyāhṛti*s),

*Vyāhṛti*s are three. They are *bhuḥ, bhuvaḥ,* and *suvaḥ*. This is very well known.

**Vaikhānasa** – Friend, very happy. But I will now tell you about the fourth *vyāhṛti.* Its name is *maha.*

तासामु ह स्मैतां चतुर्थीम्। माहाचमस्यः प्रवेदयते। मह इति।

*tāsāmu ha smaitāṁ caturthīm Mahācamasyaḥ pravedayate* । *maha iti* ।

Mahācamasya (a *ṛṣi*) knew the fourth one. It is *maha* by name.

**Prācīnayogya** – Fourth one! I have not heard it so far. It is sounding new.

**Vaikhānasa** – Yes. It is new indeed. Some days before only it was discovered.

**Prācīnayogya** – I am very happy to know that. Who is the *mahān* who came to know the fourth *vyāhṛti* and released it? Where is he? My mind desires to see him, serve him, get his blessings and preaching.

**Vaikhānasa** – You don't have to go anywhere for that. One of our friends only discovered it. Our *guru* gave that information yesterday only.

**Prācīnayogya** – Is it one of our friends? Is it Bhṛgu? If he is the one, he would have told in the beginning itself this matter to me. Perhaps it is Triśaṅku. He only remains in meditation always.

**Four *vyāhṛtis* — four worlds**

**Vaikhānasa** – It is not the two people whom you mentioned. It is Mahācamasya who found the fourth *vyāhṛti*. Hence our *guru* ordered to give the name *mahaḥ* to it.

**Prācīnayogya** – I am very happy to know. The greatness of *medhakāma japa* is known here.

**Vaikhānasa** – Friend! I am taking leave.

**Prācīnayogya** – You did not tell the reason as to why I am brought here. Are you leaving me alone and going?

**Vaikhānasa** – Friend! *guru*'s order was to tell you this information and leave you near Mahācamasya. Other matters

Mahācamasya will preach to you. Now let me leave. **(He goes)** (Prācīnayogya goes near Mahācamasya and gives his salutations.)

**Mahācamasya** – **(Opens his eyes after some time)** Is it Prācīnayogya? Come, kindly sit.

**Prācīnayogya** – **(Sitting down)** Svāmī! You must preach to me about *vyāhṛtis*.

**Mahācamasya** – Let it be so.

तद्ब्रह्म। स आत्मा। अङ्गान्यन्या देवताः। भूरिति वा अयं लोकः। भुव इत्यन्तरिक्षम्। सुवरित्यसौ लोकः। मह इत्यादित्यः। आदित्येन वाव सर्वे लोका महीयन्ते। ॥५.१॥

*tad brahma* I *sa ātmā* I *aṅgānyanyā devatāḥ* I *bhūriti vā ayaṁ lokaḥ* I *bhuva ityantarikṣam* I *suvarityasau lokaḥ* I *maha ityādityaḥ* I *ādityena vāva sarve lokā mahīyante* I I5.1I I

That is *Brahman* (the Absolute). That is *ātman* (the Self). The other gods are its limbs only. *Bhuḥ* indeed is the world. *Bhuvaḥ* is the intermediate space. *Suvaḥ* is the other world. *Mahaḥ* is the Sun. Through the Sun indeed all these worlds become great.

*Bhuḥ, bhuvaḥ, suvaḥ,* these three *vyāhṛtis* are well known. The fourth *vyāhṛti* is *mahaḥ*. That is only *Brahman*. Like *Brahman* it is very big. The other *devatās* are like its organs. Just like *chetana* (the main energy) in the body is more important than organs in the body, similarly *ātmā* is supreme. In the same way in comparison to other *vyāhṛtis,* the fourth one, *mahaḥ vyāhṛti* is supreme. *Bhuḥ* is this *loka, bhuvaḥ* is *antarikṣa* (space), *suvaḥ* is *svargaloka, mahaḥ* is Āditya. Because of Āditya only all the three worlds get their greatness, hence it is supreme. These *vyāhṛtis* should be done *upāsanā* in this manner.

**Prācīnayogya** – Kindly explain the *adhijyautiṣam* state and other states in which the *upāsanā* of these *vyāhṛtis* to be done.

**Mahācamasya** –

भूरिति वा अग्निः। भुव इति वायुः। सुवरित्यादित्यः। मह इति चन्द्रमाः।
चन्द्रमसा वाव सर्वाणि ज्योतीꣳषि महीयन्ते। ॥५.२॥
भूरिति वा ऋचः। भुव इति सामानि। सुवरिति यजूꣳषि। मह इति ब्रह्म।
ब्रह्मणा वाव सर्वे वेदा महीयन्ते। ॥५.३॥
भूरिति वै प्राणः। भुव इत्यपानः। सुवरिति व्यानः। मह इत्यन्नम्। अन्नेन
वाव सर्वे प्राणा महीयन्ते। ॥५.४॥
ता वा एताश्चतस्रश्चतुर्धा। चतस्रश्चतस्रो व्याहृतयः। ता यो वेद। स वेद
ब्रह्म। सर्वेऽस्मै देवाः बलिमावहन्ति। ॥५.५॥

*bhūriti vā agniḥ* | *bhuva iti vāyuḥ* | *suvarityādityaḥ* | *maha iti candramāḥ* | *candramasā vāva sarvāṇi jyotīm̐ṣi mahīyante* | 5.2 |

*bhūriti vā ṛcaḥ* | *bhuva iti sāmāni* | *suvariti yajūm̐ṣi* | *maha iti brahma* | *brahmaṇā vāva sarve vedā mahīyante* | 5.3 |

*bhūriti vai prāṇaḥ* | *bhuva ityapānaḥ* | *suvariti vyānaḥ* | *maha ityannam* | *annena vāva sarve prāṇā mahīyante* | 5.4 |

*tā vā etāścatasraścaturdhā* | *catasraścatasro vyāhṛtayaḥ* | *tā yo veda* | *sa veda brahma* | *sarve 'smai devāḥ balimāvahanti* | 5.5 |

*Bhuḥ agniḥ, bhuvaḥ vāyu, suvaḥ ādityaḥ, mahaḥ candraḥ.* Because of *Chandra* all *jyotiṣ* (lights) get their importance.

*Bhuḥ ṛgveda bhuvaḥ sāmāveda, suvaḥ yajurveda, mahaḥ Brahman,* that is *oṁkāra.* Because of *praṇavam* all Vedas get this importance.

Bhuḥ *prāṇavāyu, bhuvaḥ apāna-vāyu, suvaḥ vyāna-vāyu, mahaḥ annam.* Because of *annam* only all *prāṇa*s get their importances.

These four *vyāhṛti*s only, each one is shown separately here as four.

Whoever understands this and does *upāsanā* he will know *Brahman.* For a person of this capacity *deva*s will come and crown him. That is, whatever he wants *deva*s will bring it as offering.

**Prācīnayogya** – Svāmī! The fourth part having four divisions, kindly explain it in some more detail.

**Mahācamasya** – I will do so.

*Bhuḥ vyāhṛti* considered as *bhūloka, agni, Ṛgveda and prāṇa vāyu.*

*Bhuvaḥ vyāhṛti* is considered as *antarikṣa, vāyu, Sāmaveda* and *apāna vāyu.*

*Suvaḥ vyāhṛti* is considered as *svargaloka,* sun, *Yajurveda* and *vyāna vāyu.*

*Mahaḥ vyāhṛti* is considered as *āditya, chandra, praṇavam* and *annam.*

The *Brahman* which is the source of these *vyāhṛti*s should be kept in place of heart and *upāsanā* has to be done.

**Prācīnayogya** – Kindly explain this in detail.

**Mahācamasya** – I will do so.

स य एषोऽन्तर्हृदय आकाशः। तस्मिन्नयं पुरुषो मनोमयः। अमृतो हिरण्मयः। अन्तरेण तालुके। य एष स्तन इवावलम्बते। सेन्द्रयोनिः। यत्रासौ केशान्तो विवर्तते। व्यपोह्य शीर्षकपाले। भूरित्यग्नौ प्रतितिष्ठति। भुव इति वायौ ॥६.१॥

*sa ya eṣo 'ntarhṛdaya ākāśaḥ* | *tasminnayaṁ puruṣo manomayaḥ* | *amṛto hiraṇmayaḥ* | *antareṇa tāluke* | *ya eṣa stana ivāvalambate* | *sendrayoniḥ* | *yatrāsau keśānto vivartate* | *vyapohya śīrṣakapāle* | *bhūrityagnau pratitiṣṭhati* | *bhuva iti vāyau* ||6.1||

This space that is within the heart therein is the Person of great mental strength immortal and resplendent. That which hangs down between the palates like a nipple, that is the source of Indra (or *AUM*), where the hairs split apart, it exits separating the skull of the head. He is well founded in fire as the *vyāhṛti bhuḥ*. He is well founded in air as the *vyāhṛti bhuvaḥ*.

सुवरित्यादित्ये। मह इति ब्रह्मणि। आप्नोति स्वाराज्यम्। आप्नोति मनसस्पतिम्। वाक्पतिश्चक्षुष्पतिः। श्रोत्रपतिर्विज्ञानपतिः। एतत्ततो भवति। आकाशशरीरं ब्रह्म। सत्यात्म प्राणारामं मनआनन्दम्। शान्तिसमृद्धम-मृतम्। इति प्राचीनयोग्योपास्व ॥६.२॥

*suvarityāditye | maha iti brahmaṇi | āpnoti svārājyam | āpnoti manasaspatim | vākpatiścakṣuṣpatiḥ | śrotrapatirvijñānapatiḥ | etattato bhavati | ākāśa śarīraṁ brahma | satyātma prāṇārāmaṁ mana ānandam | śānti samṛddham amṛtam | iti prācīnayogyopāsva* ||6.2||

He is well founded in the Sun as the *vyāhṛti suvaḥ*. He is well founded in *Brahman* as the *vyāhṛti mahaḥ*. He attains to selfhood. He attains to the lord of the mind. He attains to the lord of speech, the lord of sight, the lord of hearing, the lord of specific knowledge. He becomes that Supreme which is beyond that. He becomes *Brahman* whose body is space. He has self-content for reality, the *prāṇa* for pleasure grove, mind for bliss, the abundance of immortality for the experiencing of peace. O Prācīnayogya, thus do you contemplate.

Prācīnayogya! You do *upāsanā* like this. Inside your heart there is *ākāśa* (space). There in the centre of the mind like a bright gold piece, indestructible *puruṣa* is present.

The person who does *upāsanā* of this *puruṣa* will reach *Brahman,* the route of which I will tell you. Starting from heart, the *suṣumnā nāḍī* goes along the piece of flesh (small inner tongue) located between the two jaws in an upward direction. This then reaches *mūrta;* there it divides along the skull into two routes and further rises up.

Along this *suṣumnā nāḍī* if one does *upāsanā* one can reach the *Brahman*. That is, the one who worships the *puruṣa* who is in the heart. At the time of death the *Brahman* leaves from the heart and along the *suṣumnā nāḍī* rises up, meets the *mūrta* and comes out.

**Prācīnayogya** – It is surprising to hear. Do tell the other places of destination of *Brahman* in detail.

**Mahācamasya** – Thus coming out He joins the *vyāhṛti bhuḥ* which is *agni-rūpa*. Then He reaches the *vyāhṛti bhuvaḥ* which is *vāyu-rūpa* and the *vyāhṛti suvaḥ* which is *āditya-rūpa*. Then He becomes one with *mahaḥ* which is *brahma-rūpa*. By reaching the *Brahman* he is deemed to have obtained the *svarājyam* (his own kingdom). He is the lord of all minds. He is also the lord of speech, eye, ear, *vijñānam,* etc. He becomes *brahma-svarūpa* which is *sarvātmā* and He is the *svarūpa* form of all *prāṇas* (living things). He does not possess any sense organs by himself. However through other's sense organs. He comes to know everything. Also He reaches a state above that. That is, He becomes *Brahman* itself which is indestructible, filled with supreme peace, gives bliss to the mind, gives quietude to the *prāṇa* and that which is truth personification and one which has the sky as the body.

**Prācīnayogya** – Svāmī! I became blessed. I will conduct myself as per your preachings.

**Mahācamasya** – I am very happy to hear that. If you have any doubts you can ask. To the extent I know I will answer. Whatever I don't know we can ask our revered *guru.*

**Prācīnayogya** – Svāmī! In *medhakāma japa* the *praṇava* body of *Brahman* is described. Now here, the *vyāhṛtis* as to where it is found and the ways to reach it have been preached. There is no special doubt, however. . . .

**Mahācamasya** – However what?

**Prācīnayogya** – That is *tat brahma sa ātmā* (तत् ब्रह्म स आत्मा) which means "That only is *Brahman,* that only is *ātmā.*"

*Atha yo veda sa veda brahma* (अथ यो वेद स वेद ब्रह्म) which means "whoever knows that, comes to know *Brahman.*" Is telling as thus alright? There creeps an element of doubt in that statement.

**Mahācamasya** – There is nothing wrong in telling like that. The fourth *vyāhṛti rūpa* is *Brahman,* that only one comes to know. It is established in the heart and it has characteristic of a *manomaya.* A person who does *upāsanā* knowing these characteristics reaches *Brahman.*

**Prācīnayogya** – Svāmī, by this *upāsanā* like a gooseberry kept in the palm the truth was shown very clearly. My salutations to you.

**Mahācamasya** – Let us go to the *āśrama,* come down.

***(Curtain falls.)***

## SCENE 5

***(Curtain opens.)***

(It is Maharṣi Vaiśampāyana's *āśrama. Maharṣi* is teaching the disciples.)

**Vaiśampāyana** – Children! Let all good tidings befall you. Try to recollect whatever I have taught. Hey Triśaṅku, tell about them in brief.

**Triśaṅku** – Bhagavān! Accept my *namaskārams.* At the beginning *śīkṣā adhyayaṁ* was preached. After that *Śrikāma homa* was explained. Through *vyāhṛti* basis you preached *upāsanā Brahman.*

**Vaiśampāyana** – Child! You told it admiringly short and also without leaving a single one. I am very happy. I am thinking of five *pāṅktams* and am teaching today *pāṅkta svarūpa upāsanā* — doing method.

**Triśaṅku** – Respected Sir, do bless us with your holy words. We are waiting to hear.

**Bhṛgu** – What is the meaning of *pāṅktam*? Kindly explain, Revered Guru.

**Five *Pāṅktams***

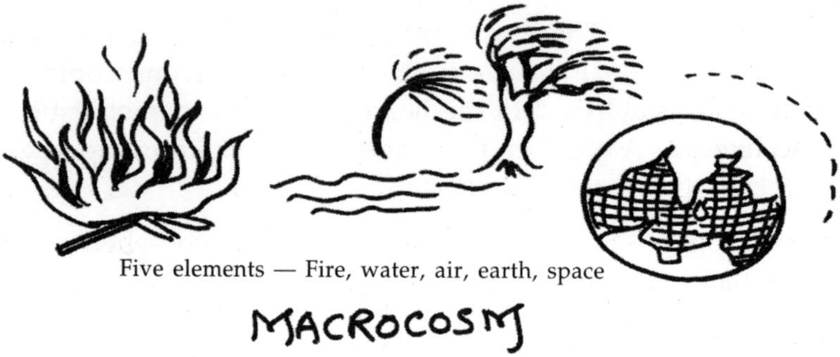


Five elements — Fire, water, air, earth, space

*fig.*: **Five sense organs — sight, taste, touch, smell and sound.**

**Vaiśampāyana** – Child! *pāṅkti* is a *chandhas* having five words. Whichever is made of the five substances is all grouped under *pāṅktam*. Now wife (*patnī*), the master, the son, wisdom, wealth with these five *yajña* gets completed. Hence this *yajña* is called *pāṅktam*. In the *adhyātmam* (body) itself three *pāṅktams* are there.

**Vaikhānasa** – Kindly inform us about *pāṅktam* like this, group-wise in *adhibhūtam*.

**Vaiśampāyana** – Child! Alright I will tell so.

पृथिव्यन्तरिक्षं द्यौर्दिशोऽवान्तरदिशः। अग्निर्वायुरादित्यश्चन्द्रमा नक्षत्राणि।

*pṛthivyantarikṣaṁ dyaurdiśo 'vāntaradiśaḥ* |
*agnirvāyurādityaścandramā nakṣatrāṇi* |

आप ओषधयो वनस्पतय आकाश आत्मा। इत्यधिभूतम्।

*āpa oṣadhayo vanaspataya ākāśa ātmā* |
*ityadhibhūtam* |

The earth, atmosphere, heaven, the (main) quarters and the intermediate quarters (thus five); fire, air, sun, moon and stars (thus five); water, plants, trees, space and the body (thus five); thus with regard to the generic material existence.

Earth, *antarikṣa* (space), sky, directions, corners of direction these five are wordly *pāṅktams*.

In the same way *agni, vāyu*, sun, moon and stars are *deva pāṅktams*.

Water, plants, trees, sky, *ātmā* (*virāṭ svarūpa*) these five are *bhūta* (element) *pāṅktams*.

These three groups can be termed as *adibhūtams*.

**Bodhāyana** – Svāmī! We understand in detail about *pāṅktams*. Now how to do *upāsanā* of them as *Brahman*, that also you must kindly explain.

**Vaiśampāyana** – The five in the sky, the five in the earth, the five in the body, these three sets of *pāṅktams*, when we understand them and their relationships clearly we will feel a great happiness.

To understand outside *pāṅktam* there are five related parts in the *adyātmam* (body).

अथाध्यात्मम्। प्राणो व्यानोऽपान उदानः समानः। चक्षुः श्रोत्रं मनो वाक् त्वक्। चर्म मा२ँस२ँ स्नावाऽस्थि मज्जा। एतदधिविधाय ऋषिरवोचत्। पाङ्क्तं वा इद२ँ सर्वम्। पाङ्क्तेनैव पाङ्क्त२ँ स्पृणोतीति॥७॥

*athādhyātmam | prāṇo vyāno 'pāna udānaḥ samānaḥ | cakṣuḥ śrotraṁ mano vāk tvak | carma māṁsaṁ snāvā 'sthi majjā | etaddhividhāya ṛṣiravocat | pāṅktaṁ vā idaṁ sarvam | pāṅktenaiva pāṅktaṁ spṛṇotīti | |7| |*

Now with regard to the individual existence: *prāṇa, vyāna, apāna, udāna,* and *samāna* (thus five); sight, hearing, mind, speech and touch (thus five); skin, flesh, muscle, bone and marrow (thus five); thus understanding these wih a structural scheme, the *ṛṣi* said, "All this is constituted of five factors.

The fivefold is supported by the fivefold indeed."

Relating to five parts in *adhibhūtam* inside the body there are five sense organs. From this we can deduce *adhibhūtam* and *adhyātmam* (macrocosm and microcosm) are the same; knowing this the *upāsanā* has to be performed.

**Prācīnayogya** – Yes, in *aṇḍam* (macrocosm) and *piṇḍam* (microcosm) same thing is there.

**Vaiśampāyana** – Outside these are three groups of *pāṅktam*. The *loka, devatā* and *bhūta*. In the same way, inside the body also three groups of *pāṅktam* are there. The *vāyu*, sense organs and *dhātu*. Thus like outside *pāṅktam*, the inside *pāṅktam* also are three. Because of the inside *pāṅktam* the outside *pāṅktam* also get fulfilment. Thus all the *pāṅktams* are seen as one *svarūpa* (form) and the entire world is contained in these six *pāṅktams*. Thus if a person does meditation as "I am *Brahma* the *jagat* (world)" then he becomes the Prajāpati.

**Bhṛgu** – Reverend Guru! All are *pāṅktams* (*idam sarvam pāṅktam*). A person knowing this becomes Prajāpati. This we have understood. Further whatever we have to know you must kindly preach to us.

**Vaiśampāyana** – Child! I will preach. You all listen carefully.

ओमिति ब्रह्म। ओमितिदꣳ सर्वम्। ओमित्येतदनुकृतिर्ह स्म वा अप्योश्रावयेत्याश्रावयन्ति। ओमिति सामानि गायन्ति। ओꣳशोमिति शस्त्राणि शꣳसन्ति। ओमित्यध्वर्युः प्रतिगरं प्रतिगृणाति। ओमिति ब्रह्मा प्रसौति। ओमित्याग्निहोत्रमनुजानाति। ओमिति ब्राह्मणः प्रवक्ष्यन्नाह ब्रह्मोपाप्नवानीति। ब्रह्मैवोपाप्नोति ॥८॥

*om iti brahma* | *omitidaṁ sarvam* | *omit etat anukṛtir ha sma vā apyo śrāvayetyāśrāvayanti* | *omiti sāmāni gāyanti* | *oṁśomiti śastrāṇi śaṁsanti* | *omity adhvaryuḥ pratigaraṁ pratigṛṇāti* | *omiti brahmā prasauti* | *omityāgnihotramanujānāti* | *omiti brāhmaṇaḥ pravakṣyannāha brahmopāpnavānīti* | *brahmaivopāpnoti* ||8||

> *AUM* is *Brahman. AUM* is this all. *AUM* is well known as a word of compliance. *AUM* make the gods hear. With these words they make them recite. With *AUM* they start singing the *sāma* chants. With *AUM* the *adhvaryu* (priest) utters encouraging chants. With *AUM* the Brahmā gives approval. With *AUM* the fire sacrifice is permitted to begin. A *brahman* a (the knower of *Brahman*) wishing to say, "May I obtain *Brahman*"; utters *AUM* he verily obtains *Brahman*.

Now I will tell about the main supreme *upāsanā* of *oṁkāra. Oṁkāra* has to be thought as *Parabrahman* and the *upāsanā* has to be done. Even though it is in a sound form, it remains as an admirable tool to reach the *Brahman* which is seen as *parama* (one) as well as *aparama* (different). Now I will tell the meaning. "*Oṁkāra* is only *Brahman*. All these are *oṁkāra.*" If a person wants to ask permission as to do a particular job or go to a temple, etc. the other person answers telling *oṁ* and gives permission.

You might have seen *yajña* taking place in *yajñaśālā*, as to how *oṁ* is used there in different ways. It is recited *oṁ śrāvya* (listen). Here *oṁkāra* is the one who calls the *agni* and *haviṣ* offering is being asked to be informed to the *devas*. After telling *oṁ* in the beginning the *sāmagāna* is sung by *Sāmavedīs*.

By telling *oṁ śom* only the *śastra mantras* of *Ṛgveda* are being recited. By chanting *oṁ* the *adhvaryu* (priest) in charge of Yajur *mantras* conveys *pratigara* rites to Hotās. Later by telling *oṁ* only, the permission is given by Brahmā for doing Agnihotra. With the intention of understanding Vedas the students who have come to learn Veda first tell *oṁ* and then start learning their lessons. Because of this students imbibe the Veda lessons more thoroughly. A person who wants to get the attitude to understand *Brahman*, to help reach such a state repeats *oṁ* several times. The *oṁkāra* helps him to attain *Brahman*-knowledge and merge with *Brahman*.

**Triśaṅku** – Svāmī! I understand the greatness of *oṁkāra*. Whatever *kriyās* (actions) undertaken by first reciting *oṁkāra* help us to get the fruits of the *kriyās*. Hence if *oṁkāra* is thought as *Brahman* and we do *upāsanā* we will reach the desired goal very soon, isn't it?

**Vaiśampāyana** – In the previous chapter it was preached that *oṁkāra* is like a sheath for *Brahman*. Here we see for all types of *upāsanās, oṁkāra* remains as the main initiator and helps us to get the result of the particular *upāsanā*. Even though it is only in sound form, that remains as the *Brahman's* staying place and the main place to reach.

**Mahācamasya** – I am eager to know the qualities of such exalted and greatness-filled *oṁkāra*. Kindly bless us more with your preachings on this, Respected Sir.

**Vaikhānasa** – Yes, I am also feeling great eagerness. You must kindly fulfil our thirst for knowledge.

**All disciples** – We too have the same feeling, Bhagavan.

**Vaiśampāyana** – Children! Seeing your eagerness for knowledge I am feeling very happy. It is not possible to tell *oṁkāras* greatness even by Ādiśeṣa. Still whatever I have learned from my *guru* I will tell you all in short.

**Bhṛgu** – Revered Guru, we will listen very carefully. Prācīnayogya what are you seeing there? Come near.

**Prācīnayogya** – Friend, I felt mother is calling from inside. I observed a little, that is all.

**Vaiśampāyana** – To you, the ones having beautiful *chit* (mind), I will tell in detail. Listen carefully. This word *oṁ* is only *Brahman*. The word only is all. Whatever happened, whatever is happening, whatever is going to happen all this is also *oṁkāra*. Whatever is happening during waking period, dream period and sleep are all *oṁkāra*.

*Oṁkāra* is the combination of the three vowels *A-kāra, U-kāra"* and *M-kāra*. For that there is another name called *praṇava*.

**Bhṛgu** – Well the greatness of *oṁkāra* is really supreme. Svāmī, preach to us further about this.

**Vaiśampāyana** – The mind should be concentrated on *praṇava*. *Praṇava* is *brahmarūpa* which is fearless. There is no need to be scared to meditate on *praṇava*. *Oṁkāra* is only *apara Brahman* and *para Brahman*. There is no cause for it. No destruction. It has no inside and no outside. *Oṁkāra* only shines within all the living things. It is non-dual and spread eveywhere. A man of wisdom who knows about *praṇava* which is spread everywhere need not ever be sad. You also do *upāsanā* of *oṁkāra* and know the true state of *Brahman*. I am giving my complete blessing to you all.

(All disciples get up to tell *abhivādaye* and do *namaskāram*s falling prostrate on the ground. The *guru* does *āśīrvādam*s individually.)

**Ṛṣipatnī** – (**Comes out from inside**) Āryaputra! Everything is ready for *vaiśvadevam*. All the things are made for *bhojanam* (food) also. The food is getting cold. Only if eaten hot it will be tasty, isn't it? Do come.

**Vaiśampāyana** – *Priye*! Here I am coming. Children! The lessons are over. Let us go to eat. Dear, even if the food gets cold there is nothing to equal the food made by your hand.

**Ṛṣipatnī** – There is no shortage of light talk. However, in my life of routine there is no *vrata* completion, no pilgrimage, no *melā* visit (**she gives a long sigh.**)

**Vaiśampāyana** – (**Goes near and comforts her**) Dear, now what did I tell which made you lament? You were born in Bhāratadeśam as a chieftain's daughter and where you have come after marriage is also not a very bad place.

**Ṛṣipatnī** – I did not tell anything critical now about the place I am married into. Everyday routine of *pūjā*, *puraṣkāra*, service to the guests, thus life is getting monotonous and won't a person get tired of this routine? Can't we do some pilgrimage and *pūrtta karma*s? It has become 24 years after coming to the *āśrama*. Have we ever gone crossing this Mithilā-nagara.

**Vaiśampāyana** – What? You are talking like this? Did we not go to Kāśī and Haridwar last year? During holy days like *sūrya-grahaṇam* and *mahālaya-amāvāsyā* did we not go and take bath in holy rivers of Gaṅgā, Yamunā and Phālgunī at confluence?

**Ṛṣipatnī** – Prāṇanātha! Was it last year? It was when Yājñavalkya was there, he had taken us. After he left it must be ten years now.

**Vaiśampāyana** – Yes (**wiping the eyes**). Ten years are over, but it feels like yesterday. What to do? All are plays of destiny. I also should not have become so angry.

**Ṛṣipatnī** – It is told the quarrel intiated by Nārada will only end in goodness. As per that everything had ended well. Because of this incident *Taittirīya Upaniṣad* also has been obtained.

**Vaiśampāyana** – Yes, Everything ended well. Bhṛgu is also not an ordinary one. I will ask him to accompany us on the pilgrimage.

**Ṛṣipatnī** – Let it be so. However you also should come.

**Vaiśampāyana** – Of course, I will also come. Where do we have to go first?

**Ṛṣipatnī** – The holy waters of Kāverī have to be visited. The *darśana* of Śrī Raṅganātha and Śrī Rāmanātha has to be done. Dhanuṣkoṭi has to be visited.

**Vaiśampāyana** – We will do so. In the month of Makara (January–February) after finishing the teachings we will go on a pilgrimage. On the *amāvāsyā* of Kātaka (July–August) we will be in Dhanuṣkoṭi. Now are you satisfied? (**pinches the cheeks**).

**Ṛṣipatnī** – (**Shies away**) Prāṇanātha! Indeed I am very happy. Your *chit* is my fortune. Come for food now. (**They are going**).

***(Curtain closes.)***

***(First part is complete.)***

## Part II

### SCENE 1

***(Curtain opens.)***

(It is the *āśrama* of Vaiśampāyana. On one side Triśaṅku is sitting in *padmāsana* and doing *dhyāna-samādhi*. In other place Vaiśampāyana is preaching to the disciples.)

**Vaiśampāyana** – Children! Did you notice the state of Triśaṅku? Last one month he is in *dhyāna* continuously like this.

**Bhr̥gu** – Respected Sir! We saw that. You must bless us also to get that state.

**Vaiśampāyana** – Child Bhr̥gu, I am very happy to know your desire. You will also get *brahmasākṣāt* state. There is no doubt about it. Why only you, my disciples, all of you will definitely get it. Not only that, whoever desires and tries for it will get it. This is definite. *Svarājyam,* that is *Brahman*-state, is our birth right. Nobody can stop it.

**Prācīnayogya** – Revered Guru! You had told previously also one can obtain *svarājyam* by *vijñānam*. Hence is it not necessary to do *śrauta smārtta karma*s?

**Vaiśampāyana** – Dear, the one having beautiful *chit* (mind), it is necessary to do those *karma*s. By following that the *chit* becomes pure. Thus they are also a tool to reach the *puruṣa* inside.

**Bodhāyana** – Svāmī! Kindly tell the important *karma*s which we have to follow.

**Vaiśampāyana** – I will do so, listen carefully.

ऋतं च स्वाध्यायप्रवचने च। सत्यं च स्वाध्यायप्रवचने च। तपश्च स्वाध्यायप्रवचने च। दमश्च स्वाध्यायप्रवचने च। शमश्च स्वाध्यायप्रवचने च। अग्नयश्च स्वाध्यायप्रवचने च। अग्निहोत्रं च स्वाध्यायप्रवचने च। अतिथयश्च स्वाध्यायप्रवचने च। मानुषं च स्वाध्यायप्रवचने च। प्रजा च स्वाध्यायप्रवचने च। प्रजनश्च स्वाध्यायप्रवचने च। प्रजातिश्च स्वाध्यायप्रवचने च। सत्यमिति सत्यवचा राथीतरः। तप इति तपोनित्यः पौरुशिष्टिः। स्वाध्यायप्रवचने एवेति नाको मौद्गल्यः। तद्धि तपस्तद्धि तपः। ॥९॥

*ṛtaṁ ca svādhyāya pravacane ca | satyaṁ ca svādhyāya pravacane ca | tapaśca svādhyāya pravacane ca | damaśca svādhyāya pravacane ca | śamaśca svādhyāya pravacane ca | agnayaśca svādhyāya pravacane ca | agnihotraṁ ca svādhyāya pravacane ca | atithayaśca svādhyāya pravacane ca | mānuṣaṁ ca svādhyāya pravacane ca | prajā ca svādhyāya pravacane ca | prajanaśca svādhyāya pravacane ca | prajātiśca svādhyāya pravacane ca | satyamiti satyavacā rāthītaraḥ | tapa iti taponityaḥ pauruśiṣṭiḥ | svādhyāya pravacane eveti nāko maudgalyaḥ | taddhi tāpastaddhi tapaḥ| |9| |*

Righteousness together with self-study and listening to the exposition of the *guru* is to be understood as *Brahman*. Truth together with self-study and listening to the exposition of the *guru* is to be understood as *Brahman*. Austerity together with self-study and listening to the exposition of the *guru* is to be understood as *Brahman*. Withdrawal of the sense organs together with self-study and listening to exposition of the *guru* is to be understood as *Brahman*. Withdrawal of the mind together with self-study and listening to exposition of the *guru* is to be understood as *Brahman*. The lighting of the sacrificial fire together with self-study and listening to the exposition of the *guru* is to be understood as *Brahman*. The performance of the fire sacrifice together with self-study and listening to the expostion of the *guru* is to be understood as *Brahman.* Entertaining guests together with self-study and listening to the expostion of the *guru* is to be understood as *Brahman.* Humanness together with self-study and listening to the expostion of the *guru* is to be understood as *Brahman.*

Procreation together with self-study and listening to the exposition of the *guru* is to be understood as *Brahman.* Propagation of the race together with self-study and listening to the exposition of the *guru* is to be understood as *Brahman.* Truth is what matters, says Satyavacas (one who says truth only), the son of Rāthītara. Austerity is what matters, says Taponitya (one consistently engaged in austerity), the son of Pauruśiṣṭi Self-study and listening to the exposition of the *guru* are what matter, says Nāka, the son of Mudgala. That verily is austerity.

*Ṛtaṁ* means a determined intellect which follows the precepts written in Śāstras and does them in an orderly manner. *Svādhyāya* means to tell Vedas and understand the meaning. *Pravacanam* means teaching to the disciples.

These three should be followed. Further it is also necessary to be truthful, to speak truth.

To undertake *tapas* means to follow the *vrata*s like *kūcāram, cāndrāyaṇam,* etc. *Tamam* means the outside sense-organs have to be controlled and *śamam* means the inside sense-organs also should be kept under check. The *kriyā*s connected with *agni* have to be done. The *Agnihotra homa* should be followed. The guests or the people coming to your doorstep have to be respected and done *pūjā.* At the time of social function like marriage the relations should be entertained and other worldly affairs have to be undertaken. For the birth of the child the *karma*s like *iṣṭi* have to be done. Only at *ṛtu* period connection has to be kept with the wife. The son has to be married and the religious *karma*s required for the birth of the grandson have to be done. Along with *svādhyāyam, pravacanam* has to be done without fail continuously.

**Bhṛgu** – Is it to show that *svādhyāyam* and *pravacanam* are important that behind every word, like, for example, in word truth (*satyam*) it is connected and told *svādhyāya pravacane ca*.

**Vaiśampāyana** – Yes, my child, usually in Veda it is never considered wrong to repeat the once-told *śruti*s again and again. Especially in this context to show the importance it is repeated again and again.

**Vaikhānasa** – The names Rāthītara, Pauruśiṣṭi and Nāka coming in *mantra*s are sounding familiar. I feel they have been heard somewhere.

**Bodhāyana** – I also feel they are familiar names, but I am not able to remember.

**Vaiśampāyana** – Children! Those *ṛṣi*s are very much known to us. Does anybody else among you remember?

**Bhṛgu** – Respected Sir, some months back for *vana bhojana* three *ṛṣi*s had come. Isn't that? I think they are only these.

**Vaiśampāyana** – *Sabhāsa*! I appreciate you. They are only these *ṛṣi*s.

**Prācīnayogya** – What are these *ṛṣi*s telling? You must kindly tell the meaning.

**Vaiśampāyana** – Mahācamasya! Do tell your friends the meaning clearly.

**Mahācamasya** – Rāthītara, the *maharṣi* who was established in truth has told that the truth is more important to reach the *Brahman*. Pauruśiṣṭi who had established himself in *tapas* has told that *tapas* is more important. Mudgala's son Nāka, stressed *svādhyāyam* and *pravacanam* are more important. He has told that it is necessary to recite Veda and to make the other person understand veda as the best form of *tapa*. "That is only *tapa*, that is only *tapa*," he has said.

**Vaiśampāyana** – Children! In whatever state or whatever *āśrama* one is, a person inclined to acquire *Brahman*-knowledge should not leave *svādhyāya* and *pravacanam*. That is only *tapas*.

To tell in short, the life itself has to be led as *ṛta* and truth. One has to recite the vedas. Make others recite the vedas. The *yajñas* to understand *Brahman*-knowledge have to be done without fail. The sense organs have to be won, and in a peaceful state *agni kriyās*, hospitality and *pūjā* to the guests have to be followed. Along with *tapas* the duties for the welfare of general public have to be done. After begetting children and after the birth of grandchildren too *svādhyāya* and *pravacanam* should be consistently followed. Persons who are inclined to Maharṣi Nāka's concepts can follow *svādhyāya* and *pravacanam* as important *tapas*. All depends on their mental make-up, character and convenience.

**Bhṛgu** – Respected Sir, are there any *mahāns* who have followed these *karmas* and attained realization of *puruṣa*.

**Vaiśampāyana** – Child! What doubt about it? There are crores of *maharṣis*, all the head *gurus* (*kulapatis*) belong to that group only. Triśaṅku who has attained the exalted state by *svādhyāya* and *pravacanam* is right in front of you. (Triśaṅku comes out of *samādhi* state, tells *oṁkāra*, gets up and gives his *praṇāmas* to the *guru*).

**Triśaṅku** – Gurudeva, many many *namaskārams* to you. I am taking leave. Please allow me.

अहं वृक्षस्य रेरिवा। कीर्तिः पृष्ठं गिरेरिव। ऊर्ध्वपवित्रो वाजिनीव स्वमृतमस्मि। द्रविणꣳसवर्चसम्। सुमेधा अमृतोक्षितः। इति त्रिशङ्कोर्वेदानुवचनम् ॥१०॥

*aham vṛkṣasya rerivā* । *kīrtiḥ pṛṣṭhaṁ gireriva* । *ūrdhvapavitro vājinīva svamṛtamasmi* । *draviṇaṁsavarcasam* । *sumedhā amṛtokṣitaḥ iti triśaṅkorvedānuvacanam* ॥10॥

I am the invigorator of the tree. My fame is like the ridge of a mountain. I am purified by the exalted one. Like the Sun, I am my own inherent righteousness. I am my own lustrous wealth. I am wise, I am immortal. I am undecaying. Such was the teaching of Triśaṅku on attaining Wisdom.

**Vaiśampāyana** – My dear disciple! May good tidings come to you. You have reached a very exalted state. You have become one with *Brahman.* Go carefully my, child.

(Triśaṅku gives his respects to every one and leaves.)

(Vaiśampāyana wiping the tears, speaks within himself.) The *kulapati*'s life is indeed very sad. He has to take leave of his dear disciples.

**Bodhāyana** – Svāmī! You must kindly tell the meaning of the *mantra*s recited by Triśaṅku.

**Vaiśampāyana** – *iti triśaṅkorvedanuvacanam* (इति त्रिशङ्कोर्वेदानुवचनम्) Such was the teaching of Triśaṅku on attaining Wisdom.

These are the blessed words which sprung out of Triśaṅku's experience. The meaning of it is as follows. "I am the higher state of the tree. Like the peak of the mountain my fame is shining. I am the *para Brahman* which is the cause and sacred. I am like the *ātma-tattvam* (concept of *ātmā*) like the one present in lord Sūrya. The brightness of the wisdom is my wealth. A good *chit* is the wealth which is like a never depleting nectar.

**Bhr̥gu** – We are highly pleased to know Triśaṅku's words after experiencing *Brahman.* However, what you mentioned as the higher state of tree, this concept is not very clear. Kindly explain.

**Vaiśampāyana** – Children, hear. The tree mentioned here is *saṁsāra* tree. It is the tradition of veda to describe the *saṁsāra* world as *aśvattha* tree having the roots above and the branches below. These *mantra*s which Triśaṅku had recited were when he was in the state of *para Brahman*. Mahācamasya, do give the explanation.

**Mahācamasya** – I who is *Brahman* is the *antaryāmi* of this *saṁsāra* tree, that is, I am the all-knowing and conducting the matters of the world. My fame has risen high like the peak of the mountain. I am the *Brahman* which is very pure and the cause of all. Like in Sūrya, in me also the *ātmā*-knowledge is shining. I am only *tat*. I am the existing brightness, prosperity and goodness. I am not bound by *dharma* of death. I am without blemish. These are the words which help to attain the state that self and *ātmā* are one.

**Vaiśampāyana** – Children! You must do *japa* of this *mantra* everyday without fail. The students who are seeking *Brahman*-knowledge are sure to realize it by doing this *japa*. Others will get knowledge of Vedas and fruits of one's action. The purity of *chit* also will happen.

**Bhṛgu** – Respected Sir, as per your orders whatever Triśaṅku told we will also recite daily.

**Vaikhānasa** – By doing that we will reach *ātmā*-realization.

**Vaiśampāyana** – Disciples! If you do *japa* of this your eye of wisdom will open. Triśaṅku's Vedic words have been pronounced after knowing *Brahman* and being immersed in *Brahman*. Those who repeat these words will also reach *Brahman*-knowledge. There is no doubt about this. The fruits one gets by doing Veda *adyayanam* daily can be reached by this *mantra jāpa* also.

**Ṛṣipatnī** – (**enters**) Engrossed in teaching, you have not realized the passing of time. The afternoon time has taken over. Do come inside.

**Vaiśampāyana** – Dear, here we are coming. Children, today let us stop the lessons here.

***(Curtain falls.)***

SCENE 2

***(Curtain opens.)***

(It is the *āśrama* of Vaiśampāyana Maharṣi. *Maharṣi* is preaching to the disciples.)

**Vaiśampāyana** – Children! The recital of Vedas is over. Now I will tell you some important teachings. *Vedamanūcyācāryo 'ntevāsina manuśāsti* (वेदमनूच्याचार्योऽन्तेवासिन मनुशास्ति). Listen carefully.

वेदमनूच्याचार्योऽन्तेवासिनमनुशास्ति। सत्यं वद। धर्मं चर। स्वाध्यायान्मा प्रमदः। आचार्याय प्रियं धनमाहृत्य प्रजातन्तुं मा व्यवच्छेत्सीः। सत्यान्न प्रमदितव्यम्। धर्मान्न प्रमदितव्यम्। कुशलान्न प्रमदितव्यम्। भूत्यै न प्रमदितव्यम्। स्वाध्यायप्रवचाभ्यां न प्रमदितव्यम्। देवपितृकार्याभ्यां न प्रमदितव्यम्। मातृदेवो भव। पितृदेवो भव। आचार्यदेवो भव। अतिथिदेवो भव। ॥११.१॥

*vedamanūcyācāryo 'ntevāsinamanuśāsti* | *satyaṁ vada* | *dharmaṁ cara* | *svādhyāyānmā pramadaḥ* | *ācāryāya priyaṁ dhanamāhṛtya prajātantuṁ mā vyavacchetsīḥ* | *satyānna pramadītavyam* | *dharmānna pramaditavyam* | *kuśalānna pramaditavyam* | *bhūtyai na pramaditavyam* | *svādhyāyapravacābhyāṁ na pramaditavyam* | *devapitṛkāryābhyāṁ na pramaditavyam* | *mātṛdevo bhava* | *pitṛdevo bhava* | *ācāryadevo bhava* | *atithidevo bhava* ||11.1||

Speak out the Truth. Practise righteousness. Do not neglect your self-study. Having brought to the teacher the wealth that is pleasing (to him), don't cut-off the line of progeny. Let there be no neglect of Truth. Let there be no neglect of righteousness. Let there be no neglect of protecting yourself. Let there be no neglect of property. Let there be no neglect of self-study and teaching. Let there be no neglect of the duties to the gods and ancestors. Be one to whom the mother is a god. Be one to whom the father is a god. Be one to whom the teacher is a god. Be one to whom the guest is a god.

Speak truth. Walk on the path of *dharma.* Don't slip from *svādhyāyam.* That is, never remain without doing regular practice of scriptures. Further whatever Veda you have learned by regular recitals, never forget it. Daily do Veda *parāyaṇam* in *brahma-jñānam.* Bring the *dakṣiṇā* to *guru* and offer it to him. Later, after taking leave of him don't act in a way that the coming generations of yours have no connection. That is, after getting married entering *gṛhastha āśrama* continue your race.

From truth don't slip even once. Also don't slip from *dharma* even once. Don't slip from acts required to protect the body. Don't slip from acts which give you prosperity and good tidings. Don't ever slip from *svādhyāya* and *pravacanam.*

By mistake or forgetting, one should not slip from work destined to *deva* and *pitṛ*. The mother has to be thought of as God and shown respect. The father has to be thought of as God and shown respect. The *ācārya* has to be thought of as God and shown respect. The guests have to be thought of as God and shown respect.

**Prācīnayogya** – Svāmī! A person who is going to become *jñānī* of *ātmā,* is it necessary for him to enter *gṛhastha āśrama*?

**Bhṛgu** – Respected Sir, a person who wants to be a *naiśtika brahmachārī,* for him how the order *prajātantuṁ mā vyavacchetsīḥ,* (प्रजातन्तुं मा व्यवच्छेत्सीः) — continue your lineage — will be appropriate? Kindly explain.

**Vaikhānasa** – Children! Your doubt is a legitimate one. I will answer. There is a duty we and our group have to do for public welfare. We are born with three debts. Debt for *deva*s, debt for *ṛṣi*s, and debt to *pitṛ*s/ancestors. We pay the debt to the *deva*s by act of *tapas, yajña,* etc. We pay the debt to the *ṛṣi*s by *svādhyāya, pravacanam*s/preachings, etc. By making good *praja*s and increasing the family we are fulfilling the debt due to ancestors. It is our duty to make good children, protect them, and train them. That only is the important service for the society. If we don't do it we will fail to give back our debt to human beings. Our debt to ancestors get removed and without any obstruction we can easily go towards *mokṣa mārga.* However a person who wants to be a *naiśtika brahmachārī* need not enter *gṛhastha āśrama.* Even if he doesn't want to bring out progenies, it is his duty to prepare good disciple dynasty and offer his services. In his case *prajātantu* will imply good disciple dynasty.

**Bodhāyana** – Respected Sir! The doubt is cleared. However if a person does not beget children even after marriage what will he do? Poor thing, he is to be pitied.

**Vaiśampāyana** – Child! If a progeny is not born he must not keep quiet. He must put in efforts and do *karmas, yajñas* like *putra-kāmeṣṭi* and try to get progenies.

**Vaikhānasa** – You must kindly further preach the things to be done by us, Gurujī.

**Vaiśampāyana** – Alright. Listen carefully.

*fig.:* **The three debts of human being.**

यान्यनवद्यानि कर्माणि। तानि सेवितव्यानि। नो इतराणि।
यान्यस्माकꣳसुचरितानि। तानि त्वयोपास्यानि। नो इतराणि। ॥११.२॥

*yānyanavadyāni karmaṇi | tāni sevitavyāni | no itarāṇi* |

*yānyasmākaṁsucaritāni* । *tāni tvayopāsyāni* । *no itarāṇi*।।11.2।।

Whatever deeds are blameless, they should be practised, not others. Whatever good practices there are among us, they are to be adopted by you, not others.

Do the *karma*s which are blemishless. Don't join hands with persons doing lowly or doubtful *karmas*. Do other good *karmas*. Follow the good conduct alone. If a *karma* is done by the *guru* don't follow it blindly as the *guru* is doing. Examine it, if the *karma* acrues good for you then follow it.

**Bhṛgu** – We became blessed hearing the preachings leading to the good path for the disciples. Kindly further bless us with your knowledgeable words.

**Vaikhānasa** – You told us clearly how to conduct ourselves in the country, in the house, in the society, etc. Now kindly tell us how to conduct ourselves in a big *sabhā* (gatherings in front of kings) and in front of *mahān*s (exalted beings).

**Vaiśampāyana** - My dear disciples, I will tell, listen.

ये के चास्मच्छ्रेयाꣳसो ब्राह्मणाः। तेषां त्वयाऽऽसनेन प्रश्वसितव्यम्।

*ye ke cāsmacchreyāṁso brāhmaṇāḥ* । *teṣām tvayāsanena praśvasitavyam* ।

Those brāhmaṇas who are superior to us, should be comforted by you by offering a seat.

If you have come to a *sabhā* of exalted *brāhmaṇa*s you must give them seat and entertain them. You must stand in front of them in reverence and listen to their talk attentively with *bhakti* and humility. These two qualities are similar to protection worn in the feet. You must wear them at a young age itself.

**Bodhāyana** – Svāmī! Kindly tell of the mental make-up at the time of doing charity.

**Vaiśampāyana** – To give help is a higher state of quality. However to do the help with pride will be improper. I will tell you what Veda tells about this.

**Bhṛgu** – We will listen carefully, Gurujī.

**Vaiśampāyana** –

श्रद्धया देयम्। अश्रद्धयादेयम्। श्रिया देयम्। ह्रिया देयम्। भिया देयम्।
संविदा देयम्॥

*śraddhayā deyam* । *aśraddhayā 'deyam* । *śriyā deyam* ।
*hriyā deyam* । *bhiyā deyam* । *saṁvidā deyam* ।

A gift is to offered with full faith. It should never be offered without full faith. Gifts should be offered in plenty. Gifts should be offered with modesty. Gifts should be offered with awe. Gifts should be offered with sympathy.

Whatever is given in charity should be given with *śraddhā.* It should not be given with lack of concern, and as per one's wealth it should be given generously. Give it with some shyness. Give it with some fear. Give it with affection.

**Bodhāyana** – I can understand that the charity has to be given with *śraddhā,* and generously. But why to be shy and why to be afraid when giving charity?

**Vaiśampāyana** – Child! Mahācamasya will answer your question.

**Mahācamasya** – Alright sir! When you are giving generously to someone, perhaps the thought of not giving sufficiently will bring shyness. When one gives with doubt, as to whether sufficient amount is given then hesitation and shyness naturally creep in. Such pride that "I am the giver" will also leave. We should think then, is my giving correct? Am I giving at the correct place? Then only the receiver's status can be gauged. When you think about the receiver being not so deserving in status, then fear creeps in. Hence without grandeur or excitement the charity should be given with humility and shyness. It should be given in the deserving place with love and affection and with a fear of not giving at a wrong place as that will be a mistake. That alone will be good charity. This will be a *puṇya karma* which will raise the level of the donor and receiver.

**Vaiśampāyana –**

> अथ यदि ते कर्मविचिकित्सा वा वृत्तविचिकित्सा वा स्यात्। ये तत्र ब्राह्मणाः सम्मर्शिनः। युक्ता आयुक्ताः। अलूक्षा धर्मकामाः स्युः। यथा ते तत्र वर्त्तेरन्। तथा तत्र वर्तेथाः। अथाभ्याख्यातेषु। ये तत्र ब्राह्मणाः संमर्शिनः। युक्ता आयुक्ताः। अलूक्षा धर्मकामाः स्युः। यथा ते तेषु वर्तेरन्। तथा तेषु वर्तेथाः। ॥११.३॥
>
> *atha yadi te karmavicikitsā vā vṛttavicikitsā vā syāt ye tatra brāhmaṇāḥ sammarśinaḥ* । *yuktā āyuktāḥ* । *alūkṣā dharmakāmāḥ syuḥ* । *yathā te tatra vartteran* । *tathā tatra vartethāḥ* । *athābhyākhyāteṣu* । *ye tatra brāhmaṇāḥ saṁmarśinaḥ* । *yuktā āyuktāḥ* । *alūkṣā dharmakāmāḥ syuḥ* । *yathā te teṣu varteran* । *tathā teṣu vartethāḥ* ।।11.3।।
>
> Then, if there is any doubt regarding any deed, any doubt regarding conduct, one should behave on such occasions as the brāhmaṇas at that time and place do, as they are able deliberators, are unitively balanced, who need no direction from others, and who are not harsh, and who love righteousness.

In case there is doubt in the work to be done or the way to conduct oneself then learn this from the righteous brāhmaṇas there, who observe the *karma*s and tradition in a proper manner and are devoid of any crude mentality. Those brāhmaṇas have the capacity to do keen enquiry and understand the situation. They are not of a nature that they get carried away by others' proddings. They do not covet for money or fame and are God-fearing, doing their *karma*s with strong attachment to *dharma*. People of such character should be considered as role models and you should follow in their foot-steps. Also, as for your behaviour with people who have wronged and whose conduct is doubtful, one should observe how the pure *dhārmika* brāhmaṇa souls are behaving and should follow their example.

**Bhr̥gu** – Instead of telling "you must conduct yourself as written in Śāstras" why are you instructing us to follow the rules and traditions of brāhmaṇas? What is the reason for this?

**Vaiśampāyana** – Child Bhr̥gu! In life during problematic times doubts will arise, this is but common. When situations are very difficult and when one is unable to decide the course of action, to clear the doubts Śāstras may be referred to. However our country is a very big one. Many kinds of traditions and customs are being followed in different parts of the country. Argument will not bring stability to the situation. There are different rhythms in different places. There are many *r̥ṣi*s who speak and interpret scriptures. At times the concept of *dharma* is hidden behind the intellect. Hence whichever way the *mahāpuruṣa*s have gone that way is the best one. The brāhmaṇas who are staunch followers of *dharma* and who are kind-hearted, their life path will help to clear the doubts as to the right conduct. It is not enough to just ask from the scriptures and get an answer for a problem, but it will be more prudent to follow the way of the *dhārmika* brāhmaṇas.

**Vaikhānasa** – We heard the exalted teaching from the exalted *guru*. Further the routes which we have to know and follow, you must kindly preach.

**Vaiśampāyana** –

> एष आदेशः। एष उपदेशः। एषा वेदोपनिषत्। एतदनुशासनम्।
> एवमुपासितव्यम्। एवमुचैतदुपास्यम् ॥११.४॥
>
> *eṣa ādeśaḥ* | *eṣa upadeśaḥ* | *eṣā vedopaniṣat* |
> *etadanuśāsanam* | *evamupāsitavyam* |
> *evamucaitadupāsyam* | |11.4| |
>
> This is the injunction. This is the instruction. This is the secret wisdom of the Vedas. This is the behest. Thus should one meditate. Thus indeed one should meditate.

My dear children! We have come to the last part of this

chapter. There are no more preachings. This is the only order. This is the only preaching. This is the secret of Veda. This is the order of gods. It has to be followed like this. It is only proper to do like this. Child Mahācamasya! Do tell a short synopsis of today's lessons to your friends.

**Mahācamasya** – Respected Sir, as per your order I will tell. After hearing the Vedic lessons when you leave the *gurkula*, it is important to know the meanings well and they have to be well digested. Before coming to understand *Brahman*-knowledge it is necessary to do *śrauta smārtta karma*s. When daily *saṁskāra* is done by these *karmas*, the person's *chit* will become pure and he will get *sattva* (pure) *buddhi*. Such a person alone can expect to get *Brahman*-knowledge.

Here seven types of preachings are given:

1. About oneself.
2. When interacting with others the conduct to be adopted.
3. To live in the world with good conduct.
4. How to interact with *mahān*s, the great people.
5. The conduct in doing charity.
6. In which contexts, discipline and proper tradition become like words from scriptures.
7. The teachings given above should be taken as the order from God or secret of Vedas and *upāsanā* should be done. This is the proper *upāsanā*.

**Vaiśampāyana** – Children! Now we will tell *śānti-pāṭha*.

**(All chant together.)**

ॐ शं नो मित्रः शं वरुणः। शं नो भवत्वर्यमा। शं न इन्द्रो बृहस्पतिः। शं नो विष्णुरुरुक्रमः। नमो ब्रह्मणे। नमस्ते वायो। त्वमेव प्रत्यक्षं ब्रह्मासि। त्वामेव प्रत्यक्षं ब्रह्मावादिषम्। ऋतमवादिषम्। सत्यमवादिषम्। तन्मामावीत्। तद्वक्तारमावीत्। आवीन्माम्। आवीद्वक्तारम्।

ॐ शान्तिः शान्तिः शान्तिः।

*oṁ śaṁ no mitraḥ śaṁ varuṇaḥ । śaṁ no bhavatvaryamā । śaṁ na indro bṛhaspatiḥ । śaṁ no viṣṇururukhramaḥ । namo brahmaṇe । namaste vāyo। tvameva pratyakṣaṁ brahmāsi । tvāmeva pratyakṣaṁ brahmāvādiṣam । ṛtamavādiṣam । satyamavādiṣam । tanmāmāvīt । tadvaktāramāvīt । āvīnmām । āvīdvaktāram । oṁ śāntiḥ śāntiḥ śāntiḥ ।*

*AUM* May Mitra (the Sun) be propitious to us. May Varuṇa (be) propitious (to us). May Aryamā (a form of the Sun) be propitious to us. May Indra and Bṛhaspati be propitious to us.

May Viṣṇu of wide strides be propitious to us. Salutations to *Brahman*. Salutations to you. O Vāyu. You indeed are the perceptible *Brahman*. Of you indeed, the perceptible *Brahman*, will I speak of the right. I'll speak of the truth. May that protect me. May that protect the speaker.

Let that protect me. Let that protect the speaker. *AUM* Peace! Peace! Peace!

**Vaiśampāyana** – My child Bhṛgu! Did you clearly understand the meaning of *śānti-pāṭha*?

**Bhṛgu** – Yes Respected Sir.

**Vaiśampāyana** – Do tell, I am eager to listen.

**Bhṛgu** – May Mitra bring good tidings to us. Varuṇa should bring prosperity. Aryamā should bless us well. Indra and Bṛhaspati should do good turn to us. Viṣṇu who has feet to measure should be benevolent to us. We are giving our *namaskārams* to *Brahman*. Vāyu! I am giving my salutations to you. You are only the *Brahman* which I can see. Hence I am worshipping you as the visible *Brahman*. That should protect me. That should protect my *guru*. Again and again I pray that should protect me and protect the teacher. Let *śānti* prevail on all three fronts.

**Vaiśampāyana** – Child! Bhṛgu! You told the meaning very well. You will get the ability to write interpretation of Veda at a later time. You will live in your later life as a great teacher and earn name and fame. (That time an *āśrama* dweller comes in haste and tells something in the ear of the Guru). Children! I am going to tell you a very good news. Child! Bhr̥gu! For you also a very dear news is this.

**All the disciples** – (**with great enthusiasm**) What is that? What is that?

**Vaiśampāyana** – In our *āśrama* tomorrow Lord Varuṇa is going to bless us with his presence. He is coming to meet us, to see his son and impart his precious knowledge to us. He is coming with lot of kindness. In a proper manner we have to do respects to him, do *atithi* (guest) *pūjā* and accord proper reception to him. All of you should in unity do the *pūjā* and give an exemplary reception to him. Like the statement *na bhūto na bhaviśyati* (न भूतो न भविश्यति) (not happened like that before nor will it happen in future) the *pūjā* should be done very well.

**Disciples** – As per your order we will do. We do not need much coaxing for doing a good deed. Svāmī! Your *chit* is our fortune.

**Vaiśampāyana** – Good, let us go now.

***(Curtain falls.)***

SCENE 3

***(Curtain opens.)***

(It is *yajñaśālā* in Vaiśampāyana's *āśrama*. Vaiśampāyana Maharṣi and Lord Varuṇa are sitting in the *vīrāsana* and conversation is taking place.)

**Varuṇa** – Friend! I am greatly indebted to the hospitality offered to me on coming. In a very elaborate manner with *pūrṇa kumbha* I was welcomed. Above all, the great affection you and the other *āśramavāsīs* showed me has drowned me in a sea of happiness. Once again I want to express my gratitude with humility.

**Vaiśampāyana** – Revered Varuṇa! There is nothing we have

done which warrants for such a praise. We only did our duty. Your showing great regard for us shows only your generosity and good nature. When we were doing *gurukula* stay do you remember Maharṣi Bṛhaspati's visit? Do you remember the *atithi pūjā* done at that time?

**Varuṇa** – Are you asking if I remember? Only if I forget, it is necessary to recall. The respect I got here is nothing less than the welcome Vedavyāsa got at that time.

**Vaiśampāyana** – Friend! It is not possible to forget those days. The incidents of those times were such that they are periods to be written in golden letters.

**Varuṇa** – Those times when we were learning Vedas, Paila, Jaimini, Sumantu and so many others, each one of them great disciples and men of high intellect, were with us. That time we stayed as one community and one family. Now we are scattered in a number of places. Is it possible to get back those days? (**sighs deeply**)

**Vaiśampāyana** – Why won't it come? All incidents in life are again and again happening in the same way, only the charactors differ. As per the climatic conditions and as per the place or country, present conditions and some incidents might change. However generally the drama continues to take place as before. The actors only get changed. That time Vedavyāsa was the *kulapati.* Jaimini and Paila were learning the lessons. Today Varuṇa is the *kulapati* and other students are learning Veda.

**Varuṇa** – Friend! What you are telling is also correct. However, I feel the olden times were good. Let that be so. There will be difference of opinion. I heard you and your wife are going on a pilgrimage. Prācīnayogya told me this morning. When do you plan to start? Where are you all going? When will you be back?

**Vaiśampāyana** – Friend! Yes I am planning to go on a pilgrimage. That is correct. This has been a long-standing demand. During Āṣādha *amāvasyā* I want to go to Rāmeśvaram. The journey will take one year (*saṁvatsaram*). However only if you give two boons we can immediately start.

**Varuṇa** – What is that? You are talking in riddles. Like the boons asked by Kaikeyī from Daśaratha, you are talking of two boons. Do tell your request.

**Vaiśampāyana** – My wife desires to take child Bhṛgu along. However much I try to stop her she does not listen. The first boon is you must send your child Bhṛgu along with us.

**Varuṇa** – *Sabhāsa*. Like separating Śrī Rāma from Daśaratha, the first boon involves separating child Bhṛgu from me. It is alright for me. But should we not ask him also.

**Vaiśampāyana** – Till *avabhṛta* bath gets over he is our child. Is it not that? We have asked him already. He is completely ready for the trip. But he is putting one condition.

**Varuṇa** – What is that condition?

**Vaiśampāyana** – Nothing much. He insists Prācīnayogya should come along. We have agreed to that.

**Varuṇa** – Like Śrī Rāma's brother Lakṣmaṇa went along with him. Alright, what is the second boon? Whom you are going to crown here in this *āśrama*?

**Vaiśampāyana** – Why, you only. Till we come back you must rule the *āśrama* taking charge as *kulapati*. You must give teachings to Mahācamasya, Bodhāyana, Vaikhānasa and other disciples. Kindly without denying you must take up this post and show your consideration.

**Varuṇa** – Very good job, Sir. Where I came to take some rest and thought of spending time with my son, you have put on me this load of teaching and all. Like Daśaratha I also accepted to grant the boons without thinking left or right. Now I have to agree. Are you satisfied now my friend?

**Vaiśampāyana** – Very happy. I know my friend won't let me down. Now I can do the preparation for the journey.

**Varuṇa** – Alright, you can make the arrangements now quickly. I am getting an opportunity to stay here, I should be fortunate. I can see Mahārājā Janaka from time to time and converse with him. In Haridwar who else is there other than *avadhūtas*?

**Vaiśampāyana** – Friend! I never thought even in my dreams that you would so easily accept. However, my partner, my wife was hopeful you would definitely agree. Let us go for food. (**They are going.**)

***(Curtain falls.)***

SCENE 4

***(Curtain opens.)***

(It is the *āśrama* of Vaiśampāyana. *Maharṣi* is sitting in *padmāsana*. Nearby the disciples are sitting. The sounds of things being packed are heard from inside the *āśrama*.)

**Vaiśampāyana** – Child! Bhṛgu! Dear Prācīnayogya! You both go inside and keep the things for travel. Tell mother to keep without fail my *pūjā* vessels, *kamaṇḍala*, etc. In the *muhūrtta* (good period) of *abhijīta* we must start.

(Bhṛgu and Prācīnayogya get up and giving their *praṇāmas*, tell "We will do as you bid" and leave.)

My disciples! the one having beautiful *chit* (mind), here Śrī Varuṇa will stay and give you lessons. You also study very carefully. Do you all remember the advice that I gave? You must act as per that.

**Vaikhānasa** – Gurujī, we remember very well your preachings and advices. We will act with great humility as per your saying.

**Vaiśampāyana** – Bodhāyana! Tell the preachings taught by me.

**Bodhāyana** – Let it be so, Respected Sir.

ये के चास्मच्छ्रेयाꣳसो ब्राह्मणाः। तेषां त्वयासनेन प्रश्वसितव्यम्।

*ye ke cāsmacchreyāṁso brāhmaṇāḥ | teṣāṁ tvayāsanena*

*praśvasitavyam* ।

Those brāmaṇas who are superior to us, should be comforted by you by offering a seat.

**Vaiśampāyana** – I am very glad children! Till now to reach *brahma-jñāna* I have told you the *upāsanā* ways. In order for the *chit* to become pure I also explained the necessity to do *śrauta smārtta karma*s and other *karmas*. Now in order to know *Brahman*'s true state *pūjya* Śrī Varuṇa will teach its characteristics and its state of existence, etc.

**Bodhāyana** – Respected Sir, one request.

**Vaiśampāyana** – Child! What is that?

**Bodhāyana** – Before Pūjya Śrī Varuṇa will preach to us, I would like to hear from you the introduction to that.

**Mahācamasya and Vaikhānasa** – We also pray the same way to you.

**Vaiśampāyana** – In case all of you wish that, I will tell you in short, listen. To know a concept clearly it is necessary to understand its characteristic (*lakṣaṇa*). The *lakṣaṇa* is of two types – 1. *svarūpa lakṣaṇa,* 2. *taṭastha lakṣaṇa.*

The *taṭastha lakṣaṇa* is of two types — 1. *upa lakṣaṇa,* 2. *upādhi.*

*Svarūpa lakṣaṇa* is the one which is attached always to the subject and speaks about its natural characteristics. *Upa lakṣaṇa* is not the naturally present characteristic but has got attached to it presently and temporarily and will vanish after some time.

**Vaikhānasa** – Gurudeva, you must tell one example and explain it.

## Brahmānanda Vallī

**Vaiśampāyana** – Say, a new person is coming to Mithilā-nagara from outside. Somehow he has managed to enquire and arrived. He has to go to the minister's house on a particular street. Again with enquiry he reaches the street. Now in the street he does not know the house. Hence he enquires a passerby as to where the ministers house is. The passerby answers, "there can you see a cuckoo over that roof and outside that house a plantain tree has been tied; further in front of that house a brāhmaṇa is standing and asking for charity by saying *bhavatī bhikṣāṁ dehi*. That is the house." Thus he shows the landmark with references. These references are temporary. They do not belong to the house permanently. The cuckoo over the roof, the plantain tree and the brāhmaṇa outside the house are *upa lakṣaṇa*s. They are there only for a short while and are temporary to show the identity of the house. That is all. As against this, a trunk on the front of an elephant can be considered as *svarūpa lakṣaṇa.*

**Mahācamasya** – We understand what is *svarūpa lakṣaṇa* and what is *upa lakṣaṇa*. Now kindly tell about *upādhi* in detail.

**Vaiśampāyana** – *Saumya*! Listen carefully. The *upādhi* is not connected with the thing either naturally or temporarily. Still using that we understand the concept.

**Mahācamasya** – Respected Sir. How is that possible?

**Vaikhānasa** – We pray, you kindly give an example for it.

**Vaiśampāyana** – Child! Mahārājā Janaka's palace tower is seen far away isn't it? To show to a child what we do? Child! See there is an *aśvattha* tree, and between the branches of the tree a bit higher you can see the tower which is *mahārājā*'s palace tower. Now in truth, there is no connection between the palace tower and the tree.

**Bodhāyana** – We understand very well, Svāmī.

**Vaiśampāyana** – In the same way the concept of *Brahman* can be understood by the three methods of reference such as *svarūpa lakṣaṇa, upa lakṣaṇa* and *upādhi*. Generally in Vedas the concept of *Brahman* is explained by *taṭastha lakṣaṇa.* However Śrī Varuṇa will make you understand it by *svarūpa lakṣaṇa*. This is a rare opportunity. He is very good in teaching this.

**Disciples** – Gurujī! We are thankful. With your blessing we are going to be gifted with a great knowledge. Our *praṇāmas* to you.

(Mahārājā Janaka's charioteer comes and gives his salutations.)

**Charioteer** – Svāmī! The chariot is ready. All the things are loaded. Shall we start for the pilgrimage.

**Vaiśampāyana** — First you go and have your food and take some rest. Give fodder to the horses. Allow them some time to roam on the river sand. We will start in the *abhijit muhūrtta* (auspicious period). Children, let us go inside.

***(They are leaving, the curtain falls.)***

***The Second Part Gets Over.***

## Part – III

### SCENE – I

(Behind the scene *oṁ śaṁ no mitraḥ śaḥ varuṇaḥ . . .* , the *śānti-pāṭha japa* is being recited. As the *japa* gets over in Maharṣi Vaiśampāyana's *āśrama* the screen is raised. The disciples Bodhāyana, Mahācamasya, Vaikhānasa are all sitting and conversing.)

**Vaikhānasa** – Friends, after our *gurujī* has left on his pilgrimage only one week has passed. However it looks like one *saṁvatsaram* (one year) has gone past.

**Bodhāyana** – Yes, because of the sadness of separation the time period will appear as long. Hasn't Śrī Varuṇa told he would be starting the lessons from today?

**Mahācamasya** – Pūjya Guru Varuṇa has said that he will come after his early morning duties. He has asked us to come here and wait for him. He will come now.

**Bodhāyana** – Yes, my friend. I can hear the footsteps. Is it *pūjya gurujī* coming? (turns around) There, do you all see who is coming? (**Everybody turns around, sees and runs towards him.**)

Our friend Triśaṅku is coming. O! What a surprise. (**They run and embrace him and bring him inside.**)

**Vaikhānasa** – Friend! It has been a long time since you have left us and gone. At least now you remembered and came.

**Mahācamasya** – Dearest friend, please take your seat. Our *gurujī* has gone on pilgrimage along with his family.

**Bodhāyana** – Bhr̥gu and Prācīnayogya have also gone together. Pūjya Śrī Varuṇa has come.

**Vaikhānasa** – Now Pūjya Śrī Varuṇa is our *āśrama*'s *kulapati.*

**Triśaṅku** – Friend! I am very happy to see you all. I am aware of all the matters.

**Disciples** – (**surprised**) How is that? By any divine knowledge or just by luck?

**Triśaṅku** – It is neither divine knowledge nor luck. All is due to blessing of the *guru.*

**Bodhāyana** – What is that? We are not able to understand.

**Triśaṅku** – When I was coming I met our *guru* and his entourage on the way. They had taken bath in Prayāga and were moving towards Naimiṣāraṇya. They explained everything. He also told that Pūjya Śrī Varuṇa is going to give teachings and advised me to hurry and join. Hence I came running. I met Pūjya Śrī Varuṇa and gave my *praṇāma*s to him. Now I have come to see you all.

**Mahācamasya** – When we were to hear some important preachings we thought our good friend was not there and were feeling a bit sad. Now that has been removed.

**Bodhāyana** – (एक स्वदु न भुञ्जीता – *eka svadu na bhuñjītā*) That is "one person alone should not enjoy what is of interest to everyone." Our friend thought as such and it is only just.

**Vaikhānasa** – For that he has brought disciples from the near-by *āśrama* also to join in Śrī Varuṇa's teachings.

**Triśaṅku** – Is that so! I am very happy. Now stop the conversation. Pūjya Guru Varuṇa is coming there.

*fig.:* **Varuṇa received in Vaiaśampāyana's Āśrama**

(Everybody gets up and give their respects, then *pūjās* like *arghya, pādya,* etc. are done to show further mark of respect. Śrī Varuṇa is sitting on a tiger-skin seat. Others with his permission sit on either side.)

**Varuṇa** – Children! Let all good tidings befall on you. Let us tell *śānti-pāṭha* before starting the preachings.

ॐ सह नाववतु। सह नौ भुनक्तु। सह वीर्यं करवावहै। तेजस्वि नावधीतमस्तु। मा विद्विषावहै।

ॐ शान्तिः शान्तिः शान्तिः।

*oṁ saha nāvavatu | saha nau bhunatku | saha vīryaṁ karavāvahai | tejasvi nāvadhītamastu | mā vidviṣāvahai |*

*oṁ śāntiḥ, śāntiḥ, śāntiḥ |*

May he protect us both together. May he nourish us both together. May we work together with vigour. Let what is learnt by us be luminous. May there be no dislike between us. *AUM*, peace! peace! peace!

(First the *guru* tells then the disciples tell together.)

**Varuṇa** – Children! Let me tell the meaning of *śānti-pāṭha* first. Let the *Brahman* protect us together (both *guru* and disciples). Let it give us food and nourish us. Let us work together with strength. Our education, that is learning of *brahma-vidyā*, let it be bright and sharp. Let no hostility or enmity enter in between us. Let *śānti* prevail on all fronts. Let peace prevail.

**Bodhāyana** – Gurujī, one doubt.

**Varuṇa** – Child! Bodhāyana! What is that? Ask immediately.

**Bodhāyana** – I understand *śānti-pāṭha* very well. However in the end it is told let no hostility happen between *guru* and disciple. Is such a prayer essential? A student who has come in search of the *guru* to get education, why will he become hostile with the *guru*? In the same way a disciple who has come in the asylum of the *guru* having full belief, why the *guru* will become hostile with the student.

**Varuṇa** – *Sabhāsa*! Saumya! It is a good question. I have also learnt a lesson that I should teach you all carefully. You are the disciples of Vaiśampāyana. Isn't that so? I will answer, now, your question. When the lessons are being taught there are reasons to develop hostility. First the teacher may not have the capacity to tell in short and precisely to make the students understand. As per the disciple's social status he may develop fondness or dislike. All these can be the mistakes on the side of the *guru*.

Then in between disciples unnecessary arguments can crop up. Due to jealousy a disciple can develop anger with another disciple and through that on the teacher. Then due to lesser capacity to learn time may elapse. This way the disciples also can have many mistakes and deficiencies. Due to this, hostility should not develop in between and be an obstacle to the learning process. This is being prayed for. Instead of spending time and brain on insignificant things to learn the important *brahma-jñāna* this prayer is being done. Further the most important concept of this is that both *guru* and disciple should not show hostility to any living being. This is the important meaning of this sentence.

**Bodhāyana** – Gurujī, we understand it very well. Kindly proceed further.

**Varuṇa** – Children! Do tell whatever you have learnt so far in short.

**Mahācamasya** – Respected Sir, as per your order I will tell. We have learnt about *saṁhitā* which does not obstruct *karma*. Then we have learnt about *ātmā* having *upādhi* (blemishes). Also about *vyāhṛti*s.

**Bodhāyana** – We have also learnt about the *upāsanā* of *oṁkāra*. Further we learned the particular *japa*s aiding *brahma-vidyā*.

**Varuṇa** – Now I will teach you how to completely annihilate *saṁsāra* and how to obtain blemishless (without *upādhi*) *ātma-darśana*. What is required for *brahma-vidyā* is removal of ignorance. Then destruction of *saṁsāra*. Now if you are learning about one *vidyā* (education) it is necessary to know the fruits of the learning. Hence first I will tell you the fruits of *brahma-vidyā* learning. Then I will teach you the same step by step so that it becomes clear like lotus in the hand.

ॐ ब्रह्मविदाप्नोति परम्।

*oṁ brahmavidāpnoti param* |

*AUM.* The knower of *Brahman* attains the Supreme.

That is, one who knows *Brahman* reaches the state of *Brahman* itself. It is bigger than everything, hence it is called as *Brahman.* Whoever knows it well he becomes *brahmavit*. That *brahmavit* is the knower of *Brahman.* He reaches the *Brahman* which is *parama* (ultimate).

**Triśaṅku** – Respected Sir, *Brahman* is present everywhere. Not that it is here and there but everywhere. That being so, how can one tell about *Brahman* that a person is obtaining it like obtaining a piece of furniture.

**Bodhāyana** – Svāmī! Here there is *kamaṇḍala*. I understand it clearly as *kamaṇḍala*. However due to this knowledge I cannot become *kamaṇḍala*.

**Vaikhānasa** – You must kindly explain this concept clearly along with examples.

**Varuṇa** – I am very happy to preach to disciples like you. I will explain clearly each of your questions. Listen carefully.

**Mahācamasya** – Respected Sir, we will listen as per your order. Kindly you must bless us with your knowledgable words.

**Varuṇa** – With the help of a story I will answer your question. Ten travellers together had to cross a river. Entering the river, they crossed it and then they tried to count and see if all ten have reached the other bank. The persons who counted each one of them did the counting leaving out himself. Hence the count came as nine. Again and again counting in the same way the count came as nine. They decided one among them has been carried away by the river and they became very sad. That time one clever person came there. Hearing the matter he made them stand in a line and with a small stick touching each one of them he counted 1, 2, 3, 4, 5, 6, 7, 8, 9, 10 and showed there are ten. The tenth count is none but oneself they realized. The false assumption (*bhramī*) left them. They came to know that by concentrating in counting others one has left counting himself. In the same way the *jivātmā* (living thing) coming under the influence of ignorance does not realize *Brahman* which is in oneself. Later hearing the preachings of the *guru* he gets back the memory and realizes *Brahman*. Even though *Brahman* is within himself always, he had not understood that before but later he realizes it through *guru*'s teachings. Before the learned one comes, they do not realize themselves. Later they come to know themselves. This is only the answer.

**Triśaṅku** – Respected Sir, I understand the concept very well now.

**Bodhāyana** – You must kindly clear my doubt in detail, Svāmī.

**Varuṇa** – Whatever we see around us is all *Brahman*. What is seen as human being, and various other forms seen differently are all *Brahman* only. Hence the *brahmavit* (one who has realized *Brahman*) sees *Brahman* alone in the human being. The ignorant sees the human beings as different beings. The *jñānī* (knowledgable) understands everything as *Brahman*.

**Bodhāyana** – Respected Sir! The doubt is cleared. Further kindly continue to educate us.

**Varuṇa** –

> ब्रह्मविदाप्नोति परम्। तदेषाभ्युक्ता सत्यं ज्ञानमनन्तं ब्रह्म। यो वेद निहितं गुहायां परमे व्योमन्। सोऽश्नुते सर्वान् कामान् सह ब्रह्मणा विपश्चितेति।
>
> *brahmavidāpnoti param* | *tadeṣābhyuktā satyaṁ jñānamanantaṁ brahma* | *yo veda nihitaṁ guhāyāṁ parame vyoman* | *so 'śnute sarvān kāmān saha brahmaṇā vipaściteti* |
>
> The knower of *Brahman* attains the supreme state. He who knows *Brahman* as the Real, as Knowledge and as the Infinite, as placed in the transcendental space within the secret cavern, enjoys all desires along with the attainment of *Brahman*, the all-knowing.

The thing which is truth, knowledge and endless is *Brahman*. Whoever realizes it he becomes the all-knowing *Brahman* itself and enjoys all desires.

**Triśaṅku** – Gurujī! truth, knowledge and infinite, what is the meaning of these words. You must explain in detail.

**Varuṇa** – The thing which does not change at any time is the true thing. Not only it does not change during anytime but also does not change in any way. Since the *Brahman* is the only one which does not change with time in any way and does not become distorted it is termed as truth. *Jñāna* means knowledge. Like the brightness and heat in the burning wick, the knowledge or *jñāna* cannot be separated from *Brahman*. Actually *Brahman* is the only main knowledge form. *Anantaṁ* means infinite. That is the one which cannot be measured and is seamless. It is endless and remains so with these charecteristics at any time period, in any province, and in any thing. *Satya, jñāna* and *ananta* (truth, knowledge and infinite), these three words are the attributes of *Brahman*.

**Mahācamasya** – Kindly explain the meaning, Svāmī.

**Varuṇa** – Here there is a mud pot and also a plate made of mud. For one the name is pot and another it is called the plate. In the pot and plate the name gets changed because of the use for which it is made and they are temporary. But the cause in them, the mud, does not change and hence that is the truth.

वाचारम्भ्यणं विकारो नामधेयं मृत्तिकेत्येव सत्यम्।

*vācārabhyaṇaṁ vikāro nāmadheyaṁ mṛttiketyeva satyam* ।

Thus in all the things of the world since the name and form keep changing all these are temporary. The cause of all that, the *Brahman*, is always the same without any change; hence it is the truth. Here since mud is shown as an example some people may think, like the mud the *Brahman* is also lifeless. Hence to remove that misconcept the *Brahman* is also described as *jñāna* (knowledge). *Brahman* is personification of knowledge. Since the knowledge in the world also comes to an end, one can think that the knowledge personified as *Brahman* also may come to an end. Hence the description of *anantaṁ* (infinite) is used to describe it. The end of one thing can come with time, or by end of a place to which it belongs, or end of the thing in which it is present. *Brahman* does not end in these three ways. *Brahman* is present in all places, at all times and in all things. This is the meaning of *ananta Brahman.*

**Bodhāyana** – Gurujī, we understand very well. You must kindly explain the meaning for other parts.

**Varuṇa** – Saumya, listen carefully. The *paramānanda* is filled everywhere. A miniscule of its part is experienced in worldly matters as bliss or happiness. The *Brahman* is shining within the heart in each individual. A person who realizes this becomes the all-knowing *Brahman* and enjoys all the happiness at the same time.

**Vaikhānasa** – It is difficult to comprehend this concept that the enjoyment we get in the things is a part of *brahmānanda.* Kindly explain and bless us.

**Varuṇa** – The happiness is not present in the outside things. This is because all the things don't give the same kind of happiness to everyone. One may be liking pancake, another may like sweetened rice. One may be keen to swim in the Ganges river. Another may be wishing to drink sweetened water. Thus it can be seen the happiness does not lie in things. That it is lying in the person experiencing is clear. The happiness one perceives through one's self belongs to *brahmānanda* (that is, happiness through *Brahman*).

**Mahācamasya** – Gurujī, we have become blessed. Kindly preach us more things we ought to know.

**Varuṇa** – Children, the time has exceeded. Let us stop the lesson here. It is not enough just listening to the lessons. It is necessary to contemplate and think deeply on them. Haven't you seen the cows chewing their cud? In the same way you also should go alone and whatever you have listened, bring it to the mind enquire properly about it and consider all aspects. Any doubts you can ask me tomorrow when the lessons start, don't feel hesitant. I consider it a great fortune to teach you all lessons.

**Disciples** – Respected Sir! We will do as advised by you.

***(Curtain falls.)***

## SCENE 2

(As the curtain opens, Pūjya Guru Varuṇa and the disciples are sitting and conversing.)

**Varuṇa** – Children! bring to memory whatever you have learned so far. Let me see, let each person tell one by one.

**Mahācamasya** – First you preached that the one who comes to know the *Brahman* reaches the *parā* state itself.

**Vaikhānasa** – Then you blessed us with the words that *Brahman* is truth, knowledge and infinite.

**Bodhāyana** – A person who is able to see the *Brahman* which is found everywhere and also in one's heart-cave he becomes *Brahma-svarūpa* and bound to enjoy all kind of happiness.

**Varuṇa** – Children! I am very happy. You have listened very carefully. You have also thought and contemplated properly. Now listen carefully to what is being told further.

**Disciples** – Respected Sir, we will do as per your order.

**Varuṇa** –

तस्माद्वा एतस्मादात्मन आकाशः संभूतः। आकाशाद्वायुः। वायोरग्निः अग्नेरापः। अद्भ्यः पृथिवी। पृथिव्या ओषधयः। ओषधीभ्योऽन्नम्। अन्नात्पुरुषः। स वा एष पुरुषोऽन्नरसमयः। तस्येदमेव शिरः। अयं दक्षिणः पक्षः। अयमुत्तरः पक्षः। अयमात्मा। इदं पुच्छं प्रतिष्ठा। तदप्येष श्लोको भवति॥

*tasmādvā etasmādātman ākāśaḥ saṁbhūtaḥ | ākāśādvāyuḥ | vāyoragniḥ| agnerāpaḥ | adbhyaḥ pṛthivī | pṛthivyā oṣadhayaḥ | oṣadhībhyo 'nnam | annātpuruṣaḥ | sa vā eṣa puruṣo 'nnarasamayaḥ | tasyedameva śiraḥ | ayaṁ dakṣiṇaḥ pakṣaḥ | ayamuttaraḥ pakṣaḥ | ayamātmā | idaṁ pucchaṁ pratiṣṭhā | tadapyeṣa śloko bhavati ||*

From such a Self, *Brahman* verily, space came into existence. From space emerged air. From air the fire; from fire the water;

> from water the earth; from the earth, plants; from plants, food; from food, the person (man); This person verily consists of the essence of food. The head; the right side; the left side; the heart and the tail end, have all come out of the essence of food.

(Raising up the index finger and showing it) From this *Brahman* (then pointing to one's chest) which is also this *ātmā,* the space came into existence. This space has seven *guṇa*s and has the essence for making the gross body with form. From the space, the air came into existence which has two qualities — sound and touch. From air the fire came into existence which has three qualities, the sound, touch and form. From fire water has formed with four *guṇa*s — sound, touch, form and essence. From water, the earth came into existence having five *guṇa*s, the sound, touch, form, essence and smell.

From the earth the trees and plants came into existence; from plants came food. From food the *puruṣa* seed (*vīryam*) came into existence. From that man came about with organs like head, leg, and sides as the essence of food.

**Bodhāyana** – Whatever you told now kindly explain it in detail so that we can understand clearly.

**Varuṇa** – Have you seen the statue of Indra made of bronze kept in *yajñaśālā*? Intially the figure is made of mud, later bronze is melted and poured over it. In a similar way here *Brahman* is said to have five coverings, five envelopes, that is, five dresses. First the one which we can see with our eyes, the gross body made of food (*annam*). Now step by step *prāṇamaya, manomaya, vijñanamaya,* and *ānandamaya* envelopes will be described. Listen carefully. Ask the meaning in the end.

**Vaikhānasa** – Respected Sir, let it be so.

**Triśaṅku** – Gurujī, kindly preach further.

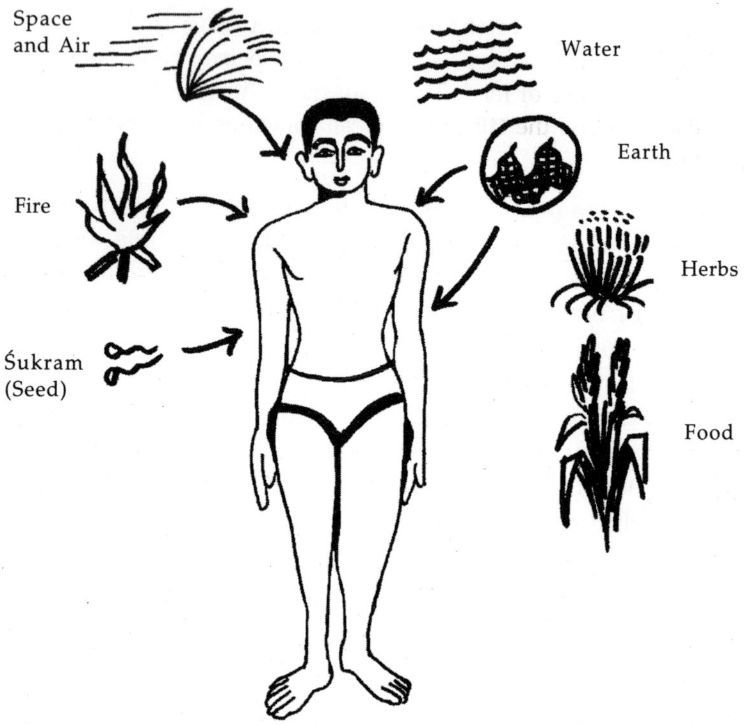


*fig.:* **Formation of human being**

**Varuṇa –**

अन्नाद्वै प्रजाः प्रजायन्ते। याः काश्च पृथिवीꣳश्रिताः। अथो अन्नेनैव जीवन्ति। अथैनदपि यन्त्यन्ततः। अन्नꣳहि भूतानां ज्येष्ठम्। तस्मात्सर्वौषधमुच्यते। सर्वं वै तेऽन्नमाप्नुवन्ति येऽन्नं ब्रह्मोपासते। अन्नꣳहि भूतानां ज्येष्ठम्। तस्मात्सर्वौषधमुच्यते। अन्नाद्भूतानि जायन्ते। जातान्यन्नेन वर्धन्ते। अद्यतेऽत्ति च भूतानि। तस्मादन्नं तदुच्यत इति।

*annādvai prajāḥ prajāyante | yāḥ kāśca pṛthivīm̐śritāḥ | atho annenaiva jīvanti | athainadapi yantyantataḥ | annam̐hi bhūtānāṁ jyeṣṭham | tasmātsarvauṣadhamucyate | sarvaṁ vai te 'nnamāpnuvanti ye 'nnaṁ brahmopāsate | annam̐hi bhūtānāṁ jyeṣṭham | tasmātsarvauṣadhamucyate |*

*annādbhūtāni jāyante | jātānyannena vardhante | adyate 'tti ca bhūtāni | tasmādannaṁ taducyata iti |*

All beings that dwell on the earth are verily born from food. Moreover, by food alone they live and die without it and then they also pass as food at the end. Food, verily, is the eldest born of beings. Therefore, it is called the medicine for all (or, the all-curing medicine). Verily, those who worship food as *Brahman* acquire all food. From food are living beings born. When born, they grow by food. It is eaten by beings. Therefore it is called food.

All the people in the earth are made from food. Later they live by the food. Finally they end as food. For all the things formed *annam* is the important source. Since it is made first it is the cause of everything. Hence it remains for everyone elixir. The one who does *upāsanā* of food as *Brahman* reaches all the food.

**Mahācamasya** – Gurujī! How to do *upāsanā* of food as *Brahman*?

**Varuṇa** – We came into being from food. We live by eating it. In the end we end in that. Thinking that way we should do *upāsanā* of food as *Brahman*.

**Bodhāyana** – Respected Sir! It is not clearly understood that we are born out of food and we are going to end in food. Hence, make that clear.

**Varuṇa** – Saumya! A person grows up eating food. There is no doubt about this. The food he eats gets converted to *vīryam* (the seed) and makes another *praja* (human being). Hence it becomes clear the *prajas* (human beings) come out of food. Later, when the person dies is buried or he is burnt. His body combines with the earth, fertilizes the food being made and becomes the food itself. Thus it is clear the *prajas* finally end as food. I will tell another example. Here is a mud pot. Initially it was just mud. Now it is converted into pot. Thus the pot originated from the mud. If the pot is broken it again becomes mud. That is, in the end it becomes the mud.

**Disciples** – We understand clearly. Kindly teach further.

**Varuṇa** – Whoever does *upāsanā* of food as *Brahman* they attain all the food. Food only came about before everything else and is termed as elixir of life. From food the living things came about. Then they grow by food. Food is eaten by all living things and one eating the living things is also food. Thus the one eaten by living things is food and the one eating the living things is also food. It is thus the cause of everything.

**Vaikhānasa** – Do tell us about other envelopes, O! Lord.

**Varuṇa** – Children

तस्माद्वा एतस्मादन्नरसमयात् अन्योऽन्तर आत्मा प्राणमयः। तेनैष पूर्णः। स वा एष पुरुषविध एव। तस्य पुरुषविधताम्। अन्वयं पुरुषविधः। तस्य प्राण एव शिरः। व्यानो दक्षिणः पक्षः। अपान उत्तरः पक्षः। आकाश आत्मा। पृथिवी पुच्छं प्रतिष्ठा। तदप्येष श्लोको भवति॥

*tasmādvā etasmādannarasamayāt anyo 'ntara ātmā prāṇamayaḥ | tenaiṣa pūrṇaḥ | sa vā eṣa puruṣavidha eva | tasya puruṣavidhatām | anvayaṁ puruṣavidhaḥ | tasya prāṇa eva śiraḥ | vyāno dakṣiṇaḥ pakṣaḥ | apāna uttara pakṣaḥ | ākāśa ātmā | pṛthivī pucchaṁ pratiṣṭhā | tadapyeṣa śloko bhavati ||*

Verily different from and within that which consists of the essence of food is the Self which consists of vital breath (*prāṇa*). By that (by the Self which consists of vital breath) this (the Self which consists of the essence of food) is filled. This Self too is of the form of the (human) person. Following that human form (of the Self-consisting of the essence of food) is this human form. Of this human form *prāṇa* is the head; *vyāna* is the right side; *apāna* is the left side; space is the body; the earth is the tail end, the foundation.

Inside the *annamaya-kośa* (food envelope) is the *prāṇamaya ātmā*. The *prāṇamaya* envelope is different than the *annamaya* envelope. It is more subtle than that. The *annamaya* envelope is filled with *prāṇamaya* envelope. This body filled with *prāṇa* follows the form of *annamaya* envelope and gets the human (*puruṣa*) form. There is no separate form for the *prāṇamaya* envelope. For this *prāṇamaya puruṣa* form the head is *prāṇa*. *Vyāna* is the right side wing. *Apāna* is the left side wing. The *ākāśa* (space) is *samāna* in the middle. The earth is the lower portion (tail). There is a *mantra* connected to this.

**Bodhāyana** – Sadguru! If the description follows the imagination, where it will go and end?

**Vaikhānasa** – Friend! Don't be scared. Gurujī will explain everything. Be patient and listen.

**Varuṇa** – The *Brahman* which is inside the cave of the heart can be equated to the main idol which is in the *sanctum sanctorum* of a temple. Surrounding it there are five *prakārams* (courtyards). In the same way around the *Brahman* there are five envelopes. The envelope made of food (*annam*) is the outside courtyard. The second courtyard is the *prāṇa* envelope. Now we have come to the second round. After crossing the next three courtyards one can reach the chief idol. There is no need to hurry. No need to doubt.

**Bodhāyana** – Kindly tell the *śloka* describing the *prāṇamaya* envelope.

**Varuṇa** –

प्राणं देवा अनु प्राणन्ति। मनुष्याः पशवश्च ये। प्राणो हि भूतानामायुः। तस्मात्सर्वायुषमुच्यते। सर्वमेव त आयुर्यन्ति। ये प्राणं ब्रह्मोपासते। प्राणो हि भूतानामायुः। तस्मात्सर्वायुषमुच्यत इति।

*prāṇaṁ deva anu prāṇanti | manuṣyāḥ paśavaśca ye | prāṇo hi bhūtānāmāyuḥ | tasmāt sarvāyuṣamucyate | sarvameva ta āyuryanti | ye prāṇaṁ brahmopāsate | prāṇo hi bhūtānāmāyuḥ | tasmāt sarvāyuṣamucyata iti |*

The gods live following the function of the vital breath, as also human beings and beasts. Since the vital breath is the lifespan of all beings, it is called the lifespan of all. Those who worship the vital breath as *Brahman* attain their full span of life, for the vital breath is the life of all beings, and therefore, it is called the lifespan of all.

I will tell the meaning of the *śloka,* listen. The *deva*s like Agni and other *deva*s do their respective work as per directions of *vāyu* (wind). When talking about body *deva*s means the sense organs. Senses follow the *vāyu* which is the *prāṇa*'s form. The people and the cattle (other living things) do the same. The *prāṇa* is the life period of the living things. It is thus the life period of all and termed as *sarva āyuṣam* (the life period of everything). Whoever worships *prāṇa* as *Brahman* will get complete or full life. There is no fear of death (*apamṛtyu*). The *prāṇa* is the life of all the living things.

**Triśaṅku** – Sadguru. Kindly explain the envelope present inside the *prāṇamaya-kośa.*

**Varuṇa** –

तस्यैष एव शारीर आत्मा। यः पूर्वस्य। तस्माद्वा एतस्मात् प्राणमयात् अन्योऽन्तर आत्मा मनोमयः। तेनैष पूर्णः। स वा एष पुरुषविध एव। तस्य पुरुषविधताम्। अन्वयं पुरुषविधः। तस्य यजुरेव शिरः। ऋग् दक्षिणः पक्षः। सामोत्तर पक्षः। आदेश आत्मा। अथर्वाङ्गीरसः पुच्छं प्रतिष्ठा। तदप्येष श्लोको भवति॥

*tasyaiṣa eva śārīra ātmā* । *yaḥ pūrvasya* । *tasmādvā etasmāt prāṇamayāt* । *anyo 'ntara ātmā manomayaḥ* । *tenaiṣa pūrṇaḥ* । *sa vā eṣa puruṣavidha eva* । *tasya puruṣavidhatām* । *anvayaṁ puruṣavidhaḥ* । *tasya yajureva śiraḥ* । *ṛg dakṣiṇaḥ pakṣaḥ* । *sāmottara pakṣaḥ* । *ādeśa ātmā* । *atharvāṅgīrasaḥ pucchaṁ pratiṣṭhā* । *tadapyeṣa śloko bhavati* ।।

This indeed is the embodied Self of the former. Verily, different from and within that which consists of the vital breaths is the Self that consists of mind. By that (by the Self-consisting of mind) this (the Self-consisting of the vital breaths) is filled. This Self too is of the form of the person (human). Following that human form (of the Self-consisting

> of the vital breaths) is this human form. Of this human form the *Yajurveda* is the head; the *Ṛgveda* is the right side; the *Sāmaveda* is the left side; teaching is its soul, and the hymns of the *Atharvaveda* are its tail end, the foundation.

This *prāṇamaya-kośa* is the *ātmā* of the previous *annamaya* body. More subtle than this *prāṇamaya* there is an envelope. But it is inside it. That is *manomaya-kośa*. The *prāṇamaya* is filled with the *manomaya*. Hence this also gets the form of *puruṣa* (human being). For this *manomaya-kośa* also there are head, sides, centre and lower portion. For this *manomaya* human form (*puruṣa* form) *Yajurveda* is the head, *Ṛgveda* is the right side, *Sāma- veda* is the left side. The centre portion (soul) is *ādeśa* (teaching). *Atharvaveda* is the lower side (tail).

> यतो वाचो निवर्त्तन्ते। अप्राप्य मनसा सह। आनन्दं ब्रह्मणो विद्वान्। न बिभेति कदाचनेति।
>
> *yato vāco nivarttante* । *aprāpya manasā saha* । *ānandaṁ brahmaṇo vidvān* । *na bibheti kadācaneti* ।
>
> Whence words return with the mind, not attaining it, he who knows that Bliss-content of *Brahman* fears not at any time.

"A person knowing the *Brahman* which cannot be reached by words and thoughts, such a person will realize happiness in that *Brahman* and will never be scared." (The disciples look at each other in surprise). Children, now we have come to the most important stage. I will tell the meaning of the *mantra* once again. "Unable to reach the *Brahman,* words from the mouth come back, the mind also goes, fails and comes back. If one knows that *brahmānanda* state he will not be scared of anything." You think about this properly. Let us stop it today over here.

***(Everybody gets up.)***

***(The curtain falls.)***

## SCENE 3

(As the curtain opens in Maharṣi Vaiśampāyana's *āśrama* the scene of Gurujī Varuṇa giving teachings to the disciples can be seen.)

**Varuṇa** – Child! Bodhāyana! We should start the lessons from where we left yesterday. Where we stopped yesterday do tell?

**Bodhāyana** – Svāmī!

यतो वाचो निवर्त्तन्ते। अप्राप्य मनसा सह। आनन्दं ब्रह्मणो विद्वान्। न बिभेति कदाचनेति।

*yato vāco nivarttante | aprāpya manasā saha | ānandaṁ brahmaṇo vidvān | na bibheti kadācaneti |*

You told this *śloka* and also the meaning.

**Varuṇa** – Child! Very correct.

**Mahācamasya** – We couldn't follow the meaning properly. Once again can you tell in detail, respected Sir?

**Varuṇa** – Children! Let it be so, listen carefully. Initially the *annamaya-kośa* was described. If the *upāsanā* of it is done as *Brahman* the fruits of it also were told. Then *prāṇamaya-kośa* was described and that also if *upāsanā* is done as *Brahman* the result of it was told. Then *manomaya-kośa* was explained. If that is considered as *Brahman* and *upāsanā* is done the results accrued are described in this *śloka*. That is, *Brahman* is beyond the words and mind. It is pure bliss form. A person who does *upāsanā* of that and realizes it will get complete bliss and will be without any fear.

**Triśaṅku** – Gurujī! If *Brahman* is beyond mind and words how to know that?

**Vaikhānasa** – Respected Sir. If anything has to be known by oneself it is due to mind only, isn't it? If it has to be known from others it is by words. If the help of both is not there how to know that?

**Varuṇa** – Children! I am happy to hear such scholarly questions. First let me tell you why the mind was not able to know it. That is because the *Brahman* only thinks. It is cause of the mind and its thoughts. For us the mind is personalized. We tell, it is your mind, my mind, his mind and so on. Hence we perceive there is another power ruling the mind. This is definite. Well, that power only is *Brahman.* Hence the mind cannot know *Brahman.* For *Brahman* the mind is like the body. The one who rules the mind is sitting inside it and it is the *Brahman*. What is seen as *manomaya-kośa* and being mind of the mind is *Brahman*. Hence mind also keeps trying to look for *Brahman* but gets defeated and comes back.

**Vaikhānasa** – Kindly tell how the words withdraw and come back.

**Varuṇa** – Saumya! I will tell, listen carefully. How the major in the army sends his soldiers first to the war front and then he also follows, in the same way sending the words first and later the mind goes behind. However both fail and come back. As per the status of the official the mind which is in that category was first told and its defeat described. Now I will tell how the words and sentences returned. The words can be divided into four types:

1. The one denoting name of the thing, that is man, cow, tree, *kamaṇḍala*, cereal, etc.
2. The one denoting the quality of a thing, that is goodness, evil, black, blue, anger, peace, and so on.
3. The one denoting action, that is cooking, running, bathing, breathing, giving alms, laughing, and so on.
4. The one denoting connection (relation), that is father, mother, *guru*, husband, and so on.

However *Brahman* cannot be explained by these four types of words. What name does it possess? What quality? What action? Since it stands alone as the only one, how is it possible to connect it to something and call a name. Since it does not come under the four parts of the words we are not able to know it. That is, the words also get defeated and return.

**Triśaṅku** – Gurujī! Very wonderfully and in a rare manner you described it. We understand very clearly. Kindly you must preach further.

**Mahācamasya** – Sadguru! We understand that mind is not able to know it, and for it mind is like a body. The one which cannot be clarified by word and mind but which prompts them is *Brahman*, we understood.

**Bodhāyana** – Respected Sir, kindly show consideration on us and continue to further preach to us.

**Varuṇa** – Let it be so, my children.

तस्यैष एव शरीर आत्मा। यः पूर्वस्य।

*tasyaiṣa eva śarīra ātmā | yaḥ pūrvasya |*

For the *prāṇamaya-kośa* told before this *manomaya-kośa* is only *ātmā* inside the body.

यतो वाचो निवर्त्तन्ते। अप्राप्य मनसा सह। आनन्दं ब्रह्मणो विद्वान्। न बिभेति कदाचनेति। तस्यैष एव शारीर आत्मा। यः पूर्वस्य। तस्माद्वा एतस्मान्मनोमयात्। अन्योऽन्तर आत्मा विज्ञानमयः। तेनैष पूर्णः। स वा एष पुरुषविध एव। तस्य पुरुषविधताम्। अन्वयं पुरुषविधः। तस्य श्रद्धैव शिरः। ऋतं दक्षिणः पक्षः। सत्यमुत्तरः पक्षः। योग आत्मा। महः पुच्छ प्रतिष्ठा। तदप्येष श्लोको भवति॥

*yato vāco nivartante | aprāpya manasā saha | ānandaṁ brahmaṇo vidvān | na bibheti kadācaneti | tasyaiṣa eva śārīra ātmā | yaḥ pūrvasya | tasmādvā etasmānmanomayāt anyo 'ntara ātmā vijñānamayaḥ | tenaiṣa pūrṇaḥ | sa vā eṣa puruṣavidha eva | tasya puruṣavidhatām anvayaṁ puruṣavidhaḥ | tasya śraddhaiva śiraḥ | ṛtaṁ dakṣiṇaḥ pakṣaḥ | satyamuttaraḥ pakṣaḥ | yoga ātmā | mahaḥ puccham pratiṣṭhā | tadapyeṣa śloko bhavati ||*

> This indeed is the embodied Self of the former. Verily, different from and within that which consists of mind is the Self that consists of applied knowledge. By that (the Self-consisting of applied knowledge) this (the Self-consisting of mind) is filled. This Self too is of the form of the person (human). Following that human form (of the Self-consisting of mind) is this human form. Of this human form faith (*śraddhā*) is the head; *ṛtam* or discipline is the right side; Truth is the left side; unitiveness (*yoga*) is the body; the Great (*mahaḥ*) is the tail-end, the foundation.

Different from *manomaya-kośa* and being further inside is *vijñānamaya ātmā*. Because of that the *manomaya-kośa* is filled. Hence its form also, like before, is the *puruṣa* form. For this *śraddhā* is the head, *ṛtam* meaning discipline is the right side, the truth is the left side, *yoga* is the centre body. *Mahat* concept is the lower portion.

**Bodhāyana** – *Yoga, mahat, tattva* all these means what? *vijñānam* means what?

**Varuṇa** – The *karmas* have to be done along with *vijñānam*. For those *karmas śraddhā* is very important. Hence *śraddhā* as head is told first. *Karmas* have to be done in the proper order and truthfully. Hence those are described as *puruṣa*'s, two parts — wings. *Yoga* means humility, to hold oneself without crossing limits. The *manomaya-kośa* is described as Veda *rūpam*, isn't it? The steady intellect to understand the meaning of the Vedas is told here as *vijñānam*. *Mahat* is the concept which came out of *Brahman* first. It is fundamental for everything.

**Vaikhānasa** – Respected Sir, kindly tell us the *śloka* describing *vijñānamaya kośa* and its meaning.

**Varuṇa** –

> विज्ञानं यज्ञं तनुते। कर्माणि तनुतेऽपि च। विज्ञानं देवाः सर्वे। ब्रह्म ज्येष्ठमुपासते। विज्ञानं ब्रह्म चेद्वेद। तस्माच्चेन्न प्रमाद्यति। शरीरे पाप्मनो हित्वा। सर्वान् कामान् समश्नुत इति।

*vijñānaṁ yajñaṁ tanute । karmāṇi tanute 'pi ca ।*
*vijñānaṁ devaḥ sarve । brahma jyeṣṭhamupāsate ।*
*vijñānaṁ brahma cedveda । tasmāccenna pramādyati।*
*śarīre pāpmano hitvā । sarvān kāmān samaśnuta iti।*

Applied wisdom actualizes the sacrifice. It actualizes actions too. All the gods meditate on the primeval applied wisdom as *Brahman*. If one knows *Brahman* as applied wisdom and if one does not swerve from it, he leaves his sins while in the body and attains all desires.

*Vijñānam* is the one which does the *yajña*. It does other *karmas* also. All *devas* consider *vijñānam* as the first-seen *Brahman* and do *upāsanā*. A person who comes to know this and who does not slip from that *Brahman* gets rid of all *pāpas* (sins) and realizes happiness or bliss. The *manomaya-kośa* is the body; *vijñānam* is its *ātmā*.

**Bodhāyana** – When a person does *karma, puṇyas* and *pāpas* (sins) do happen. How to get rid of them?

**Varuṇa** – Due to ego of the person all *puṇyas* and *pāpas* happen. When ego takes leave, all *karmas* become *niṣkāmya* (without desire for result) *karmas*. That time all *puṇyas* and *pāpas* get annihilated.

**Vaikhānasa** – Do continue to preach to us, respected Sir.

**Varuṇa** – Saumya! Listen.

तस्यैष एव शारीर आत्मा। यः पूर्वस्य। तस्माद्वा एतस्माद्विज्ञानमयात्। अन्योऽन्तर आत्मानन्दमयः। तेनैष पूर्णः। स वा एष पुरुषविध एव। तस्य पुरुषविधताम्। अन्वयं पुरुषविधः। तस्य प्रियमेव शिरः। मोदो दक्षिणः पक्षः। प्रमोद उत्तरः पक्षः। आनन्द आत्मा। ब्रह्म पुच्छं प्रतिष्ठा। तदप्येष श्लोको भवति॥५॥

*tasyaiṣa eva śārīra ātmā । yaḥ pūrvasya । tasmādvā etasmād vijñānamayāt anyo 'ntara ātmānandamayaḥ । tenaiṣa pūrṇaḥ । sa vā eṣa puruṣavidha eva । tasya puruṣavidhatām । anvayaṁ puruṣavidhaḥ । tasya priyameva śiraḥ । modo dakṣiṇaḥ pakṣaḥ । pramoda uttaraḥ pakṣaḥ । ānanda ātmā । brahma pucchaṁ pratiṣṭhā | tadapyeṣa śloko bhavati ||5||*

> This indeed is the embodied Self of the former. Verily different from and within that which consists of applied wisdom is the Self that consists of bliss (the ultimate value). By that (by the Self-consisting of Value) this (the Self-consisting of applied wisdom) is filled. This Self too is of the form of a person (human). Following that human form (of the Self-consisting of applied wisdom) is this human form. Of this human form happiness (*priyam*) is the head; *moda* is the right side; *pramoda* is the left side; value (*ānanda*) is the soul *Brahman* is the tail-end, the foundation.

Different from *vijñānamayam* but being inside it is *ānandamaya ātmā*. Due to *ānandamaya ātmā* the previously described *vijñānamaya-kośa* is filled up. Its form is similar to the previous *puruṣa* form. For the *ānandamaya puruṣa* the happiness is the head, *moda* is the right side, *pramoda* is the left side. Value (*ānanda*) is the soul. *Brahman* is the lower portion (tail).

**Mahācamasya** – *Priya, moda* and *pramoda* what do these terms mean? Kindly explain the difference of these words.

**Varuṇa** – All these words point to happiness but differ in degree. The happiness one gets seeing the thing one desired can be equated to *priya*. The happiness one gets on acquiring the thing desired is *moda*. The happiness one gets when he enjoys the acquired thing is *pramoda*. Going through the three kinds of happiness described above is the *ānanda* happiness. Due to penance (*tapa*), *brahmacaryam, upāsanā, śraddhā*, learning of Vedas, etc. the inner parts become purified. The more they get purified the more is the happiness (*ānanda*). However this happiness is only but a part of *paramānandam*. The *ātmā is* filled with happiness and the *jīva* is a *saṁsārī*. The *puccha* (tail) which is the main base (foundation) represents *paramātmā Brahman*. There is nothing further to it. Children, think well what you have heard today. I am closing the lesson here. The afternoon prayer-time is nearing. Let us go (All of them get up and go).

***(Curtain falls.)***

## SCENE 4

(Curtain is raised. In Vaiśampāyana's *āśrama* Pūjya Guru Varuṇa and disciples are sitting.)

**Varuṇa** – Children! Did you think over and exercise well on the lessons taught yesterday. If any doubts are there do ask without hesitation and fear. I will clear your doubts.

**Triśaṅku** – Gurujī, we came to know without any doubt. Do kindly preach to us further on this.

**Varuṇa** – Alright, I will teach you. Listen carefully.

असन्नेव स भवति। असद् ब्रह्मेति वेद चेत्। अस्ति ब्रह्मेति चेद्वेद।
सन्तमेनं ततो विदुरिति। तस्यैष एव शारीर आत्मा। यः पूर्वस्य।

*asanneva sa bhavati | asad brahmeti veda cet | asti brahmeti cedveda | santamenaṁ tato viduriti | tasyaiṣa eva śārīra ātmā | yaḥ pūrvasya |*

One does become verily non-existent, if he feels *Brahman* as non-existent, when one knows *Brahman* exists in everything, such a person is known as existent. This is, indeed, the embodied Self of the former.

Whoever thinks there is no *Brahman* he becomes *asat* (non-true person). That is, if one thinks *Brahman* is not there he becomes a completely fallen person. If he thinks *Brahman* is there in a true manner then he experiences truth, that is *Brahman* itself, thus thinks the *brahmavit* (one who has attained *Brahman*).

For the previous *vijñānamaya* body this *ānandamaya* body becomes the *ātmā*.

**Bodhāyana** – If we hear the meaning it appears we have understood it well. However it is not very clear. A little more explanation to make it clear will be helpful, Gurujī.

**Varuṇa** – In the world the only true thing is *Brahman*. Only by knowing this *Brahman* a person reaches the state of *mokṣa* (liberation) which is the true *puruṣārtha*. If one decides there is no *Brahman* he will never try to know *Brahman*, then how can he attain *Brahman*? To attain *Brahman* should be the aim of a true *puruṣottama*. If one knows that *Brahman* is there then he tries to realize it and ultimately he can become one with *Brahman*. *Brahmavit* (knowledgeable people) will know him as true *Brahman*. If *sat* (truth) is known as *Brahman* this explanation holds good. However if the *sat* (truth) word is interpreted as *sādhu* and *asat* is interpreted as *asādhu*, it can be explained in a different manner. That is, whoever thinks *Brahman* is not there, he will also maintain that the path of knowing *Brahman* is not there. He won't have belief in such *dhārmika* path. Hence the *nāstika* (non-believer) will be termed by elders as *asādhu*. Instead if he knows that the *Brahman* truth is there he will with *śraddhā* go in search of understanding *Brahman* and follow *varṇāśramādi dharma* (वर्णाश्रमादि धर्म). The *āstika* (believer) will be termed as *sādhu* (a person going on a good path) by elders. Hence to reach the exalted *puruṣottama* state and to earn a good name *sādhu*, it is basically required to believe staunchly that *Brahman* is there. Since it cannot be reached by mind and words, even persons having good brains can decide *Brahman* is not there. Hence Vedas are continuously and repeatedly telling *Brahman* is there.

**Triśaṅku** – Respected Sir! Now can I ask questions connected to this?

अथातोऽनुप्रश्नाः ।

*athāto 'nupraśnāḥ* ।

Now, then, the subsequent questions.

**Varuṇa** – Child! By all means you can ask.

**Triśaṅku** –

उताविद्वानमुं लोकं प्रेत्य। कश्चन गच्छति ३। आहो विद्वानमुं लोकं प्रेत्य। कश्चित्स्मश्नुता ३ उ।

*utāvidvānamuṁ lokaṁ pretya* । *kaścana gacchati* 3 ।
*āho vidvānamuṁ lokaṁ pretya* । *kaścitsmaśnutā* 3 U ।

> Does anyone who knows not, on departing from this life, go to the yonder world? Or, is it that anyone who knows, on departing from this life, attains that world?

A person who does not know *Brahman,* after leaving the body, will he reach the other world and get united with *paramātmā?*

**Varuṇa** – *Sabhāsa* Triśaṅku! A very good question. These questions can be asked further separating them. Mahācamasya, make it into four parts and tell.

**Mahācamasya** – Gurujī, I will do so.

1. A person having no knowledge of *Brahman* who does not possess that *vidyā,* will he reach that *loka* (*brahma-loka*) after leaving this world?
2. Or does it happen that a non-knowledgable person will not reach there?
3. The *vidvān* and *brahma-jñānī,* does he reach the *loka* (world) of *paramātmā*?
4. Or does it happen that a *brahma-jñānī* does not reach the world of *paramātmā*?

**Varuṇa** – Children! For these questions, I don't want to tell in a few words, as to whether there is an answer or there is no answer. I want to tell clearly and in detail. Further when I started the lessons on the first day itself I had told an answer you can recall. Now I will tell you clearly, listen carefully.

**Bodhāyana** – Respected Sir! Let it be so.

**Varuṇa** –

> सोऽकामयत। बहु स्यां प्रजायेयेति। स तपोऽतप्यत। स तपस्तप्त्वा। इदꣳसर्वमसृजत। यदिदं किं च। तत्सृष्ट्वा। तदेवानुप्राविशत्। तदनुप्रविश्य। सच्चत्यच्चाभवत्। निरुक्तं चानिरुक्तं च। निलयनं चानिलयनं च। विज्ञानं चाविज्ञानं च। सत्यं चानृतं च सत्यमभवत्। यदिदं किं च। तत्सत्यमित्याचक्षते। तदप्येष श्लोको भवति॥६॥

> *so 'kāmayata | bahu syāṁ prajāyeyeti | sa tapo 'tapyata |*

*sa tapastaptvā idaṁsarvamasṛjata | yadidaṁ kiṁ ca | tatsṛṣṭvā | tadevanuprāviśat | tadanupraviśya | saccatyaccābhavat | niruktaṁ cāniruktaṁ ca | nilayanaṁ cānilayanaṁ ca | vijñānaṁ cāvijñānaṁ ca | satyaṁ cānṛtaṁ ca satyamabhavat | yadidaṁ kiṁ ca | tatsatyamityācakṣate | tadapyeṣa śloko bhavati ||6||*

> He desired: Let me become many. Let me be born. He heated himself upon this desire. On being heated up, he created all this, whatever is here. Having created it, into it, indeed, he entered. Thus he became both the actual and the beyond, the defined and the undefined, the founded and the unfounded, knowledge and non-knowledge, the true and the untrue. The real became whatever is here. That is why everything here is called real.

The *Brahman* which is the cause of *paramātmā, ākāśa*, etc. decided to grow fast and in a vast manner. For that it did *tapa* (penance). Doing the *tapa*, it created whatever is there around. After creating it, it entered into that and became form and formless.

It became *sarvaguṇa* with (good qualities) and *nirguṇa* (with no qualities). It became as a thing occupying place and not occupying place. It became *chit* and *achit*. It became the truth and untruth. The truth only became all that which is here. Hence it is called truth of the truth.

**Triśaṅku** – Svāmī! You have told that *Brahman* did *tapa* with determination telling "I will enlarge and become more vast and varied." What kind of *tapa* the *Brahman* did? You must kindly explain.

**Varuṇa** – Here *tapa* by *Brahman* does not mean that it did *tapa* (penance) like us. Hence the question of directing the *tapa* towards a particular person does not arise. It did *tapa* means it spread the light of knowledge. The world which has to be created, the order of creation, the method to create all these things were thought out deeply. That is the penance. Thinking thus "It" created whatever is seen around here. Later as per the requirement of the fruits of *karma* of living things, this world was made.

**Mahācamasya** – Gurujī! We understand that the creation was made because of *Brahman*'s *tapa*. Since *Brahman* is omnipresent, found everywhere, after creation, it may not be correct to tell it entered the creation. Isn't that so? Did it enter in its own form? Or in any other form?

**Vaikhānasa** – The things which are not inside but out, only those can enter inside. This being so how it can be told that *Brahman* entered the creation? *Brahman* only has taken the form of the world. In that world the *Brahman* is present inside, outside, everywhere and all the time. Thus if we say *Brahman* entered the creation, how will it be apt? In that case it has to be assumed that before entering inside, the *Brahman* was not there inside. That way it will sound as though *Brahman* is not all-pervading.

**Varuṇa** – It is not that the world is different and *Brahman* is different. It cannot be imagined like a person making a house and doing *gṛhapraveśaṁ* (house warming cermony), that *Brahman* makes the world and enters into it. When we see in the still, clear waters of a pond the reflection of the sun, we assume the sun has entered the water, isn't it? It is the same way here. It is not truly there but only appears to have entered. That is all. *Brahman* is the cause of all divergent creation. Even though it is undifferentiated, without any blemish and is whole, due to its *saṁkalpa* (determination) it took the shapes of various beings and forms. By itself though undifferentiated it brought about a differentiated universe. After bringing about the universe it entered into the living things, heart and the true *parama* thing became things having form and also formless things. Thus it became things which are specific and things which are not specific. It became things which are intelligent and non-intelligent. It became all things which are connected with daily living and also things in the universe which are not connected with daily living. This alone is the true substance.

**Triśaṅku** – Gurujī, we followed about the creation of the universe and how, the *Brahman* became everything. Kindly continue with your preachings.

**Bodhāyana** – Svāmī! We have become blessed. The *Brahman* which is the cause of *pañcabhūta* created all beings and in the intelligent beings it acts as the one who can see, one who can hear, etc. and further in all kinds of ways it is being seen and felt. This we have understood. However, one doubt.

**Varuṇa** – What is that? Child, do ask.

**Bodhāyana** – Respected Sir! you told about Truth in *vyavahāram* (daily living) and untruth in daily living. Further you told truth is *pāramārthika satya*. Those things we were not able to follow properly. Kindly tell in detail.

**Varuṇa** – The *pāramārthika* truth is *Brahman*. The facts like *rajju sarpam* (the rope which is seen as snake) and *sūkti rajatam* (the silver seen over the shell) are untruths. The truth in comparison to that is the real snake and the real silver. In fact, they are also in a way untruths but they are truths in daily life.

**Vaikhānasa** – Respected Sir, kindly tell the *mantra*s and their meaning.

असद्वा इदमग्र आसीत्। ततो वै सदजायत। तदात्मानꣳस्वयमकुरुत। तस्मात्तत्सुकृतमुच्यत इति। यद्वै तत्सुकृतम्। रसो वै सः। रसꣳ ह्येवायं लब्ध्वानन्दी भवति। को ह्येवान्यात् कः प्राण्यात् । यदेष आकाश आनन्दो न स्यात्। एष ह्येवानन्दयाति। यदा ह्येवैष एतस्मिन्नदृश्येऽनात्म्येऽनिरुक्तेऽनिलयनेऽभयं प्रतिष्ठां विन्दते। अथ सोऽभयं गतो भवति। यदा ह्येवैष एतस्मिन्नुदरमन्तरं कुरुते। अथ तस्य भयं भवति। तत्त्वेव भयं विदुषोऽमन्वानस्य। तदप्येष श्लोको भवति॥७॥

*asad vā idamagra āsīt | tato vai sadajāyata | tadātmānam̐svayamakuruta | tasmāt tatsukṛtamucyata iti | yad vai tatsukṛtam | raso vai saḥ | rasam̐hyevāyam labdhvānandī bhavati | ko hyevānyāt kaḥ prāṇyāt | yadeṣa ākāśa ānando na syāt | eṣa hyevānandayāti | yadā hyevaiṣa etasminnadṛśye 'nātmye 'nirukte 'nilayane 'bhayam pratiṣṭhāṁ vindate | atha so 'bhayaṁ gato bhavati | yadā hyevaiṣa etasminnudaramantaraṁ kurute | atha tasya bhayaṁ bhavati | tattveva bhayaṁ viduṣo 'manvānasya | tadapyeṣa śloko bhavati||7||*

This world in the beginning verily was non-existent. Therefrom, indeed, was the existent born. It (*Brahman*) created itself by itself. Therefore it is called the self-made. Verily what is self-made is joy in essence. For truly, on attaining one's own essence one becomes happy. For who indeed could live, who could breathe, if it were not this happiness in the pure space? This One, indeed, makes people attain happiness. When one finds this fearlessness, which is invisible, bodiless, undefined and abodeless, as one's firm support, then he has reached fearlessness. When, however, this one differs even slightly in this, for him, there is fear. That verily is the fear of the learned lacking contemplation.

Before creation initially this universe was *asat* that is, it was devoid of differentiation of name and form. It was only *Brahman.* From the *Brahman* the *sat,* that is, differentiated world of beings and forms came about. That *asat Brahman* by itself modulated into different things. Hence it is called *svakr̥tam.* The meaning of *svakr̥tam* is self-created. The *Brahman* which has become all is the *puṇya rūpam* and it gives us many benefits. Hence *puṇya* is also called *svakr̥tam. Brahman* is the one which is present everywhere and at all times, doing *chetana* (action) and is the cause of the universe. This *Brahman,* that is, *svakr̥tam,* is the essence of happiness. It shines in the sky of the heart as happiness personified. Even though there is no intoxicating thing still the wise ones remain in a state of perpetual happiness. It is due to the *Brahman* which is settled in their minds. Further if it is not there how the action of *prāṇa, apāna,* etc. will function? In the body the organs functions due to Him. That only gives all happiness in this world. When a *sādhaka* (practitioner) will stabilize himself in this *parama* thing which has no form or body, no changes on itself, he will reach a fearless state. If he sees even slight change between Him and the ultimate thing (*Brahman*) he will have fear. Once he feels "I am different, the *ātmā* is different" then immediately the fear enters there. Even if he is *vidvān* (educated man) if he sees the *Brahman* as a different entity then he will get fear.

**Triśaṅku** – Sadguru, kindly tell the *mantra.*

**Varuṇa** –

> भीषाऽस्माद्वातः पवते। भीषोदेति सूर्यः। भीषाऽस्मादग्निश्चेन्द्रश्च। मृत्युर्धावति पञ्चम इति।
>
> *bhīṣā 'smādvātaḥ pavate* । *bhīṣodeti sūryaḥ* ।
> *bhīṣā 'smādagniścendraśca* । *mṛtyurdhāvati pañcama iti* ।।
>
> Being afraid of Him the wind blows. Being afraid (of Him) the sun rises. Being afraid of Him the fire and Indra function. And death too runs as the fifth. Thus (is the stanza).

Due to the fear of this *Brahman* the wind blows. Due to Its fear the sun rises. Agni and Indra likewise fearing do their respective jobs. The Lord Yama also functions due to its fear. For all, the cause is *Brahman. Niyanta* (नियन्त) is *Brahman.* Vāyu and Sūrya though themselves are gods still prompted by fear do their actions without fail, without delay, in proper time. The reason for the fear is *Brahman.* He is the master.

**Triśaṅku** – *Gurujī*! kindly answer in detail these smaller questions.

**Varuṇa** – *Brahman* is present everywhere and is the being of everything. That is the *parama* thing which is *ānanda* (happiness). It is self-created and self-creator. It is the only essence (*rasa*) when a person is alive which nourishes him. In every breath, every action, every thought, each and every word it is present. It is the essence of happiness. If it is not there life will ebb away. *Brahman* is the same for the knowledgeable and non-knowledgeable. The difference is a *vidvān* comes to know "It." In leaving the body It does not mean death. It is only leaving the body-connected things or *saṁsāra*-connected things. That is, relinquishing the present *jīva* (life) or attaining *jīvanmukti* state.

**Bodhāyana** – The ignorant does not know. The wise knows, you told. But is the happiness they get the same?

**Varuṇa** – Yes, my child.

**Bodhāyana** – If that is so, you told the *pañcabhūta* — the five elements and *deva*s get scared. What is the meaning of that? Aren't *deva*s the wise ones?

**Varuṇa** – Child! The *deva*s are very intelligent and knowledgeable indeed. However, only as long as they don't see a difference between themselves and *Brahman,* they get installed in the state of fearlessness in a steady manner. Even if he is an expert in Śāstras still if he does not realize that he and *paramātmā* are one, he cannot reach the *mukti* state. It is realization of the unity with *Brahman* which removes all fear from the mind of the wise ones. That only creates the fear for the ignorant as also the knowledgeable who sees the difference. Till he sees the difference he will see the fear. As as he sees the fear he cannot reach *Brahman,* and even the knowledgeable will remain far from *Brahman.*

**Vaikhānasa** – The cause for everything, the one who is present everywhere and shines, the one who induces fear as well as one who is the cause of removing fear, all are *paramātmā,* thus we have come to know.

**Varuṇa** – Children! Get your asylum in fearlessness. Get your happiness in fearlessness. That is the essence. That is the explanation in short. I will tell you the limits of this *ānanda* (happiness) tomorrow. Let us go now.

***(As everybody gets up, curtain falls.)***

## SCENE 5

(Curtain opens. In Vaiśampāyana's *āśrama.* Lord Varuṇa is teaching the disciples.)

**Triśaṅku** – Respected Sir, you told us that today you will bless us and tell about the limits of *parama ānadam.* Kindly do tell us.

**Varuṇa** – Children! Before I tell about *parama ānandam*, I will tell about *laukika* (worldly) happiness. This is easy to understand. Hence let us know about worldly happiness.

**Mahācamasya** – Svāmī! I am having a doubt.

**Varuṇa** – What is that?

**Mahācamasya** – The worldly happiness is the stimulant for the senses. It happens with things which are outside. Knowing this, is it possible to know about *parama ānandam* from worldly happiness?

**Varuṇa** – Child, it is possible because it is also a part of *brahmānandam.*

**Vaikhānasa** – Gurujī! Kindly continue your preachings.

**Varuṇa** – I am telling. Listen carefully.

सैषानन्दस्य मीमाꣳसा भवति। युवा स्यात्साधुयुवाऽध्यायकः। आशिष्ठो दृढिष्ठो बलिष्ठः। तस्येयं पृथिवी सर्वा वित्तस्य पूर्णा स्यात्। स एको मानुष आनन्दः। ते ये शतं मानुषा आनन्दाः। स एको मनुष्यगन्धर्वाणामानन्दः। श्रोत्रियस्य चाकामहतस्य।

*saiṣānandasya mīmāṁsā bhavati | yuvā syātsādhu yuvā 'dhyāyakaḥ | āśiṣṭho dṛḍhiṣṭho baliṣṭhaḥ | tasyeyaṁ pṛthivī sarvā vittasya pūrṇā syāt | sa eko mānuṣa ānandaḥ | te ye śataṁ mānuṣā ānandāḥ | sa eko manuṣya-gandharvāṇāmānandaḥ | śrotriyasya cākāmahatasya |*

This is the critical enquiry concerning ultimate value (*ānanda*). Let there be a youth, a good youth, well read, full of aspirations, steady in mind, and strong in body. Let this whole earth full of wealth be for him. That is one human happiness. What is hundred times the human happiness, that is one happiness of human *gandharva*s (fairies). Also of the one well-versed in scriptures.

There should be a yardstick to determine the amount of happiness, isn't it? The happiness evaluation is as follows. Youth, goodness, knowledge of Vedas, the ability to act at the correct time, bravery, strength, and the ability to rule this world which is filled with all the wealth. If a person has all this in full the happiness he attains is the human happiness. This can be taken as a standard or yardstick and let us enquire about other greater happiness. In comparison to this happiness the human *gandharva*'s happiness is hundred times more.

**Bodhāyana** – Who is human *gandharva*? Kindly explain in detail, Gurudeva.

**Varuṇa** – Saumya! Being a human person if he follows the *karma*s and *upāsanā*s as told in the Śāstras, then he gets the birth of a *gandharva* and he is known as human *gandharva*. *Gandharva*s have the *antardhyāna* capacity, that is to be invisible to others. Their body is very subtle. Hence changes in weather and other difficulties do not affect their body very quickly. Even if at times some small difficulties tend to happen, there is ability to easily get rid of them. Further they will be having plenty of things for pleasure and comfort. Always finely dressed up they will be involved in dance and music. Because of these reasons their happiness is hundred times more than human happiness. The first measure is the previously described human happiness. In comparison to this step by step the amount of other happiness has to be understood. The one which is hundred times the first-told happiness, that is human *gandharva* happiness is the standard. However, a person who knows the meaning of Vedas, a person who has not done any *pāpa*s and one who has relinquished the desire in the human happiness, such a *śrotriya* also reaches this hundredfold happiness of human *gandharva*, even though he is still in human state.

**Vaikhānasa** – You did not tell that the *śrotriya* also enjoys the human happiness.

**Varuṇa** – The *śrotriya* who has no desire in human happiness even in human birth, gets happiness hundred times more than human happiness. Since his happiness is so great it was not mentioned that he gets the little human happiness. A person getting thousand coins has also the experience of enjoying hundred coins. However he has still desire in human *gandharva* state. Hence he gets only that. He does not get happiness above that. But a *śrotriya* just by relinquishing desire in that happiness and who has no desire in human *gandharva* state, in this world itself, gets hundred times more happiness than human being and equal to that of human *gandharva*. The happiness one gets after being born in the respective births, the *śrotriya* gets without taking those respective births. Others who do not reach the desireless state, they do not get happiness beyond the prescribed level of their births. The *brahmavit* (a person knowing about *Brahman*) who has relinquished everything gets all the happiness. However a person having desire in enjoyment should still be a knower of Vedas and blemishless (not having done any sins). In this way in every stage by evaluation of desires the amount of happiness enjoyed also gets multiplied.

**Bodhāyana** – Respected Sir, do continue to preach.

**Varuṇa** –

ते ये शतं मनुष्यगन्धर्वाणामानन्दाः। स एको देवगन्धर्वाणामानन्दः। श्रोत्रियस्य चाकामहतस्य। ते ये शतं देवगन्धर्वाणामानन्दाः। स एकः पितृणां चिरलोकलोकानामानन्दः। श्रोत्रियस्य चाकामहतस्य। ते ये शतं पितृणां चिरलोकलोकानामानन्दाः। स एकः आजानजानां देवानामानन्दः। श्रोत्रियस्य चाकामहतस्य।

*te ye śataṁ manuṣyagandharvāṇāmānandāḥ | sa eko devagandharvāṇāmānandaḥ | śrotriyasya cākāmahatasya | te ye śataṁ devagandharvāṇāmānandāḥ | sa ekaḥ pitṝṇāṁ ciralokalokānāmānandaḥ | śrotriyasya cākāmahatasya | te ye śataṁ pitṝṇāṁ ciralokalokānāmānandāḥ | sa ekaḥ ājānajānāṁ devānāmānandaḥ* | *śrotriyasya cākāmahatasya* |

> What is hundred times happiness of human *gandharvas*, that is one happiness of divine *gandharvas*. Also of the one well-versed in scriptures, who is not smitten with desires. What is a hundred times the happiness of divine *gandharvas*, that is one happiness of the human beings (ancestors) in their long enduring world that is one happiness of gods who are so by birth. Also of the one well-versed in scriptures, who is not smitten with desires.

The hundred times happiness of human *gandharva* is *deva gandharva* happiness. That happiness the *śrotriya* will also get who has relinquished worldly desires. Hundred times *deva gandharva's* happiness is the happiness of ancestors (*pitṛs*) who stay in long lasting worlds. A person who does exercise of Vedas and who is not bound by desires, the *śrotriya*, also experiences this happiness. In this same way the happiness of *devas* who are born in *devaloka* is hundred times the happiness of the *pitṛs*. This happiness is also experienced by the *śrotriya* who has relinquished worldly desires.

**Mahācamasya** – Kindly tell us the difference between human *gandharva* and *deva gandharva*.

**Varuṇa** – A person born in this *kalpa* as a human being takes birth as *gandharva* as a result of doing good *karmas*. After staying for some time as *gandharvas*, the ones who come back to the human world are human *gandharvas*. However persons who have done good *karmas* in the previous *kalpa* get *gandharva* body in the beginning of this *kalpa* and stay like that in this entire *kalpa* and are called *deva gandharvas*. Children, I will tell you further, listen carefully.

ते ये शतमाजानजानां देवानामानन्दाः। स एकः कर्मदेवानां देवानामानन्दः। ये कर्मणा देवानपियन्ति। श्रोत्रियस्य चाकामहतस्य। ते ये शतं कर्मदेवानां देवानामानन्दाः। स एको देवानामानन्दः। श्रोत्रियस्य चाकामहतस्य। ते ये शतं देवानामानन्दाः। स एक इन्द्रस्यानन्दः। श्रोत्रियस्य चाकामहतस्य।
*te ye śatamājānajānāṁ devānāmānandāḥ* | *sa ekaḥ*

*karmadevānāṁ devanāmānandaḥ | ye karmaṇā devānapiyanti | śrotriyasya cākāmahatasya | te ye śataṁ karmadevānāṁ devānāmānandāḥ | sa eko devānāmānandaḥ | śrotriyasya cākāmahatasya | te ye śataṁ devānāmānandāḥ | sa eka indrasyānandaḥ | śrotriyasya cākāmahatasya |*

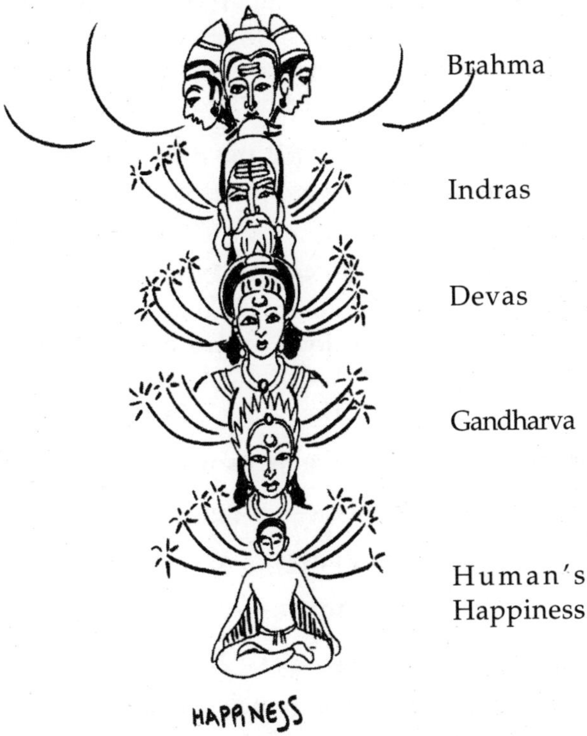


*fig.:* **Measure of happiness.**

What is a hundred times the happiness of the gods who are so by birth, that is one happiness of the gods by rites; also of the one well-versed in scriptures, who is not smitten with desires. What is a hundred times the happiness of the gods by rites, that is one happiness of the gods; also of the one well-versed in scriptures, who is not smitten with desires. What is a hundred times the happiness of the gods, that is one happiness of Indra. Also of the one well-versed in scriptures, who is not smitten with desires. Hundred times more the happiness of *ajānaja deva*s (gods by birth) is *karma deva*s (gods by rites) happiness. This happiness, as previously told, the *vedavit* also gets. Hundred items more happiness of *karma deva*s is enjoyed by *deva*s who have right to get *havir bhāga* (*havis* from the *homa*s performed). Further lord Indra's happiness is hundred times more than these *deva*'s happiness. The *śrotriya* who is well-versed in scriptures and who is not smitten by desires also gets the level of happiness enjoyed by lord Indra.

**Triśaṅku** – Svāmī! kindly tell the difference between the *deva* clans whom you describe as *ajānaja deva*s, *karma deva*s and just *deva*s.

**Varuṇa** – People who do *smārtta karma*s and get *puṇya* and as a result of that get born in *devaloka* they are *ajānaja deva*s. People who do Agnihotra religious *karma*s and get born in *devaloka* are *karma deva*s. The *deva*s who get *havir bhāga* from *yajña* are really known as *deva*s. They have come up stage by stage.

**Vaikhānasa** – Who are the *deva*s who consume *havis*?

**Varuṇa** – *Aṣṭa* Vasus – eight

*Ekādaśa* Rudras, – eleven

*Dvādaśa* Ādityas – twelve

lord Indra – thus total 32.

ते ये शतमिन्द्रस्यानन्दाः। स एको बृहस्पतेरानन्दः। श्रोत्रियस्य चाकामहतस्य। ते ये शतं बृहस्पतेरानन्दाः। स एकः प्रजापतेरानन्दः। श्रोत्रियस्य चाकामहतस्य। ते ये शतं प्रजापतेरानन्दाः। स एको ब्रह्मण आनन्दः। श्रोत्रियस्य चाकामहतस्य।

*ṭe ye śatamindrasyānandāḥ* । *sa eko bṛhaspaterānandaḥ* । *śrotriyasya cākāmahatasya* । *te ye śataṁ bṛhaspaterānandāḥ* । *sa ekaḥ prajāpaterānandaḥ* । *śrotriyasya cākāmahatasya* । *te ye śataṁ prajāpaterānandāḥ* | *sa eko brahmaṇa ānandaḥ* | *śrotriyasya cākāmahatasya* |

What is a hundred times the happiness of Indra, that is one happiness of Bṛhaspati. So Also of the one well-versed in scriptures, who is not smitten by desires. What is a hundred times the happiness of Bṛhaspati, that is one happiness of Prajāpati. So also of the one well-versed in scriptures, who is not smitten by desires. What is a hundred times the happiness of Prajāpati, that is one happiness of *Brahman*. So also of the one well-versed in scriptures, who is not smitten by desires.

Hundred times more than Indra's happiness is Indra's *guru* Bṛhaspati's happiness. This happiness *śrotriya* also experiences. More than hundred times happiness of Bṛhaspati is experienced by Prajāpati (*virāṭ puruṣa*). This also the *śrotriya* experiences. Hundred times more than Prajāpati's happiness is lord Brahmā (Hiraṇyagarbha's) happiness. A *śrotriya* who has no desires also gets all the happiness from human being-happiness to different stages of happiness as described here in this world itself. Among all happiness, starting from human happiness to Brahmā's happiness, the most highest form of happiness is Brahmā's *ānanda*. However this exalted Brahmā's *ānanda* is like a drop in the ocean of *brahmānanda*. Hence it is not possible to measure *brahmānanda*. Just to show its magnitude, different happiness and their measures have been discussed here.

**Vaikhānasa** – The enquiry of the happiness is very wonderful indeed. Kindly give us more preachings in this direction.

**Varuṇa** –

स यश्चायं पुरुषे। स एकः। यश्चासावादित्ये। स य एवंवित्अस्माल्लोकात् प्रेत्य। एतमन्नमयमात्मानमुपसंक्रामति। एतं प्राणमयमात्मानमुपसंक्रामति। एतं मनोमयमात्मानमुपसंक्रामति। एतं विज्ञानमयमात्मानमुपसंक्रामति। एतमानन्दमयमात्मानमुपसंक्रामति। तदप्येष श्लोको भवति॥८॥

*sa yaścāyaṁ puruṣe* | *sa ekaḥ* | *yaścāsāvāditye* | *sa ya evaṁvid asmāllokāt pretya* | *etamannamayamātmā-*

*namupasaṁkrāmati* | *etaṁ prāṇamayamā-tmānamupasaṁkrāmati* | *etaṁ manomayamātmāna-mupasaṁkrāmati* | *etaṁ vijñānamayamātmā-namupasaṁkrāmati etamānandamayamā-tmānamupasaṁkrāmati* | *tadapyeṣa śloko bhavati* | |8| |

And the one who is in this person, and the one who is in the sun.

He is the One. He who knows thus, on going forward from this world; Attains with close proximity the Self-consisting of the stuff of food; Attains with close proximity the Self-consisting of the stuff of mind; Attains with close proximity the Self-consisting of the stuff of understanding; Attains with close proximity the Self-consisting of the stuff of *ānanda* (Bliss or Supreme Value).

That *Brahman* stays in the *puruṣa*'s heart-cave. It is also in the Āditya (sun) shining in the sky. Thus the one in the heart cave and one giving *chetana* to the sun are one and the same. A person who realizes that alone is *Brahman*, relinquishes this world, leaving attachment on all matters in this world and with intense *vairāgyam* (detachment) crosses the *ātmā* which is *annam* personified. Then in due course he crosses the *ātmā* which is *prāṇa* personified, *vijñāna* personified, and *ānanda* personified.

**Bodhāyana** – Gurujī, we understand the enquiries and explanations about happiness. However we did not follow what you have told us subsequently. Kindly tell it in detail.

**Varuṇa** – Saumya! Let it be so. The *Brahman* which shines in the heart cave known as *brahma-vyoma* is the creator of *kārya* world from the sky up to *annamaya-kośa.* That only entered the living things which are *annamaya*. It is a limitless bliss form. The essence of it, a small fraction of it brings immense happiness in the world. It is only the cause of both sun's brightness and man's intellect. That alone is the truth, knowledge, happiness and the supreme being. We undertstood it so. Step by step we did our enquiries about the happiness. This *brahmānanda* in different format and the happiness (*ānanda*) were described. A person knowing it thus leaves the attachment to worldly things and reaches the *annamaya ātmā*. Then leaving that he reaches *prāṇamaya, manomaya, vijñānamaya* and *ānandamaya kośa*s.

**Vaikhānasa** – The *Brahman* which is the cause and effect of everything reached one layer after another layer does not sounding correct. Only if it is an outside thing it can reach and leave the *kośa*s. This you kindly explain.

**Varuṇa** – The meaning of *saṅkramaṇa* is *prāpti* or to get it. However this meaning cannot be accepted here. The *ātmā* which is *annamaya,* how it can reach *annamayam*? Hence the fact that by knowing the truth the false assumptions get removed is the meaning of *saṅkramaṇa* here. There is nothing apart from *Brahman*. Hence the different characteristics like becoming many, enters into the creation, attains the happiness, gives asylum, step by step spreads to all *kośa*s, etc. are all told in imagination. In truth for the *Brahman* which is blemishless there cannot be any change. Hence the person who is enquiring should first leave the *vyaṣṭi,* the body ego form of limited *Brahman* equation and understand that the *virāṭ puruṣa* is both *samiṣṭi* (the *virāṭ* form) and *vyaṣṭi* (the gross body, ego form). In the same way leaving the *vyaṣṭi* feeling of separateness, understand the *prāṇamaya, manomaya, vijñānamaya,* and *ānandamaya* as *samaṣṭi rūpa*. Then realize *satya ānanda* characterstic of *Brahman* which is the basis of *ānandamaya.* Later he becomes the *Brahman* himself.

The afternoon prayer time is nearing. Let us stop today's lessons here.

(He gets up. The disciples also get up and give their salutations.)

***(Curtain falls.)***

## SCENE 6

(Curtain opens, Maharṣi Vaiśampāyana's *āśrama* is seen. Pūjya Guru Varuṇa, and disciples Triśaṅku and other disciples are sitting.)

**Varuṇa** – Children, have you properly understood the lessons so far learned. Can you tell them in short, but clearly. Hey Bodhāyana! Do tell! Let us see.

**Bodhāyana** – We listened properly. We thought about it and understood it. However our expertise is not so much as to tell others, Svāmī!

**Varuṇa** – Is that so? A filled vessel does not spill over. You talk with humility. I am happy. Hey Triśaṅku! You tell, let us see.

**Triśaṅku** – Respected Sir! I will do so as per your order. Whatever we see around us has come out of *Brahman*. The sky, *vāyu, agni*, water, earth, plants, food, all of them, step by step has come out of *Brahman*. The body which is the essence of food is like a sheath to the *ātmā*. This body hence is called *annamaya-kośa*. More subtle than *annamaya-kośa* is the *prāṇamaya-kośa* which is described as contained in that; within that is *manomaya-kośa*, with in that is *vijñānamaya-kośa* and with in that *ānandamaya-kośa*, so it is described. It can be understood the basis for all the five *kośa*s is *Brahman*. As the seed is there within the fruit, we should understand the *Brahman* is with the *kośa*s and that alone is the truth. Thus if a person understands the *Brahman* he himself becomes *sat*. A person not knowing this becomes *asat*. *Brahman* by Its own *saṁkalpa* (decision) enters everything. In life It forms both essence as also happiness. *Brahman* itself is the form and formless, *saguṇa* and *nirguṇa*, *chit* and *achit*, stable and unstable. Its *ānanda svarūpa* is in every breath, in every act and each person reaches it in every breath, in every act, and every moment without fail.

Further you taught us about the various yardsticks of happiness also.

**Varuṇa** – *Sabhāsa,* Triśaṅku! You told very beautifully and in detail. I am very happy. I want to tell you all a happy news.

**Disciples** – **(with great interest)** What is that?

**Varuṇa** – Maharṣi Vaiśampāyana and his entourage who had gone on piligrimage are coming tomorrow here. The news has been received some time back. The king's soldiers came and told.

**Mahācamasya** – Svāmī! We are very happy. Kindly continue the lessons further.

**Varuṇa** – Children, listen carefully. Today's lessons will be my last lesson, tomorrow when my friend comes I have to take leave of him and go to my place.

> यतो वाचो निवर्तन्ते। अप्राप्य मनसा सह। आनन्दं ब्रह्मणो विद्वान्। न बिभेति कुतश्चनेति।
>
> *yato vāco nivartante* | *aprāpya manasā saha* | *ānandaṁ brahmaṇo vidvān* | *na bibheti kutascaneti* |
>
> He who is aware of the happiness of *Brahman,* from where all words, along with the mind, recede not attaining it, is not afraid of anything at all. Such is the verse.

As previously described the words from the mouth and the thoughts from the mind unable to reach even the borders of *brahmānandam* come back. Knowing such a *brahmānandam* the wise one never get scared for any reason.

**Vaikhānasa** – Gurujī, we seem to remember of having heard these *ṛk*s before.

**Varuṇa** – Yes, correct. I have told it before in another context. Can you make out the difference between that and this context?

**Mahācamasya** – Respected Sir! You told this while describing *manomaya-kośa*. The difference is not known. Kindly tell clearly.

**Varuṇa** – Alright! Child! Tell the *ṛk*s which I told then.

**Mahācamasya** –

> यतो वाचो निवर्तन्ते। अप्राप्य मनसा सह। आनन्दं ब्रह्मणो विद्वान्। न बिभेति कदाचनेति।
>
> *yato vāco nivartante | aprāpya manasā saha | ānandaṁ brahmaṇo vidvān na bibheti kadācaneti |*

Is it correct?

**Varuṇa** – Yes, it is correct. I will now tell the difference between the two, listen carefully. That time *kadācaneti* (कदाचनेति) was the word and now *kutaścaneti* (कुतश्चनेति) is the word. Child Vaikhānasa! Tell the meaning of the words.

**Vaikhānasa** – *Kadācaneti* (कदाचनेति) means any time and *kutaścaneti* (कुतश्चनेति) means any reason. These are ordinary meanings.

**Varuṇa** – Child! You told correctly. When explaining in context of *manomaya-kośa* it was told, a person knowing the *Brahman* of *manomaya-kośa* will not be scared of anything. For *brahma-jñānī* mind is the most important tool, hence it is told here *Brahman* should be taken in mind and contemplated. The feeling of fear also gets annihilated once the realization dawns that there is nothing else apart from *Brahman*. For *ātma-jñāni* who sees the centre of universe as *ātmā* form and since there is nothing apart from oneself, how he will be scared about anything? The *śrotriya* also realizes this *Brahman* which cannot be described by mind or words. The one who is sinless, one who has no desire, a wise one of that nature will not be afraid, any time and for any reason. For example, a person having double vision (eye disease) the moon will be seen as two. Once the disease becomes alright the moon will be seen as one. In the same manner, once ignorance is removed the variety of differences seen will be removed. Hence for the knowledgeable there is no fear for any reason from anything.

**Bodhāyana** – Won't the knowledgable (*jñānī*) have the fear of not doing good *karma*s and doing sinful deeds lest the fruits of his deed catch up with him?

**Varuṇa** – Child! That fear also he won't have.

एतꣳह वाव न तपति। किमहꣳसाधु नाकरवम्। किमहं पापमकरवमिति।
स य एवं विद्वानेते आत्मानꣳस्पृणुते। उभे ह्येवैष एते आत्मानꣳस्पृणुते।
य एवं वेद। इत्युपनिषत्॥९॥

*etaṁ̐ha vāva na tapati | kimahaṁ̐sādhu nākaravam | kimahaṁ pāpamakaravamiti | sa ya evaṁ vidvānete ātmānaṁ̐spr̥̥ṇute | ubhe hyevaiṣa ete ātmānaṁ̐spr̥̥ṇute | ya evaṁ veda | ityupaniṣat||9||*

The thought "why have I not done the right thing? Why have I done the sinful?" does not torment such a one. He who knows thus cherishes both these as if it is the Self verily; such is the secret doctrine (Upaniṣad).

Like the ignorant, the knowledgeable is not bothered by the thought as, "why I did not do good, why I did sins?" That is because the *ātma-jñānī* (self-knowledgeable person) sees the *puṇya*s and *pāpa*s as his own *ātmā*. Due to the strength of knowledge of *ātmā* the fear of doing good and bad does not trouble him. This is the secret of *Upaniṣad*.

**Vaikhānasa** – Gurujī! It is very surprising indeed.

**Varuṇa** – There is nothing to be surprised in this. Whichever person gets his happiness in *ātmā*, and satisfied in *ātmā* for him there is no work to be done. For him doing any *karma* here does not fetch any fruits, and even if he does not do there is no loss. This is only the *Brahman* state. A person who reaches this will not be immersed in the sea of *puṇya*s and *pāpa*s, as these are worldly effects of *karma*.

**Vaikhānasa** – This way why should he be discarding the *dharma* rules and regular order and discipline?

**Varuṇa** – For him there is no *dharma*, no order and no discipline. There is no desire for *svarga* or *naraka* (heaven or hell). Even in getting *mukti* he has no desire.

**Bodhāyana** – Even in *mukti* he has no desire? Doesn't he have to get free from bondage, Svāmī?

**Varuṇa** – There is nothing like knowledge or ignorance for him. There is no intellect, no universe, no bondage, hence no *mukti* from bondage. The truth beyond the twin sides of every matter is known to him. Having known the attachment to *puṇya* and *pāpa* is the cause of all problems, and knowing that the knowledge of *ātmā* will wipe off the difficulties and sadness, he with the wisdom, annihilates the *puṇya*s and *pāpa*s. He praises the *ātmā* and keeps in regard the *ātmā* alone. This is the main essence of Upaniṣad's preaching.

**Triśaṅku** – (**gets up and gives his salutations**) Respected Sir, we became very much blessed. I have no bondage with the *saṁsāra* and no *mokṣa*. I have no *śāstra,* no *guru*. All these have come about by *māyā.* I have come out of *māyā*. I am leaving, Svāmī.

(He takes leave from others also and goes.)

**Varuṇa** – Children! Triśaṅku is a big *ātma-jñānī*. It is not easy for everyone to reach the state that he has reached.

**Vaikhānasa** – Svāmī! Kindly tell the meaning of the word *upaniṣad*.

**Varuṇa** – Child! Mahācamasya! Tell the meaning as far as you know.

**Mahācamasya** – I shall tell as direced by you. The *brahma-vidyā* is also called *upaniṣad*. It can be divided into three parts — *upa-ni-ṣat*.

*upa* – with the help of the teachers' preachings to reach the *brahma-jñāna*.

*ni* – to remain stable in that and for those who do daily exercise of that knowledge.

*ṣat* – since *avidyā* is removed the *brahma-vidyā* is *upaniṣad*.

**Varuṇa** – You told very well. The last word *sat* has three kinds of meanings. They are –

1. *Vicaraṇa* (complete annihilation) – Annihilation of scattering thoughts, the differentiations of the world's appearance due to ignorance and fears.

2. *Avasādhana* (complete destruction) – Destruction from roots of the *saṁsāra.* That is the birth pains, death, sorrow, the body-connected difficulties all of them get completely destroyed.
3. *Kadhi* (the final route) – It shows the path and takes a person to its ideal.
4. In short *Upaniṣad* removes the ignorance, annihilates the *saṁsāra* and takes us to the Advaita *Brahman.*

**Bodhāyana** – We are very fortunate. From your mouth we have heard great and precious teachings. We will never forget our gratitude to you.

**Vaikhānasa** – Svāmī! You have come and preached us such *ātmā rahasya* (secret) which is *brahma-jñāna,* the one which is worthy of learning and to know which people go from place to place in search of it. Your kindness is really great. It is bigger than the sea. We salute you again and again and express our thanks to you. (**The disciples, all of them, get up and do *namaskāram* by fully prostrating themselves in front of the *guru.***)

**Varuṇa** – Children! I consider it my great fortune to give lessons to disciples like you. This light of Vedānta now will never be put off. For your generations it will give its light. The sun though ancient looks new everyday. In the same way the *Upaniṣad* will also shine for ever and become common to all human race. Like today it will be describing the Supreme thing which is never changing. Child Mahācamasya! With today's lessons my teaching itself is getting completed. Whatever you have learnt today, tell it in short.

**Mahācamasya** – I will tell so. "That from which the words and mind come back unable to reach it, that *Brahman* knowing *vidvān* won't have any fear about anything. Such a person even if he does not do *puṇya* and even if he does *pāpa* (sins) he will not be affected. That is because the *vidvān* sees *puṇya* and *pāpa* (good and bad deeds) as his own *ātmā*. That is, the *ātmā* stands apart and deeds get annihilated.

**Varuṇa** – Child you told very beautifully. Now only *śānti-*

*pāṭha* has to be told.

**Bodhāyana** – Tomorrow Bhṛgu and Prācīnayogya will come and get disappointed. They lost a rare opportunity. When I think about it, I feel very sad.

**Vaikhānasa** – I also feel sad, but what to do.

**Mahācamasya** – Friends! There is no need to feel sad. The benevolent *gurujī* will go and preach to them after going to his place. There is no need for doubt or fear in this.

**Varuṇa** – You told properly Mahācamasya. However it is not that I will preach only to them. Whoever comes and asks I will teach the lessons. Being my child, Bhṛgu won't get any separate favouritism. Like other disciples if he also takes asylum in me and wishes to get preachings from me I will teach with great happiness. I consider teaching lessons as my life's work and a great fortune. That too if I get good students like you I am ready to teach, sacrificing even food and sleep.

**Vaikhānasa** – Friend Bhṛgu is a great scholar, isn't that so? He will prove to be an exalted disciple.

**Bodhāyana** – Further he has gone for a pilgrimage. After that he will shine like gold, which has gone through fire.

**Varuṇa** – Children, let us tell *śānti-pāṭha* together. Let Vedamātā give you all good tidings. Let blessed things happen.

**(All are telling *śānti-pāṭha* together.)**

ॐ सह नाववतु। सह नौ भुनक्तु। सह वीर्यं करवावहै।
तेजस्विनावधीतमस्तु। मा विद्विषावहै।
ॐ शान्तिः शान्तिः शान्तिः।

*oṁ saha nāvavatu | saha nau bhunaktu | saha vīryaṁ karavāvahai | tejasvināvadhītamastu | mā vidviṣāvahai |*

*oṁ śāntiḥ śāntiḥ śāntiḥ |*

***(Third Part Ends)***

# PART – IV

## Bhṛgu-Vallī

(Curtain opens. In Haridwar Pūjya Guru Varuṇa's *āśrama*. On the tiger skin seat Varuṇa is sitting. His son is entering. He tells *abhivādaye* and prostrates on the ground offering his salutations. The *maharṣi* lifts his son and kisses him. Asks him to sit near him. Then sitting near, the conversation takes place).

**Bhṛgu** – Father!

**Varuṇa** – Child!

**Bhṛgu** – Father! I have a doubt.

**Varuṇa** – Child! What is the hesitation? Ask.

**Bhṛgu** – Father, I wanted to ask you right from the time I came from Mithilā; since there was a big crowd who had come for some *yajña*, there was no way to ask the doubt immediately.

**Varuṇa** – Is that so, *saumya*? Ask now, I will tell.

**Bhṛgu** – Respected Sir, you must tell me in detail about *Brahman*.

**Varuṇa** – **(smiling)** Child! Didn't Vaiśampāyana teach you? Apart from what he taught what more am I going to tell?

**Bhṛgu** – Father! We were taught in Mithilā lessons for a number of days. We received many rare teachings. Still in the end we did not have the opportunity to get your teachings. Further I went to the piligrimage, isn't it? At that time I missed your teachings and I am eager to hear those words.

**Varuṇa** – Child! Very happily will I tell you. However, before preaching about *Brahman* it is necessary to know the ability of the disciple. You are my son, I know you well but on this criterion alone to preach will be wrong. The disciple should have required good habits and tradition. Good conduct and *brahmacarya* are among the prerequisites. He should have great interest to learn *brahma-vidyā*. You have all these qualities. Hence without any reservations I will teach you.

**Bhṛgu** – Respected Father, I am very glad. That day by preaching Gāyatrī *mantra* you made me holy. Today with great consideration you are going to tell about *Brahman*. I am again prostrating and giving my salutations at your lotus feet. (**gets up and does *namaskārams*.**)

**Varuṇa** – May good tidings befall you. May you live a long life, *Saumya*. You tell me in short as to what you learned in Mithila.

**Bhṛgu** – Respected Sir! We were taught as to how a disciple when staying in *gurukula* has to study, the *upāsanās* to be done, the *oṁkāra* meditation to be done and after leaving *gurukula* the way he has to conduct himself in the world. Now kindly give me the preachings of *Brahman* and bless me.

**Varuṇa** – Child! I will give you some hints. You make your own enquiries and try to know it, that will be good. In *brahma-vidyā* learning from *guru* and contemplation are very important. They are like two eyes.

**Bhṛgu** – Your will is my command. Do command me Sir.

**Varuṇa** – Child Bhṛgu! Listen carefully. The different ways to know *Brahman* are through *annam, prāṇa, dṛṣṭi, śrotriya, manas* or *vāk*. Further I will tell you about *Brahman*'s characteristics. That from which everything is born, because of which everything born lives, and into which everything goes back and merges, that is *Brahman*. That *Brahman* as I previously told can be known by *annam* or other routes.

(**From behind the screen *ṛṣipatnī*'s voice.**)

Hey Bhṛgu, for *viśvadeva* everything is ready, tell your father.

**Varuṇa** – Child! I am going inside. You contemplate on what I have told you now.

**(Varuṇa is going.)**

**Bhṛgu** – (**walking about**) Father has posed a riddle and gone. From which everything has come about? (**He thinks**) Here this body is here, this is made from *annam*. It is then stabilized by *annam* (food). There is no doubt about it. Then during destruction time what happens? (**he walks, thinking**). It is buried or it is burnt (**thinks again**) finally it becomes again *annam* (food). It loses itself in that, there is no doubt about it. In that case I have come to know that *annam* is only *Brahman*. Yes, I have understood (**with great happiness jumps around**).

*Annam* is *Brahman* that only brings about life.
*Annam* is the protector and that only is the destroyer.
*Annam* is *Brahman* that is only everything.

**(Then sits and thinks again.)**

Everything is made from *annam*, it is stabilized by *annam* and loses itself in *annam*. Due to this one has to reach the answer as *annam* is only *Brahman*. Is it correct or wrong? One more doubt! *Annam* is a temporary thing, how can it be the *Brahman* which cannot be destroyed? My decision is not correct. Any way let me ask father. How about doing penance before that? By controlling the senses and by disciplining the mind let me think. That only is the best penance. Is there anything which cannot be reached by penance? Let me take my friend Prācīnayogya, and going to Rishikesh let me do penance and come back succeeding in this enquiry.

Good question! Thinking about the proper answer the complications are mounting. The answer is in the enquiry only. Let me do penance in solitude and get *siddhi*. Dear father, my salutations to you (**looks at the direction and does *praṇāmas*.**) Today itself, now only I will go (**He goes**).

***(Curtain falls.)***

## SCENE 2

(On the banks of Gaṅgā it is the *sandhyā maṇḍapa*.

Prācīnayogya and two *āśrama* residents are sitting and conversing.)

**The first āśrama resident** – Friends, when did you come from Rishikesh? Has Bhr̥gu come?

**Prācīnayogya** – I came yesterday. Bhr̥gu is coming tomorrow.

**The second āśrama resident** – When are lord Varuṇa and the entourage coming?

**The first āśrama resident** – Where has lord Varuṇa gone? To come back?

**The second āśrama resident** – Don't you know? Even though you are the resident of the neighbouring *āśrama*, it is surprising you don't know the news.

**The first āśrama resident** – What is surprising about it? I am staying peacefully attending to my routine. If I go to gossip like you I will know the happenings of the place.

**The second āśrama resident** – What did you tell? You are staying very calmly and composed. I am going and talking gossip? You are insulting me and insinuating that I am, in comparison to you, inferior in following discipline and order. That is not becoming of you. It is not fair.

**The first āśrama resident** – If I tell the truth —

**Prācīnayogya** – Friends! *śānti, śānti, śānti.* Become peaceful. As soon as myself and Bhr̥gu went to Rishikesh, the next day itself Pūjya Gurujī Varuṇa and his followers came there. All of us stayed in Kapila's *āśrama* for all these days. In the summer the Gaṅgā was very majestic and playful. Due to heat the snow had melted increasing the flow. It was a very pleasing sight to the mind. Tomorrow they are all coming back.

**The first āśrama resident** – Is that so? I am very happy. Where the Gaṅgā is not beautiful? Here also what is lacking in her beauty? Now though it is rainy season she with her tumultuous flow gives happiness to the mind. Did you see the boats going there? We can imagine them like the boats of *bhakti* which are attempting to cross the sea of *saṁsāra* (worldly affairs).

**The second resident** – Here the Gaṅgā is flowing turbid like a person prone to quick anger, like a person having lost his humility due to pride in his learning.

**Prācīnayogya** – We cannot comment about Mother Gaṅgā. She is non-chalant in her flow. We, who are staying on her banks, saluting her, praying to her and dipping in her holy waters, are only remaining without peace.

**The first āśrama resident** – Yes, it is not the fault of Mother Gaṅgā, it is our fault only. Let it be so. We are interested to know the happenings in Rishikesh. Kindly tell everything in detail.

**The second one** – Friend, I also like to hear, kindly tell.

**Prācīnayogya** – My dear friend, I will tell, listen.

भृगुर्वै वारुणिः। वरुणं पितरमुपससार। अधीहि भगवो ब्रह्मेति। तस्मा एतत् प्रोवाच। अन्नं प्राणं चक्षुः श्रोत्रं मनो वाचमिति। तꣳहोवाच। यतो वा इमानि भूतानि जायन्ते। येन जातानि जीवन्ति। यत्प्रयन्त्यभिसंविशन्ति। तद्विजिज्ञासस्व। तद्ब्रह्मेति। स तपोऽतप्यत। स तपस्तप्त्वा ॥१॥

*bhṛgurvai vāruṇiḥ | varuṇaṁ pitaramupasasāra | adhīhi bhagavo brahmeti | tasmā etat provāca | annaṁ prāṇaṁ cakṣuḥ śrotraṁ mano vācamiti | taṁhovāca | yato vā imāni bhūtāni jāyante | yena jātāni jīvanti | yat prayantyabhisaṁviśanti | tad vijijñāsasva | tad brahmeti | sa tapo 'tapyata | sa tapastaptvā ||1||*

Bhṛgu the son of Varuṇa approached his father Varuṇa and said "Venerable Sir, teach me *Brahman*."

To him he said thus: "(Understand) food, vital breath (*prāṇa*), sight, hearing, mind, speech (as *Brahman*)."

To him he said further: "That verily from which beings are born, that by which those that are born live, into which they finally reach and merge — seek to know That. That is *Brahman.* He underwent an austere enquiry (*tapas*) (keeping the above preahings in mind).

Our best friend Bhr̥gu went to his father Varuṇa and told "Respected Sir, kindly preach to me about *Brahman.*" Lord Varuṇa told as follows to Bhr̥gu: "*annam, prāṇa,* sight, hearing, speech, these are the routes to know *Brahman.*" Further he told: "That from which everything is born, because of which everything born lives, and into which everything goes back and merges, what is that? Think deeply about this and try to know it. That only is *Brahman.*" Keeping these teachings in mind Bhr̥gu did penance.

**The first resident** – You told the meaning of the *śloka*. Kindly give an explanation in detail.

**Prācīnayogya** – Alright, here is the meaning of the *śloka*. To his son who was eager to know about *Brahman* and who enquired in a proper way, lord Varuṇa said "Child! What we see as the gross world through that only we should see the subtle. This body is due to *annam* (food); inside is the *prāṇa* and the organs to know about external things, like eyes, ears, mind, and speech, these are the tools to understand *Brahman*. From whichever all the living things came about, taking support of which they live and grow, later during the time of destruction, that is, after death go and join the supreme, that only is *Brahman.* The meaning of *tātparyam* means during production, stability, living times, from whichever form (*svarūpa*) it does not move off, that only is *Brahman.* This is the characteristic of *Brahman.* It should be understood. That is the one which is *prāṇa* to *prāṇa*, eye to the eye, ear to the ear, *annam* to *annam*, mind to the mind that thing you must try to know."

**The second one** – Dear friend! Later what did Bhr̥gu do?

**Prācīnayogya** – Then he did penance for knowing the truth of *Brahman*.

**The first resident** – His father did not tell him to perform penance. Then why did he do?

**Prācīnayogya** – It is true that his father did not tell. Varuṇa who is *sadguru* did not want to thrust all his opinions on the disciple. He explained the characteristics and told him to understand by himself and left him. Bhṛgu chose the exalted tool of that time which was penance. It is better than all other tools. It leads the person to *siddhi*. Hence he chose penance (*tapa*) to further know the matter.

**The second one** – What penance did he do?

**The first one** – Did he go to places like Gaṅgotrī, Kedāra, etc.?

**Prācīnayogya** – He did not go anywhere. He stayed put in his place itself. He controlled the senses and he immersed into the inner space. By controlling the senses and mind he made them focused. He went into *samādhi* and thought deeply. This was the only penance he did.

**The first one** – I don't feel it is a difficult penance, what was the fruit of it?

**Prācīnayogya** – Is there doubt in the results? The fruits of penance were there immediately.

अन्नं ब्रह्मेति व्यजानात्। अन्नाद्ध्येव खल्विमानि भूतानि जायन्ते। अन्नेन जातानि जीवन्ति। अन्नं प्रयन्त्यभिसंविशन्तीति। तद्विज्ञाय। पुनरेव वरुणं पितरमुपससार। अधीहि भगवो ब्रह्मेति। तꣳहोवाच। तपसा ब्रह्म विजिज्ञासस्व। तपो ब्रह्मेति। स तपोऽतप्यत। स तपस्तप्त्वा ॥२॥

*annaṁ brahmeti vyajānāt | annāddhyeva khalvimāni bhūtāni jāyante | annena jātāni jīvanti | annaṁ prayantyabhisaṁviśantīti | tadvijñāya | punareva varuṇaṁ pitaramupasasāra | adhīhi bhagavo brahmeti | taṁ̐hovāca | tapasā brahma vijijñāsasva | tapo brahmeti | sa tapo 'tapyata | sa tapastaptvā ||2||*

He understood, food is *Brahman*. For truly, beings here are reborn from food; those that are born live because of food; and into food they finally reach and merge.

> Having understood that, he again approached his father Varuṇa and said, "Venerable Sir, teach me *Brahman.*" To him he said "Through austere self-enquiry seek to know *Brahman.* the very austere self-enquiry is *Brahman.*"

He did austere self-enquiry. Having done austere self-enquiry, Bhr̥gu did *tapa* and realised that the *annam* (food) is *Brahman.* From food only all these living beings come about. After being born they live due to food. Finally they meet their end and then merge with food. This way the *Brahman* characteristics described by his father are to be found in the food (*annam*). Having realized this, he found the *Brahman* in that. Still he approached his father Varuṇa.

**The first resident** – After knowing the *Brahman,* why did he go to his father?

**Prācīnayogya** – Even when Bhr̥gu came to know *annam* (food) is *Brahman,* Bhr̥gu had a doubt which was not cleared. The *annam* can be produced and destroyed; however *Brahman* is indestructible. Thus there is a difference between *annam* and *Brahman.*" Let me again approach my father and clear the doubt," thus thinking he approached his father and told "Respected Sir, kindly bless me by preaching to me about *Brahman*" and went on to explain to his father whatever happened in detail. With great consideration Varuṇa told, "Your decision is not wrong. What you realized as *annam* is *Brahman* is correct." Still by penance you must try to go higher. With penance only try to know *Brahman,* my child Bhr̥gu, the path by which you are going is correct." Thus he encouraged him and preached to him. As per that Bhr̥gu did penance again.

**The first resident** – It is very interesting friend, do tell further.

**The second resident** – Bhr̥gu is an apt son of the father. The conversation and the way you are narrating it are wonderful. Tell further in detail.

**Prācīnayogya** –

प्राणो ब्रह्मेति व्यजानात्। प्राणाद्ध्येव खल्विमानि भूतानि जायन्ते। प्राणेन जातानि जीवन्ति। प्राणं प्रयन्त्यभिसंविशन्तीति। तद्विज्ञाय। पुनरेव वरुणं पितरमुपससार। अधीहि भगवो ब्रह्मेति। तꣳहोवाच। तपसा ब्रह्म विजिज्ञासस्व। तपो ब्रह्मेति। स तपोऽतप्यत। स तपस्तप्त्वा ॥३॥

*prāṇo brahmeti vyajānāt | prāṇāddhyeva khalvimāni bhūtāni jāyante | prāṇena jātāni jīvanti | prāṇaṁ prayantyabhisaṁviśantīti | tadvijñāya | punareva varuṇaṁ pitaramupasasāra | adhīhi bhagavo brahmeti | taṁhovāca | tapasā brahma vijijñāsasva | tapo brahmeti | sa tapo 'tapyata | sa tapastaptvā ||3||*

He understood, vital breath is *Brahman.* For truly, beings are born from vital breath; they finally reach and merge into vital breath. Having understood that, he again approached his father Varuṇa and said "Venerable Sir, teach me *Brahman.*" To him he said, "Through austere self-enquiry seek to know *Brahman*. The very austere self-enquiry is *Brahman.*" He did austere self-enquiry. Having done austere self-enquiry.. . .

Bhṛgu came to know *prāṇa* is *Brahman.* Due to the power of *prāṇa* all the elements are formed. The elements exist due to *prāṇa.* When they end they merge into *prāṇa-śakti.* "Hence *prāṇa* is only *Brahman,* he concluded. However as *prāṇa-śakti* is non-living and without intelligence it has no independence. Hence it is not wholly true that *prāṇa* alone is *Brahman.* To clear the doubt, again approaching father Bhṛgu requested "Respected Sir, kindly preach about *Brahman.*" The father also seeing the son progressing in the correct path became happy and told "The *Brahman* has to be known by penance. The penance is *Brahman.*" Bhṛgu also as per the order of father again did *tapa.* That is, he made further enquiry. He thought deeply about the matter and contemplated.

**The first resident** – What conclusion did he come to?

**Prācīnayogya** –

मनो ब्रह्मेति व्यजानात्। मनसो ह्येव खल्विमानि भूतानि जायन्ते। मनसा जातानि जीवन्ति। मनः प्रयन्त्यभिसंविशन्तीति। तद्विज्ञाय। पुनरेव वरुणं पितरमुपससार। अधीहि भगवो ब्रह्मेति। तꣳहोवाच। तपसा ब्रह्म विजिज्ञासस्व। तपो ब्रह्मेति। स तपोऽतप्यत। स तपस्तप्त्वा ॥४॥

*mano brahmeti vyajānāt | manaso hyeva khalvimāni bhūtāni jāyante | manasā jātāni jīvanti | manaḥ prayantyabhi-saṁviśantīti | tadvijñāya | punareva-varuṇaṁ pitaramupasasāra | adhīhi bhagavo brahmeti | taṁ̐hovāca | tapasā brahma vijijñāsasva | tapo brahmeti | sa tapo 'tapyata | sa tapastaptvā ||4||*

He understood, mind is *Brahman*. For, truly, beings here are born from mind; those that are born live because of mind; and into mind they finally reach and merge. Having understood that, he again approached his father Varuṇa and said, "Venerable Sir, teach me *Brahman*."

To him he said, "Through austere self-enquiry seek to know *Brahman*. The very austere self-enquiry is *Brahman*". He did austere self-enquiry.

After much research he understood that the mind is *Brahman*. By the power of mind alone all these living things come about. After coming about they live due to the mind. Finally they end by reaching the mind. Hence mind is only *Brahman,* thus Bhr̥gu knew. After knowing that he felt it is not wholly correct. Again he approached his father "Svāmī you must preach to me about *Brahman,*" he further asked. Lord Varuṇa further told "Child, the *tapa* is *Brahman,* do *tapa* to know *Brahman* fully" thus he blessed. Bhr̥gu did *tapa* as per his father's direction.

**The first āśrama resident** – Friend! The conch-shell of Viśvanātha temple is sounding announcing the afternoon time is nearing. I have to go immediately, or else I won't get today's food. We will meet tomorrow.

**The second resident** – I am also having some important work.

We will come back here tomorrow. Kindy you must come to the same place tomorrow and tell us.

**Prācīnayogya** – Friends! Getting involved in the talk we did not realize how time flew by. The interest in the matter is also such. As per your wish we will meet tomorrow. My *namaskāram*.

**The other two** – *Namaskāram*, our heartfelt thanks.

(**They are leaving**.)

***(Curtain falls.)***

SCENE 3

(Like the previous scene on the banks of river Gaṅgā in the *sandhyā maṇḍapa*, Prācīnayogya and two *āśrama* residents are sitting and conversing).

**The first resident** – Friends! Yesterday you told that Bhṛgu realized step by step that *annam* is *Brahman*, *prāṇa* is *Brahman* and *manas* is *Brahman*. As per the order of his father, he did penance and later what other conclusions he came to? Kindly, you must tell in detail.

**The second resident** – I am also eager to hear. I have even kept aside the important jobs to be done in the *āśrama* and have come running. You must be considerate and tell us.

**Prācīnayogya** – Later he did penance and came to know the truth. In the same way you can also know all. There is no doubt about it. However I will tell about what Bhṛgu understood. Listen.

विज्ञानं ब्रह्मेति व्यजानात्। विज्ञानाद्ध्येव खल्विमानि भूतानि जायन्ते। विज्ञानेन जातानि जीवन्ति। विज्ञानं प्रत्यन्त्यभिसंविशन्तीति। तद्विज्ञाय। पुनरेव वरुणं पितरमुपससार। अधीहि भगवो ब्रह्मेति। तꣳहोवाच। तपसा ब्रह्म विजिज्ञासस्व। तपो ब्रह्मेति। स तपोऽतप्यत। स तपस्तप्त्वा ॥५॥

*vijñānaṁ brahmeti vyajānāt | vijñānāddhyeva*

*khalvimāni bhūtāni jāyante* I *vijñānena jātāni jīvanti* I *vijñānaṁ pratyantyabhisaṁviśantīti* I *tadvijñāya* I *punareva varuṇaṁ pitaramupasasāra* I *adhīhi bhagavo brahmeti* I *taṁhovāca* I *tapasā brahma vijijñāsasva* I *tapo brahmeti* I *sa tapo 'tapyata* I *sa tapastaptvā* I I5I I

He came to understand that knowledge is *Brahman.* For, truly, beings here are born from knowledge; that are born live because of knowledge; and into knowledge they finally reach and merge.

Having understood that, he again approached his father Varuṇa and said "Venerable Sir, teach me *Brahman.*"

To him he said, "Through austere self-enquiry seek to know *Brahman.* The very austere self-enquiry is *Brahman.*"

He did further austere self-enquiry.

He came to know by research that knowledge is *Brahman*. That is, only by strength of knowledge all the living things came to exist. All the things which came about live by knowledge. Finally in knowledge they disappear and go. Hence knowledge is *Brahman*. However, this way after knowing this also, still his doubts have not been cleared and he approaches the father and tells, "You must kindly preach about *Brahman*." For which Lord Varuṇa again replies, "*Brahman* has to be known by penance only, I bless you for further penance." As per that Bhṛgu took to further penance rigorously.

**The second resident** – That time what did he come to know?

**The first resident** – Did he approach the truth?

**Prācīnayogya** – Yes! He came to know *Brahman*. Listen.

आनन्दो ब्रह्मेति व्यजानात्। आनन्दाद्ध्येव खल्विमानि भूतानि जायन्ते। आनन्देन जातानि जीवन्ति। आनन्दं प्रत्यन्त्यभिसंविशन्तीति। सैषा भार्गवी

वारुणी विद्या। परमे व्योमन् प्रतिष्ठिता। य एवं वेद प्रतितिष्ठति। अन्नवानन्नादो भवति। महान् भवति प्रजया पशुभिर्ब्रह्मवर्चसेन। महान् कीर्त्या ॥६॥

*ānando brahmeti vyajānāt । ānandāddhyeva khalvimāni bhūtāni jāyante । ānandena jātāni jīvanti । ānandaṁ pratyantyabhisaṁviśantīti । saiṣā bhārgavī vāruṇī vidyā । parame vyoman pratiṣṭhitā । ya evaṁ veda pratitiṣṭhati । annavānannādo bhavati । mahān bhavati prajayā paśurbhirbrahmavarcasena । mahān kīrtyā* ।।6।।

He understood, Happiness is *Brahman*. For truly, beings here are born from Happiness; those are born live because of Happiness; and into Happiness they finally reach and merge. This wisdom of Bhṛgu and Varuṇa is in the supreme heaven. He who knows this becomes well founded. He becomes the possessor of food and the eater of food. He becomes great with progeny, with cattle (wealth) and with the splendour of sacred Wisdom; great in fame.

He realized *ānandam* (Supreme happiness) is *Brahman*. All the living things came about due to *ānandam,* isn't that so? They live by *ānandam* (happiness) and they get merged into *ānandam* when they die. After knowing this Bhṛgu came out of his doubts. After reaching *ānandamaya-kośa* and seeing the *Brahman* inside it a normal *sādhaka* would have come out of all his doubts. Only a person like Bhṛgu does his research by *tapa* (penance) will get to reach the *Brahman.*

**The first āśrama resident** – Friend! I am very happy we came to know about these wonderful teachings. You must continue to give these explanations.

**Prācīnayogya** – This *vidyā* which is described by me is called *bhārgavī-vidyā*. This only is what Varuṇa preached and Bhṛgu realized. Bhṛgu also got stabilized in *Brahman*. Everybody has a right on this. Whoever like this with penance and with full determination and deep concentration (*śraddhā*) enquires, he will get stabilized in *Brahman*. He stays in this world with no dearth of *annam* (food). He also eats his food well and relishes it. He becomes great with a lot of good progeny, cattle and other wealth and the light of knowledge. His fame rises and he becomes a *mahān* (great).

**The first āśrama resident** – Friend! *parame vyoman*, for this, I pray you tell the meaning in detail.

**Prācīnayogya** – Friend! *vyoma* means sky. It is of three types. The one we see outside is *mahā ākāśa* (this is gross). In dream, thought and mind what we see is *chit ākāśa* (subtle). The witness of mind settles in the cave of intellect. The one inside this cave of intellect is *chit ākāśa.* This only is called *parame vyoman* as told here.

**The second āśrama resident** – I have heard the *Brahman* is in the cave found in the heart sky. You are telling intellect cave.

**Prācīnayogya** – Both are the same. The bliss-personified *Brahman* which is installed in the cave of intellect is found in the sky of the heart. The one who realizes it becomes *Brahman* itself. Further he comes to get a lot of *annam* (food). To consume the *annam* he gets lot of fire in his system and he becomes the *mahāpuruṣa* having lot of cattle, progeny and fame.

**The first resident** – Friend! I am getting some doubts. Can I ask?

**The second resident** – I also have some doubts. You must kindly clear them, friend.

**Prācīnayogya** – You can ask one by one. As much as I know I will tell. If I am not knowing, I will take you to Bhṛgu. If necessary we can ask the revered *gurujī*. Even in ordinary things the doubts should not be left. Without any reservation you must understand the matter. *Saṁsayātmā vinaśyati*, doubting minds gets destroyed, so goes an old saying. That too in *brahma-vidyā* there should not be any doubts. In the beginning itself it should be uprooted. Friend! What is your doubt?

**The first resident** – Sir, you said that Bhr̥gu first came to know *annam* is *Brahman*. But he understood it is temporary, hence cannot be *Brahman*. In the same way *prāṇa*, mind, knowledge, in that order he came to know that they are *Brahman*. Later he realized they also cannot be *Brahman*. This you told us but kindly tell the reason for this.

**Prācīnayogya** – It is a good question. The *prāṇa-śakti* which controls the *annam*, will that be *Brahman*? he initially thought. However he found it is not so. Because even though it is subtle like *annam*, that also is temporary. Life starts with *prāṇa*. It continues in it, then it ends in that. Still *prāṇa* is non-living and without intellect. Hence that cannot be the cause. It has beginning and end. Hence it cannot be *Brahman*. In the same way, mind. Though mind is one step above *prāṇa*, still it is only a part. It is not whole. Like other sense organs it is also a sense-giving part. It functions as such. Its knowledge also it has borrowed from intellect. Thoughts sharpen in mind. After some time they change. Then they just vanish without a trace. Hence mind is also not *Brahman*. Then the knowledge (*vijñānam*) is there. That is very powerful. It controls the mind, *prāṇa* and body and rules it. Still it has production and destruction. Hence that is also not *Brahman*. Our friend Bhr̥gu then step by step crosses *annamaya-kośa, manomaya-kośa, prāṇamaya-kośa, vijñānamaya-kośa* and reaches *ānandamaya-kośa* and comes to know true *Brahman*. Like him, we also, by doing penance with the help of *prāṇāyāma, brahmacaryam*, silence, *vrata, dhyāna* (meditation), control of our mind and one-pointed research, then can get that knowledge.

**The second āśrama resident** – It is told that to cross the five *kośa*s he did penance five times separately.

**Prācīnayogya** – Yes, it appears so. What is your doubt my dear friend?

**The second āśrama resident** – Initially *annam, prāṇa*, eye, ear, mind, speach these are the routes to *Brahman*, you told, isn't it? The *annamaya-kośa, prāṇamaya-kośa* and *manomaya-kośa* (the envelopes made of food, *prāṇa* and *manas*) these are understood from the words which used to denote them. Here nothing has been told about *vijñānamaya-kośa,* why?

**Prācīnayogya** – Mind: the word itself will apply to the two *kośa*s (envelopes) — *manomaya* and *vijñānamaya*. Eye, ear and speech, these are the characteristics of other sense organs. These will be contained in those particular *kośa*s.

**The first one** – Alright, friend! Our doubts have been cleared. Kindly, you must preach further.

**Prācīnayogya** – I myself don't know the continuation. *Gurujī* has told he will tell tomorrow. You also come and listen.

**The second one** – Can we come? Can you recommend our names beforehand itself?

**Prācīnayogya** – Everyone can come by all means. For disciples our *āśrama* door will always be open. Whoever comes will be accepted with affection. As per their ability the proper preachings will also be received. You all can come. We will meet tomorrow morning.

**The first one** – Both of us will definitely come. Still please tell Bhṛgu and Pūjya Gurujī Varuṇa beforehand.

**The second one** – Friend, you must kindly be considerate. We will also bring *samidhā* (firewood) and come.

**Prācīnayogya** – Friends! I am very happy. Bring properly dried *samidhā*. When we were not in the *āśrama,* in the rain all the *samidhā* got wet. Even when we do a small *homa* the place gets filled with smoke. Hence we require well-dried *samidhā*. I myself wanted to tell. As you have yourself remembered, you try to bring it. We will meet tomorrow.

**The first one** – We are taking leave.

**The second one** – *Namaskārams*.

***(They are going in different directions.)***

***(Curtain closes.)***

## SCENE – 4

(Curtain opens, Guru Varuṇa's *āśrama* is seen. Varuṇa is sitting on tiger skin seat. On both the sides Bhṛgu, Prācīnayogya and other disciples and *āśrama* residents are sitting. Conversation is taking place.)

**Varuṇa** – Welcome to every one. Children, today I am going to tell about some rare matters and methods to do *upāsanā*. Listen carefully.

**Bhṛgu** – Father, we will do so. About what you are going to tell?

**Varuṇa** – Child, the first route of the *Brahman* is through *annam* (food). *Annam* is very important. From *annam* one gets *prāṇa,* from *prāṇa* one gets strength, from strength one gets *tapa* (concentration), from *tapa* one gets *śraddhā*, from *śraddhā* one gets sharpness of brain, from sharpness of brain one gets mental determination, from that peace, from peace one gets *chit* (mind), from *chit* one gets memory, from memory one gets stable nature, from stable nature one gets knowledge, from knowledge one gets *Brahman.* Only if the wall is there one can draw a picture. In the same way giving *annam* (food) is like giving all the things. Hence I am starting the preaching *annam* of this today.

अन्नं न निन्द्यात्। तद्व्रतम्। प्राणो वा अन्नम्। शरीरमन्नादम्। प्राणे शरीरं प्रतिष्ठितम्। शरीरे प्राणः प्रतिष्ठितः। तदेतदन्नमन्ने प्रतिष्ठितम्। स य एतदन्नमन्ने प्रतिष्ठितं वेद प्रतितिष्ठति। अन्नवानन्नादो भवति। महान् भवति प्रजया पशुभिर्ब्रह्मवर्चसेन। महान् कीर्त्या ॥७॥

*annaṁ na nindyāt* | *tad vratam* | *prāṇo vā annam* | *śarīramannādam* | *prāṇe śarīraṁ pratiṣṭhitam* | *śarīre prāṇaḥ pratiṣṭhitaḥ* | *tadetadannamanne pratiṣṭhitam* | *sa ya etadannamanne pratiṣṭhitaṁ veda pratitiṣṭhati* | *annavānannādo bhavati* | *mahān bhavati prajayā paśubhirbrahmavarcasena* | *mahān kīrtyā* ||7||

Do not speak ill of food. That shall be a vow. Vital breath, verily, is food. The body is the eater of food. The body is well founded in the vital breath, and the vital breath is well founded in the body. Thus food is well founded in food. He who knows that food is thus well founded in food, becomes well founded. He becomes the possessor of food and the eater of food. He becomes great with progeny, with wealth, and with the splendour of sacred Wisdom; great in fame.

**Prācīnayogya** – Svāmī! Kindly explain the meaning in detail.

**Varuṇa** – One must never insult *annam*. It is a *vrata* (vow) for the *upāsaka*. *Prāṇa* is only *annam*, the body is eater of food and gets nourished by it. In the *prāṇa* the body is contained. Thus the *annam* (food) is contained in *annam* (food) itself. A person who realizes this reaches a stable state. He becomes the one who creates the *annam* and has the ability to eat *annam* and enjoy it. He gets exalted by progeny, wealth and by illuminated knowledge of *Brahman* and he reaches a higher state. In fame also he becomes *mahān* (achieve greatness).

**The first resident** – Respected Sir, *annam* means it is a thing to eat. That is what we understand, but what is *annādam*?

**The second resident** – It is correct that one should not insult *annam*, but how can it be a *vrata*?

**Varuṇa** – *Annādam* means the person who eats. Whoever eats *annam* is called *annādam*. One should not belittle *annam*. This should be considered as an important message, as a preaching. Without fail, with *śraddhā*, it should be followed like a *vrata* (vow). This discipline would never be given away. At any time without insulting the *annam*, this discipline should be followed very carefully.

**Varuṇa** –

अन्नं न परिचक्षीत। तद्व्रतम्। आपो वा अन्नम्। ज्योतिरन्नादम्। अप्सु ज्योतिः प्रतिष्ठितम्। ज्योतिष्यापः प्रतिष्ठिताः। तदेतदन्नमन्ने प्रतिष्ठितम्। स य एतदन्नमन्ने प्रतिष्ठितं वेद प्रतितिष्ठति। अन्नवानन्नादो भवति। महान् भवति प्रजया पशुभिर्ब्रह्मवर्चसेन। महान् कीर्त्या॥८॥

*annaṁ na paricakṣīta* I *tad vratam* I *āpo vā annam* I *jyotirannādam* I *apsu jyotiḥ pratiṣṭhitam* I *jyotiṣyāpaḥ pratiṣṭhitāḥ* I *tadetadannamanne pratiṣṭhitam* I *sa ya etadannamanne pratiṣṭhitaṁ veda pratitiṣṭhati* I *annavānannādo bhavati* I *mahān bhavati prajayā paśubhirbrahmavarcasena* I *mahān kīrtyā* I I8I I

Do not despise food. That shall be a vow. Water verily is food. Fire is the eater of food. Fire is well founded in water, and water is well founded in fire. Thus food is well founded in food. He who knows that food is well founded thus, in food, becomes well founded. He becomes the possessor of food and the eater of food. He becomes great with progeny, with wealth, and with the splendour of sacred Wisdom; great in fame.

*Annam* should not be despised and wasted at any time. This also should be taken as a discipline. The water is *annam.* The fire can be seen in *annādam.* In water fire and in fire the water can be seen. One supports another. In the same way *annam* is seen in *annādam.* A person knowing this will live in greatness (*mahān*) along with a number of progeny, wealth and gets lot of fame as possessor of illuminated knowledge of *Brahman.*

**Prācīnayogya** – Gurujī! as you told us, water is *annam,* fire is *annādam.* This is not understood clearly. Kindly explain in detail.

**Varuṇa** – Child Bhr̥gu! Clear the doubt of your friend.

**Bhr̥gu** – Respected Father, with your blessings I will give the explanation. The heat of the sun and the digestive fire in the stomach consume the water. Hence water is *annam,* the heat is *annādam.* Due to the heat of the sun the rain and the sweat happens. Due to rain and sweat the heat gets decreased. Hence one contains another. As how this *āśrama*'s doors, pillars, roof, etc. are supportive of one another, in the same way the fire and water are contained in one another and remains supportive of one another.

**Prācīnayogya** – Friend! The doubt is cleared, many thanks.

**Prācīnayogya** – Svāmī, please continue to preach to us.

**Varuṇa** –

अन्नं बहु कुर्वीत। तद्व्रतम्। पृथिवी वा अन्नम्। आकाशोऽन्नादः। पृथिव्यामाकाशः प्रतिष्ठितः। आकाशे पृथिवी प्रतिष्ठिता। तदेतदन्नमन्ने प्रतिष्ठितम्। स य एतदन्नमन्ने प्रतिष्ठितं वेद प्रतितिष्ठति। अन्नवानन्नादो भवति। महान् भवति प्रजया पशुभिर्ब्रह्मवर्चसेन। महान् कीर्त्या॥९॥

*annaṁ bahu kurvīnta | tad vratam | pṛthivī vā annam |ākāśo 'nnādaḥ | pṛthivyāmākāśaḥ pratiṣṭhitaḥ | ākāśe pṛthivī pratiṣṭhitā | tadetadannamanne pratiṣṭhitam | sa ya etadannamanne pratiṣṭhitaṁ veda pratitiṣṭhati |annavānannādo bhavati | mahān bhavati prajayā paśubhirbrahmavarcasena | mahān kīrtyā ||9||*

Make food in plenty. That shall be a vow. The earth, verily is food. Space is the eater of food. Space is well founded in the earth, and the earth is well founded in space. Thus food is well founded in food. He who knows that food is well founded thus in food, becomes well founded. He becomes the possessor of food and the eater of food. He becomes great with progeny, with wealth, and with the splendour of sacred Wisdom, great in fame.

*Annam* has to be produced in plenty. That is a vow. The earth and sky become *annam* and *annādam*. In the earth the sky is contained. A person knowing this will reach a stable state. He gets the capacity to produce more *annam* and he enjoys eating that. He begets enough children, wealth and blessed with the brightness of knowledge, he reaches a higher state. He becomes *mahān* with great deeds and fame.

**The first one** – One should not insult *annam*. *Annam* has to be made in enough quantity. These statements are the usual ordinary information everyone knows. In the context of preaching about *Brahman*, to tell about these, is it apt? What philosophical concept is present in this? Gurujī, you must clear this doubt.

**The second one** – When taking food, to belittle the food, to talk insultingly about it, blame it or to doubt it and find mistakes with it, is not a healthy way to take food. This food is very good. It will give health, it will give comfort, it will give strength, it will purify the mind. With these good thoughts the food has to be taken. This is what the medicine *śāstra* is telling. Further the food should not be thrown and wasted; this also everybody knows. "This food is not good," thus telling it should not be thrown and wasted; this also everybody knows. The food which is good also should not be taken more and later discarded. The food which protects the life is a dear thing. It should be produced more. Not only for self-use but for everybody on the earth it should be made in plenty. These principles are ordinary concepts. To talk about this here in this context of explaining about *Brahman*, this I am not able to understand. Kindly clear the doubts, Svāmī.

**Varuṇa** – From the doubts you are getting, it is clear you are keenly following it. I will tell this *ṛk* and clear the doubts.

**Bhṛgu** – Father, do continue to tell.

न कंचन वसतौ प्रत्याचक्षीत। तद्व्रतम्। तस्माद्यया कया च विधया बह्वन्नं प्राप्नुयात्। अराध्यस्मा अन्नमित्याचक्षते। एतद्वै मुखतोऽन्नꣳराद्धम्। मुखतोऽस्मा अन्नꣳराध्यते। एतद्वै मध्यतोऽन्नꣳराद्धम्। मध्यतोऽस्मा अन्नꣳराध्यते। एतद्वा अन्ततोऽन्नꣳराद्धम्। अन्ततोऽस्मा अन्नꣳराध्यते ॥१०.१॥

*na kañcana vasatau pratyācakṣīta | tad vratam | tasmād yayā kayā ca vidhayā bahvannaṁ prāpnuyāt | arādhyasmā annamityācakṣate | etad vai mukhato 'nnaṁrāddham | mukhato 'smā annaṁrādhyate | etad vai madhyato 'nnaṁrāddham | madhyato 'smā annaṁ rādhyate | etad vā antato 'nnaṁrāddham | antato 'smā annaṁrādhyate* ||10.1||

Do not turn away anyone (without giving food) in the

> residence. That shall be a vow. Therefore, by whatever means, one should acquire plenty of food. They say, "Food is prepared for Him."
>
> For the one who prepares food (for guests) with the highest care, is food ready for him. For the one who prepares food (for guests) in mediocre way is the food ready for him. For the one who prepares food (for guests) with the lowest care, at the lowest is food ready for him.

Whoever comes home they should not be told to go. That is a vow. The visitor who has come should be praised and entertained. This is a big discipline. Hence for that more food should be collected and kept. Any time if guests come they should not be denied food. The elders have told that. The one who receive the guests well and give them food in a good manner will receive food in the same way along with regard and honour. In case the guests are welcomed in an ordinary way he also will be getting food in the same ordinary way or else if a person chooses to treat the guests in a low way he also will be getting food in the same low way. In whatever way one chooses to give, in the same way he also gets. A person who knows this truth will, as told in the previous paragraph, become a person having lot of food, a person who has the capacity to enjoy the food and becomes a *mahan* with abundance of progeny, wealth, wisdom and good name.

**Bhṛgu** – We considered food as an ordinary thing, but how much deep concept is contained in this?

**Varuṇa** – Child Bhṛgu, you try to clear further doubts of your friends.

**Bhṛgu** – No Father, you only should clear it. If you with great consideration bless us with your holy words it has a separate importance. Kindly you should tell us.

**Others** – Respected Sir, you should clear the doubts. We are requesting. You must show your good will kindly.

**Varuṇa** – Children! If it is the wish of everyone let it be so.

Like what *āśrama* residents told, these are ordinary concepts. However the meaning of *upāsanā* is to find special wisdom from ordinary things. As how in a small *liṅga* one sees and meditates the god *parameśvara*, in the same way to realize *Brahman*, in the first step *annam* has to be done *upāsanā*. Hence so much importance of *annam* is told here. Like, before entering a temple, the temple entrance is first worshipped, in the same way the *sādhaka* should think *annam* as the entrance of *brahma-jñāna* and should not belittle *annam* but keep it in exalted position and praise it. It is wrong to throw it, abuse it and to waste it. The food which saves and protects the life is the food which we can see. That should be protected and increased and not abused. Lot of food has to be made. The medical discipline (Āyurveda) is also a Veda. What is told in those medical books are as important as told in the Veda. The same thing since it has been told in the Veda, its importance increases. Since *annam* is a tool to reach *Brahman* it has to be worshipped. The *annam* which is on equal level to *guru* and *Brahman*-knowledgeable person, it should be honoured and kept in high praise. Through *anna kośa* (envelope) only we have to reach *Brahman* which is inside. A person who defiles these rules, the results for him are also told. With this today's lesson is getting completed.

***(The curtain falls.)***

## SCENE 5

(Behind the screen like the previous scene all are sitting.)

**Guru Varuṇa** – Children! Before starting today's lessons if any doubt is there you all can ask.

**Prācīnayogya** – You described giving food to the guests in three ways: *uttamam* (the best), *madhyamam* (ordinary way), *adhamam* (degraded way). Can you please explain this in detail?

**Varuṇa** – Child! It is an important matter which has to be known properly. I will tell, listen. Whoever asks food it should never be denied. Yes! It is there it must be told. Like some misers tell the guests "I suppose you have taken food isn't it? Or asking will you be going to your house for the food? Such a way the guests should never be treated. It is our duty to entertain the guests. Without entertaining if the visitor gets back that house is like staying place of a jackal. If the guests are properly entertained, considering them as *bhagavān* and kept in that state then one will get *svarga*. By whichever way a lot of food has to be collected and kept.

**The first resident** – Respected Sir! In whichever way means even by bad ways?

**Varuṇa** – Saumya! It is not meaning that. Only by good means. By making money and increasing the food collection the person should be ready for charity. In whichever way during whichever time he does charity, in a similar way during those periods he will get the right fruits. That is, if a person does charity during his youth, he will get back its fruits during that period; in the same way a person giving charity during middle age or old age, he will get back the results of the deed during those periods either in the present life or in the lives which he will bear in future. Further, a person giving food in *sāttvika* manner will get back results in *sāttvika* manner. Similarly *rajas, tamas* ways of giving food will fetch results in *rajas, tamas* ways.

**Bhṛgu** – Father, please continue to give your preachings.

**Prācīnayogya** – Respected Sir, the doubts have been cleared. We are eager to know more preachings from your learned mouth.

**Varuṇa** – Now I will tell about *ādhyātma upāsanā*. Listen carefully.

> य एवं वेद। क्षेम इति वाचि। योगक्षेम इति प्राणापानयोः। कर्मेति हस्तयोः।
> गतिरिति पादयोः। विमुक्तिरिति पायौ। इति मानुषी समाज्ञाः ॥१० ॥१ ॥
>
> *ya evaṁ veda | kṣema iti vāci | yogakṣema iti prāṇāpānayoḥ | karmeti hastayoḥ | gatiriti pādayoḥ | vimuktiriti pāyau | iti mānuṣī samājñāḥ ||10.1||*

> For him who knows the food thus, it becomes the well-being in words, the unitive well-being in *prāṇa* and *apāna*, work in the hands, movement in the feet, evacuation in the anus. Such is food when contemplated with reference to a human being.

*Brahman* is in a productive manner in the words, in *prāṇa, apāna* and *śakti*s it is in the form of *yoga* and well-being, in the hand it is *karma-rūpī,* in the legs it is in the form of walk, in the anus it is the waste product; thus the *upāsanā* of it should be done. This is the *upāsanā* of human body. This *upāsanā* helps the *sādhaka* to purify the mind. Talking, breathing, the action of hand and legs and passing stools are all important works of the body. Hence the *śloka* is telling to feel *Brahman* in those day-to-day acts.

**Bhṛgu** – Respected Sir, we understand the *upāsanā* of the human body. Further whatever we have to know kindly preach us.

**Varuṇa** – Disciples, it is said to be fortunate to earn what is not there. To take care of what is obtained in prosperity and well-being. From words also well-being happens. From the strength of *prāṇa* and *apāna,* fortunate and good happenings come to everybody. However the words, *prāṇa* and *apāna* get their strength from *Brahman*. Hence *Brahman* is established in words and in *prāṇa* and *apāna*.

अथ दैवीः। तृप्तिरिति वृष्टौ। बलमिति विद्युति ॥१०.२॥
यश इति पशुषु। ज्योतिरिति नक्षत्रेषु। प्रजातिरमृतमानन्द इत्युपस्थे।
सर्वमित्याकाशे। तत्प्रतिष्ठेत्युपासीत। प्रतिष्ठावान् भवति। तन्मह इत्युपासीत।
महान् भवति। तन्मन इत्युपासीत। मानवान् भवति ॥१०.३॥
तन्नम इत्युपासीत। नम्यन्तेऽस्मै कामाः। तद्ब्रह्मेत्युपासीत। ब्रह्मवान् भवति।
तद्ब्रह्मणः परिमर इत्युपासीत। पर्येणं म्रियन्ते द्विषन्तः सपत्नाः। परियेऽप्रिया
भ्रातृव्याः। स यश्चायं पुरुषे। यश्चासावादित्ये। स एकः ॥१०.४॥

*atha daivīḥ* | *tṛptiriti vṛṣṭau* | *balamiti vidyuti* ||10.2||

*yaśa iti paśuṣu | jyotiriti nakṣatreṣu | prajātiramṛtamānanda ityupasye | sarvamityākāśe | tatpratiṣṭhetyupāsīta | pratiṣṭhāvān bhavati | tanmaha ityupāsīta | mahān bhavati | tanmana ityupāsīta | mānavān bhavati ||10.3||*

*tannama ityupāsīta | namyante 'smai kāmāḥ | tad brahmetyupāsīta | brahmavān bhavati | tad brahmaṇaḥ parimara ityupāsīta | paryeṇaṁ mriyante dviṣantaḥ sapatnāḥ | pariye 'priyā bhrātṛvyāḥ | sa yaścāyaṁ puruṣe | yaścāsāvāditye | sa ekaḥ ||10.4||*

Now with reference to the divine entities: It becomes satisfaction in rain, strength in lightning.

Fame in cattle, light in the stars, the immortal bliss of procreation in genitals, and everything in space. Let one contemplate That as the support; he becomes the possessor of supports. Let one contemplate That as the great; he becomes great. Let one contemplate That as thought; he becomes thoughtful.

Let one contemplate That as obeisance; desires pay obeisance to him. Let one contemplate That as *Brahman*, he becomes possessed of *Brahman*. Let one contemplate That as the destructive power of *Brahman;* his hateful adversaries are destroyed, and also those whom he does not like. He who is here in the person and he who is in the yonder sun — He is One.

Now the *ādideva upāsanā* is as follows. That is the wisdom connected with the *devatās*. In rains consider *Brahman* as satisfaction, in lightening one should consider *Brahman* as big strength. In cows as prosperity, in stars as light, in genitals as bliss of procreation, in sky as everything. Thus thinking, the *upāsanā* has to be done.

If one thinks *Brahman* as the foundation and do *upāsanā* he becomes the *Brahman* of foundation. If *Brahman* is done *upāsanā* as having great qualities, he acquires the greatness and becomes a *mahān*. If he worships as mind then he gets mental strength, if he worships it as *kāma*, then the desires too worship him. If he does *upāsanā* of it as *Brahman* then he becomes *Brahman* itself. If he worships as *parimaram* (as a destructive force) the enemies around and people who have hostility will be destroyed. What is inside this body and what is present in god Sūrya, they both are the same, that is *Brahman*.

**Prācīnayogya** – Respected Sir! We heard the explanation. However we could not follow it very well. Kindly explain it some more.

**The first resident** – What is the meaning of *parimaram*?

**Varuṇa** – My Dear Disciples, I will explain it in detail. *Brahman* is filled everywhere. There is no place or nothing where It is not present. Here, there, everywhere in all places It is present. It is *Brahman* which makes all things function. It is not enough that we know the truth. This has to be constantly thought about and realized. To stabilize this knowledge in oneself these *upāsanās* are prescribed. Taking into account the *sādhaka*'s requirement and the possibility to do *upāsanā*, Vedamātā is preaching with lot of consideration different *upāsanā* methods. In the hands it is action, in the legs it is walk, in the words it is prosperity or well-being, in the anus it is *vimukti rūpa* as told in the previous *ṛk* (evacuation). In the lightning it is strength and in the rains it is satisfaction, thus the *śruti* tells us. The rains give coolness and happiness at the same time. Is there anyone who is not satisfied by rains? Not anyone. More than wealth from material things getting blessings is a better wealth. To get blessings the cows are being used. With *yajñas* and charity one gets fame and greatness. In that cows are imperative, this is a known thing. If one worships the *Brahman* as *mahat* (greatness) he becomes *mahān* (great). As per universal justice whatever a person thinks, he becomes that only. Hence if a person thinks himself as *Brahman* he becomes *Brahman*. If he worships as *kāma* all the desires will worship him. It will stay in his command. He will become *avāpta samasta kāma* (all desires fulfilled) person. *Brahman*'s destructive force is called *parimaram*. That is lightening, rain, *chandra*, *sūrya*, *agni*, destroying these five is *vāyu* which is called *parimaram*. The one which is attached to *vāyu* is *ākāśa*. If *ākāśa* is worshipped as *Brahman*'s destructive force the enemies of the *sādhaka* will get destroyed. Further, those whom he does not like also will be destroyed. Here it does not mean the enemies will be destroyed. The hostility, enmity, dislike, these will be destroyed, the meaning has to be understood that way.

**Bhṛgu** – Dear father! A person who worships like this how he looks in this world? What he talks? Can we know him differently from other persons? You must describe it, father.

**Varuṇa** – Disciples, I will continue to preach. The answer for Bhṛgu's question will be continued in this.

स य एवंवित्। अस्माल्लोकात् प्रेत्य। एतमन्नमयमात्मानमुपसꣳक्रम्य। एतं प्राणमयमात्मानमुपसंक्रम्य। एतं मनोमयमात्मानमुपसंक्रम्य। एतं विज्ञानमयमात्मानमुपसंक्रम्य। एतमानन्दमयमात्मानमुपसंक्रम्य। इमाँल्लोकान् कामान्नी कामरूप्यनुसंरन्। एतत् साम गायन्नास्ते। हाꣳवु। हाꣳवु। हाꣳवु ॥१०.५॥

*sa ya evaṁvit | asmāllokāt pretya | etamannamayamātmānamupasaṁkramya | etaṁ prāṇamayamātmānamupasaṁkramya | etaṁ manomayamātmānamupasaṁkramya | etaṁ vijñānamayamātmānamupasaṁkramya | etamānandamayamātmānamupasaṁkramya | imām̐llokān kāmānnī kāmarūpyanusañcaran | etat sāma gāyannāste | hśu | hśu | hśu ||10.5||*

He who knows thus, on going forward from this world, reaching on intimately to that Self-consisting of food, reaching on intimately to that Self-consisting of vital breath, reaching on intimately to that Self-consisting of understanding, reaching on intimately to that Self-consisting of happiness (*ānanda*) moves around these worlds, eating

> the food he desires, assuming the form he desires. He sits singing this chant O Wonderful! O Wonderful! O Wonderful!

A person knowing this crosses this *prapañca* (universe) having *prāṇamaya* and other envelopes. That is, due to ignorance whatever seen as *ātmā* here all those things are discarded as non-*ātmā* and he becomes independent and *Brahman-svarūpa*. Crossing everything he becomes *kāmānnī,* that is a person eating whatever he likes, getting whatever form he wants and moves in different worlds, singing the *Sāmaveda* and lives a happy carefree life. That *sāmagānam* (*sāma* song) is *hāśvu, hāśvu, hāśvu,* meaning "surprise, surprise, surprise." Whosoever's mind is kept maintained in a stable state, only those will get stabilized in *brahman.* In whatever direction I see, whatever I see is all myself, apart from me there is none. Knowing this fills one with great happiness. As I see and continue to see, it is a great bliss; the joy overflows. Wonder, wonder he tells and he sings. It is difficult to know him from others.

> (That time Vaiśampāyana's disciples Triṣaṅku, Bodhāyana, Vaikhānasa, and Mahācamasya are entering. They prostrate and do *namaskārams* to Guru Varuṇa and get *āśīrvāda* (blessings). Then they are conversing with Bhṛgu and other friends. With *guru*'s permission all are sitting.)

**Varuṇa** – (**addressing Triśaṅku and others**) Now you have come at the correct stage. Whatever I preached you all when Bhṛgu and others had gone on pilgrimage, now I am telling them.)

**Triśaṅku** – Gurujī! When we were entering we heard the words "surprise, surprise." Why it was told like that?

**Varuṇa** – A person who crosses the *annamaya-kośa* and other *kośa*s in line and becomes *brahma-jñānī* and *kāma-rūpī,* attains all *bhoga*s and moves around this world and in other worlds doing *sāmagāna* with great happiness. That *sāmagānī*'s first line is O! wonder, wonder, wonder. (**Overwhelmed with wonder he tells three times.**)

**Bhṛgu** – Respected Sir, You must continue to tell the *sāmam* and also the meaning.

**Varuṇa** –

> अहमन्नमहमन्नमहमन्नम्। अहमन्नदो३ऽहमन्नादो ३ऽहमन्नादः।
> अह१ँश्लोककृदह१ँश्लोककृदह१ँश्लोककृत्। अहमस्मि प्रथमजा ऋता३स्य।
> पूर्वं देवेभ्योमृतस्य ना३भायि। यो मा ददाति स इदेव मा३वाः।
> अहमन्नमन्नमदन्तमा३द्मि। अहं विश्वं भुवनमभ्यभवा३म्। सुवर्न ज्योतीः।
> य एवं वेद। इत्युपनिषत्॥१०.६॥
>
> *aham annam aham annam aham annam | aham annado 'hamannādo 'hamannādaḥ | ahaṁ̐ślokakṛdahaṁ̐ ślokakṛdahaṁ̐ ślokakṛt | ahamasmi prathamajā ṛtā ३ sya | pūrvaṁ devebhyo amūtasya nā ३ bhāyi | yo mā dadāti sa ideva mā 'vāḥ | aham annam annamadantamā ३dmi | ahaṁ viśvaṁ bhuvanamabhyabhavā ३m | suvarna jyotīḥ | ya evaṁ veda | ityupaniṣat ||10.6||*
>
> I am food, I am food, I am food. I am the food-eater, I am the food-eater, I am the food-eater. I am the maker of stanzas, I am the maker of stanzas, I am the maker of stanzas. I am she who was the first born of the world-order. I am the one who was even prior to the gods. I am the locus of immortality. Whoever gives me, he surely does save me thus. I, who is food, am the eater of the food, I become manifest as the entire world. My splendour is as of the Sun, One who knows thus, becomes thus. Such is the secret teaching.

I am only *annam,* I am only *annam,* I am only *annam.* I am only *annādaḥ,* I am only *annādaḥ,* I'm only *annādaḥ.* I am maker of *śloka* I am only maker of *śloka,* I am only maker of *śloka.* I am here before this world came about. I am the centre of the indestructible state. Whosever gives away *annam* (that is *annarūpa Brahman*), he becomes protector of *ātmā.* A person not doing that I eat him up. I am the entire world. My brightness is like the Sun's brightness. The one who knows it like previously told becomes *Brahman*. Thus the *Upaniṣad* says.

**Vaikhānasa** – Kindly give a detailed explanation for this song.

**Varuṇa** – As explained before, after crossing *annamaya* and the five *kośa*s, it reaches the *Brahman* which is the basis of all and apart from this, a person who has reached this state of *Brahman* gets out of all bondage and becomes happiness-personified. His *svarūpa* quality is all happiness. Hence he will take the form he wishes to have. As per his wish he will enjoy the *bhoga*s (the enjoyable things). He will move everywhere. Leaving likes and dislikes, needs and non-needs and leaving other attractions, he will move as per his wish. That time he sings this *sāmagāna*. This way he sings about "It is the *Brahman* which is everywhere equal and is the seed of everything." What does he tell? I am only everything apart from me nothing is there. I am the nectar form which the living things finally reach. I am the person who eats the food. I am the one who creates the relation between food and the person who eats which is the *chaitanyam*. I have come before. This is *prapañca* having beauty and order. I am the Hiraṇyagarbha, a person who thinks he is everything and filled with pride. If he does not give food, he gets destroyed. A person having clear mind, a *Brahman*-knowledgeable person, reaches the worlds wished by Indra and gets the pleasures aspired by the mind.

**Bodhāyana** – Gurujī! These are really wonderful preachings. We came in good time. We became blessed.

**Mahācamasya** – Respected Sir! Our *gurujī* and your dear friend Vaiśampāyana has gone to Kedāra. This you must be knowing. We also are going there. On the way unexpectedly we got wonderful preachings. It is like the precious herb you went in search of was found under your feet itself. We came to know the true knowledge of *Brahman* clearly like a gooseberry in the palm of the hand. Our birth's real objective we have achieved. We also got the gift of not-to-be-born again. We came to know the path of living proper life. We offer our thanks with humility.

**Varuṇa** - My dear disciples! With this the *Upaniṣad* is completed. Child Bhṛgu! You and your friends should live properly as you learned. You must set an example to others. The great thoughts of Upaniṣads should be spread everywhere. **(All disciples get up and tell *abhivādhye . . . aśmibho* and each of them goes in front of Pūjya Guru Varuṇa and does *namaskārams* by prostrating on the ground. Varuṇa blesses them *dīrghāyuṣmān bhava, saumya*. That time word from the sky is heard as "With Vedamātā's great consideration, and blessings of Maharṣi Vyāsa you all have reached *Brahman* state.)** As all of you have *Brahman* state and reached great happiness, you all can dance in this state which cannot be described. With wonder-expressing words, losing yourself in a rare and wonderful state you can move around."

**Another scene** – Now in shadow scene Pūjya Guru Varuṇa standing in the centre, the disciples are joining hands and make a circle around and dance. They sing like in *rāsa* with great enthusiasm.

*********

॥ कठोपनिषत् ॥

# Kaṭha Upaniṣad

## Introduction

*Kaṭha Upaniṣad* belongs to the *Kaṭha Śākhā* of *Kṛṣṇa Yajurveda* hence, it is known by the name of *Kaṭha Upaniṣad.*

*Kaṭha Upaniṣad* is one of the well known, much read Upaniṣads. Perhaps the story content of the Upaniṣad is captivating to human mind.

PART I

A young lad, Naciketā, by sheer power of his righteousness reaches the portals of the awesome and feared *yamaloka* to meet Lord Yama. He had undertaken the journey, to offer himself to Lord Yama to redeem an unworthy act of charity done by his father Maharṣi Gautama (the father of Naciketā is known by three other names: Auddalaki, Āruṇi (son of Aruṇa), and Vājaśravas) during a *mahāyajña* named Viśvajīta conducted by him at his *āśrama* in Haridwar. At that time along with various charities given to the assembled Veda *paṇḍits*, brāhmaṇas and others, the Maharṣi gifts some old cows which were weak and incapable of producing milk. When this was brought to the notice of the righteous son Naciketā, he ventures to question his father on this lapse, an unbecoming act. Father Gautama in a fit of anger retorts that there is nothing else left to be given. But on repeated prodding he tells his son, "as you are the only one left I will give you to Yama." These words are taken to heart by the young lad Naciketā.

PART II

Naciketā prays ardently to be taken to *yamaloka*. On the strength of his prayers he miraculously gets transported to *yamaloka* in the human form itself. On reaching *yamaloka*, he found Lord Yama is out of his kingdom. However he is received by *yamadūtas* wondering as to who he is — a *deva* or one of the gods. They take him hence to Chitragupta, the prime administrator in the kingdom of Yamarāja. Chitragupta receives him well and tells him to wait for Yamarāja. Naciketā then settles down to meditation and prayer under a *pārijāta* tree. Lord Yamarāja arrives after his sojourn, three days later. He is informed about the arrival of a brāhmaṇa lad from *bhūloka*. Yama immediately goes to receive him and is aghast that a brāhmaṇa lad, a guest of honour, stayed in his kingdom without food for three complete days. To redeem this lapse he, after taking Naciketā to his palace, grants three boons for the three days' act of omission. Naciketā then puts his request for the three boons granted to him.

First he asks, when he gets back to *bhūloka*, his father and family should receive him back without any anger or bitterness. This gets immediately granted by Lord Yamarāja.

The second boon he asks, is to be preached the *agni-vidyā* which will take him to *svargaloka*. This again is immediately granted by Lord Yama. He then goes to impart this rare knowledge and also names the *agni-vidyā* as Naciketā-*agni*.

Then comes the third boon. This time Naciketā chooses to ask, what happens to the soul after death. A question of this magnitude is not expected by Lord Yama from a young lad. To answer that he may have to preach *brahma-vidyā* itself. He decides to lure the lad away from such a question and offers him many attractions. He offers to give him unlimited wealth, kingdoms, luxuries, children and, to enjoy all these along with life having lasting youth. However Naciketā refuses to be attracted to all these glittering goods kept in front of him and sticks to his demand to know the fate of the soul on embracing death.

On seeing the unwavering determination of the young lad to know the truth, Dharmarāja accepts him as a suitable disciple to learn the exalted knowledge of *brahma-vidyā*.

PART III

This part of the drama unfolds a scene in *yamaloka* where the treatment meted out to *pāpa* and *puṇya jīva*s on arriving in *yamaloka* is seen. To the court of Dharmarāja (Lord Yama) is bought a *pāpa jīva* in a pathetic condition, dragged and beaten by the *yamadūta*s. Chitragupta reads the account of his life which is full of misdeeds. The *jīva* is wailing and seeking for compassion. Lord Yama with unwavering justice sends the *jīva* to hell for further punishments.

Then a *puṇya jīva* is brought, this time with great honour. Dharmarāja himself gets up with respect to receive him while Chitragupta reads the good deeds done by the *jīva*. He is then sent heavenwards to the land of *deva*s.

Naciketā witnessing this scene feels great sympathy for the *pāpa jīva*. His tender heart is shaken with compassion. He then thinks he should do all his might to help the *pāpa jīva* to reduce its suffering.

The scene then shifts to the palace of Yamarāja. In right earnest Yamarāja tries to tell the deserving disciple Naciketā about the soul and the ways it travels after death.

The Dharmarāja first tells the ways open for the soul to operate as *jīva* in *bhūloka*. One is the *śreyas* way, which is the good and correct path leading one to *vidyā* and *mokṣa*. The other is *preyas* which is a pleasant and desirable path leading one to *avidyā*. Here by *vidyā* it is meant the knowledge or *jñāna* of *ātmā*. A person striving to get *ātma-jñāna* is the true seeker. The *jīva* carries the soul within him. This is the *ātmā* in each person. This *ātmā* is immortal having no birth and death. It is only the body which experiences birth and death. The *ātmā* is stabilized in the cave of the intellect of a person. One can realize the presence of this *ātmā*, by turning the mind inside and concentrating. The realization of this *ātmā* is called *mokṣa,* when one gets released from the bonds of pain-pleasure and *pāpa-puṇya* and becomes free. All the persons we see around are *jīva*s holding the *ātmā* within them. It is the *ātmā* which operates through the five sense organs and mind. However because of different mindsets, each *jīva* gets different characteristics and body forms. Hence, we consider them as different persons. But it is the same *ātmā* which is operating in them.

Lord Yamarāja tells, in each *jīva* the *ātmā* appears both as *jīvātmā* and *Īśvara* or God. While *jīvātmā* is the experiencer going through pleasure and pain of living, *Īśvara* stands as a witness. They are like shadow and light. Then Dharmarāja explains it by another familiar picture. The body is equated to a chariot. The intellect of the *jīva* is compared to the charioteer. The *ātmā* is the master inside the chariot. The five horses tied to the chariot are the sense organs, and mind the reins. Thus the path the sense organs take is controlled by the intellect and mind (charioteer and reins). Hence it is essential to drive the sense organs wisely to reach the exalted *parama padam.* To realize and reach the *paramātmā* is the primary goal of every *jīva.* Only then the *jīva* gets freedom from *saṁsāra* (worldly bondage) and becomes a free *ātmā.*

PART IV

Naciketā, the good ardent and intelligent student imbibes the preaching and starts understanding the *ātmā svarūpa.* However his mind also dwells in the fate of the *pāpa jīva.* His mind yearns to see him and comfort him. Hence taking the permission of Yamarāja, accompanied by *yamadūta* Pāśahasta, he goes to visit the hell. There he sees terrible scenes of torture of *jīva*s. Some are hung upside down, while some are beaten repeatedly. As they cry out in pain, some are left to be eaten by scorpions and white ants.

The *jīva* whom Naciketā came to see is in a deep *kumbhaka* part of the hell. He is led to the place. As Naciketā tries to have a look at the *jīva* the *yamadūta* Pāśahasta who holds a grudge against Naciketā for being a mere human being yet getting an honoured place in Yamapurī takes his revenge now. He pushes Naciketā too into the hell. And look at the miracle! The purity and *tejas* of Naciketā purifies all the *pāpa jīva*s inside. They get released of their sins, and entire hell with the inmates immediately get transported to *svarga* as they have become *puṇya ātmā*s.

After this wondrous event, the ability of Naciketā to absorb the profound truth preached by Dharmarāja became evident. The next day hence Dharmarāja continues the preaching more emphatically.

Naciketā is anxious. Lord Dharmarāja has asked him to have an one-pointed concentration to get *ātmā svarūpa* but his senses always are attracted to things outside. Is it possible at all to stop the outgoing senses which obstruct the focus of looking inside? "Yes, it can be done" tells Yamarāja. With determination the senses can be controlled to look inside. It can also be done by going to a *guru* and taking his guidance. By steady practice the magnanimous and resplendent state will be realized. Later the *jīvātmā* will become one with the *paramātmā* and become immortal.

This *ātmā* is hidden inside every *jīva* like fire hidden inside wood. It is *paramātmā* shining in all the things we see around in the universe right from the sky, the stars to all worldly things around us. Understanding this, differentiations get mitigated and the sun of wisdom dawns.

*Yamarāja* also tells Naciketā the importance of the stay in *bhūloka*. It is the place where *ātma-darśana* can be obtained. It is also a place to do *karma* whose results are augured by the individual soul. Whereas in *pitṛloka* and other *gandharva loka*s the *ātma-darśana* is not seen with clarity.

The *ātma-darśana* in *bhūloka* can be obtained by *yoga*. Here the state of *yoga* is, after controlling the senses when mind and intellect remain steady, the mind gets freed from all wrong knowledge and gets united with *ātmā*. This is the true *yoga* and the individual gets *ātma-darśana*.

After getting the answer to his question and the third boon thus granted Naciketā with great reverence takes leave of Dharmarāja and everyone at *yamaloka*. He is sent back home in *puṣpaka vimāna* (celestial plane) along with Chitragupta.

PART V

Here at the *āśrama* at Haridwar the parents of Naciketā, mother Vasumatī and father Vājaśravas are beside themselves with grief thinking about the dear child Naciketā. The mother in anguish even desires to end her life. In the agonizing state, suddenly she gets a ray of hope as she sees a dream that her son is coming back from *yamaloka*. Soon her dream becomes true. Their child Naciketā comes resplendent with *tejas* and gets down from the *puṣpaka vimāna*. The entire *āśrama* residents are electrified and overwhelmed with happiness seeing Naciketā back. They all rush to meet him. They sing and dance in great happiness. Naciketā gives his respects to the parents and embraces his friends. Soon a great welcoming ceremony is arranged near the *āśrama*. All the learned scholars as well as the gentry assemble in large numbers to see and hear this young boy Naciketā, who has accomplished the impossible, who has returned back alive from the world of death the *yamaloka*. The scholars term it as a victory to human race. They request Naciketā to tell them what he learned in his own words. The young lad addresses the learned gathering with all humility and informs them all he learned with clarity.

The *ātma-jñāna* imparted to Naciketā thus spreads to all *jīva*s. Everyone of the *jīva* who is keenly tuned to this truth can also realize his true state, as a representative of *ātmā* which is immortal. On completely knowing his true state as one is none but *ātmā*, he gets released from the shackles of mind and senses, and gets off from the ever fluctuating state of pain and pleasure, *pāpa* and *puṇya*, life and death and becomes one with the *paramātmā*.

# The Drama

<u>**Characters:**</u>

| | | |
|---|---|---|
| **Yamarāja** | – | *Mr̥tyudevatā*, he is the lord of *yamaloka* |
| **Chitragupta** | – | The main chief of *yamaloka* |
| **Gautama** | – | Father of Naciketā, a *maharṣi* staying in the Himālayas. Also called Vājaśravas, Auddalaki, and Āruṇi (son of Aruṇa) |
| **Vasumatī** | – | Wife of Maharṣi Gautama |
| **Naciketā** | – | A young lad, son of Maharṣi Gautama |
| **Agniveśa, Satyakṣada** | – | *Brahmachārī*s, the friends of Naciketā |
| **Pāsāhasta, Vajradanta** | – | The messengers of lord Yama |
| **Ghorarūpa, Śoṇitākṣa** | – | The soldiers of lord Yama |
| **Śravaṇa 1**<br>**Śravaṇa 2** | – | Scholars at Lord Yama's *sabhā* |
| **Sūtradhāra** | – | The narrator |
| **Śairandhrī** | – | The actress helping |

(Further *āśrama* residents, *r̥ṣis*, *r̥ṣipatnī*s, the brāhmaṇas who collect alms, cows and other articles of charity, soldiers, disciples, country folk, *deva*s and others.)

(The first and fourth part is set in *bhūloka* (earth), while the second and third parts in *yamaloka*.)

## SCENE 1

(**The first curtain is raised**. The *sūtradhāra* and Śairandhrī are entering from either side and are facing one another.)

**Sūtradhāra** – Sister! My *praṇāmas*. The arrangements of the stage are over. The decorations are complete. Are the actors ready with their costumes?

**Śairandhrī** – *Namaskāra*, yes sir. All are set and ready. All the actors are ready in their costumes and are eager to play their roles in a realistic manner. We are waiting for your orders and the blessings of the elders assembled here.

**Sūtradhāra** – The appreciative audience are also increasing day by day like the waxing moon. They are eager to see our Upaniṣadic drama.

**Śairandhrī** – Svāmī! What is the drama scheduled for today? I forgot the name.

**Sūtradhāra** – Today the drama which we are going to submit in front of the *mahāns* is called *Kaṭhavallī*.

**Śairandhrī** – What! The name sounds strange. You had said that it is an Upaniṣad story but it sounds like the present-day modern dramas.

**Sūtradhāra** – There is nothing modern about the name. Actually we are going to stage the *Kaṭha Upaniṣad* drama. In this there are six sections. This belongs to *Kṛṣṇa Yajurveda*'s last part. Hence it is named as *Kaṭha Upaniṣad* (*Kaṭha* — last) and also *Kaṭhavallī* (last six sections). It has another name — *Naciketā Bhāṣyam* (the explanation of Naciketā).

**Śairandhrī** – Very happy to know all this. Respected Sir, let us not stand in between and lose further time. Our audience are waiting eagerly.

**Sūtradhāra** – Whatever you are saying is very correct. Let us go inside.

(Addressing the audience) — Respected gentry! Many many *namaskārams*. We, who are younger in age and intellect, request you most humbly to see the drama enacted by us with patience. Kindly then tell us the drawbacks and good things about it and bless us.

***(Both leave and the curtain falls.)***

## SCENE 2

(In the foothills of the Himālayas along the banks of Gaṅgā is the path leading to the *āśrama* of Auddalaki Āruṇī.)

(It is a forest route with dense deodar trees on either side. Agniveśa and Satyakṣada are talking and walking along the narrow path. Everywhere there is the pleasant smell of *kastūrī*, and pure *ghee* derived from cow's milk. Behind the curtain the sound of feast and festivity is heard.)

**Agniveśa** – Friend! Today's food was really wonderful (**tapping the stomach**). Whatever events Pūjyaśrī Gautama conducts in the culmination of *Viśvajīta yajña*, they are conducted in an excellent manner.

**Satyakṣada** –

ॐ अशन् ह वै वाजश्रवसः सर्ववेदसं ददौ।
तस्य ह नचिकेता नाम पुत्र आस ॥१॥

*oṁ aśan ha vai Vājaśravasaḥ sarvavedasaṁ dadau* |
*tasya ha Naciketā nāma putra āsa* ||1||

Desirous of the fruits (of the Viśvajīta sacrifice) Vājaśravas, as the story goes, gave away all his wealth (after the sacrifice). He had a son, Naciketā by name.

Yes, fitting to be Vājaśrava (*vāja* — food, *śravā* — fame), he has raised his flag of charity by providing food to thousands of people and has achieved lasting fame. He had a son by name Naciketā.

**Agniveśa** – All are praising and saying that this kind of feast has not taken place not only on these sides but also in the entire Bhārata country, *na bhūto na bhaviśyati* (neither in the past, nor in the future). Even if we have thousand stomachs we can say we are not having enough space to eat such a delicious meal.

**Satyakṣada** – Friend, as per your name, the strength of your *jaṭharāgni* (stomach fire) is very strong. It is truly said that brāhmaṇas are fond of food.

**Agniveśa** – You also don't seem to be lagging behind in relishing food. Let it be. Did you notice another thing?

**Satyakṣada** – Do tell me what is that.

**Agniveśa** – That is regarding our friend Naciketā. I was thinking till now that he is only well educated. Today, I have discovered that he is also good in performing religious rites. He performed them with great *śraddhā* and in an exemplary manner. In welcoming the guests and inviting them with grace, nobody can equal him.

**Satyakṣada** – I also noticed that he was moving here and there helping his father and was attending to all the things very well. He was seen everywhere. A son should be like this, as a great help to the father.

**Agniveśa** – Yes friend, a son like Naciketā who understands the work and assists his father can be got only by the good *karma* of previous births. Everyone is not so fortunate.

**Satyakṣada** – Yes, what will happen to this *yajña*, if one were to get lazy progeny like us, who are in the front only for eating and lag behind for work?

**Agniveśa** – This *yajña* called *Viśvajīta* would not have been completed. Also the correct result would not have been obtained. Only due to Naciketā's inspiration and industry it is happening. But one thing . . .

**Satyakṣada** – Why are you not completing what you propose to say.

**Agniveśa** – Well, it is a matter of big places. Why should we invite trouble? Still my mind could not contain it hence I am telling you.

**Satyakṣada** - Do tell, you have kindled my curiosity and now try to satisfy it. If you tell me, am I going to broadcast it outside? Do tell me boldly.

**Agniveśa** – Actually the act of charity is done as per rule. Still the same can be done in a little more magnanimous manner.

Doing like that will be good. It will shine forth still better.

**Satyakṣada** – I also noticed. What you are saying is correct. It is a great *yajña*. It is being done with great expenditure, aiming at some big exalted benefits. Even their personal possessions are given in charity. Still in the midst of all this, ungracious act of charity is also being done. Hence let us tell Naciketā and do the needful.

**Agniveśa** – No. No. There is no need to tell him. If I had known that you would rake up this matter, I would not have talked to you about this.

**Satyakṣada** – There is no need to fear, my friend. What is there in correcting a drawback which is quite obviously visible. I can't understand as to why we should keep quiet.

**Agniveśa** – If Naciketā takes what we tell in a wrong manner? At least silence will fetch no trouble. It is better to keep quiet.

**Satyakṣada** – That is not correct. When a friend is going on a wrong path it is our duty to tell him good words of advice. This matter is definitely to be reported to Naciketā and the required corrective action has to be advised. Our friend won't think anything bad about it.

**Agniveśa** – All right, let us do as per your wish. Let us go.

**(They leave, the curtain falls.)**

## SCENE 3

(**The curtain opens**. The *āśrama* of Gautama is seen. The arrangements of the *yajña* have been properly done. Gautama, Vasumatī, *ṛṣis*, *ṛṣipatnī*s are all sitting in their respective seats. The *ṛtvig*s are doing *homa* in the *homakuṇḍa*. Veda *mantra*s are being recited. Naciketā is near his father giving a supportive role to all the rites. Satyakṣada and Agniveśa are sitting on one side. The brāhmaṇas are coming one by one and collecting the alms.)

**The first ṛṣi** – Gautama! You are a meritorious person having done a lot of *puṇya karma*. You have done a big *yajña* called *Viśvajīta*. You have won all the *puṇyaloka*s.

**Gautama** – Maharṣi! *Namaskāra*. It is all due to your blessings only.

**Vasumatī** – Āryaputra! What you are telling is very good. All this is due to these *mahān*s' blessings. Our family has got grace with good tidings and has obtained everlasting fame.

**The second ṛṣi** – Everything went off well. You have donated all the horses you got for *Aśvamedha yajña* from the king of Aṅga to the brāhmaṇa Anandavīrya.

**The first ṛṣi** – Not only that, you also gave the costly silk and gold you got from Kashmir to Veda Paṇḍit Gaurī Śaṅkara.

**Gautama** – Yes, also we gave all the pearls obtained from the Pāṇḍya kingdom to Padmapāda!

**The second ṛṣi** – Mother Vasumatī! Your fortune is indeed great. You could participate in this exalted *Viśvajīta yajña* as the wife of Dīkṣitar. You must have done special *puṇya* in your last birth.

**Vasumatī** – Svāmī! All these are due to the *śraddhā* of my husband and your kind blessings.

**The second ṛṣi** – you donated the cows you brought from Gokarṇa to the brāhmaṇa who came from Kurukṣetra.

**Gautama** – I think all the charity work connected with this *yajña Viśvajīta* is over. (**Addressing his wife**)

तꣳह कुमारꣳ सन्तं दक्षिणासु नीयमानासु श्रद्धाऽऽविवेश सोऽमन्यत ॥२॥

*taṁ ha kumāraṁ santaṁ dakṣiṇāsu nīyamānāsu śraddhā 'viveśa so 'manyata* | |2| |

Dear, I think we have given away all our possessions as charity. He thought that faith (*śraddhā*) took possession of the good youngster as the gifts were being taken away by the priests.

**Naciketā** – **(within himself)** What my friends told me is indeed correct. When giving charity there does not appear to be any *śraddhā* or *bhakti*. By getting these old cows what benefit will Kauśika get.

**(speaks out)** Respected Father, my *namaskārams*. There is nothing of benefit in giving away these cows. They have no strength even to drink water. Since the teeth are not strong they cannot eat grass. They have lost strength in all their organs. They cannot also yield milk. Father, giving such cows with only skin and bones, having no capacity to yield any milk, one may not be able to reach any *puṇyaloka*. One can only reach worlds bereft of happiness. There is no doubt about it.

**Vasumatī** – Child Naciketā. Don't talk in between.

**Naciketā** – **(he thought)**

पीतोदका जग्धतृणा दुग्धदोहा निरिन्द्रियाः।
अनन्दा नाम ते लोकास्तान् स गच्छति ता ददत्॥३॥

*pītodakā jagdhatṛṇā dugdhadohā nirindriyāḥ* I
*anandā nāma te lokāstān sa gacchati tā dadat* I I3I I

Joyless are the worlds one goes to on giving away as gifts cows that have stopped drinking water, eating food, and yielding milk and lost vitality.

**Naciketā** – **(spoke thus)** No mother, giving these old cows will definitely incur sins. In order to correct the mistakes committed in charity, you must give the most exalted thing in your possession as charity. Father, can you do that?

**Gautama** – Child! Everything has been given in charity. Now there is nothing in our possession which remains. What can be given away now?

**Naciketā** – Father, I am here, your most valued possession. It will be best to give in charity a thing, which is most dear to you. Father, to whom are you going to give me in charity?

**Vasumatī** – Child Naciketā! You please keep quiet.

**Naciketā** – Father, to whom are you going to give me in charity?

**Gautama** – Child, don't disturb us like this when *dakṣiṇā*s (offerings) are being given.

**Vasumatī** – My child, don't ask foolish questions like this. Your father is a very angry person.

**Naciketā** – (**going near**) Father, to whom are you going to give me in charity?

स होवाच पितरं तत कस्मै मां दास्यसीति। द्वितीयं तृतीयं तꣳ होवाच।

*sa hovācha pitaraṁ tata kasmai māṁ dāsyasīti* ǀ
*dvitīyaṁ tṛtīyaṁ taṁ̐ hovāca*

(**He asks his father**)"O Father, to whom are you going to offer me?" (**He asks him a second time, a third time. Then the father says.**)

*fig.:* **Old cows given as charity.**

**Gautama** –

मृत्यवे त्वा ददामीति ॥४॥

*mṛtyave tvā dadāmīti* |

"To Death I offer you." ||4||

**(angrily)** I will give you to Lord Yama (king of death).

(Hearing this everyone in the *yajñaśālā* is stunned. Vasumatī swoons and falls down. The ladies in the *āśrama* bring her back to senses. She exclaims (Oh! what will happen!)

**Naciketā** – **(thinks)**

बहूनामेमि प्रथमो बहूनामेमि मध्यमः।
किꣳ स्विद्यमस्य कर्त्तव्यं यन्मयाद्य करिष्यति ॥५॥

*bahūnāmemi prathamo bahūnāmemi madhyamaḥ* |
*kiṁ svidyamasya karttavyaṁ yanmayādya karişyati* | |5| |

I am the first (of first grade conduct) among many of the disciples; I stand in the middle (my conduct was never of the lowest grade. Then why did father say so). What purpose there may be that father will fulfil through me by offering me to Yama?

**(Then with bright countenance he gives his *praṇāmas* to his father and says)** Elders! Nobody need to feel sad on hearing what my father has said. Whoever is born has to die some time or the other. Nobody can escape death.

**Vasumatī** – O My husand! Listen to the child saying this and that. Do please forgive him and call him back.

**Gautama** – **(thinking for some time)** *Munis*, learned ones, what should I do in this difficult situation? My words should not go wrong. At the same time my son also should not leave me and go. Kindly find some way and save my family.

**Vasumatī** – Great souls! You all only should kindly show grace and help us. By some way save my only son. Will a mother be ready to part wih a son who is not even ten years old? Svāmī! Do forgive us and order the needful. (**She prostrates to the** ***munis*****.**) Child Naciketā! Do come near me (**she embraces him**).

**Agniveśa and Satyakṣada** – (**troubled**) All this happened because of us. If we had not told you this, you would not have got excited and spoken out.

**Naciketā** – Friends, don't worry. Everything happens as per God's will.

**Ṛṣis** – Let good tidings fall on everyone! Let not anybody get scared. Child Naciketā, you should not go to Yama's kingdom leaving your mother, father and others in sorrow. Instead of you, a cow or a big black bull can be offered as charity keeping in mind Lord Yamarāja. There is a rule in the Śāstras for that.

**Vasumatī** – Respected *muni*s, many thousand *namaskāram*s to you all. Now only my mind cooled hearing these words of compensation as allowed by the Śāstras.

**Agniveśa and Satyakṣada** – *Maharṣi*s, you can give us instead of Naciketā. We are ready to go instead of our friend to Lord Yama.

**Vasumatī** – Come here, you are also my children, aren't you?

**Naciketā** – Elders! mother! friends! My dear father! My *namaskaram*s to everyone. Please allow me to go. I won't allow other things to be given instead of me. If others get some things instead of me they can use it. What is the purpose of giving Lord Yama those things? To Lord Yama who has everything, even what I can do? Still if my father offers me in charity I will definitely go. What else can I do for my father? The only proper thing for me to do is, as per his order, go to Lord Yama. That is the best thing. My father's words should not become false.

**Gautama** – Child! I said some things foolishly in a hurry, without being able to control my anger. For that, should you be so insistent to follow it?

**Vasumatī** – Child, you need not go. Otherwise take me also along with you.

**Naciketā** –

अनुपश्य यथा पूर्वे प्रतिपश्य तथापरे।
सस्यमिव मर्त्यः पच्यते सस्यमिवाजायते पुनः ॥६॥

*anupaśya yathā pūrve pratipaśya tathāpare* |
*sasyamiva marttyaḥ pacyate sasyamivājāyate punaḥ* | |6| |

Father, look back and see what happened to your ancestors; look around and see what happens to others. Man decays and dies like corn; man emerges again like corn.

How did our ancestors live? We should think keenly. In the same way we should also be righteous and follow a sincere path. Men get destroyed like vegetation and again germinate and rise like vegetation.

*punarapi jananam, punarapi maraṇam*
(again and again birth and again and again death take place).

My dear parents, don't worry. A person can meet his death at the age of six or hundred. What is there to worry about a thing which cannot be avoided? Hence, let us leave the fear of death. Let us think about reaching the feet of the Lord. Father, with your blessings, I will go. Your words should become true. It is the most important *dharma* to follow the words of one's father. Hence, dear father, my dear mother, elders, friends! Do allow me to leave. All of you give me permission to go with all your heart.

**Gautama** – (**with eyes filled with tears**) Child! Young one! Do go happily. Convey my respects to Lord Yamarāja.

**Vasumatī** – Child! Don't disobey my words. There are no words above the words of a mother. Don't you know that?

Don't go my child.

**Āśrama residents** – Naciketā. You don't have to go.

**Ṛṣis** – How can Naciketā go?

**Ṛtvigs** – Going to *yamaloka* is not as easy as plucking flowers from a tree. One has to travel thousands of *yojanas*. How can he go to Yama's capital travelling thousands of *yojanas*?

**Friends** – Naciketā, what they are saying is correct. You don't have to go. Return back. See the bull Śiva-prasada which you reared fondly feeding tender grass, it is not able to bear your going and it is shedding tears.

(However, Naciketā does not listen to whatever they say and goes around the *yajña kuṇḍa*, father and mother three times and falls prostrate to everyone. Then he takes a handful of sanctified water (*ācamanam*), picks the *samidhā* (holy twigs) and resolves:

"Myself, if I have done my duties to my parents correctly let my wish be fulfilled. Respected Sir! Lord Yamarāja! If I have done my service to my forefathers correctly and followed that *dharma* in proper order, also if I have followed the *brahmacharya vrata* without fail in proper discipline and with my full mind, if I have done service to my mother, and if there had been any unfailing result for all those *dharmas* I have followed, as per that I must now only, without loss of time, reach your kingdom.

"O Lord Yamarāja! If I had done *upāsanā* of Gāyatrī without fail three times, O Lord Sūrya! as a reward for it, I must reach the kingdom of your son Lord Yama without fail. If without failing even for half a second if I had adhered to *brahmacharya vrata*, then my aim should be fulfilled immediately. This moment itself without any further obstruction I must reach the kingdom of Lord Yama.

"I completely surrender to you Sūryaputra who is the witness to all that is happening in the world. Holding truth as the basis of my life, believing that as the main help of life and strength to hold on, and upholding truth as the most exalted path, if these beliefs of mine are correct, do take me to your abode. In the eyes and presence of the entire world I have been offered to you by my father. You are Svāmī and my keeper. I am your slave. Do take me to you with all your grace. Do take me to you immediately."

***fig.:* Naciketā goes up, Mother Vasumatī swoons and falls down.**

(At that time a great miracle happens there. As everybody is watching, Naciketā rises up. Others are absolutely wonderstruck and spellbound seeing this sight. Vasumatī swoons and falls down. Gautama sits down with great anguish.)

*(The screen closes.)*

*(End of Part I.)*

## PART II

### SCENE 1

(Naciketā is seen going swiftly up along the sky (**should be shown in shadows**). Inside the screen the scenes are seen. Outside the Sūtradhāra and Śairandhrī are giving explanations. As soon as the screen opens, both Sūtradhāra and Śairandhrī enter.)

**(They are singing)**

ओं नमो भगवते वैवस्वताय मृत्यवे ब्रह्मविध्याचार्याय नचिकेतसे च।
यस्मेन सर्वं यथ सर्वं य सर्वं सर्वध्य्क् सदा।
सर्वभावपथातीतं स्वात्मानं तं स्मराम्यहम्

*oṁ namo bhagavate vaivasvatāya mṛtyave*
*brahmavidyācāryāya naciketase ca* |

*yasmena sarvaṁ yatha sarvaṁ ya sarvaṁ*
*sarvadhyksadā* |

*sarvabhāvapathātītaṁ svātmānaṁ taṁ*
*smarāmyaham*

Salutations to Vaivasa (son of sun god), lord of time, *guru* of *brahmavidyā* and to Naciketā prayers to the *ātmā* which is present in everything, which is everything, which is spread everywhere. Prayers to the *ātmā* which is beyond thoughts and actions.

**Sūtradhāra** – Sister, did you see our Naciketā? He is going along the route where *devas*, *vidyadharas*, *apsarases*, *siddhas* and *chāraṇas* travel. Due to his unparalleled goodness and glory, he is now going up in the sky close to the clouds like a *brahmāstra* (weapon), which has been released, from the bow of Atiratha.

**Śairandhrī** – Yes respected Sir! How majestically does he go? Just as an offering done in a *homa*, in the name of a *devatā*, is taken up by Agni in great speed, in the same way Naciketā is rising up and going.

**Sūtradhāra** – The sun has cooled down and is shining in tolerable warmth. The wind is also blowing cool breeze. The *munis* and immortals are praising Naciketā and encouraging him.

**Śairandhrī** – The blessings of Devī Gāyatrī are indeed great. Can anything be equivalent to that prayer of Gāyatrī? Due to its greatness today, Naciketā is crossing the boundaries of the sky and is going higher and higher.

**Sūtradhāra** – See that! *Deva*s and *siddha*s are offering sweet tasting herbs, roots and fruits and are welcoming him. Isn't the *dharma* of following one's ancestors' and parents' words an exalted virtue?

**Śairandhrī** – Sir, what is that? Suddenly the route itself has become darkened. Is it eclipse time? It is very smoky, isn't it?

**Sūtradhāra** – No, it is not an eclipse. Naciketā is now going along the smoky route — along the *pitṛyāna* path. "Dark smoke, night, *kṛṣṇapakṣa*, six months of *dakṣiṇāyana* (the Sun travelling along the southern route)" a *yogī* going on this route receives the moon's rays and returns back.

**Śairandhrī** – I have a doubt. Isn't Naciketā a blessed *puṇya* soul? I thought he had to go along the *deva*s' route.

**Sūtradhāra** – It is not like that. The ones who go along the *jyoti* route do not return. However Naciketā will come back after meeting the Dharmarāja, isn't it?

**Śairandhrī** – Svāmī! What is this? All the trees and leaves are like sharp knives. It is like the end of the world, with the Sun also blazing with such intense heat. Who are the small people crying and going with limbs as small as a thumb? Who are the ones who are taking them around and scolding them in such an authoritative manner?

**Sūtradhāra** – Dear child, these fearful forests are treacherous. They belong to *yamaloka* and are called *asapatra* forest. *Jiva*s (dead ones) who are suffering from hunger and thirst are being dragged for 240 miles along this forest by Yama's messengers. Our Naciketā crossed the fearful *asapatra* forest in a few seconds without any hindrance. Yama's messengers gave way, going to a side with fear, did you notice?

**Śairandhrī** – Yes respected Sir. What is this? A huge river is coming in between. How to cross that? Seeing that itself is scary. It is filled not only with water, but with blood also. The bad smell is intolerable. How to cross this river?

**Sūtradhāra** – Kalyāṇī! Don't be disturbed. This is only Vaitaraṇī River. If in life one has done charity of a cow, a cow now will come and help one to cross this river. For persons who have done *puṇya karma,* many boatmen are coming and helping them to cross the river, did you see that? The persons who have sinned are pushed into the river pressed down till *pātāla,* deep down and tortured, did you see that? But Naciketā considered this troublesome huge river Vaitaraṇī as a small pool and crossed over it without any effort. Did you notice it?

**Śairandhrī** – Yes, I also saw a cow coming to help him. Did you notice how healthy and strong it was, Svāmī?

**Sūtradhāra** – Yes, though his father donated very feeble and diseased cows, due to his adherence to truthfulness those became many times stronger and came to help him. See that, my daughter, how Naciketā goes forward at great speed, crossing Sūryamaṇḍala, Chandramaṇḍala, going around Puṣya and Śravaṇa group of stars.

**Śairandhrī** – What is this? There is something very bright and red in the sky. Who is that coming on an elephant?

**Sūtradhāra** – Those red rings belong to planet Mars. When he is crossing those planets, the lord Devendra is coming on his elephant Airāvata and blessing Naciketā. Imagine a harsh sea with huge disturbing waves and how a ship sails smoothly along without any obstacles. In the same way, our Naciketā is going magnificently through the troubled route without any obstacles.

**Śairandhrī** – Here the city that is seen, does it belong to Kubera? Or is it Amarāvatī? This palace having golden walls, diamond pillars and provided with numerous windows shining brightly like a bright lamp, to whom does it belong? A cool and pleasant smelling breeze is blowing. Everywhere good music is heard. Which is this *puṇyaloka* Svāmī?

**Sūtradhāra** – This is the Vaivastha city. It is the capital of Yamarāja. It is shining with *gandharva*s and *apsaras*es. Filled with song and dance this palace indeed belongs to Lord Yama. The palace near it belongs to Chitragupta. Chitragupta is writing the accounts of *pāpa* and *puṇya* of all *jīva*s meticulously without any mistakes. There is no chance of any mistakes. Whatever happens in *bhūloka* cannot escape his eyes.

**Śairandhrī** – Respected Sir! I am surprised seeing all these. Has Naciketā reached the entrance of the palace? Does Chitragupta write these conversations also?

**Sūtradhāra** – Where is the doubt about that? Definitely it will be added to his account. Look! Naciketā is moving with the speed of bird Garuḍa crossing the sky route, *vāyu* route, going around the planets, shining with the glow of *ātmā*, crossing places with *tejas* where *deva*s move around, getting down in the Vaivastha city. The fragrant *pārijāta* flowers are falling on him and welcoming him. In the sky, everywhere sounds of hailing him with joy are heard. What happiness is seen in the faces of everybody assembled. Everywhere there is joy.

**Śairandhrī** – Respected Sir, let us also go inside and see what else is happening. Do come.

**Sūtradhāra** – Sister! Let us do so.

***(They go inside. The curtain falls.)***

## SCENE 2

***(The curtain opens.)***

(*Yamaloka*. It is a city filled with palaces, castles and domes. The flags are shining like the bright rays of the sun.

Everywhere cool-shaded trees, sacred streams like the mind of the *ṛṣis* are found. Naciketā enters in and goes around the streets. With great happiness looks around on all sides.)

**Naciketā** – **(within himself)** Due to the blessings of my Respected Father and due to the grace of Gāyatrī Devī I came to *yamaloka* without any problem and any undue strain. For all these, strong belief and grace of the God are the main cause. If strength of mind is there what cannot be achieved? To reach *yamaloka* was as easy as climbing a tree and plucking flowers for *Śiva-pūjā* **(gets down in the stream and does *ācamanam*)**. These lakes are still bigger than Mānasarovara lake found on the earth. The *maṇi-maṇḍapa* here looks really distinguished. Have I by any chance taken a different route and come to Devendra's city, instead of going to *yamaloka*? Well seeing the persons coming there, I feel they look like *yamadūtas*. They are having in hand the binding rope for tying humans. However seeing them I am not having any fear in my mind.

(The soldiers of Yama by name Pāśahasta, Vajradanta and Conitākṣa are entering.)

**Vajradanta** – Who is that? Did you see him? What *tejas*? What magnetism is seen in his face?

**Pāśahasta** – Yes, I am also surprised. How has he come here without invitation.

**Śoṇitākṣa**– Yes, without our permission how did he enter? What a surprise it is?

**Naciketā** – **(within himself)** This majestic palace with many open windows, embedded with precious pearls, pillars made of diamonds, adorned with fluttering flags, is definitely of king Yamarāja. The soldiers are carefully guarding the entrance whose steps are shining as though laid in brightly molten gold.

**Vajradanta** – Looking at him he appears like a person who follows very austere *vratas*. Let us go near and enquire.

**Pāśahasta** – Let us do so.

**(They go near.)**

**Naciketā** – Groups of *yamadūtas* are seen moving here and there. Some of them are coming towards me. I will tell them the intention of my coming here.

(Naciketā first does *namaskāra* to them and gives his respects. Except Pāśahasta all others reciprocate with *namaskāra* to him.)

**Vajradanta** – Svāmī, who are you? You appear to be a big *mahān* (great soul). Are you Dhruva Bhagavān having come from Dhruva-maṇḍala to shower your grace or are you one of the *sanakādis* (enlightened ones) who has come to show your grace to us.

**Śoṇitākṣa** – Respected being, are you the Bāla Subramaṇya playing near Lord Śiva's abode at Kailāsa and have you come here losing your way? You must kindly inform us as to who you are?

**Vajradanta** – O Great one! If you tell us we will listen to it with happiness. Do grace us and tell.

**Naciketā** – I think you are all *yamadūtas*. As you are thinking I am neither a *deva* nor a *yakṣa*, nor a *gandharva*. I am a human being, and no *deva* sent me here.

**Pāśahasta** – Friends, what I thought was correct. When I was coming from *bhūloka* today I remembered having seen him. He was moving fast like Garuḍa and many were giving way to him, in fact avoiding him like a hot cinder. Did you notice?

**Vajradanta** – Yes, I remember now.

**Pāśahasta** – Vajradanta! We have understood who is this being. He is only one of the humanoids who gets scared just by hearing our name. Knowing it still I can't understand why you are all standing spell-bound. Let us drive him out.

**Śoṇitākṣa** – Have patience. Let us ask the reason of his coming. Svāmī! What is the reason for your showing your graceful presence here?

**Naciketā** – I am the son of the exalted brāhmaṇa Vājaśravas who is a great *paṇḍit*, prime in giving charities and has done many *yajñas*. I came to see Yamarāja. You all should kindly take me to his Majesty.

**Pāśahasta** – *Sabhāsa*! This insignificant insect belonging to human race who gets scared just hearing the first name of our master now wants to see him. It is indeed a good joke. Friends! Let us drive him out or we will catch him and close him up in the Kumbhibaka city.

**Vajradanta** – Friend! Don't show your colours to everyone. Do have control on yourself.

**Śoṇitākṣa** – Pāśahasta! Be a bit subdued. Once before you got insulted by Ajāmila. Have you forgotten it by now?

**Vajradanta** – Have you forgotten the advices revered Mahaśavahana gave us that time. Like Ajāmila he may also be a *Viṣṇu-bhakta*.

**Śoṇitākṣa** – He looks indeed like a great (*mahān*). No doubt about it. Pāśahasta, why unnecessarily invite trouble. Let Vajradanta and others stay here. We will go and tell Chitragupta. (**Both leave.**)

**Vajradanta** – Svāmī! Our friend Pāśahasta is always a hasty person. Do forgive him.

**Naciketā** – He did not do any harm to me for me to forgive. If a new person comes it is common to get doubtful. Where has your king gone? When will he be back?

**Vajradanta** – Our king has gone to *sūryaloka*. It will take three days for him to come back (**Chitragupta enters**).

**Chitragupta** – (**To himself**) He looks like Mārkaṇḍeya. What brightness is seen on his face. Has Mārkaṇḍeya completed his lifespan or has he surrendered to Lord Śiva, or has he accepted death by himself? He is not in our account, isn't he? Now I remember, his lifespan would not have got completed. Has Lord Brahmā only taken a different form and come to greet us. Let us go inside and enquire. (**As Chitragupta comes near, both are giving salutations to one another.**)

**Chitragupta** – Svāmī, let your arrival be good. You are like the Upendramūrti who has been separated from Devendra. Welcome, what is your honoured name? You, who are possessing a great matchless form. Who is the one who has sent you here? Are they Rudras? Or Mārutas? Or Viṣṇu Bhagavān, else are you among the eight *bālaka*s? (apart from our master is it one of the seven *bālaka*s?) Do tell us the details.

**Naciketā** – I have come from *bhūloka*. My name is Naciketā, I have not been sent here by any *deva*s. My father only sent me here.

**Chitragupta** – You belong to human race? I am happy to know that. Doing the *karma*s and earning *puṇya*s, a human birth which is worthy of that, is to be respected. That is our opinion. Which *brahmarṣi*'s dynasty is proud of your presence? The people of which country are suffering in your absence? Do tell in detail; what is the reason for your father sending you at this tender age. Kindly enlighten us as to these details.

**Naciketā** – I belong to Auddālaki Āruṇi's dynasty which is in the foothills of Himālayas. I am the eldest son of exalted Vipraśreṣṭha Gautama. In the *yajña* of *Viśvajīta* I have been given in charity to Lord Yama by my father. I have come here to see him in person and give my salutations. In this Yamapurī as a brother I am giving my *praṇāma*s to you on behalf of persons staying in *bhūloka*.

**Chitragupta** – Svāmī! This Yamapurī got brightened with your arrival. We have also become blessed. However there is a request we are making in a humble manner. At present the king is not here. It may take minimum three days for him to return from *sūryaloka*. You must kindly come to our humble abode. We will take care of you there and see that your daily disciplines and rituals are carried on without any difficulties.

**Naciketā** – Chitragupta, I am grateful for your affections. Your kind words itself have given me the required respect.

**Chitragupta** – If you so wish you can stay in the guesthouse. We are waiting to render the required help and take care of your comforts. O Exalted brāhmaṇa! You must grace us.

(Under the *pārijāta* tree, sitting in *padmāsana,* Naciketā is doing *japa* of *Gāyatrī mantra*. Others are coming and doing *namaskāra*. *Pāśahasta* also finally comes and gives his salutations.)

***(The curtain falls.)***

## SCENE 3

***(The curtain opens.)***

(The palace of Yamarāja is seen. At the entrance, the soldiers of Yama are guarding it holding spears, knives, armour, etc. (**The sound of Yamarāja approaching is heard from behind the screen.**) The soldiers Ghorarūpa and others are surrounding the person who is sitting on *mahiṣa* (buffalo). Some people are blowing conch-shells. Some are fanning him with feather-headed fans. Some are holding up colourful umbrellas. Yamarāja comes and gets down in front of the palace. The soldiers are shouting, "Hail Dharmarāja, hail his rule of punishing the *pāpī*s (sinners) and making them holy. Hail the one, who gives the fruits of *karma*! Hail the one, who has the power to destroy many worlds. Long live the friend of *puṇya* (good deeds). Let his justice be given without prejudice! Let the exalted one who gives justice live long!" They cry out thus. Opening the palace door Yamarajā's wife and friends and ministers enter. The serving girls follow with the required things to perform *arghya-pūjā* for him.)

**Yamarāja's wife** – Āryaputra! *Namaskāra*. Was the journey comfortable? Are my father-in-law and mother-in-law doing well?

**Yamarāja** – Dear one, everything was comfortable, all are keeping well? (**Yamarāja's wife washes her husband's feet and does *pūjā*. Chitragupta comes running and yelling.**)

**Chitragupta** – Mahārāja! Welcome, welcome. When you were away (**pointing to Naciketā who is sitting under the *pārijāta* tree in a corner and doing *pūjā***) he came from *bhūloka*. He is the son of a brāhmaṇa Vājaśravas. His name is Naciketā. He has been donated to you by his father and he is keen on meeting you. He has been waiting for the last three days without partaking of any food.

वैश्वानरः प्रविशत्यतिथिर्ब्राह्मणो गृहान्।
तस्यैतां शान्तिं कुर्वन्ति हर वैवस्वतोदकम् ॥७॥

*vaiśvānaraḥ praviśatyatithirbrāhmaṇo gṛhān |*
*tasyaitāṁ śāntiṁ kurvanti hara*
*vaivasvatodakam | |7| |*

A brāhmaṇa guest entering a house is like fire; hosts, to put the fire down, make pacifying offerings. O Death, please bring water for him.

A guest in a brāhmaṇa's form is equal to Agni's form, *sādhaka*s here are doing *śānti-pūjā* equivalent to *arghya-pūjā* or else Vaiśvānara (Agni) will burn everything. Hence Vaisvānara! First bring the holy water, do *atithi-pūjā* to Naciketā. It is not that you are unaware of these things. I am only reminding you, as is my duty.

**Dharmarāja** – Chitragupta! What you said is very correct. (**addressing his wife**) Dear, we too will go and do *atithi-pūjā* to this brāhmaṇa boy.

**Yama's wife** – Āryaputra, O! I did not see him at all.

आशाप्रतीक्षे संङ्गतं सूनृतां च इष्टापूर्त्ते पुत्रपशूंश्च सर्वान्।
एतद् वृङ्क्ते पुरुषस्याल्पमेधसो यस्याश्नन् वसति ब्राह्मणो गृहे ॥८॥

*āśāpratīkṣe saṁṅgataṁ sūnṛtāṁ ca iṣṭāpūrtte*
*putrapaśūṁśca sarvān* ।
*etad vṛṅkte puruṣasyālpamedhaso yasyāśnan vasati*
*brāhmaṇo gṛhe* ।।8।।

Hopes and aspirations, fruits of noble speech and noble acts such as sacrifice and charities, sons and cattle and all else are taken away from the person in whose house a brāhmaṇa had to remain unfed.

Isn't it a great sin to keep a brāhmaṇa without food? A person in whose house a brāhmaṇa guest stays without food accumulates a great sin, so say the Śāstras. His desires, resolutions, connections with good things, good words, *pūjā* to *deva*s, service to human beings, his children, cow, everything and all goodness accrued through *iṣṭa* and *pūrtta* deeds get burnt off by the *atithi* who is *agnirūpa*. It is Agni only who has come in an *atithi*'s form.

**Dharmarāja** – Dear! What you say is very correct. In our house this brāhmaṇa boy was staying without being fed. Due to this we have lost all our fortunes and goodness accrued through good deeds. We have now accumulated sin. Let us now itself entertain the *atithi* and compensate for our lapses.

(All go towards Naciketā. Naciketā gets up after finishing *japa*. Seeing Yama, he realizes who it is, gets up and gives his salutations.)

**Naciketā** –

यमाय धर्मराजाय मृत्यवे च अन्तकाय च।
वैवस्वताय कालाय सर्वभूतक्षयाय च।
औदुम्बराय दध्नाय नीलाय परमेष्ठिने।
वृकोदराय चित्राय चित्रगुप्ताय वै नम॥

*yamāya dharmarājāya mrtyave ca antakāya ca* ।
*vaivasvatāya kālāya sarvabhūtakṣayāya ca* ।

*audumbarāya dadhnāya nīlāya parameṣṭhine* |
*vr̥kodarāya citrāya citraguptāya vai nama* ||

My salutations to lord Yama, Dharamarāja, lord of death and finality.

Salutations to vaivasvatāya (son of the sun), lord of time, mitigater of all lives.

My salutations to audumbarāya (son of the sun), dadhnāya, lord of blue, lord of sky.

My salutations vr̥kodarāya (the one who devours all), chitra, and chitragupta.

**(Yamarāja blesses him and embraces Naciketā)**

**Naciketā** – Svāmī! By your *darśana* I have become very blessed. To make my father's promise come true and for his *yajña* to be completed I have come seeking you. Please accept me.

**Yamarāja** – Child! Naciketā! Let your arrival bring good tidings. We are all very happy at your arrival. This Yamapurī itself has become blessed by your arrival. *Svāgatam dvijottama* (Welcome the best of brahmins) **(Yamarāja and his wife perform *pūjā* with *arghyapāda* and other welcoming rituals.)**

तिस्रो रात्रीर्यदवात्सीगृहे मेऽ अनश्नन् ब्रह्मन्नतिथिर्नमस्यः ।
नमस्तेऽस्तु ब्रह्मन् स्वस्ति मेऽस्तु तस्मात्प्रति त्रीन् वरान् वृणीष्व ॥९॥

*tistro rātrīryadavātsīgr̥he me 'anaśnan brahmannatithirnamasyaḥ* |
*namaste 'stu brahman svasti me 'stu tasmāt prati trīn varān vr̥ṇīṣva* ||9||

I make obeisance to you, O brāhmaṇa, a guest of honour, who had to stay three nights in my residence unfed. May well-being be unto me. To make amends for the wrong, please choose three boons.

Naciketā! Revered brāhmaṇa! You are an *atithi* worthy of worship. However for three days you stayed in my house without partaking of any food. To absolve that sin I do *namaskāras* to you. O brāhmaṇa! let goodness happen to me. To compensate for the sins committed by keeping you hungry for three nights I will give you three boons with my heartfelt feelings. You must accept them. Let good tidings be bestowed on me. You can ask whatever you wish. I am ready to give you.

*fig.:* **Yamarāja granting three boons to Naciketā**

**Yamapatnī** – Respected Husband, for how long are you going to keep the person who has arrived at our doorstep outside and talk? Let all of you come inside and after taking food, you can rest and continue the conversation.

**Yamarāja** – Dear! What you say is correct. Let us all go inside. O revered brāhmaṇa! come inside.

***(All of them go inside the palace. The curtain falls.)***

## SCENE 4

(The inside of Yamarāja's palace is very huge and spread out. It has lots of sculptures. In the *maṇḍapa* made of clear marble on a raised throne Lord Yamarāja is seated. Facing the east, on his right side on a smaller seat Naciketā is sitting. On the left side two disciples are sitting in their respective seats. The soldiers like Ghorarūpa and others bearing spears are guarding the entrance.)

**Yamarāja** – *Dvijottama*! (best of brāhmaṇs) You can immediately ask for the three boons I granted you, and receive them. Relieve me from the debt. Receive the boons and go back to *bhūloka* and stay happily with your parents.

**Naciketā** – (**within himself**) Going back? Even if I go will my parents take me back? If a dead person goes they may think he is a ghost and drive him away. Even if my father comes to know it is me, he may still be angry with me, will he be willing to accept back, what was given in charity? Hence the first boon I ask, should be able to solve these problems (**thinking**) "Yes I will ask as such" (**then looking at Yama**).

शान्तसङ्कल्पः सुमना यथा स्यात् वीतमन्युर्गौतमो माऽभिमृत्यो ।
त्वत्प्रसृष्टं माऽभिवदेत् प्रतीतः एतत्त्रयाणां प्रथमं वरं वृणे ॥ १० ॥

*śāntasaṁkalpaḥ sumanā yathā syāt*
*vītamanyurgautamo mābhi 'mṛtyo* |
*tvatprasṛṣṭaṁ mā 'bhivadet pratītaḥ etattrayāṇāṁ*
*prathamaṁ varaṁ vṛṇe* ||10||

Let Gautama (my father) with allayed anxiety, anger gone, gracious towards me, recognizing me greet me and speak to me with joy when set free by you. This I choose as the first of the three boons.

O *deva* of death! My father Gautama should become of peaceful temperament, good mind and devoid of anger towards me. If sent back by you, he must receive me with love and bless me. As soon as I go, my father, mother and others should accept me and greet me with happiness and bless me. Only this I ask as the first boon of the three.

**Yamarāja** – Kumāra! I am very happy, so be it.

यथा परस्ताद्भविता प्रतीत औद्दालकिरारुणिर्मत्प्रसृष्टः।
सुखꣳ रात्री शयिता वीतमन्युः त्वां ददृशिवान् मृत्युमुखान् प्रमुक्तम् ॥११॥

*yathā parastād bhavitā pratīta*
*auddālakirāruṇirmatprasr̥ṣṭaḥ* ।
*sūkhaṁ rātrī śayitā vītamanyuḥ tvāṁ dadr̥śivān*
*mr̥tyumūkhātn pramuktam* ।।11।।

As he had been before, Auddālaki Āruṇi, your father, seeing you released from the jaws of death, his anger gone, through my favour will sleep happily many a night.

Your father Auddālaki Āruṇi (due to the boon I give) will leave his worries and become a person like before. He will look at you, who have come back from the door of death, with great affection and will be without anger. Till now, as he has been separated from you, he has lost his sleep and is in a worried state. From now on in the night time he will get a good sleep. Hence you don't have to worry. As soon as you return when he sees you he will remember all the past and receive you with affection, embrace you and will become very happy. Child, now you may ask for the second boon.

**Naciketā** – (**within himself**) What to ask for? What I immediately wanted was the blessings of my parents and I have asked for it. Now I will ask for something for use at a later time (**aloud**).

स्वर्गे लोके न भयं किञ्चनास्ति न तत्र त्वं न जरया बिभेति।
उभे तीर्त्वाऽशनायापिपासे शोकातिगो मोदते स्वर्गलोके ॥१२॥

*svarge loke na bhayaṁ kiñcanāsti na tatra tvaṁ na*
*jarayā bibheti* ।
*ubhe tīrtvā 'śanāyāpipāse śokātigo modate svargaloke*
।।12।।

> No fear prevails in the heavenly world. You (death) too do not exist there; nor is there the fear of old-age. Having crossed over both hunger and thirst, leaving sorrow behind, one rejoices in that world.

Svāmī! It is said that in *svargaloka* there is no fear at all; that is because there nobody has to be afraid of death. As everyone is in a constant state of youth they don't have to be scared about getting old. As they have partaken the nectar, there is no hunger and thirst. Without any worries they are always immersed in happiness.

> स त्वमग्निꣳ स्वर्ग्यमध्येषि मृत्यो प्रब्रूहि तꣳ श्रद्दधानाय मह्यम्।
> स्वर्गलोकाः अमृतत्त्वं भजन्ते एतद्द्वितीयेन वृणे वरेण ॥१३॥

> *sa tvamagniṁ svargyamadhyeṣi mṛtyo prabrūhi taṁ śraddadhānāya mahyam* |
> *svargalokāḥ amṛtattvaṁ bhajante etad dvitīyena vṛṇe vareṇa* ||13||

> O Death, such as you are, you know the fire (sacrifice) that leads one to heaven. Please teach me that (fire sacrifice) owing to which the dwellers of heaven gain immortality. This I choose as my second boon.

To reach this astonishing place having all kinds of comforts, you must preach to me about the helping tool, the *agni-vidyā*, that is the second boon I ask. Svāmī! You are well versed in this *agni-vidyā* practice with which one can attain *svargaloka*. I am asking you that boon with great *śraddhā*. You must kindly preach to me that. At *svargaloka* it is said that a person becomes free from pangs of hunger, thirst, old-age, different diseases, becoming grey, having diminishing vision and many more difficulties. A place where there is always *bhoga* (enjoyment), happy experiences and abundant nectar. People who have reached such a *svargaloka* attain a divine state. You must kindly preach to me the *agni-vidyā* which will help me reach such a state. I ask for this as my second boon.

**Yamarāja** –

प्र ते ब्रवीमि तदु मे निबोध स्वर्ग्यमग्निं नचिकेतः प्रजानन्।
अनन्तलोकाप्तिमथो प्रतिष्ठां विद्धि त्वमेतन्निहितं निहितं गुहायाम् ॥१४॥

*pra te bravīmi tadu me nibodha svargyamagniṁ*
*naciketaḥ prajānan* |
*anantalokāptimatho pratiṣṭhāṁ viddhi tvametan*
*nihitaṁ guhāyām* | |14| |

(Yama said:) Knowing well as I do, that heaven-reaching fire, I shall instruct you on it. Learn it from me. Know it, the means of attaining the boundless world, its support too, as abiding in the secret abode (of understanding).

Naciketā! What you have asked for is very apt. I know *agni-vidyā* well which is the route to *svargaloka*. I will preach to you. Listen carefully and understand that. Listen to it with complete concentration. This *agni-vidyā* is a very rare knowledge. It is the tool to reach *svarga*. Further Agni which is *virāṭ rūpa* (all encompassing) is found in the *upāsaka*'s *buddhi*'s cave. You must realize that and protect it with great care.

**Naciketā** – I am very happy. I will protect it with great *śraddhā*.

लोकादिमग्निं तमुवाच तस्मै या इष्टका यावतीर्वा यथा वा।
स चापि तत्प्रत्यवदद्यथोक्तं अथास्य मृत्युः पुनरेवाह तुष्टः ॥१५॥

*lokādimagniṁ tamuvāca tasmai yā iṣṭakā yāvatīrvā yathā*
*vā* |
*sa cāpi tat pratyavadad yathoktaṁ athāsya mṛtyuḥ*
*punarevāha tuṣṭaḥ* | |15| |

The Yama taught him the *agni-vidyā*, the source of heaven; (he narrated) what type of and how many bricks are necessary for building the sacrificial pit; and how they may be selected; (thereafter) that Naciketā also reproduced what he heard from Yamarāja; after that the fully gratified Yamarāja said again —

Then Yamarāja preaches to Naciketā the *agni-vidyā*. He tells him for that *pūjā* how many bricks, what sort of bricks, in what arrangement they have to be kept and in what way they have to be used. He also shows him how to make the *agnikuṇḍa*. All these Yamarāja tells Naciketā in detail. He learns with concentration and repeats it.

**Yamarāja – (Surprised and happy at the disciple's sharp intellect.)**

> तमब्रवीत् प्रीयमाणो महात्मा वरं तवेहाद्य ददामि भूयः।
> तवैव नाम्ना भविताऽयमग्निः सृङ्कां चेमामनेकरूपां गृहाण॥ १६॥
>
> *tamabravīt prīyamāṇo mahātmā varaṁ tavehādya*
> *dadāmi bhūyaḥ* ।
> *tavaiva nāmnā bhavitā 'yamagniḥ sṛṅkāṁ*
> *cemāmanekarūpāṁ gṛhāṇa* ।।16।।

Delighted extremely, the great-minded (Yama) told him: I give you now one more boon: by your name shall this (sacrificial) fire be known. Also take this necklace of multiple beauty as a gift.

Child! I appreciate your quick grasping power. Now I give you yet another boon. Let the *agni-vidyā* get known in the world by your name. Also I am giving you this precious bejewelled necklace made of *ratna*s and glittering work with many colours. This *agni-vidyā* which I have taught you will henceforth be known as Naciketā *agni*.

**Śravaṇa 1** – O Mahārāja! Mahātmā (great soul)! What are the benefits accrued by following Naciketā *agni-vidyā*?

**Yamarāja –**

> त्रिणाचिकेतस्त्रिभिरेत्य सन्धिं त्रिकर्मकृत्तरति जन्ममृत्यू।
> ब्रह्मजज्ञं देवमीड्यं विदित्वा निचाय्येमाँ शान्तिमत्यन्तमेति ॥१७॥
>
> *triṇāciketastribhiretya sandhiṁ trikarmakṛt tarati*
> *janmamṛtyū* ।
> *brahmajajñaṁ devamīḍyaṁ viditvā nicāyyemām̐*
> *śāntimatyantameti* ।।17।।

(He) transcends birth and death; who worships this fire (in the manner enjoined by Śāstras) three times; who establishes his relations with three (mother, father, and teacher), who performs three acts (*yajña*, *dāna* and *tapas*), in an unattached way; he who fully knows this adorable Fire god — the knower of the reason made by Brahmā; (and) collecting (erecting) this fire; attains this eternal peace.

A person who knows this *vidyā* and follows it three times ritually, and also one who is obedient to the words of his mother, father and *guru,* and has connection with Veda, Smṛti, regular daily discipline and follows the *yajña* and charities as ordered in the scriptures, crosses birth and death. He crosses the cycle of rebirth and reaches *svarga* and remains happily there. He does not have any fear of death.

**Śravaṇa 2** –

त्रिणाचिकेतस्त्रयमेतद्विदित्वा य एवं विद्वाꣳश्चिनुते नाचिकेतम्।
स मृत्युपाशान् पुरतः प्रणोद्य शोकातिगो मोदते स्वर्गलोके ॥१८॥

*triṇāciketastrayam etad viditvā ya evaṁ vidvāṁścinute nāciketam* ।
*sa mṛtyupāśān puratan praṇodya śokātigo modate svargaloke* ।।18।।

The wise one who, knowing the three factors, who performs three times this sacrificial knowledge; who worships this Naciketā fire; he cuts the noose of death in his very lifetime; crosses all sorrows and enjoys in the heaven.

Yes, yes! A person doing *upāsanā* of this *agni* three times gets the name Tri Naciketā and gets rid of shackles like *adharma,* ignorance, desire and hatred and becomes free and remains without any worries. He reaches *svargaloka* and enjoys there.

**Yamarāja** – A person who does *upāsanā* like that becomes pure like one having come out of Hiraṇyagarbha, gets knowledge of everything under the sun, becomes a person worthy of praise, gets realization of the Almighty, the *virāṭ svarūpa*. He realizes the *ātmā* and gets absolute peace. As fruits for his *karma* and *upāsanā*s he reaches *Virājasthāna*.

एष तेऽग्निर्नचिकेतः स्वर्ग्यो यमवृणीथा द्वितीयेन वरेण।
एतमग्निं तवैव प्रवक्ष्यन्ति जनासः तृतीयं वरं नचिकेतो वृणीष्व ॥१९॥

*eṣa te 'agnirnaciketaḥ svargyo yamavr̥ṇīthā dvitīyena varena* |
*etamagniṁ tavaiva pravakṣyanti janāsaḥ tr̥tīyaṁ varaṁ naciketo vr̥ṇīṣva* ||19||

O Naciketā! this fire (*agni-vidyā*) capable of providing you heaven; which you desired as your second boon; people will call this fire associating with your name; now ask for the third boon.

O Naciketā! Whatever you asked for as the second boon, that is *agni-vidyā*, which is requisite knowledge for reaching *svarga-loka* has been given to you. The people will know this by your name (Naciketā-*agni*) itself. Now you can ask for the third boon.

**Naciketā** – (**within himself**) I have asked a boon for the *bhūloka* and another for *svargaloka*. Now the fear, which vexes all human beings, is their state after death. That will be the one I should ask about.

**Yamarāja** – Come forth with the third request. By granting you that boon I will be freed of my debts.

**Naciketā** –

येयं प्रेते विचिकित्सा मनुष्ये अस्तीत्येके नायमस्तीति चैके।
एतद्विद्यामनुशिष्टस्त्वयाऽहं वराणामेष वरस्तृतीयः ॥२०॥

*yeyaṁ prete vicikitsā manuṣye astītyeke nāyamastīti caike* |
*etad vidyāmanuśiṣṭastvayā 'haṁ varāṇāmeṣa varastr̥tīyaḥ* ||20||

This doubt after the death of man; some say that this *ātmā* continues after death; some say that it ceases to be; taught by you I must know it fully well; this is the third of my boons.

Respected Sir! When a person leaves his body in the *bhūloka* then people say, "he later becomes like 'this'," or some people comment "no, he does not become later like 'this.'" I would like to know the truth by your preachings. This is the third boon I am asking for.

O Yamarāja! A person has, apart from his body, sense organs, and mind, intellect, a thing called *ātmā*, which also leaves his body when he dies. Some people say that *ātmā* reaches another body and some others dispute it saying there is nothing like an *ātmā*. Kindly explain, what is the truth behind it. It is not possible to know about this in any way by direct experience or by guesswork. I would like to know it clearly. You must preach me this secret of the *ātmā* knowledge with kind consideration. Respected Sir, that is my last request.

**Śravaṇa 1** – **(addressing the other *Śravaṇa*)** Brother! Did you see! The third request crossed even Vāmanamūrti's third step.

**Śravaṇa 2** – Yes, let us hear what our king is going to say for this.

**Yamarāja** – **(within himself)** Finally he asked what should not be asked. However, does he have the proper capacity to take the *ātma-jñāna*?

देवैरत्रापि विचिकित्सितं पुरा न हि सुविज्ञेयमणुरेष धर्मः।
अन्यं वरं नचिकेतो वृणीष्व मा मोपरोत्सीरति मा सृजैनम् ॥२१॥

*devairatrāpi vicikitsitaṁ purā na hi suvijñeyamaṇureṣa dharmaḥ* |
*anyaṁ varaṁ naciketo vṛṇīṣva mā moparotsīrati mā sṛjainam* ||21||

O Naciketā; on this subject; in the time of yore even gods were in doubt (they could not come to any decision); because the subject is very subtle; not easy to comprehend; ask another boon; do not pressurize me.

This boon in regard of the knowledge of self; return to me (**addressing Naciketā**) Child Naciketā, leave this and ask for some other boon. I will grant you anything else happily. This is a thing which cannot be understood by ordinary people. Don't ask for a boon, which will give you doubtful results. Ask something which will give you definite results. Like a rich person troubling the indebted person, don't insist on asking me such boons.

**Naciketā** –

देवैरत्रापि विचिकित्सितं किल त्वं च मृत्यो यं न सुज्ञेयमात्थ।
वक्ता चास्य त्वादृगन्यो न लभ्यो नान्यो वरस्तुल्य एतस्य कश्चित् ॥२२॥

*devairatrāpi vicikitsitaṁ kila tvaṁ ca mṛtyo yaṁ na sujñeyamāttha* |
*vaktā cāsya tvādṛganyo na labhyo nānyo varastulya etasya kaścit* | | 22 | |

Naciketā said: That even gods have doubts as to this, you yourself say, O Death, and that it is not easy to comprehend. No better teacher than you therefore is available; no better boon to choose either.

O Mṛtyudevatā! You are saying that it is a matter which even *devas* find it difficult to understand and get doubts. I won't get anyone like you to explain such a rare and difficult matter with clarity. Hence you must kindly be considerate to me and preach to me that knowledge. There is no boon I can think of which is equal to this. I don't want to leave this opportunity.

**Śravaṇa 1** – Brother, did you notice the stable intellect of Naciketā.

**Śravaṇa 2** – Yes, a person who is steadfast in his intentions alone can advance in obtaining *ātmā* knowledge.

**Yamarāja** –

शतायुषः पुत्रपौत्रान् वृणीष्व बहून् पशून् हस्तिहिरण्यमश्वान्।
भूमेर्महदायतनं वृणीष्व स्वयं च जीव शरदो यावदिच्छसि ॥ २३॥

*śatāyuṣaḥ putrapautrān vṛṇīṣva bahūn paśūn*
*hastihiraṇyamaśvān* |
*bhūmermahadāyatanaṁ vṛṇīṣva svayaṁ ca jīva śarado*
*yāvadicchasi* | | 23 | |

Choose children and grandchildren of a hundred years' life, cattle in plenty, elephants, gold and horses. A very very big piece of land (kingdom) ask for; hundreds of years aṣ long as you desire you may live Kumāra! There is no need for this boon for you.

I will give you children, grandchildren who will live for hundreds of years, many cows, elephants, horses, gold, etc. Take it with pleasure. I will give you a big kingdom in the *bhūloka*. Further after getting all this, if one passes away in a short time then all that would be unwanted, isn't it? Hence to enjoy these comfort I will grant you a long life span so that you can live as long as you choose to. Also you don't have to be scared of living till an old age. Along with all the perceivable comforts and wealth ruling a huge kingdom in good strength, I can grant you the boon to live as long as you wish in youth. If you don't want this you can also ask for similar boons like this. I can grant you whatever you wisḥ for.

**Śravaṇa 2** – Yes, it is the normal thing to first probe the mind and then to preach. Just as the fire is probed and stimulated before performing the *homa*.

**Naciketā** – Svāmī! If you wish to give the boon I asked for kindly grant it. By showing other glittering things I don't get attracted. I won't get anywhere else a *paṇḍit* like you to preach *ātma-tattva*. Hence this is the thing I aspire for.

**Yamarāja – (Again tempts him by offering him more and different wealths he can grant.)**

एतत्तुल्यं यदि मन्यसे वरं वृणीष्व वित्तं चिरजीविकां च।
महाभूमौ नचिकेतस्त्वमेधि कामानां त्वा कामभाजं करोमि ॥२४॥

*etat tulyaṁ yadi manyase varaṁ vr̥ṇīṣva vittaṁ*
*cirajīvikāṁ ca* |
*mahābhūmau naciketastvamedhi kāmānāṁ tvā*
*kāmabhājaṁ karomi* ||24||

If you think of some other boon equally good, wealth or long life, choose it. O Naciketā! prosper thus on this vast region. I shall make you the enjoyer of all such desires.

O Naciketā! Receive a huge wide kingdom and rule it for a long time living as *chiranjīvī*. All the *bhoga*s which both human beings and *deva*s can obtain I will grant you. You can enjoy them. Don't think I'm just telling something to sidetrack you.

ये ये कामा दुर्लभा मर्त्त्यलोके सर्वान् कामांश्छन्दतः प्रार्थयस्व ।
इमा रामाः सरथाः सतूर्य्या न हीदृशा लम्भनीया मनुष्यैः ॥
आभिर्मत्प्रत्ताभिः परिचारयस्व नचिकेतो मरणं माऽनुप्राक्षीः ॥२५॥

*ye ye kāmā durlabhā marttyaloke sarvān*
*kāmāṁśchandataḥ prārthayasva* |
*imā rāmāḥ sarathāḥ satūryyā na hīdr̥śā lambhanīyā*
*manuṣyaiḥ* ||
*ābhirmatprattābhiḥ paricārayasva naciketo maraṇaṁ*
*mā 'nuprākṣīḥ* ||25||

Whatever objects of enjoyment are rare in the mortal world; ask for them unhesitatingly; these nymphs with chariots and musical instruments (take them with you); such nymphs are unobtainable to the mortal men; get yourself nursed by these given by me; do not ask what happens after death.

I am a person who truthfully abides by his words. I will grant you everything as promised. I will grant you the *bhoga*s not possible to get in *bhūloka*. These nymphs with chariots and musical instruments, *apsaras*es which men may not even imagine in their dreams, I will grant you. Since I am granting you, they will come with you and serve you. See these beautiful nymphs that sing and dance with pleasing music. If only you just say, all these will belong to you. Are you out of your mind to throw away these luxuries and comforts which are real? Don't be obstinate Kumāra. Take them with satisfaction and live well. But don't ask me anything concerning death, what is behind death? and such questions.

**Naciketā** –

श्वोभावा मर्त्यस्य यदन्तकैतत् सर्वेन्द्रियाणां जरयन्ति तेजः ।
अपि सर्वं जीवितमल्पमेव तवैव वाहास्तव नृत्यगीते ॥ २६ ॥

*śvobhāvā martyasya yadantakaitat sarvendriyāṇāṁ jarayanti tejaḥ* |
*api sarvaṁ jīvitamalpameva tavaiva vāhāstava nṛtyagīte* ||26||

O Yamarāja!, these momentary enjoyments (and pleasure derived from them) weaken the vitality of man and all his sense organs; apart from that the life period is very small (howsoever big it may be); let your chariots, the music and musical instruments remain with you (I don't want them).

Revered Yamarāja! The things you promised such as *ratna* necklace, horses, chariots, elephants, gold, kingdom, *apsaras*es, all these I don't want. All these get destroyed if not today, by tomorrow. Not only they finish off, they also take away the strength of the sense organs. However strong the *indriya*s are, due to *bhoga*s they get burnt out, isnt it? However long a life, it is till limited. Even *pitāmāha* who creates everything also possesses a limited living period. That being so, the long life you propose to grant me should indeed be very limited. Hence the necklace, nymphs, chariots, dances, and songs let all these be here with you.

**Yamarāja** – Hey Naciketā! However much I explain to you, still you are not ready to listen. I am telling you for your good only.

**Naciketā** –

न वित्तेन तर्पणीयो मनुष्यो लप्स्यामहे वित्तमद्राक्ष्म चेत्त्वा ।
जीविष्यामो यावदीशिष्यसि त्वं वरस्तु मे वरणीयः स एव ॥ २७ ॥

*na vittena tarpaṇīyo manuṣyo lapsyāmahe*
*vittamadrākṣma cettvā* |
*jīviṣyāmo yāvadīśiṣyasi tvaṁ varastu me varaṇīyaḥ sa*
*eva* ||27||

"Man can never get contented with wealth; when I have had your vision, I shall certainly get wealth; (and) so long as you will rule over the world," I shall be living, it is unnecessary to ask such things; the boon worth asking is the one I had asked for.

Svāmī! A person will never be satisfied getting wealth. If we are in need of wealth we can request you to grant some. Being our well-wisher I am sure you would do it. There is no need to get it separately as a boon. As long as you bless us, we can also get a long life and enjoy the same. After getting your *darśana* will anyone end up living a short life amidst poverty? However all these are temporary, not permanent. They don't give lasting happiness. I am steadfast in the boon I am asking for.

**Śravaṇa 1** – Naciketā is like a huge lake which cannot be moved by the wind and in which no disturbing waves are there.

**Śravaṇa 2** – Yes, he seems to be filled with all the *sādhanā*s and means a *mumukti* possesses. Now what is the obstacle in giving the preachings?

**Naciketā** – Svāmī! It may appear like giving but finally you draw the thing to yourself. Like giving with the right hand and taking back with the left. In effect all these are yours only. It may appear like you are giving us and one day you may throw the noose and take back everything. Hence all these are not the boons which you really give. You are the one who takes away life and things.

अजीर्यताममृतानामुपेत्य जीर्यन् मर्त्यः क्वधःस्थः प्रजानन्।
अभिध्यायन् वर्णरतिप्रमोदान् अतिदीर्घे जीविते को रमेत ॥२८॥

*ajīryatāmamṛtānāmupetya jīryan martyaḥ kvadhaḥ sthaḥ prajānan* |
*abhidhyāyan varṇaratipramodān atidīrghe jīvite ko rameta* ||28||

Having approached the undecaying state of the immortals, which mortal, aware of and deliberating on the nature of pleasures of beauty and love, will find joy in an over-long life?

Once realizing about the ones having no old-age and death, that is, the *amaratva* (*deva*s), will man again be tempted to the route where he habitually gets lured and falls prey to pleasures, old-age and death? Persons having a narrow outlook may do it, not a learned wise person.

**Yamarāja** – O child Naciketā! However much I tell you, you are not ready to listen. I have done my duty. Finally, what is your opinion?

**Naciketā** – Svāmī! I don't want the *bhoga*s, which you said you were going to give me. I don't want the pleasure of beauty and love nor kingship of any kingdom. I am also not desirous of ruling the skies surrounded by enchanting *apsarase*s who with their slender waist and beautiful form like Menakā entertain with their sweet songs and captivating dances. I also don't desire to be an emperor sitting under a raised throne surrounded by persons honouring me by fanning *cāmara*s and holding umbrellas.

यस्मिन्निदं विचिकित्सन्ति मृत्यो यत्साम्पराये महति ब्रूहि नस्तत्।
योऽयं वरो गूढमनुप्रविष्टो नान्यं तस्मान्नचिकेता वृणीते ॥२९॥

*yasminnidaṁ vicikitsanti mṛtyo yatsāmparāye mahati brūhi nastat* |
*yo 'yaṁ varo gūḍhamanupraviṣṭo nānyaṁ tasmānnaciketā vṛṇīte* ||29||

O Yamarāja! tell me of the beyond about which there has

been much doubt prevailing — the knowledge which is followed by great results. Apart from this knowledge that penetrates the mystery, no other boon does this Naciketā choose.

However, you must bless me with the knowledge about life after death, about which people at *paraloka* are afraid and confused. Apart from the words of explanation about the state, which is not easily understood by intellect, I have no desire for anything else. Kindly grace me and preach this to me.

**Yamarāja** – **(to himself)** He is an *uttama adhikārī* (most deserving person). He is worthy of being preached. There is no doubt about it. **(aloud)** O child! till now I was testing you. You have passed in that. Now I will preach to you.

**Naciketā** – **(Getting up and giving his *praṇāmas*)** Gurudeva, I have become very blessed. I will listen carefully what you are going to say. **(Chitragupta enters)**

**Chitragupta** – Mahārāja! It is time for you to address the court. Your majesty kindly come over and show your grace.

**Yamarāja** – All right, let us go. Naciketā! You also can come to the court along with us.

***(All leave. The curtain closes.)***

***IInd Part Over.***

## Part III

### SCENE 1

***(The curtain rises)***

(In the city of Samyamaṇi belonging to Yamarāja, there is the ancient and famous hall *taijasī*. It has many thousand diamond pillars, adorned by flags embedded with bunches of pearls and other precious stones. It is shining with the golden lustre. A breeze is blowing laden with *chaitanya*. Fine pleasant music is heard. In the centre of a *maṇḍapa* on big throne Lord Yama is seated. Messengers like Vajradanta are standing around holding different weapons. All different diseases are standing having gruesome faces. On one side Śravaṇas and Chitragupta are sitting. Naciketā also sitting on a seat, is looking at the proceedings full of wonder. Pāśahasta is bringing one sinner dragging him along. Behind *yamadūta*s are beating him well and coming. That *jīva* seeing the court and Yamarāja, is scared and crying in fear.)

**Pāpa jīva** – Oh! Alas, what sin did I do that they are beating me like this! Is there no one to question this? Is there no end to this suffering which I am experiencing? Like a sweltering wound being pricked with a spear, they are torturing me, who is already crestfallen having left my children, wife and property in the *bhūloka*. Instead of giving me some solace, they are beating me like this. Oh! I am not able to bear these pangs of hunger and thirst. Is there no one who can save me? Oh! Alas!.

**Yamarāja** – Chitragupta, what are the misdeeds this *jīva* has committed? Do tell in detail.

**Chitragupta** – Svāmī! (**turning and seeing the accounts**) he is a great sinner. He has done five big sins. He was a highly short-tempered person and was full of greed. He had many illicit relationships with other women. He had collected wealth in a wrongful deceitful *adhārmika* way. He troubled the poor to no end. He has never spoken a good sweet word with his tongue.

**Yamarāja** – Has he done any good deeds?

**Chitragupta** – Never! Even in his dreams he has not done any *dharma*.

**Yamarāja** – In that case it is a sin to even look at this *mahāpāpī*'s face. Take him immediately and put him in the pit of burning cinders. Later beat him well with heavy wooden sticks. Make him embrace a well-heated iron statue and tie him up to it by iron chains. Denying him food, ask him to eat his own flesh. If he refuses tie him up to an iron rod and roast him in fire. For using bad words towards his elders make the germ gnaw his tongue.

**Yama's soldiers** – We will do so, Svāmī.

**The sinned jīva** – (**trembling with fear**) Alas! Dharmarāja, kindly save me. Show sympathy on me. For once pardon me, I will change forever. Kindly show consideration. Don't torture me.

**Yamarāja** – Hey *jīva*! I am a judge pronouncing judgement without any prejudice. Being a fair and just judge here is no place for personal likes and dislikes. This harsh punishment is only to correct you. You will be given a chance in the next birth. Hence now you can go.

**The sinned jīva** – Is this the verdict? What justice is this? Can justice not mixed with compassion be proper justice? Repentance is the redemption for sins, isn't it? I can't understand anything. My head is reeling. (He falls down. The messengers beat him with leather belt, drag him and take him away. Naciketā tries to control his tears and wipes them.)

*fig:* **Papātmā brought to Lord Yama**

(Dharmathvā is bringing one *jīva* who has done good deed, with great respect. For the eyes of *puṇya jīva* everything seen appears beautiful and blessed. The gruesome faces are not seen. Yamarāja is also looking gracious and in peaceful form. Seeing the *puṇyātmā* everyone gets up and welcomes him. They invite him saying pleasant words of welcome.)

*fig:* **Puṇyātmā brought to Lord Yama**

**Yamarāja** – Do come *puṇyātmā*! Let your coming bring good tidings. Do come and take this seat. (**As the *jīva* sits Dharmarāja's attendent fans him with *cāmara*.**)

**Śravaṇa 1** – (**getting up**) Dharmarāja, I am pleased to narrate his *karmas*. He is a learned *paṇḍit* of Vedas and Śāstras As he learnt them he followed its concepts too. He wrote himself by hand great Purāṇas like *Rāmāyaṇa, Mahābhārata, Śrīmad Bhāgavatam*, etc., made others read and taught persons aspiring to learn. He is a person who has helped others greatly. Whoever went to his door and asked for charity, has never gone back empty-handed.

**Śravaṇa 2** – Not only that. He has done *upavāsa* (eaten only once) during *ekādaśī* (waxing and waning moon of the 11th day). During *dvādaśī* (12th day of the moon) he has fed brāhmaṇas. He has dug wells and ponds for the welfare of the common people. He has built beautiful gardens. Also he has done many charities. Further he has established institutes for doing *dhārmika* works.

**Puṇya jīva** – (**with humility**) I have not done anything special. I only did my duty. All these happened due to the grace of God, blessings of elders and co-operation of the public. I have only been trying to be just and proper, nothing else.

**Yamarāja** – Chitragupta! Has he commited any sins? Why is there silence regarding that?

**Chitragupta** – Knowingly he has not commited any sins. Unknowingly he has committed some small sins. However as a redemption to the sins he seeks forgiveness and had done compensatory deeds with a good mind. Also he has given away a lot in charity for good deeds and has become purified with that.

**Yamarāja** – Is that so? I am very happy. The requisite blessing should be passed on to him.

**Chitragupta** – As a final act for all good deeds, his death occurred at the holy pilgrimage place Kāśī. Lord Viśvanātha himself uttered the *tāraka mantra* into his ears. Immediately he came here in a *puṣpaka* plane.

**Yamarāja** – I am very happy. Due to his coming this city itself has become holy. Give him the due respects and we will send him to *svargaloka*. With this let today's court be dispersed. (**Yamarāja gets up and goes. All get up and go along. Naciketā is standing and thinking.**)

**Naciketā** – (**within himself**) Everything, which happens here is very surprising. Though there are punishments like this why are people committing sins? If they know that, they will never do it. (**He walks around**) Though the Purāṇas instruct about these still it is not possible for humans to live without committing sins. What is that, without oneself being aware of prods one to sin? Is it not possible to avoid it? What is the one which makes one do *puṇya*? Everything is a mystery. Only Yamarāja should clear the doubts. He has agreed to preach, that itself is the first victory. Is it somehow possible to save the sinner who came today? He kept looking at me with his pitiful looks again and again. The torture he bore moved my heart (**wiping his tears**). O Alas! he is in great agony. Somehow I should save him. Dharmarāja will not break the rule. He is a witness for everything. He has worn the armour of justice to show the way to the sinners by punishment. Hence there is no point asking him. Then what is the way? Let me ask the Śravaṇas, if there is a way. That is only right. Let me go.

***(He goes, curtain falls.)***

SCENE 2

***(The curtain opens.)***

(It is the palace of Yamarāja. It has a vast sprawling *maṇḍapam*. Yamarāja is sitting facing east. Śravaṇas are sitting nearby. Naciketā also is sitting facing north.)

**Naciketā** – O Paramaguru! you must kindly show grace and preach to this humble one.

**Yamarāja** – I will preach to you indeed. You are a disciple close to my heart. I will tell you. Listen carefully.

**Naciketā** – As per your order Svāmī. I shall carefully listen.

**Yamarāja** –

अन्यच्छ्रेयोऽन्यदुतैव प्रेयः ते उभे नानार्थे पुरुषꣳ सिनीतः।
तयोः श्रेय आददानस्य साधु भवति हीयतेऽर्थाद्य उ प्रेयो वृणीते ॥१॥

*anyacchreyo 'nyadutaiva preyaḥ te ubhe nānārthe puruṣaṁ sinītaḥ* |
*tayoḥ śreya ādadānasya sādhu bhavati hīyate 'rthādya u preyo vṛṇīte* ||1||

That which is of the highest value (*śreyas*) is one; that which is pleasant here and now (*preyas*) is another. Serving different purposes, the two make men blind. Of the two, well is it for him who chooses *śreyas*. He fails his aim who chooses *preyas*.

Child, there is one thing called *śreyas* and another thing called *preyas*. *Śreyas* is goodness that is the correct path. *Preyas* is pleasant and that is the desire path. Goodness is one thing, pleasantness is another. Both of them take hold of the human mind and lead him to different paths. The one who follows *śreyas* reaps goodness. The one who follows *preyas* slips from path of truth.

**Naciketā** – If one discriminates between *śreyas* and *preyas* and follows the path of *śreyas* alone, then he moves from strength to strength as told by you. However still why does a person not take to *śreyas* ways? Why does he leave goodness and follow not-so-good ways?

**Yamarāja** –

श्रेयश्च प्रेयश्च मनुष्यमेतः स्तौ सम्परीत्य विविनक्ति धीरः।
श्रेयो हि धीरोऽभिप्रेयसो वृणीते प्रेयो मन्दो योगक्षेमाद्वृणीते ॥२॥

*śreyaśca preyaśca manuṣyametaḥ stau samparītya vivinakti dhīraḥ* |
*śreyo hi dhīro 'bhi preyaso vṛṇīte preyo mando yogakṣemād vṛṇīte* ||2||

*Śreyas* and *preyas* both come before a man; the wise distinguishes between the two; the wise prefers the *śreyas* in comparison to *preyas*; the dull witted chooses the *preyas* as a means of mundane prosperity.

As such both the ways are open for him. A person of superior virtue examining them both will reject the pleasant but impermanent ways and adopt goodness or *śreyas*. However a person of lesser intellect will spend his time in collecting wealth and taking care of it. The fool throws away the better thing and catches the pleasures. Just as a swan can delineate the milk from a mixture of milk and water, a person of intelligence will leave *preyas* and take *śreyas*. However a person of lesser intellect pays attention and gets attached with his cattle, wealth, wife, children, and comforts and seeks *preyas*.

स त्वं प्रियान् प्रियरूपाꣳश्च कामान् अभिध्यायन्नचिकेतोऽत्यस्राक्षीः।
नैताꣳ सृङ्कां वित्तमयीमवाप्तो यस्यां मज्जन्ति बहवो मनुष्याः ॥ ३॥

*sa tvaṁ priyān priyarūpām̐śca kāmān abhidhyāyan naciketo 'tyasrākṣīḥ* |
*naitām̐ sṛṅkāṁ vittamayīmavāpto yasyāṁ majjanti bahavo manuṣyāḥ* ||3||

O Naciketā! you being such, when pleasant and beautiful desirables presented themselves, rightly reflecting on, have rejected them. You did not choose the garland of wealth that chains you up. Many are who sink therein.

Hey Naciketā, don't be scared. You have left the coveted things as insignificant. Though I tempted you variedly about things connected with *preyas* and prodded you to accept them, understanding their temporary nature, you discarded them. You have great *viveka* (discrimination). You didn't step on the path of the *bhoga*s (enjoyment) in which many people drown and die. You are a very strong-willed person.

**Naciketā** – Svāmī! You must tell me about *śreyas* in greater detail.

**Yamarāja** –

दूरमेते विपरीते विषूची अविद्या या च विद्येति ज्ञाता।
विद्याभीप्सिनं नचिकेतसं मन्ये न त्वा कामा बहवोऽलोलुपन्त ॥४॥

*dūramete viparīte viṣūcī avidyā yā ca vidyeti jñātā* |
*vidyābhīpsinaṁ naciketasaṁ manye na tvā kāmā bahavo 'lolupanta* || 4||

These two *avidyā* and *vidyā* are to a very great exent contradictory to each other, yielding entirely different fruits; I regard you, Naciketā as desirous of *vidyā*; all these allurements did not entice you.

*Avidyā* is *preyas, vidyā* is *śreyas*. One should realize that they are dramatically different from one another. It is like darkness and brightness. The result accrued from them is also different.

The result of one is *mokṣa* and the other one *saṁsāra* (worldly life). Naciketā I think you are the one who yearns for *vidyā*. *Śreyas* is the tool for the most exalted benefit of *mokṣa*. People having narrow vision will get attracted to *preyas*. A person who has not left the desire for *avidyā* cannot get attracted to *vidyā*. You did not aspire for the *bhoga*s (enjoyments), which bind men like animals. The different desires and *bhoga*s did not attract you. Hence you will receive a lot of *śreyas*. There is no doubt about it.

**Naciketā** – I am very happy to hear the nectar-like words of yours. O Pūjya Guru! you must tell me in detail the state of those who follow *preyas*.

**Śravaṇa 1** – Naciketā's question is very good. To leave the attracting nature of *avidyā* it is necessary to know its ill effects.

**Yamarāja** –

अविद्यायामन्तरे वर्तमानाः स्वयं धीराः पण्डितम्मन्यमानाः ।
दन्द्रम्यमाणाः परियन्ति मूढाः अन्धेनैव नीयमाना यथाऽन्धाः ॥५॥

*avidyāyāmantare vartamānāḥ svayaṁ dhīrāḥ*
*paṇḍitammanyamānāḥ* ।
*dandramyamāṇāḥ pariyanti mūḍhāḥ andhenaiva*
*nīyamānā yathā 'ndhāḥ* ।।5।।

Living within *avidyā*, still regarding themselves as wise and learned, such fools (desirous of earthly pleasures) get stumbled while wandering in various wombs; like blind led by another blind (having been lost and not reaching their goal, they suffer).

Persons having dimmed intellect are fools. They are the ones having narrow mentalities. They welcome easy pleasures and embrace *preyas*. The fools who are immersed in that think they are only the *paṇḍit*s. They assume that they are the strong ones and struggle in that *preyas*. Like persons following the path of blind people they get confused and go round in circles. These dim-witted people lose their *ātmā* knowledge. They end up doing bad deeds, become enemies of the world, and are born, die and remain in this cycle constantly.

न साम्परायः प्रतिभाति बालं प्रमाद्यन्तं वित्तमोहेन मूढम्।
अयं लोको नास्ति पर इति मानी पुनः पुनर्वशमापद्यते मे ॥६॥

*na sāmparāyaḥ pratibhāti bālaṁ pramādyantaṁ*
*vittamohena mūḍham* |
*ayaṁ loko nāsti para iti mānī punaḥ*
*punarvaśamāpadyate me* ||6||

The beyond is not visible to the ignorant, heedless, deluded by the glamour of wealth, thinking, "This world is what exists, nothing beyond." Again and again he reaches me (death).

**Two paths of life: *śreyas* and *preyas***

They, being blinded by the darkness of desire, remain in an illusory world and can't understand about *ātma-jñāna* or matters of other world. "This is the only world, there is no other world" thinking thus an *avivekī* (unwise person) again and again dies and thus falls into my net. He gets caught in this cycle of birth and death.

**Śravaṇa 2** – "This earth, the wealth, the women, the children and all the things seen on earth are permanent and there is no other world," thinking thus they get immersed in that cycle. Hence it is said that this *saṁsāra* is a big ocean.

**Naciketā** – What you are saying is very correct. Because of that only I want to come out of this sea of *saṁsāra*. I am approaching wise elders like you and trying to know the truth.

**Yamarāja** –

> श्रवणायापि बहुभिर्यो न लभ्यः शृण्वन्तोऽपि बहवो यं न विद्युः।
> आश्चर्यो वक्ता कुशलोऽस्य लब्धा ऽश्चर्यो ज्ञाता कुशलानुशिष्टः ॥७॥
>
> *śravaṇāyāpi bahubhiryo na labhyaḥ śṛṇvanto 'pi bahavo yaṁ na vidyuḥ* |
> *āścaryo vaktā kuśalo 'sya labdhā 'ścaryo jñātā kuśalānuśiṣṭaḥ* ||7||
>
> That which many people do not have opportunity to hear; that which many people even after hearing do not comprehend; the expounder of such a subject is rare; the gainer of this is rare; and one who is taught by a realized great soul and becomes well-versed and thus the knower of this subject is also very rare (a surprise).

It is rare to get a disciple like you who has an ardent yearning to know *ātma-jñāna*. Out of thousand one may think of it. In most persons' minds even questions do not arise and even if the question arises for very few, such a person of yearning reaching a knowledgable person is also rare.

It is not the work to be explained by a person of less virtue who has no qualification to teach it. It is a very rare opportunity to be taught by an expert *ācārya* and a deserving disciple to understand it. These prerequisites are important. It has to be learnt from a qualified teacher alone. That is because different people teach that which is unknown differently. If taught by less knowledgeable persons it will again become distorted.

**Naciketā** – Pūjya Guru, how does the *ātma-jñāna* get distorted? How to know it correctly? Kindly tell me in detail.

**Yamarāja** –

न नरेणावरेण प्रोक्त एषः सुविज्ञेयो बहुधा चिन्त्यमानः।
अनन्यप्रोक्ते गतिरत्र नास्त्यणीयान् ह्यतर्क्यमणुप्रमाणात् ॥ ८॥

*na nareṇāvareṇa prokta eṣaḥ suvijñeyo bahudhā cintyamānaḥ* |
*ananyaprokte gatiratra nāstyaṇīyān hyatarkyamaṇupramāṇāt* ||8||

The *ātma-tattva* is not easy to understand if it is narrated by a person of low standard and of shallow knowledge; and even if contemplated much by the listener, if it is not taught by a wise person, it cannot be grasped. Because it is subtler than the subtlest, it is inaccessible to reasoning.

Since *ātmā* is a component of the smallest atom it cannot be known by discussion. Ordinary persons can never come to know about it. Some say there is *ātmā,* and some say *ātmā* is not there. Thus persons capable of speech, speak of it in several ways: "It is there, it is not there; it is the doer, it is not the doer, it is pure, it is not pure; it is a thing of wonderment, what knowledge (*vidyā*) is this?" Yet, one, hearing all these, will remain ignorant. It can only be preached as "not this, not this" (*neti, neti*).

**Śravaṇa 1** – Among thousands of persons only some attempt to get *ātma-jñāna*, and among the some only one may get the *ātma-jñāna*. Naciketā! you belong to the class of fortunate persons.

**Yamarāja** –

नैषा तर्केण मतिरापनेया प्रोक्तान्येनैव सुज्ञानाय प्रेष्ठ।
यां त्वमापः सत्यधृतिर्बतासि त्वादृङ्नो भूयान्नचिकेतः प्रष्टा ॥९॥

*naiṣā tarkeṇa matirāpaneyā proktānyenaiva sujñānāya preṣṭha* |
*yāṁ tvamāpaḥ satyadhṛtirbatāsi tvādṛṅno bhūyānnaciketaḥ praṣṭā* ||9||

This wisdom is not obtainable through logic or argument. Only the teaching of a competent person is instrumental in getting self-knowledge; really you are bestowed with perseverence of a high order. O Naciketā! I wish to have a questioner like you.

Naciketā! you who are worthy of my affection! The *samyak-jñāna*, which you have obtained, cannot be obtained by discussion. You are a person having true determination, let us get more disciples like you who come seeking this knowledge.

जानाम्यहꣳ शेवधिरित्यनित्यं न ह्यध्रुवैः प्राप्यते हि ध्रुवं तत्।
ततो मया नाचिकेतश्चितोऽग्निरनित्यैर्द्रव्यैः प्राप्तवानस्मि नित्यम् ॥१०॥

*jānāmyahaṁ̐ śevadhirityanityaṁ na hyadhruvaiḥ*
*prāpyate hi dhruvaṁ tat* |
*tato mayā nāciketaścito 'gniranityairdravyaiḥ*
*prāptavānasmi nityam* ||10||

I know the fruit of *karma* in the form of treasure is ephemeral; because that imperishable permanent object (God) cannot be obtained through perishable objects. I myself, though collected this Naciketā *agni* with the help of these perishable worldly objects by virtue of the matchless power of desirelssness I obtained that Permanent *paramātmā*.

Child! I know this fact that as the result of one's deeds, whatever treasure, i.e. pleasure of this world, one gets, it has to perish one day and is temporary. By temporary things one cannot obtain the permanent wealth of *ātma-jñāna*. Only afer knowing this secret I have arranged this Naciketā *agni* and whatever sacrifices in the form of duty I have performed, it was all without desire and attachment but only with the sense of duty. It is due to the glory of this desirelessness and performing duty, which was my adoration to God, that I attained Him, the eternal bliss.

कामस्याप्तिं जगतः प्रतिष्ठां क्रतोरानन्त्यमभयस्य पारम्।
स्तोमं महदुरुगायं प्रतिष्ठां दृष्ट्वा धृत्या धीरो नचिकेतोऽत्यस्राक्षीः ॥११॥

*kāmasyāptiṁ jagataḥ pratiṣṭhāṁ kratorānant-*
*yamabhayasya pāram* ।
*stomaṁ mahadurugāyaṁ pratiṣṭhāṁ dṛṣṭvā dhṛtyā*
*dhīro naciketo 'tyasrākṣīḥ* ।।11।।

The foundation of the world, the best of all desires, the endlessness of sacrifices, the ultimate limit of fearlessness, that which holds within it limitless creativity — having visualized That, you with perseverence, have let all else go.

However you relinquished even the *hiraṇyagarbha* status, which is the culmination of all desires in all the worlds, the end benefits of all *upāsanā*s, lasting for a long time and being praised and sought by everyone, filled with all the wealth and prosperity. Such a status also you refused knowing it as not significant and that its ultimate nature is not permanent. Due to your intense yearning you felt *vairāgya* (lack of desire) in the entire universe, which is the creation of Brahmā and termed as *brahmaloka*. You are an extremely strong person.

तं दुर्दर्शं गूढमनुप्रविष्टं गुहाहितं गह्वरेष्ठं पुराणम् ।
अध्यात्मयोगाधिगमेन देवं मत्वा धीरो हर्षशोकौ जहाति ॥१२॥

*taṁ durdarśaṁ gūḍhamanupraviṣṭaṁ guhāhitaṁ*
*gahvareṣṭhaṁ purāṇam* ।
*adhyātmayogādhigamena devaṁ matvā dhīro*
*harṣaśokau jahāti* ।।12।।

He who is hidden behind the curtain of *yoga-māyā*, who is all permeating, who is situated in the cave of the heart of all beings, who lives in the forest of the world, who is ancient; such deity who is difficult to perceive; knowing Him through the *adhyātma-yoga*, the wise *sādhaka* renounces pleasure and sorrow both.

Naciketā! though this world is full of Supreme *Brahman* and He is found in every particle, still the world is like a dense inaccessible forest as He is hidden behind the curtain of *māyā*. Thus, though He is present and living with everyone, people do not perceive Him easily. His vision is extremely difficult. However the *sādhaka* having pure intellect and who always uses his mind and intellect in meditating upon Him attains Him. He then comes out of the twin emotions of sorrow and pleasure and obtains eternal bliss.

**Śravaṇa 2 –**

एतच्छ्रुत्वा सम्परिगृह्य मर्त्यः प्रवृह्य धर्म्यमणुमेतमाप्य।
स मोदते मोदनीयꣳ हि लब्ध्वा विवृतꣳ सद्म नचिकेतसं मन्ये ॥१३॥

*etat śrutvā samparigṛhya martyaḥ pravṛhya dharmyamaṇumetamāpya* |
*sa modate modanīyaṁ hi labdhvā vivṛtaṁ sadma naciketasaṁ manye* ||13||

Having heard this and comprehending this, extracting the all-sustaining essence and attaining its subtle secret, man, the mortal, rejoices on attaining what really makes him happy. That mansion, I feel, is now wide open to Naciketā.

After hearing this from an experienced person with extreme faith, one should ponder over the subject, understand and hold the understanding close to heart. By practising this way he comes to realize the Self, i.e. knows the Self in reality. Then he attains the Supreme *Brahman* — the bliss incarnate. Naciketā, the doors of the Supreme abode are open for you. None can stop you from going there.

**Naciketā –**

अन्यत्र धर्मादन्यत्राधर्मादन्यत्रास्मात् कृताकृतात्।
अन्यत्र भूताच्च भव्याच्च यत्तत् पश्यसि तद्वद ॥१४॥

*anyatra dharmādanyatrādharmādanyatrāsmāt kṛtākṛtāt* |
*anyatra bhūtācca bhavyācca yattat paśyasi tadvada* ||14||

Please tell me that, which you consider different from and beyond *dharma* and *adharma* both; different from the whole

> of the world in the form of cause and effect both; different from the past, present and future and the objects concerned with them as you see.

Svāmī! Dharmarāja! "That, which is beyond cause and effect, that which is beyond time, that which is beyond goodness and evil, that which is beyond what is created and also beyond things yet to be created," you must tell me about that *Brahman* and bless me.

**Yamarāja** –

> सर्वे वेदा यत् पदमामनन्ति तपांऽसि सर्वाणि च यद्वदन्ति।
> यदिच्छन्तो ब्रह्मचर्यं चरन्ति तत्ते पदऽ संग्रहेण ब्रवीमि ओमित्येतत्॥१५॥

> *sarve vedā yat padamāmananti tapāṁsi sarvāṇi ca yadvadanti* |
> *yadicchanto brahmacaryaṁ caranti tat te padaṁ saṅgraheṇa bravīmi omityetat* ||15||

> The supreme abode which all the Vedas describe again and again; the supreme state which is aimed at by all penances; desiring which, people adopt and practise celibacy I will speak to you about that in brief; It is *oṁ*.

I will tell you in short about that which all the Vedas praise, which all penances seek, seeking which men follow *brahmacharya* penance. That is called the word *oṁ*.

**(Śravaṇas are singing)**

> *oṁ, oṁ, oṁ, oṁ, oṁ* || *oṁ sat oṁ* || *oṁ cit oṁ* || *oṁ ānanda oṁ* || *oṁ oṁ bhaje oṁ oṁ.*

**Yamarāja** –

> एतद्ध्येवाक्षरं ब्रह्म एतदेवाक्षरं परम्।
> एतद्ध्येवाक्षरं ज्ञात्वा यो यदिच्छति तस्य तत् ॥१६॥

> *etaddhyevākṣaraṁ brahma etadevākṣaraṁ param* |
> *etaddhyevākṣaraṁ jñātvā yo yadicchati tasya tat* ||16||

This imperishable syllable is *Brahman*; The imperishable syllable is the Transcendental; Knowing this imperishable syllable, whatever one desires will indeed be his.

The word *akṣara*, as is used here signifies both syllable *oṁ* as well as the imperishable reality signified by it. Knowing this if a *sādhaka* meditates on this, he realizes his own substance. Finding this identity with the Real, one discovers the will and desire of the Real, the will and desire of nature, and one's own will and desire are the same.

एतदालम्बनꣳ श्रेष्ठमेतदालम्बनं परम्।
एतदालम्बनं ज्ञात्वा ब्रह्मलोके महीयते ॥१७॥

*etadālambanaṁ̐ śreṣṭhametadālambanaṁ param* ।
*etadālambanaṁ jñātvā brahmaloke mahīyate* ।।17।।

It is the best support of all; it is the ultimate centre of all; by knowing it one gets glorified in the Supreme Abode of *Brahman*.

This *oṁkāra* is the best among all means to realize Supreme *Brahman*. Knowing this secret if one faithfully depends on this, he undoubtedly gains the glorious position of God-realization.

न जायते म्रियते वा विपश्चिन्नायं कुतश्चिन्न बभूव कश्चित्।
अजो नित्यः शाश्वतोऽयं पुराणो न हन्यते हन्यमाने शरीरे ॥१८॥

*na jāyate mriyate vā vipaścinnāyaṁ kutaścinna babhūva kaścit* ।
*ajo nityaḥ śāśvato 'yaṁ purāṇo na hanyate hanyamāne śarīre* ।।18।।

The all-knowing one (the Self) is never born nor does it die. Not originating from anywhere, nothing originates from it. Unborn, everlasting, eternal, the most ancient, it is not destroyed on the destruction of the body.

This *ātmā* is neither born nor does it die. This *ātmā* does not become anything else apart from its true Self. *Ātma* is without birth, has no destruction, it does not decrease or get consumed. It is ancient and was there before all things known. When the body gets annihilated, the *ātmā* remains undestroyed and constant like the sky, and like the sky it is present everywhere.

**Naciketā** – If the *ātmā* is like the sky filled everywhere and has no coming or going then how does it leave one body and enter another body.

**Yamarāja** –

हन्ता चेन्मन्यते हन्तुꣳ हतश्चेन्मन्यते हतम्।
उभौ तौ न विजानीतो नायꣳ हन्ति न हन्यते॥१९॥

*hantā cenmanyate hantuṁ hataścenmanyate hatam* |
*ubhau tau na vijānīto nāyaṁ hanti na hanyate* ||19||

If somebody regards himself as capable of killing; if the killed regards himself to have been killed; both of them do not know the *ātmā* in reality; This *ātmā* neither kills nor is killed.

Truly *ātmā* does not leave one body and enter some other body. The sun does not rise and set yet we feel as if the sun rises and sets everyday; in the same way this *ātmā*, which does not have birth and death, due to its connection with *prakṛti*, appears as if it leaves a body and enters some other body. Considering the body as *ātmā*, people think that *ātmā* is the murderer or *ātmā* was killed. However *ātmā* is never killed, nor does it kill any one.

**Naciketā** – O Parama Guru! you must tell me about *ātmasvarūpa* in greater detail.

**Yamarāja** –

अणोरणीयान्महतो महीयानात्मास्य जन्तोर्निहितो गुहायाम्।
तमक्रतुः पश्यति वीतशोको धातुः प्रसादान्महिमानमात्मनः॥२०॥

*aṇoraṇīyān mahato mahīyānātmāsya jantornihito guhāyām* |

*tamakratuḥ paśyati vītaśoko dhātuḥ*
*prasādānmahimānamātmanaḥ* ||20||

Minuter than the minutest, greater than the greatest, the Self (*ātman*) abides hidden in all beings. One without active will, freed from sorrow, beholds the glory of the Self, by the grace of the all-sustaining One.

The *ātmā* is difficult to see. It penetrates in all things but unseen it is stabilized in the core of the intellect, it is spread all over the body. It is an ancient divine light. This *ātmā* is the atom to the atom itself. It is larger than the largest thing. It stabilizes in the mind of living things. A person who is not captivated by desires is able to see it. At that time he gets rid of sorrow and has a clear vision of the inner Self. He then comes to know the greatness of the *ātmā*.

Here, the *jīvātmā* is referred to as *jantu* — a creature or being. Even though in human guise, human beings are wasting the precious human life like the low-born creatures such as insects and moths. One has to strive to realize this ultimate truth. It can be realized only by *adhyātma yoga* (अद्यात्म योग). A person realizing it as such is not affected by happiness or sorrow.

**Śravaṇa 1** – Child, Naciketā, to turn the mind from external matters and concentrate it inside into the *ātmā* is *adhyātma yoga*. After following the *ātmā*'s true *svarūpa* within oneself, both sorrow and happiness will become nullified. For the Supreme thing, what is goodness and what is evil? Though *ātmā* is present in us our desires and affections do not affect it. To see and realize such an *ātmā* is attaining *mokṣa*.

**Yamarāja** –

आसीनो दूरं व्रजति शयानो याति सर्वतः।
कस्तं मदामदं देवं मदन्यो ज्ञातुमर्हति ॥२१॥

*āsīno dūraṁ vrajati śayāno yāti sarvataḥ* |
*kastaṁ madāmadaṁ devaṁ madanyo*
*jñātumarhati* ||21||

He (the *paramātmā*) while sitting, travels far; while sleeping, reaches everywhere; who but me can know that Supreme Deity who is never intoxicaed by his sovereign power.

He is present always everywhere and in every form with all His glory. Even though He is the Supreme ruler yet He does not feel any pride because of His sovereign power.

अशरीरꣳ शरीरेष्वनवस्थेष्ववस्थितम्।
महान्तं विभुमात्मानं मत्वा धीरो न शोचति ॥२२॥

*aśarīraṁ śarīreṣvanavastheṣvavasthitam* |
*mahāntaṁ vibhumātmānaṁ matvā dhīro na śocati* ||22||

The wise person does not grieve, (as he) knows (that) the all-prevading, the greatest Supreme Self is present, without body, among the perishable bodies.

Knowing this from our *ācārya* (teacher) and realizing it, as one's own *svarūpa* and understanding this subtle *ātmā* by one's wisdom as different from the body, one becomes blissful. I think for Naciketā the gates of *mokṣa* are open.

**Naciketā** – Dharmarāja, after listening to what you have been telling me, I realize this *ātmā* is very much different from the body. Till now I was thinking that the *ātmā* and the body are one and I was immersed in ignorance. Because of you my doubts have been cleared. Further kindly tell me the things I should know.

**Yamarāja** –

नायमात्मा प्रवचनेन लभ्यो न मेधया न बहुना श्रुतेन।
यमेवैष वृणुते तेन लभ्यस्तस्यैष आत्मा विवृणुते तनूꣳ स्वाम् ॥ २३॥

*nāyamātmā pravacanena labhyo na medhayā na bahunā śrutena* |
*yamevaiṣa vṛṇute tena labhyastasyaiṣa ātmā vivṛṇute tanūṁ svām* ||23||

This Self is not obtained through discourses; nor through

intellect; nor through hearing scriptures. It is attainable to one it chooses; to such a person it reveals itself wholly. This *ātmā* however cannot be reached by learning Vedas or by collecting lot of knowledge.

**Naciketā** – Then how does one know the *ātmā*, which cannot be understood by constant studies or wide scholarship?

**Yamarāja** – Without allowing the mind to run after anything else if a *sādhaka* dwells with one-minded concentration on the *ātmā* he will be able to reach it. That is, when the *sādhaka*, to know *ātmā*, surrenders himself to the *ātmā*, the *ātmā* itself will show its true *svarūpa* to him.

**Naciketā** – Svāmī, is there any code of conduct to be followed in this?

**Yamarāja** –

नाविरतो दुश्चरितान्नाशान्तो नासमाहितः।
नाशान्तमानसो वापि प्रज्ञानेनैनमाप्नुयात् ॥२४॥

*nāvirato duścaritānnāśānto nāsamāhitaḥ* |
*nāśāntamānaso vāpi prajñānenainamāpnuyāt* ||24||

He who has not abandoned evil conduct, he who is not calm, nor he whose senses and mind are unbridled, nor he, whose mind is not peaceful, cannot perceive *ātmā*, Him even though having subtle intellect.

A person who has not left doing sinful deeds or evil ways of living, a person who has not attained peace to concentrate his mind in one direction, cannot know the *ātmā*. They are not the deserving persons to know *ātmā*.

**Naciketā** – *Guru*, in knowing the *ātmā* knowledge, is there any caste differentiation?

**Yamarāja** –

यस्य ब्रह्म च क्षत्रं च उभे भवत ओदनः।
मृत्युर्यस्योपसेचनं क इत्था वेद यत्र सः ॥२५॥

*yasya brahma ca kṣatraṁ ca ubhe bhavata odanaḥ* |
*mr̥tyuryasyopasecanaṁ ka itthā veda yatra saḥ* ||25||

Brāhmaṇas and kṣatriyas, i.e. all beings are staple food for it, and death its sauce. What and how great is Lord; who knows this in reality?

Child, it is brāhmaṇas and kṣatriyas who nurture and follow the *dharma* and protect the world. Though they are mentioned in particular, *Brahman* does not distinguish between people as this entire world becomes the food for it. The all-consuming death is also a process of consuming creation. Who is capable of knowing Him, who knows all? Therefore on whom the Lord bestows His favour only he can know Him.

**Śravaṇa 2** – Very correct. If life is *annam* (offering) the death which happens in between, is like a sauce (also an offering).

**Yamarāja** – Naciketā! Listen carefully; this *ātmā* when sitting near goes very far. Lying here it can still run a long distance. It is full of happiness and also bereft of happiness.

**Naciketā** – What is this? What you are saying is very mysterious. Please elaborate.

**Yamarāja** – Though this *ātmā* is motionless due to *upādhi* (disturbances in it) it can move very far. Even if it is in one place it can reach all directions. It is filled with happiness and unhappiness. Such an *ātmā* can be known only by ones who have understanding of subtle knowledge, who are having *sūkṣma* intellect. To control the senses alone is called lying still in one place. All the names and forms, which we see around us is *ātmā* only. As *ātmā* gets *upādhi* (disturbances) in it, it develops different *lakṣaṇa*s (characteristics) from which arise different forms having different nature and character.

**Naciketā** – Svāmī! You must kindly tell me about the *oṁkāra* a little more in detail.

**Yamarāja** – Child! For *ātmā*, *pratīka* is *oṁkāra*. *Akṣara* is *Parabrahman*. That only is *aparabrahman*. Doing *upāsanā* of this *akṣara*, a person desirous of reaching *parā* or *aparā-vidyā* can reach it. This is the exalted *ālāpana* for *Brahman prāpti*. A person gets welcomed and is thought of highly in *Brahmaloka* if he considers the *oṁkāra* as *ālāpana*. I shall tell you in brief what I have said so far. Listen.

O Naciketā! it's not that at one time myself, you, these Śravaṇas were not there and now only we are present, and when this life and our actions are over we will be destroyed. This *ātmā* within us, which constitutes our life, is not born nor does it die. It is not that it was not there and it was born, and also not that it was present and later it died. This surprising *ātmā* is not born, does not die, does not decrease and does not grow. Even when the body dies *ātmā* is not destroyed. It is not possible to reach *ātmā* by our trials or by the power of our brain. A person who surrenders to the *ātmā* he alone will come to know it. It is motionless, it is spread everywhere equally. When the body enjoys, it appears as if it also enjoys together. However it stays in the status of witness and hence it actually does not participate in the happiness and the sorrow. *Oṁkāra* is the one which stands for it. Think over clearly whatever has been taught today. Other matters I shall tell you in the next conversation.

(Naciketā gets up and salutes. **All are singing together.**)

***(Curtain falls)***

## SCENE 3

(It is the capital of Lord Yamarāja. Close to the palace in a vast garden on one side are many *maṇḍapa*s for gatherings (*sabhā maṇḍapa*s). In the middle at the centre of a pool is a *vasanta maṇḍapa*. Everywhere pleasant music is heard. The divine smell of sweet smelling *pārijāta* flowers is spread everywhere. In the *vasanta maṇḍapa* there is a huge throne. Near that Śravaṇas and Chitragupta are sitting in their respective seats. Pāśahasta is standing outside with the spear and guarding the *vasanta maṇḍapa*. A Śravaṇa and Naciketā enter the scene.)

**Śravaṇa 1** – Child Naciketā, do you like life in this city?

**Naciketā** – Respected elder! I like it very much. However the things happening here are strange and a wonder to my eyes.

**Śravaṇa 1** – Dear one! Do you remember your father and mother who are in *bhūloka?*

**Naciketā** – Initially for some days, their thoughts were coming often and because of that my mind was getting disturbed and I was feeling sad about parting with them. However after Dharmarāja started his teachings those thoughts have subsided. But . . .

**Śravaṇa 1** – But what? Why did you stop? Now what is troubling your mind?

**Naciketā** – Svāmī, today when I came to the *rājasabhā* hearing the punishments awarded to the sinners, it made my mind feel very sad.

**Śravaṇa 1** – Seeing someone in trouble and hearing about them it is but natural to feel compassion. That day itself I saw your eyes filled with tears. I also at times, like you, feel very unhappy. However, what can we do? Seeing the circumstances and keeping in mind the duties the mind has to be made stubborn and whatever has to be done has to be done.

**Naciketā** – Respected Sir, those sinners have to be somehow relieved from hell and its punishments. This thought is rising in my mind again and again. You only have to tell me a way out.

**Śravaṇa 1** – Child! You are not realizing what you are saying and are not understanding what to ask? You are asking whatever is coming to your mind. Here everything is happening as per God's will. We cannot change the rules and regulations. Nobody can change it. (**Seeing here and there**) Why! Even Yamarāja is bound by rules and regulations.

**Naciketā** – Svāmī, I know Yamarāja will never agree to this.

Still I have taken a *saṁkalpa* (decision) in my mind to save the sinners. Hence you must kindly show me grace and a way out. If the mind wills, a way will be found.

**Śravaṇa 1** – That is not a thing which can happen. Leave that thought. Here the rule of God is taking place. Against nature's law, the one who crosses its rules and regulations will have to suffer the punishments for it. Unlike *bhūloka* here the rule is not by human beings who can change the law as they desire. Here everyone has the same rule. There is no difference from person to person.

**Naciketā** – Svāmī! please do not give me any excuses. Somehow you should show me a way. Otherwise I wont leave your feet. (Falls down and prostrates in front of the Śravaṇa, begging for a way out. Śravaṇa picks him up and embraces him.)

**Śravaṇa 1** – (**thinking deeply**) Child, get up, I will find a way out.

**Naciketā** – Oh! Is that so? Do tell me about it quickly.

**Śravaṇa 1** – Naciketā, this should be a secret. My name should not come out by any chance.

**Naciketā** – Svāmī! Do bless me soon. I will keep it a secret.

**Śravaṇa 1** – (**calling him near, whispers in his ears**) Today as soon as the preaching of Dharmarāja is over, you should ask him like this.

**Naciketā** – (**A bit doubtful**) Will the king agree? Even if he agrees, will our work be done?

**Śravaṇa 1** – Child, you should not have doubts. The king will agree. Then see what happens. Definitely you will achieve victory.

**Naciketā** – (**very happily**) I will never forget the help you have given me. I give you many thousand thanks, Svāmī (**gives his *praṇāmas***).

**Pāśahasta** – (**within himself**) This nitwit, why does he fall at the Śravaṇa's feet from time to time? It is all fraught with fraud. If only he comes to my hand alone, I will teach him a lesson. Hmm . . . (**In anger bites his teeth**)

**Śravaṇa 1** – Dear Naciketā! Today, Lord Yamarāja is going to preach in this *vasanta maṇḍapa* only. Let us go.

**Naciketā** – Yes I was told. I am going there only. I seemed to have achieved what I was seeking. It is indeed my fortune.

(Both enter the *vasanta maṇḍapa* and are sitting on their seats. Pāśahasta is staring at them with objections.)

**Pāśahasta** – (**within himself**) This insignificant human insect is given such an honour! It is like giving bath to a dog and making him ascend the throne. Look at the status this low creature has attained! It is very unfortunate. A time will come when he will be shown his place. (**The bell sound of a chariot is being heard then**) O! It's a good omen. The bell sound is heard, which says that my thoughts are correct. This boy will definitely get caught in my hands once. Then he will be finished off. Well this is the bell sound of our master's chariot.

(They are hailing *jaya vijaya bhava*, in a chariot drawn by five horses Dharmarāja is coming. The charioteer skilfully pulls the reins and stops the chariot. Though they are swift horses they listen obediently to the charioteer. Chitragupta comes running and holds Yamarāja's hand for getting down, Yamarāja gets down. The charioteer parks the chariot to one side. Dharmarāja enters *vasanta maṇḍapa* and sits on the throne. After he sits all give their *praṇāma*s to him and sit on their respective seats. Pāśahasta is fanning him with the white *chāmara*.)

**Yamarāja** – Child Naciketā, did you think about the matters told till now? Have you any doubts? Do ask without any reservations.

**Naciketā** – Parama Guru, my *praṇāma*s. I did think and contemplated on it well. I seem to have understood everything, at the same time it appears like I have not understood anything. If you can explain a little more with examples it may become easier.

**Yamarāja** – So be it child. To make you understand, I have come in the chariot. I will explain with examples. Listen.

**Naciketā** – Svāmī, I will listen very carefully.

**Yamarāja** –

ऋतं पिबन्तौ सुकृतस्य लोके गुहां प्रविष्टौ परमे परार्द्धे।
छायातपौ ब्रह्मविदो वदन्ति पञ्चाग्नयो ये च त्रिणाचिकेताः ॥१॥

*ṛtaṁ pibantau sukṛtasya loke guhāṁ praviṣṭau parame parārdhe* |
*chāyātapau brahmavido vadanti pañcāgnayo ye ca triṇāciketāḥ* ||1||

In the human body as the result of good deeds, two enjoyers are there, hidden in the cave of intellect, drinking the truth, different from each other like sun and shade, the knowers of *Brahman* say, and so do householders who maintain the five sacrificial fires, and those too who perform the triple Naciketā fire.

In this world (in each body), there are two who are staying and experiencing the results of the *karma*s done. They both stabilize in the sky of the heart inside the cave of the intellect. They are compared to the sun and the shadow by the *brahma-jñānī*s, the *upāsaka*s of *pañcāgni*, the *gṛhastha*s (householders) and the strong ones who have done *upāsanā* of Naciketā *agni* three times everyday.

यः सेतुरीजानानामक्षरं ब्रह्म यत्परम्।
अभयं तितीर्षतां पारं नाचिकेतꣳ शकेमहि ॥२॥

*yaḥ seturījānānāmakṣaraṁ brahma yatparam* |
*abhayaṁ titīrṣatāṁ pāraṁ nāciketaṁ̐ śakemahi* ||2||

Which is a bridge for sacrifices to cross the ocean of misery, for those desirous of crossing over to the fearless farther

> shore and reach the imperishable Supreme *Brahman*, it is that Naciketā *agni.* May we possess the capability to attain Him.

O Naciketā! the sure way to reach the Supreme abode is to pray to the Lord to bestow the potency to know Him. The best and easiest means of knowing and attaining God is only to pray to Him.

**Śravaṇa 1** – Mahārāja! of the two it is the *jīva* alone which experiences the *karma* result, the other one, *Īśvara* does not experience *kārmika* results, isn't it? That being so, is it correct to say that both are experiencing it?

**Yamarāja** – I told you as per "umbrella dictum."

**Naciketā** – What is "umbrella dictum"?

**Śravaṇa 2** – In a crowd, if some hold umbrellas and some don't hold umbrellas, still talking about the crowd we say that here is a group of people who are holding umbrellas and going. This general statement is called "umbrella dictum."

**Yamarāja** – As *jīvātmā* experiences the results *Īśvara* (*paramātmā*) stands as a witness. It is often told, *paramātmā* and *jīvātmā* are like light and shadow. Factually, it is not as if light and shadow are different. The light is brightness; the thing, which diminished the light, is called the shadow. The obstruction to the light produces shadow. The light (*paramātmā*) has no form, the shadow has a form — *jīvātmā* has a body. As soon as the obstruction gets removed, the light and shadow become one. This is in brief the concept of the *Brahman* and the *jīva*.

**Naciketā** – Respected Sir! By your preaching I become blessed. I would like to know its details further.

**Yamarāja** –

> आत्मानꣳ रथिनं विद्धि शरीरꣳ रथमेव तु ।
> बुद्धिं तु सारथिं विद्धि मनः प्रग्रहमेव च ॥३॥

*ātmānaṁ rathinaṁ viddhi śarīraṁ rathameva tu* |

*buddhiṁ tu sārathiṁ viddhi manaḥ pragrahameva ca* ||3||

Know the *jīvātmā* as rider; and this body as chariot; intellect as charioteer and mind as rein.

This *jīvātmā* is the master sitting in the chariot, the body is the chariot, the intellect is the charioteer, the mind is the rein, and the sense organs are the horses.

**Śravaṇa 1** – What a wonderful comparison! Naciketā, look at the chariot parked here. (Naciketā looks at the chariot with wonder. Yamarāja continues.)

**Yamarāja** –

इन्द्रियाणि हयानाहुर्विषयाꣳस्तेषु गोचरान्।
आत्मेन्द्रियमनोयुक्तं भोक्तेत्याहुर्मनीषिणः ॥४॥

*indriyāṇi hayānāhurviṣayām̐steṣu gocarān* |
*ātmendriyamanoyuktaṁ bhoktetyāhurmanīṣiṇaḥ* ||4||

Senses are said to be the horses, and sense-objects, what they range over. The Self, united with senses and mind, wise men say, is the enjoyer.

The body is the chariot. The sense organs (five senses) are the five horses tied to that. The path along which the sense organs take us is the way along which the chariot moves. The mind holds the reins, which controls the sense organs. The intellect is the charioteer.

**Naciketā** – Svāmī, the example you told is very apt. How to control these senses and how can our aim be reached? What do we have to do for that? Kindly explain in detail.

**Yamarāja** –

यस्त्वविज्ञानवान् भवत्ययुक्तेन मनसा सदा।
तस्येन्द्रियाण्यवश्यानि दुष्टाश्वा इव सारथेः ॥५॥

*yastvavijñānavān bhavatyayuktena manasā sadā* |
*tasyendriyāṇyavaśyāni duṣṭāśvā iva sāratheḥ* ||5||

He who is always without discriminating fault, whose mind is uncontrolled, his sense organs are never in his control like the wicked horses under a careless charioteer.

यस्तु विज्ञानवान् भवति युक्तेन मनसा सदा।
तस्येन्द्रियाणि वश्यानि सदश्वा इव सारथेः ॥ ६ ॥

*yastu vijñānavān bhavati yuktena manasā sadā* |
*tasyendriyāṇi vaśyāni sadaśvā iva sāratheḥ* ||6||

He who is always with discriminating intellect, controlled mind, his senses are fully controlled, like disciplined horses under a skilled charioteer.

यस्त्वविज्ञानवान् भवत्यमनस्कः सदाशुचिः।
न स तत्पदमाप्नोति संसारं चाधिगच्छति ॥७॥

*yastvavijñānavān bhavatyamanaskaḥ sadāśuciḥ* |
*na sa tatpadamāpnoti saṁsāraṁ cādhigacchati* ||7||

Whose intellect is indiscriminate, whose mind is uncontrolled, who is impure, he does not attain to that supreme place. On the contrary he always wanders in the worldly circle of birth and death.

यस्तु विज्ञानवान् भवति समनस्कः सदा शुचिः।
स तु तत्पदमाप्नोति यस्माद्भूयो न जायते ॥८॥

*yastu vijñānavān bhavati samanaskaḥ sadā śuciḥ* |
*sa tu tatpadamāpnoti yasmādbhūyo na jāyate* ||8||

He who possesses discriminating intellect, has a restrained mind, pure, attains to the supreme abode, from where he does not have to take birth again.

The *jīva* having the body, mind and sense organs is called *bhoktā* (experiencer) by the *vivekīs* (wise ones). For a person who does not control the mind and whose intellect is not wise, the sense organs, like the untamed horses under the control of the unwise charioteer, won't be under control. Hence, if a person makes a wise intellect as his charioteer and a controlled mind as his reins and drives the chariot in the difficult path of *saṁsāra* and leads his life as such, he will reach the end he seeks. That is, he can become one with the supreme thing which is present everywhere and thus reaches the status of *paramapadam*. As just I started from the palace and reached this *vasanta maṇḍapam*, in the same way easily speedily and without any difficulty he will reach *Vaiṣṇava padam*. Hence like the intelligent charioteer you must learn to drive the chariot using the reins and controlling the horses. If the horses are not kept under the reins, they can run amuck taking the charioteer with them and can even dump him in a ditch. He, along with the chariot, can fall deep down and won't be able to reach his destination. Not only that, he may end up accumulating unnecessary bad *karma*s. Hence child! You must learn to drive the chariot properly. This is only my important preaching.

| | |
|---|---|
| Body | — chariot |
| intellect | — charioteer |
| Mind | — Rein |
| Sense Organ | — horses |

*fig* : **Jīvātmā in the chariot**

**Naciketā** – What is meant by Vaiṣṇava *padam*?

**Yamarāja** –

विज्ञानसारथिर्यस्तु मनः प्रग्रहवान्नरः ।
सोऽध्वनः पारमाप्नोति तद्विष्णोः परमं पदम् ॥९॥

*vijñānasārathiryastu manaḥ pragrahavānnaraḥ* |
*so 'dhvanaḥ pāramāpnoti tadviṣṇoḥ paramaṁ padam* ||9||

He who has the discriminating intellect as his charioteer; a restrained mind to hold reins; reaches the other end of the world; and the supreme abode of Lord Viṣṇu.

A wise charioteer with a determined mind of pure *chitta*, driving the chariot (leads his life) crosses the *saṁsāra sāgara* and reaches *paramātmā*. He is released of all *saṁsāra* (worldly) bondages and reaches the most exalted and all encompassing Vaiṣṇava *padam* (all are Vāsudeva's *chaitanya*). However, a foolish charioteer goes as his mind works, becomes unholy, ignorant and instead of reaching *parama padam* remains in the ocean of birth and death.

**Naciketā** – What are the subtle equations for the gross sense organs? Kindly bless me with that knowledge, *parama guru*.

**Yamarāja** –

इन्द्रियेभ्यः परा ह्यर्था अर्थेभ्यश्च परं मनः ।
मनसस्तु परा बुद्धिर्बुद्धेरात्मा महान् परः ॥१०॥

*indriyebhyaḥ parā hyarthā arthebhyaśca paraṁ manaḥ* |
*manasastu parā buddhirbuddherātmā mahān paraḥ* ||10||

The sense-objects are stronger than the senses; mind is stronger than the sense-objects; intellect is still stronger than even the mind; the *ātmā* is greater and stronger even than the intellect.

महतः परमव्यक्तमव्यक्तात् पुरुषः परः ।
पुरुषान्न परं किंचित्सा काष्ठा सा परा गतिः ॥११॥

*mahataḥ paramavyaktamavyaktāt puruṣaḥ paraḥ* |
*puruṣānna paraṁ kiñcitsā kāṣṭhā sā parā gatiḥ* ||11||

The unmanifested deluding power of the Lord is stronger than *jīvātmā*; the *puruṣa*, the Supreme person is stronger than unmanifested *māyā*. Beyond *puruṣa* nothing is there. That is the destination; that is the final refuge.

Child, higher than the sense organs are the cause of it, the subtle meaning behind it, higher than those subtle things is the mind. Above that is the intellect. Above the intellect is its *samaśṇi*, the concept of *hiraṇyagarbha* (creator of all things). Above *hiraṇyagarbha* is the basic concept (*mūla prakṛti*). Above the *mūla prakṛti* is the *parama puruṣa*. Since he is filled everywhere, he is called *puruṣa*. There is no more subtle representation of *ātmā* apart from this. All these though present in the sense organs to certain extent the one which has reached its complete limit is the *puruṣa*. Reaching Him, is the highest state. After going there one does not have to return.

**Śravaṇa 2** – From where people once go don't return, about which the sun, moon and fire cannot explain, that only is *parama padam*.

**Naciketā** – *Parama guru*! The sense organs are at a higher order than the body, higher to that is the mind and then intellect. Above all that is *ātmā*. This I have understood well. However there is another doubt cropping up. If in the world a person goes to a new place, we find him returning from there. In the same way when a person reaches Vaiṣṇava *padam* from here later he has to come back, isn't it? How is it possible that he won't come back?

**Yamarāja** –

एष सर्वेषु भूतेषु गुढोऽत्मा न प्रकाशते।
दृश्यते त्वग्रयया बुद्धया सूक्ष्मया सूक्ष्मदर्शिभिः ॥१२॥

*eṣa sarveṣu bhūteṣu guḍho 'tmā na prakāśate* |
*dṛśyate tvagrayyā buddhyā sūkṣmayā sūkṣmadarśibhiḥ* ||12||

The Supreme person as soul in all beings is hidden in all and does not shine forth. It is not visible to anybody. Only persons having sharpened intellect capable of realizing the subtle principles can see it through very subtle and sharp intellect.

यच्छेद्वाङ्मनसी प्राज्ञस्तद्यच्छेज्ज्ञान आत्मनि।
ज्ञानमात्मनि महति नियच्छेत्तद्यच्छेच्छान्त आत्मनि ॥१३॥

*yacchedvāṅmanasī prajñastad yacchejjñāna ātmani* |
*jñānamātmani mahati niyacchet tad yacchecchānta ātmani* | |13| |

A wise striver should fully hold in his mind all senses like speech, etc. That mind he should merge into the knowledge that is intellect itself. (Again) he sould merge that intellect in the great *ātmā*, and that *ātmā* he should merge into the peaceful Supreme person.

You have asked well, Naciketā. In all lives this *parama puruṣa* is there but hidden. It is not seen outside. However, persons with keen intellect, with one-minded concentration can see this *ātmā* through their subtle senses. Thus, a wise person should control his senses by the mind and the mind has to be controlled by the higher intellect. The intellect should be kept in check by wisdom, and all that has to be surrendered to the *paramātmā* or *parama puruṣa*. Then the screen of ignorance will open up and he realizes himself as *paramātmā svarūpa*. To bring these to an understandable level, one is said to reach *paramātmā*. Apart from that, there is nothing like going and coming, my dear son. You must try as I have directed. You will then realize the *ātmā*.

**Naciketā** – Svāmī, as you explain more and more, it appears difficult. It does not seem easy to get *ātma-jñāna*.

**Śravaṇa 1** – Young one, yes! What you are saying is correct. The chariot runs because the wheel moves. However, if the chariot tries to drive the wheel? It will appear an impossible proposition. Likewise, we are trying to understand *ātmā* by our brain. It is a very complicated path, my dear.

**Yamarāja** –

उत्तिष्ठत जाग्रत प्राप्य वरान् निबोधत ।
क्षुरस्य धारा निशिता दुरत्यया दुर्गं पथस्तत् कवयो वदन्ति ॥१४॥

*uttiṣṭhata jāgrata prāpya varān nibodhata* |
*kṣurasya dhārā niśitā duratyayā durgaṁ pathastat kavayo vadanti* ||14||

Get up; wake up (be vigilant); approaching the best of masters, do get enlightened. Difficult to cross and hard to tread, like a razor's sharpened edge, is that path: so the wise proclaim.

O Human Beings! who are immersed in *avidyā*, get up, open your eyes, reach good teachers and get *jñāna* of *ātmā*. The path may be sharp like the edge of a knife. It may be a difficult path to walk and cross. So say the *jñānī*s (learned ones).

**Śravaṇa 2** – Vedamātā is waking us with great compassion like a mother with great love waking up her child, she calls out why this deep sleep, do get up?

**Śravaṇa 1** – Get up from the sleep of *moha* (desire), don't sleep, the sun of knowledge has risen. The sun is telling *suprabhātam* (good morning) to everyone.

**Yamarāja** – Child Naciketā, it is not easy to get up from the sorrow created by *saṁsāra* (worldly illusion), for that, there should be great determination. Just as a person walking on the edge of a knife is very careful — even if he wavers a little he can get hurt badly — with the same carefulness one should control the mind and senses and keep hold on good conduct and habits keeping the mind pure. Removing all feelings of differences and reaching a proper exalted *guru* one should obtain wisdom. This should be done persistently without saying it can be done tomorrow. It should not be postponed. Today itself it has to be started. It should be known now itself.

**Naciketā** – Hearing your words of teaching I have become very pure. Just as the crops, which are withering due to lack of rain, again get rejuvenated by rain, in the same way my intellect has also become fertile. Svāmī I will follow your words and live accordingly.

**Yamarāja** –

अशब्दमस्पर्शमरूपमव्ययं तथारसं नित्यमगन्धवच्च यत्।
अनाद्यनन्तं महतः परं ध्रुवं निचाय्य तं मृत्युमुखात् प्रमुच्यते ॥१५॥

*aśabdam asparśam arūpam avyayaṁ tathā 'rasaṁ nityamagandhavacca yat* ।
*anādyanantaṁ mahataḥ paraṁ dhruvaṁ nicāyya taṁ mṛtyumūkhāt pramucyate* ।।15।।

That, which is beyond sound, beyond touch, beyond form, beyond taste, beyond smell, beyond mutation, eternal, beginningless, endless (limitless), beyond and superior to the great *ātmā* even, all truth, knowing that supreme Lord, the striver is released from the jaws of death.

Beyond the *śabda* (sound), *sparśa* (touch), *rūpa* (form), *rasa* (taste), *gandha* (smell), what stays changeless without any beginning or end and never loses its state is the *paramātmā*. Knowing that a *mumukṣu* (a person who aspires to get *mokṣa*) escapes from the jaws of death.

**Śravaṇa 2** –

नाचिकेतामुपाख्यानं मृत्युप्रोक्तꣳ सनातनम्।
उक्तवा श्रुत्वा च मेधावी ब्रह्मलोके महीयते ॥१६॥

*nāciketāmupākhyānaṁ mṛtyuproktaṁ sanātanam* ।
*uktvā śrutvā ca medhāvī brahmaloke mahīyate* ।।16।।

By reciting and hearing this eternal tale of Naciketā, narrated by the Lord Yama, the wise person is glorified in *brahmaloka*.

य इमं परमं गुह्यं श्रावयेद्ब्रह्मसंसदि।
प्रयतः श्राद्धकाले वा तदानन्त्याय कल्पते।
तदानन्त्याय कल्पत इति ॥१७॥

*ya imaṁ paramaṁ guhyaṁ śrāvayed brahmasaṁsadi* |
*prayataḥ śrāddhakāle vā tadānantyāya kalpate*
*tadānantyāya kalpata iti* | |17| |

The man who, purified in all respects, narrates this supreme secret in an assembly of *Brahman* seekers, or at the ceremony for the dead, this supreme secret makes for everlastingness.

Any person narrating or hearing this discussion between you and *Mahārājā* will also reach *brahmaloka* and will be held in high regard. Further, if this is read in front of brāhmaṇas who are sitting for food during *śrāddha* (death rites) time that *śrāddha* will fetch good results.

**Naciketā** – Svāmī, kindly summarize the teachings.

**Yamarāja** – Only the strong one who is indifferent about *bhoga*s (enjoyment), which, one gets from senses will be able to get *ātma-darśana*. He should have a blemishless mind. He should be able to control the desires and get out of attachments. Just as how fire is hidden inside a wooden piece, the *ātmā* is hidden in the body. Just as fire possessing brightness and strength is hidden inside the wooden piece, the *ātmā*, which is bright and deathless, is hidden inside the body. The body has to be considered as a chariot. The senses as the horses, which draw the chariot. The experiencing of the things as the path by which the chariot has to move, and the master sitting in the chariot as *ātmā*. If the journey has to go properly the charioteer has to carefully pull the reins, control the horses and has to drive the chariot, or else, the horses, will run amok and fall into the ocean of birth and death and go round in cycles.

Hence without sleeping further, one should get a good teacher and get *ātma-jñāna*. Till the objective is achieved one should not rest. One should try again and again. Though this *jñāna-mārga* is the best, still it is not easy. It is like walking on the edge of a knife. The *ātmā* does not have *śabda, sparśa, rūpa, rasa* and *gandha*. It does not have a beginning or ending. Thus knowing this *ātma-tattva*, one should come out of the noose of death.

**Naciketā** – Gurujī! One request.

**Yamarāja** – Child! What do you want to ask.

**Naciketā** – Svāmī! I am very much eager to see this city. I want to see the high raised buildings, other places and the beautiful gardens. You must give me permission.

**Śravaṇa 1** – **(within himself)** Naciketā is a young boy and he has enthusiasm to see these places. He is asking with humility. I should show him the places.

**Yamarāja** – Is anybody there? **(Pāśahasta comes and bows)** Pāśahasta! Tomorrow morning take him and show him the sights of our place.

**Pāśahasta** – Mahārāja, as your order. Should I take him to hell also?

**Yamarāja** – No need Pāśahasta. Other than hell show all other places in our city.

**Naciketā** – Gurujī! I am keen on seeing hell also. You must kindly give me permission.

**Yamarāja** – Why do you want to see hell? It is not the place where people like you should go. Even in your dreams you need not see those sights.

**Naciketā** – Svāmī! I want to go to hell. Please give me permission.

**Yamarāja** – I don't want to foil your wish. Hey Pāśahasta! Take him and show him the different hells and bring him safely back to the palace.

**Pāśahasta** – Mahārāja! I will do as you order. **(Within himself)** A good opportunity has been obtained. It is the best time to teach him a lesson.

*(All are singing jointly)*

*(Curtain falls)*

***End of Part III.***

## Part IV

### SCENE 1

***(Curtain opens)***

(In *yamaloka* it is the route for going to hell. Both Pāśahasta and Naciketā are conversing and coming.)

**Pāśahasta** – Brāhmaṇa boy, I have shown you almost all the places.

**Naciketā** – Thanks for everything, respected sir. The palaces, cultural centres, the prominent buildings, the armouries, the different orchards, gardens, vehicular roads, smaller lanes, I have seen everything. Are we now nearing hell?

**Pāśahasta** – Now we are going there directly.

**Naciketā** – Messenger of the king! Further do continue to tell me the wonderful places and things found enroute.

**Pāśahasta** – So be it. What we crossed just now was the palace of Chitragupta. In a house to its south, *vicāra* disease and other skin related diseases are staying. The one seen in the north is the palace of stomach-ache. There, in the house found a little on the east side fever and cold are staying. In the house facing west delirium and dizziness are staying.

**Naciketā** – What are the jobs they do? Can I know?

**Pāśahasta** – These diseases are under the orders of Dharmarāja. It attacks the *jīva* and causes their death. When it is time for the end of a *jīva*'s life then these diseases are used as the cause to end his life. That is because Lord Yama won't be the direct one to attack the *jīva* and take his life. Here! We have come close to the entrance of hell.

The scene changes. (**Showing the scene in shadow play**)

(Hell is seen. Around hell are huge walls made of black stones. Yama's soldiers are guarding the gates. There is foul smell emitted everywhere from the ground. Yama's men in hell are punishing the *jīva* in severe manner. They are shouting atrociously, hitting him, beating him, catching him, kicking him, crushing him, etc. The *jīva*s are crying pathetically, "Oh! it is unbearable; It is beyond endurance, it is injustice. Have mercy on us. Please leave us." Śoṇitākṣa is standing at the entrance.)

**Naciketā** – Pāśahasta! Let us go inside. That day a *jīva* cried and asked for mercy in the king's court. Do you know where he is?

**Pāśahasta** – As you wish you can go inside and see. I took so much pains only for that. Let that be so. Do tell me, are you not afraid to see them?

**Naciketā** – I am not scared even one bit. But I feel great compassion seeing the state of the *jīva*s. I am feeling very earnestly to save them. Now let us go. Let us not delay further. (**Pāśahasta is showing hand and calling Śoṇitākṣa near.**)

**Pāśahasta** – (**Talking to Śoṇitākṣa in private**) "He wants to see the *pāpa jīva*s in hell. Take him to the *kumbhika* part of the hell and push him there." Now open the gate.

**Śoṇitākṣa** – Why to invite unnecessary trouble? He is a guest in our palace. If something untoward happens who will take the responsibility?

**Pāśahasta** – You need not be scared of anything. We are acting according to Naciketā's wish. Further the orders of *mahārāja* are that we should show him everything.

**Śoṇitākṣa** – Well, I will do as you say (**looking at Naciketā**), Do come, Respected Sir. Let us go inside. (**They go inside.**)

**Śoṇitākṣa** – Naciketā, this is the *vahnikuṇḍa*. What you see there is *celakṣama kuṇḍa*, this is *dhūmanta kuṇḍa*. Those who have not done their daily disciplines of living are made to stay here for hundred years and made to drink smoke. Here we see *jīva*s who are hung upside down and suffering.

**Pāśahasta** – There, the *kumbhika* part of hell has come. It is a very cruel and treacherous part. Here the prostitutes or those who seek prostitutes are locked and kept. Among the 86 different kinds of cells in hell, here the torture is more. The *jīva* whom you are asking for is somewhere out there. Go and see.

**Naciketā** – Is that so? They are all very surprising to hear as well as looking scary. However, in my mind, more than fear, it is compassion, which is welling up. (**Bends down and looks at the deeply built hell hole**) but the *jīva* he was looking for is not seen.

**Pāśahasta** – This *kumbhika* is very deep. Hence if you try to observe from the outer end, nothing will be visible. Go inside and see. (**He catches Naciketā by his hair and pushes him into the *kumbhika* hell.**)

**Śoṇitākṣa** – Oh! Oh! What have you done? Very atrocious. If a *puṇya jīva* is pushed into hell, I don't know what calamity will befall us. You may have become the cause of instigating *mahārāja*'s anger.

**Pāśahasta** – Keep quiet, "I only did what Naciketā wanted. I helped him to see the *pāpa jīva*, "thus saying, I will escape (**bends down and sees**). Well, he is not seen. Hā! Hā! He was keen to see hell. I suppose the tongue which was repeatedly saying. "I want to see hell, I want to see the hell" must have been gnawed and eaten by scorpions and white ants by now. A good punishment for the human being who talked like this.

**(He claps his hands and laughs with glee.)**

(As soon as Naciketā falls inside, a wonderful thing happens. Even as Yama's men were seeing, to their utter surprise and as the people in hell are gaping, hell itself becomes heaven. Because of the *brahma-jñānī*'s *darśana* all *pāpī*s become holy and pure. As his feet touched hell, a place of sinners becomes a *puṇyaloka*. The *yamadūtas*, *kiṅkaras* including Pāśahasta are running for cover.)

(The scene changes.)

(The sound of trumpets of *devaloka* is heard. The sweet

fragrance of *pārijāta* flowers is spread everywhere. Pleasant, pure music is heard. As *gandharvas* play on the music strings, the Rambhā and other *apsarases* dance around. Lord Devendra, surrounded by *ṛṣis* is going in procession. Flower petals are raining down. The young *deva* lasses come carrying the scented perfumes and lighted lamps and welcome the *jīvas* to receive them in heaven.)

**Devas** – *Puṇyātmās* do come. We welcome you to this heaven world with great pleasure. We have decorated the way with arches and are looking forward eagerly to your arrival.

**Vasus** – Welcome, welcome, with your arrival we have become very happy. (**They are saying words of welcome and sprinkling the fragrant *parijāta* and other scented flowers on them.**)

**Rudras** – Do come this way, this is the route.

**Ādityas** – Welcome, welcome! Let your coming bring good tidings. (**They are hailing them with gusto.**)

(The *munis* are leading in the front. The *kinnaras* are singing songs. Some are blowing conch-shells.)

**Arambaiyar (heavenly nymphs)** – The ones ruling the skies have come. (**They are blessing them.**)

(The Marutas and Vasus are reciting *ślokas*. The *devas* come in the front and welcome them. The Lord Devendra comes and washes their feet in a gesture of welcome. The *saptarṣis* welcome them with *pūrṇa kumbha*. Ladies such as Saśidevī, Urvaśī perform *āratī* and invite the new entrants. All the *jīvas* praise Naciketā and reach *svargaloka*.)

***(The scene changes.)***

***(Only Naciketā is standing.)***

**Naciketā** – What a surprise? I don't understand anything clearly. Is whatever I am seeing, a dream or real?

(Śravaṇas are coming)

**Śravaṇa 1** – Dear Naciketā! You are indeed a great soul. Due to the strength of your *puṇya,* all *the jīva*s went to heaven.

**Dharmadhvaja** – Svāmī! The *mahārāja* also is coming here to bless us with his *darśana.*

**Śravaṇa 2** – Child Naciketā! For some time to come our *kiṅkara*s won't have any work.

**Śravaṇa 1** – Brother! Here also, like in *bhūloka,* will the unemployment problem come up?

**Naciketā** – (Prostrating fully at the feet of the first Śravaṇa) Svāmī! Everything has happened due to your blessing. What you told me was really the best way. It fetched results too. I am full of gratitude to you. Many thanks for making it happen. My *namaskāram*s to you.

(That time Pāśahasta comes with great humility. Fully humbled, he falls at Naciketā's feet.)

**Pāśahasta** – Svāmī! Kindly forgive me for my lapses. My faults are really very bad and punishable. Even in comparison to the grave crime called *pañca aparādha* this *aparādha* (mistake) is of a higher order.

"O Brāhmaṇa! you who have knowledge, good speech, purity, love, good blessings, wisdom, learning, great penance, good conduct, good strength, good morals! I prostrate in front of you. O noble soul, who gives asylum to the needy! Show mercy on me, forgive me and kindly save me."

**Naciketā** – Pāśahasta, get up. Everything happens according to the will of God. We are all but instruments of God. In this play you did your part as ordained. That is all; there is nothing to worry.

**Śravaṇa 1** – Pāśahasta! Initially itself we advised you to leave your hasty ways. You didn't listen. That also was correct in a way. If you were not there, would Naciketā have gone to hell? Could all the sinners have gone to heaven?

**Naciketā at the hell**

**Pāpījīvas are blessed by Naciketā**

**Śravaṇa 2** – But for you, would we have known Naciketā's greatness and his strength? Whatever happens is for the good. There is no doubt about it.

**Naciketā** – We are only dice who are rolled in this game of *prapañca* (universe). Isn't that so?

(Yamarāja is coming along with his entourage. Naciketā does *abhivādaye* and tells his *praṇāmas*. Yamarāja embraces him with great affection.)

**Yamarāja** – Dear child! It is not possible to measure your greatness. Even for the thousand-tongued Ādiśeṣa (snake god) it may not be possible to tell the details of your strength. You are a *brahma-jñānī*. An ardent worshipper of Almighty. An exalted *bhakta*. Everything happened with the lord's great blessings. I am feeling great affection and happiness on seeing you.

**Naciketā** – (**feeling a bit embarrassed**) Gurudeva! It is all due to your blessings.

(As Dharmarāja signals, the Śravaṇas take Naciketā and go.)

(Yamarāja calls his soldiers, messengers and *kiṅkaras* close and whispers something in their ears.)

**Yamarāja** – My dear messengers, O *kiṅkaras* who are always dutiful and earnest in doing their duty, I am telling you an important matter. Listen . . .

**All the soldiers** – As you order Mahārāja! We are listening keenly.

**Yamarāja** – Did you all see the danger which came to our job today? Now you all should be very careful. You should not go in the direction of *bhaktas*, *brahma-jñānīs*, etc.

**Yama's soldiers** – Yes, Svāmī, we will follow your orders. But what is the reason for this?

**Yama** – I am not their Lord at any time. My authority and power will not be of any effect on them, do remember always. The lesson you all learnt today in person, don't forget it.

**Yama's soldiers** – We wont forget Mahārāja! We will never ever forget it.

**Yamarāja** – I am now relieved. My fears are removed. If you commit a mistake it will be a setback for you all and also for me. Why? Our world itself will be endangered due to that. Hence, if you meet *bhaktas* and *brahma-jñānīs*, keep a long distance and move away. My advice is that you follow your jobs very carefully as ordered.

(The soldiers are singing.)

Naciketā! O Naciketā!
You won over hell Naciketā
Knowledger of four Vedas Naciketā
Ahiṁsāmūrti! Naciketā
Pinnacle of love! Naciketā

Nurture of dharma! Naciketā
Destroyer of evil! Naciketā
Brahmajñānī Naciketā
Worshipper of the Lord, Naciketā

*(All are leaving.)*

*(The curtain falls.)*

## SCENE 2

(A spacious *maṇḍapa* in Yamarāja's palace. There is a prominent seat where Yamarāja is sitting. On another side Naciketā is sitting.)

**Yamarāja** – Child Naciketā! I suppose till now whatever has been told you must have thought well, contemplated on it and brought to realization.

**Naciketā** – Gurudeva! I have been listening attentively to your preaching. I have been bringing it to memory. I am kindly requesting you to preach further the important preachings and bless me.

**Yamarāja** – My dear disciple! If you have any doubts you are free to ask me.

**Naciketā** – Svāmī! You told me to see the *ātmā*, which is found in all lives but hidden and which is found everywhere. One has to have a one-pointed mind. But it is difficult to get one-pointed concentration of the mind. What is the thing, which causes obstructions to it?

**Śravaṇa 1** – A good question. Only if one knows the cause of a problem one can try to find the solution for it.

**Yamarāja** –

पराञ्चि खानि व्यतृणत् स्वयम्भूस्तस्मात् पराङ् पश्यति नान्तरात्मन्।
कश्चिद्धीरः प्रत्यगात्मानमैक्षदावृत्तचक्षुरमृतत्वमिच्छन् ॥१॥

*parāñci khāni vyatṛṇat svayambhūstasmāt parāñ*
*paśyati nāntarātman* |

*kaściddhīraḥ pratyagātmānamaikṣadāvṛtta-*
*cakṣuramṛtattvamicchan* | |1| |

> The self-born Lord made the doors of sense organs opening towards outside; therefore the man through his sense organs looks only outer objects and not the inner self; rarely any wise person alone, desirous of immortality, diverts his eyes interiorized, and visualizes the inner self.

Child! I am very happy that you have asked this question. I will explain. Listen carefully. The Lord Parameśvara made the sense organs facing the outer world, hence, man sees constantly the external scenes. Thus, enjoying the outer world through the outgoing senses, he more and more seeks the enjoyment of the outer world. But one strong person among them (one in many thousands) wishing for a deathless state, stops the senses from going outside. By that, he develops a pure one-pointed mind and is able to see the *ātmasvarūpa*, the *pratyagātmā*.

**Śravaṇa 2** – That wise person, like one swimming against the current, with determination turns the senses from going outside and going against their natural tendency. And with consistency, he finally succeeds in his trials.

**Naciketā** – What is the meaning of *pratyagātmā*?

**Yamarāja** – The *ātmā*, which is inside everything and all lives and by its self-effulgence, brightens all matters, is called *pratyagātmā*. A determined person sees this *ātma-svarūpa* of himself by stopping his senses from going outside and trying to direct them inside in one-pointed concentration and as he desires, he reaches the immortal state.

पराचः कामाननुयन्ति बालास्ते मृत्योर्यन्ति विततस्य पाशम्।
अथ धीरा अमृतत्वं विदित्वा ध्रुवमध्रुवेष्विह न प्रार्थयन्ते॥२॥

*parācaḥ kāmānanuyanti bālāste mṛtyoryanti vitatasya*
*pāśam* |

*atha dhīrā amṛtattvaṁ viditvā dhruvamadhruveṣviha*
*na prārthayante* | |2| |

The foolish who are after the outer enjoyments fall into the clutches of eternal death, but the wise ones grasp the immortality by knowing it through their discriminating faculty and shun this world which is unstable.

However, persons with less intellect and having minds seeking small temporary pleasures, seek to get their happiness outside and in doing so fall into the net of death.

**Śravaṇa 1** – Getting pulled by desires they fall in the net laid for them, by the Lord of Death. They get caught and suffer endlessly.

**Yamarāja** – However, the determined and courageous souls, who have one-pointed minds, come to know the real true thing which has no destruction. Having known that they do not fall into the net laid for them. In the world, which is temporary and has no lasting presence they don't consider anything as permanent and they don't seek anything which is not of lasting value.

**Śravaṇa 2** – Yes, they don't have any benefit of even doing *karmas*. If they don't do them also they don't get affected. They don't have to seek anything for their benefit. That is because they have seen and realized the *pratyagātmā*, which is the reality of the world.

**Śravaṇa 1** – Those wise souls leave their desire on the temporary things and remain away from the attraction of children, family, property, etc.

**Naciketā** – Gurudeva! I have learnt the way to get an one-pointed mind. Do tell me more about the route to reach *pratyagātmā*.

**Yamarāja** –

येन रूपं रसं गन्धं शब्दान् स्पर्श्रांश्च मैथुनान्।
एतेनैव विजानाति किमत्र परिशिष्यते। एतद्वै तत् ॥३॥

*yena rūpaṁ rasaṁ gandhaṁ śabdān sparścāṁśca maithunān* ।
*etenaiva vijānāti kimatra pariśiṣyate* । *etad vai tat* ।।3।।

By whose grace a person grasps the sound, the touch, the form, the taste, the smell and the copulation, by the grace of the same (he knows) what remains (after these) is that very *paramātmā*.

The knowledge behind senses like sound, touch, form, taste, and smell is *ātmā*. There is nothing that the *ātmā* will not know. Is it this all-knowing *ātmā*, about which you asked? There is nothing beyond this. You asked about this only which is *sākṣī* (the witness), *sarvajñānī* (knowledge of everything), and *sarvavyāpī* (found everywhere).

**Śravaṇa 2** – The *ātmā* about which you asked is beyond *dharma* and *adharma*, above which nothing else exists, which for *deva*s also, is of a doubtful knowledge.

**Yamarāja** – I will further explain this concept to you by an example.

**Naciketā** - Kindly do so, Svāmī. Whatever you have told is still a mystery. By examples I can understand the same with more clarity and incisively.

**Yamarāja** –

स्वप्नान्तं जागरितान्तं चोभौ येनानुपश्यति ।
महान्तं विभुमात्मानं मत्वा धीरे न शोचति ॥४॥

*svapnāntaṁ jāgaritāntaṁ cobhau yenānupaśyati* ।
*mahāntaṁ vibhumātmānaṁ matvā dhīre na śocati* ।।4।।

Because of which the man perceives both the experiences of dream and wakeful state, the wise one knowing fully the greatest, all-prevading *ātmā,* does not feel sorry.

Whatever a person sees in his dreams, waking state and sleep is due to this *ātmā*. A person who realizes the truth that it is none but the *ātmā*, which sees in *svapna* state, *jāgarita* state and *suṣupti* state will become a realized person. He then never gets engulfed in sufferings and sorrow. The *ātmā* is only the master who rules in the three states, in three different periods. A person who realizes this, has no desire or worries about his well-being at the present.

**Śravaṇa 1** –

य इमं मध्वदं वेद आत्मानं जीवमन्तिकात्।
ईशानं भूतभव्यस्य न ततो विजुगुप्सते। एतद्वै तत् ॥५॥

*ya imaṁ madhvadaṁ veda ātmānaṁ jīvamantikāt* |
*īśānaṁ bhūtabhavyasya na tato vijugupsate* | *etad vai tat* | |5| |

He who knows from close quarters, this *ātmā* as the life-giver of all, the ruler of past and future; he would not desire to protect himself from it. This verily is that.

The *jīva* which holds the *prāṇa*, sense organs, etc. is none but the *svarūpa* of *paramātmā* who rules the three states and three time periods namely, past, present and future. Once a person realizes this, he gets freed from fear. Knowing that he is none but the *āṭmā*, which is permanent, having no duality of birth and death, he comes out of fears caused by unknown things. He thinks about what he has to fear? For what does he have to be protected? From what, what has to be protected, since all are but one *paramātmā*? Thus, one should realize *ātmā* very clearly. What you asked for, is this only.

**Yamarāja** –

यः पूर्वं तपसो जातमद्भ्यः पूर्वमजायत।
गुहां प्रविश्य तिष्ठन्तं यो भूतेभिर्व्यपश्यत। एतद्वै तत् ॥६॥

*yaḥ pūrvaṁ tapaso jātamadbhyaḥ pūrvamajāyata* |
*guhāṁ praviśya tiṣṭhantaṁ yo bhūtebhirvyapaśyata* | *etad vai tat* | |6| |

That which in the beginning brought forth the world from itself through *tapas*, was existing even before the creation of five great elements; who abides along with the *jīvātmās*; by entering into the cavity of hearts; it is he, who perceives rightly. This is the Lord about whom you have enquired.

In the beginning of creation, even before water and other free elements came about, the one, which came from *Brahman* initially, was *hiraṇyagarbha*. Since he is *samaṣṭi*, he remains in the cave of the heart of all *jīvas*, *devas*, all entities and He is the one who shines in *jīva-svarūpa*. The one who is able to see the Hiraṇyagarbha (the creator), who has come from Brahmā, sees *Brahman* itself. This is the meaning of the concept you asked about.

**Śravaṇa 2** – The eyes, ears and other sense organs operate by that supreme entity's working.

**Śravaṇa 1** – Child! It is not by the eyes that a thing is seen. It is not by the ears that a thing is heard. It is the supreme thing which does all these actions. The *ātmā* is the one which sees, hears and other senses too, function through the *ātmā*.

**Yamarāja** –

या प्राणेन सम्भवत्यदितिर्देवतामयी :
गुहां प्रविश्य तिष्ठन्तीं या भूतेभिर्व्यजायत। एतद्वै तत्॥७॥

*yā prāṇena sambhavatyaditirdevatāmayī* |
*guhāṁ praviśya tiṣṭhantīṁ yā bhūtebhirvyajāyata* |
*etad vai tat* ||7||

That Aditi comprising deities born along with *prāṇa*, who came out along with all creatures, who is seated in the cave of heart, that is He.

Like the foetus that grows hidden in the mother's womb, like the fire hidden inside the coal, in all *jīva*'s mind the *ātmā* is staying hidden.

**Śravaṇa 2** – Just as the foetus emerges from the pregnant woman's womb at the correct time, from the *uttama adhikārī* (deserving person) the *ātmā* reveals itself when he reaches the proper stage of maturity.

**Śravaṇa 1** – Just as a pregnant mother takes proper care of her foetus by good food and proper nurturing, the *yogīs* who do *yajña* nurture the *homa agni* (fire) by pure ghee, dry twigs and other things required for performing a proper *homa*. They consider the Agni *devatā* as *virāṭ-svarūpa* and hold it in their heart and worship it. You also understand such an Agni as the Supreme Being.

**Yamarāja** – Just as from the coal, the Agni (fire) is extracted, from the mind the *ātmā* has to be taken out. Then it can be seen.

**Naciketā** – To my limited intellect the simile between Agni (fire) and *ātmā* is not clearly understood. Kindly explain the same a little more elaborately.

**Yamarāja** –

अरण्योर्निहितो जातवेदा गर्भ इव सुभृतो गर्भिणीभिः।
दिवे दिव ईड्यो जागृवद्भिर्हविष्मद्भिर्मनुष्येभिरग्निः।
एतद्वै तत् ॥८॥

*araṇyornihito jātavedā garbha iva subhr̥to garbhiṇībhiḥ* |
*dive diva īḍyo jāgr̥vadbhirhaviṣmadbhir manuṣyebhir agniḥ* | *etad vai tat* ||8||

The fire, hiding in the pair of fire-sticks, like an embryo well-cared-for by a pregnant woman, is to be adored with oblations day after day by the needful, and is to be preserved by them. This verily is that.

In all the firewood it is the same kind of Agni which is hidden. When it is properly heated the fire emits out. In the same way in all live forms the *ātmā* is present. The Agni takes the form of the things in which it burns. As per the wick and oil in lamp, the lamp may burn dimly or brightly. The same Agni becomes cooking fire, fire in *homa*, forest fire and stomach fire (*jaṭharāgni*). Thus it takes the form of the thing in which it burns. In the same way, the *ātmā* also takes different forms. However it never loses its true state but resides in different bodies in different forms and appears as many as different lifes.

**Śravaṇa 2** – The Agni and the wood, as well as other things which act as fodder for the fire become one. Likewise, lives finally get merged into *para-Brahmam*.

**Yamarāja** –

यतश्चोदेति सूर्योऽस्तं यत्र य गच्छति।
तं देवाः सर्वेऽर्पितास्तदु नात्येति कश्चन। एतद्वै तत् ॥ ९॥

*yataścodeti sūryo 'staṁ yatra ya gacchati* ।
*taṁ devāḥ sarver 'pitāstadu nātyeti kaścana* । *etad vai tat* ।।9।।

From where the sun rises and where the sun sets; all gods are dedicated to Him; none can overtake Him; it is He.

Hiraṇyagarbha is the *samaṣṭi rūpa* of all *devatā*s. From Him only, everyday the sun comes out to rise as well as sets. Like the spokes of a wheel emerging from the axle, all *devatā*s emerge from Him. Such a *samaṣṭi* Hiraṇyagarbha is Brahmā-*svarūpa*. Apart from Brahmā-*svarūpa* there are no other things in the world.

**Naciketā** – Svāmī! I have become blessed hearing your words. I am eager to hear more from you.

**Yamarāja** –

यदेवेह तदमुत्र यदमुत्र तदन्विह।
मृत्योः स मृत्युमाप्नोति य इह नानेव पश्यति ॥१०॥

*yadeveha tadamutra yadamutra tadanviha* ।
*mṛtyoḥ sa mṛtyumāpnoti ya iha nāneva paśyati* ।।10।।

That *Brahman* which is here, the same is there (other world); that which is there, the same is here (this world); he suffers death after death, who perceives the Lord as many.

मनसैवेदमाप्तव्यं नेह नानास्ति किञ्चन।
मृत्योः स मृत्युं गच्छति य इह नानेव पश्यति ॥११॥

*manasaivedamāptavyaṁ neha nānāsti kiñcana* |
*mṛtyoḥ sa mṛtyuṁ gacchati ya iha nāneva paśyati* ||11||

By intuitive mind indeed, one perceives that many do not exist at all; one who perceives many as existing, he goes from death to death.

Whatever we are seeing around us is all one. It is all *ātmā*; apart from the *ātmā* there is nothing else. In everything there is only *ātmā*. Whatever is there is here. The *ātmā*, which is seen in all bodies, and the *paramātmā*, which is the cause of the universe, is all one. There is not a little difference between both. Not understanding this, a person who sees them as different gets entangled in the cycle of birth and death and repeatedly meets death.

**Śravaṇa 1** – What is the microcosm is the macrocosm and vice versa. Hence there is no need to see I, that, this, this person, that person, etc. as varied things and get disturbed. The feelings of varied things and differentiation in names and forms have to be removed from the mind.

**Śravaṇa 2** – Till the wisdom and realization does not seep in that there is nothing apart from the Supreme Being everywhere, a person does not come out of the circle of birth and death and *saṁsāra*. Once the feeling of differentiation is removed then the sun of wisdom will rise. In the lives that look different and all the minds that are split, there resides the same *ātmā* which is undifferentiated and indestructible, permanent. At that time there is no difference as *jīva* and *Īśvara*, no difference as *deva* and human, no difference as *guru* and *śiṣya*. A person who has acquired learning and education and a person who is ignorant without education look the same.

Feelings such as he is higher and he is lower will be removed.

**Naciketā** – I understand it very well. Where a person sees unity in everything, he will get happiness. Others will meet suffering. A person not seeing unity but differences will never get happiness.

**Yamarāja** –

अङ्गुष्ठमात्रः पुरुषो मध्य आत्मनि तिष्ठति।
ईशानो भूतभव्यस्य न ततो विजुगुप्सते। एतद्वै तत् ॥१२॥

*aṅguṣṭhamātraḥ puruṣo madhya ātmani tiṣṭhati* |
*īśāno bhūtabhavyasya na tato vijugupsate* |
*etad vai tat* ||12||

*Puruṣa*, the size of a thumb, resides as the core of one's own being, who is the controller of the past and the future, after knowing Him one would not desire to save oneself from; it is He whom you have enquired about.

अङ्गुष्ठमात्रः पुरुषो ज्योतिरिवाधूमकः।
ईशानो भूतभव्यस्य स एवाद्य स उ श्वः। एतद्वै तत् ॥१३॥

*aṅguṣṭhamātraḥ puruṣo jyotirivādhūmakaḥ* |
*īśāno bhūtabhavyasya sa evādya sa u śvaḥ* |
*etad vai tat* ||13||

The thumb-sized *puruṣa* is like smokeless fire; Supreme controller of past and future; that very *puruṣa* is present today; that very *puruṣa* will be present tomorrow; it is He about whom you have enquired.

The *puruṣa* in the size of a thumb stays in the place of the heart. This *puruṣa* shines like a lamp without smoke. He is the Lord/*Īśvara* for whatever happened, whatever happens and whatever is going to happen. All happiness and sorrow depend upon his state. A person who is aware of these things does not require any protection and need not be scared of anything. He is the one found today, will be present tomorrow and master of both states. He is the Supreme being about which we are discussing now.

**Śravaṇa 1** – The human body changes every minute but the thing which remains in a changeless manner in the body is the *puruṣa*, which is the *ātmā*.

**Śravaṇa 2** – The thoughts and emotions that change from time to time cannot be considered as *ātmā*. Further, the body gets destroyed at the time of death. Hence, that also is not the *ātmā*. Thus the *ātmā* is apart from the body, sense organs, mind, etc. It is a permanent Supreme Being and is the Brahmā-*svarūpa* (the *Brahman*'s form). One can understand this by the preaching of a teacher, by contemplations and study of Upaniṣads, etc. Once that is known, the *avidyā* or ignorance gets removed and the differences get erased. Till it is not known, the differences will be felt in different life forms and a person caught in ignorance gets born and dies again and again.

**Yamarāja** –

यथोदकं दुर्गे वृष्टं पर्वतेषु विधावति ।
एवं धर्मान् पृथक् पस्यंस्तानेवानुविधावति ॥१४ ॥

*yathodakaṁ durge vṛṣṭaṁ parvateṣu vidhāvati |*
*evaṁ dharmān pṛthak pasyaṁstānevānuvidhāvati ||14||*

Water rained in ravines runs to waste among hills; so too he who sees qualities as existing on their own runs to waste after them.

Just as the rain which falls in the high mountains, separates into various waterways and moves in different directions as different rivers, in the same way the *ātmā* also is seen as different *jīva*s. Seeing this without knowing the truth the ignorant person sees them as different forms. Seeing the water in the river the foolish person forgets the rain. Likewise the person of less wisdom seeing the *jīva*s forgets the *ātmā*. Seeing the same one-*parama* thing differently he cultivates the notion that there are many things around him.

**Śravaṇa 1** – We forget the rain given by the lord Parameśvara with great compassion. But seeing the various rivers which have originated from the rain as the Kāverī, Gaṅgā, Alakanandā, Sarasvatī, Narmadā, we see them as different rivers. In the same way, forgetting the *ātmā*, seeing the various names and forms, we think they are the true forms of the world. This is utter foolishness. We have to get out of this.

**Yamarāja** –

यथोदकं शुद्धे शुद्धमासिक्तं तादृगेव भवति।
एवं मुनेर्विजानत आत्मा भवति गौतम ॥१५॥

*yathodakaṁ śuddhe śuddhamāsiktaṁ tādṛgeva bhavati* |
*evaṁ munervijānata ātmā bhavati gautama* | | 15 | |

When Pure water is mixed with another portion of pure water, both become one undifferentiated unit. In the same way the *muni* who has realized the true wisdom combines his *ātmā* with the Supreme thing and becomes one.

Hey Gautama! You have also reached that unity. Everyone similarly should leave the differentially viewing perspective that is very argumentative. Leave the *nāstika* (one bereft of belief), cultivate faith in Vedamātā's preaching and obtain *ātma-jñāna*.

Hence Gautama (Naciketā)! Overcome the nature of the senses, which are outward-facing and turn your view towards inside. Realize that *ātmā* is indestructible and deathless in nature. One has to leave enjoyments, which are temporary and short-lived, and also the feeling of differentiation. Like the foetus hidden in the womb of the mother, like the fire hidden in a piece of coal, it lies hidden in the mind. It is there inside you too, like a bright burning lamp, small in size of a thumb. It is the master of the present and future. Whatever we see is one. Once one attains this wisdom one can be free from the shackles of *saṁsāra-chakra*. Just as the rain falls in the mountains and runs as different rivers *paramātmā* is seen differently in various forms and names. You also must get away from this world of differences and realize the unity. And like pure water mixing with another pure water in a unified manner, become one with the *paramātmā*.

**Naciketā** – Svāmī! I am indeed very happy. I am very grateful to your preaching.

**Yamarāja** – Child! Let us stop today's conversation with this.

**Śravaṇas** – *Mahārāja*'s will is our fortune.

***(Everybody gets up and sings)***

SCENE 3

***(The curtain opens)***

(Everybody is sitting like in the previous scene.)

**Naciketā** – Gurudeva! *Namaskāra*. As I keep hearing your precious words, I am getting filled with great happiness and bliss. Kindly show your grace further.

**Yamarāja** –

पुरमेकादशद्वारमजस्यावक्रचेतसः ।
अनुष्ठाय न शोचति विमुक्तश्च विमुच्यते । एतद्वै तत् ॥१॥

*puramekādaśadvāramajasyāvakracetasaḥ* ।
*anuṣṭhāya na śocati vimuktaśca vimucyate* ।
*etad vai tat* ।।1।।

The *Brahman* which has no birth, which is changeless and which is unflickering and pure knowledge itself, has a city with eleven gates (human body); (while living in this city), practising the proper discipline, one never grieves; freed of grief, one becomes liberated. This indeed is that.

Child! It is very difficult to know this *ātmā*. Hence I will explain to you in yet another way. This *ātmā* which has no birth and which is changeless has come to stay in a city having eleven gates or openings. Don't think anything less of this body. Think of it as the king *paramātmā*'s dwelling place. However, a person who thinks this body as *ātmā* is equal to the person who thinks of the city itself as the king.

**Śravaṇa 1** – Two eyes, two ears, two nostrils, one mouth, one navel, two urine and stool passing openings, one *brahmarandhra* on top of the head making a total eleven. The body having these eleven openings is equal to a capital city (*rājadhānī*) having eleven gates for movement. The *ātmā* inside the body is equal to the king who sits in his throne in the *rājadhānī*. He is the one having no birth. With great *bhakti,* surrender to Him and being courageous, you will never come to grief anymore.

**Yamarāja** – A person who thinks, understands and realizes the *ātmā* will never again be sorrowful for anything. He is relieved from birth and death and attains *mukti*. This is the one, which you asked about.

**Śravaṇa 2** – Leaving desires and attachment, relinquishing all *karmas* from the mind, meditating on the *ātmā* staying in this city a person who does not do anything, nor is the cause for anything is the realized person. He is the one who has attained *mukti* (salvation) for the *jīva*. He is the one having no birth or death.

**Yamarāja**

हꣳसः शुचिषद्वसुरन्तरिक्षसद्धोता वेदिषदतिथिर्दुरोणसत् ।
नृषद्वरसदृतसद्व्योमसदब्जा गोजा ऋतजा अद्रिजा ऋतं बृहत् ॥२॥

*haṁsaḥ śuciṣadvasurantarikṣasaddhotā vediṣadati-thirduroṇasat* |
*nṛṣad varasadṛtasad vyomasadabjā gojā ṛtajā adrijā ṛtaṁ bṛhat* | |2| |

It appears like a swan (like the sun) in the clear sky, the Vasu in the atmosphere, priest at the altar, guest in the house. It dwells in man, in gods, in the world order (*ṛta*), in the sky. It is all that is born of the world order, born of mountains. It is the Truth, It is the Great!.

Naciketā! Don't think this *ātmā* is the one who stays only in the city of the body. He is everywhere. He goes everywhere. There is no movement without his reach. He is the sun in the sky. He is inside the Self of everyone. He is the *vāyu* (air) in the *antarikṣa* (space). He is the *agni* (fire), which is worshipped in the *yajña*. He is the *somarasa*, which is kept in the *kalaśa* (holy pot). He is the one who comes to the house as the guest. He is in the mind of the persons as well as in the minds of the *devas*. He is the one fixed in truth. He is the one seen as different life forms. All the things created on earth are He alone. He is the rivers and the rivulets, which start from the mountains, and is found everywhere. This way He stays as *sarvātmā* (*ātmā* of everyone) without difference. He is the great thing and Supreme thing, which is in all creation. He alone is the true thing.

**Śravaṇa 1** – Child! The short of it is, It is *ātmā* which is spread in all the world. There is no difference in It as it is present in all things.

**Naciketā** – Svāmī! The *ātmā*, which is spread everywhere, is also found in the body, which is *ātmā*'s dwelling city. This being so is it not true that a man stays alive due to the strength given by he *ātmā*?

**Yamarāja** –

ऊर्ध्वं प्राणमुन्नयत्यपानं प्रत्यगस्यति ।
मध्ये वामनमासीनं विश्वे देवा उपासते ॥ ३ ॥

*ūrdhvaṁ prāṇamunnayatyapānaṁ pratyagasyati* |
*madhye vāmanamāsīnaṁ viśve devā upāsate* ||3||

It is the one that leads *prāṇa* upwards it is the one that brings down *apāna*, It is the one seated in the middle as worthy of adoration. It is the one all the gods (senses) adore.

Gautama! What you are telling is very correct. It is not that a man stays alive by *prāṇa* or *apāna vāyu*, but the foundation of these is the *ātmā*. Because of this only he stays alive. It is *ātmā* which draws the air up, it is the same *ātmā* which allows the air to go down. It is in the form of Vāmana found in the middle of the body that is in the heart and being prayed to by the senses.

**Śravaṇa 2** – The mind is like a temple for *ātmā* and it rules from there. All the senses obediently follow the master and remain worshipping Him.

**Yamarāja** –

अस्य विस्रंसमानस्य शरीरस्थस्य देहिनः।
देहाद्विमुच्यमानस्य किमत्र परिशिष्यते। एतद्वै तत् ॥४॥

*asya visraṁsamānasya śarīrasthasya dehinaḥ* |
*dehād vimucyamānasya kimatra pariśiṣyate* |
*etad vai tat* ||4||

(When) the *ātmā* seated in this body drops the body down and gets released from it, what remains here? It is indeed that *Brahman* about which you have enquired.

न प्राणेन नापानेन मर्त्यो जीवति कश्चन।
इतरेण तु जीवन्ति यस्मिन्नेतावुपाश्रितौ ॥५॥

*na prāṇena nāpānena martyo jīvati kaścana* |
*itareṇa tu jīvanti yasminnetāvupāśritau* ||5||

Any mortal creature lives neither through *prāṇa* nor through *apāna*; they live on account of someone else; on whom these two depend and take shelter.

Once the *ātmā* goes out of the body, the body becomes the corpse. See that! What is remaining then? The senses, which work according to the orders of the king, become powerless and quiete. After He leaves, what is there for them? After the head of the country departs, the countrymen reach an unfortunate state. In the same way, the sense organs also lose strength and ebb away when *ātmā* takes leave of the body.

Without *ātmā* the sense organs get weakened. The *prāṇa vāyu* and *apāna vāyu* also leave a body bereft of *ātmā*'s presence.

**Naciketā** – Gurudeva! When a *jīva* dies what happens to the *ātmā*?

**Yamarāja** –

> हन्त त इदं प्रवक्ष्यामि गुह्यं ब्रह्म सनातनम्।
> यथा च मरणं प्राप्य आत्मा भवति गौतम ॥६॥
>
> *hanta ta idaṁ pravakṣyāmi guhyaṁ brahma sanātanam* ।
> *yathā ca maraṇaṁ prāpya ātmā bhavati gautama* ॥6॥
>
> O Gautama! how that mysterious and eternal *Brahman* is; and how the *jīvātmā* after death becomes; I will again tell you.

Hey Gautama! Listen carefully. I will tell you some thing about the very mysterious and ancient *Brahman*. Also I will tell you how a *jīvātmā* suffers after death without knowing this. The *jīvātmā* gets caught in the *saṁsāra* of birth and death and continuously suffers.

> योनिमन्ये प्रपद्यन्ते शरीरत्वाय देहिनः।
> स्थाणुमन्येऽनुसंयन्ति यथाकर्म यथाश्रुतम् ॥७॥
>
> *yonimanye prapadyante śarīratvāya dehinaḥ* ।
> *sthāṇumanye 'nusaṁyanti yathākarma yathāśrutam* ॥7॥
>
> Some *jīvātmā*s go to the wombs for assuming bodies as mobile ones; others go to immobile wombs; as per their deeds, according to one's learning.

When death comes the *ātmā* leaves the body but, according to the *karmas* done and the knowledge obtained, goes in search of different bodies and enters the womb of different living beings. Out of these, whose virtues and vices are in equal balance they get human birth; whose virtues are less and sins are more, they are born in subhuman species; whose sins are excessive they become immobile, i.e. trees, creepers, grass and mountain, etc. Accordingly it gets the form of animal or human and is reborn.

**Śravaṇa 1** – Some persons leaving the human body get similar human bodies. Some get the form of plants too. As per one's action and knowledge, the kind of living form is determined. Persons doing good deeds get good birth; persons doing bad deeds obtain bad *yoni*s (form) and suffer.

**Śravaṇa 2** – Persons having *satguṇa* (good nature) go further up. They obtain higher births. They get born in *yogī*s and rich persons' houses and scholars' houses. They increase their wisdom, do good deeds and find ways to get *mukti* (salvation). Persons having *rajoguṇa* stay in the centre. Persons, who have *tāmasa guṇa* go down, take birth of low status, in *yoni*s which are low down in living form and suffer in their next births. For the question you asked as to what happens to the *ātmā* trapped in the body, well here is the answer.

**Yamarāja** –

य एष सुप्तेषु जागर्ति कामंकामं पुरुषो निर्मिमाणः।
तदेव शुक्रं तद्ब्रह्म तदेवामृतमुच्यते।
तस्मिँल्लोकाः श्रिताः सर्वे तदु नात्येति कश्चन। एतद्वै तत्॥८॥

*ya eṣa supteṣu jāgarti kāmaṁ kāmaṁ puruṣo nirmimāṇaḥ* |
*tadeva śukraṁ tad brahma tadevāmṛtamucyate* |
*tasmiṁllokāḥ śritāḥ sarve tadu nātyeti kaścana* |
*etad vai tat* ||8||

The *paramātmā* who made different types of enjoyments in accordance with the deeds of individuals, keeps awake while all others sleep (final dissolution); He alone is pure; He indeed is *Brahman*; He indeed is immortal. On Him alone all the worlds get shelter; and none ever goes beyond Him. It is indeed that God about whom you have enquired.

When everything else is sleeping in the body, the one who prepares for the things, which are desired for, and keeps awake, he alone is pure *Brahman*. He only is called nectar. In him only is contained all the worlds. There is none who goes beyond him. He is only That, the *Brahman* which we are enquiring about.

**Śravaṇa 1** – Nothing can go beyond this *Brahman*, which has no death. This only is the *ātmā*. As the worlds are held in its foundation, there is nothing else beyond This.

**Yamarāja** –

अग्निर्यथैको भुवनं प्रविष्टो रूपं रूपं प्रतिरूपो बभूव।
एकस्तथा सर्वभूतान्तरात्मा रूपं रूपं प्रतिरूपो बहिश्च ॥९॥

*agniryathaiko bhuvanaṁ praviṣṭo rūpaṁ rūpaṁ pratirūpo babhūva* |
*ekastathā sarvabhūtāntarātmā rūpaṁ rūpaṁ pratirūpo bahiśca* | |9| |

Just as one and the same fire present in the whole universe appears in different form as the form of the object may be, similarly the indwelling *ātmā* of all creatures, even though one, appears exactly in the same form in different objects which form they possess; and He is wihout also.

As just one universal fire enters all the things in the world and according to the form of the thing, takes multiple forms, in the same way one *ātmā* enters all lives as *antarātmā* and according to the form of the living being takes that shape. It is there outside the living being too. Its names are many, its forms are many. As per the name and form you aspire to see the *ātmā*, it will be seen in the same name and form.

**Śravaṇa 2** – Even though it is seen in many forms there is only one Supreme thing. It is only attached to different bodies and appears differently, However, whatever, inside is the same.

That only is *Brahman*. Though It is seen in all forms, still It is beyond them. It is different, the forms are different.

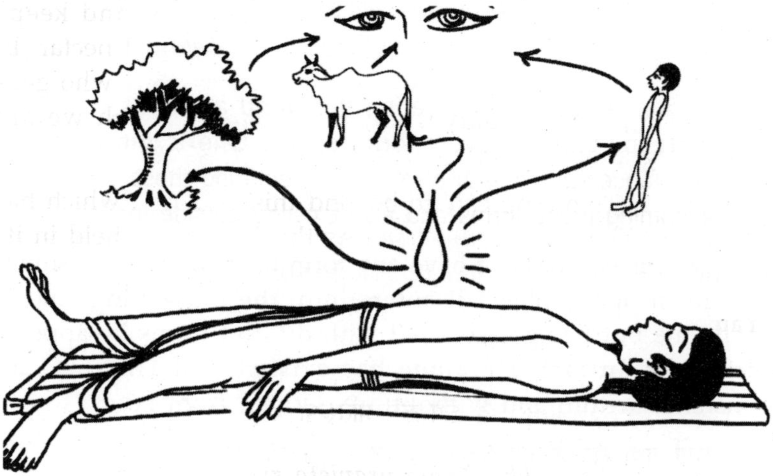

*fig* : **Ātmā leaves the body and becomes — human, animal, plant**

**Yamarāja** – Child! I will tell you another example. Listen, as the same *vāyu* enters the body and according to its position it is called *prāṇa* and other *vāyu*s. In the same way *ātmā* enters different bodies and obtains different names and forms.

**Śravaṇa 1** – In the body the different *vāyu*s called *prāṇa, apāna, samāna*, etc. are all but the same *vāyu*. That *vāyu* is not only inside but also all outside. In the same way, the *ātmā* is also found inside and outside.

**Yamarāja** – Till now I told you about the sameness of *Brahman*. Now I am going to tell about its blemishless characteristics.

**Naciketā** – As you explain with examples, it is becoming increasingly clear.

**Yamarāja** –

वायुर्यथैको भुवनं प्रविष्टो रूपं रूपं प्रतिरूपो बभूव।
एकस्तथा सर्वभूतान्तरात्मा रूपं रूपं प्रतिरूपो बहिश्च ॥१०॥

*vāyuryathaiko bhuvanaṁ praviṣṭo rūpaṁ rūpaṁ*
*pratirūpo babhūva* |
*ekastathā sarvabhūtāntarātmā rūpaṁ rūpaṁ pratirūpo*
*bahiśca* | |10| |

As air, though one, entering the world assumes forms corresponding to every form, so the One is the inner substance (*antarātmā*) of all things, entering those things, assuming those forms and also existing outside them.

Just as the air does not have any form of its own but assumes the form of the object it enters into, the indwelling God is only one but being associated with differnt forms he appears different. In fact, He alone has existence of His own, all existence within and without are derived from Him.

सूर्यो यथा सर्वलोकस्य चक्षुर्न लिप्यते चाक्षुषैर्बाह्यदोषैः।
एकस्तथा सर्वभूतान्तरात्मा न लिप्यते लोकदुःखेन बाह्यः ॥११॥

*sūryo yathā sarvalokasya cakṣurna lipyate*
*cākṣuṣairbāhyadoṣaiḥ* |
*ekastathā sarvabhūtāntarātmā na lipyate lokaduḥkhena*
*bāhyaḥ* | |11| |

Just as the Sun-god, the very eye of the entire universe (the illuminator), remains untainted by the defects of the eyes of people, similarly the indwelling *ātmā* of all beings, the one *paramātmā*, is not tainted by the sufferings of the world; though permeating everything he is above and beyond.

Just as the Sun which is the eye for the entire world, but does not get affected by the diseases which the eye may get affected with, in the same way the *ātmā* which is present in all lives created does not get affected by the sorrows of the world. It is beyond all that. The Sun helps one to see the good as well as bad things, however, the impurity in these things does not reach him. Likewise though the same *ātmā* is present in *sarvabhūta* (all living beings), the *ātmā* does not get affected by the happenings and sorrows of the beings. It stands apart from that. It remains pure and unaffected.

**Naciketā** – If It is the one present in all the living things then is it not necessary for It to get affected by the joys and sorrows of beings.

**Yamarāja** – No, it isn't so. The happiness and sorrows touch only living beings. However these passing phases do not touch the *antarātmā,* which is responsible for the life in living beings. As soon as the differences, which have come about due to ignorance, get removed the blemishless and pure state of *ātmā* is known.

**Śravaṇa 1** – Due to ignorance we see the rope as the snake and the shining shell as silver. When Truth is known ignorance is removed, the rope and shell become visible. By any amount of imagination the rope cannot be changed into a snake, and the shining shell cannot be converted into silver. The characteristics of a snake and silver will never come to the rope and the shell.

**Yamarāja** –

एको वशी सर्वभूतान्तरात्मा एकं रूपं बहुधा यः करोति।
तमात्मस्थं येऽनुपश्यन्ति धीरास्तेषां सुखं शाश्वतं नेतरेषाम् ॥१२॥

*eko vaśī sarvabhūtāntarātmā ekaṁ rūpaṁ bahudhā yaḥ karoti* ।
*tamātmasthaṁ ye 'nupaśyanti dhīrāsteṣāṁ sukhaṁ śāśvataṁ netareṣām* ।।12।।

The Almighty and *antarātmā*, which is but one, get, differentiated into different forms and appear differently. The determined enlightened one who sees Him within himself reaches the immortal state and gets bliss. The others don't get it.

**Śravaṇa 1** – *Ātmā* is one. He is the master of all. He is independent. He is spread everywhere. There is no one who is equal to Him or above Him. He is the protector of the entire world. He is the *antarātmā* of everyone. He who is *ekamūrti* (one form) also manifests as many forms.

**Śravaṇa 2** – He is the basis of everything. There is no further source for Him. Since He appears in the mind we cannot consider that He is the basis of the mind. Though we see our reflection in the mirror, the mirror is not the basis for our face. A person who thus sees Him and realizes Him gets unlimited happiness. Others that are not realized souls struggle in the world of joys and sorrows not reaching the limitless bliss.

**Yamarāja** –

नित्योनित्यानां चेतनश्चेतनानामेको बहूनां यो विदधाति कामान्।
तमात्मस्थं येऽनुपश्यन्ति धीरास्तेषां शान्तिः शाश्वती नेतरेषाम् ॥१३॥

*nityo nityānāṁ cetanaścetanānāmeko bahūnāṁ yo vidadhāti kāmān* ।
*tamātmasthaṁ ye 'nupaśyanti dhīrāsteṣāṁ śāntiḥ śāśvatī netareṣām* ।।13।।

The everlasting in all that is ephemeral, the consciousness in all that is conscious, the one in all the many, the dispenser of all desires — the wise who constantly perceive Him as abiding in themselves, alone, and no others, have eternal peace.

**Yamarāja** –

तदेतदिति मन्यन्तेऽनिर्देश्यं परमं सुखम्।
कथं नु तद्विजानीयां किमु भाति विभाति वा॥१४॥

*tadetaditi manyante 'nirdeśyaṁ paramaṁ sukham* ।
*kathaṁ nu tadvijānīyāṁ kimu bhāti vibhāti vā* ।।14।।

(Wise) think that supreme bliss, which cannot be described, to be this (individual soul). How then shall I know it? Does it manifest or does it not manifest?

Further, among the imperishable things He is the stable aspect, and He is the intelligence in intelligent beings. He fulfils singlehandedly everybody's desires. A person who realizes His presence in him gets permanent peace.

**Śravaṇa 1** – All the things of the world are perishable. Being in those perishable things the *ātmā* remains imperishable. Just as *agni* (fire) gives warmth to the water, He is the one who gives intelligence to all living beings while He remains intelligence personified. He who is *sarvātmā, sarveśvara* blesses all living things and fulfils their desires. The one who sees Him inside his mind and realizes His presence gets permanent happiness and peace. Others don't get it.

**Śravaṇa 2** – A person stabilized in this wisdom sees himself in all living beings and also sees all living things in himself. Such a realized wise person does not lose sight of *ātmā*; the *ātmā* also does not lose track of Him. A person who is stabilized in the knowledge that everything is one, stays fixed in *ātmā* in different conditions. He maintains peace and attains happiness.

**Yamarāja** – The happiness the realized one attains cannot be measured or pointed at. But one should strive to get answers to these questions. Is such bliss like a lamp, which is self-effulgent, or does it shine by any reflected light? How to understand It by the intellect? One should strive to get answers to these questions. Having to known the answers they should then be explained to others.

**Śravaṇa 1** – Through this exalted bliss obtained by realization cannot be described, still its presence is very evident and obvious, thus consider the wise ones. Such an all-encompassing brightness does not emit from the sun, moon or *agni*. It is definite that it shines by itself. It only brightens everything else.

**Yamarāja** –

न तत्र सूर्यों भाति न चन्द्रतारकं नेमा विद्युतो भान्ति कुतोऽयमग्निः।
तमेव भान्तमनुभाति सर्वं तस्य भासा सर्वमिदं विभाति ॥१५॥

*na tatra sūryo bhāti na candratārakaṁ nemā vidyuto bhānti kuto 'yamagniḥ |*
*tameva bhāntamanubhāti sarvaṁ tasya bhāsā sarvamidaṁ vibhāti* | |15| |

There the sun shines not, nor the moon, nor the stars, nor these lightning flashes, then how can the earthly fire show its luminosity? All these shine only after He shines, it is only through His luminosity that this all illumines.

Yes, that is the correct understanding. The brightness created by the divine beings such as sun, moon, stars and lightening obtain their power form *Brahman*. The *agni* (fire) whom we talk about cannot stand anywhere to its own. Taking the help of the self-effulgent *ātmā* only all other things get their brightness. Due to Its light only all other things come into being.

**Śravaṇa 2** – The *ātmā* shines by its own light. It shines in a very special and different manner and cannot be compared to the brightness of the sun and the moon. It shines by itself and also makes other things to shine. All the brightness we see in the universe is the brightness borrowed from the Supreme thing. All the light we see around us is only reflected light. The brightness seen in our inner mind is also the Supreme thing's brightness.

**Yamarāja** – Child Naciketā! I will tell things in short. Listen. In this body, which can be called a city, the heart (mind) can be aligned to a palace. The king who is residing there is the Supreme thing. He is present in your mind also. At the same time he is present in all the things, which you see around you in complete absoluteness. Everywhere it is He. Everything is Him. Everything operates on His strength. Your breath is also His action only. After death, according to the good and bad deeds committed, It takes another birth. Though It is in all, It remains apart from them. The sorrow or happiness of living things does not affect It. The sun by its rays ripens the fruits.

The fruit, which has a quality of sweetness, becomes sweet. The fruit, which is bitter, does not acquire sweetness. The sun's rays do not condition the fruit's sweetness and bitterness. In the same way the *ātmā* also remains without blemish. A person who is aware and realizes this all-pervading *ātmā* is a wise and strong person. He is the all-knowing *jñānī*. Once a person realizes Its presence in him he can get liberation. He can get happiness and bliss together. The *antarātmā* shines by Its own light. The bright stellar objects like sun, moon, stars and lightening do not brighten the *ātmā*. Their light is not required when the *ātmā* shines. As just the fireflies do not shine in front of the sun, in the same way in front of *ātmā*'s brightness the planet's brightness is not seen. They are able to shine only from the brightness they have borrowed from the Supreme thing as *prasāda* (offering). Knowing such a light, leave sorrow and attain happiness.

**Naciketā** – Svāmī! I now understand that the brightness of *antarātmā* which illuminates steadily my mind is none but the light of *paramātmā*. I am very happy knowing this.

**Yamarāja** – Alright. With this we will end today's teachings.

(First Yamarāja gets up. Then all others get up and sing together.)

***(The cutain falls.)***

## SCENE 4

***(The curtain opens.)***

(Like the previous scene all are sitting and the teachings are continuing).

**Yamarāja** – Child! Today I will explain to you *Brahman* in a different manner, listen.

**Naciketā** – Svāmī, I will listen carefully.

**Yamarāja** –

ऊर्ध्वमूलोऽवाक्शाख एषोऽश्वत्थः सनातनः ।

तदेव शुक्रं तद्ब्रह्म तदेवामृतमुच्यते।
तस्मिल्लोकाः श्रिताः सर्वे तदु नात्येति कश्चन। एतद्वै तत् ॥१॥

*ūrdhvamūlo 'rvākśākha eṣo 'śvatthaḥ sanātanaḥ* |
*tadeva śukraṁ tad brahma tadevāmṛtamucyate* |
*tasmilokāḥ śritāḥ sarve tadu nātyeti kaścana* |
*etad vai tat* ||1||

Rooted above with branches downwards is this eternal *pīpala* tree; that indeed is the supreme Lord, the purest *tattva*; that indeed is *Brahman*; that indeed is the immortal; all the worlds are dependent upon Him; no one goes beyond It. It is indeed that Lord about whom you have enquired.

This *saṁsāra* can be compared to an *aśvattha* tree, which has roots above and branches below. That *aśvattha* tree is very old. In that only all the worlds are getting stabilized. That is the Supreme thing we are trying to understand.

**Naciketā** – Why is the *aśvattha* tree given as an example? What is the concept behind it?

**Yamarāja** – The word *aśvattham* means : *a* — not, *śva* — tomorrow, *sttham* — existence, i.e. it has no existence tomorrow, or there is no permanence. This is only *saṁsāra*.

**Śravaṇa 1** – There is a saying "this world is known for it, what was present yesterday is not today."

**Yamarāja** – For this *saṁsāra* tree, the root, that is the foundation is *Brahman*, the branches are *liṅga* (bodies), the stem is the sense aspects like sight, smell, etc. the leaves are the Śruti, Smṛti, etc. the fruits are experiences like happiness and sorrow, the hanging roots are the *vāsanā*s (attitudes) which have come out of previous *karma*s. This comes again and again, grows, gets destroyed and this cycle continues unabated. To remove it, it should be cut by the sword of dispassion or non-attachment. By that the tree can be cut and discarded. At that time the person will get liberated from *saṁsāra* or else he will again and again get bodies and get caught in this cycle. To cut this tree and to see the foundation of it (that is the *Brahman*) is the main objective of this birth.

यदिदं किञ्च जगत्सर्वं प्राण एजति निःसृतम्।
महद्भयं वज्रमुद्यतं य एतद्विदुरमृतास्ते भवन्ति ॥२॥

*yadidaṁ kiñca jagat sarvaṁ prāṇa ejati niḥsṛtam* |
*mahad bhayaṁ vajramudyataṁ ya etad viduramṛtāste bhavanti* ||2||

Whatever there is as this changeful world had emerged from and moves within this *prāṇa*, the great awesome, upraised thunder-bolt-like. Knowing It one becomes immortal.

By the wisdom obtained, he can reach the imperishable, deathless state. It is only by the orders of this *Brahman* that the entire world operates. Afraid of its strong diamond-like cutting sword the universe acts. Everything is under the control of its rule. A person knowing this gets united with the *ātmā* and becomes immortal.

**Śravaṇa 2** – The fire burns in obedience to this great power. The sun shines without fail spreading its warmth everywhere, again as per the dictates of this power. The falling of rain and blowing of wind are all under the command of this power. The Death taking away our lives is also by the supreme power's command.

**Śravaṇa 1** –

भयादस्याग्निस्तपति भयात्तपति सूर्यः।
भयादिन्द्रश्च वायुश्च मृत्युर्धावति पञ्चमः ॥३॥

*bhayādasyāgnistapati bhayāttapati sūryaḥ* |
*bhayādindraśca vāyuśca mṛtyurdhāvati pañcamaḥ* ||3||

From its fear the fire burns; from its fear the sun causes heat, again from its fear Indra and Vāyu and Death, the fifth, does speed along.

All the acts of nature are going on in obedience to that supreme commander. The protectors or guards of the world Indra, Vāyu (air), Kāla (death god), Agni (fire), Sūrya (sun) all work ceaselessly at His orders. Afraid of the supreme commander *Brahman* they like servants work ceaselessly and unerringly. Thus the master is *Brahman*.

**Yamarāja** –

इह चेदशकद्बोद्धुं प्राक् शरीरस्य विस्रसः।
ततः सर्गेषु लोकेषु शरीरत्वाय कल्पते ॥४॥

*iha cedaśakad boddhuṁ prāk śarīrasya visrasaḥ* ।
*tataḥ sargeṣu lokeṣu śarīratvāya kalpate* ।।4।।

If before the fall of this human body (the striver could realize God) here in this human birth (it is well and good), otherwise again one has to be born in the different worlds and wombs, for many *kalpa*s.

Here itself, before the body gets destroyed one should strive to reach the *ātmā*. If a person does not do it, or even after trying is unable to succeed and without finishing the task he passes away, then he takes birth again in different forms. Hence he must obtain *ātma-jñāna* now itself in this human birth only.

**Naciketā** – What is the significance of this world Gurudeva? Is it not possible to get *ātma-jñāna* in the heavens where *devā*s and ancestors reside.

**Yamarāja** –

यथादर्शे तथात्मनि यथा स्वप्ने तथा पितृलोके।
यथाप्सु परीव ददृशे तथा गन्धर्वलोके छायातपयोरिव ब्रह्मलोके ॥५॥

*yathādarśe tathātmani yathā svapne tathā pitṛloke* ।
*yathāpsu parīva dadṛśe tathā gandharvaloke*
*chāyātapayoriva brahmaloke* ।।5।।

Just as in a mirror, in the same way in the purified heart (*Brahman* is seen); just as in a dream, so is seen in the human world; just as in shallow water so is seen in *gandharvaloka* and in *brahmaloka* like shade and light.

In the human birth it is possible to see *Brahman* very clearly and easily as we see our face in the mirror. In ancestral world it is seen like things we see in the dream very vaguely. In *gandharva* world it is seen like reflections seen in water. However in *brahmaloka* the *ātmā* is again seen clearly like sun and shade. But it is best and possible to get *ātma-darśana* in this world where it can be seen very clearly. It is not so easy in other worlds.

**Śravaṇa 2** – The *bhūloka* is a place to do *karma*s (action) whose results can be realized by the individual soul. Other worlds are only *bhoga* (enjoyment). The other worlds are made to experience the result of *karma* done here. Hence to do penanace, *yajñas*, and different *karma*s as well as to understand about *Brahman* from preachings, this *bhūloka* is the correct place. There is no doubt about it.

**Śravaṇa 1** – Here in this *bhūloka* that is in human birth *ātma-darśana* is seen very clearly. In *pitṛloka* (ancestors world) it is seen not so clearly. Likewise in *gandharvaloka* also it is seen without much clarity. But in *brahmaloka* it is seen very clearly like sunrays and shadows.

**Naciketā** – If that is so, won't it be more prudent to try to see it in *brahmaloka* ?

**Yamarāja** – Only after doing most exalted *karma*s and *dhyāna* (meditations) one can go to *brahmaloka*. Thus since going to *brahmaloka* is so difficult, it is our duty to strive for *ātma-darśana* in the human world and in the human birth.

**Naciketā** – Svāmī! You must tell us about the way to get that *ātma-darśana* and the benefits on getting it.

**Yamarāja** –

इन्द्रियाणां पृथग्भावमुदयास्तमयौ च यत्।
पृथगुत्पद्यमानानां मत्वा धीरो न शोचति ॥६॥

*indriyāṇāṁ pṛthagbhāvamudayāstamayau ca yat* |
*pṛthagutpadyamānānāṁ matvā dhīro na śocati* ||6||

The senses, one different from the other, emanate (from Him). The wise and firm one who knows their state of being so, and how do they emerge and re-merge, he is not touched by sorrows.

Child! The happiness and sorrow we experience are through the sense organs. Since we can experience these emotions only while awake and during sleep they completely melt away we can understand that the senses are not fundamental things. We come to realize there is something else, some other power which operates these senses. That is only the *ātmā*. If a person realizes this clearly and becomes wise, such a person crosses all sorrows.

इन्द्रियेभ्यः परं मनो मनसः सत्त्वमुत्तमम्।
सत्त्वादधि महानात्मा महतोऽव्यक्तमुत्तमम्॥७॥

*indriyebhyaḥ paraṁ mano manasaḥ sattvamuttamam* |
*sattvādadhi mahānātmā*
*mahato 'vyaktamuttamam* ||7||

The mind is superior to senses; the intellect superior to the mind; even to the intellect the great *jīvātmā* is superior; the unmanifest power is superior even to the *jīvātmā*.

Now since *ātmā* is different from the sense organs, one should not assume it is somewhere far. It is a thing which penetrates into everything and is called *antarātmā*. The mind is higher than the sense organs, above that is intellect, that intellect, which is termed *sattvam*, above that, is *mahat*. The intellect does service to the *mahat*. Above that *mahat* is the *avyakta* thing.

अव्यक्तात्तु परः पुरुषो व्यापकोऽलिङ्ग एव च।
यज्ज्ञात्वा मुच्यते जन्तुरमृतत्वं च गच्छति ॥८॥

*avyaktāt tu paraḥ puruṣo vyāpako 'liṅga eva ca* |
*yaj jñātvā mucyate janturamṛtattvaṁ ca gacchati* ||8||

Still beyond the unmanifested is *puruṣa*, the all-prevading with no distinguishing mark. Knowing Him, any living being gets liberated and attains immortality.

Beyond that is *puruṣottama*. He is spread everywhere and remains without form. A person knowing or realizing Him gets *mukti* (salvation). He attains the deathless immortal state.

**Naciketā** – Is it not correct that the stage of salvation comes later and the deathless state comes before?

**Yamarāja** – It is a good question, Naciketā. I am very happy. As soon as a person realizes the *puruṣa* which is not confined by any rules and which is apart from *saṁsāra dharma*s but which is understood from preachings and study of scriptures, he gets free from the knots of ignorance which bind his heart and gets liberated. This is only *mukti* of the *jīva*. Then he leaves the body and becomes immortal.

**Naciketā** – How to reach the *puruṣa*, which is not described by any characteristics?

**Yamarāja** –

न सन्दृशे तिष्ठति रूपमस्य न चक्षुषा पश्यति कश्चनैनम्।
हृदा मनीषा मनसाभिक्लृप्तो य एतद्विदुरमृतास्ते भवन्ति ॥९॥

*na sandṛśe tiṣṭhati rūpamasya na cakṣuṣā paśyati kaścanainam* |
*hṛdā manīṣā manasābhiklṛpto ya etad viduramṛtāste bhavanti* | |9| |

Not within the range of vison, His form is visible to the eyes of none; those who contemplate repeatedly and know Him through taintless and unwavering heart and purified intellect; they become immortal.

Nobody sees Him by his or her eyes. His form does not come in front of the eyes. It is not possible to know him by other senses. With a steady intellect and mind one can know him and reach him. Persons knowing Him obtain a deathless state.

**Śravaṇa 2** – The *ātmā* which cannot be seen by sight, which is not seen as a form by anyone, can be seen in the heart by an intellect which is not disturbed and by a mind, which is steady. Without any desire distracting the mind, channellizing the intellect and steadily holding it in the heart, if a person meditates, he can know the *ātmā*. A person who realizes that *ātmā* is only *Brahman*, becomes immortal.

**Yamarāja** –

यदा पञ्चावतिष्ठन्ते ज्ञानानि मनसा सह ।
बुद्धिश्च न विचेष्टति तामाहुः परमां गतिम् ॥१०॥

*yadā pañcāvatiṣṭhante jñānāni manasā saha* |
*buddhiśca na viceṣṭati tāmāhuḥ paramāṁ gatim* | |10| |

When all the five senses along with the mind become steady, and intellect stops its activites, that state is called Supreme state.

To control the intellect and mind thus, one has to learn *yoga*. All the five sense organs have to be kept steady along with the mind. Then the intellect won't have any work. The mind turns inwards. A person in that state is not influenced by the senses and is very careful.

**Śravaṇa 1** – Thus controlling the senses, if the mind and intellect remain steady that is the state of *yoga*. That state is the highest state. In that state the mind gets freed from all wrong knowledge and gets united with the *ātmā*. That only is *yoga*. At that time the *sādhaka* should be careful without going overboard. That is because, along with *yoga* a person may reach the highest state, but to hold on to that there may be many difficulties and dangers.

**Śravaṇa 2** – The senses will again draw the mind and take it away. The mind will pull the intellect. Hence being very careful, the mind and intellect once controlled should be kept in that state. On reaching that highest state the *ātmā* can be seen.

However that *ātmā* will show itself and vanish like the sun coming and going. It is very difficult to remain in the state of *yoga* always.

**Yamarāja** –

तां योगमिति मन्यन्ते स्थिरामिन्द्रियधारणाम्।
अप्रमत्तस्तदा भवति योगो हि प्रभवाप्ययौ ॥११॥

*tāṁ yogamiti manyante sthirāmindriyadhāraṇām* |
*apramattastadā bhavati yogo hi prabhavāpyayau* ||11||

The constant holding back of senses is considered *yoga*; at that time the striver becomes completely devoid of absentmindedness. *Yoga* is of the nature of being created and dissolved (subject to rising and setting).

The *sādhaka* will reach a state of *yoga* or union and will see the *ātmā*. He may again come back to worldly matters and can slip back to *saṁsāra*. This will go on till the bodily journey continues. Hence a person reaching the state of *yoga* should be very careful. He should not slip from that state, and should try to protect and hold on to the state.

नैव वाचा न मनसा प्राप्तुं शक्यो न चक्षुषा।
अस्तीति ब्रुवतोऽन्यत्र कथं तदुपलभ्यते ॥१२॥

*naiva vācā na manasā prāptuṁ śakyo na cakṣuṣā* |
*astīti bruvato 'nyatra kathaṁ tadupalabhyate* ||12||

The Supreme Lord is not attainabie either through speech or mind or eyes. Apart from the one who utters, "It is what exists" how is It obtainable.

That *ātmā* cannot be seen by words, mind and eyes. However, it can be known from the wise ones, who emphatically state that there is something called *ātmā*. There is no other way apart from this.

**Śravaṇa 1** – Though we are not able to know this *ātmā* through our sense organs, still, knowing that there is a true thing which is the cause of this wide universe and without which this world would not have come about, and with such a thought stabilized in the mind, one goes in search of It. Only then it is possible to obtain It. Then he will realize Its true concept. That it is in a *nirguṇa* (having no characteristics) state will be known. However if a person thinks there is no *paramātmā* then it is not possible to realize It. How can such a person reach the *ātmā*?

**Śravaṇa 2** – This true thing is apart from word, thought, and sight. Only by seeing it in one's mind, and confirming that it is there, one has to realize it. It is not possible to know It in any other way. How can a thing, which is the cause of the five senses, be known by the senses? It is not possible. Once a *sādhaka* understands and agrees that there is a true Supreme Being behind all the created things, he first aspires to see It as *saguṇa Brahman* (*Brahman* with attributes). However finally he comes to know it as the *nirguṇa Brahman*, that is, beyond all forms beyond all thought and speech. That too happens only when It comes forth by Itself and reveals Itself.

**Yamarāja** –

अस्तीत्येवोपलब्धव्यस्तत्त्वभावेन चोभयोः ।
अस्तीत्येवोपलब्धस्य तत्त्वभावः प्रसीदति ॥१३॥

*astītyevopalabdhavyastattvabhāvena cobhayoḥ* |
*astītyevopalabdhasya tattvabhāvaḥ prasīdati* ||13||

First of all having firm faith in His existence, He should be strived to be reached; after that He should be attained with *tattva-bhāva*; for such a striver the real aspect of the Lord is manifested by Itself.

In this way, by variously thinking and analysing, we have come to the conclusion that there is a Supreme Being, the *Brahman*. Once such a thought gets rooted in our mind, then it may be possible to see It. However, not by this handicapped eye. In the normal way, It will not be visible through our eyesight. It is not possible to comprehend It by the mind. It cannot be described by any language.

यदा सर्वे प्रमुच्यन्ते कामा येऽस्य हृदि श्रिताः।
अथ मर्त्योऽमृतो भवत्यत्र ब्रह्म समश्नुते ॥१४॥

*yadā sarve pramucyante kāmā ye 'sya hṛdi śritāḥ* |
*atha martyo 'mṛto bhavatyatra brahma samaśnute* | | 14 | |

When all desires present in the heart of a man are destroyed branch and root; then the mortal man becomes immortal and thoroughly enjoys *Brahman*.

Only when all desires hidden in the heart are annihilated a person, whose tendency is towards *Brahman*, reaches a deathless state. He experiences the *Brahman*. He becomes blissful. Like a lamp, which is put off, if a person comes out of all attachments, he can hope to reach *Brahman*. On realizing *Brahman* he becomes *Brahman* itself.

**Śravaṇa 1** – When emotions of desires and hatred gripping the heart leaves a person, he achieves immortal state and becomes *Brahman*. Before realizing the *ātmā*, he was conditioned by *dharma* of life and death. However as soon as he gets *ātma-jñāna*, the life-death cycle consisting of ignorance, desires and *karma*s leaves him and he becomes immortal.

**Naciketā** – Is it enough if only desires leave him? Is it not necessary for *vāsanā*s (aptitudes, latent desires) also to leave him from the root?

**Yamarāja** –

यदा सर्वे प्रभिद्यन्ते हृदयस्येह ग्रन्थयः।
अथ मर्त्योऽमृतो भवत्येतावदनुशासनम् ॥१५॥

*yadā sarve prabhidyante hṛdayasyeha granthayaḥ* |
*atha martyo 'mṛto bhavatyetāvadanuśāsanam* | | 15 | |

When all the knots of the heart are cut-off, then the mortal man, in the body itself, becomes immortal, this much is the eternal instruction.

Yes. It is necessary to loosen all the knots, which control the heart. Once all the *granthis*, knots are slackened he is liberated. He leaves the *dharma* of life and death and reaches a deathless state. This alone is the preaching of all the Vedas.

**Śravaṇa 2** – The knots are nothing but attachments, attractions and desires. As these leave, the bondage also goes away. *Vāsanās* (aptitudes) also get destroyed. He reaches the *Brahman*.

**Yamarāja** – "I am this body, this is my wealth, I am very happy," such kinds of thought which stem from ignorance have to be kept away. The thoughts like "I am the *Brahman* who is not a *saṁsārī*" should be entertained. Then the knots, which bind the heart, will get broken and he will become immortal.

शतं चैका च हृदयस्य नाड्यस्तासां मूर्धानमभिनिःसृतैका ।
तयोर्ध्वमायन्नमृतत्वमेति विष्वङ्ङन्या उत्क्रमणे भवन्ति ॥१६॥

*śataṁ caikā ca hṛdayasya nāḍyastāsāṁ*
*mūrdhānamabhiniḥ sṛtaikā* |
*tayordhvamāyannamṛtatvameti viṣvaṅṅanyā*
*utkramaṇe bhavanti* | | 16 | |

Further in the heart there are 101 *nāḍī*s. Of them one goes towards the top of the head. If the *prāṇa* escapes along that, then one can reach the permanent *Brahmaloka*. The other *nāḍī*s are the cause of birth and death.

**Śravaṇa 1** – Among the 101 *nāḍī*s, the *suṣumnā nāḍī* alone takes one to *Brahmaloka*, while the others will be attached to different desires. If the *jīva*'s *prāṇa* goes along those ways and escapes, then there is no liberation. That is, if the life is ended without leaving the desires and attachments then again one has to take birth, death and get caught in that cycle. However, if one's *prāṇa* seeking *Brahman* escapes through the *nāḍī*s at the top of the head, then, one can go to *brahmaloka* and reach *Brahman*. However this also is for the *upāsaka* who meditates on *saguṇa Brahman*.

**Yamarāja** –

> अङ्गुष्ठमात्रः पुरुषोऽन्तरात्मा सदा जनानां हृदये सन्निविष्टः।
> तं स्वाच्छरीरात् प्रवृहेन्मुञ्जादिवेषीकां धैर्येण।
> तं विद्याच्छुक्रममृतं तं विद्याच्छुक्रममृतमिति ॥१७॥
>
> *aṅguṣṭhamātraḥ puruṣo 'ntarātmā sadā janānāṁ hṛdaye sanniviṣṭaḥ* |
> *taṁ svāccharīrāt pravṛhenmuñjādiveṣīkāṁ dhairyeṇa*
> *taṁ vidyācchukramamṛtaṁ taṁ vidyācchukram amṛtamiti* | | 17 | |

The *antarātmā* who is *puruṣa* present in the body of the size of a thumb, is seated in the heart of all living beings. Like separating the straw from the grass, he has to separate from the body and realize the *ātmā* as pure form of nector. A person knowing this gets *mukti* here itself without going to any place.

**Śravaṇa 2** – The *puruṣa* staying inside the human being does so by constricting his form and strength. As just a snake leaves its skin, desires and attachments which bind human beings have to be removed one by one and one, has to see the Supreme Being which is blemishless. That is only *Brahman*.

**Naciketā** – (**Gets up and does *abhivādaye* to Yamarāja**) Gurudeva, I obtained wisdom. My attractions have gone away. The knots of my heart have melted away. Without any doubts and with confidence, I am stabilized in the *Brahman*. I will follow your words sincerely. I give my *namaskārams* to you many times.

**Yamarāja** –

> मृत्युप्रोक्तां नचिकेतोऽथ लब्ध्वा विद्यामेतां योगविधिं च कृत्स्नम्।
> ब्रह्म प्राप्तो विरजोऽभूद्विमृत्युरन्योऽप्येवं यो विदध्यात्ममेव ॥ १८॥
>
> *mṛtyuproktāṁ naciketo 'tha labdhvā vidyāmetāṁ yogavidhiṁ ca kṛtsnam* |
> *brahma prāpto virajo 'bhūd vimṛtyuranyo 'pyevaṁ yo vidadhyātmameva* | | 18 | |

Naciketā, having gained that science declared by Death, and also the whole rule of concentration, obtained *Brahman*, and hence was without passion and immortal; thus also any other (will obtain *Brahman*) who knows in the same manner the unchangeable soul.

*fig* : **Naciketā leaves Yamaloka**

After hearing the above discourse delivered by Yamarāja, Naciketā learnt and absorbed this entire science and grasping the process of *yoga* became immortal and free from all mutations; he realized God. The other persons also who grasped this spiritual science in this way became the same, i.e. free from death and mutation, they realize God.

Child! Naciketā! I gave this preaching to you as a boon with pleasure. However you should not give this to a person who has not done the required penance, who has no *bhakti* (devotion), who has no feeling for service, who ridicules me (here 'me' denotes *ātmā*). A person preaching this to deserving persons reaches the exalted state. There is no doubt about it.

**Śravaṇa** 1 – A person realizing this concept of the *ātmā* reaches *Brahman*, gets removed of blemishes and crosses death also.

***(All get up and sing.)***

***(Curtain closes.)***

## SCENE 5

(In front of Yamarāja's palace, a plane well decorated with flowers is standing in the street. Naciketā is taking leave from Yamarāja, his wife and others. Naciketā is giving salutations to everybody separately.)

**Naciketā** – Gurudeva! Mother! Elders! To all of you my *praṇāmas*. If I have done any wrong actions either knowingly or unknowingly kindly pardon me for the same and bless me with *āśīrvāda*. Kindly give me leave.

**Yamarāja** – Child! Let all good tidings befall you. As long as the Vedas are present, as long as Veda songs are present, as long as *nāda* (sounds) are present, as long as the tongue is there, your good fame will spread in all four directions. You may go comfortably in this plane. Chitragupta you also go along with him and leave him.

**The wife of Yamarāja** – Child! I can never forget you. Though you stayed here for just a few days, I feel so close with you as though I have known you for *yugas*. It is now very difficult to give you a send-off. However, when I think of your parents who are pining for you, it is necessary that you should go to *bhūloka* without fail and quickly. My love and respect to you will always be there. Do give my *praṇāmas* to your mother, who is most fortunate to have you as her child.

**Naciketā** – As you will, respected mother.

**Yamarāja** – Child! In the first day itself, you must wear this *ratnamāla* which I have given you as a present. (He puts it around his neck) Śravaṇa! Did you see! now these *ratnas* (precious stones) are shining with more sheen like the *kaustubha* pearls, which are worn by Upendramūrti.

**Śravaṇas** - Yes Mahārāja! Naciketā! Do convey our humble *namaskārams* to your parents as soon as you reach home. Our heartfelt blessings to you, you will always have. Preach the *brahma-vidyā* you learnt from the *mahārāja* to the deserving disciples.

**Chitragupta** – Respected Brāhmaṇa! After you leave, this city itself will loose its shine. Like a city not bathed by the rays of the moon, like a cloud not visited by lightning, this city will feel deprived. I am also feeling sad. However, what can one do? You reach your place safely and well. I will also come in the plane and leave you at your destination.

**Pāśahasta and other soldiers** – Svāmī! Please accept our most affectionate *praṇāma*s. Kindly pardon whatever mistakes we have done knowingly and unknowingly and do give your *āśīrvāda*s to us.

**(All are saluting Naciketā.)**

**Naciketā** – Gurudeva! My dear mother, my affectionate friends and messengers, I am starting on my journey. Do give me leave. (So saying he climbs into the plane along with Chitragupta).

**(That time Yama's soldiers cry out victory calls.)**

**Yama's soldiers** – Victory to Naciketā.

**Pāśahasta** – *Jaya bhava, Vijayī bhava*! Let the fame of Naciketā rise.

**(Yamarāja's wife wipes her eyes with the end of her *saree*)**

**Others** – Let Naciketā's name and fame spread. Let the Naciketā *agni* grow, Victory to Naciketā. *Jaya bhava, Vijayī bhava.*

***(Showers the flower petals.)***

***(The plane starts. The curtain falls.)***

***(Part IV Ends.)***

## Part V

### SCENE 1

(In the foothills of the Himālayas it is the *āśrama* of Vājaśravas. Outside on the *verāṇḍā*, Vājaśravas and Vasumatī immersed in great sorrow are conversing. Agniveśa is feeding grass to the male calf, which is tied below the *arjuna* tree. Satyakṣada is pouring water to the flowering plants nearby. The *āśrama* and the place surrounding it appears lack-lusture. It must be about ten hours after the rise of the sun.)

**Vasumatī** – Āryaputra! I am not able to stay anymore without seeing my dear son. I am ready to leave this life if it is possible to see him that way. My *prāṇanātha*! with great anguish I am waiting for permission from you. Kindly show mercy on this poor soul and grant me permission.

**Vājaśravas** – Dear one! Is it just for you to go leaving me alone to suffer here? This may not be proper for a *dharmapatnī*. In human life birth and death happen as fate wills. Will that become false?

**Vasumatī** – For the last three years, I was thinking everyday that he would be coming. But I was disappointed. By now I am in a state of intolerable suffering like burning in hell-fire. Can't you see that, Svāmī?

**Vājaśravas** – Vasumatī! Am I not suffering? I am only keeping my feelings bottled up lest I exhibit them in front of you and disturb you further. It has been a long time since I have slept in the nights.

**Vasumatī** – My Prāṇanātha! I am aware that you are suffering in the night without sleep. Is it not through Lord Yama that we got initiated into this *yajña* of *Viśvajīta*? Look at what the fruits this *yajña* has given us.

**Vājaśravas** – (**angrily**) Vasumatī! What did you say? Don't lose your balance. Whatever has to happen is bound to happen. Nothing is in our hands. For that, don't blabber as your mind dictates.

O Naciketā! Satyavrata! Has my *dharma* got wasted! Fortunately last night I slept well and saw a good dream. Vasumatī you also hear that. All of you come (**calls the *āśrama* residents who come close by**) I saw in the dream that our son was praised by Lord Yama. He gave him several boons and then with honour he sent him back here in a plane. Then I suddenly opened my eyes. Since it was *brahmamuhūrtta*, I went outside to do my morning duties.

**Agniveśa** – Gurudeva! The dream seen early in the morning, it is said, it will definitely come true, isn't it?

**Satyakṣada** – Without Naciketā this *āśrama* itself is looking deserted.

**Agniveśa** – Without our friend, these places look bereft and lack-lusture, like a flower without smell, like a musical instrument without strings, like a *yajña* conducted without the rules of Vedas.

**Satyakṣada** – My mind says something strongly. I feel he will come today. O Lord Yajñeśvara! Do make it come true.

**Vasumatī** – O alas! My child has not yet come. I am not able to control my overwhelming anguish. My heart is getting choked with sorrow.

(She collapses and falls. The *āśrama* residents rush and try to revive her back. She gets up, does *ācamanam* and applies holy ash on her forehead and meditates. Then she brightens up as she sees some good omens.)

**Vasumatī** – My Prāṇanātha! My face has brightened up suddenly and my left eye and shoulder are twitching. My mind also feels clear and happy. O *Vanadevatā*s! Do show your mercy. Kindly protect my son. Svāmī! All these good omens tell me, that, our son will be back definitely. There is no doubt about it.

**Vājaśravas** – Dear! What you are saying is very correct. I am also seeing many good signs. My right eye, right shoulders and right thigh are twitching. The *dharma*, which we followed, won't become useless. Our Naciketā will come now. This is definite.

**Agniveśa** – There the bird on the top branch also is singing in a sweet voice and informing us of the arrival of a relation.

**Satyakṣada** – Not only that, see above there, the bird Garuḍa is flying and circling around. O Our friend! has indeed come here.

(A little far off a plane lands. Naciketā gets down. Naciketā folds his hands and does *praṇāmas* to Chitragupta. Chitragupta also reciprocates. The plane takes off and goes back with Chitragupta. Naciketā comes running towards the *āśrama*. Agniveśa takes him and goes. The young *Ṛṣabha* unties its knots and runs towards Naciketā.)

**Satyakṣada** – (Overwhelmed with happiness, he dances and sings.)

The one who comes is a blessing for our deeds.
The one who comes is the God whom we worship.
The one who comes is our colourful friend.
The respected one comes! The Ārya comes!
The Gautama comes! The blissful one comes!
The pure one comes! The dear friend comes.
The *Godilan* come! Let the dynasty prosper.

**The parents** – Child! Dear one!

**Naciketā** – Father! Mother!

(Naciketā falls at the feet of his parents. Both of them lift him up, embrace him and overwhelmed, shed tears of joy.)

**Vājaśravas** – Vasumatī, did you see our child's face? Like a full moon, like a lotus flower blossomed now, his face is shining with a new light and *tejas*.

**Agniveśa** – Yes, what a *tejas*! What majesty! I think he has drunk nectar from heaven.

**Vasumatī** – The saying that an unfortunate person who is in darkness for many years will eventually see the light and obtain happiness has come true in my case. Naciketā! My wealth! My dearest one! Come, do come! Talk to me your sweet words. Let both my ears get filled with your voice. Let me embrace you to my heart's content. Let you the honey-filled one come.

(Naciketā does salutation to everyone and embraces his friends. All of them go together to the *āśrama*. Naciketā comes out, pats and fondles the male calf and enters inside.)

***(The curtain falls.)***

## SCENE 2

(On the banks of Ganges a great *paṇḍāla* (closed enclosure) has been erected and it is decorated with festoons made of mango leaves, coconut leaves and banana plants. In a high seat both Vājaśravas and his wife are sitting. Nearby Naciketā and some disciples are standing. Next to that on a reed seat, a Munipuṅgava, a Brāhmaṇottama and a Dīkṣita are sitting. (On another side *ṛṣipatni*s, *dīkṣitapatnī*s and other ladies are sitting. The disciples and small children are sitting in a disciplined manner. Outside the *paṇḍāla* also many people are standing in groups. Even though there is a large gathering still it is very quiet and calm. *Pūrṇakumbha,* flowers and other auspicious objects are kept).

**First Ṛṣi** – (getting up) Elders! I welcome everyone who has assembled here. You all know why we have assembled here. The one who is the focus of all our love and respect, *ciraṅjīvī* Naciketā and the fortunate parents who have given birth to such a child, the *kulapati* Vājaśravas couple are present here. We want to honour them as well as to shower our blessings on them. My heart felt good wishes and blessings.

**Brahmarṣi** – Today is a great day for our human population itself. This is a golden day, when we propose to honour Naciketā who has come back from *yamaloka.* It is like honouring the human race. The benefits of that can be obtained by the entire human society. Let his fame spread.

**Dīkṣita** – It is a great wonder and happiness to know the welcome and the boons our Naciketā received in Yamarāja's kingdom. We all can obtain *svarga* by doing the *yajña* of *Naciketāgni*. Our gratitude and blessings will always be given to Naciketā. By doing this *yajña* three times, is there any *loka,* which we cannot reach? Its greatness indeed is indescribable.

**Second ṛṣi** – Apart from the boons Naciketā has obtained for this world and other worlds, he has also obtained *brahma-jñana*. It is our good fortune that he has come back. With compassion for us he has preached *Kaṭha Upaniṣad* to Agniveśa and Satyakṣada. Now through *guru* and *śiṣya* lineages, the knowledge can be obtained by all of us and we can reap its fruits. Is it proper to leave this golden opportunity? We should send our children also to the *gurukula* of Vājaśravas. Let everyone obtain wisdom and get exalted. My heart felt blessing for all that.

**Munipuṅgava** – Our minds yearn to hear the preachings of Dharmarāja through the words of *ciraṅjīvī* Naciketā himself. We request him to tell it in a way it can be easily understood by the ladies and children assembled here. Child, Naciketā! Do come here. Stand on this platform and tell us about the teachings you received.

**Everyone** – Yes that is right. If Naciketā climbs the platform we all can see him. Do come and pour down your nectar-filled words.

> (Naciketā does *namaskārams* to all elders by falling prostrate at their feet. Then he gives salutations to his parents. He further glances in the direction of Lord Yama and does meditation in the mind itself. Then he addresses the gathering without embarrassment and speaks in an easy way that everyone understands.)

**Naciketā** – Elders, mothers, friends! My heartfelt thanks to everyone. It indeed shows the great regard you have for me by asking me to talk in the group consisting of Veda exponents, *Vedāntakesarīs* who are experts in explanations, exponents of *mīmāṁsās* and authority in argumentative discussions. In comparison, what do I know? Is it possible for a small tree to grow under a banyan tree? In front of you learned *paṇḍits* I must only be quiet. Still as you all have prompted me to talk, I am holding your orders as my strength and am standing in front of you. Now your blessing alone will make me talk. I give my *praṇāmas* to my *gurus* and *devatās* who are dear to me. Let them shower their grace on me.

*fig.:* **Naciketā addressing *āśrama* residents**

First let me give my *namaskārams* to the *bīja* (seed) which, in an astonishing way, without changing its status, with no one planting it or watering it, forms crops of *jīvas* having different forms and characteristics. It is the one which does not change and with any passing season and situations remains the fundamental cause of everything. Let us meditate on this *ātmā* thing.

*Ātmā*, which is the inner knowledge, please do enter my insides and pour your grace unto me. Let us all immerse in that and lose ourselves in its bliss. It is the exalted *Brahman*, which is the scene of all that we see. It is the one which shows all that we see by being our sight. Like the foetus hidden in the womb of the mother who is pregnant, as the fire is hidden in a wooden piece, the *ātmā* is hidden in our minds. This will emerge at the right time like the child coming out of the womb. Just as how the fire is drawn out of the wood in the same way it has to be drawn from the mind. First the thought as seed should be planted in the mind and the desire should arise that one has to be connected with it. Then the mind has to be chained with the wisdom (that is enquiry of *Brahman*) and then alone the *ātmā* will reveal itself.

That *ātmā,* like a king, is seated in the heart, which is its palace, and it is ruling us. It is beyond birth and death. Under its directions only the sun shines and the wind blows. He is the master of everything. The rain falling is also under its sovereignty. The god of death takes the lives back under its orders only. All the matters happen under its rule. Nobody can cross its orders.

As the rain falling in the mountain divides into many rivers with different names, the Supreme Being separates into different *jīva*s. Seeing the various *jīva*s we should not forget the original single unit. Though in the water routes there are big rivers, small rivers, deep ones, shallow ones, streams, pools, etc. it is the same water in all of them. In the same way, the *ātmā* also takes different forms which are short, tall, minister, servant, man, woman, animal, tree, and so on. But in all, the same *ātmā* is present. It is the master of whatever has happened, whatever happens, and whatever is going to happen. In both sleep and wakefulness. It is only functioning. It decreases to small miniscule size and dwells in the heart and rules from there. We should know the Supreme Being, who is the cause of anything and everything. It cannot be reached by knowledge of books. By repeating the Veda *mantra*s also it cannot be reached. Even learned *paṇḍit*s cannot understand it. Will the animal which carries the fragrant saffron flowers know its smell? Only when a person leaves attachment for things in this world and desires for experience in other worlds he will be ready to see the *ātmā*. That alone is permanent bliss.

To meditate on the *mantra oṁ* is also a way to reach It. This *oṁ mantra* is the basis of the entire Veda. Getting tuned to this *mantra* and repeating this one can reach the exalted state. The *saṁsāra* tree is akin to the *aśvattha* tree having its roots above and branches below and that, which is spread widely, can be cut and thrown off only by the sword of detachment. All our senses always travel outwards. They roam outside in search of sensory pleasures. They do not have the capacity to go inside and look at the *antarātmā*. We have to build that capacity in them. That only is strength. We should change our character of looking out and learn to look inside. Then all senses, both *karma indriya*s (leading to action) and *jñāna indriya*s (leading to knowledge) will be quietened. The intellect also won't be disturbed. This only is *yoga*. Then *ātma-jñāna* will rise up. There is no need of any light to see this *ātma-jñāna*. It is self-effulgent. It is the light of all lights.

If we consider our body as a chariot, the master who is sitting inside is the *ātmā*. The charioteer is the intellect, the mind is the rein, and the horses are the five senses. Just as the chariot when driven properly will reach its destination, we should drive the chariot, which is the body. If we pull the rein, which is equated to the mind, properly, then the five senses can be controlled, the chariot will be properly driven and we can reach our destination, which is reaching the *paramātmā*, or else we will be embroiled in the cycle of *saṁsāra*. Let us come out of our sleep of ignorance. Let us reach the known souls and hear their preaching. Just like walking on a sharp knife the yogic path may be difficult. But if we proceed without losing heart then we are sure to get wisdom.

A person should be charged with the desire that he must know the *ātmā*, and with earnest mind and yearning to get *ātma-jñāna*, leaving all other desires and without getting drawn in worldly attractions, controlling the mind and purifying it, he can come out of aptitude towards material life, then the *yoga* state will naturally reach him. The knots, which control the mind, have to be loosened. Then the *upāsaka* will escape from the *suṣumnā nāḍī* at the time of death and reach *brahmaloka*. Thus the wise person will get mingled with the *paramātmā*, like a river getting mixed with the ocean, and gets liberated.

The eyes cannot see this *ātmā*. It cannot be talked about and described. It cannot be thought of by the mind. Hence it is not proper that I tell you these things and you can understand by hearing the truth. How can I describe a thing, which is apart from the senses, and how can you hear about it and know it? How can that, which is apart from minds, be thought about by mind and meditated upon? Only if *ātmā* shines by itself can it be known. It is not correct to say that one can see it. Non-attachment is the only route to freedom. Remove the blemishes and embrace the good. With that I seek your blessings. To the elders my *namaskāram*s.

(Naciketā once more prostrates and gives his salutations to every one.)

**First ṛṣi** – Child! Your preaching was indeed very good. Like a gooseberry kept in the palm of the hand you showed the truth very clearly. You will be a *ciraṅjīvī* (live for ever).

**Munipuṅgava** – Kumāra! We are happy hearing your preaching. If you had done this in king's court you would have been done *kanakābhiṣeka* (you would have been showered with gold coins). However, what do we poor people have? I give this hide of deer to you as an offering.

**Brahmarṣi** – Child! I give you this reed mat. Do accept it.

**Dīkṣita** – Child, here take this *prasāda* of *iṣṭi yajña* performed this morning.

**Second ṛṣi** – Naciketā! You showed clearly how to destroy the route of *saṁsāra*, which is highly temporary, and the way to reach the *ātmā*. Do accept this *kamaṇḍala* as my gift.

(Naciketā accepts everything with great humility. The ladies come and shower holy grains and do *āratī*.)

***(Curtain falls.)***

## SCENE-3

***(The curtain opens.)***

(It is the *āśrama* site of Gautama *ṛṣi*. Śairandhrī and Sūtradhāra are coming.)

**Sūtradhāra** – Dear friend! With the end of this scene our drama is over. I don't know how the viewers enjoyed it.

**Śairandhrī** – Sir! I can only see question marks on their faces.

**Sūtradhāra** – Yes I also noticed. To enjoy a new attempt one should have a proper attitude and open mind. Only persons who have a capacity to appreciate could have enjoyed it.

**Śairandhrī** – Could everybody have understood the concept of this drama? Or else what is the way?

**Sūtradhāra** – Again and again it should be read along with the original Upaniṣad and the *bhāṣya* explanations Śaṅkarācārya had written for it.

**Śairandhrī** – What! The list seems to be quite long.

**Sūtradhāra** – Dear girl, it is not so. If the *Bhagavad-Gītā* also is studied along with this, one can obtain *ātma-jñāna* easily.

**Śairandhrī** – Sir! Though so many books of knowledge and treasures of wisdom are there why are you in particular telling about the *Gītā*? What is the connection between this and the *Gītā*? Do tell.

**Sūtradhāra** – O colourful girl! This *Kaṭha Upaniṣad* is the mother scripture. The *Bhagavat-Gīta* is the child scripture. The palace called *Gītā* is built upon the foundation of this *Upaniṣad* only. In the *Kaṭha Upaniṣad* there is description of the chariot. Lord Kṛṣṇa takes that description only as example to preach Arjuna. Further many *śloka*s of *Kaṭha Upaniṣad* are taken as such and appear in the *Gītā*.

**Śairandhrī** – Is that so? I did not know this till now.

**Sūtradhāra** – There are many like you who don't know. To give them the gift of knowledge and give them good life only our Śaṅkara-kṛpā is taking all the efforts. There is such a close connection between *Gītā* and *Kaṭha Upaniṣad*. Hence for the drama to be known well, I advised that the *Gītā* has to be read. If it is read as such, everyone will obtain *brahma-jñāna*.

**Śairandhrī** – Will it not be proper to tell the viewers well in advance?

**Sūtradhāra** – Next it should be *Praśna Upaniṣad*. The fans should give support, enthusiasm and blessings for it to go well. Everyone who has heard, read, listened to this *Upaniṣad* will leave the sea of birth and death and get salvation. The Vedamātā's compassion is greater than that of the mother who has given birth. She will give the treasure of wisdom in great bounty and bless us all.

**Śairandhrī** – My dear ones! Dear fans! Even if you concentrate on one part of the scripture and learn it thoroughly you can reach a higher state. It will give blessings in this life and the next lives. My humble request to you all is to read this Upaniṣad.

**Sūtradhāra** – Dear viewers, our salutations. For the time being we are taking leave of you with the faith that your support and blessings are always there.

**Śairandhrī** – To everyone in the gathering *namaskārams*. Do give us leave till the next drama. We have to part. Elders do give us your blessings. Our *praṇāmas* to you all.

***(The curtain falls.)***

# Bibliography


Chinmayananda, Swami, *Īśavāsya Upaniṣad*, New Delhi: Central Chinmaya Mission Trust, 2001.

———, *Māṇḍūkya Upaniṣad*, Mumbai: Central Chinmaya Mission Trust, 2003.

Gambhirananda, Swami, *Eight Upaniṣads*, Calcutta: Advaita Ashrama, 1998.

Mehta, Rohit, *Upaniṣads*, Delhi: Motilal Banarsidass, 1999.

Prasad, Narayana Swami Muni, *Kena Upaniṣad*, New Delhi: D.K. Printworld, 1994.

———, *Muṇḍaka Upaniṣad*, New Delhi: D.K. Printworld, 1998.

———, *Taittirīya Upaniṣad*, New Delhi: D.K. Printworld, 1994.

———, *Praśna Upaniṣad*, New Delhi: D.K. Printworld, 1999.